P9-DMY-672

RESPONDING to
DOMESTIC VIOLENCE

4 EDITION

*To the millions who endure and survive and
to those who protect and support.*

RESPONDING to
DOMESTIC VIOLENCE
The Integration of Criminal Justice and Human Services

Eve S. Buzawa ▪ Carl G. Buzawa ▪ Evan Stark

4 EDITION

Los Angeles | London | New Delhi
Singapore | Washington DC

9/16/11
Lin
$49.95

Copyright © 2012 by SAGE Publications, Inc.

All rights reserved. No part of this book may be reproduced or utilized in any form or by any means, electronic or mechanical, including photocopying, recording, or by any information storage and retrieval system, without permission in writing from the publisher.

For information:

SAGE Publications, Inc.
2455 Teller Road
Thousand Oaks, California 91320
E-mail: order@sagepub.com

SAGE Publications India Pvt. Ltd.
B 1/I 1 Mohan Cooperative Industrial Area
Mathura Road, New Delhi 110 044
India

SAGE Publications Ltd.
1 Oliver's Yard
55 City Road
London EC1Y 1SP
United Kingdom

SAGE Publications Asia-Pacific Pte. Ltd.
33 Pekin Street #02-01
Far East Square
Singapore 048763

Printed in the United States of America

Library of Congress Cataloging-in-Publication Data

Buzawa, Eva Schlesinger.
Responding to domestic violence: the integration of criminal justice and human services / Eve S. Buzawa, Carl G. Buzawa, Evan Stark.—4th ed.
   p. cm.
Rev. ed. of: Domestic violence. 3rd ed. c2003.
Includes bibliographical references and index.
ISBN 978-1-4129-5639-0 (cloth)
ISBN 978-1-4129-5640-6 (pbk.)
   1. Wife abuse—United States. 2. Family violence—United States—Prevention. 3. Criminal justice, Administration of—United States. I. Buzawa, Carl G. II. Stark, Evan. III. Buzawa, Eva Schlesinger. Domestic violence. IV. Title.

HV6626.2.B89 2011
364.15′5530973—dc22   2010046454

This book is printed on acid-free paper.

11   12   13   14   15   10   9   8   7   6   5   4   3   2   1

Acquisitions Editor:	Jerry Westby
Editorial Assistant:	Nichole O'Grady
Production Editor:	Karen Wiley
Copy Editor:	Sheree VanVreede
Typesetter:	C&M Digitals (P) Ltd.
Proofreader:	Penelope Sippel
Indexer:	Sheila Bodell
Cover Designer:	Candice Harman
Marketing Manager:	Erica DeLuca
Permissions Editor:	Karen Ehrmann

Brief Contents

Detailed Contents

Introduction 1

The Role and Context of Agency Responses to Domestic Violence

Purpose and Overview

The movement to end domestic violence in the United States began more than a century ago. In 1885, volunteers working with a coalition of women's organizations in Chicago started a "court watch" project designed to monitor proceedings that involved female and child victims of abuse and rape. In addition to providing legal aid and personal assistance, they also sent abused women to a shelter run by the Women's Club of Chicago, the first shelter of its kind. The Chicago initiative was short-lived, however, and the idea of using emergency housing as a first-line protection did not take hold until a May afternoon in 1972 when the first call to a shelter was made to Women's Advocates in St. Paul, Minnesota. As recalled by Sharon Vaughan (2009), a founder of the St. Paul program and a pioneer in the battered women's movement:

> The call was . . . from Emergency Social Services. A worker said a woman was at the St. Paul Greyhound bus station with a two-year-old child. To get a job, she had traveled 150 miles from Superior, Wisconsin, with two dollars in her pocket. What were we expected to do? Where would they stay after two days at the Grand Hotel? One of the advocates borrowed a high chair and stroller and we took them to the apartment that was our office. These were the first residents we sheltered. The two-year-old destroyed the office in one night because all the papers were tacked on low shelves held up by bricks. His mother didn't talk about being battered; she said she wanted to go to secretarial school to make a life for her and her son. She tried to get a place to live, but no one would rent to her without a deposit, which she didn't have. . . . After a couple of weeks, she went back to Superior, and every Christmas for several years sent a card thanking Women's Advocates for being there and enclosed $2.00, the amount she had when she came to town. (p. 3)

During the next 3 decades, the use of shelters for women escaping abusive partners became widespread in the United States and in dozens of other countries. The shelter movement helped to stimulate a revolution in the societal response to domestic violence victims and offenders that has circled the globe, stirring women from all walks of life; of all races, religions, and ages; and in thousands of neighborhoods, to challenge

1

men's age-old prerogative to hurt, demean, or otherwise subjugate their female partners virtually at will. In addition to the proliferation of community-based services for victims, the revolution consists of the three other major components that are the focus of this text: (1) the criminalization of domestic violence; (2) the mobilization of a range of legal resources to protect abused women and their children and to arrest, sanction, and/or counsel perpetrators; and (3) the development of a vast base of knowledge describing virtually every facet of abuse and the societal response. By 2010, police in the United States were arresting more than a million offenders for domestic violence crimes annually, and shelters and related programs for battered women in more than 2,000 communities were serving over 3 million women and children. Most of those arrested for domestic violence are male, although a large number of females also are arrested for abusing male or female partners and both partners are arrested in many cases. So-called dual arrests are a controversial practice that has stimulated much debate.

The Domestic Violence Revolution: Taking Stock

At the heart of public reforms is an ambitious conceit, that violence in intimate relationships can be significantly reduced or even ended if it is treated as criminal behavior and punished accordingly. Given this goal, it is not surprising that the societal response has rested so heavily on reforming criminal justice and legal intervention with offenders and victims. From the start, it was assumed that the primary responsibility for supporting individual victims would be borne by domestic violence organizations and other community-based services and that the role of public agencies like the police and the courts was to provide the legal framework for this support and to manage offenders through some combination of arrest, prosecution, punishment, rehabilitation, and monitoring (i.e., much in the way that other criminal populations are managed). An unfortunate side effect of the focus on individual offenders and victims is that relatively little attention has been paid to identifying and modifying the structural and cultural sources of abusive behavior. Mapping the societal response to domestic violence requires that we place the criminal justice and legal systems center stage. But it also means recognizing the limits of addressing a major societal problem like abuse with a criminal justice approach to individual wrong-doing.

Since the opening and diffusion of shelters, the policies, programs, and legal landscape affecting victims and perpetrators of partner abuse have changed dramatically. Reforms run the gamut from those designed to facilitate victim access to services or to strengthen the criminal justice response to those aimed at preventing future violence by rehabilitating offenders. A range of new protections is available for victims from civil or criminal courts. Conversely, a distinct domestic violence function has been identified in numerous justice agencies and is increasingly being carried out by specialized personnel. Examples include "dedicated" domestic violence prosecutors, domestic violence courts, and domestic violence police units. Complementary reforms have attempted to enhance the predictability and consistency of the justice response by restricting discretion in decisions about whether to arrest or prosecute offenders, making domestic violence a factor in decisions regarding custody or divorce, integrating the criminal and family court response to domestic violence by creating "consolidated" courts, and constructing "one-stop" models of service delivery for victims. In hundreds of communities, once perpetrators are arrested, they are offered counseling as an alternative to jail through "batterer intervention programs" (BIPs). Several thousand localities now host collaborative efforts to reduce or prevent abuse in which community-based services such as shelters join with courts, law enforcement, local businesses, child protection agencies, and a range of health and other service organizations. The rationale for these reforms in the United States is straightforward: Under the Equal Protection Clause of the Fourteenth Amendment to the Constitution, women assaulted by present or former partners are entitled to the same protections as persons assaulted by strangers.

At the basis of these reforms is the hope that they will make the societal response to domestic violence more effective. But the efficacy of new laws, practices, or programs is hard to measure directly. Moreover, there is only a tenuous link between whether a program is effective and whether it receives institutional support. Legal and criminal justice agencies have a variety of interests in new policies, programs, or practices other than whether they meet the goals of protection and accountability. To win acceptance by the criminal justice or legal systems, institutional reforms must meet a variety of internal or system needs as well as satisfy public demands. These needs include facilitating an agency's capacity to attract resources or to add personnel or to achieve greater public visibility and political support. Conversely, police and other public agencies may continue to promote programs or policies that meet these needs long after they have been proved ineffective. Understanding why the police and other justice agencies respond to domestic violence as they do means appreciating how the given practice converges with the agency's norms, values, and system needs as well as how it is received by the public or affects the problem at hand.

This point is illustrated by the propensity for courts, police, or prosecution to develop specialized functions when confronted with high-demand problems like domestic violence. Examples of specialization in the domestic violence field include consolidated domestic violence courts as well as police teams or prosecutorial units "dedicated" to misdemeanor domestic violence cases. In theory, these reforms benefit victims by standardizing and streamlining arrest, processing, and case disposition. The assumption is that better outcomes will result from case handling by more knowledgeable and experienced agents. Regardless of whether this assumption is supported by evaluation research, specialization is appealing because it serves the system maintenance functions described earlier. For example, specialization helps ration scarce resources by making expenditures on a problem predictable, attracts new resources, adds status to routine functions by reframing them as "special," and helps protect other elements of the system from being overwhelmed. In the past, the large proportion of police calls involving domestic violence posed little threat to routine policing because these cases could be dismissed as "just domestics." If they reached the courts, they received the lowest priority and were routinely dismissed. But as public pressure raised the profile of this class of criminal behaviors and agencies were held accountable for intervention, it was increasingly difficult to respond appropriately while maintaining business as usual with respect to other types of crime. Specialization has helped criminal justice and law enforcement manage this problem, albeit with added costs for administration and training. Thirty years ago, few justice officials would have openly identified themselves with domestic violence cases. Today, being an expert in this area has become an important route to promotion and professional recognition.

A major limit of services for domestic violence victims is that they are delivered piecemeal, forcing victims to negotiate for needed resources at multiple and often distal sites. Moreover, the lack of dialogue or coordination between service providers often means that systems respond in very different and even contradictory ways to victims and offenders. A common example are cases where the child welfare system threatens to place children in foster care whose mothers continue contact with an abusive father while the custody court threatens them with contempt if they deny the father access. Furthermore, there is a growing appreciation that things can be made worse if one element of the system improves its response, but others do not. For instance, a victim's risk of being seriously injured or killed may increase if she is encouraged to seek a protection order but police and the court fail to enforce it.

A recent round of programs has attempted to address the fragmentation and lack of coordination of services in the field as well as the obvious obstacles to access created when victims must traverse multiple portals to get the support they need to be safe. Since the late 1990s, several thousand localities have initiated a "coordinated community response," where shelters and a range of local agencies meet regularly to plan the local response. Meanwhile, more than 60 communities have used federal funds to support "Family Justice Centers," a one-stop model of service delivery originally developed in Alameda County, California. These centers bring crisis intervention together in one building with medical and mental health services, legal assistance, law enforcement, and often employment help as well. Prevention, too, has commanded increased attention. In 2002, the Centers for Disease Control and Prevention (CDC) funded 14 state coalitions to implement the Domestic Violence Prevention Enhancement and Leadership Through Alliances (DELTA) program, which focuses on reducing first-time perpetration by addressing the risk factors associated with domestic violence and by enhancing protective factors. A secondary effect of this initiative has been to foster evidence-based strategic planning by the state coalitions as well as closer working relationships with researchers.

The success of these efforts at coordination and planning, like the durability of programmatic reform within agencies, depends on the larger political and economic context as well as on a substantive commitment to end domestic violence. Currently, the United States is in the midst of a prolonged recession. In the current climate of austerity, an ideal response would involve economies of scale, where agencies sustain cooperative work by eliminating duplication, pooling resources, and sharing personnel. Far more often, however, austerity fosters a much more short-sighted strategy in which funders hone in on sustaining traditional or basic services, local agencies return to a self-protective stance of competing for scarce resources against their erstwhile partners, and policymakers redraw their priorities in response to political pressure. In this climate, cooperation and coordination are put off as desirable in the long run, but unrealistic in the near future, and whatever benefits they may have provided for victim groups can erode quickly.

Is the Domestic Violence Revolution a Success?

Never before has such an array of resources and interventions been brought to bear on abuse in relationships or families. But are these interventions effective?

By most conventional standards, the domestic violence revolution has been an unqualified success. This is true whether we look at the amount of public money directed at the problem, the degree to which politicians across a broad spectrum have embraced its core imagery of male violence and female victimization, the vast knowledge base that has accumulated about abuse, or the degree to which law and criminal justice (and, to a lesser extent, health and child welfare) have moved the heretofore low-status crime of domestic violence to the top of their agenda. Indeed, it would be hard to find another criminal activity in these last decades that has commanded anything like the resources or manpower that have flowed to law enforcement on behalf of abuse victims.

A persuasive case also could be made that the revolution has shifted the normative climate, if ever so slightly, so that partner violence has become a litmus test for the integrity of relationships. Male violence against women (as well as against other men) continues to be a media staple, as the durability of the James Bond, *Rambo, Halloween,* and *Scream* franchises illustrate. Even when a slasher takes an equal-opportunity approach to his victims (as Freddie Kruger does occasionally in the *Nightmare on Elm Street* movies) or violence against women is treated ironically, as it was in the *Scream* trilogy or *I Know What You Did Last Summer* and its sequel, woman killing tends to be protracted and sexualized in ways that the killing of men is not, pointing to the underlying stereotypes perpetuated by this work (Boyle, 2005). Moreover, rape and woman killing remain key themes in other forms of mass culture, most notably in video games (Dill, 2009) and in the brand of rap known as "gangsta rap," which peaked in the songs of Eminem (1999–2005) (Armstrong, 2009).

But if violence continues to compete with sexual conquest as the ultimate test of manhood, male violence against women has increasingly had to share the media stage with images of women as independent actors in their own right who are equally capable of using force and of abusive men as purposeful, obsessive, and cruel. Classic cinema depicted rape victims as viragos getting their just deserts or as helpless victims of brutes who themselves could only be punished by male heroes. Starting with *Thelma & Louise* (1991), however, a series of films pictured women as fully capable of exacting revenge on their assailants, usually by killing them. The idea that women can be *both* victimized and heroic was dramatically presented in *Sleeping with the Enemy,* a 1991 film in which the battered wife (Julia Roberts) is stalked by, but then kills, her husband. Arguably, television has taken the lead in its willingness to provide realistic portraits of abusive men and victimized women on everything from the day-time soaps to evening dramas about hospitals (like *ER*), courts (*The Good Wife*), police (*CSI*), or prosecutors (*Law and Order*). This is a major change from the days when audiences were encouraged to identify with an aggressive James Cagney squeezing a grapefruit in his girlfriend's face (*Public Enemy,* 1931) or even with Jackie Gleason's apparent ability to stop just short of abuse when Ralph Cramden famously threatened to send his wife Alice "to the moon." Of course, this was no joking matter to millions of battered wives in the audience for *The Honeymooners.* For much of the media, and presumably then for their audience, violence against a wife or partner has become the social problem of choice, a mixed blessing perhaps, but a direct reflection of its currency among the general public.

Ironically, both the nadir and the zenith of the domestic violence revolution occurred in close chronological proximity. If we had to pick a single event that could be considered the nadir of the domestic violence revolution, it might be the 1994 murder of Nicole Brown Simpson and her friend, Ron Goldman, and the 1995 trial—and acquittal—of O.J. Simpson for these homicides. The zenith of the revolution also occurred in 1994, when Congress passed, and President Clinton signed, the Violence Against Women Act (VAWA).

Previous legislation lacked the scope, ambition, or funding levels of VAWA. Its passage—and its reauthorization in 2000 and 2005—signaled a growing national consensus that domestic violence and rape merited a nationally coordinated effort focused on safety for victims and accountability for "batterers," both to be achieved through some combination of arrest, prosecution, counseling for offenders, and the delivery of a broad, if poorly defined, range of community-based and traditional services. It was assumed that states would use VAWA funding to expand training programs for criminal justice personnel, refine criminal justice data collection and processing, and build bridges between law enforcement and domestic violence services. During the first 5 years of VAWA, more than $1.8 billion was appropriated for grant programs, primarily in criminal justice, and administered by the Department of Justice and the Department of Health and Human Services. Through the STOP (Services*Training*Officers* and Prosecutors) Formula Grant Program alone, from 1995 to 2000, in excess of $440 million was awarded to support 9,000 projects.

In the wake of VAWA's passage, there was widespread optimism that a broadly based criminal justice response would contain and significantly reduce the incidence of domestic violence, if not prevent it altogether. As the original authorization period for the VAWA came to a close, it was widely assumed that the sheer quantity of the resources committed would have positive effects. As a September 1999 report issued by then Senator Biden stated, "we have successfully begun to change attitudes, perceptions, and behaviors related to violence against women" (p. 5). The report also claimed that, "[f]ive years after the Violence Against Women Act became law, it is demonstrably true that the state of affairs that existed before its enactment has changed for the better" (p. 9). In making his assessment, Senator Biden highlighted "attitudes, perceptions[,]" and "behaviors related to violence against women." The implication was that violence against women had dropped as a direct result of new policies and programs.

To some extent, official figures support Senator Biden's optimism. The last three decades have witnessed a decline in the most serious forms of partner assault, including partner homicides, and for some groups, this decline has been dramatic. What is less clear is whether the changes are in the direction we would expect if interventions were effective or are the result of changes in policy or intervention. For example, other than arrest and prosecution, most reforms have sought to enhance the safety of female victims, starting with shelters. Interestingly, however, men rather than women have benefited most from the declines in partner homicide, particularly Black men. Since the mid-1970s, when the first shelters opened, the number of males killed by female partners has dropped 70% (and an astounding 82% among Blacks). This is a far greater drop than the overall drop in homicides during this period, suggesting that domestic violence interventions may have contributed to the decline. The number of females killed by partners also has dropped during this period but by only 30% on average and a mere 5% for White women, the largest group of victims. Indeed, until very recently, partner homicides actually increased among women who have never married, which is a substantial subgroup (Uniform Crime Reports, 2006).

It may seem strange that more men than women have been saved by new programs and interventions designed to protect women. This positive, but unintended, effect is explained by the different circumstances in which men and women kill their partners. Abusive males tend to kill partners when they fear they will leave them or the women actually do so. Since virtually all the new protections for women involve separation from an abusive partner, these protections may threaten men's control, causing some abusers to escalate their violence. In this line of reasoning, women's continued vulnerability to male partner violence is the result of another fact, that available protections tend to be short term and fragmented and that no effective means has been found to deny abusive partners from accessing their former victims, at least in the long term. By contrast, female partners tend to kill males when they fear for their own or their children's safety, although not necessarily in self-defense. The same options that seem to intensify men's propensity for partner violence may defuse women's feelings of having no way out of their abusive relationship, making it less likely they will kill male partners.

Measuring how our efforts have affected aggregate changes in domestic violence is difficult. Some studies of individual interventions discussed in this text show high success rates, particularly when a broad spectrum of integrated services is at work. Even here, however, the declines documented are not always uniform. Nor is it clear which element or which enhanced program or effort explains reported declines. To illustrate, we return to partner homicide. A retrospective study published in 2001 and sponsored by the National Institute of Justice (NIJ) assessed whether reductions in partner homicide reported in 48 of the 50 largest U.S. cities could be linked to the changing societal response, specifically recently enacted amendments to state statutes, enhanced local police and prosecution policies, legal advocacy programs, or the prevalence of hotlines. The study attempted to link these data during a 20-year time frame (1976–1996) that encompassed the period before and after the enactment of these initiatives (Dugan, Nagin, & Rosenfeld, 2001). The findings provided some support for optimistic projections like Senator Biden's. In slightly more than half of the jurisdictions, an increase in available resources correlated with lower rates of domestic homicide. Ironically, however, in the other jurisdictions, increased resources were correlated with *increased* homicide rates, especially for certain categories of victims. These findings persisted even after population mix, demographic trends, and patterns of economic growth or decline were controlled.

These examples illustrate a conservative theme that runs through this book: that it is naive to assume that simply increasing the resources or personnel dedicated to domestic violence, adding more dollars to policing or assigning more police or prosecutors or judges to the problem, will lead automatically to a decrease in domestic violence. Even if domestic violence of certain types does decline, this may or may not be the result of the intervention. The corollary of this caution is the importance of specificity: We are at a point in the development of the field when we need to replace the heady generalizations of its early days (such as "arrest works") with carefully hewn, scientifically grounded observations about which elements of which interventions are effective for which subgroups. This text should help move readers in this direction.

However effective some interventions may be, there can be no question that violence against women remains a major problem affecting a significant proportion of the female population and, by extension, the families and communities in which these families live. Based on extrapolations from the 8,000 women questioned by the highly regarded National Violence Against Women Survey (NVAWS), conducted in 2006, approximately 25,677,735 women in the United States have been assaulted, raped, or stalked as adults, while slightly less than 2 million women reported being abused in these ways in the last year (Tjaden & Thoennes, 2000). We know from other research that the average duration of abusive relationships is between 5.5 and 7 years (Stark, 2007). This average includes the small proportion for whom a single assault is the sole act of abuse and the millions of abusive relationships that last considerably longer than 7 years. Applying a simple formula of prevalence from public health ($P = I \times D$) generates a conservative estimate that approximately 15.3 million women in the United States were in abusive relationships in 2010. Whatever the trends in domestic violence, these numbers should justify the important place of intervening and/or ending domestic violence on the public agenda.

The Challenges Before Us

Domestic violence intervention was at a crossroads. Mounting evidence suggests that criminal justice intervention alone has a limited effect on the size and nature of the domestic violence problem and that the most effective approaches involve cross-agency and cross-community alliances and coordination. Despite this understanding, budgetary pressures are dashing society's capacity and perhaps also its willingness to fund alternatives to a strict law-and-order approach. For example, California has long been recognized as having one of the best programs for proactively addressing social problems, including domestic violence. It was here that the Family Justice Centers were first imagined and implemented. Throughout the state, criminal justice agencies have practiced an integrated approach using community resources to assist victims and to rehabilitate or control offenders. These efforts are now seriously at risk. To balance the state's budget, Governor Arnold Schwarzenegger eliminated the remaining $16 million of financing for his state's domestic violence programs. These cuts equate to approximately $200,000 for each of the state's 94 nonprofit programs involved in sheltering victims. One result is that many programs must now turn away victims in crisis, close transitional shelters, or simply put vulnerable victims and their families in cheap hotels where they are unlikely to get the resources or support they need to remain independent.

California's attempts to balance its budget at the expense of domestic violence services is extreme. But other states, such as New Jersey and Illinois, also have struggled to keep domestic violence services open. The irony is that cutbacks to established and relatively successful programs are occurring on the 15th anniversary of the passage of VAWA.

Discrimination against domestic violence victims is another major challenge. Until this practice was outlawed by the Health Care Reform Bill passed in 2010, Washington, D.C., and seven states allowed insurance companies to consider domestic violence as a "preexisting condition" and as a reason to deny health coverage to women they believed to be victimized. As several congressional representatives observed, this form of discrimination was the equivalent of defining being female as a preexisting condition.

Domestic violence victims can lawfully leave a rental property without notice and get top priority in public housing in Connecticut and several other states. Still, the number of instances where families have been evicted from public housing because of abuse is on the rise as is the adaptation of antiviolence policies and their use against victims by local housing authorities.

Fundamental issues that many thought would have long been settled remain on the table alongside the emergence of new questions and challenges that concern the preferred method of intervention. An issue that seemed to be settled in the early 1990s, the appropriate response to domestic violence and the role of criminal justice intervention as part of this response, is once again being hotly debated.

In the United States, the criminal justice system has spearheaded the response to domestic violence. The dissemination of mandatory arrest and "no-drop" prosecution in the 1980s and early 1990s reflected a consensus that arrest and prosecution were not merely proper but the preferred response in abuse cases. Starting in the late 1990s, however, there was a growing sentiment in the field that criminal justice intervention alone was not an adequate or even a desirable approach to the problem (see, e.g., Mills, 1999, 2006). Even some advocates warned that the reliance on arrest had gone too far, causing the original emphasis on victim empowerment to wane. Today, even those who support a lead role for criminal justice realize that the response by police, prosecution, or criminal courts is merely one piece of society's overall reaction to domestic violence.

It is important to appreciate that the demand to provide equal protection to victims of partner assault from advocates was not the only source of pressure for criminal justice intervention in the United States To the contrary, support for a criminal justice response to domestic violence was also part of a long-term trend in the United States toward "law-and-order" approaches to social problems. This trend is reflected in domestic funding priorities and in polling data probing how U.S. citizens believe the government should react to "social deviance." The propensity to rely on coercive legal powers to "solve" multidimensional social problems is illustrated by the "war on drugs," "get-tough" policies on juvenile crime, and the treatment of drunk driving as a law enforcement issue primarily. In each case, there is little evidence that criminal justice intervention is particularly effective, particularly when compared with alternative prevention and treatment models. Of course, this does not mean criminal justice intervention is not effective with domestic violence. But it does remind us of a point we made earlier, that efficacy is not the sole factor that is sustaining the current emphasis.

The overall approach to domestic violence also reflects broader societal trends. One such trend is to seek official retribution for a range of acts that were once considered "private" or "outside the law" because they occurred in family life. Child abuse and homosexuality fall into this category as well as domestic violence. A concurrent trend involves a shift in decision making in these cases. In the past, it was assumed that justice was best served when police, prosecutors, judges, or other professionals allocated resources or sanctions based on their review of individual circumstances. Today, however, it is increasingly common to find these actors constrained by legislative mandates in decisions that range from whether to arrest and whom to sentence and for how long they should be imprisoned and whom should be released. Interestingly, although there is a new political imperative to protect victims and provide a forum where they can express their fear, hurt, or anger, as Garland (2001) points out, "the crime victim now is a much more representative character whose experience is taken to be common and collective rather than individual and atypical" (p. 144). Thus, domestic violence victims often are viewed as part of a generic group exhibiting typical traits rather than as unique individuals who have been harmed in specific ways by identifiable offenders.

Several other basic questions that were first raised in the 1980s have still not been answered definitively, including when police should arrest offenders, the conditions under which prosecutors should charge or refuse to drop cases, and when and how judges should sentence offenders rather than send them to counseling. Even so, our understanding of domestic violence has been considerably advanced by recently developed typologies of offenders and by a deeper appreciation for the range of tactics deployed by offenders, many of which have yet to be incorporated into criminal law. The most popular of these typologies was developed by sociologist Michael Johnson (1995, 2008). Johnson set out to reconcile discrepancies between population-based surveys and point-of-service data drawn from courts, arrest statistics, and shelters. Where the former reported high rates of perpetration by female partners as well as of "mutual" abuse, the latter left a consistent picture of domestic violence as a crime committed largely by men. Johnson argued that the discrepant findings reflected two different general types of abuse. The first type of abuse he described was "common" or "situational" couple violence and was largely limited to physical assault and emotional abuse. The second involved a range of control tactics in addition to physical assault. He termed the latter behavioral dynamic "intimate terrorism." Either or both partners might engage in "situational" violence, although women were more likely to sustain injuries in these cases. But men were the primary perpetrators of "intimate terrorism," the type of abuse most likely to prompt help-seeking. Johnson used the term "violent resistance" to characterize situations where victims used force in response to a partner who was violent and controlling and termed situations where both partners were violent and controlling "mutual violent control."

A similar distinction was offered by Evan Stark (2007). Stark subdivided situational couple violence into two separate, but occasionally overlapping, dynamics, one of which he termed "fights" and the other "partner assaults." For Stark, assaults are distinguished from fights by the intent for which force is employed (to instill fear, hurt, control, and dominate a partner rather than to express anger or resolve differences, for example) and the perception of victimization by the targeted party. Although "fights" may come to police attention as a form of domestic violence, Stark does not consider them a type of abuse for which domestic violence intervention is properly applied. Stark used "coercive control" rather than "intimate terrorism" to describe the use of multiple tactics (such as intimidation, isolation, and control) alongside physical assault, and argued that coercive control may exist even in the absence of physical assault. Like Johnson, Stark contended that coercive control was a tactic used by male offenders primarily, largely because they played off existing sexual inequalities. But he placed a greater emphasis than Johnson on the structural deprivations that partners use to establish control (such as taking a partner's money or depriving her of access to transportation or communication). Several other typologies are reviewed in this book. Suffice it to say that much empirical work must be done before we can determine the utility and applicability of these categories or whether subdividing domestic violence in these ways moves us toward or away from more definitive and nuanced interventions. In any case, the work on typologies introduces an argument we will make in the subsequent discussion, that a straightforward equation of partner abuse with physical violence may not accurately reflect the dynamics in many, perhaps most, abusive relationships or fully capture the harms inflicted or the motivation that causes victims to call police or seek other types of assistance.

We have many more clues today than we did 30 years ago about which facets of our response are most helpful. We believe that literally thousands of women, men, and children owe the fact that they are alive to the overwhelming shift in legal reforms in this field and the improved responsiveness of criminal justice agencies, the availability of shelters, and shifts in the response by health care and social service agencies. There are now a broad spectrum of innovative programs to protect, assist, or otherwise support abused women and their children. Unfortunately, these programs are not universally available and most remain vulnerable to the vagaries of local, state, and federal budgets.

Challenges to a Criminal Justice Approach

An important question we address in this book is what the impact has been of relying so heavily on criminal justice intervention to limit domestic violence. Part of the answer involves changes in rates of partner abuse as a result of criminal justice intervention, an issue to which we give considerable attention. But equally important is how this emphasis has shaped societal perceptions of the problem, including the willingness of individuals to accept responsibility for addressing abuse in their own lives and communities or for supporting local efforts at mitigation or prevention. Does the view of domestic violence as a crime make it more or less likely that hospital patients will discuss it with their health providers, for instance? A related issue involves how the primacy of criminal justice affects the decision of other public or community-based institutions to intervene. Are health providers or child welfare workers likely to make domestic violence a priority if they believe it falls solely in the province of criminal justice or that they may be called as witnesses in abuse cases?

Relegating domestic violence to the criminal justice and legal system also has another unintended effect with far-reaching implications for intervention. Filtering the societal response to domestic violence through the criminal justice system reinforces a widespread proclivity to equate partner abuse with discrete assaults and then to measure the seriousness of these assaults by the level of injury inflicted. This occurs because violence falls squarely in the comfort zone of policing and because prosecution and the criminal courts function best when they target specific acts with tangible consequences. Domestic violence statutes define partner abuse as a form of assault that is only different from stranger assault because of the offender's relationship to the victim. Although few such statutes include the infliction of injury as part of the definition of a domestic violence crime, as a practical matter, criminal justice and legal resources often are rationed based on a crude calculus of physical harms.

There are at least three problems with equating domestic violence with discrete or injurious criminal assaults. The most obvious is that abuse is repeated in most cases. Although this often is ascribed to "recidivism," the proportion of offenders who "repeat" is so high—much more than 90% according to some estimates—that it may be both more accurate and more useful to frame domestic violence as a chronic or ongoing behavioral pattern that has more in common with a chronic health problem like diabetes or heart disease than with an acute and time-limited problem like the flu. The reconceptualization of domestic violence as ongoing may be hard to reconcile with traditional models of crime that highlight isolated offenses. But it has far-reaching implications for intervention. To continue our medical analogy, imagine the costs as well as the problems created if physicians did a full medical evaluation every time a patient with a diagnosis of heart disease presented with one of the symptoms. By contrast, once the chronic nature of the problem is recognized, intervention can be proactive as well as comprehensive. At present, victims who repeatedly call the police may be labeled as "repeaters" whose complaints can be taken less and less seriously as abuse escalates. By contrast, if its ongoing nature is incorporated into the definition of abuse, then, continuing and even proactive contact with victims would be viewed as a critical facet of help.

Serious injury and fatality are tragic outcomes of domestic violence. But a second problem with the violent incident definition develops because most abuse incidents are noninjurious and seem relatively minor from a criminal justice or legal standpoint if observed in isolation. For many victims, the significance of these violent acts may have less to do with the emergent nature of a given incident than with the cumulative effect of multiple incidents on their sense of autonomy and security in the world. Victims who experience multiple, but low-level assaults may experience high levels of entrapment and fear. But when justice professionals view these effects only in relation to a given abuse incident (which is usually relatively minor), the victim may seem to be exaggerating the situation and not be taken seriously. Victims also may minimize abuse if they equate "real" domestic violence with an injurious assault.

A third problem with the violent incident definition develops because the emphasis on discrete assaults can mask the co-occurrence of a range of other harmful tactics that may compliment physical abuse in establishing one partner's domination of the other and compromise a victim's capacity to escape or resist abuse. These complimentary tactics also may be minimized because the need for "proof beyond a reasonable doubt" in a criminal justice system tends to bring injurious violence to the fore rather than the multifaceted behavior that comprises the abuse for victims and their children.

These points are meant to illustrate an important point in the book, that however necessary or important, the criminal justice framework can be a very blunt and inexact instrument to rely on to stop or prevent the ongoing pattern of coercion and control in relationships.

Should Criminal Justice Intervention Be Victim-Centered?

At the heart of the criminal justice response is the dichotomy between "victim" and "offender." Given the mission of criminal justice, including the belief by key actors that the primary role of police and prosecution is to protect society as a whole from crimes against the public order, it is hardly surprising that the justice system has emphasized the identification, arrest, deterrence, and rehabilitation of offenders. But there also has been immense pressure for the system to assist and empower domestic violence victims. Whether to be victim-centered and how to do this in a way that does not undermine other goals of criminal justice presents another set of challenges addressed in the book.

In keeping with a "tough-on-crime" approach and deterrence-based theories of offending and reoffending, the emphasis in criminal justice intervention has been on tactical issues such as the certainty of apprehension, deterrence via arrest, aggressive prosecution, forced attendance in batterer treatment programs, and "target hardening" via issuance of restraining orders. The general premise behind this emphasis is that crime is an offense against the state, hence, that the interests of any given victim are secondary. The result is that victim assistance has been relegated to an ancillary status in criminal proceedings and that relatively little funding is available for direct victim support. Unfortunately, this model fails to empower, or even protect, many victims of domestic violence. As this book will explore in detail, victims whose preferences are not followed, whether it be to arrest or not arrest, are those who are most dissatisfied. The lack of sensitivity to a victim's wishes comes into play when a policy determination is made to process all offenders through mandatory arrest and/or mandatory prosecution even if such a course is not a victim's preference or even, for a variety of reasons, is not objectively in her best interests.

In this book, we argue that this "mission-centric" emphasis can be shortsighted and that the criminal justice system *should* consider the impact of intervention on individual victims. Unlike bank robbery or even stranger assault where the crime is an isolated event against a victim who is relatively anonymous, in "private" crimes such as domestic violence, victims disproportionately bear a crime's "costs." Interestingly, the fact that the largest burden of abuse falls on individual victims was an implicit rationale for nonintervention early on. Some believed that partner violence was a "private matter" and a by-product of family conflicts that participants could and should resolve "informally." Some observers believed that because victims had entered the abusive relationship voluntarily, they had "made their bed" and now should "lie in it." There also were positive rationales for noninterference based on respect for the right of adult women to make their own decisions about the sort of troubles they dealt with in their personal lives. Another reason why listening to victim voices is imperative originates from the fact that we have yet to find a foolproof way to deny an offender access to the partner he victimized. The "privilege" of intimacy often affords offenders a special knowledge of a victim's whereabouts and vulnerabilities that is rarely available in anonymous crimes. Since most offenders remain at large for some period of time, even if they are eventually convicted and sent to jail, or receive relatively minor sanctions, arrest may not enhance victim safety, even if it is followed by conviction and/or assignment to a BIP. It is a well-tested adage of the advocacy movement that victims themselves are the best judge of what keeps them safe. Finally, as we explain in the text, enormous burdens often are placed on victims at each stage of criminal justice processing.

Following a victim's wishes with respect to arrest or prosecution need not mean doing nothing. Once victims initiate contact with the justice or court system, they should have access to a range of supports and resources regardless of whether an offender is arrested or prosecuted. In opposition to our view, some respected researchers argue that, given the structural and organizational capacities of justice agencies, a traditional crime-fighting approach is preferable to a victim-centered, multipronged approach to domestic violence. Jeffrey Fagan (1996), for example, argues that the criminal justice system functions best when its primary focus is on the detection, control, and punishment of offenders, batterers in this instance, and it has minimal and only indirect involvement in providing services to victims (i.e., battered women). His reasoning is that trying to factor in victim experiences and rights or the rehabilitation of offenders conflicts with the primary mission of these institutions and confounds their efficacy. Ironically, this broad emphasis on serving victims as well as on punishing offenders can inadvertently make it easier for these agencies to marginalize "domestic" cases as they did in the past, turning case handling into low-status "social work" rather than "crime fighting."

Another challenge posed by the prevailing economy of offenders and victims originates from the complexity and ambiguity of many abusive relationships. For the criminal justice system to operate within statutory requirements, crimes must have offenders and victims who can be clearly demarcated based on objective criteria. This determination, in turn, implies that the status of the persons involved is not only identifiable but also constant. Unfortunately, research suggests that the offender–victim dichotomy is hard to sustain in a significant proportion of abusive relationships. For example, in an examination of 2,000 police reports during a 10-year period for *all* assaults (not just domestic), researchers found that 18% to 20% (depending on the year examined) of victims also had been seen by the criminal justice system as offenders (Hotaling & Buzawa, 2001).

Because the law's definition of a domestic violence assault relies so heavily on violent acts, it is hard to distinguish abusive assaults that merit police intervention from mere fights, where the use of force is typically noninjurious and may reflect a maladaptive response to family conflicts rather than an effort to coerce, control, or dominate a partner. Once persons are publicly recognized as participants in violence, they may suffer the stigma associated with being labeled. Everyone is familiar with the negative effects of being labeled a "wife beater." But being identified as an abuse "victim" also can have a downside. However sympathetic the general public may be with persons who have been victimized, in certain communities, being a "victim" may signal that the particular person "can be had" (i.e., exploited) by others. Individuals may resist the label "victim" because they associate it with weakness. Moreover, a range of characteristics and behaviors may be associated in the public's mind with being a "worthy" victim, including a person's race, age, social class, looks, and their propensity for self-assertion or aggression. Moreover, once someone is a "victim," he or she may be expected to enact these stereotypes, which is a constraint that often extends to their perceived eligibility for vital services (Wuest & Merritt-Gray, 1999).

The Evolution of This Text

This is the fourth edition of this text. Each edition has been updated and revised, and in this edition, we go even further by complementing the emphasis on criminal justice and law with chapters on how domestic violence affects children and health and on the roles played by the health care system, child welfare, and family court in the societal response. In part, we have broadened the focus to reflect a growing realization that relying so heavily on criminal justice and law may not have proved as effective as was initially hoped.

Interestingly, each edition of this text has appeared at a watershed of sorts in the history of the domestic violence revolution. We try to capture these moments for our readers, particularly in terms of what they imply for the criminal justice response to domestic violence, as well as to anticipate where things are headed.

The first edition of this text was published in 1990, 3 years before the historical signing of VAWA by President Clinton. In a very small way, the goal of the text, to synthesize existing knowledge about the criminal justice response, was the intellectual counterpart to the political goal of VAWA, namely, to bring together the diverse strands of criminal justice intervention under a single-policy umbrella.

The target audiences for the first edition of this text included students and practitioners in criminal justice and other social sciences who had little prior knowledge about domestic violence and those who had a substantive interest in domestic violence but little sense of how the response by police and the courts fit into the broader workings of the criminal justice system. The initial focus solely on criminal justice reflected the over-all societal emphasis in the United States on defining domestic violence as a criminal assault involving partners or other family members, the propensity to frame the participants as "offenders" and "victims," the widespread reliance on court orders to protect victims and on police intervention, and primarily on arrest, as the front-line intervention that would complement the safety afforded by shelters. The focus on criminal justice also reflected another reality: Starting with hearings and a report by the U.S. Commission on Civil Rights in 1978, the criminal justice system also had borne the brunt of criticism for the inadequate societal response to domestic violence.

By 1993, most localities had already adapted so-called mandatory arrest policies, although debate about the wisdom and efficacy of these policies was still widespread. Although some commentators questioned whether domestic violence should be treated as a crime rather than as a problem in family dynamics, the most trenchant criticism highlighted the threat these policies posed to victim autonomy and police discretion and the possibility that making arrest standard procedure might exacerbate racial bias in policing. Many jurisdictions also had initiated BIPs, although criminal courts were not yet relying on referrals to counseling as the preferred alternative to jail to nearly the extent they are today. Although some research suggested these programs could reduce subsequent violence, the quality of evaluations was poor. Moreover, advocacy organizations remained skeptical about BIPs, both because they questioned their efficacy in reducing violence and because they worried that money spent to rehabilitate offenders might draw funds away from front-line protections for victims, including shelters. In addition to mandatory arrest, many cutting-edge issues of the day involved the sensitivity of police, prosecutors, judges, and other front-line providers to victims, the wisdom of so-called dedicated domestic violence prosecution, the interstate enforcement of protection orders issued by civil or criminal courts, and whether "no-drop" prosecution should be widely adapted.

The second edition, published in 1996, focused on the nature and extent of the rapidly evolving criminal justice system and offered tentative observations about the opportunities and limitations of the various approaches being attempted at the time of its publication.

In the third edition, published in 2003, we noted a proliferation of research evaluating the impact of innovative intervention strategies and the unanticipated problems originating from aggressive intervention.

In the decade since the first edition was released, it also had become clear that the efficacy of arrest, prosecution, and other components of the criminal justice response depend on their interplay with other components of the societal response, including health, child welfare, and the family courts. The third edition presented the various elements of the criminal justice response as if each could be evaluated in isolation (as if we could answer questions, like "Does arrest end violence?" solely by comparing the propensity for continued violence among arrested offenders with offenders who are not arrested, for instance). This was the dominant approach in the field, and we felt we should reflect it. In reality, however, there are few communities in the United States where "arrest" exists in a vacuum. Even if an individual offender is not deterred by arrest, for instance, the police response may open a door to a range of services for victims as well as to counseling for the batterer. Thus, the question of whether arrest is an effective deterrent is increasingly secondary to the assessment of which "package" of services is available, and which supports are most likely to inhibit subsequent abuse. This is why the fourth edition includes chapters on key non–criminal justice responses by BIPs, the child welfare system, family courts, and health care agencies. We cover both the strategies that guide intervention by these agencies and the knowledge base that supports these interventions. We also identify the limits of these interventions. Key issues in these chapters are the health dimensions and consequences of adult and child victimization; the institutional response by health care, child welfare, and the family court; and whether and how the harms caused by domestic violence are ameliorated by these institutional responses. As with criminal justice, an outstanding question is whether certain interventions do more harm to victims than good. Examples include mandatory reporting of domestic violence by health providers and the removal of children from mothers who have been abused.

A primary goal of this edition, as with the earlier editions, is to assist the reader to understand the cultural, political, and organizational contexts that shape how criminal justice agencies relate to one another as well as to other societal agencies or institutions, historically and at the present time. This edition will explore the individual components of the criminal justice system, how these components interact, and how these interactions affect outcomes.

Organization of This Edition

Most chapters have been substantially rewritten from the earlier editions. An obvious exception are the chapters on the historical precedents and the classic response to domestic violence. In accordance with the sweeping changes undertaken by the criminal justice system, we have significantly expanded our emphasis on efforts made by the prosecutors' offices and courts as well as on strategies to protect victims through victim advocacy and other services. We also have provided expanded coverage of the empirical research on the efficacy of such interventions with offenders, and of the risk factors that predict both offending and reoffending behaviors.

Perhaps the most significant addition to the original text is the new chapter on the impact of domestic violence on children and on the responses to the threats by two institutions that are most directly concerned with protecting children, the child welfare system and the family court. Research on how abuse affects children has been a major subsection of the domestic violence field for several decades at least. But earlier research was deficient in many respects. For one thing, estimates of the "overlap" of domestic violence and harms to children varied from a relatively modest 6.5% to a staggering 82%, and the number of children affected from 3.3 million to 10 million. For another, definitions of harms to children ran the gamut from physical harms to long-term behavioral changes that were difficult to link etiologically to abuse exposure. Moreover, generalizations about the harms to children were often based on unsubstantiated reports from mothers in shelter or, conversely, on the results of psychological tests that were not verified for individual children or compared with scores before exposure occurred. Perhaps most importantly, few studies factored out the possible role of other forms of potentially traumatic exposure (such as divorce, actual child abuse, or community violence) with similar effects. Research has improved considerably since these earlier editions. There is now credible evidence regarding the extent of children's exposure—with recent studies showing that nearly one-in-four intimate partner violence cases involved a child witness (Finkelhor, Turner, Ormrod, Hamby, & Kracke, 2009). Moreover, these harms to children have been increasingly targeted by a range of institutional actors, including those in criminal justice and the law. Finally, although a causal link between childhood exposure to partner violence and adult violence is almost certainly weaker than is generally believed and may not even rank among the most important etiological factors in domestic violence, even if a small proportion of exposed children develop psychological or behavioral problems as a result of living in a home where partner violence occurs, it is significant numerically, which justifies our concern.

This text is structurally organized as follows:

Chapter 2 explores why the definition of domestic abuse, perhaps more than any criminal act, should encompass a very wide range of behaviors and apply to all forms of intimacy, regardless of marital or living status. We will discuss how, along with the direct impact of enforcement actions, case processing requirements might have indirectly defined the parameters of "permissible" contact by only criminalizing certain violent conduct, while conversely, tacitly condoning harassment or other strategies of coercive control—actions that in practice rarely result in arrest or prosecution. Thus, definitions are important not merely for what they highlight, but also for the sorts of behaviors, relationships, and consequences they throw into the shadows.

Chapter 2 identifies gaps in the behaviors and relationships covered by domestic violence criminal codes. We contrast the propensity for criminal codes to define violence as *individual acts,* usually a physical assault or threat of physical harm intended to cause physical harm, with the growing realization by researchers that domestic violence is more accurately conceptualized as including a range of behaviors that coerce and control victims, many of which currently are not recognized as criminal. These behaviors may entail isolating victims from resources or supports; exploiting them financially, sexually, or emotionally; humiliating them; intimidating them through a range of threatening behaviors; and using various means to control them physically or psychologically. Although not directly causing physical injury, by undermining a victim's ability to resist or escape abuse, these behaviors can greatly increase the likelihood that a victim will be vulnerable to injury or even death. In this perspective, it is the *pattern* of violent and abusive behavior within the relationship that constitutes domestic violence rather than the individual acts of perpetrators. The relationships included under these acts also vary from state to state, sometimes only including married individuals, or alternatively, including some or all of the following: current and past intimate partners, anyone living in the same residence, children, siblings, any other "family members," and/or any relative. Nothing we say here or elsewhere in the text suggests ending or even significantly limiting the role of criminal justice intervention. However, we do suggest that criminal justice and law enforcement are unlikely to prevent domestic violence or even revictimization unless their focus is clear and consistent and they are parts of a comprehensive societal response.

Chapter 3 discusses the historical context of domestic violence. There have been significant variations in how societies have responded to domestic violence, starting with ancient peoples. But close inspection reveals these responses to have revolved around a single theme, the right of the male patriarch or his surrogate to use violence and other means to enforce his will on the women and children under his control. Male domination in family or intimate relationships was alternately sanctioned by culture, religion, law, or some combination, making governmental support for abuse implicit, and faced periodic challenges from liberal governments, social critics, or movements to improve women's lot. Nevertheless, the domestic violence revolution that sets the stage for this book has been far and away the most effective in eliciting reform.

Chapter 4 posits that actual acts of violence often are merely a part of an overall pattern of behavior. Although a given offender may select a particular means of coercion or control from all available options, the chronic nature of most abuse and the complexity of the dynamic that typically unfolds makes it unrealistic to hope that either party will simply stop or withdraw "in the moment." Conversely, any effective societal intervention must confront this complexity either by complementing situational sanctions with a larger strategy of prevention, building from the bottom-up so to speak, or as part of a coordinated community response in which criminal justice is deployed, as needed, as part of a multi-institutional strategy designed to prevent revictimization and reoffending. We see funding for prevention and for criminal justice intervention as part of a piece rather than as alternative policy initiatives.

Chapter 5 discusses the long history of societal neglect of this problem. Prior to the 1970s, the statutory structure for handling domestic violence could charitably be described as "benevolent neglect" of "family problems." State assistance for victims, if any, went to traditional social welfare agencies that handled a variety of family problems, most of which were assumed to originate from poverty, ignorance, or ill-breeding. Not only did these agencies lack expertise in domestic violence, but also they often took the occurrence of violence as an occasion to strengthen family bonds, in many cases exacerbating women's abuse. Managing violence against women was considered beyond the purview of government; as a result, the failure of government to assume responsibility for the safety of women and children in their homes was not noticed. To the contrary, it was widely believed that intervening to protect women and children except in the most egregious cases could do incalculable harms to family structure and so, by extension, to society as a whole.

Chapter 6 identifies the factors that changed the traditional criminal justice response. The frequency of calls for help to police suggests that the general public viewed domestic violence as a problem meriting state intervention. Nevertheless, little was done to address it, let alone to control its incidence. By the early 1970s, however, the climate had changed and a range of publications, including research monographs, news articles, and advocacy papers criticized justice agencies for their failure to deter future acts of violence or respond to requests for assistance from victims. Changing the criminal justice response proved much more difficult than criticizing it, however.

Reforms in the criminal justice system were elicited by a historically unique constellation of the grassroots activists who formed the battered women's movement, policymakers across a broad political spectrum, and those law professors Elizabeth Schneider (2000) called "feminist lawmakers." Resistance to change was deeply rooted in organizational culture. Police and prosecution were committed to using their discretion to filter out cases that lacked sufficient public purpose to merit a major expenditure of resources. In effect, they had used this discretion historically to eliminate not only cases where there was insufficient evidence for an arrest or conviction, but also those considered unimportant or unworthy of their time. Domestic violence fell squarely in this latter group, making police arrest-averse and instilling a strong bias in favor of dismissal among prosecutors.

Chapter 7 hones in on a core issue, how the criminalization of domestic violence led first to an emphasis on arrest as the "solution" to domestic violence and, more recently, as a required initial response. The immediate effect of such legislation was to give primary responsibility for the suppression of ongoing domestic violence to the criminal justice system, the very institution that had neglected the problem historically, and to do so by constraining discretion in the decision to arrest, which is a core value in policing.

Chapter 8 focuses on the implementation and the diverse impact of the new pro-arrest statutes on police arrest practices. We argue that some proponents of more aggressive intervention had a limited understanding of how laws or policies that mandated a particular response would affect victims, especially in those states or police departments that *require* officers to make an arrest in cases of intimate partner violence. The chapter highlights an unintended consequence of these policies, that many victims feel disempowered by their inability to control the outcome of a call for police assistance. To reiterate earlier points, some victims may feel control over the arrest decision provides bargaining room with an abusive partner or may fear the financial consequences of arrest for themselves or their abusive partner, particularly if he is unable to work or she must miss work to appear in court. In addition, victims who choose to remain with offenders may find their relationship harmed, whereas those leaving may find themselves in greater danger from the offender. As a result, victim reporting may diminish, and in such jurisdictions, a smaller population of victims may actually be served than are served if police discretion is exercised in the victim's interest. This chapter also addresses another serious and unintended consequence of current arrest policies, the dramatic increase in the arrest of women as well as an increase in dual arrests (e.g., the arrest of both parties).

Chapter 9 focuses on the breadth of statutory changes since the 1970s, including legislative reform in all 50 states. Although the new statutes differed markedly in their scope and substance, they were designed to effect profound structural changes in the response of government agencies to domestic violence. Such changes have primarily been concentrated in three areas: (1) the police response, (2) the handling of cases by prosecutors, and to a lesser extent, the (3) judiciary methods of educating the public about the problem and providing state funding for shelters and direct assistance to its victims. An additional set of reforms supported batterer intervention. More recently, criminal codes have evolved to include "stalking" or "harassment" as forms of abuse. These statutes move beyond the equation of domestic violent with physical assault. But they are not as widely used as the original statutes, often are inconsistent, and are set standards of proof that are difficult to meet. Little is known about whether these statutes are an effective way to combat abuse or even whether their use is an improvement over the statutes focused only on violent incidents. We conclude this chapter by asking whether the focus on identifying violent offenders, determining guilt, and using criminal justice sanctions to prevent reoffending have clarified or obscured the larger societal concerns about the control of domestic violence.

Chapter 10 focuses on the increasing attention and significance attributed to the role of the prosecutor. As practitioners and policymakers realized that the mere arrest of an offender was rarely sufficient to deter reoffending and/or protect victims, the focus shifted to the practices and efficacy of prosecutors. As with police, so here too have changed expectations led to attempts to mandate aggressive prosecution in domestic violence cases. Although legislative mandates with respect to prosecution are more problematic than similar mandates for police, there has been a massive increase in the proportion of cases prosecuted. However, victim cooperation continues to be a key factor in determining whether prosecution is successful.

Even more than police, prosecutors have the capacity to provide key services for victims other than taking a case to trial. Specifically, they can help reduce victim fear, provide a degree of ongoing protection, and facilitate access to needed services, including advocacy. Many victims may be safer as the result of prosecution. But most offenders continue their abuse, many are undeterred by conviction, and some become even more violent. The solution is not to forego prosecution but to combine aggressive prosecution of high-risk offenders with enhanced efforts to ensure victim safety. There is some evidence that we can identify a subpopulation of low-risk offenders who are unlikely to reoffend, regardless of whether the case is prosecuted. In these instances, the best course from the standpoint of both the victim and society may be to follow a victim's preference.

Chapter 11 discusses restraining orders and how civil courts work to address elements of domestic violence that are not specified in criminal statutes. Even more effective relief might be provided by expanding the application of other statutes not expressly linked to domestic violence at the moment, including harassment or stalking laws.

Chapter 12 covers the role of the judiciary. Determining the extent and nature of judicial intervention depends on which of many conflicting goals is considered paramount: retribution, rehabilitation, or satisfaction and safety of the victim. Historically, the response fluctuated between punitive responses to domestic violence—ensure arrest, prosecution, and conviction—and violence suppression strategies to deter aggressive behavior without regard to their punitive nature.

There have been tremendous changes in the judicial response, but the diversity and inconsistency of these responses make it hard to generalize across jurisdictions. Some jurisdictions prefer the traditional model, with domestic violence cases heard in a criminal court setting where the offender and victim can be clearly demarcated. Other jurisdictions favor a more holistic approach, hearing all misdemeanor domestic violence cases in a single venue or "domestic violence court," for instance, or combining all matters pertaining to the couple in a single proceeding, including family matters, the "integrated" domestic violence court. This chapter explores these alternative approaches, identifies their varied goals and procedures, and highlights the need for research that explores their relative efficacy.

Chapter 13 focuses on the courts' most common disposition, mandated attendance at a BIP. Currently, most batterers attending these programs are there as part of a judicial sentence. We assess the general efficacy of such programs in reducing violence as well as their relative success with specific types of offenders. Proponents of these programs continue to insist on their general efficacy, at least in reducing repeat violence in the long term. Our conclusion, however, is that these programs do not seem to deter many types of offenders, specifically those who are chronic and severe batterers. In response to these concerns, there is a growing trend to use these programs to ensure "offender accountability" rather than to "rehabilitate" offenders. We assess the wisdom of this approach.

Research since the publication of our third edition continues to show that, no matter how innovative or enhanced, serious domestic violence cannot be effectively addressed unless the criminal justice system works in concert with the range of government, nonprofit, and community-based agencies and programs. Chapters 14 and 15 address the three other institutions that are central in the lives of domestic violence victims, the health care, child welfare, and family court systems.

It was by no means inevitable that the domestic violence revolution in the United States would rely so heavily on the criminal justice system. In countries where the welfare state is more developed than it is in the United States, England, or Scotland, for instance, arrest is just one piece of a complex web of services to which domestic violence victims have access. In Scandinavia, support for victims plays a more important role than sanctioning offenders. So it is worth asking why police were so central to the societal response in the United States. One obvious reason is that, with the exception of health crises, the police are the default agency contacted in the midst of an emergency. A related factor is that their services are free and are available 24/7, which is an important fact since only a small proportion of family assault calls occur on weekdays during "office hours" between 8:00 a.m. and 5:00 p.m. Also important is the nature of the crisis precipitated by domestic violence. In the midst of an assault, many victims want police intervention: Police are easy to contact, respond relatively quickly, make "home visits," and provide a highly visible authority figure to counter the raw power of the abuser. These factors mean that the police often are the source of the family's contact with other local government agencies such as health care or child welfare and that these agencies, in turn, often depend on police referrals for their clientele.

Chapter 14 covers the health dimensions and consequences of domestic violence, the subsequent utilization of health services by victims and related costs, and the development of a health care response. Starting in the late 1970s, a substantial body of research documented the significance of abuse for women's health. Early work focused on physical injury as the most obvious symptom of abusive relationships, showing, for example, that domestic violence was the leading cause of injury for which women sought medical attention (Stark & Flitcraft, 1996). However, comparisons of health utilization by battered and nonbattered women also showed that victims suffered disproportionately from a range of medical, behavioral, and mental health problems in addition to injury, including most notably substance abuse, attempted suicide, depression, and a range of disorders related to the fear and entrapment established by abuse. Although the emphasis on injury pointed toward intervention in hospital emergency rooms, a larger picture of its health consequences suggested that domestic violence required clinical violence intervention across the board, ranging from health to mental health to public health services.

Many of the same factors that defined the police as first responders in domestic violence cases disqualified other services, at least initially, including health care. Although hospital emergency rooms are usually open around the clock 7 days a week, they present victims with any number of obstacles to access. These obstacles include long waits, the need for self-transport, ambiguity about where domestic violence ranks in relation to the sorts of trauma for which emergency medicine was established, and limited services for the uninsured or underinsured. Through much of the 1970s and 1980s, medical providers were much less likely to be aware of domestic violence than the police and even more reluctant to become involved with "family problems." Thus, they responded symptomatically, providing medication for pain but doing nothing to enhance women's awareness or safety.

Today, some, but by no means all, of the barriers to accessing health services have been removed. Starting with the introduction of domestic violence into professional education and training, medicine, nursing, psychology, psychiatry, and social work have introduced a range of innovative programs to identify and respond more appropriately to the adult and child victims of abuse. Most agencies where these professionals work have adapted formal protocols for recognizing, assessing, and providing services to victims as well as for interfacing with the criminal justice system, shelters, and other service agencies where appropriate. Still, major challenges to mounting an appropriate health system response remain.

Chapter 15 starts with a remarkable fact, that domestic violence may be the most prevalent context for child abuse and neglect. We explore the many ways in which exposure to abuse can harm children as well as the resiliency of battered mothers and their children in the face of abuse. Despite the importance of domestic violence for children's well-being, the child welfare system and the family court—the two institutions most directly charged with protecting children and their "best interest"—have hesitated to get involved in partner abuse, in part because they have feared that doing so would embroil them in political controversy. The traditional focus of child welfare on women as "mothers" and its historical move away from criminal justice toward counseling and parent education has left enormous ambiguity about whether its function in these cases was to protect children by removing them from the potential danger posed by abuse or to broaden its perspective to encompass women's safety as well. A similar dilemma has faced the family court. Following congressional guidance, many states have adapted rules mandating that their family courts give significant weight to domestic violence in custody disputes. But many of these same states also have emphasized shared or co-parenting as the most desirable outcome of divorce for children. The dilemmas faced by the child welfare and family court systems often are borne by victimized women.

Conclusion

The goal of this edition is to track the domestic violence revolution largely, but not exclusively, through the prism of the criminal justice and legal response. The text has evolved alongside the societal response. In an ideal world, three decades of intervention would yield a finite picture of what works and what does not, and we could simply embrace those programs identified as "best practices" and move on to eliminate partner violence against women. This is not the world in which we live. Some of what has been done to end domestic violence seems to help. However, the effect of much of what has been done remains unclear, with equivocal findings suggesting that the organizational, social, and cultural context in which interventions operate may be as important to their outcome as their content. And some interventions that are widely thought to be effective are probably not. We take a victim-friendly approach and suggest where we *should* go next in our support for victims and our efforts to sanction or otherwise manage offenders. But this text is not designed to promote one type of program, solution, political direction, or philosophy. Rather, it takes stock, asking how we got where we are in our societal response to domestic violence and where we are likely to go next. We will be satisfied if the text helps readers locate these points on their social compass.

The Scope of the Problem

Defining and Measuring Domestic Violence

Chapter Overview

What is the scope of the domestic violence problem? Official data show that despite a period of notable decrease, the trend is now indicating an increase in an already major problem. Moreover official data do not disclose the full extent of the problem as victims often fail to report abuse. This is partially a result of uncertainty over what is meant by domestic violence and how we define it, which has been the topic of considerable discussion among practitioners, researchers, policymakers, feminists, and victim advocates. There are inherent judgments implicit in how we define domestic violence and the limitations imposed by legal definitions. These judgments include variations in the relationships between domestic violence victims and offenders and the types of acts that current definitions encompass. As a result, researchers and government agencies measure domestic violence in different ways. Therefore, this chapter will discuss what we know about factors impacting victim decisions to report domestic abuse.

Survivor

Falling

My mother never told me how it happened—her fall from grace. In high school she was a beauty queen—beautiful, popular, fun. We would look at her scrapbooks together and for a few minutes her eyes would shine, making her look more like the girl in the pictures. Once, I asked her why she didn't have fun like that anymore. She stopped smiling and went back to the ironing.

(Continued)

(Continued)

    I was in high school when I learned the real story—how she had shocked everyone by coming up pregnant in her senior year.

    I was in college when I learned that my dad wasn't the father. He'd married my mother later, to "make an honest woman of her."

    I was working at a shelter when I learned how she'd paid for her respectability. How he'd beaten her up on their wedding night. How he'd knocked her down the stairs when she was eight months pregnant with me.

    Somehow she forgave him, and they went on. But somewhere between the fall from grace and the fall down the stairs, the light left my mother's eyes. I'll never get to ask her about it, though. Twenty-six years later, after an argument with my father, she shot herself in the head.

Source: Artwork and text from *Beating Hearts: Stories of Domestic Violence* featuring "Survivor" by Kate Sartor Hilburn. http://www.beatinghearts.net/exhibit/window.html

What Is Domestic Violence?

Researchers define domestic violence through a wide variety of instruments that the general public depends on to understand the incidence and prevalence of domestic violence, as well as its patterns and trends. Furthermore, there is wide variation in reported rates of intimate partner violence based on the type of survey used and the year(s) it was administered. Although many such studies have been published, we will concentrate on data from several "official sources" and one widely published, if dated, "unofficial" national study that seemed to show a far higher rate of domestic abuse.

Official Survey Data on Domestic Violence

    The National Crime Victimization Survey (NCVS), supported by the Bureau of Justice Statistics (BJS), is the most comprehensive source for data on victimization for individuals 12 years of age and older. Its sample draws on U.S. Census Bureau data and is address based. The same sample is used for 3 years and sampled seven times at 6-month intervals. In 2008, the NCVS reported an average rate of interpersonal, non-fatal victimization as 4.3% for females compared with 0.8% for males (Catalano, Smith, Snyder, & Rand, 2009).

    Available data demonstrate that violence between intimates is a serious long-term problem facing the United States. As shown in Figure 2.1, homicide, the most serious form of domestic violence, remains a persistent problem.

Figure 2.1   Homicides of Intimate Partners by Gender of Victim, 1993–2007

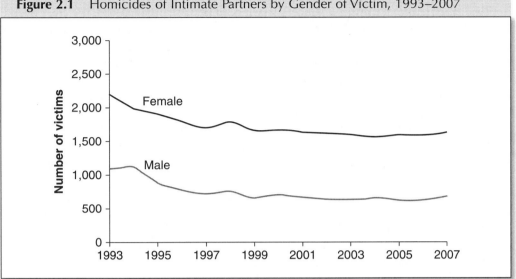

Source: Bureau of Justice Statistics' analysis of the FBI Uniform Crime Reporting Program's Supplementary Homicide Reports, 1993–2007.

Note: Homicide data are voluntarily reported to the FBI by law enforcement agencies active in the Uniform Crime Reporting Program. Offender information (and, therefore, information on the victim-offender relationship) is missing in about 1 in every 3 murders reported. This information is missing because either no offender was identified or information on the identified offender was not sent to the FBI. For this report, missing victim-offender relationships were estimated by assuming that the distribution of relationships in murders for which the relationship was known was the same as in murders for which the relationship information was missing.

This figure demonstrates that despite massive statutory overhauls and a large influx of resources, the number of domestic violence homicides has not declined at all during the last 10 years of available data, 1997–2007.

Data on homicides are perhaps the most complete as the crime is more apparent and easier for officials to identify. Domestic violence clearly plays a major role in homicide. Approximately 33% of female victims of homicides are killed by an intimate partner compared with approximately 4% of male murder victims (Rand & Rennison, 2004). Furthermore, although official BJS data end at calendar year 2007, available figures from early reporting states and municipalities suggest that the rates of domestic homicides have resumed increasing. For example, in 2007, Utah had 18 domestic homicides. In 2008, the number increased to 22 and in 2009 jumped to 27. In accordance with State Coalitions Against Domestic Violence, the State of Maryland increased reported domestic homicides from 52 in 2008 to 75 in 2009.

Several trends seem to be occurring. The economic decline now known as the "Great Recession" has increased the number of individuals and families that are under economic distress. At the same time, police have shown far more relative ability to intervene successfully prior to other types of homicides. As a result, the relative percentage of total homicides related to domestic violence is soaring. In Philadelphia in 2009, the city's overall homicide rate declined 23%, whereas rates for domestic violence homicides increased by 67%. Although that is probably an extreme example, it may show that the relative importance of domestic violence is markedly increasing. Finally, a growing trend, which has been widely televised in the national media, has been former spouses or boyfriends committing domestic homicide (including killing relatives) and then committing suicide nearly immediately afterward. Realistically, if someone is willing to commit such a crime, and to immediately die thereafter, intervention possibilities are, to say the least, rather limited.

Similarly, "official" data on rates of nonfatal violent victimization show that the relative importance of domestic violence compared with other violent crimes has markedly increased even before the full effects of the Great Recession have been tabulated.

The data in Figure 2.2 were provided by BJS, a division of the U.S. Department of Justice charged with maintaining official crime survey statistics. The data show that during a 15-year period, nonfatal assaults against strangers and "friends" or acquaintances have dramatically declined. Meanwhile, measures of violence against intimates, although somewhat declining, do not show nearly as great a decline as other groups. One could state that the good news is that between 1993 and 2008, intimate partner violence against females declined 53% and for males, it declined 54% (Catalano et al., 2009). However, in reality, this decline really occurred between 1993 and 2000. Since 2000, the actual officially reported rates of female domestic violence has, at best, stayed the same and recently has appeared to increase since 2005. As we will see later from more recent data, although they relate to specific communities, an overall increase is shown.

This result is surprising, given that society has placed considerable effort into reforming its responses toward domestic violence—far more than any other specified violent crime. Despite disproportionate efforts directed at limiting domestic violence, official statistics do not really demonstrate a significant impact in reducing domestic violence offenses. It is anticipated that rates for domestic assault in 2009 and 2010 will

Figure 2.2 Nonfatal Violent Victimization Rate by Victim/Offender Relationship and Victim Gender, 1993–2008

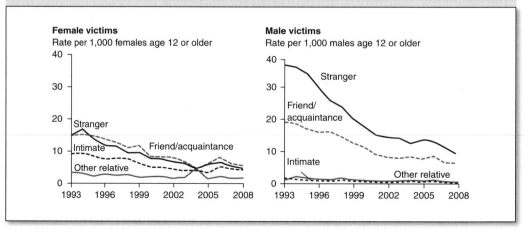

Source: Bureau of Justice Statistics, National Crime Victimization Survey, 1993–2008.

increase when actually published, as rates of domestic violence often are correlated with economic distress (Green, 2010).

Similarly, Figure 2.3 provides official data on the types and numbers of victims of domestic violence through CY2008.

Figure 2.3   Violence by Intimate Partners, by Type of Crime and Gender of the Victim, 2008

	Total		Female		Male	
	Number	Rate	Number	Rate	Number	Rate
Overall violent crime	652,660	2.6	551,590	4.3	101,050	0.8
Rape/sexual assault	44,000	0.2	35,690	0.3^	8,310	0.1^
Robbery	38,820	0.2^	38,820	0.3^	–	–
Aggravated assault	111,530	0.4	70,550	0.5	40,970	0.3^
Simple assault	458,310	1.8	406,530	3.1	51,770	0.4

Source: Bureau of Justice Statistics, National Crime Victimization Survey, 2008.

Note: Victimization rates are per 1,000 persons age 12 or order. The differece in male and female intimate partner victimization rates is significant at the 95% confidence level for overall violent crime, robbery, and simple assault. There is no significant difference in the rate of male and female intimate partner victimization for aggravated assault.

^ Based on 10 or fewer sample cases.

– No cases were present for this category.

As shown in Figure 2.3, women as expected are far more likely than men to be victims of crimes committed by their partners. In approximately 90% of the cases, females are the victims of assaults, with the remainder split fairly evenly between those that are robbed and those that are sexually assaulted.

These figures are clearly underreported. As we will discuss later in this chapter, it is well known that domestic violence crimes tend as a group to be among the crimes least reported to the police. Within the overall category of overall underreported domestic abuse cases, the number of marital sexual assaults is especially likely to be grossly underreported, as numerous studies have shown that sexual assaults by an intimate partner are even less likely than other sexual assaults to be reported by women—especially by women subjected to so-called marital rape.

It also is worthwhile to note that although it is far more prevalent among women, men report being victimized at a rate of 4 per 1,000 persons over the age of 12 years compared with a rate of 3.1 per 1,000 persons for women.

Figure 2.3 highlights that the high number of assaults has resulted in massive numbers of injured and dead victims. It has been estimated that women were injured in approximately half of the domestic assaults committed between 1993 and 2004 (Catalano, 2006; Rennison & Welchans, 2000) and that one third were male victims (Catalano, 2006). The rate of serious injury was approximately 5% for both females and males and 43% and 31% for minor injuries, respectively (Catalano, 2006). However, we also know that the number of incidents coming to police attention has grown considerably in recent years. Legislation, departmental policies, changing public values, increased criminal justice personnel, and resources have all contributed to an increase in assaults reported to police as well as recorded.

Controversies Over Definitions

Before going farther and commenting on the prevalence of domestic violence, we need to discuss the fundamental controversies regarding the definition of domestic violence. These continue despite years of public attention, much research, and an active legislative effort to develop explicit statutory definitions. There are societal definitions, legal definitions, and research definitions—all of which differ. However, they all involve two primary considerations. First, *what are the relationships considered in identifying cases of "domestic violence"?* Second, *what acts actually should be defined as "domestic violence" or perhaps as "domestic abuse"?*

Statutorily Defined Relationships

What is not often acknowledged is the complexity of diverse relationships that domestic violence statutes encompass. Most people believe that "domestic violence" should be interchangeable with, and limited to, "wife battering" or "spousal abuse" (e.g., an assault between intimate or perhaps prior intimate partners). However, as we shall see, a variety of domestic violence statutes use definitions that cover a far broader range of relationships.

Initial domestic violence statutes did limit relationships by marital status. Only married or previously married couples were covered. Most states have long since revised initial statutes to encompass offenses involving parent(s) or caretakers(s), dependent children, siblings, grandparents, and grandchildren. Therefore, it is safe to say that currently state domestic violence statutes address a far broader range of relationships than simply intimate partner violence.

This is troublesome in that "official statistics" unless carefully scrubbed may be inaccurate. Also, other intrafamily violence may be severe and require intervention. However, the characteristics, causes, and intervention for violence against children or elderly parents may differ markedly from intimate partner violence. Moreover, although it is important to place intimate partner violence in the broader context of violent behavior, as we will see, there are different historical and societal bases for such violence and there are different overall patterns of occurrence that distinguish this type of violence from violence in these other relationships.

Normally, we would not care about the legislature use of definitional "shorthand" to aggregate most nonstranger violent crimes under the rubric of "domestic violence." Unfortunately, official data on domestic violence often suffer from aggregating these other problems.

As a result, conclusions drawn about intimate partner violence from official data remain questionable on a variety of critical variables, such as injury, criminal justice decision making, and revictimization. In addition, it is very difficult to comparatively use overall rates of victimization and comparisons based on official data.

Fortunately, the federal government has relied on different sources for data. Using the National Incident Based Reporting System (NIBRS) data, which are police data collected by the Federal Bureau of Investigation (FBI), Greenfeld and colleagues (1998) found that only a little more than half (53%) of domestic violence cases involved spouses, 5% involved ex-spouses, and 42% involved "other intimates." NIBRS defines "other intimates" as current or past boyfriend or girlfriend relationships, common-law spouses, or homosexual relationships. A more recent study of 2003 NIBRS data reported similar findings: 47.5% of domestic violence cases involved spouses, 4% involved ex-spouses, and 48.5% involved "other intimates" (Hirschel, Buzawa, Pattavina, Faggiani, & Reuland, 2007).

Of the intimate partner cases falling under the category of "other intimates," there is great room for interpretation. What type of relationship between a male and a female constitutes a boyfriend or girlfriend? When classifying a call, do police routinely ask such couples if they have ever resided together or if they have been sexually intimate?

Domestic Violence Offenses

Domestic violence, especially when used by the public and most media as opposed to the legal system and academic publications, now encompasses different acts and behaviors. There are huge differences in how the legal system defines domestic violence and how practitioners, researchers, and many victim advocates define an abusive relationship. Unlike many crimes such as murder, robbery, or burglary, there has never been agreement about the proper crimes of domestic violence. Many members of the public still consider that only extreme physical abuse or sexual assault should qualify. Others argue that it should include coercive control if one party can successfully intimidate another.

There is, however, a growing recognition that a strict dichotomy between acceptable intimate partner behavior and violent physical acts fails to address the totality and complexity of domestic violence. Hence, a more comprehensive view of domestic violence probably should include controlling behaviors that encompass psychological, verbal, and economic abuse. These behaviors are typically not expressly included in criminal domestic violence statutes as they are perceived as ambiguous and difficult to identify and perhaps not worthy of criminal sanction even if proven.

Our discussion of these acts, as well as of direct physical abuse, is not intended to minimize the trauma of actual physical abuse. Instead it seeks to recognize that violence typically occurs in the context of a far broader relationship where there is an ongoing pattern of total submission by one party, and complete domination and control by the other party, using a variety of techniques (Gordon, 2000).

These types of controlling behaviors are now commonly referred to as *coercive control*. Perhaps the earliest definition of this concept that is still widely used today was provided by Evan Stark and his wife, Prof. Anne Flitcraft (1996). They define coercive control as follows:

> [A] pattern of coercion characterized by the use of threats, intimidation, isolation, and emotional abuse, as well as a pattern of control over sexuality and social life, including . . . relationships with family and friends; material resources (such as money food, or transportation); and various facets of everyday life (such as coming and going, shopping, cleaning, and so forth). (pp. 166–167)

Using such techniques, batterers may micromanage the victim's activity through the use of physical and sexual violence, and this can be perceived as a pattern of controlling behaviors more akin to terrorism and hostage-taking (Stark, 2009b).

As Angela Moore Parmley (2004) of the U.S. Department of Justice noted,

> The two perspectives are not diametrically opposed . . . to accept a narrow definition of violence against women would deny the totality of the vast majority of those women who are victimized by their intimate partners on a daily basis . . . adopting a broad definition that includes various types of abuse, control and coercive behavior means incorporating some behavior . . . that has not been legally proscribed and thus not sanctioned. (p. 1419)

The significance of this dilemma can be seen in our later discussion on how prevalent domestic violence actually is, who commits these acts, and domestic violence's impact and consequences to society in general.

The term "domestic violence" as we use it in this book encompasses a broad range of maltreatment by intimates. We include (1) physical violence, including an assault or a homicide; (2) sexual violence; (3) threats of physical and/or sexual violence; (4) severe emotional or psychological abuse; and (5) stalking, by former intimates for the express purpose of committing domestic violence.

France provides an interesting example of efforts to address psychological abuse through its legal system. It is the first country in the world to criminalize psychological abuse. The law is expected to include "repeated rude remarks about a partner's appearance, false allegations of infidelity and threats of physical violence" (Allen, 2010, para. 4).

"According to government statistics, 10% of women in France are victims of domestic mistreatment of some kind, and 80% of women who make calls to state-funded help lines complain of severe verbal abuse compared to 77% who report physical violence. . . . [T]here is growing sentiment that something must be done to halt the emotional and mental trauma that continues unabated" (Crumley, 2010, para. 5).

It is recognized that there has yet to be overall agreement regarding the harm caused by coercive control, and in all likelihood, a consensus may never be reached. Nonetheless, there are admitted problems with aggregating what most people consider serious acts of violence with behaviors considered more ambiguous. If threats and coercive control are included in the definition of "domestic violence," many might dismiss as hyperbole any findings regarding the overall prevalence of domestic violence. Therefore, although we include such conduct in the definition, we will, whenever possible, try to segregate specific acts when measuring rates of occurrence.

Stalking as Coercive Control

Having stated this, and regardless of whether it is called "domestic violence," there is a growing trend to recognize the seriousness of this type of coercive "proto-violent" behavior. In addition to coercive control, when the parties live together, a growing phenomenon has involved attempts by abusive personalities who have been forced out of the relationship by protective orders, divorces, or simply the spouse herself to circumvent explicit statutes on domestic violence through "stalking." Stalking can be defined as the act of deliberately and repeatedly following or harassing another to create fear or to coerce the victim to accede to the wishes of the stalker. Stalking is sometimes considered a separate phenomenon, but it is often closely related, and sometimes a precursor, to physical assaults and is therefore properly included in many domestic violence statutes. Although many in the general public consider this behavior as a mere nuisance or inconvenience, the reality of stalking is far different and, in the context of former intimate partners, is potentially very dangerous to the target.

One of the primary difficulties many agencies face, especially criminal justice bureaucracies such as the police, prosecutors, and the judiciary, is the confusion between patterns of behavior and violent acts. Specifically, *the criminal justice system does not adequately address patterns of abusive behavior, but it is systematically biased to address specific illegal acts.* After all, individuals are charged with a specific offense that must be proven "beyond a reasonable doubt." This inherently separates how the legal system defines domestic violence from the more inclusive definitions preferred by most social scientists.

In addition, there is confusion between committing violent acts and actually inflicting an observable injury. Many people incorrectly believe that the sole legal criterion for measuring a violent act should be injury. However, even domestic violence statutes do not require physical contact as an element of a criminal assault. Placing someone in "reasonable fear" of such an assault is legally sufficient. Criminal law acknowledges differences in assault severity only by a dichotomy that distinguishes among simple assault, aggravated assault, and sexual assault. Researchers, however, often use the umbrella term "assault" to measure a wide range of behaviors, from a continuum ranging from minor threats to serious violent behavior resulting in injury.

Similarly, for estimation purposes, the U.S. Justice Department's Bureau of Justice Statistics' NCVS adopted an inclusive definition that acknowledges that an "assault" may range from a minor threat to incidents that are nearly fatal.

State statutes regularly redefine what constitutes legal criteria for "attempts" as well as "acts." Most surveys take a much broader view of assault that goes beyond simply measuring injuries. Assault incidents may therefore range from face-to-face verbal threats to an attack resulting in extensive injuries. An even wider net can be cast in defining assault by arguing for the inclusion of behaviors such as verbal aggression, harassment, or other behaviors that are emotionally distressing.

The NVAWS was a national telephone survey supported by the BJS conducted from November 1995 to May 1996. The survey represented an effort to improve on the NCVS by focusing specifically on violence against women (Tjaden & Thoennes, 2000). The study collected data between 1995 and 1996 and only included individuals 18 years and older; it employed a methodology that differed from the one used in the NCVS.

The NVAWS reported that 1 out of every 5 women compared with 1 out of every 14 men were physically assaulted by a partner during their lifetime. Therefore, the results are not directly comparable. However, unlike many other national surveys, they also reported the prevalence of stalking as a separate phenomenon. They estimated that 4.8% of women had been stalked by an intimate in their lifetime and that 0.5% of women had been stalked in the past year. In comparison, they estimated that 0.6% of men had been stalked by an intimate during their lifetime and that 0.2% of the men had been stalked by an intimate in the last 12 months.

The number of violent acts committed by a stranger often is reported as an indicator of the relative seriousness of intimate partner violence, compared with total violent acts. For example, in 2007, 28% of violent acts against women were committed by a stranger, 8% were committed by "other relative," and 38% by a "friend or acquaintance." The percentage of violent crimes against women by an intimate partner was 23% compared with 3 of all men (Rand, 2009).

One conclusion that can be drawn with obvious certainty is that studies report wide variation in domestic violence rates, partially originating from differences in the age of the sample population, how the sample was selected, as well as other methodological artifacts. Therefore, an immediate comparison of the NVAWS data from 1995 with the more current NCVS data would have little utility. This can be highlighted in a report issued by the Bureau of Justice Statistics where it was observed that the victimization rate for women aged 12 years or older declined from 10 in 1,000 in 1993 to 4 in 1,000 in 2005.

It is equally unclear whether different findings in these studies reflect not only differences in methodology but also real differences in rates of occurrence. For example, according to the then current NCVS studies reported between 1993 and 2003, domestic violence rates fell by more than 50%, paralleling a similar reduction in all violent offenses. Moreover, it is premature to conclude that any official statistics showing a drop in domestic violence rates are related to recent more proactive efforts to combat such offenses. It was encouraging to observe a drop in both fatal and nonfatal domestic violence between 1993 and 2003 of simple assault by two thirds, and aggravated assault by one third (Catalano, 2006).

Definitions of domestic violence are largely dependent on descriptions by the police, assailants, victims, and witnesses. Hence, the definition of domestic violence also is largely based on then prevalent societal values. Many people assume assaults are physical acts that result in injuries. However, physical contact is not the sole legal criterion for assault. For example, the Uniform Crime Reports program includes "attempts" in its definition of aggravated assault. The NCVS definition of an assault encompasses acts that range from minor threats to incidents that are nearly fatal (Dunrose et al., 2005).

Unfortunately, we cannot uncritically accept official data in this area. Researchers know that official data measuring many "minor crimes" like domestic violence are critically dependent on a series of problematic assumptions, that the police are called for each incident, that the police respond in time to intervene, the police accurately fill out official reports, and finally that departments submit these data to the FBI. Unfortunately in crimes that are considered by the police to be relatively minor, each of these critical assumptions tends to be unrealistic. As a result, *official statistics dramatically understate real incidence rates.*

Unofficial Survey Data

The National Surveys of Family Violence (NSFV) relied on data generated by the Conflict Tactics Scale (CTS) and its revision (Straus & Gelles, 1990). These "unofficial" but highly comprehensive studies of victimization reported overall physical violence rates of 12.1% for women and 11.6% for men in the late 1970s, climbing to 12.3% for women and 12.1% for men in the mid-1980s. The key is that these data suggest a lifetime exposure that is approximately 30 times the rate reported by the NCVS. It is doubtful that stark differences can be accounted for simply by the reporting period. However, the NFVS study intended to examine how conflict and violence is expressed in families and has not been administered on a national basis since 1985—25 years ago.

The NFVS survey has been the source of considerable controversy. Researchers have questioned reliance on the CTS as an adequate and accurate measure of domestic violence. Its critics question the lack of understanding as to context, motivations, meanings, and outcome of violence, which is not encompassed by its scale (Belknap, Fleury, Melton, Sullivan, & Leisenring, 2001; Belknap & Potter, 2005; DeKeseredy, 1995; DeKeseredy & Schwartz, 1998; Stark, 2007; Stark & Flitcraft, 1983; Yllö, 1984).

As we will explore in the next section of this chapter, particularly severe criticism has been leveled by those who believe "family violence" studies inappropriately equate rates of violence by heterosexual women against their partners as being substantially similar to rates of violence committed by heterosexual men.

Furthermore, both sexes report violence in different ways. It has been argued that males are more likely to underreport abuse than females, whereas females are more likely to report but to minimize the actual abuse perpetrated against them (Belknap & Potter, 2005; Berns, 2000; Campbell, 1995; Heckert & Gondolf, 2000). Female underreporting of domestic violence has been attributed to fear of retaliation, suffer from embarrassment, view the violence as a private matter, or distrust the interviewer (Belknap & Potter, 2005; Smith, 1994). However, Hamel (2007) discusses several research studies arguing that male victims have a far greater likelihood of fearing embarrassment as it is contradictory to cultural expectations of male strength.

The National Survey of Family Violence, although dated and with some severe methodological assumptions, provides tantalizing support for the thesis that domestic violence, especially if relatively low levels of force are used, is far more common in society than officially reported. An easy assumption that males commit virtually all acts of domestic violence seems unwarranted. However, as will be discussed, women tend to be overwhelmingly the victims of serious violence.

Who Are the Victims?

National-level aggregate data often tend to mask major differences among various subgroups in the United States. These variations are now being identified, and their significance for practitioners and policymakers is being explored further. When domestic violence first became recognized as a national problem, researchers and advocates emphasized that it was equally prevalent among all groups of women. Pragmatically, this made sense. If domestic violence was considered primarily a problem of specific racial and/or ethnic groups, or the poor in general, it risked being marginalized as an important societal issue—simply another seemingly intractable problem of these subgroups within society. Like poverty itself, poor housing, or inadequate medical care, such problems if they did not involve the middle class could politically be set aside. The fact that it was better known among victims of lower socioeconomic or racial minority status was attributed solely to its visibility in this group, compared with more affluent, white victims, who tend to keep such incidents hidden from the public eye. However, the differential impact of domestic violence on groups is now widely acknowledged (Buzawa & Buzawa, 2003; Stanko, 2004).

The Role of Gender

Does the use of violence by women have the same meaning as violence used by men? A continuing source of controversy is whether there is gender symmetry in the perpetration of intimate partner assaults or whether there is a distinct and far more severe problem of females being the victims of male violence. Some researchers and many "men's advocacy groups" contend that numerous studies indicate gender symmetry, suggesting that women initiate as many, if not more, acts of violence compared with men. This perspective examines the number of incidents where women initiate violence and does not focus on the effects or understanding of the context of the violent act nor the degree of injury inflicted. The National Family Violence Survey as well as more than 100 additional studies that used the CTS tended as a group to report rates of violence committed by women to be as high as men (Straus, 1999). Straus believes this reflects the critical differences between crime studies and conflict studies. Research by Straus and his colleagues suggests that only approximately 2% of incidents of domestic assault are reported to police (compared with 53% according to the NCVS, as discussed earlier) and that those reported are likely to be the more serious assaults or those for which there is greatest fear of serious injury—most likely by a male perpetrator (Straus & Gelles, 1986, 1990).

Resolution of this issue is important not just for its academic merit but also primarily because statutory criminal penalties may be differentially applied if this is treated as a crime against women. Perhaps even more importantly, huge federal funding is granted to combat male-on-female violence under VAWA with no direct analog to the reverse sequence or, for that matter, violence against male intimates in same-sex relationships.

Figure 2.2, as shown earlier, fairly clearly demonstrates that officially reported rates of nonfatal domestic violence are very heavily skewed toward women as victims. This pattern is not a 1-year phenomenon, but it has continued during the past 15 years with approximately a 5-to-1 ratio of "officially reported" female-to-male victims reported for most years.

Advocates of a "gender-neutral" approach to intimate violence conclude that violence perpetrated by females against males is widely underreported to the police for a variety of reasons. They do acknowledge that the injury and level of violence is far greater in cases of male against female violence, but they believe that law enforcement should treat the commission of interpersonal violence by anyone as a problem, and not just focus on male against female violence. They also note that official statistics are suspect because male victims of abuse tend not to report as frequently as females, out of embarrassment, or because they are aware that police frequently do not take such complaints as seriously as violence against women.

Both sides have some validity. Male against female violence is the more serious problem both in terms of frequency and in terms of rates of serious crime. Official BJS data show how domestic violence is proportionately a far greater concern to women than to men relative to other violent victimizations. In one study comparing multiple data sets, 22% of all violent offenses against women were committed by intimates versus only 4% of all victimized men (Catalano, 2006).

Another valid indicator is the seriousness of victim injuries. The more serious the nature of the injury, the more likely the crime is to be reported. The most serious of all is, of course, a homicide. Figure 2.1, as reported earlier, discusses the sex of victims of intimate homicides. Such crimes are, for obvious reasons, not likely to not be reported, or "recategorized." The figure still shows a 3:1 ratio of female-to-male victims making the crime still more likely to be committed against women, but having a substantial cohort of male victims. Similarly, since proportionately fewer overall homicides are committed against females compared with males (less gang, prison, and drug violence), the proportion of intimate homicides to total homicides is much greater for women, 30% of the total homicides compared with 5% of the total for men.

Is a Woman Who Fights Back Considered a Victim?

The image of a victim of domestic violence morphed from a low-income woman of color to a passive, middle-class, White woman cowering in the corner as her enraged husband prepares to beat her again. This woman never fights back. Because this woman is the one whom lawyers want to present and judges expect to see in their courtrooms, women who fight back are at a distinct disadvantage when they turn to the civil legal system for assistance. The battered woman who fights back simply is not a victim in the eyes of many in the legal system. (Goodmark, 2008, p. 78)

Virtually all researchers now believe that female-initiated violence poses less of a problem to society than male-on-female violence. As we have shown, their rates of violence are somewhat lower, and when violence is used by women, it is often related in some manner to self-defense. Furthermore, they unequivocally account for far less severe injuries to their victims than heterosexual men. Therefore, although our legal system supports a definition of intimate partner violence that is gender neutral, women are clearly at a disproportionate amount of risk for serious victimization. Their risks for intimate partner violence, sexual assault, and stalking simply are greater than for men. They also are at greater risk for multiple types of victimization as well as for recurrent violent victimization within relationships.

The flawed but "official" data sources, the NCVS and the NVAWS, have consistently reported higher rates of female compared with male intimate partner victimization (Bachman & Saltzman, 1995; Tjaden & Thoennes, 2000). The NVAWS, based on survey information with 8,000 representative men and women, reported that nearly 25% of surveyed women and approximately 8% of surveyed men said that they were raped or physically assaulted (or both) by a current or former spouse, a cohabiting partner, or a date at some point in their lifetime. From this, they extrapolated that approximately 4.8 million intimate partner rapes and physical assaults were perpetrated against U.S. women annually and that approximately 2.9 million intimate partner assaults were committed against men annually (Tjaden & Thoennes, 2000).

In addition to controversy over which data source more accurately reflects women's use of violence, many independent researchers argue that the number of violent acts alone should not be the basis for judging female violence in comparison with that committed by males but that the outcome and the context of their violent acts also should be considered. They believe this for a variety of good reasons.

First, as Stets and Straus (1990) emphasized, the *comparative rates of injury clearly demonstrate that women use less force than men.* They reported that the rate of injury-inflicted assaults was 3.5 per 1,000 for men against women, compared with 0.6 per 1,000 for women against men—six times the rate of injury of men. Similarly, the National Family Violence Survey (NFVS) found the injury rate for women was six times higher than it was for men (3% and 0.5%, respectively).

Similarly, the NVAWS reported that 42% of women who were assaulted since the age of 18 years were injured in their most recent assault; however, most injuries were relatively minor (Tjaden & Thoennes, 2000). The NCVS found that approximately half of female domestic violence victims reported physical injury compared with 32% of male victims. The rates of serious injury were similar (4% for men and 5% for women), but women are significantly more likely to incur minor injuries (more than 4 in 10 women compared with fewer than 3 in 10 men; Rennison & Welchans, 2000).

The NVAWS also found that gender differences became even more pronounced when the severity of the injury was measured. Of the 4.8 million rapes and physical assaults perpetrated against women annually, approximately 2 million resulted in an injury to the victim, and more than 550,000 required some type of medical treatment for female victims. In contrast, of the approximately 2.9 million intimate partner physical assaults perpetrated against men annually, approximately 580,000 resulted in injuries and only 125,000 required medical treatments. Therefore, although the total overall number of injuries—4.8 million compared with 2.9 million—may not be remarkably dissimilar, the difference between the 550,000 women requiring medical care compared with the 125,000 men reveals considerably greater risk to women. In addition, because the NVAWS study included same-sex violence, where a far larger percentage of men were far more likely to be abused by a male partner, the difference in injuries sustained by each sex at the hands of the other is even greater.

Second, although the overall rate of violence against women may be less than violence against males (as a result of staggering levels of male-on-male violence), the *relative impact of intimate partner violence on each group is different.* In the year 2000, the NCVS reported that the 20% of violence against women was committed by an intimate partner, compared with only 3% of males (Rennison, 2001). In a real sense, violence committed by women against their heterosexual partners is only a small incremental risk factor to men, whereas it is a large component of the overall risk to women. In addition, although both men and women initiate violence, in most cases, violence initiated by women is far less severe and is often in response to actual or anticipated male violence.

Third, as noted earlier, it has long been suggested that *there are major differences in the use of violence between men and women in their relationships.* Since the early 1980s, some researchers have suggested that women may initiate violence more often than men as a tactical strategy to avoid an imminent violent act against them (Bowker, 1983; Feld & Straus, 1989). In addition, many women may be acting in self-defense or simply fighting back (Barnett, Lee, & Thelen, 1997; Chesney-Lind, 2002; Hanmer & Saunders, 1984; Miller, 2005; Renzetti, 1999; Renzetti, Goodstein, & Miller, 2005; Stark, 2007; Stark & Flitcraft, 1996).

This argument is further substantiated by empirical data from a national study of dating violence in Canada, which reported that most women who used violence were acting in self-defense or fighting back (DeKeseredy, Saunders, Schwartz, & Alvi, 1997). A study by Swan and Snow (2002) studied women who had used physical violence with a male partner. They reported that "almost all of the women committed moderate physical violence, 57% committed severe violence, 54% injured their partner, 28% used sexual coercion, and 86% used some form of coercive control" (Swan & Snow, 2002, p. 311). Almost all these women also experienced physical violence from their male partners. They ultimately reported that only 12% of women were aggressors; the remaining women reported that the men committed significantly more acts of violence against them with less than 6% experiencing no physical violence by their partner.

Similarly, Swan, Gambone, Fields, Sullivan, and Snow (2005) reported that close to 92% of the women they studied used violence against male partners who had physically or sexually abused them.

Although women committed significantly more acts of moderate physical violence against male partners than their partners committed against them, their partners committed almost 1.5 times the number of severe physical acts against them (although only moderately significant), committed 2.5 times the rate of sexual coercion, and caused 1.5 times as much injury. Also of interest is that although there were many relationships in which women were more physically aggressive, their male partner was more controlling (50% of relationships). The researchers suggested that this indicates these women were not necessarily in control of their partner's behavior despite the fact that they used more severe violence (Swan & Snow, 2002).

Belknap and Melton (2004) provided four reasons that they suggest represent a feminist rationale for defining the primary problem as one of violence against women rather than as a gender-neutral "domestic violence." First, they believe that the CTS leads to inaccurate results as it is incapable of measuring the "context, motivations, meanings and consequences" ("Varied Findings on the Prevalence of Female Perpetration of IPA" section, para. 5). Hence, these studies cannot distinguish a primarily female victim from a male victim, who may be subject to violence but is likely to have initiated the overall sequence by his prior abusive behavior. Thus, only a few situations would be considered "female-initiated" or mutually combative domestic violence. In support of this, they note that the most serious violence is committed against women, and in studies using shelter samples, police reports, and hospitals, as many as 90% to 95% are male-on-female violence.

Second, it is argued that research demonstrates that we are in a societal environment in which females are more likely to minimize victimization, and where males are more likely to minimize their violent offending (Campbell, 1995; Dobash, Dobash, Cavanagh, & Lewis, 1998; Goodrum, Umberson, & Anderson, 2001; Heckert & Gondolf, 2000).

Third, the data collection methods for studies using the CTS are critiqued since subjects are not questioned in a private, safe environment such as a shelter or hospital. If measures are not taken to ensure that the abuser is not present and/or the victim does not fear his learning about an interview, they will be afraid to disclose abuse or provide candid accounts.

Fourth, these researchers believe that "common couple violence" as reported by the gender-neutral theorists is only occasionally correct. They will acknowledge that in some cases, each family member may use occasional outbursts of abuse, but this phenomenon is qualitatively different from "patriarchal terrorism" where a man uses much more serious violence to maintain control. Therefore, what they consider problematic behavior is limited to cases of patriarchal terrorism rather than to use of violence in general.

There is validity to the foregoing commentary. Violence committed against women by male abusers causes far more injuries and has been documented as posing a far more significant societal problem. Nevertheless, limiting the problem of partner violence almost exclusively to that of female victimization may be criticized. First, the "context, meanings and consequences" of violence can rarely be determined in any circumstance. There are often divergent perspectives as to the underlying cause and intermediary variables and the actual trigger for violence. To imply that it is typically a case of male domination over a female is a political perspective, and it is not necessarily borne out by empirical research. Furthermore, it does not encompass the role of critical risk factors for offending such as substance abuse and mental health or, alternatively, implicitly generalizes them as primarily "male problems."

Claire Renzetti (1999), although clearly bringing a feminist view to the problem, moderates this approach by noting the need to acknowledge that some women do use violence, if only to remain credible to others. The historic reluctance of many victim advocates to hold women accountable for acts of violence could have contributed to the backlash expressed by many men's organizations. Women do initiate acts of domestic assault, and these are not always the result of self-defense (Moore Parmley, 2004).

Second, issues of "control" and implicit domination are unclear. If one party verbally abuses the other, some will argue that this is part of a pattern of patriarchal intimidation and hence essential to violence against women, which is different than the pattern of verbal abuse initiated by a woman against a male partner. In reality, when one party consistently verbally harasses and the other uses physical violence because of an inability to be able to defend himself verbally, the person actually in control of the relationship may not really be clear; the line between physical and psychological abuse may become less distinct.

This is especially true when the definition of domestic violence is broadened to include a pattern of emotional abuse. One must then be ideologically certain that a patriarchal society has similarly conditioned the behavior of both genders, all immigrant, racial, and ethnic groups, and that such behavior patterns have remained unchanged during the past decades despite major societal changes. In this case, might not chronic verbal abuse be initiated by the woman?

Another point many people raise is that comments made at victim shelters, to victim advocates, hospital personnel, and police contradict the rough "parity" of violence. However, there are few, if any, shelters available for male victims of female violence, and few victim service agencies handle problems of male victims. Meanwhile, the police, as will be noted in subsequent chapters, are less likely to be sympathetic to complaints of female violence against male partners. It would seem that the more impartial format of a well-designed telephone survey bears some distinct advantages.

One in-depth study that does present an interesting view of female-on-male violence examined a representative sample of 360 couples. These couples were interviewed as young adults when the incidence of partner violence is greatest. In addition, partners corroborated each others' reports of abuse, and all reports were examined for reliability (Moffitt, Robins, & Caspi, 2001). Moffitt and colleagues' research did not support a male aggressor model of violence. Instead, these researchers found that the range and distribution of abusive acts did not significantly differ by gender. In addition, their findings did not support the belief that women's use of violence is usually motivated by self-defense. The researchers reported that a substantial number of women committed one-sided violent acts during the study period that exceeded the number of male acts. Furthermore, 18% of women initiated assaults despite the fact that both parties agreed that the male partner had committed no acts of abuse, a fact true for only 6% of the male respondents.

Moffitt and colleagues (2001) also reported that women in the study who were abusive toward their partners were four times more likely to have been violent toward someone other than an intimate partner in the same year. What is interesting is that longitudinal studies have suggested that there are relationships in which women are the initially aggressive partner but that at a later point in time, men become physically abusive— "men do abuse women who abuse them" (p. 23).

The preceding recent studies collectively suggest that the extent of female-on-male violence is highly dependent on how violence is defined. If "common couple violence" is eliminated from the definition (Belknap & Melton, 2004), *because* it is not typically gender related and its outcome is less injurious and/or non-life-threatening (Johnson, 1995), then it is likely that the actual data would be in agreement. Researchers from either orientation emphasize that females are at much greater rate of risk of severe victimization. However, disagreement remains on whether the use of any violence in interpersonal relationships should be sanctioned. Alternatively, should "common couple" violence be deemed acceptable, and only serious acts of violence addressed, primarily because female-on-male violence does not fit into the image that many authors, activists, and politicians have of a crime that is almost exclusively committed by men?

Finally, if common acts of violence in "battling family structure are to be tolerated because they do not fit into a mold of male repression of women, should they be equally tolerated for both males and females? It can be argued that domestic violence varies in its type, severity, and degree of mutuality, and that reliance on any one perspective impacts our ability to effectively intervene (Hamel & Nicholls, 2006).

Same-Sex Violence

Data also suggest that lifetime domestic violence is experienced by a large percentage of lesbian and gay individuals, although there is considerable variation in the estimates of violent attacks that occur in these groups (Pattavina, Hirschel, Buzawa, Faggiani, &

Bentley, 2007). Early research was limited to small, unrepresentative samples of same-sex partner violence. Not only did this make it difficult to generalize from their findings, but the estimates of prevalence varied tremendously, ranging from 17% (Loulan, 1987) to 74% (Lie, Schilit, Bush, Montagne, & Reyes, 1991) depending on the measures used and the time period measured.

The NVAWS was the first study to include same-sex violence as part of a large-scale national survey. It reported that approximately 11% of women in a lesbian relationship reported being raped, physically assaulted, or stalked by their partner. Although a significant percentage, this number was less than the 30% of women who reported such violence when living with a man in a heterosexual relationship. In contrast, in male same-sex couples, the rate of violence was approximately 15% against a partner, whereas men in heterosexual relationships were physically abused by women at a rate slightly less than 8%. Hence, although same-sex violence is clearly an underaddressed issue, the research suggests that men perpetrate more violence in both same-sex and heterosexual relationships, with the highest rates of male violence occurring in heterosexual relationships (Tjaden & Thoennes, 2000).

More recent research has reexamined national-level official statistics for 2005 and has concluded that intimate partner violence between same-sex couples was at least as frequent and severe as heterosexual couples (Pattavina, Hirschel, et al., 2007; Seelau & Seelau, 2005). Another recently published study found that lifetime rates of interpersonal violence for female same-sex violence reached a staggering 41% to 68% lifetime prevalence (Eaton et al., 2008; Simpson & Helfrich, 2005). In some ways, the problem for such victims is even more severe than among heterosexual females because often they accurately fear that no one will believe that their abuse was genuine (Simpson & Helfrich, 2005).

Profiles of victims of same-sex violence may not fit common stereotypes. The difficulty in reporting this type of partner violence is that it does not fit the narrative of a socially marginalized woman. As such, it does not fit traditional feminist theory (Simpson & Helfrich, 2005). In fact, the battered women's movement historically viewed lesbian relationships as a safe haven where they would be free from male violence and patriarchal ideals (Hassouneh & Glass, 2008).

This theoretical framework will be discussed in the next chapter. What it does show, however, is that the dynamics within a relationship between same-sex partner violence parallels that of a heterosexual relationship. Most violence occurs against victims who have less power in their relationships and less power in sexual decision making (Eaton et al., 2006; Glass et al., 2008). The fact is that in society as a whole, despite marked social change in recent decades, this still means that heterosexual women are more likely to be victimized by males than the converse.

Age

Victims' ages also seems to affect the incidence and reports of domestic violence. Data are somewhat difficult to analyze because there is some overlap in the studies between domestic violence and "child abuse" typically committed in families. The NCVS addresses all women 12 years and older, many of whom are not likely to be at risk of violence by an "intimate." In contrast, the Uniform Crime Reports program (UCR) published by the U.S. Department of Justice, addresses adults aged 18 years and older, as does the National Family Violence Survey. To further confuse the issue, the NVAWS, sponsored by the National Institute of Justice and the Centers for Disease Control and Prevention consisting of a survey of 8,000 women and 8,000 men, addressed violence committed against women ages 16 years and older (Tjaden & Thoennes, 1998). Because parental violence against teens in this country is at least as prevalent, these studies may be capturing and reporting this phenomenon as domestic violence. Similarly, the more age-restricted studies largely fail to report violence committed between teen partners, which are relationships that can be violent according to statistics.

In an examination of NCVS data from 1993 to 2004, Catalano (2006) reports that in general, females in the youngest age group (12–15 years) had the least risk of domestic assault. However, this may be a function of reporting. Finkelhor, Cross, and Cantor (2005) argue that the rate of juvenile victimization for such crimes is vastly underreported. They further note that NCVS survey data stated that only 28% of incidents for juveniles ages 12–17 years were reported to police, which is a rate substantially lower than for adults.

To some extent, definitions of abuse toward children and adolescents impact reporting. Children and juveniles are less likely than their parents or other adults to report intimate violence especially if in the form of violence in an ongoing dating relationship. Many teens simply do not trust their parents or other adults to handle appropriately complaints of violence committed by intimate friends. Instead, they worry that if they discuss being abused these adults are equally likely to blame the adolescent victim for having sexual relations in the first place.

If we discard as unreliable the somewhat questionable survey data involving intimate violence against children, most available data show that violence among intimates peaks in early adulthood and then declines. For example, the NCVS reported that between 1993 and 2003, females between the ages of 20 and 24 years were at the greatest risk of domestic violence, whereas females older than 50 years were at the lowest risk and for all females in all age categories, domestic assault victimization is inversely correlated with age.

Marital Status

Marital status has a significant, although complex, relationship to rates of violence. Currently married victims reported the lowest rates of intimate partner violence. However, females who have separated reported higher victimization rates compared with females in other relationships. However, most intimate partner homicides involved spouses, although the number of deaths by boyfriends and girlfriends has remained stable in recent years (Catalano, 2006). These data may simply be explained by the fact that when a husband uses violence against family members, including their intimate partner, a growing tendency exists for women to leave such relationships and possibly secure a protective order against their abusers. The alternative explanation, undoubtedly true for some abusers, is that when they "lose control" over their previous spouse, that is the time that they are more likely to start becoming physically abusive in an escalating pattern to try to reestablish control.

Socioeconomic Status

Women with less income have higher rates of victimization (Catalano, 2006). For example, the NCVS data reported that women in low-income households with annual incomes less than $7,500 reported a rate of nonlethal violence committed against them at a rate 10 times greater than those with an income of $75,000 or more. Women who are supported by welfare experience higher rates of abuse than women in a similarly low socioeconomic bracket. One estimate reports that approximately one third of women on welfare are current victims of abuse, whereas slightly more than half had been victims of abuse during their lifetime (Tolman & Raphael, 2000). Undoubtedly showing an overlap of such population sets, the BJS reported that from 1993 to 2004, both females and males living in rental housing were three times more likely to be victims of domestic violence than those living in their own homes. This factor may become significant as the current recession exacts an increasing toll on the economics of many families.

Racial and Ethnic Variations

Before the birth of the battered women's movement, the assumption was that domestic violence happened to "them"—poor African American women who lived in slums. Advocacy by the battered women's movement around the idea that domestic violence is endemic to all races, ethnicities, religions, and socioeconomic brackets, coupled with the introduction of "battered woman syndrome" and its reliance on the theory of learned helplessness to explain why battered women remain in abusive relationships, changed the portrait of the victim of intimate partner violence. The image of a victim of domestic violence morphed from a low-income woman of color to a passive, middle-class, white woman cowering in the corner as her enraged husband prepares to beat her again. (Goodmark, 2008, p. 76)

The popular press still seems obsessed with violence among high-profile, primarily White victims. Similarly, popular movies and television programs, in an effort to appeal to their viewers, often highlight victims that are White, heterosexual, and middle class. During the last decade, research has, however, allowed for the development of a more balanced picture that can penetrate some stereotypes and examine past overly broad generalizations. As we will see in detail, racial and ethnic minorities are more likely to be victims (Bent-Goodley, 2001; Frye, Wilt, & Schomberg, 2000). In Chapter 3, we will discuss the likely reasons for this variance. In this chapter, it is sufficient to note that available data show a significant racial and ethnic variance. Efforts at data collection often have contributed to overly simplistic characterizations as well.

Violence Among Black Americans

Coker (2000) discussed how research simplifies the diverse experience of women in the United States. She observed that studies purporting to examine "women of color" have relied primarily on African American women, whereas research on White women in many smaller-scale studies has become the surrogate for all women. Even domestic violence among intimate partners is primarily intraracial in nature, as with other forms of nonfatal victimization (Catalano, 2006). Catalano (2006) reported that approximately 89% of White victims were victimized by White offenders, whereas approximately 95% of Black victims were victimized by Black offenders.

Data on intimate partner violence among Blacks as compared with the general population consistently show a larger pattern of victimization. In one of the earliest studies, Straus and Gelles (1986) reported that African Americans had four times the rate of partner violence compared with Whites. Moreover, injuries within that group tend to be disproportionately severe and actual homicides are more frequent (Bent-Goodley, 2001). Hence, as a social pathology, intimate partner violence victimizes African Americans at rates significantly higher than any other group (Bent-Goodley, 2001; Rennison & Welchans, 2000).

NCVS data suggest that the comparative rates of domestic violence between African American and White women decreased between 1990 and 2003. However, this downward trend reversed between 2003 and 2004, and the rates for Black females increased 3.8 to 6.6 victimizations per 2,000 people age 12 years or older. Domestic violence for Whites also increased that year from 0.5 to 1.1 victimizations per 1,000 males age 12 years or older (Catalano, 2006).

Violence Among Hispanic Americans

Many studies have attempted to identify rates of violence in this community. The earliest studies suffered from severe methodological difficulties. For example, Coker (2000) performed one of the largest studies at that time to examine domestic violence rates among Latino women; the study included only women who spoke English, obviously limiting participation.

Second, one of the largest problems when addressing violence in the Hispanic population is that the term "Hispanic" simply defines one characteristic of this population, the language spoken by their immigrant ancestors. We are just now beginning to see research that does a good job in differentiating between such disparate groups as those whose parents may have emigrated from Puerto Rico, Cuba and other Caribbean Islands, Mexico, Central America, and South America. It should be intuitively obvious that these cultural backgrounds are extremely diverse. The immigrant families may have originated from different socioeconomic groups within their countries, and in many cases, the assumption of a Catholic upbringing is incorrect, as there has been a growth of evangelical Christians and other denominations.

Interpreting overall rates of intimate partner violence among Hispanics as a defined population subset also needs special care because most large-scale "official" studies fail to differentiate between native born and immigrant, and they do not differentiate as to whether immigrant status is legal or illegal. Specifically, many surveys combined the population of Hispanic immigrants with Hispanics born in the United States, whose families may have been raised in the United States for generations.

We know that measuring overall rates of intimate partner violence among immigrant groups as a defined subset of the population subset is extremely difficult. A national survey of criminal justice officials and leaders of six ethnic communities (not just Hispanic) suggest that many recent immigrants fail to report crimes. In fact, 67% of the officials in the national survey believed that they were less likely to report crimes compared with other victims, and only 12% thought they were as or more likely to report offenses to the police. In addition, domestic violence victims were less likely to report their victimizations, making an overall appraisal of the rates of domestic violence in this group especially problematic. This has been especially true as the federal, along with some state, governments have made it a point of deporting individuals charged with crimes. Unless the woman is terrified for her life or the lives of her children, this is a huge deterrent to reporting a crime committed by her husband.

A recent study by the Family Violence Prevention Fund (2009) provides a comprehensive literature review on interpersonal violence in immigrant and refugee communities. They point out the continued lack of data. Their review of the literature suggests that nonfatal domestic violence is not more prevalent and is possibly less prevalent among immigrant and refugee populations; however, they are overrepresented in the homicide data compared with American-born individuals. However, as the authors note, there are numerous methodological problems with the data. Not all the studies cited separate out first-born immigrants. Furthermore, how violence becomes known in order for data to be generated is problematic. Thus, we believe it is unclear whether nonfatal rates are in fact lower, especially when coupled with their increased risk for homicides—where the incident is far more likely to be identified.

Given these severe methodological problems, at this stage, we can simply report on the results of individual studies that have focused on Hispanic Americans. More general observations will need to wait until the next edition of this treatise.

The available data are inconsistent. One large-scale national study of lifetime risks of victimization, the NVAWS, reported little difference in intimate partner physical violence and stalking between Hispanic and non-Hispanic women, but it did find significant differences in rape reported by a current or former partner in these populations.

The researchers highlighted the significance of this finding because Hispanic women are less likely than other women to be sexually assaulted by a nonintimate or former nonintimate partner (Tjaden & Thoennes, 2000). Meanwhile, a study of 292 Latina women who were U.S.-born, immigrant, or seasonal migrant workers was conducted in San Diego in 2002 and reported a different, higher risk profile (Hazen & Soriano, 2007). They reported a higher rate of physical violence than the NVAWS rates with a reported lifetime prevalence rate of 34% for physical violence, 21% for sexual coercion, and 83% for psychological aggression.

Also, Frias and Angel (2005) reported that the risk of reported victimization by foreign-born Mexicans and Puerto Ricans was lower than for those born in the United States. In addition, Dominican, Puerto Rican, and other Hispanic women reported significantly lower rates of violence than African American women, whereas Mexican-born women reported rates similar to African American women. However, they were properly cautious in drawing conclusions regarding citizenship status (Davis & Erez, 1998).

Other Ethnic Groups

Significant differences in intimate partner violence also have been reported among other racial groups; however, the data are inconsistent and frankly suspect. The NVAWS study found that American Indian/Alaska Native women reported significantly higher rates of intimate partner violence than women of other racial backgrounds. The researchers noted that American Indian/Alaska Native women could have been more willing to report victimization to interviewers than other victims (Tjaden & Thoennes, 2000). NCVS data from 1993 to 2004 also reported that this population had the highest rates of domestic violence with 11.1 out of 1,000 American Indian women reporting being victimized and 5.3 out of 1,000 American Indian men reporting being victimized compared with 4 and 0.8 per 1,000, respectively, for their White counterparts (Catalano, 2006).

Another rapidly growing population is that of Asian Americans. Research on domestic violence within this group shares somewhat the same methodological problems as with Hispanics. Specifically, there may be marked differences based on whether Asian Americans were born in this country compared with first-generation immigrants. In addition, other than racial identity, we suspect there is little, if any, commonality in cultural experience between immigrants from Japan and Korea compared with less economically developed countries in Southeast Asia. Even when a group emigrates from an individual country such as India, there could theoretically be major differences between rates of domestic violence based on whether they were Indian Muslims or Hindus. We do not believe that these disparities can ever be fully addressed as the cultural backgrounds are simply not analogous except on a superficial racial level. Therefore, the best data that we can hope to achieve will be the reporting of the results of studies that carefully differentiate rates of domestic violence between immigrants from a specific country and the general population. To have external validity, such studies also would need to control the legal status of the participants and the number of years in which they were immersed into U.S. culture.

Having stated these severe limitations, some data are available. Markedly higher rates of physical and/or sexual violence by an intimate partner within the Asian population in the United States have been reported (Yoshihama & Dabby, 2009). We appreciate the work done by the Asian and Pacific Islander Institute on Domestic Violence that has carefully summarized several diverse studies at the community level, which show markedly different results. Given the disparity, it is there that studies of individual communities are typically done at the level of a particular ethnic group within a particular U.S. city. These small-scale studies may be instructive, but generalizability to the overall population is suspect.

For example, the Asian American Task Force on Domestic Violence in Boston using a self-administered questionnaire at ethnic fairs reported that 44% to 47% of Cambodians interviewed said they knew a woman who had experienced domestic violence (Yoshioka & Dang, 2000). Similarly, random telephone surveys of the Chinese community in Los Angeles reported lifetime violence rates of between 18% (minor physical violence) and 8% (severe physical violence) (Yick, 2000). Similarly, 20% of a survey population of 54 undocumented Filipinos living in San Francisco reported some form of domestic violence (Hoagland & Rosen, 1990), whereas in 1995, in a random sample of 211 Japanese immigrants, 61% reported some form of physical, emotional, or sexual partner violence and 52% reported lifetime physical violence (Shimtuh, 2000). In a 1986 study of 150 Koreans living in Chicago, 60% reported lifetime prevalence of physical abuse (Kim & Sung, 2000). A study of 160 South Asian women in Greater Boston reported that 41% experienced lifetime physical or sexual abuse from their current male partners. This study also showed far higher rates of current abuse given that 37% reported having been so victimized in the last year (Raj & Silverman, 2002a). In addition, 65% of the women reporting physical abuse also reported sexual abuse, and 30% reporting sexual abuse reported injuries (Raj & Silverman, 2002a).

Similarly another high-risk group may be the Vietnamese, where in a study of 30 Vietnamese women in Boston, 47% reported intimate physical violence in their lifetime and 30% reported intimate physical violence in the past year (Tran, 1997).

The victim-related needs of many ethnic groups of women also have not been fully recognized. The country's increasing ethnic diversity necessitates an understanding of *the additional* challenges facing these groups of domestic violence victims. Although specific interventions and services will be discussed in a later chapter, efforts first need to be made to improve our identification of these victims.

The Impact of Domestic Violence

Injuries

It has been estimated that 41.5% of women who were physically assaulted and 36.2% of women who were sexually assaulted by an intimate partner were injured. They also reported that nearly 15,000 of the rapes and 240,000 of the physical assaults resulted in emergency room visits (Tjaden & Thoennes, 2000).

Sexual assault as a component of domestic violence also is common, but it is less frequently reported and there is a lack of empirical data. Although it may occur in isolation from physical and other forms of abuse, it often is observed in cases in which there also is severe physical abuse (Gordon, 2000; Painter & Farrington, 1998). This form of victimization can be particularly harmful for victims and can lead to other chronic health problems (Foa & Riggs, 1994; Riggs, Kilpatrick, & Resnick, 1992).

Acute physical injury resulting from a domestic assault may lead to long-term physical health problems for the victim. These problems include chronic pain, sexually transmitted diseases, miscarriages, gastrointestinal disorders, genitourinary tract problems, and a variety of other disorders (Walker, Logan, Jordan, & Campbell, 2004). Although many women receive medical treatment for their problems, many others are denied access for a variety of reasons, including assistance in obtaining care, financial constraints, and/or prohibitions placed on them by their abuser.

Psychological and Quality-of-Life Effects on Victims

Many researchers and practitioners believe that emotional and psychological adjustments typically precede physical separation (Theran, Sutherland, Sullivan, & Bogat, 2006;

Walker et al., 2004). The impact of domestic violence is far greater than the individual acts. Severe physical abuse is more likely to result in greater psychological impact. The degree of psychological impact may not be totally a result of measures of violence such as the amount of force used or injuries sustained but based in part on individual subjective factors. Victims become emotionally traumatized. The battering syndrome has been found to result in high rates of seemingly unrelated medical complaints (Stark & Flitcraft, 1988), depression and low self-esteem (Campbell, Kub, Belknap, & Templin, 1997; Campbell & Soeken, 1999; Zlotnick, Kohn, Peterson, & Pearlstein, 1998), psychosocial problems, and later disproportionate risks of rape, miscarriage, abortion, alcohol and drug abuse, attempted suicide (Stets & Straus, 1990), and general emotional well-being including posttraumatic stress disorder (PTSD) resulting from severe stress (Campbell & Soeken, 1999; Stark & Flitcraft, 1988).

The impact of these problems is difficult to exaggerate. Suicide rates for battered women are almost five times as high as in nonbattered populations (Stark, 1984). Furthermore, it seems that many of these problems begin *after* the abuse, not as a cluster of which abuse is merely one factor (Holtzworth-Munroe, Smutzler, & Sandin, 1997; Stark, 1984; Woods, 1999). The emotional toll of domestic violence also may be greatly increased if a psychological assault is part of the pattern of abuse. Some researchers have reported that many women find psychological, verbal, and emotional abuse more harmful and of far greater duration than physical abuse (DeKeseredy & MacLeod, 1997; Fitzpatrick & Halliday, 1992).

The severity and extent of abuse is highly related to the victims showing symptoms of PTSD. In fact, not only do large proportions of victims of sexual, physical, and psychological assault suffer from PTSD, these individuals also constitute a significant proportion of the total number of people who experience these symptoms.

Monetary Costs

When examining costs, there have been actual dollar figures attributed in an effort to better determine the impact of domestic violence on society. The CDC estimates that physical and mental health care costs for interpersonal violence are close to $4.1 billion. They place an additional productivity cost of $858.6 million for days of employment and household chores lost (CDC, 2003).

The Impact on Children and Adolescents

In Chapter 3 we will discuss in detail how childhood exposure to domestic violence may create a lifetime cycle of domestic violence in future generations. Here we will talk about the general consequences of childhood exposure to such trauma. Children in abusive families seem to be psychologically vulnerable. It is significant that large numbers of this especially vulnerable group regularly witness violence in the family. One estimate (using data derived from total instances of domestic violence and "adjusted" for the number of children in the household) is that approximately 3.3 million children witness acts of domestic violence each year (Carlson, 1984). Straus and Gelles (1990) using the

Family Violence Survey suggested an even higher figure of 10 million or 1/3 of American children who witness violence each year between parents. More recently, the National Survey of Children's Exposure to Violence (NatSCEV) estimated that 9.8% of children are exposed to domestic violence each year (Finkelhor, Turner, Ormrod, Hamby, & Kracke, 2009). This is considerably different than estimates from NCVS data, which found that between 1993 and 2004, children were residents in households where domestic violence occurred in 43% of the incidents involving females and in 25% of the incidents involving males (Catalano, 2006). This disparity could be because the latter does not distinguish children who are present from those who actually witness the incident.

These figures are only estimates and are dependent on definitions (Edleson, 2007). Researchers still disagree as to whether estimates should include only serious incidents of domestic violence or a broad set of behaviors including slaps, pushing, or shoving (see also Kracke & Hahn, 2008; Osthoff, 2002).

What impact does witnessing violence have on children? Could such an impact manifest itself in the context of general behavioral problems or in a tendency to be a victim or a victimizer? These questions are important in the context of theories of the generation of long-term social and behavioral problems and the possible intergenerational transfer of violence.

An extensive body of literature now exists with more than 100 studies trying to determine the impact of family violence on children and approximately one third dealing solely with children witnessing violence as opposed to being battered themselves (Edleson, 2001). Edleson reported that several studies found that "externalized" behaviors such as aggression and antisocial behavior were more common in children, especially boys, exposed to domestic violence; "internalized" behaviors such as unusual fears and inhibitions also were common, especially among girls (Fantuzzo et al., 1991). Other studies have reported a variety of adverse effects with children who have witnessed domestic violence, including that, in general, they score lower on tests of social competency and higher on depression, anxiety, aggression, shyness, and school-related problems (Adamson & Thompson, 1998; Fantuzzo et al., 1991; Silvern et al., 1995). Another study indicates that these children score lower on tests of cognitive functioning (Rossman, 1998).

These attitudes can potentially result in a series of behavioral problems. One study of violent teenage boys reported that exposure to family violence apparently was associated with the development of positive feelings toward using violence to "solve" problems and hence indirectly to violent offending (Spaccarelli, Coatworth, & Bowden, 1995).

In addition—and perhaps this is the most chilling prospect—witnessing parental violence is highly correlated with subsequent suicide attempts of children. One study found that 65% of children who had attempted suicide had previously witnessed family violence (Kosky, 1983). Although Edleson (2001) correctly noted that solely using this factor to predict individual attitudes or behavior would be wrong, he also noted that within the highly variable individual experiences and reactions, most studies show group trends in which adverse impact may be observed.

Some children and teens are more affected by exposure to violence than others. Resilience may be a result of several factors. First, a child's relationship with a caring adult, usually a parent, may reduce the negative impact of exposure. Second, characteristics of the victim have been found to be of significance. Children with average or above average intelligence and strong interpersonal skills are more likely to have increased resilience. Additional factors include self-esteem and other personality traits, socioeconomic background, religion, and contact with supportive people (Osofsky, 1999).

Children and teens exposed to this violence are also at greater risk for exposure to other types of violence. Often, they reside in communities with high rates of community violence. Youth growing up in such neighborhoods are regularly exposed to the use of drugs, guns and other weapons, and random acts of violence. One report states that children in urban schools who have not received such exposure are the exception, not the norm (Osofsky, 1999). In fact, the Juvenile Victimization Questionnaire (JVQ) reported that the average child experienced three different direct or indirect victimizations in a 1-year time frame and only 29% of children had none (Finkelhor et al., 2005).

Although research regarding the impact of childhood and adolescent exposure to violence is now emerging, findings still need more development. We lack an understanding of what the link is between witnessing violence and subsequent victimization and offending. Many witnesses of early violence do not become either victims or offenders as adults. Others become offenders, and still others become victims. Also, some children become both victims and offenders. A better understanding of how these behaviors evolve is needed. We also need an increased understanding of how to intervene successfully with children and adolescents to decrease the likelihood of negative consequences. At this point in time, we simply know we need to intervene, but we lack an empirical understanding of how best to provide assistance.

The Specialized Problem of Stalking in Intimate Relationships

Stalking is a relatively new concept that has become increasingly prevalent in the context of domestic abuse because of the increased tendency of judges to order abusers to leave their family abode and restrain themselves from any contact. Many such abusers react by plotting a campaign either to reinsert themselves into the lives of their former intimates or in essence to terrorize them into submission.

Many definitions have been proposed for the term "stalking." We will use the definition proposed by the National Center for Victims of Crime (NCVC). In 2007, they published the revised Model Stalking Code. It defined stalking as follows:

> Any person who purposefully engages in a course of conduct directed at a specific person and knows or should know that the course of conduct would cause a reasonable person to fear for his or her safety or the safety of a third person or suffer emotional distress is guilty of the crime of stalking.
>
> (a) "Course of conduct" means two or more acts, including, but not limited to, acts in which the stalker directly, indirectly, or through third parties, by any action, method, device, or means, follows, monitors, observes, surveils, threatens, or communicates to or about, a person, or interferes with a person's property.
>
> (b) "Emotional distress" means significant mental suffering or distress that may, but does not necessarily, require medical or other professional treatment or counseling.
>
> (c) "Reasonable person" means a reasonable person in the victim's circumstances. (NCVC, 2007, p. 44)

Estimates of the prevalence of stalking vary. There are significant difficulties in determining the rates of stalking. The percentage of stalking incidents reported to police is even lower than is the case when an actual assault or an assault involving an injury has occurred. As a result, recent survey research that is not dependent on police reports has revealed prevalence rates for stalking that are far higher than previously considered.

It has been reported that almost 5% of women and 0.6% of men were stalked by a current or former spouse, cohabiting partner, or date during their lifetime. In addition, 0.5% of the women and 0.2% of the men were stalked within the last 12 months. They extrapolated these figures to result in approximately 504,000 women and 185,000 men being stalked annually by intimate partners in the United States (Tjaden & Thoennes, 2000).

Recently, a meta-analysis was performed of 175 studies of stalking. The results demonstrated far greater prevalence than we would have anticipated. Various studies showed a lifetime prevalence rate between 2% and 13% for males, whereas lifetime victimization rates for females were 8% to 32%. Furthermore, although many studies covered nonrelationship stalking such as celebrity stalking, the meta-analysis shows that approximately 80% of stalkers were known by the victim and approximately half occurred in the context of some form of romantic relationship (Botuck et al., 2009; Spitzberg & Cupach, 2007).

Unfortunately, most studies included in the meta-analysis were not exclusively focused on intimate partner stalking. This may be because stalking is considered ancillary or simply a part of an overall partner of intimate partner violence and studied in that context rather than as a separate phenomenon with potentially different causal factors and perhaps different effects on victims (Stark, 2007).

Not surprisingly, research has suggested that college women may be at increased risk for stalking victimization compared with the general population (Fisher, Cullen, & Turner, 2002; Schwartz & DeKeseredy, 1997). Fisher and colleagues (2002) conducted a national telephone survey of 4,446 women attending 2- and 4-year colleges and universities in 1997. They reported that 13.1% of women were stalked during a 7-month period, which is a figure considerably higher than the national average. Of those women, 12.7% experienced two incidents, and 2.3% experienced three or more incidents. Victims were threatened or an assault was attempted in 15.3% of the cases.

The Impact of Stalking

As mentioned earlier, stalking is part of the definition of domestic violence, either in the context of being part of an ongoing pattern of a variety of types of abuse, of becoming an alternative to earlier physical abuse, or as the only type of behavior the offender displays. In the case of its becoming an alternative form of abuse, the methods chosen continue at long range the control tactics that had been finely honed previously. Stalking has been concisely described as "psychological war" (Geberth, 1992), and it instills tremendous terror in victims. Tactics vary enormously. Some stalkers simply trail their victims continuously. Others destroy or vandalize property; send packages or deliveries (often of inappropriate or bizarre items); poison or kill pets; use phone threats; and contact employers, neighbors, and relatives, making normal life impossible.

Danger in stalking is an ever-present threat. In this context, the behavior of O. J. Simpson in stalking his ex-wife Nicole Brown Simpson is a typical pattern, even if the outcome was extreme. Although research in this field is in its infancy, we know that stalking by itself is a strong predictor of subsequent, often uncontrolled, violence against the victim, her (or his) family, bystanders, and even the offender. Mass murder and suicidal rage are not uncommon, although difficult to predict. The public is familiar with headlines in which both celebrities and others have been stalked and sometimes killed. Others have been attacked and permanently injured or disfigured. In the context of the psychopathological stalker, this is explainable; he seeks to retain control. Such violence may be used as either a tactic (to keep control) or a spasmodic response to the realization that he has utterly "lost it," perhaps when the victim finally rebuffs him (or her) or becomes involved with another. The best evidence of this is the often expressed stalker statement, "If I can't have her, no one else will."

In addition, stalking affects the mental health of victims (Davis & Freeze, 2000; Turmanis & Brown, 2006). The NVAWS reported that one third of female stalking victims sought psychological counseling. Victims often suffer "social damage" (Knoll and Resnick, 2007, p. 16; Logan, Walker, Stewart, & Allen, 2006) and often are forced to make major lifestyle changes that can include relocating, not working or seeking new employment resulting in monetary costs to these victims. In fact, more than a quarter of the victims reported losing time from their current employment because of stalking, and 7% gave up their job altogether (Tjaden & Thoennes, 1998).

Victims also suffer from increased emotional stress that increases their risk for anxiety disorders, substance abuse, PTSD, and depression (Knoll & Resnick, 2007).

SUMMARY

As discussed, intimate partner and domestic violence is a huge problem in terms of the number of incidents and its effects on victims. Disparities in definitions of domestic violence have at times resulted in conflicting reports of its incidence and trends. There is considerable variation in the relationships considered, and one must consider the variations among legal, research, and societal definitions. Legal definitions shape our official response by defining the acts and behaviors that are criminalized. Thus, surveys by government agencies such as the UCR and NCVS frame and measure the problem differently than other sources such as the NFVS and NVAWS.

Furthermore, this remains a highly controversial topic among researchers, and this is reflected in the diverse range of findings among their studies (e.g., the NFVS and NVAWS, victim advocates, and practitioners). These data sources help us frame and understand the problem of domestic violence. It further impacts how policymakers address the problem. Therefore, definitions do matter and is worth our careful consideration.

Available evidence suggests that rates may vary among different subpopulations with many minorities and ethnic groups being particularly vulnerable. Finally, stalking may be regarded as a newly identified variant of domestic violence or, perhaps more appropriately, coercive control. Even though it may have been present for some time, rates may be increasing as abusive partners are evicted from their homes.

DISCUSSION QUESTIONS

1. How would you define domestic violence? What relationships and acts do you think should be included? Should stalking be viewed as part of domestic violence or as a separate problem?

2. When is mutual violence self-defense against an aggressor, and when is it retaliation?

3. If violence is committed in self-defense, should this make a difference in how we intervene? In other words, if a woman prefers to respond to a violent attack with reciprocal violence rather than seeking police assistance, should she be considered an aggressor as well?

4. If one party uses physical violence, and the other party uses extreme coercion and psychological abuse, is only the perpetrator of physical violence considered the offender?

5. What are the policy implications in how we define domestic violence in the allocation of victim services?

6. How do we respond to cases where victims and offenders change roles?

7. John Hamel (2007) has typologized people in what he terms the "Gender Camp" and the "Conflict Tactics Camp." Those in the "Gender Camp" believe that the domestic violence is primarily a crime committed by men against women and that women are more likely to be subjected to serious violence and in fear of their abuser. Conversely, those in the "Conflict Tactics Camp" believe that men and women are equally likely to be victims and offenders for a variety of reasons. Do you think domestic violence is gender neutral?

Matters of History, Faith, and Society 3

Chapter Overview

Why do we care about historical attitudes and precedents toward women or religion in what is now a secular society? Are religious doctrines and attitudes still important in the context of a modern society? Simply put, we believe an understanding of domestic violence also must include a macrolevel analysis to explain the structural violence considered by many to be endemic against women in most societies. This chapter will discuss how socially sanctioned violence against women has been persistent since ancient times. Christianity, Judaism, Islam, and other religions simply have affirmed ancient male-dominated family structures. The results can be found in the official discrimination and tolerance of domestic violence exemplified by English common law in the history and practices of the United States at least until the enactment of modern reforms. Although most societies have the same—or even significantly worse—issues with official and tacit tolerance toward domestic violence, this chapter will focus on historical and religious antecedents that have shaped the "traditional" U.S. tolerance of domestic violence. Furthermore, we will explore how these might still impact how our society treats this problem.

Historic Attitudes on Domestic Violence

Domestic violence has long been a feature of both ancient and modern societies. From the earliest record, most societies to varying extents have given the male patriarch of a family the right to use force against women and children under his control.

The basis for patriarchal power often was a desire to maintain social order extending to defined relations within the family. One graphic example is Roman civil law, which gave legal guardianship of a wife to her husband. This concept, *patria potestas*, included the largely unfettered ability of the husband to beat his wife, who became, in legal effect, his "daughter." Such rights were theoretically not necessarily for her well-being since they extended to the right to sell a wife into slavery or, under certain limited circumstances, to put her to death (Pleck, 1989). This was codified in the earliest known example of a written marital code (753 BC); Roman law stated simply that wives were "to conform themselves entirely to the temper of their husbands and the husbands to rule their wives as necessary and inseparable possessions" (Pressman, 1984, p. 18). Similar codes or judicial doctrines were enacted in ancient Western societies where women, whether slave, concubine, or wife, were under the authority of men. In law, they were treated as property (Anderson & Zinsser, 1989) or "as men ruled in government and society, so husbands ruled in the home" (Lentz, 1999, p. 10). Ancient historical precedents can therefore best be summarized by the concept of the natural inferiority of women, the natural authority of the male head of the household, and at its extreme, the "property" rights of the head of the household over everyone in his domain.

English Common Law and European History

English common law, the predecessor to many U.S. statutes, followed a variant of the well-recognized custom of male control over women. English feudal law reinforced religious edicts holding forth the concept of male property rights over women and the right of men to beat "their women" if needed. In English society, "property rights" were the key denominator of social status. Class or heredity determined far more than personal achievement in setting the potential limits for what a person could attain. Hence, one was either bred into nobility with the numerous rights thereof or one was a commoner. Each group had clearly defined property rights and behavioral expectations with regard to the other. Within such a charged atmosphere, the characterization of one's rights over property was perhaps the most important attribute of a person's status. In feudal times, women became "a femme covert" according to common law. This meant women were under the protection and control of their husbands. There also were risks for the men in this allocation of responsibilities as under the law of covertures, husbands were legally responsible for the actions of their wives. However, women incurred the far greater loss as they relinquished property rights in favor of their husbands, even if it was inherited from their families (Frey & Morton, 1986; Lentz, 1999; Salmon, 1986).

The implications of a man's "property rights" and his reaction to the violation of such rights was acknowledged in the British judiciary's reaction to adultery by each gender. English common law differentiated between the "reasonable reactions" of a husband to his spouse's adultery and those of a similarly situated wife.

From the 17th century through the mid-20th century, British common law endorsed conceptions of men having a natural dominance over their wives and, hence, a "normal" reaction to their violation. Under this conception of dominance, adultery by the wife constituted adequate provocation to mitigate murder to manslaughter (a lesser crime not punished by death) regardless of whether a husband killed the wife or her lover. Because adultery was viewed as violating a husband's property rights in his wife's body and his family name, the common law recognized allegations of infidelity as the most severe form of provocation. As the court opined in *Regina v. Mawgridge* (as cited in Miccio, 2000, p. 161), "Jealousy is the rage of a man, and adultery is the highest invasion of property. . . . [A] man cannot receive a higher provocation."

Although spousal infidelity might be considered a severe betrayal, the law of adultery was totally gendered in its application. Until 1946, English courts assumed that wives did not experience rage as men did. Therefore, women who killed philandering husbands could not use adultery as a justification to reduce a murder charge to manslaughter.

This exemption for killing in defense of a man's honor—and in effect, in defense of his property—was carried forth from common law and widely recognized in the United States as well, both by state statutes (four of which made it a complete defense to criminal charges of killing a wife's lover) and more commonly by judicial notice (Miccio, 2000).

Some historical progress, however, was evident beginning in the 1500s. English common law began the process of introducing some limits on a man's rights over his wife. The concept of restraint was introduced to place some control on the largely unfettered rights of the husband. Under later English common law, husbands were to "dominate" wives using violence "with restraint" (e.g., the theory of "moderate chastisement"). The power of "life and death" over his wife was taken away—at least officially. In practice, however, few if any restraints short of sanctioning murder were imposed on the husband's ability to chastise his wife (Gamache, Edelson, & Schock, 1988; Oppenlander, 1982; Sigler, 1989; Walker, 1990).

It was not until the late 1500s, however, that the British jurisprudence began debating whether there were limits to the theory of "chastisement." Public debate began as to whether God or the state sanctioned physical beatings (Doggett, 1992; Fletcher, 1995; Lentz, 1999). In this regard, courts began to be more concerned about the reasons for the beating and the extent of the physical damage inflicted. Hence, it held the women somehow "responsible" for the beating—if a woman was an "adulteress," or even a "nag," more physical punishment would be permitted. From this perspective, the concept of restricting beating to particular acts as well as the physical punishment inflicted became key limitations on the common law right to "chastise" one's wife.

Furthermore, up to the period immediately before England began its colonial era, "wife beating," although widespread, came to be viewed as a mark of the lower class—at least by members of the upper classes, who increasingly disdained such violence. In reality, now that records exist, we might surmise that beatings in upper-class families, although perhaps rarer than in the lower classes, simply were veiled in silence (Fletcher, 1995; Lentz, 1999). Such limiting rights were perhaps most graphically illustrated by the often-stated, if somewhat allegorical, concept of the rule of thumb, which purported to allow husbands to beat their wives with a rod or stick no thicker than his thumb. The probability that a whipping with such an instrument could still cause serious injury or even death illustrates how maintenance of the family unit was more important than stopping violence. As such, one 18th-century court ruling gave authority to the husband to punish his wife as long as it was confined to "blows, thumps, kicks or punches in the back which did not leave marks" (Dobash & Dobash, 1979, p. 40).

Other societies adopted similar theories that limited the application of the husband's violence while in effect condoning his right as the family patriarch to engage in violence to promote family values. For example, a 16th-century Russian ordinance expressly listed the methods by which a man could beat his wife (Quinn, 1985). When violence became too serious, laws against assault and battery were typically not invoked. Instead, informal sanctions by family, friends, the church, and perhaps vigilantes were undertaken. Such sanctions included social ostracism, lectures by the clergy, or retaliatory beatings of an offender (Pleck, 1979).

The fact is that in virtually every society we have examined, proverbs, jokes, and laws indicate strong cultural acceptance and even approval of the beating of women by their husbands. Any effort to list them all would be futile, but two examples are illustrative of the extent of such beliefs:

> A wife is not a jug . . . she won't crack if you hit her 10 times. (Russian proverb)

> A spaniel, a woman, and a walnut tree—the more they're beaten, the better they be. (English proverb)

In addition, English comic plays used wife beating as a recurrent comic theme. One obvious example is William Shakespeare's witty comedy, *The Taming of the Shrew,* where the woman's desire to test the limits and her acceptance of a beating were comedic.

Certainly U.S. culture is no less inundated with messages of this nature. Until at least the 1970s, American pop culture often trivialized domestic violence. Consider television programs such as *I Love Lucy,* in which Ricky Ricardo regularly "spanked" Lucille Ball, for comic effect, or *The Honeymooners,* in which Jackie Gleason's arguments with his wife, Alice, typically ended with his catch phrase, "One of these days, Alice . . . pow, zoom, right to the moon." John Wayne movies similarly used spanking as a staple strategy in many movies to "tame" a spouse or even to "win over" independent, strong women—usually in front of the entire town. Notably, such taming did not stop until the woman stopped struggling. Although the spanking might have been perceived as trivial, and no injuries ever resulted, at least on camera, in effect women were perceived to encourage "moderate" violence by taunting the male until he gave her the beating she tacitly desired. The reality of serious domestic violence was simply never addressed.

Early American Strategies and Interventions

The Massachusetts Body of Laws and Liberties, enacted by the Puritans in 1641, were the first laws in the world expressly making domestic violence illegal. This statute provided that "every married woman shall be free from bodily correction or stripes [lashing] by her husband, unless it be in his own defense upon her assault" (Pleck, 1987, pp. 21–22). Similarly, in 1672, the Pilgrims of Plymouth Plantation made wife beating illegal, punishable by fine or a whipping (Pleck, 1987). The limitations of this first U.S. intervention, however, should be clearly understood. Puritans and Pilgrims did not object to moderate violence under religious law, and over time, the practices sanctioned (or tolerated by the Pilgrims and Puritans) began to evolve into the more definitive boundaries for permissible levels of violence that became the historical antecedents for the experience in the United States.

Within these sects, the family patriarch not only retained the responsibility but also the duty to enforce rules of conduct within the family. Therefore, they largely concurred, perhaps unknowingly, with European thinking regarding violence in the family. Moderate force was necessary and proper to ensure that women, as well as children, followed the correct path to salvation. In effect, the right to use violence was sanctioned, but only if it was for the benefit of the family—and hence of the colony's social stability (Koehler, 1980; Pleck, 1979).

Also, the effect of these laws was largely symbolic, defining acceptable conduct and not often enforced by the public floggings or the other more draconian criminal justice punishments then in vogue. One exhaustive research project found that from 1633 to 1802 (169 years), only 12 cases of wife abuse were ever brought in Plymouth Colony (Pleck, 1989). In addition, although these statutes might have "influenced" other colonies, they were confined to the more religious New England colonies and were not extended to the larger and more religiously representative Southern and Mid-Atlantic settlements. Finally, because these were primarily based on religion, determining the appropriateness of conduct that was "suitable in the Eyes of the Lord" became even more problematic as American society, in common with most of Europe, became more secularized. For these reasons, enforcement of such laws largely disappeared before the American Revolution.

During the period between the late 1700s and the 1850s, there were virtually no recorded initiatives by society to control domestic violence, and despite a detailed search, it seems that a legislative vacuum existed (Pleck, 1989). In fact, in the early 1800s throughout the United States, judges commonly dismissed infrequent criminal charges of spousal violence because a husband was legally permitted to chastise his wife without being prosecuted for assault and battery (Lerman, 1981).

Furthermore, although not codified into law, state courts as early as the 1824 Supreme Court of Mississippi decision in *Bradley v. State* (1824) expressly reiterated the English common law principle that a husband could beat his wife "with a rod no thicker than his thumb." Some court decisions of this period, although using extreme language, illustrate the prevailing judicial sentiments toward intervening in domestic matters.

One court clearly focused on how the wife brought punishment down on herself (Hirschel, Hutchison, Dean, & Mills, 1992): "The law gives the husband power to use such a degree of force as is necessary to make the wife behave herself and know her place" (p. 251). The same court made it clear that it was even immaterial whether the husband used a whip or another weapon on his wife "if she deserved it," and this gave her no authority to abandon her husband, *an offense for which she could be prosecuted* (Hirschel et al., 1992, pp. 252–253, emphasis in original).

In reality, a woman could not be viewed as being autonomous or being an "adult" in most popular conceptions of the word. Until the start of the 20th century, she had few legal rights. As noted, a husband owned all of a family's property and assets and was allowed to chastise his wife physically. He also had the right to force her to accept new domiciles even if this meant uprooting the family. Not surprisingly, in the closely related context of marital rape, legislatures and courts viewed the husband as having an unfettered right to the sexual enjoyment of his wife with or without her consent.

This acceptance of marital rape changed only in the last century. In *Oppenheimer v. Kridel* (1923), the court abridged this right, noting that in the past in New York State,

> [t]he marriage contract vested in husbands a limited property interest in the wife's body with the concomitant right to "the personal enjoyment" of his wife. Consequently, in exchange for shelter and protection from external forms of violence, the wife gave over her body. If wives refused conveyance of the self, husbands enforced compliance by force. Marital status conferred upon husbands the right to violate the bodily integrity of their wives. (Miccio, 2000, p. 157, emphasis added)

Why did judges condone obvious violence? Well, it helped that for centuries all judges were men, but we believe it simply reflected the widely held belief that a woman, with an inferior mind and countenance, needed the protection of her spouse, regardless of the possible harm inflicted by a few that used such powers to abuse their spouse. It also is probable that larger societal trends were at work. As society became more secularized, the enforcement of community moral standards in private conduct became considered an improper state activity—an overreaching use of governmental power (Hartog, 1976).

In this regard, the operations of the legal systems of the new U.S. Republic (as well as Great Britain) reflected the philosophies and teachings of classic liberal philosophers. For example, John Locke, the British philosopher, strongly believed that society should restrict its concerns to the maintenance of public order and abjure both trying to regulate the private order and to eliminate private vice (Pleck, 1989). Jean-Jacques Rousseau, the French philosopher, had a strong intellectual influence in the United States on the importance of equality and the "role of the state." His beliefs did not extend his concept of equality to women, however, whom he viewed as inferior and as having interests confined to "women's functions" (Miccio, 2000).

Enforcement in the Mid-1800s

In the United States, the second period of criminal justice enforcement against domestic violence occurred in the context of the major societal upheavals of the latter part of the 19th century. Laws passed and cases decided during or immediately after the Civil War reflected a new willingness to impose restrictions typical of a more urban environment and of an enhanced government willingness to regulate families. Some legislation began to erode the husband's unfettered authority over his spouse (Pleck, 1989).

Did such new enforcement occur because of an enhanced appreciation of the rights of women? Perhaps, but frankly, we believe that we cannot underestimate the force of society's reaction at that time to the lifestyles and mores of new immigrants and the lower social classes—long a theme of American "reformers." At this time, the emerging financial elite, as well as the professional and middle classes, were frightened over their perception of uncontrollable crime waves committed by the "lower classes." This was exacerbated by hysteria over the threatened demise of American civilization resulting from progressive waves of immigrants with markedly different—and supposedly more brutal—cultural backgrounds (Boyer, 1978).

In any event, by 1871, the Supreme Court of Alabama became the first appellate court in the United States to rescind the common law rights of a husband to beat his wife as follows:

> The privilege, ancient though it may be, to beat [one's wife] with a stick, to pull her hair, choke her, spit in her face or kick her about the floor, or to inflict upon her like indignities, is not now acknowledged by our law. . . . In person, the wife is entitled to the same protection of the law that the husband can invoke for himself. (Hart, 1992, p. 22)

In sharp contrast, the North Carolina Supreme Court had rejected a similar case just 3 years earlier in 1868: "If no permanent injury has been inflicted, nor malice, cruelty nor dangerous violence shown by the husband, it is better to draw the civilian, shut out the public gaze, and leave the parties to forget and forgive" (*State v. Rhodes*, 1868).

In addition to growing judicial limits on a husband's authority to "chastise" his wife, concerns about physical abuse were beginning to be expressed by the nascent women's advocacy movement. Upper-class and highly religious women began organizing to achieve political purposes. The first of these organizations were the Temperance Leagues. The Temperance Leagues saw their primary mission as stamping out the most visible cause of societal problems, "demon rum," especially when used by immigrants and the lower classes. Out of these early movements, a new phenomenon, "Suffragettes," evolved into the effort to gain women's voting rights. Although this was their primary mission, they also organized activities designed to help women more generally, which included efforts to lift the numerous legal restrictions on women's freedom, such as the right to own property in their own name.

In the last decades of the 19th century, women began to achieve some modest degree of financial freedom and protection of their property rights. Divorce became at least theoretically possible. Although there were legislative "reforms" to "protect women" by limiting their ability to work in difficult, but well-paying, positions, there was a gradual acceptance of women in the workforce, at least in what we now view as traditional female occupations such as teaching, nursing, and other skilled services. Also, with the widespread passage in all states of Married Women's Property Acts, the most restrictive limits on women holding property in their own name were lifted throughout the country. Women thus began the process of accumulating wealth and some degree of economic—and later political—power.

In addition to the right to own property in their own name, women's groups did, indeed, affect official attitudes toward domestic violence. By the end of the 19th century, "chastisement" as an official defense to a charge of assault largely ended. Twelve states considered, and three adopted, a stronger position containing explicit laws against wife beating. In these three states, Maryland (1882), Delaware (1881), and Oregon (1886), the crime of wife beating became officially punishable at the whipping post.

Although these statutes demonstrated a new level of societal concern, we believe that they were rarely officially enforced. In a far more problematic manner, some regions' vigilantes, including the Ku Klux Klan, supplanted official sanctions by using beatings against alleged offenders, primarily Blacks, to control such behavior (Pleck, 1989). One can obviously question their real motivation in that such actions naturally had the effect of maintaining the enforcers' claim as final arbiter of permissible conduct—powers dramatically abused since their formation.

The Continuing Importance of History

Does pre-1900 history still matter? Although it would be easy to dismiss its relevance to the present, several recurrent patterns between domestic violence and the criminal justice system seem to carry over. First, restrictive laws nominally on statute books were not equated with real enforcement policies. Although they might exist, criminal sanctions were infrequently imposed. Instead, they were tacitly deployed to control the fringes of clearly improper conduct. The excess had to become impossible to ignore because of a victim's recurrent severe injuries or public breaches of the peace. Instead, as we discuss later in this chapter, informal methods of control became the primary vehicle for enforcing basic societal norms.

Second, when official punishment was deployed, it was far more extensively used against Blacks, immigrants, vagrants, and other groups without political, economic, or social power. In these cases, it is debatable whether societal interventions were primarily out of concern to assist men's wives or intimate partners, or instead became an additional method to enforce the existing social order against these disfavored minority groups.

Third, the contemplated use of highly visible and emotionally charged punishments such as the whipping post, even though infrequently applied, might be considered an attempt to deter future criminal activity with the prospect of public humiliation. As such, it might have been the logical precursor to modern efforts to use arrest without subsequent conviction as a mechanism for deterrence via public humiliation rather than relying on the ultimate exercise of criminal punishment.

The Historical Pull Back

In any event, just as domestic violence as an issue seemed to have gained a foothold in the national consciousness, the second great experiment of using societal sanctions to combat domestic violence had largely ended by the start of the 1900s. By several accounts, domestic violence as an officially punished crime virtually disappeared from the public view (Pleck, 1979, 1989; Rothman, 1980). This was probably inevitable. After a series of financial panics in the late 1800s and early 1900s, economic rather than social issues became the focal point of concern for middle-class Americans. Also, female activists were focusing their efforts on their primary goals: suffrage and, subsequently, temperance, and not domestic violence.

During this period, the criminal justice system and other social institutions rapidly evolved away from enforcing crimes committed in the home. Political theorists instead began to fear the possibility of coercive use of police, a characteristic rapidly increasing in the emerging authoritarian states of Prussia and czarist (and later Soviet) Russia. Excesses of police use of force in Europe greatly contributed to a countertradition in the United States. U.S. politicians and commentators contrasted their supposedly superior respect of family privacy compared to authoritarian Europe. Not surprisingly, this so-called concern for family privacy minimized societal intrusion into the family, even if there were severe abuse in the family (Rothman, 1980).

In this context, in the early 20th century, case law and statutory restrictions developed that severely restricted the previously growing power of the police. The impact of these restrictions, perhaps unintended, was to limit dramatically any interference with violent families. In one highly significant development, virtually all states codified and then reinforced common law requirements that forbade police from making arrests in misdemeanor cases without witnesses. Hence, a perverse American outcome to the international growth of police state abuse was to limit society's ability to react to families in trouble.

Furthermore, as with the police, the judicial trend moved *away* from criminalizing domestic violence. Americans also were concerned about overreaching criminal courts that served to repress individual freedom. They saw, in the authoritarian states of Europe, courts that suppressed dissent by sentencing large numbers of people on pre-textual crimes. The United States' reaction was to try to limit the role of criminal courts and to divert as many cases as possible away from the criminal justice system. Family disputes were a key area for such diversion. In the first several decades of the 20th century, the development of family courts was expressly designed to eliminate family troubles from criminal court dockets and instead provide a specialized forum that would deal with family crises. Although these courts could frequently grant divorce, the typically expressed goals of such courts were to assist couples to work out problems within the family structure and seek reconciliation. In this context, their mission did not usually include efforts to sentence for criminal behavior within the family (Pleck, 1987).

These courts, as well as courts of general jurisdiction, also began to be influenced by the nascent social work movement. Although perhaps simplistic, at least in the early years, these professionals might have viewed the criminal prosecution of domestic violence cases as "unprofessional" or as largely the result of society's overall preference to stamp its own normative behavioral models coercively onto those of the "lower classes" and minorities. The rehabilitative model used by social workers was viewed as vastly superior in that it tried to help dysfunctional family units or rehabilitate an offender's behavior. Thus, early social workers attempted to develop a consistent intervention strategy for all batterers (as compared with current approaches that acknowledge vast differences among batterers) (Saunders, 1993).

This period of criminal justice dormancy had a profound impact on current criminal justice operational practices. Although less true than reported in the earlier editions of this treatise, and despite nearly universal policies to the contrary, some police officers, prosecutors, and judges still privately hold that society should not customarily intervene in domestic disputes except in cases of dire violence.

As we explore in subsequent chapters, until recently, procedural requirements adopted by bureaucratized and highly controlled police forces virtually eliminated criminal justice intervention. At the same time, there was a largely unexplored but probably real increase in the tendency of police to mete out "street level" justice to minor miscreants, by giving stern lectures, or even an occasional beating, to drunk domestic violence offenders to "teach them a lesson" while avoiding making an actual arrest.

The restrictions on misdemeanor arrests without a warrant were probably the key legal impediment to the use of arrest; however, the restrictive policies of prosecutors adopted in the 1900s also made use of criminal sanctions even more problematic. The combined effect of these procedural barriers made the actual intervention of the criminal justice system far more remote than the crime would otherwise warrant based on victim injuries or offender intent and conduct.

The Biblical and Koranic Basis for Abuse

Traditions subordinating women have a long religious history rooted in a literal biblical understanding of "patriarchy"—the institutional rule of men. Much of the Bible portrays women as naturally inferior, both physically and intellectually. As we all know from the Old Testament, the foundation for all of the Judeo-Christian as well as the Islamic faith starts in Genesis. Within this book, it is strongly suggested that women should be subordinate to men and that they are potentially untrustworthy. In this story, God creates Adam in his likeness, while Eve was created solely from a rib or appendage of Adam, marking her as a subordinate both in time and in stature. "And the rib that the Lord God had taken from the man he made into a woman" (Genesis 2:22; note that all biblical text references herein are to the New King James Version Bible published in 1975). Why is this passage important? Because in medieval times, God was the center of "all good" and people rightly wanted to be considered in his image. Hence, in early church law, it often was explicitly stated that women were one step removed from the image of God.

Eve also then fell first prey to the Devil, successfully tempting Adam to partake of her sin. (Then to Adam He said, "Because you have heeded the voice of your wife and have eaten from the tree . . . in toil you shall eat of it All the days of your life.") Thus, the first sin of the woman ultimately led to the expulsion of mankind from the Garden of Eden and to mankind's fall from grace.

Therefore, in a literal sense, Adam, although made in the image of God, was led away from the Garden of Eden ("paradise on earth") by the transgressions of his "wife," Eve. Therefore, it seems that because a woman had already led to the "fall" of man once, it was right that he whom the woman had led into wrongdoing should have her under his direction so that they might not fail a second time.

Thus, the Bible repeatedly sets forth that women should suffer for this original sin. "I will greatly multiply your (woman's) sorrow, and your conception; in pain you shall bring forth children; your desire shall be to thy husband, *and he shall rule over you*" (Genesis 3:16, emphasis added).

This passage clearly sets the tone for much of the later writings and indicates that God deliberately sought to extract special punishment on women; also, in a very literal sense, it specifically gives the authority of a husband to rule over his wife. No chapter or verse in the Bible ever contradicts this very direct subservient role of women. It is not surprising, then, that throughout recorded history, Judeo-Christian writings have been used to reinforce the subordination of women and, in effect, have condoned any measures used to support the primacy of males.

Therefore, when looking at responses to abuse, we need to consider how ecclesiastical or religious law treated family control and responsibility. Throughout recorded history, we know that deeply held religious beliefs have strongly influenced and, in many societies, have governed political and social attitudes. In this regard, the impact of the religious experience on domestic violence can be huge. Although this subject can be oversimplified, at a minimum, we can say that Judeo-Christian religions have reinforced a husband's right to control his wife since, as we will show, many passages in the Bible repeatedly justify man's primacy. In fact, as the patriarch of the family, the husband was to enforce the law against his spouse.

Consider the following passage:

[W]hen a wife while under her husband's authority, goes astray and defiles herself or when the spirit of jealousy comes on a man and he is jealous of his wife; then he shall stand the woman before the Lord and the priest shall execute all this law upon her. Then the man shall be free from iniquity, but that woman shall bear her guilt. (Numbers 5:29–32++)

Other biblical passages are even more explicit in promulgating the husband as an agent of the state to both interpret and enforce the law. The husband was given the authority to interpret the wife's actions as improper and therefore to invoke religious law against her. "Wives be subject to your husbands as you are to the Lord. For the husband is the head of the wife just as Christ is the head of the Church, his body, of which he is the Savior" (Ephesians 5:22–23). Although we doubt most women ever "worshipped" their husbands, the husband's authority over his wife is clear. See also Number 5:15, where it is clear the husband can go to the priest to bring forth an allegation of infidelity (due simply to a "spirit of jealousy"), whereas no parallel "authority" is *ever* given to a woman.

Priestly, and hence societal, authoritative interpretations of the Bible have reinforced the subordinate role of women. St. Augustine in the 5th century wrote of the natural order of a man and woman's respective duties:

> For domestic peace . . . they who care for the rest rule—the husband: the wife, the parents: the children, the masters: the servants; and *they who are cared for obey*—the women their husbands, the children their parents, the servants their masters. (Lentz, 1999, p. 11)

In this Christian family and household, rule was not ostensibly for any male love of power but from a "sense of duty." According to St. Augustine, "[i]f any member of the family interrupts the domestic peace by disobedience, he is corrected either by word or blow, or some kind of just and legitimate punishment, such as society permits" (Lentz, 1999, p. 11).

It might not be a total coincidence that until recent times, ordained clergy in all Judeo-Christian faiths were men who might naturally wholeheartedly support the natural primacy of men. The particular Christian denomination did not matter as this attitude did not change between the Catholic writers of the Middle Ages and those of the Protestant Reformation. Martin Luther, although seeking to dispel the primacy of the Catholic Church, had no problem stating in unequivocal terms the man's right to rule over his wife and other members of his family as authority "remains with the husband and the wife is compelled to obey him" (Lentz, 1999, p. 11).

Barbara Hart has noted that violence in the context of a marriage was not recognized historically as abusive at all but, instead, simply one of the religious duties of the husband. A medieval Christian scholar even propagated rules of marriage in the late 15th century, specifying the following:

> When you see your wife commit an offense, don't rush at her with insults and violent blows . . . scold her sharply, bully and terrify her. And if this doesn't work . . . take up a stick and beat her soundly, for it is better to punish the body and correct the soul than to damage the soul and spare the body. . . . Then readily beat her, not in rage, but out of charity and concern for her soul, so that the beating will rebound to your merit and her good. (Hart, 1992, p. 3)

Similarly, the Koran in the 34th Koranic verse (Ayah) of the Al Nisa chapter contains the following verse, "As to those women on whose part ye fear disloyalty and ill conduct, admonish them, refuse to share their beds, and beat them." Nawal Ammar (2007) in a well-reasoned article reviews how this seemingly simple passage has been interpreted many different ways both to justify spousal abuse by a family patriarch or conversely to show why spouse abuse should not happen in a normal Islamic marriage.

The author finds that some more "modern" scholars note that the Prophet Mohamed never beat his wife and scorned those who felt it necessary to do so. Still, Ammar (2007) wrote that "predominant" Islamic scholarly thought holds that "beating" is still an allowable last resort but only to be used after admonishment and loss of marital cohabitation do not work to correct the "error" of the wife. In any event, beating would implicitly be preferable to terminating a marriage. Many Muslims believe that,

> [t]he superiority of men over women . . . is a natural and everlasting one . . . according to this interpretation, [it] is a God given relationship of power and authority that men are granted over women that permits men to discipline women (including wives) by beating them. (Shaikh, 1997, quoted in Ammar, 2007, p. 519)

So why are ancient biblical texts still relevant? First, as we noted above, many people of different faiths still believe in a literal interpretation of the Old Testament, uphold Christian biblical- and Koranic-based beliefs to discriminate against women, and give husbands the authority to dominate and use coercion to control their wives.

Second, male dominance can be perceived in the more secular traditions through a host of seemingly paternalistic rituals. For example, many people still consider marriage a holy institution. This belief is a concern because interpretations of holy texts often are coupled with a strong belief that marriage is a sacred institution—even if physical abuse occurs.

One key tenet in traditional Judeo-Christian faiths is that marriage is permanent and not dissolvable easily, at least by the woman. The results, when deconstructed, produce an odd language that shows the unequal social views of the responsibility of men and women in basic institutions, like marriage.

For example, readers as old as the authors might remember the vows exchanged in traditional wedding ceremonies. The bride vowed to "love, honor, and *obey*" her husband, whereas the groom vowed to "love, honor, and *cherish*" his spouse. Both parties still today agree to remain together "for better or for worse until death do us part," which in the context of a marriage with domestic violence, if taken literally, could effectively place the attacker and the victim on a similar moral plane. The difference in marital vows between "obeying" and "cherishing" (as a prize possession?) clearly have implied to some women that adversity—perhaps including being beaten—could not justify leaving a marriage. After all, children may be "cherished" by a parent but prior to modern childbearing techniques often were physically punished. At worst, relaying problems of marital conflict to a priest, pastor, rabbi, or Imam might even invoke stern lectures to the wife as to her biblical responsibility to raise the family and accede to the natural order.

Why Religion Remains Important

One could argue with reasonable validity that historical attitudes toward religion might be largely irrelevant in the context of modern, pluralistic societies. In other words, although it might have been true that the historical basis for most of the world's monotheistic religions—Judaism, Christianity, and Islam—encouraged, or at least tolerated, violence against married women as part of a patriarchal control system, this attitude largely is irrelevant in today's world. Indeed, many denominations have undertaken great effort to eliminate (or at least address) physical domination of married women.

Also, we do need to stress that religion can and has been used to try to prevent domestic violence. In fact, many pastors in virtually all denominations have denounced any type of relationship abuse. In doing so they can cite specific references in the Bible that clearly promote tolerance and would seem to denounce spousal violence. For example:

> There is neither Jew nor Greek, there is neither bond nor free, there is neither male nor female: for ye are all one in Christ Jesus. (Galatians 3:28)

Similarly, even if a literal reading of the Bible gives man "authority" over woman, this does not mean he has any right to abuse that woman:

> In the same way, husbands ought to love their wives as their own bodies. He who loves his wife loves himself. After all, no one ever hated his own body, but he feeds and cares for it, just as Christ does the church. (Ephesians 5:28-29)

From this perspective, a modern reading of the Scriptures can lead the faithful to conclude that early church leaders like St. Augustine in their zeal to assert male control over their patriarchy simply neglected to consider that giving "authority" to the husband does not mean that the husband has the right to abuse that authority. After all, unless someone likes to beat themselves, and God states that he who loves his wife loves himself, there would seem to be a fairly direct prohibition on hitting your spouse even if as the man you are the "head" of the household.

This phenomenon, however, does not involve rewriting the Scriptures themselves, is of recent origin, and has not fully penetrated popular culture in some denominations. Thus, although we can acknowledge and greatly praise the role of many religious leaders in leading the fight against domestic violence and in funding many shelters for victims of such abuse, we believe that for many reasons, historically based religious tolerance for abuse continues to some extent.

For example, we know that many subpopulations within any society retain traditional beliefs regarding the status of women. As discussed in later chapters, many immigrant families might retain belief systems more in accordance with their country of origin rather than with their country of migration. Similarly, there are many "home-grown" religious sects that maintain absolute adherence to their version of a sacred text. For these people, modernity and its rejection of the patriarchal family is regarded as an anathema.

Potter (2007, p. 268) noted the following: "Clearly there is a discouraging theme among the followers and clerics of major religious groups in the United States in their perpetuation and response to domestic violence." Similarly, it has been noted that the continuing role of religion in helping perpetuate domestic violence has not been adequately examined (Ellison, Bartkowski, & Anderson, 1999).

Domestic Violence Rates Among the Faithful

Nevertheless, evidence shows that being religious of and by itself does not apparently lead to greater levels of domestic violence. Regular attendance at services and other evidence of deeply held religious beliefs is in fact correlated to *higher* levels of marital satisfaction and happiness. One reported study found that those couples that attended religious services on a weekly basis were less than half as likely to commit violence as those that attended once a year or less, even in conservatively orientated groups (Ellison et al., 1999). As a logical corollary to this finding, then, one study reported that women with high levels of religious activity (strong beliefs, church attendance, and participation in religious activities) experience lower rates of violent victimization (Raj, Silverman, Wingood, & DiClemente, 1999).

In today's world, however, is religious commitment always a benign influence? As illustrated earlier, many seminal texts, including the Torah, the Bible, and the Koran, all contain passages that, if literally read, seem to subordinate women, or emphasize family solidarity and the preservation of family harmony to the apparent exclusion of concerns over the physical safety of the wife. The key factors toward the role of certain religious beliefs might therefore be in predisposing some male adherents of some religious groups to be violent and some women in these same groups to be more accepting of such violence.

This should not be surprising. Many modern religious scholars teach that books of such breadth as the Bible, the Koran, or the Torah have many, sometimes contradictory, themes. They understand that although some parts might be literally "written by God," others such as passages that justify slavery or family violence merely reflect the social views and historical context of the period when these great books were first written down. Based on this premise, adherents to their faiths should not adopt overly strict interpretations that might seem likely to justify the use of force inside the family. In the same vein, regular attendance at services might provide a family with the services of clergy in pastoral counseling and guidance, none of which is likely to emphasize a man's right to commit marital violence.

The Effect of Religion on Potential Batterers

Conservative evangelical and fundamentalist groups often still fairly explicitly embrace a patriarchal vision of the family (Hertel & Hughes, 1987) and have emphasized clear-cut "male" and "female" roles where the woman's participation in the workforce and public spheres are limited and "traditional" feminine pursuits in the home are "cherished." This often has the effect of tacitly or even explicitly arguing for the primacy of male authority (Ellison, Bartkowski, & Segal, 1996). Exposure to such teachings and belief of their inherent truth have been associated with both corporal punishment against children and intimate abuse by male spouses (Ellison et al., 1996).

In the case of potential batterers, it has been noted by some researchers that some conservative evangelical and Christian clergy provide advice that in effect supports the male batterers' activities—but only if it is part of a context of maintaining the primacy of the family and of the man as the head of the family (Giesbrecht & Sevcik, 2000; Horne & Levitt, 2004; Knickmeyer, Levitt, Horne, & Bayer, 2004; Pagelow, 1981; Potter, 2007).

Furthermore, some religious leaders to this day continue to support male supremacy through a literal reading of biblical text. The vehicle used might be the selected use of quotes provided here. One author referred to this as "proof texting." It has been noted that even today, "proof texting" the selective use of a text to support one's position is a common ploy by those who seek to simply justify their actions (Fortune & Enger, 2005). Today, batterers often quote the Scriptures when justifying their activities. Andrew Klein (1993), the former chief probation officer of the Quincy domestic violence court, stated that he often heard batterers defy his state's domestic violence laws, claiming that "restraining orders are against God's will because the Bible says a man should control his wife" (p. 1).

In noting this, we do not mean to imply that being a member of a fundamentalist church makes one more likely to be a batterer. In fact, such a pattern has not been documented. Instead, Ellison and colleagues (1999) found that while being a fundamentalist did not of and by itself relate to more abuse, what was correlated was that men often were more religiously "conservative" than their female partners (e.g., believing in the authority of the Bible more than their wives). Although interesting, and somewhat unexpected, perhaps this is simply because women who match their husbands' conservative religious beliefs are not predisposed to challenge their "family patriarch." While preferable to violent physical attacks, this lack of actual violence might therefore not equate to "no threat of violence" should the woman ever adopt more mainstream beliefs, especially if her husband retains the belief in his rights as the head of the household.

In 2009, former President Jimmy Carter made international news for his decision to publicize his choice to withdraw from his church.

There is neither Jew nor Greek, there is neither bond nor free, there is neither male nor female: for ye are all one in Christ Jesus. (Galatians 3:28)

I have been a practicing Christian all my life and a deacon and Bible teacher for many years. My faith is a source of strength and comfort to me, as religious beliefs are to hundreds of millions of people around the world.

So my decision to sever my ties with the Southern Baptist Convention, after six decades, was painful and difficult. It was, however, an unavoidable decision when the convention's leaders, quoting a few carefully selected Bible verses and claiming that Eve was created second to Adam and was responsible for original sin, ordained that women must be "subservient" to their husbands and prohibited from serving as deacons, pastors or chaplains in the military service. This was in conflict with my belief—confirmed in the holy scriptures—that we are all equal in the eyes of God.

This view that women are somehow inferior to men is not restricted to one religion or belief. It is widespread. Women are prevented from playing a full and equal role in many faiths. . . .

(Continued)

(Continued)

Although not having training in religion or theology, I understand that the carefully selected verses found in the holy scriptures to justify the superiority of men owe more to time and place—and the determination of male leaders to hold onto their influence—than eternal truths. Similar Biblical excerpts could be found to support the approval of slavery and the timid acquiescence to oppressive rulers.

At the same time, I am also familiar with vivid descriptions in the same scriptures in which women are revered as pre-eminent leaders. During the years of the early Christian church women served as deacons, priests, bishops, apostles, teachers and prophets. It wasn't until the fourth century that dominant Christian leaders, all men, twisted and distorted holy scriptures to perpetuate their ascendant positions within the religious hierarchy. . . .

The truth is that male religious leaders have had—and still have—an option to interpret holy teachings either to exalt or subjugate women. They have, for their own selfish ends, overwhelmingly chosen the latter.

Their continuing choice provides the foundation or justification for much of the pervasive persecution and abuse of women throughout the world. This is in clear violation not just of the Universal Declaration of Human Rights but also the teachings of Jesus Christ, the Apostle Paul, Moses and the prophets, Muhammad, and founders of other great religions—all of whom have called for proper and equitable treatment of all the children of God. It is time we had the courage to challenge these views. (Carter, 2009, para. 2–5, 16, 17, 19, & 20)

The Effect of Religion on Potential Victims

Although potential male batterers might be "tolerated" or find their beliefs reinforced in some religious communities, perhaps the more insidious effect might be on female victims of domestic violence. At times the effect is direct. We know that some religious faiths teach their female adherents that their primary responsibilities are to assume traditional roles such as childbearing, child rearing, and obeying the husband. In this context, simply being battered might result in hesitation to leave an abusive relationship (Knickmeyer et al., 2004; Potter, 2007). When these women seek counsel, some might even be admonished that they deserve "chastisement" by their husbands (Horne & Levitt, 2004). Not surprisingly, for that reason, it has long been known that religious women tend to remain in abusive relationships longer than their nonreligious cohorts (Horton, Wilkins, & Wright, 1988).

Some, but certainly not all, conservative clergy might be advising battered women to accept God's mandate to preserve their families. Several studies have been conducted where Christian women were interviewed about their experiences with pastoral counseling in the context of domestic violence. Interestingly, one study reported that approximately 70% were expressly given the responsibility to "save their husbands" spiritually (Alsdurf & Alsdurf, 1989). One woman was even told that she would be saved in heaven for enduring abuse and attempting to save her husband (Rotunda, Williamson, & Penfold, 2004).

Several common beliefs found in Christian literature might influence battered women to accept their subordinate marital status. In virtually all Christian faiths, marriage is considered to be sacrosanct. In many, such as the Catholic Church, divorces still are very difficult to obtain ecclesiastically. Furthermore, some Christian churches often treat the tolerance of suffering as a virtue, and even as an honor, "a cross to bear." This belief, coupled with the theme by the Catholic Church that a good Christian must forgive and reconcile with those who sin against them, might encourage some religious women to tolerate abuse that often their more secularly oriented sisters would reject. Collectively, these might have a profound influence on her tolerance of otherwise unacceptable and illegal behavior.

> Many scriptures are interpreted to mean that God's forgiveness of an individual depends on that person being able to forgive others. When a victim is confronted with scriptures that discourage her from seeking relief from an abusive marriage, she may be likely to stay in the relationship out of a sense of guilt. In essence, the common values of women, which include holding the family together, not wanting to hurt anyone, having faith that prayers will be answered, and not wanting to lose status in church are strong motivators to remain in abusive relationships. (Rotunda et al., 2004, pp. 355–356)

In another example, although there are no passages in the Torah that expressly promote violence against women, several scholars have reported that the concept of "Shalom Bayit" (peace in the home) places the primary responsibility on wives for preserving peace in the family. Thus, many battered Jewish women have been in effect pressured by more conservative and orthodox rabbis to stay with abusers (Graetz, 1998; Kaufman, 2003).

Evan Stark (2007) in his recent book, *Coercive Control: How Men Entrap Women in Personal Life,* provides a graphic case study of what happens when a particular group finds it difficult to accept laws and norms contradicting religious beliefs:

> A devoted Jehovah's Witness was repeatedly assaulted and emotionally abused by her husband, also a Witness. The woman reported her abuse to the church elders, an all-male body of lay ministers responsible for counseling parishioners on religious and family matters. In response, the elders advised their "sister" to try harder to please her husband and God. One consequence of following their advice—becoming more devout and accepting responsibility for her problems—was that she began to cut and starve herself, losing so much weight that she was admitted to the hospital. When she again brought her complaints of abuse to the elders, this time showing them the marks from her husband's belt, she was 'disfellowshipped,' a form of ostracism that prevented other Witnesses from communicating with her, cutting her off from her entire social network. As isolated and miserable as these experiences made her, she only took the elders to court when they made her abusive husband an elder in clear violation of the church doctrine in which she still believed. (p. 240)

Similarly, although the American Muslim community has not been as well studied in the context of domestic violence as either Judaism or Christianity, several studies have reported that abuse exists and might in fact be increasing in the community because of increased community tensions after 9/11 (Childress, 2003) and because of perceptions that the community is to some extent "at siege" from racism and xenophobia (Haddad & Smith, 2002).

Furthermore, female victims of abuse by Muslim mates might be reluctant to disclose such abuse either to other members of their religious communities or to their Imams. Researchers have reported that the community does not want to get involved in the matters of a family, and that many Imams have held victims responsible for the conduct of their husbands (Alkhateeb). In common with the context of "proof texting" noted earlier, another author reported that although the Koran did not instruct men to abuse female partners, many clergy in effect modified the Koran by focusing women's attention on sections that dealt with spousal obedience (Hassouneh-Phillips, 2003). On a more global basis, South Asian women, regardless of religion (Hindu or Muslim), reported that religious institutions made it very difficult for battered women in their communities to leave their abusers (Abraham, 2000, cited in Potter, 2007).

Can Religion Become Part of the Solution to Domestic Violence?

In some contexts, religion plays a key mediating role in the cultural component of how victims cope with or learn to tolerate an abusive relationship. Potter (2007) reported on a case study of 40 African American women, finding that reliance on spirituality facilitated their tolerance of an abusive relationship. A reasonably high percentage of those women who sought help from their clergy or other people from their religious community were told to "work things out" and remain in the relationship, thereby reifying an abusive relationship rather than seeking to terminate an abusive relationship. Although Potter had only a very small sample (5), she reported that Islamic clergy and mosques tended to provide more support for the abused women than did Christian clergy. Bowker (1988) also reported that clergy from religions other than from Christianity tended to provide more support for battered women. Not surprisingly, then, Potter concluded a higher percentage of Christian women were either disappointed in advice received from clergy or did not even seek out assistance as a result of their perception that the church would not help. Similarly, Potter (2007) reported that Muslim women were more satisfied, even though overall orientation was quite paternalistic and patriarchal. What is not clear is whether support by Muslim clergy tended to support intervention for the purposes of sustaining a relationship rather than encouraging women to leave violent partners.

Muslim Men Against Domestic Violence

Shyam K. Sriram is an Instructor of Political Science at Georgia Perimeter College, just outside of Atlanta. He is the Coordinator for Muslim Men Against Domestic Violence and the founder of the Muslim Suicide Survivors Association.

Speaking out against domestic violence amongst American Muslims is extremely difficult as the community is very diverse and heterogeneous making the adoption of a single stance or ideology is fraught with difficulty.

Can we organize, fund and maintain more shelters just for Muslim women? Can a program to rehabilitate Bosnian-American batterers work for Arab-American men as well? Can a *khutbah* (sermon) in Somali against sexual abuse be simply translated and repeated in Bengali, Spanish or Hausa? These are just some of the challenges facing domestic violence advocates in the American Muslim community.

The biggest obstacle facing the American Muslim community is the prevalence and dependence on cultural identities, traditions and customs instead of a focus on the Qur'an, *hadith* (traditions of Prophet Muhammad, peace be upon him) and Islamic scholarship. For instance, there is not a single, *sahih* (authenticated) *hadith* that describes Prophet Muhammad (peace be upon him) *ever* hitting his wives or children. And yet Muslim men, originally from Asia, Africa and even South America, to name a few, can be some of the most abusive and destructive men on the planet. Why does this happen? Why do we allow ourselves to be blinded by "spiritual amnesia" where we take only those elements of Islam that appeal to us, as men, but reject those that take away—as we perceive it—from our Muslim "manhood"?

For years, this work has been carried only on the shoulders of our sisters in the movement. But we, as men, are taking more responsibility for our actions and also starting to hold other men accountable. Some of the steps we have taken including asking imams to choose significant topics for the Friday *khutbah* including domestic violence, keys to healthy marriage, anger management, etc. We are also starting to become more involved in group counseling and therapy to learn how not to use violent and controlling behaviors in relationships. And we are also finally taking the time to really understand the Qur'an and our traditions regarding the full equality that exists and needs to be enforced between Muslim men and women.

Source: Written by Shyam Sriram.

It should also be acknowledged that although religious belief systems are correlated with lower levels of domestic violence, they might better prepare a woman who does leave such an abusive relationship to cope. This would be true since if a woman has no other source of reference other than the abusing partner, as a practical matter, she might be less able to cope with leaving a relationship compared with those with a strong religious background who might have the ties to a belief system as well as to a strong social network.

Do Societies Hold Different Standards for Some Religious Communities?

The final impact of religion is considerably more subtle: Does society turn a blind eye to abuse in minority religious communities? Clearly, some retrograde traditional practices will not be tolerated by any modern society. For example, the use of female circumcision (e.g., genital mutilation), practiced by those attempting to "protect their daughters from sexual promiscuity" by eliminating surgically the areas responsible for her sexual pleasure, would be treated as a crime in virtually all Western societies. However, some members of the majority simply tolerate abuse in immigrant communities as a result of their perceptions that historic religious or cultural history allows or encourages such behavior. In effect, such tolerance condones, tacitly, discrimination against such women.

The following is a graphic, if somewhat extreme, example of the different standards expected of a specific religious group.

Judge Tells Battered Muslim Wife: Koran Says 'Men Are in Charge of Women'

Friday, March 23, 2007

BERLIN—Politicians and Muslim leaders denounced a German judge for citing the Koran in her rejection of a Muslim woman's request for a quick divorce on grounds she was abused by her husband.

Judge Christa Datz-Winter said in a recommendation earlier this year that both partners came from a "Moroccan cultural environment in which it is not uncommon for a man to exert a right of corporal punishment over his wife," according to the court. The woman is a German of Moroccan descent married to a Moroccan citizen. The judge argued that her case was not one of exceptional hardship in which fast-track divorce proceedings would be justified. When the woman protested, Datz-Winter cited a passage from the Koran that reads in part, "men are in charge of women."

The judge was removed from the case on Wednesday and the Frankfurt administrative court said it was considering disciplinary action.

Court vice president Bernhard Olp said Thursday the judge "regrets that the impression arose that she approves of violence in marriage."

Representatives of Germany's Muslim population were also critical of the ruling. "Violence and abuse of people—whether against men or women—are, of course, naturally reasons to warrant a divorce in Islam as well," the country's Central Council of Muslims said in a statement. . . .

Source: Associated Press, 2007, para. 1–5.

The Social Critique Perspective on History and Religion

The Feminist Perspective

Some researchers have drawn on the totality of the extensive historical background of violence in families and of societies' seemingly callous disregard. These researchers look at the same history and, with some evidence, view the abuse of women and the historically meek societal reaction to male violence as a symptom of the unequal distribution of power between the sexes.

Despite numerous studies showing high levels of female-on-male violence, many researchers do not consider domestic violence to be gender neutral but merely a vehicle by which society, as an adaptive institution, maintains coercive control over the under classes, such as women, through many generations (Jones & Schechter, 1992; Ptacek, 1999; Yllö, Gary, Newberger, Pandolfino, & Schechter, 1992). This perspective views that virtually all Western societies tacitly condoned economic deprivation, sexual abuse, isolation, and terrorism of women for centuries (Yllö, 1993).

The link between violence toward women and sexual inequality finds support in some cross-cultural research on domestic violence. In one study of 90 societies worldwide, Levinson (1989) found that violence between family members was rare or nonexistent in 16 societies but prevalent in most others. In his analysis of these cultures, he observed that, in addition to the existence of natural support systems and a societal emphasis on peaceful conflict resolution and marital stability, spouses in these peaceful societies enjoy sexual equality. This equality between men and women was reflected in joint decision making in household and financial matters and in the absence of double standards with regard to premarital sex and other freedoms.

In short, some feminists have argued that a holistic view of our faiths, history, and social structure provides a more complete analysis of why violence occurs than any examination of a particular individual offender or characteristic of the family unit. From this perspective and as previously covered, the study of which particular men or family units succumb to the temptations of using violence is largely irrelevant at best and at worst detracts from "deconstructing" historical and societal institutions and practices, which feminists believe is a necessary precondition to eliminating sexism in society.

Myra Marx Ferree concisely stated the position: "Feminists agree that male dominance within families is part of a wider system of male power, is neither natural nor inevitable, and occurs at women's cost" (cited in Yllö, 1993, p. 54). In this model, law, religion, and even the behavioral sciences historically have endorsed the husband's authority and have justified use of violence to punish a disobedient wife (Freeman, 1980; Schechter, 1982; Sonkin, Martin, & Walker, 1985). In a real sense, structured gender inequality existed both in the home and in the institutions designed to maintain Western cultural and family values. Furthermore, women were forced into the role of maintaining home and family in a male-dominated society that did not value such occupations. Both men and women would implicitly recognize that economic dependence left women effectively powerless to their partners' whims.

Other critical commentators view American society as part of this pattern. According to them, sexism is merely part of a capitalist-dominated class system based on "successive domination" of one class over another—that is, men dominate women, Whites dominate minorities, and the upper class dominates all those without economic resources. In this context, these commentators reason that *all* men implicitly use the fear of potential violence to subordinate women (Schechter & Gary, 1988). Although such critiques recognize that most men do not themselves resort to violence, the perception is that men, as the dominant class, have benefited from women's continued fear of the potential violence of rape or assaults by both strangers and intimates.

Although efforts have been made to synthesize the learning of domestic violence to encompass all levels of analysis, many researchers believe that structural impediments to a gender-neutral social structure are unjustifiably minimized by a focus on the family unit. In short, by focusing on the other levels of analysis, the opportunity to change society at the structural level has been thwarted.

These researchers most commonly look at the same history and, with quite a bit of evidence, view abused females and society's tacit acceptance of male violence against intimates as a symptom of the unequal distribution of power in the relations between the sexes. Furthermore, the concept of domestic violence as primarily one of a few deranged perpetrators committing a physical attack is rejected. These researchers view all of society as tacitly condoning the power structure benefiting from the economic deprivation, sexual abuse, isolation, stalking, and terrorism of the under classes, including, but not limited to women as a group (Yllö, 1993).

Although we do not necessarily believe the entire social critique implied in the model as described earlier, we do need to recognize the significant contributions of such research. These works provide a theoretical framework for understanding how a society might be predisposed to domestic violence or, more aptly, violence against the less powerful within society. It also provides insight into why particular societal responses occur and why social and legal institutions have tacitly tolerated or at times even perpetuated domestic violence over centuries.

Is Domestic Violence Merely an Extreme Form of Social Control?

Part of the reason is perceived as the males simply acting out in what they believe are widely held and socially learned norms of male control and family dominance. Some feminists have argued that in more intimate relationships, the dominant group is motivated to control the subordinate but not in a manner that expressly uses violence (Jackman, 1994). Most men correctly perceive that violence within a relationship might lead to the subordinate simply fleeing or, in modern terms, seeking a divorce or moving out of a shared dwelling (Johnson, 2008). The relationship in nonviolent, but controlling, relationships becomes analogous to colonizer-colonized or capitalist-worker. Thus, it is the routines establishing inequality that both parties take for granted that demonstrate the continued reality of male dominance in intimate relationships (Johnson, 2006a). From this perspective, the need for violence primarily occurs when the implicit power model has broken down and the male/dominant refuses to allow the female/subordinate to act independently, or if a particularly aggressive man refuses to try control through the "softer" methods.

The Stupid List

When I got here to the shelter, I made myself a Stupid List. You know, all the things he said I was too stupid to do:

    I was too stupid to get a job.
    I was too stupid to learn to drive.

I was too stupid to handle money.

I was too stupid to make it on my own.

Well, I'll tell you this. I've done all but one thing on that Stupid List, and you know what I found out?

I'm not stupid at all.

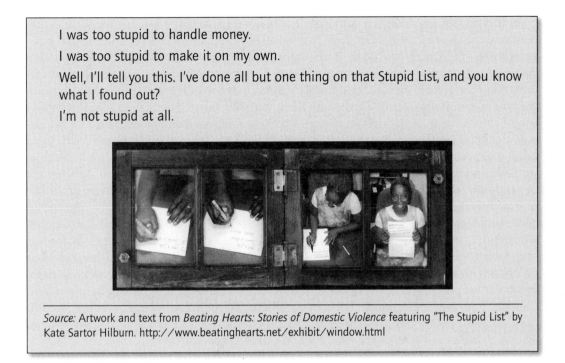

Source: Artwork and text from *Beating Hearts: Stories of Domestic Violence* featuring "The Stupid List" by Kate Sartor Hilburn. http://www.beatinghearts.net/exhibit/window.html

Domestic violence in this context does not simply mean a physical assault as defined by legal statutes. Instead, it is the logical outcome of a continuum of conduct centered on a pattern of coercive controls established by a dominant partner. Violence is simply the most visible and, hence, most objectionable way to accomplish these goals when nonviolent methods fail. The theory of coercive control has several elements: The dominant partner in the dyad (the man to feminists) makes clear what he wants the other to do. Second, he makes it clear that he can impose a punishment if the subordinate does not comply with his wishes, which as Johnson (2007) makes clear can involve not only expressed violence but also threats to take the children, leave an economically dependent woman, report her misconduct to child services, report her to immigration authorities, and so on. Third, he monitors the activities of the subordinate. Finally, he wears down the target's resistance:

Another basic element of coercive control is wearing down the target's resistance, and intimate terrorists use a variety of tactics to undermine their partner's willingness or ability to fight for freedom from control. This is the source of the emotional and psychological abuse that have been the focus of so much research in psychology and social work. Coercive partners work to convince their partners that they are lazy, incompetent, stupid, oversexed, sexually frigid, bad parents, poor wives—in a word useless. An individual who feels worthless does not have the will to resist. A related tactic . . . is legitimation, convincing the target that the intimate terrorist has the right to control and punish. The legitimation may take the form of an assertion of status as male head of household. (Johnson, 2006a, p. 11)

In this model, law, religion, and even the behavioral sciences historically have tacitly condoned such coercive control over "his woman" and have ignored the occasional publicized use of violence, especially in the lower classes, to punish a disobedient wife. In a real sense, structured gender inequality existed both in the home and in the institutions designed to maintain cultural and family values. Furthermore, women were forced into the role of maintaining home and family in a male-dominated society that did not value such roles. This, in turn, was reinforced by the somewhat solitary existence of housewives in their homes during the latter part of the 20th century because the "privatized family structure," or "nuclear family," made intimate violence a family or individual problem, not a social concern. Men and women in society each came to recognize how dependency left women effectively powerless to their partner's whims (Schechter, 1982).

The link between violence toward women and sexual inequality finds support in some cross-cultural research on domestic violence. In one early study of 90 societies worldwide, Levinson (1989) found that violence between family members was rare or nonexistent in 16 societies but prevalent in most others. In his analysis of these cultures, he observed that, in addition to the existence of natural support systems and a societal emphasis on peaceful conflict resolution and marital stability, spouses in these peaceful societies enjoy sexual equality. This equality between men and women was reflected in joint decision making in household and financial matters and in the absence of double standards with regard to premarital sex and other freedoms.

In short, some feminists have argued that a holistic view of our social structure provides a more complete analysis of why violence occurs than any examination of the individual circumstances of a particular individual offender or the characteristics of the family unit. As a result of this perspective, many feminist researchers have not been tolerant of mainstream psychological and family violence sociological theorists precisely because they do not tend to stress the historical and cultural underpinnings of violence. From this perspective, the study of which particular family units succumb to the temptations of using violence is largely irrelevant, at best, and, at worst, detracts from "deconstructing" societal institutions and practices, which as noted earlier is a necessary precondition to eliminating sexism in society. Although efforts have been made by many sociologists to synthesize the learning of domestic violence to encompass all levels of analysis, see especially Gelles (2007), many feminists believe that structural impediments to a gender-neutral social structure remain unjustifiably minimized by focusing on dysfunctional families. Similarly, they often find psychological risk factors for violence to be an excuse for countenancing the widespread nature of the behavior, thereby diverting attention from the real societal dysfunction that encourages violence by susceptible men (Yllö, 1993).

In short, the feminist critique centers on their belief that by focusing on the other levels of analysis, the opportunity to change society at the structural level has been thwarted. Although we do not necessarily believe the entire social critique implied in the model as described, everyone should recognize the significant contributions of feminist research. Such works have provided a powerful theoretical framework to understand how a society might be predisposed to domestic violence, more aptly, violence against the less powerful within society, including women as a class vis-à-vis men as well as class-based oppression. It also provides insight into why particular societal responses occur and why social and legal institutions have tacitly tolerated or at times even perpetuated domestic violence.

Modifications and Challenges to the Theory of a Sexist Society

Feminist theories, almost from their inception, have been criticized as being long on theory and ideology and short on empirical data. As Sugarman and Frankel put it in 1996, "Findings offer limited support for the ideological component of the patriarchal theory of wife assault" (p. 13). Those that batter do not seem, at least in attitudinal studies, to be particularly imbued with rabidly male dominance world views. Instead, the reasons why they batter seem to be more related to their own intrinsic issues of psychological abnormalities and/or membership in particularly violent families or more violent social groups within society. An expressly misogynist ideology, if there at all, is not at the surface of virtually any batterer. General psychology or learning theory seems to be more explanatory of their conduct.

Furthermore, the feminist "movement" cannot now, if it ever could, be accurately described as united in beliefs. Some very critical commentators with an otherwise clearly feminist perspective, place most abuse in the overall context of American society being based on "successive domination" of one class over another—that is, men dominate women using implicit threats of domestic abuse, rape, and hateful language designed to keep women in their place. Whites dominate minorities through discrimination in education, jobs, housing, and access to medical care. The upper class dominates all those with lesser resources.

From this vantage point, increasing numbers of feminist writers now distinguish the effects of various forms of oppression in society. They find that although women as a whole share a common bond of being oppressed by men, White women, particularly those in the upper and middle classes, gain from the oppression of minority and poor women by having access to cheaper household labor and the provision of less expensive goods and services throughout the economy. As such, they find that traditional feminist theory in its emphasis on the primacy of sexual oppression to be far too constraining a theoretical model, and one that perversely does not assist those statistically most victimized by domestic violence, poor urban minorities (Franklin, 2000; Oliver, 1999; Williams, 1999).

A more pointed critique has been raised by Stets and Hammons (2002) and by Felson and Outlaw (2007) who report that wives are more likely to engage in controlling behavior than husbands. Felson and Outlaw (2007) used questions from the National Violence against Women Survey (NVAWS), which asked the respondent about their partners' controlling behavior. Although the NVAWS reported higher rates of physical violence, they found that wives were more controlling than husbands in current marriages but not in prior marriages. Furthermore, Felson and Outlaw (2007) also reported that both male and female perpetrators who are controlling of their partners are much more likely to be physically assaultive (see also Hamel, 2005).

Can Feminist Insights Be Integrated Into Other Theories?

Feminists have provided a challenge to working within the context of traditional institutions as currently structured. A great debt also is owed to the feminist movement as a whole because it often has been the primary impetus for social and legal change in this area. Neither the psychological nor the sociological theories explored earlier have provided much analysis as to why society has tolerated generations of domestic violence, nor have their proponents proven to be aggressive agents for change. Although the pioneering work of sociologists from seminal articles by Gelles (1972) and by Steinmetz and Straus (1974) have played a major role in making domestic violence a salient public issue, they remain more active in academic circles and not as vocal in advocating institutional or structural changes as a mechanism to address domestic violence.

Fortunately, many of these deep philosophical rifts described earlier were more characteristic of writings in the late 1980s and early 1990s. Since our last edition, many of the writings of newer authors have combined the insights of both feminist and family researchers to achieve a more synergistic appraisal and far greater consensus on many key issues. With regard to the role of inherent sexism in our society, disagreements are now less common among feminist activists and researchers and those from other perspectives who do not believe gender and power to be the overarching features explaining intimate violence. Attempts are now being advanced to try to examine where feminist control type theories might be more salient than in other cases.

For example, Michael Johnson's writings have evolved from a perspective emphasizing patriarchal or intimate terrorism, which is consistent with feminist theories of dominance, into far more complex typologies with greater explanatory power. He now addresses and integrates the batterer typologies first proposed in the 1990s by himself and others. Most recently, he has suggested there are four types of intimate partner violence.

First, intimate terrorism is violence seeking control over a partner. That control can be psychological, physical, or some combination. This type of violence is most consistent with feminist theory since the perpetrator is violent and controlling while the victim is not.

The second type, violent resistance, is violence enacted to resist intimate terrorism. This might be the violence that Straus, Gelles, and Steinmetz (1980) have observed from women but put into the context of women that violently need to resist intimate terrorism. As such, their violence should be considered as simply a reaction and not as a type of independent domestic violence. It is important to differentiate this violence from a legal definition of self-defense, which requires an immediacy of harm and efforts to retreat from the offender. It instead focuses on the fact that this type of violence is simply a reaction to an overall pattern of male abuse that might occur in a separate incident.

The third type of violence he defines is "situational couple violence" where violence is in the context of an argument that escalates into violence via rage or an unforeseen reaction. Although severe injury and even a homicide can occur unexpectedly, most domestic assaults typically involve less severe forms of violence and might be committed by either a male or a female. We would posit that such violence might be highly correlated with substance abuse but not with psychopathology or not always with feminist theories of coercive control.

Finally, Johnson observes that a certain amount of domestic violence is the result of mutual attempts at control (e.g., the "battling spouses" of old). This mutual pattern of coercive control becomes, in effect, a battle for control of the relationship. Although these two types of domestic violence might be fully consistent with feminist theory, several others that Johnson proposes are more consistent with either psychological or family violence theories (Johnson, 2007).

We now find that a more cooperative spirit exists that seeks to understand the psychological, familial, historical, and societal risk markers for domestic violence and that focuses on strategies to ensure victim safety. As our knowledge base grows, perhaps we can focus on the need for policy changes and resources for implementation, rather than on philosophical differences as to the relative contribution of a given approach to the problem of domestic violence.

Conclusion

Clearly, there are still numerous problems with assessing the validity of these various typologies and regarding issues such as appropriate operational definitions of control and violence, as well as the interrelationship between physical aggression and control. At a minimum, we now know that batterers should not be considered a homogeneous group. It seems that life-course events and interpersonal dynamics all tend to influence milder forms of physical aggression, whereas more violent batterers are more likely to display significant psychopathological disorders. For some offenders, these violent tendencies might be limited by control of substance abuse, anger control therapy, or other behavioral modification approaches. For others, the problems are personality disorders that are not easily amenable to rehabilitation.

This perspective suggests that policies attempting a single, generic approach to controlling domestic violence are grossly unrealistic and inadequate. Instead, societal institutions (police, courts, social welfare, and medical establishments) need the resources (and the willingness) to use a variety of interventions appropriately, both punitive and therapeutic, to control domestic violence.

Similarly, it might initially seem that the diverse range of theories and risk markers for domestic violence offenders are totally fragmented. For example, psychologists might state that individual psychopathology or even biochemical characteristics are responsible for serious domestic violence. In contrast, other theories are focused on the sociological basis for abuse, including race, ethnicity, and poverty. Still other researchers have focused on family characteristics and structure that might create an intergenerational propensity toward violent offending (or victimization). Currently, many researchers are attempting to develop and test batterer typologies in which they group risk factors into categories to provide a more comprehensive understanding of offender behavior and dangerousness.

Traditional approaches to the study of batterer behavior clearly have failed to identify patterns of differences in violent relationships. Early writers instead simply reported that much domestic violence might be categorized as a pattern of destructive escalation of violence between "battling spouses." Specifically, they thought that much domestic violence by men might be precipitated by earlier aggression or conflicts by their partners. One researcher noted that often the husband is violent as a response to the "provocative antagonistic" behavior of a spouse (Faulk, 1977). The natural difficulty in applying this model to the real world is that virtually all conduct not immediately acceding to the wishes of the other party might be viewed as "provocative" or "antagonistic." In most households, this is rarely followed by violence, so this model does not explain those instances in which violence erupts.

SUMMARY

Historically, domestic violence was considered a normal part of some intimate relationships and a part of everyday life for some women. This historical context of violence against women is neither of a short time span nor of a sporadic one. It often has been explicitly stated in pronouncements and codified into numerous laws, becoming an endemic feature of most societies from the ancient world until very recent times. Religion, being a key component of, and justifying much of, social and legal attitudes toward women, has reinforced such history, although in modern times religion has shown that it can be part of the solution. Finally, as noted by many feminists and others that critique social structure, the deeply ingrained nature of domestic violence into society might serve to reinforce battering by some.

Hence, although we might punish the batterer, help the victims, and try to reform dysfunctional families, we must remember the deeply entrenched historical, religious, and societal bases of domestic violence.

DISCUSSION QUESTIONS

1. To what extent do you believe early laws contributed to the acceptance of domestic violence?

2. In what ways can you see how the attitudes of batterers and victims relate to their early laws regarding the role of women or religious beliefs?

3. In what ways do religion and spirituality increase vulnerability?

4. In what ways do religion and spirituality increase resilience?

5. How important a role do you believe religion still plays, and how could it help better support victims?

Theoretical Explanations for Domestic Violence 4

Chapter Overview

We believe that for professionals to recognize and treat domestic violence victims, it is essential that they recognize the primary theoretical frameworks for understanding the continued prevalence of domestic violence and the reasons why some people and families are more susceptible than others. Theoretical orientations, even if not acknowledged explicitly, drive policies, interventions, and allocation of resources. A growing body of research exists that can help us better understand characteristics, behaviors, and relationships that are likely to increase the probability of battering or victimization. This chapter will provide an overview of theoretical approaches that contribute to our understanding of batterer behavior. We will not attempt to persuade the reader as to their relative explanatory powers but will instead progress as follows from subsocietal microlevel to macrolevel explanations: (a) biological and genetic predispositions, (b) psychological explanations, (c) family factors, as well as (d) community and neighborhood factors.

The Complexity of Analyzing Intimate Partner Abuse

Since the 1960s, researchers have understood the abuse of intimates as a serious problem for victims, their families, and society in general. One might assume erroneously that the publication of dozens of treatises and literally hundreds of empirical studies would result in a consensus as to why domestic violence continues to plague society. This has not occurred. Furthermore, many "general" explanations fail to address adequately why certain individuals are susceptible and others are not, as well as the observed variations among specific subpopulations.

Instead of a synthesis of all approaches, currently we have a rich but disparate body of theoretical and empirical literature, all purporting to address the issue of why some batter or stalk their victims. This might loosely be divided into research that emphasizes the biology, psychological characteristics, and life experiences associated with known batterers, studies of dysfunctional family structures, and community features that correlate highly with battering. Because we are focused on batterers and victims in the context of societal interventions, a detailed study of all approaches would be beyond the scope of this book. Our primary focus instead is to understand how divergent theoretical constructs might have pragmatic utility in our efforts to stop violence and understand a victim's tolerance of this behavior. In addition, we focus on the implications for the criminal justice system and for health and social service agencies in their daily interactions with victims and offenders.

In stating this as a goal for this chapter, we understand that if any social structure such as the criminal justice system simply had a goal of punishing offenders, then an understanding of battering might be perceived as immaterial. However, as we will discuss later, most agencies have multiple goals typically far more complex than mere punishment, which include the suppression of future abuse through deterrence of potential offenders, the rehabilitation of those who offend, and victim empowerment. To accomplish these divergent goals, it is critical that we determine the reasons a particular person or family might have a tendency to become abusive. Successful interventions depend on understanding why someone batters and an acknowledgment that this reason might vary among batterers.

Simply examining an entire population of offenders and victims without understanding the diversity within that population might blur efforts to understand causative factors, or even variations, in the factors promoting violence. Although many victims and offenders share characteristics and behaviors that are similar to those not exposed to violence in the general population, it is the context of the interaction among these characteristics and behaviors that is crucial to identifying those at risk.

Without this basic understanding, criminal justice and social services might easily fail and/or serious unintended consequences might ensue. Similarly, the ability to identify key markers in an offender's history, such as criminal record or when an individual's criminal activity was first reported, might prove useful in determining how to allocate limited public resources.

Unfortunately, as in most social science research, researchers are handicapped by the inability to conduct true experiments. As is common with much pathological behavior, domestic abuse and other recognizable individual and socially deviant behaviors do not occur in a vacuum. Complex experimentation on human subjects that might actually lead to violence would be forbidden. Furthermore, research that statistically attempts to "tease out" individual causal variables is possible and often attempted, but in our opinion, it is rarely conclusive. As a result, we might never identify definitively the root causes of domestic violence because too many factors interact that have a differential impact on the particular individuals involved. This is made even more complex in cases of family abuse because in some contexts, a strict dichotomy between a victim and an offender is not necessarily an accurate portrayal of individuals over their life span. In addition, it does not accurately describe all potential intimate relationships, where an easy victim–offender dichotomy describes reality.

In addition to these difficulties, most research in this area is unable to determine the underlying "cause(s)." Whether we simply report repeatable correlates of violence or identify risk markers, it is difficult—if not impossible—to establish conclusive causal relationships. One example can illustrate this. We have long known the highly significant relationship between alcohol abuse and intimate violence. One might, therefore, conclude that a causal relationship is clear—an abuser becomes drunk and then becomes violent toward their partner. However, might *both* behaviors, becoming drunk and then, subsequently, abusing one's partner stem from social acceptance, an underlying psychological condition, a prior family experience, or a biologically based mental illness? As such, the concept of "causation" throughout this chapter should be approached only with extreme caution even when research seemingly shows definitively a causative connection between two entwined behaviors or conditions.

Despite not knowing causal relationships, simply understanding risk assessment scales provides a key tool for health care and social service providers, as well as for criminal justice agencies. As we continue to refine our knowledge of correlates that predict risk, the use of these indicators is growing rapidly as they might provide a viable mechanism for targeting interventions based on probabilities.

Individual Focused Theories of Violence

The Role and Use of Batterer Typologies

Early research conducted in the 1970s, as well as the current lay literature of some advocacy groups, tacitly views batterers as a monolithic group. Little effort was made to differentiate, and it was assumed that the only possible deterrent for a confirmed, or even latent abuser, was the threat or imposition of criminal sanctions. As Cavanaugh and Gelles (2005, p. 157) observed, "The stereotypic (if wrong) view of a batterer is that of an out-of-control, violent sociopath who is easily identifiable." These sociopaths were generally considered to have a deep-seated tendency toward abuse and were highly resistant to change.

During the past 20 years, a growing body of literature has instead recognized that distinctions among batterers exist and that the assumption of a monolithic class of "batterers" who would respond predictably to a specific intervention is inaccurate (Edleson, 1996; Gondolf, 1999; Holtzworth-Munroe & Stuart, 1994; Johnson, 2006a; Saunders, 1993; Swan & Snow, 2002).

Some batterers have a generalized history of violence and do not perpetrate violence on a single victim or class of victims. The National Family Violence Survey studied a large sample (2,291 cases) identifying 15% who had been violent during the preceding 12 months. Of those, 67% were only violent toward their wives, whereas 23% were violent against nonfamily members, and 10% were violent toward both their wives and nonfamily members (Straus & Gelles, 1990).

Furthermore, other researchers reported that roughly half of all batterers in their samples were arrested previously for violence against other victims (Fagan, Stewart, & Hansen, 1983). They refer to those batterers as "generally violent." Barnett, Lee, and colleagues (1997) referred to these offenders as being "panviolent," that is, violent both within and apart from family settings. Fagan and colleagues (1983) found that 80% of those reported to be violent with nonpartners had prior experience with the criminal justice system, having been arrested for such violence.

An understanding that batterers were not a monolithic group then opened consideration to different interventions for differing offenders, even if the result of the abusive behavior seemed the same. Although an in-depth discussion of criminal justice and treatment interventions will follow in later chapters, it is essential at this point to recognize that there are multiple ways to categorize batterers, and placement into these groups might be affected differentially by various biological, psychological, and social factors. We will illustrate two typologies that we believe have significant utility. The first typology classifies batterers by the severity and frequency of abuse, whereas the second typology focuses on the generality of violence and psychopathology.

Classifying Batterers by Severity and Frequency of Abuse

In Professor Johnson's (1995) typology, most offenders rarely, if ever, intend to injure their victims severely. Instead, they engage in what he terms "common couple violence." Acts of violence were spontaneous and often occurred while under the influence of alcohol or drugs. Such sporadic episodes were related directly to what Johnson describes as the stresses of dysfunctional families or "relationship factors." Although these abusers might act impulsively, they also might be cognizant of society's historic tolerance of moderate abuse within the family.

The second group of abusers, which includes the distinct minority, is referred to as "intimate terrorists." These offenders commit abuse more frequently and more severely. These individuals are more likely to draw the attention of law enforcement, and within law enforcement, they are more likely to be responsible for more calls for assistance. For example, Sherman (1992) found that 20% of abusive couples generated more than half of all incidents reported to the police. Furthermore, these tended to constitute the bulk of serious occurrences. Victim injuries are far more likely to occur with this group, and a pattern of escalating violence with this group is probably lacking effective societal intervention. It seems most likely that characteristics intrinsic to this type of hardcore offender (biological or psychological) might be far more important than a dysfunctional family structure or the presumed existence of a patriarchal society that allegedly condones violence against the underclass.

What these typologies also clarify is the distinction between common couple violence, which is likely to occur equally between the genders, and intimate terrorism, which is almost entirely perpetrated by male offenders. As Evan Stark (2007) noted,

> [a] key implication of Johnson's terminology is that situational violence and intimate terrorism have different dynamics and qualitative different outcomes and so should be judged by different moral yardsticks. They also require a different response. Abuse should no more be considered a simple extension of using force than a heart attack should be treated as an extreme instance of heartburn. (p. 104)

Typing Batterers by Their Generality of Violence and Psychopathology

In this typology, most abusers are violent only within the family. They can contain violent aggressive impulses, except for occasional family incidents where at least in the past, they could lash out on the family with almost total impunity. These offenders are the least violent overall and exhibit few, if any, striking psychological characteristics relative to the general population beyond somewhat lower impulse control and higher rates of substance abuse. Their violence does not tend to increase in frequency, even if there is little societal intervention. However, as we will discuss in later chapters, their violence is the easiest to deter, especially if underlying factors such as substance abuse are dealt with concurrently.

Holtzworth-Munroe and Stuart (1994) estimated that this group constituted approximately 50% of the total batterers—although far less of a percentage of total violent acts or severity of injuries. Inflicting severe victim injuries would typically be the exception for this group, and often it occurs accidentally.

These batterers exhibit low levels of violence and criminal involvement and only moderate levels of anger. There is often no discernable motive for violence. They primarily act situationally against partners or dependents (children and elderly parents); incidents involving these offenders often occur after bouts of substance abuse, conditions of extreme stress, or a loss of economic status, such as losing one's job or experiencing severe work challenges (Straus, 1996). These abusers typically do not otherwise have extensive histories of other generalized antisocial behavior. This subgroup is more likely to be employed, have other vested community ties (Sherman, 1990), and have had few adversarial contacts with law enforcement. Therefore, it is considered to be most amenable to outside interventions. The actions of this subgroup also might be explained by the "broken family" and/or feminist structural theories of violence based on the reader's view of the relative merits of a dysfunctional family or a belief in the existence of a patriarchal society that condones violence within the family.

The second group, which consists of approximately 25% at any one time (Holtzworth-Munroe & Stuart, 1994), is primarily violent toward its family members (both intimates and children) but sporadically engages in violence outside the home. Members of this group can, at times, be described as borderline personalities, ranging from mood disorder to psychotic. They have variously been termed "borderline/ dysphoric" by Holtzworth-Munroe or, far more graphically, "pit bulls" by Jacobson and Gottman (1998).

These batterers tend to engage in more serious violence inside rather than outside the home, but this might not be their only violent behavior. As a group, they tend to exhibit identifiable and easy-to-diagnose psychopathologies, including paranoia, jealousy, and other fear-based emotions described later in the chapter. Control of a victim by force is a tactic to prevent losing her as well as to keep the batterer from suffering subsequent feelings of total rejection.

As a result, an analysis of the psychological makeup of these batterers might be critical to understanding the conduct of this group. One observable characteristic we would attach to these men is that of nearly irrational jealousy toward their intimates.

Finally, the third group is more violent to the world at large. This group has been termed by Holtzworth-Munroe as "the generally violent/antisocial." Jacobson and Gottman again succinctly called members of this group "cobras." We would equally simply describe them as a subset of sociopaths. This group typically initiates criminal activity as juveniles and continues with sporadic explosive acts of rage against a variety of targets. As a group, they assault their intimates, children, friends, and strangers with little provocation. They might disproportionately come from broken families; however, their strongest identifiable trait is a history of violent crime and, when tested, observable psychological abnormalities and rage disorders. These batterers freely use violence, terrorism, and any other tactic necessary to control their social environments to achieve their highly egocentric goals of domination

A link between violence in general and partner abuse is expected. With minor exception as to the preferred target of their rage, the psychological and criminal profile of a severe batterer also presents an accurate profile of those who perpetrate violent crimes in general. The development of an antisocial personality might be the key linkage between batterers and the "generally violent." Research on batterer behavior has increasingly used research and insights from those offenders who are generally violent (Barnett & Hamberger, 1992; Dunford, Huizinga, & Elliot, 1990; Fagan & Browne, 1994; Fagan et al., 1983; also see discussion by Barnett, Miller-Perrin, et al., 1997). Hotaling, Straus, and Lincoln (1989) noted that such severe batterers typically did not limit their use of violence to family members. They reported that men who assaulted children or spouses were five times more likely than other men to have been generally violent and to have assaulted nonfamily members.

A striking illustration of the carnage brought about by a generally violent batterer can be observed in the case of John Allen Muhammad, the senior member of the so-called D.C. Snipers:

D.C. Sniper's Wife Tells All

By Nafeesa Syeed, Associated Press

As the ex-wife of the notorious D.C. sniper reflected during a 30 day fast five years ago, one question tormented her—why did he want to kill her?

Mildred Muhammad wrote about the isolation and torment for years in her journals. She began when her ex-husband, John Allen Muhammad, took their three young children from her nearly a decade ago. She continued when he was convicted of the 2002 sniper attacks in the Washington area and still jots down her emotions as her ex-husband awaits his scheduled Nov. 10 execution.

'The paper don't talk back,' the 49 year old told the Associated Press in a recent interview. 'It just lets you write down your thoughts, and you're able to express anger, shame, and guilt.'

They were all emotions that Ms. Muhammad had to purge during that 30 day fast in July 2004, just as her ex-husband's second trial was beginning. She had to understand everything she poured into the journals so she could finally move on....

Ms. Muhammad, who now lives in Prince George's County, maintains she was the target when her abusive ex-husband and his teenage accomplice, Lee Boyd Malvo, killed 10 people in Maryland, Virginia, and Washington. After their 12 year marriage fell apart in 2000, he secretly took the children to the Caribbean.

'I have come home many times and seen her in a fetal position, not knowing where her children are,' said Maisha Moses, Ms. Muhammad's older sister, who took Ms. Muhammad in at her suburban Maryland home after the children were taken.

During the 18 months the children spent with the father in Antigua, Ms. Muhammad stayed in a shelter for a time and struggled financially. A Tacoma, Wash., court eventually granted her custody of the children in 2001.

Ms. Muhammad said her ex-husband threatened to kill her and she lived in constant fear that he was after her, until he was caught and convicted....

Her Muslim faith anchored her, and as she cleansed herself by fasting, she was able to forgive her ex-husband, forgive herself and move forward.

Source: Syeed, 2009, para. 1–4 & 8–13. Reprinted by permission from Associated Press.

For this group, it is believed that the dysfunctional family is secondary to its pathology. Risk prevention, management, and treatment of these individuals is a societal priority. The proportion of this extremely violent group of abusers varies widely among studies (Johnson, 2006a). One study estimated that they were approximately 25% of all batterers (Holtzworth-Munroe & Stuart, 1994).

Why do such well-developed studies show wildly variant results for a key group of offenders? The answer might be twofold. First, in certain societies or even in a subpopulation within a country, "casual" family abuse simply might not be tolerated. Its perpetrators will be subject to ridicule or worse. The result might be societal suppression of the many potential "family-only" abusers.

Second, in some studies, the population studied includes only those differentially selected for court-ordered treatment programs. We would expect far higher rates of severe pathologies to be reported in this group, more so than in the general population of batterers, many of whom are never prosecuted because it is their first offense, did not involve serious injury, and/or their victims want the case dropped. The group going to court might, therefore, typify a more serious group of offenders. By definition, these individuals have already been arrested and, presumably, present a high risk of subsequent abuse.

Johnson (2006a) found that 60% of this domestic violence offenders best fit a profile of being generally violent and antisocial compared with the 25% figure for a general population of batterers reported by Holtzworth-Munroe and Stuart (1994). Similarly, Dunford and colleagues (1990) found that *most* abusers of women in shelters had serious criminal records. Klein (1994a) reported that most men brought for civil restraining orders had prior criminal records for assaults. In a later publication in 2004, Holtzworth-Munroe and Meehan acknowledged that these typologies are unstable over time and that a minority of offenders might shift from one group to another.

Although there might be overlap and we are uncertain of the actual numbers with categories of offenders, we believe these categorizations remain extremely helpful to our understanding of battering. This was substantiated by Dixon and Browne (2003) in their review of 12 selected studies where they reported that the threefold categorization of situational batterers, those primarily violent in their family but who exhibit some degree of violence outside the family (the borderline/pitbull), and those that are generally violent (the panviolent/cobras) proved to be the most robust model.

A Case Study of Different Offenders:
The Quincy District Court Study of Batterers

Current criminal justice polices and practices tend to treat every batterer monolithically—in many jurisdictions with neglect and in others quite aggressively so. Although a minority of abusers in total, a study sponsored by the National Institute of Justice and conducted at the Quincy District Court demonstrates how the recurrent patterns of violence in high-risk offenders can lead to their dominating court dockets.

(Continued)

(Continued)

Researchers found graphic evidence of early offender involvement in the criminal justice system (Buzawa, Hotaling, Klein, & Byrne, 1999). Although this research was limited to offenders reaching court, they found that at least 25% had juvenile records and that an additional 36% began offending by the age of 20 years. In all, more than 60% had drawn criminal charges before the age of 21 years; 90% of this sample had a first offense by age 35 years.

Research in different courts serving other Massachusetts communities also studied by Buzawa and Hotaling (2000) found that the suspect had at least one prior criminal charge at the time of the incident in most cases (58% overall). In fact, the average number of prior criminal charges of suspects was 5.9 per offender and ranged from 0 to 96 incidents per offender. The only prior criminal areas not heavily represented by the suspects were prior sex offenses, averaging only 1 per person with a range of 0 to 6, and restraining order violations, averaging 0.1 with a range of 0 to 5.

The Buzawa and Hotaling (2006) research also examined reoffending of abusers for an 11-month period after the study incident. Reoffenders of domestic violence against female partners in this sample were more likely to be young, unmarried, unemployed men with long and extensive criminal histories of personal offending. Their profile matches that of the criminal offender in general that is developed in the criminological literature.

The most important predictor of future offending against female partners was the most recent pattern of offending against female partners: The past served as a good predictor of the future. Male domestic violence offenders who were involved in two or more domestic violence incidents with the same victim were more than eight times more likely than others to reoffend during the 11-month period. Reoffending in this context seems to be another instance of offending in a continuing pattern of multiple incidents within a short period of time that was not deterred by arrest.

Reoffenders of domestic violence also were more likely to be persons with extensive personal crime histories. Reoffenders with four or more personal crime charges were more than three times more likely than the less criminally active to have reoffended. The dangerousness of this group does not seem to be directed at only one victim. Reoffenders were almost four times more likely to have had multiple individuals take out restraining orders against them over the years.

Who Is Most at Risk of Battering?

Biology and Abuse: Are Some Batterers "Pre-Wired" for Abuse?

Although many in the social sciences might find this subject disquieting, biologically based theories of domestic violence have long been asserted. It is generally acknowledged that some genetic component might predispose violence in certain individuals.

Studies of adopted male children whose biological fathers were convicted of crimes found these children more likely to commit crime than in cases where their adoptive parents had been convicted, despite the far higher degree of familial intimacy and "modeling behavior" that we would associate with the adopted parent (Mednick, Gabrielli, & Hutchison, 1987). As more fully discussed in the next section, one possible explanation for such a disparity is the largely inherited level of serum testosterone. One rigorous study of twins separated at birth found that 66% of the differences in testosterone levels were attributed to heredity, not environment, which in turn was associated strongly with self-reported levels of verbal aggression and physical violence (Soler, Vinayak, & Quadagno, 2000). Although the relative strength of the genetic linkage between higher levels of testosterone and increased rates of violence has not yet been fully explained, both theoretical (Wilson & Hernstein, 1985) and some analytic studies (Walters, 1992) conclude that such a relationship exists.

It is unclear currently whether this relationship is simply a result of genetics or whether other more subtle factors are at play and, if so, what these factors are. One possible mediating factor predisposing some to violent behavior is an abnormally high level of the hormone testosterone, levels of which often are inherited. As discussed previously, it has been established empirically that although both genders commit acts of domestic violence, men commit far more serious violence than women. Sociobiologists have hypothesized that higher natural levels of testosterone predispose many to a general latent predisposition of aggression and violence. Although men as a group have far higher levels of testosterone than women, research also has reported that higher levels of testosterone in men are associated with higher rates of committing *violent* crimes (Dabbs, Carr, Frady, & Riad, 1995; Dabbs & Dabbs, 2000).

The theoretical basis for a linkage between testosterone levels and violence has been proposed by Lee Ellis, in what he terms the evolutionary neuroandrogenic theory (ENA). It can be summarized briefly as follows: First, females within the context of a whole host of other selection criteria (presumably including regularity of features and intelligence) differentially prefer mates on the basis of their ability to provide for offspring. Second, males exhibit their ability to be good providers by employing "aggressive acquisitive behavior" exemplified by hunting and, more importantly, competing with other males for tangible supremacy within their communities. This preference directly linked the status in the tribal pecking order to their ability to find a mate and pass on their genes. Third, comparatively higher testosterone levels increased the males' desire and capability to compete successfully, and thus more aggressive males passed on genes of ever higher testosterone levels (Ellis, 2005).

The seismic shift from prehistoric to modern society has resulted in the behavioral traits correlated with higher levels of testosterone, having far less survival value and instead becoming more problematic for society. Survival no longer depends on the ability to fight off wild animals or, in most cases other males, using mere physical strength. Competitive aggressive behavior, if not mediated and channeled by intelligence and opportunity into societally sanctioned business or legal (or academic!) careers, might leave some males with a tendency to act impulsively and often violently whether in the context of criminal behavior in general or violence in the family.

This finding is not surprising given that chronic higher exposures to androgens, such as testosterone, have been associated with sudden bursts of rage, whether termed "episodic dyscontrol" (Kandel & Freed, 1989), "psychotic trigger reaction" (Pontius, 2004), or more colloquially, "Roid rage," which is the misuse of anabolic steroids that are chemically similar to testosterone. Increased levels of testosterone also emphasize brain functioning in the right hemisphere (spatial functioning and risk-based calculations) and away from the left hemisphere, which is said to be the center of language abilities, empathy, and moral reasoning (Moll et al., 2002). Since moral reasoning, language facility, and empathy all tend to check aggressive behavior and violent criminality, higher levels of testosterone in some males might predispose acts of impulsive violence if they perceive provocation (Ellis, 2005).

Criminal behavior studies documenting differences in patterns of criminal behavior based on testosterone levels, although not directly applicable to the commission of domestic violence, are suggestive of a testosterone link to violence. In one study relating types of crimes committed by male juvenile offenders with tested testosterone levels, more than 80% of the offenders with high testosterone levels committed violent crimes, whereas more than 90% of juvenile offenders with lower testosterone committed nonviolent crimes (Dabbs, Frady, Carr, & Beach, 1987; Dabbs, Jurkovic, & Frady, 1991). Similar disparities in testosterone levels and rates of violence also were found among women (Dabbs, Ruback, Frady, & Hopper, 1988), and another study found that testosterone levels were higher among violent sex offenders than others (Bradford & Bourget, 1986).

A study by George et al. (2001) examined comparative testosterone levels of batterers along with the neurotransmitter serotonin. They found abnormally high levels of testosterone in the population of batterers as well as a lower blood serum level imbalance of serotonin, which is the so-called contentment hormone. George, Phillips, Doty, Umhau, and Rawlings (2006) later concluded that malprocessing of serotonin and testosterone metabolism could contribute to excessive fear reactions and "overreactivity" to environmental stimuli, such as easily taking offense and, therefore, reacting with rage to "looks," "slights," or "tones of voice."

Batterers with such chemistry might be prone to overreacting to normal stresses in their interactions with their partners and literally reach a point where they cannot listen to reason or stop potentially violent rages. It also suggests why certain selective serotonin reuptake inhibitors (SSRIs) that increase the blood serum level of serotonin might reduce aggression with some batterers. However, evidence also suggests that randomly treating abusers with Prozac does not seem to be of value (Lee, Gollan, Kasckow, Geracioti, & Coccaro, 2006).

In presenting this linkage, we must emphasize that no one has asserted that a simple measure of testosterone (or serotonin) could be responsible for all, or even most, acts of domestic violence. In many, if not most, cases, higher levels of testosterone might simply lead to socially positive competitive behavior, such as the desire to excel or otherwise achieve a positive outcome, as predicted in Ellis's ENA model. Moreover, the theory loses some explanatory power when we recognize that some women with lower rates of testosterone than males commit serious acts of violence. However, perhaps the best use of these data would be to recognize that the largely inherited aspect of comparatively higher levels of testosterone might interact with a person's subsequent social experiences. Learned behavior, conditioned responses, and social control might suppress the negative features of high hormone levels, whereas other environments might strengthen a hormonal predisposition for aggression.

In short, biological theories might be valuable in providing an understanding of why family, social, and community variables impact individuals differentially. The acknowledged limitation of sociological explanations is its inability to provide insight into why two similarly situated individuals behave differently. Thus, the integration of biology into the other paradigms discussed next might contribute to the overall understanding of why some commit domestic violence.

A recent study asserted that the behavior of chimpanzees might help explain human domestic violence. A team of researchers led by Martin Muller, a biological anthropologist at Boston University, spent 7 years in Kibale National Park in Uganda tracking aggression in wild chimpanzees. They recorded every act of aggression, along with every act of copulation and pregnancy. They reported that male chimpanzees were highly aggressive toward female group members, even using branches as clubs to beat them. Male aggression was triggered by sexual coercion. Males were most aggressive toward the most fertile females and subsequently mated with those toward whom they had been most aggressive. Their conclusions might have some relevance to domestic abuse in humans: "[M]ale-female aggression represents an evolved strategy to constrain female sexuality, which in chimpanzees has evolved to favor promiscuous mating. . . . Chimpanzee females are highly promiscuous, and they seem to want to mate with all the males in their communities. Most of the aggression that we observed in our studies seemed to be directed toward females to prevent them from mating with other males. Thus, sexual coercion in chimpanzees more commonly involves males using force to constrain female sexuality, rather than to overcome female reluctance. Males are basically trying to force females into exclusive mating relationships. This is thus much more similar to wife-beating in humans" (Highfield, 2007, para. 5, 7, & 8).

A Question of the Mind?

A growing body of research has added to the biological analysis of the effects of hormones in predicting likely domestic violence offenders. This research is based primarily on insights into general behavior and on neurological development made by experimental and clinical neurologists.

Although a detailed discussion of the neurobiology is far beyond our skill set, the analysis is as follows: Epinephrine and norepinephrine are hormones produced by the adrenal glands, typically in response to fear or anxiety. They are the key hormones responsible for evolutionary survival because they help the mind focus on the basic survival options of "fight or flight" in connection with perceived threats.

These hormones are especially important in activating the hypothalamus, which is an area within the brain. This structure, along with the adjacent limbic structures, the hippocampus, and the amygdala, often are referred to as part of the "primitive brain" because they developed earlier in evolution than the "higher" cognitive areas of the cerebral cortex and are still disproportionately larger in less advanced species where survival is more dependent on quick, reflexive action in response to threats. Although the cerebral cortex, which is the most recently developed, and largest part of the human brain, is commonly thought to process logical thoughts and act as the primary center of who we are as individuals, the primitive brain handles the essential issues of satisfying food needs, determining whether the fight or flight reflex is needed, and maintaining the overall emotional state of mind.

Experimental research on nonhuman subjects has shown that when the hypothalamus and the adjacent structures of the limbic system, the hippocampus, and the amygdala are overstimulated by electrical impulses, extreme aggressive behavior can result. The same has been found clinically in human patients where a tumor or trials of electrical stimulation to correct abnormal behavior have resulted in "Sham rage," which is extremely aggressive impulsive behavior even in the absence of any deep-seated anger toward the person who is the object of the aggression.

When the adrenal glands continue to perceive repetitive threats, they start producing high levels of cortisol, which is another hormone closely related to epinephrine. The effects of these adrenal hormones might be extreme, and over time, they have more insidious consequences. In the extreme form, a sudden large jolt of adrenal hormones in response to something that the mind perceives as a threat might provoke a person into uncontrollable rage (e.g., the "fight" part of "fight or flight"). Hence, although seemingly a paradoxical finding, fear might actually cause violent behavior in some highly susceptible people. Those who have that condition have been referred to as having explosive anger disorder; when activated by these biochemical signals, these individuals might be unable to control their emotions and lash out at victims in violence extremely disproportionate to the stimulus. This might be one mechanism that causes a "normal" argument with a spouse to be perceived as such a threat that a violent reaction is, at the moment, the only recourse of a batterer.

We do know now that children who observe violence in their household whether against them, their siblings, or their parents have markedly higher rates of cortisol in their developing brains. Such prolonged exposure to cortisol has been demonstrated in some neurological studies to affect the architecture and the chemistry of the brain permanently, weakening cognitive development, lessening emotional control, and even if prolonged enough, reducing the actual size of the brain itself. Neuroscientists and developmental psychiatrists have long noted that the developing human brain has an extraordinary ability to adapt and respond to its environment. In normal development, exposure is an environment where rational problem solving and verbal expressions of one's needs and desires is stressed. The brain reacts to this and develops the ability to accomplish these tasks. However, exposure to violence or trauma might subvert these normal processes.

It seems that some individuals, through prolonged exposure to cortisol, especially during their brain's early development, seem to be markedly less able to control their emotions overall. This makes their behavior predictably erratic and potentially violent—characteristics of many violent offenders, including domestic abuse perpetrators. Similar findings, with victims of posttraumatic stress disorder have been observed. Furthermore, these "traumas" do seem to have an effect on adult behavior, as stated in the following quote:

The chronic overactivation of neurochemical responses to threat in the central nervous system, particularly in the earliest years of life, can result in lifelong states of either dissociation or hyperarousal (anger). (Balbernie, 2001, p. 247)

How does this apply to domestic violence? Can we say that we have unlocked a key to violent behavior? Not yet; the research simply is not that well developed. We do know that neurologists have found that childhood exposure to severe stress from either child abuse or witnessing domestic violence causes structural changes in the brain and in the brain's chemistry (Lehmann, 2002). We also know that many domestic violence offenders report exceptionally higher levels of fear and anxiety relative to the normal population.

If such childhood neurological–behavioral connections are valid, then society might have a difficult problem in rooting out domestic abuse. Research indicates that between 3.3 and 10 million American children are exposed to domestic violence or child abuse annually (Carlson, 1984). These children are at a high risk for onset of later long-term mental health disorders, including "impulse control issues, anxiety, decreased attention span, and inability to express one's self adequately" (p. 147). Violent behavior as a symptom of child exposure to violence has been well chronicled (Fantuzzo & Fusco, 2007). We also know that there are sex differences in the response to such early childhood trauma. Females are likely to withdraw or "disassociate," whereas males will tend to become far more aggressive later in life (Perry, 2001).

As we shall discuss in the next section of this chapter, psychologists often relate exactly these attributes to entire categories of domestic violence perpetrators. Hence, it is possible that biochemical triggers, especially during development, might lead people toward a path of subsequent domestic violence in later generations.

Biological- and Psychological-Based Fear and Anxiety

Violence, especially against intimates and other family members, is regarded most easily as a blatant tactic to establish absolute control over the victim. For some, that might indeed be the case. However, one recent study of abusers reached a somewhat different conclusion, finding that a common trait was excessive fear, to the point of having an identified Axis I anxiety disorder as defined in the *DSM-III-R* (the *Diagnostic and Statistical Manual of Mental Disorders* [aka *DSM*], published by the American Psychiatric Association, 1987). Typical abusers were found to have extraordinary levels of anxiety with "racing thoughts, heart palpitations, post traumatic stress disorder," and a "compelling need to defend themselves" against an enemy (George et al., 2006, p. 346). The fact that their reaction was typically not warranted or at the least far disproportionate to the "potential threat" could not be viewed for many offenders who acted "in the moment" without regard to future consequences. They fit most of the criteria for intermittent explosive disorder as defined in the *DSM-III-R* (with the exception that many might have self-medicated with drugs or alcohol—exclusionary criteria to the formal diagnosis. Perhaps this is why many offenders without self-awareness try to shift blame to their victims. It is also wholly consistent with the observation that many severe batterers are frantic about possible rejection and will use violence to control their partner violence, if necessary (Widiger & Mullins-Sweatt, 2004).

Can Psychology Explain Domestic Abuse?

Psychologically based theories of domestic violence focus on personality disorders and early experiences that increase the risk of violent behavior (Gelles & Loseke, 1993). In the context of trying to differentiate degrees of criminality, it is not surprising that research on the effects of legal sanctions for batterers often has been based on psychological typologies or on profiling (Andrews & Brewin, 1990; Holtzworth-Munroe & Stuart, 1994). This remains a popular perspective both for its commonsense explanatory power ("bad people do bad things") and because our society generally believes an individual can, or at least is legally required to, control their conduct.

Psychologists understandably have long studied idiosyncratic factors that predispose someone to batter. Unfortunately, a single personality attribute or "defect" has never been identified that adequately and completely explains battering. Instead, research has shown that a complex constellation of factors predisposes some people to batter. This finding is important because the genesis of a particular problem affects the likelihood that it might be remedied easily by societal intervention, including sanctions imposed directly by the criminal justice system or the prospects for successful rehabilitation through court-ordered counseling.

Personality Disorders and Mental Illness

Strong relationships between domestic violence and a wide variety of personality disorders and mental illness have been reported. Although such linkages have been questioned, especially by those who view domestic violence as originating largely from a dysfunctional family or culture acceptance, many studies have suggested that most male batterers have some degree of deeply rooted mental and personality disorders. Hence, for decades, severe battering has been correlated with several conditions, including depression, schizophrenia, severe personality disorders, and other cognitive or profound behavioral abnormalities.[1]

Of particular significance are the findings of the Dunedin Multidisciplinary Health and Development Study (Moffitt & Caspi, 1999). Researchers investigated a representative birth cohort starting as infants during a 21-year period with periodic reassessments. Eighty-eight percent of male perpetrators of severe physical abuse met the criteria for disorders listed by the American Psychiatric Association (1987; *DSM-III-R*). Male offenders were 13 times more likely than nonoffenders to be mentally ill. Illnesses included depression, anxiety disorders, substance abuse, antisocial personality disorder, and schizophrenia. Similarly, a study of persons who commit generalized acts of violence (not specifically limited to domestic abuse) found a high correlation between violent activity and thought disturbances, negative affect (lack of ability to respond emotionally), and earlier psychiatric hospitalization (Crocker et al., 2005).

---

[1]For further discussion, see Coates, Leong, & Lindsey, 1987; Costa & Babcock, 2008; Dutton, 1998; George et al., 2006; Hamberger & Hastings, 1986, 1993; Hotaling & Sugarman, 1986; Maiuro, Cahn, & Vitaliano, 1986; Margolin, John, & Gleberman, 1988; Ross & Babcock, 2009.

Although these studies report significant correlations between certain psychiatric conditions and domestic abuse, at least one other study of psychological characteristics of batterers has failed to disclose any singular profile of most men who batter (Koss et al., 1994; Ross & Babcock, 2009). For this reason, trying to present a unified psychological theory as the model for understanding batterers grossly simplifies reality. Instead, we find it more viable to focus on the actual observable traits that tend to correlate with domestic violence.

Anger Control and the Failure to Communicate

Perhaps the greatest marker for the potential of abuse is the presence of generalized anger and hostility. Although studies on batterers are not always conclusive (see Sellers, 1999), it seems that generalized feelings of anger or lack of self-control (or both) constitute common precursors to subsequent violence (Barnett, Fagan, & Booker, 1991; Maiuro, Cahn, Vitaliano, Wagner, & Zegree, 1988; Prince & Arias, 1994). This also can be true for offenders who express anger and violence toward children (Saunders, 1995; Straus, 1983). Naturally, if the anger is triggered specifically by the victim's real or perceived acts of rejection (Dutton & Strachan, 1987), abandonment (Holtzworth-Munroe & Hutchinson, 1993), or jealousy (Pagelow, 1981), then the likelihood that the man will target his intimate partner greatly increases.

Moffitt, Robins, and Caspi (2001) aggregated several personality traits that we might define as "anger" or "hostility" into a more generalized construct that they defined as "negative emotionality." This includes negative reactions to stress, how a person experiences emotions, a person's expectations of other people's attitudes and behaviors, and his or her attitudes toward the use of aggression to achieve certain ends. They confirmed earlier research that these attributes are more prevalent among batterers. Individuals who scored high on negative emotionality described themselves as "nervous," "vulnerable," "prone to worry," "emotionally volatile," and "unable to cope with stress," "having a low threshold for feeling tense, fearful, hostile, and angry; they feel callous and suspicious, expect mistreatment, and see the world as being peopled with potential enemies; they admit they seek revenge for slights, could enjoy frightening others, and would remorselessly take advantage of others" (Moffitt & Caspi, 1999, p. 7).

In this context, violence against an intimate partner might be a reaction to the batterer's inability to work through anger control issues. The interaction between anger control and the overall process of male socialization during and after puberty explains much of the tendency for male violence. In many subcultures within the United States, the ability to identify and express anger in a constructive manner is not generally stressed among male teenagers or, for that matter, is it even highly valued in boys during their formative years (Dutton, 1998; Hamby, Poindexter, & Gray-Little, 1996; O'Neil & Nadeau, 1999).

The broader context of potential batterers being unable to communicate effectively, especially when angry, also has been regarded as a strong factor predicting a violent outcome. An inability to argue effectively might cause the party without such skills to lash out violently to "win" or possibly to overcome a humiliating defeat (Infante & Wigley, 1986; Olsen, Fine, & Lloyd, 2005). Truly this is an example of the aphorism, "Violence is the last resort of the inept." Interestingly, this can be predictive of both a verbally inept individual becoming violent and violent couples where each of the parties resort to violence because they cannot make their points understood verbally (Ridley & Feldman, 2003).

Low Self-Esteem

Another frequently observed characteristic of batterers is a pattern of low self-esteem, which often is compounded by a perceived or real power imbalance in relationships (Barnett, Lee, et al., 1997; Green, 1984; Hamberger, Lohr, Bunge, & Tolin, 1997). The negative impact of low self-esteem might actually have intensified in recent decades as growing numbers of women have entered the workforce and have assumed management and professional positions. Some men with low self-esteem might feel threatened with a relative loss of social position compared with women who historically could not aspire to equality in the workforce, let alone to management authority directly over them. A "power loss" by individuals with low levels of self-esteem and little self-control might invite physical retaliation against any target of opportunity. Violence in this context would merely be an inappropriate effort to maintain the appearance of control, especially if the abuser is unable, as a viable alternative, to express himself verbally or against the real targets of his anger. In this context, the easiest targets of opportunity are his intimates or children because any acts of violence in public or at the workplace are more likely to be met with punishment.

Some research confirms this theory indirectly. Domestic violence has been reported to increase when measurable attributes of "power" between the couple are more evenly balanced (Coleman & Straus, 1986; Kahn, 1984; Yllö, 1984) or when the man expresses that he feels threatened by his spouse's career or income success. Not surprisingly, for some people, subjectively feeling "powerless" in a relationship might serve as a precursor to violence (Goodman, Koss, Fitzgerald, & Puryear-Keita, 1993). Similarly, the loss of self-esteem might be a key intermediate step in some batterers' decision to retaliate against a particular victim, either directly by physical attack or passive-aggressively through stalking, when a woman has challenged him by leaving the abuser or has already sought societal intervention to restrain actual physical abuse.

Conflict Resolution Capabilities and the Failure to Communicate

Obviously, most adults frequently confront circumstances that evoke anger without resorting to physical acts of aggression. Why do some individuals become violent, whereas most others resolve conflicts through alternative, socially appropriate strategies? One possibility is that batterers have poorly developed conflict resolution strategies (Hastings & Hamberger, 1988; Holtzworth-Munroe & Anglin, 1991). In fact, a growing body of evidence suggests that batterers generally are less capable or adept at argumentative self-expression (Dutton, 1987; Hotaling & Sugarman, 1986) or tend to misperceive grossly a partner's efforts at communication as constituting an outright verbal attack (Barnett, Lee, et al., 1997; Holtzworth-Munroe & Hutchinson, 1993; Langhinrichsen-Rohling, Smutzler, & Vivian, 1994).

In contrast, traditionally, women have been socialized to value communication and "sharing" and to work through conflicts. Although the point can be overgeneralized, especially in light of recent research showing that female-on-male violence is far from uncommon, gender role socialization might make women as a group more comfortable with handling loss of control and anger without physical violence. Therefore, they might be more skilled at using and expressing emotions and feelings to shape and indirectly control interpersonal relations. They also might be more adept at the use of verbal and even psychological aggression as an alternative to physical aggression during partner conflicts. In this context, many batterers have stated that they fear the woman's "feminine" capabilities of "twisting words" and manipulation. Susceptible men might express this fear inappropriately through violence.

The interaction of poor conflict resolution capabilities, fear, frustration, and an inability to control or even readily express feelings might increase the propensity of physical aggressions toward a "threatening" intimate partner in times of stress or anger. From this perspective, the act of violence for some batterers might relieve otherwise unacceptable stress and forestall emasculation of self-image. The paradox is that the manifestations of such insecurity might be violent acts that from an outside perspective often seem to be "controlling" tendencies.

A partial, but nevertheless intriguing, confirmation has been reported in one study in which certain severe batterers unexpectedly demonstrated a *decrease* in heart rates during extremely belligerent verbal behaviors, such as yelling, threatening, and demeaning their partners. This finding indicates that expressions of verbal attack served to provide a calming effect for these individuals. This physiological response contrasts with "normal" individuals who, in the midst of similar behavior, typically experience increased heart rates, evidencing a strong emotional reaction. It even differed from a third, far more dangerous, group that was diagnosed as having "antisocial personality disorders," for whom virtually no heart rate variation was observed after these batterers expressed "verbal violence" (Hare, 1993). This study provides tantalizing, albeit indirect, evidence that violence and aggression relieves or resolves anger control issues on a physical as well as a psychological level for many batterers.

"Immature" Personality

Batterers often display classic aspects of immature personalities. This includes a well-developed propensity to blame shift or to minimize the impact for their criminal actions. Many assailants immaturely externalize blame for violence to the victim with comments such as "She provoked me," thereby rationalizing otherwise inexcusable conduct. Blame shifting is common with many assailants, who repeatedly cite asserted victim "provocations" that they must know are irrational at best. These include such classics as "I told her I wanted a hot meal," "She knew she was not supposed to mouth off to me," and "She was casting eyes on another man."

A considerable amount of empirical evidence indicates that victims and offenders do not agree on the frequency and severity of violent tactics that male partners use, and this discrepancy is a result of the offender profoundly underestimating the frequency of his violent conduct (Edleson & Brygger, 1986; Sonkin, Martin, & Walker, 1985;

Szinovacz, 1983; Wetzel & Ross, 1983). Polling results from one study published in 1997 show a tendency for abusers to understate the extent of abuse (Klein, Campbell, Soler, & Ghez, 1997). Perhaps this might be best understood as a maladaptive effort to reduce the cognitive dissonance of perceiving himself or herself as a victim although, in reality, acting as the aggressor.

Is Substance Abuse the Linkage Among Sociobiological, Psychological, and Sociological Theories?

Substance abuse has long been known to lower inhibitions to violence and is associated with offender behavior (Anderson, 2002; Chermack, Booth, & Curran, 2006; Lipsey, Wilson, Cohen, & Derzon, 1997). In fact, many comprehensive studies demonstrated that acute intoxication preceded battering.

The timing of the use of the alcohol and drugs seems to be related closely to assault. An in-depth study of the correlates of domestic violence in the city of Memphis reported an overwhelming concurrency of substance abuse and domestic violence. This research reported that almost all offenders had used drugs or alcohol the day of the assault; two thirds had used a dangerous combination of cocaine and alcohol, and nearly half of all assailants (45%) were reported by families as using drugs, alcohol, or both daily to the point of intoxication for the past month (Brookoff, 1997, p. 1).

Another investigation found that 70% of the abusers, at the time of attack, were under the influence of drugs, alcohol, or both, with 32% using only drugs, 17% only alcohol, and 22% using both (Roberts, 1988). A more recent study reported that male perpetrators entering domestic violence treatment were eight times more likely to have used violence against their partner after drinking (Fals-Stewart, Golden, & Schumacher, 2003).

Most researchers have reported that high numbers of domestic violence offenders use illegal drugs or consume excessive quantities of alcohol at rates far beyond those found in the general population (Coleman & Straus, 1986; Kantor & Straus, 1987; Scott, Schafer, & Greenfield, 1999; Tolman & Bennett, 1990). Alcohol and drug abuse are among the most important variables that predict female intimate violence (Kantor & Straus, 1989). In several studies that statistically controlled for several sociodemographic variables and for hostility and marital satisfaction, the relationship of alcohol to violence remained highly significant (H. Johnson, 2001; Kaufman Kantor & Straus, 1990; Leonard, 1993; Tolman & Bennett, 1990).

The method of alcohol use also strongly impacts the likelihood that abuse will result. Individuals who have a pattern of consuming excessive amounts of alcohol at one time, but not on a consistent basis (binge drinking), are far more likely to engage in domestic violence than individuals who engage in other patterns of sustained alcohol consumption (e.g., heavy drinkers). Specifically, the National Family Violence Survey reported that domestic violence rates for high moderate drinkers were twice as high, and the rates for binge drinkers were three times as high as nondrinkers (Kaufman Kantor & Straus, 1990). The National Violence Against Women Survey estimated that binge drinkers are three to five times more likely to be violent against a female partner than those who do not drink (Tjaden & Thoennes, 2000).

In addition, substance abuse seems to be a factor for reoffending for offenders with a criminal history and without a criminal history, with one recent study of approximately 2,000 domestic violence offenders reporting reoffending rates of 58.8% and 41.2%, respectively (Hirschel, Buzawa, Pattavina, Faggiani, & Reuland, 2007). These findings suggest that this group of offenders might not be career criminals but instead more closely aligned with Holtzworth-Munroe and Stuart's (1994) typology of "domestic violence only" offenders who act situationally in the family and often have problems including substance abuse.

The age at which an individual begins abusing substances is highly correlated with the risk of violent behavior, and the probability of a drug or alcohol arrest declines as individuals age. In fact, an arrest for drug or alcohol abuse is an indicator that this substance abuse will persist and that there is an increased likelihood of a victim seeking a restraining order, the commission of violent crimes, and the probability of receiving a jail sentence (Wilson & Klein, 2006).

The use of alcohol and drugs seems to be even more common among those committing more serious acts of violence. For example, one study found that more than half of prison inmates convicted of violent crimes against intimates were drinking or using drugs at the time of the offense; the same study found that approximately 40% of intimate partner homicide offenders reportedly were drinking at the time of the incident (Greenfeld et al., 1998; Willson et al., 2000).

Other studies maintain that the evidence to date provides inadequate empirical support for the conclusion that alcohol and drug use are *causally* related to domestic violence (H. Johnson, 2000; Kantor & Asdigian, 1997; Mears, Carlson, Holden, & Harris, 2001; Miller & Wellford, 1997; Schaefer, Caetano, & Cunradi, 2004; Schwartz & DeKeseredy, 1997; Testa, 2004). In fact, a Canadian study reported that if all attitudinal and behavioral measures that predict violence against women were controlled, then the simple correlation with alcohol abuse would largely disappear (H. Johnson, 2001).

In support of this position, it has been suggested that the relationship between alcohol and domestic abuse is indirect and is a function of attitudes supporting the use of violence. Kaufman Kantor and Straus (1990) reported that rates of domestic abuse by men who supported the idea of hitting a partner but who rarely consumed alcohol had higher rates of actual violence than men who were heavy drinkers but did not approve of violence toward a partner. The highest rates of violence, however, were among men with attitudes supportive of violence against women and who also were heavy drinkers, indicating that attitudes toward violence strongly mediated any effect that the consumption of alcohol might have on committing violent acts. This finding suggests that alcohol might reduce inhibitions in people who are already attitudinally prone to violence but who in a sober state can control such behaviors.

Holly Johnson (2001) examined the role of alcohol abuse and reported that although half of assaulted women said their male attacker had been or usually was drinking at the time of assault, only 29% of victims believed alcohol was the precipitating factor in the incident. In fact, when controlling for attitudes toward the acceptability of male dominance and violence toward women, alcohol abuse was not related to violence. Nonetheless, most research reports that there is a high correlation between alcohol abuse and the perpetration of domestic abuse (Scott et al., 1999; Testa, 2004).

Part of the problem is that it is becoming clear that people react to alcohol in markedly different ways—based, once again, on brain chemistry, previous experiences, and ingrained psychological characteristics. Although it is widely believed that aggression and alcohol use are strongly related, most people who consume alcohol do so without acting aggressively. As Higley (2001) summarized, alcohol consumption increases aggressiveness in some individuals but decreases it in others. Such mixed findings might be related to researchers' lack of focus on differences among individuals. For example, research indicates a stronger relationship between alcohol consumption and aggression in subjects with certain traits, including antisocial personality, impaired cognitive functions, previous aggressive episodes, and low levels of the brain chemical serotonin in the central nervous system (Higley, 2001). Unfortunately, as we reported previously, in studying brain chemistry and psychology, these traits predict that a person will become a spouse abuser.

Hence, although a causal relationship has not been found, the fact remains that the two phenomena are correlated closely. In addition, substance abuse is associated closely with higher rates of recurrent battering. However, defining and proving a causal relationship might not be necessary for treatment. The reality of treatment is that a batterer with substance abuse problems might need concomitant help with long-standing issues of substance abuse, as well as behavior modification therapy to address his abusive tendencies, as the two behaviors do coexist and reinforce each other. Unfortunately, many court-ordered batterer treatment programs disaggregate these factors and do not provide a sustained, two-pronged treatment approach or might even disqualify substance abuse–affected offenders.

Similarly, victims of violence might need substance abuse assistance to avoid being revictimized. The role of alcohol and drug use is also a risk marker for domestic violence victims. Binge drinking by either the offender or the victim seems to place victims at increased risk (Fals-Stewart, 2003; Kantor & Straus, 1989).

Research suggests that rates of substance abuse among women with histories of victimization are higher than among women in the general population (Kaysen et al., 2007). Many studies have demonstrated that the use of alcohol and drugs by women could place them at increased risk for domestic violence (Brady & Ashley, 2005; Breslau, Davis, Andreski, & Peterson, 1991; Kantor & Straus, 1989). According to victim reports or those of family members, approximately 42% of victims used alcohol or drugs on the day of the assaults and 15% had used cocaine.

It is interesting to note that approximately half of those using cocaine said that their assailants had forced this use (Brookoff, 1997, pp. 1–2). Also significant is the increased risk for women's use of alcohol and drugs *after* abuse (Gilbert, El-Bassel, Rajajh, Foleno, & Frye, 2001; Kilpatrick, Acierno, Renick, Saunders, & Best, 1997). This relationship was significant even after controlling for a victim's substance abuse and assault history (Kilpatrick et al., 1997).

In this manner, a victim's alcohol or drug use might not be a "cause" of domestic violence but merely a consequence of repeated abuse; that is, it might simply be a reaction or a coping mechanism for abuse (Kantor & Asdigian, 1997). For example, one study reported that women's drinking was twice as likely to occur among victims compared with perpetrators after the abusive incident (Barnett & Fagan, 1993). Such substance use, in turn, also could increase the likelihood of revictimization, resulting in the continuation of a cycle of substance abuse (Kilpatrick et al., 1997) and in the creation of a pernicious feedback loop between violence and victim substance abuse.

Substance and partner abuse might spring from a personality or physiological disorder, such as a chemical imbalance in the pleasure centers of the brain, or from increased testosterone levels in males, which lead to the misuse of alcohol or illegal substances *and* to the inability to control violent tendencies (Scott et al., 1999). Hence, although H. Johnson (2001) and others have not reported a causal relationship, substance abuse is highly correlated with intimate partner violence among both batterers and their victims. However, the reason, and even the causal direction, if any, for the correlation between alcohol and substance abuse and battering is unclear.

Regardless of whether a causal relationship exists or whether substance abuse reduces inhibitions to violence and/or subverts the effectiveness of batterer intervention programs, the implication for treatment might simply be that offenders with substance abuse problems need help with both its use as well as their abusive behavior. This finding is important because many court-ordered batterer intervention programs fail to understand the importance of addressing both issues. Batterers with substance abuse histories often are disqualified from batterer intervention programs and, therefore, remain at high risk for reoffending. Similarly, victims of violence ultimately need substance abuse assistance to reduce their long-term risks for revictimization.

The pernicious effects of substance abuse and other patterns supporting abuse are not spread equally throughout the entire population. For a variety of reasons, African American, Latino, and Native American populations have been found to be at increased risk for heavy drinking, dramatically increasing the risks of domestic violence (Bachman, 1992a, 1992b; Hampton, 1987; Kaufman Kantor, 1996; West, 1998). For example, one study reported that Latinas with partners who were binge drinkers were 10 times more likely to be assaulted than those with low-to-moderate drinking partners (Kaufman Kantor & Straus, 1990).

Are Certain Families Violent?

Sociological theories might, if properly used, provide a powerful tool for understanding domestic violence or, if inaccurate, might hinder effective solutions. When the general public begins to understand the familial and social conditions that breed violence, society might decide that such conditions are both intolerable and changeable. As such, prevention efforts might be targeted to those families in which violence is likely to erupt.

Traditional sociological approaches to the study of batterer behavior prior to the 1980s were not particularly helpful. Early writers instead simply reported that much domestic violence can be categorized as a pattern of destructive escalation of violence between "battling spouses." Specifically, they thought that domestic violence was precipitated by earlier aggression or conflicts by their partner—the victim of the physical abuse. One researcher noted that often the husband was typically violent as a response to the "provocative antagonistic" behavior of a spouse (Faulk, 1977). The difficulty in applying this model to the real world is that virtually all conduct that does not immediately accede to the wishes of the other party might be viewed as "provocative" or "antagonistic." Since this is rarely followed by violence in most households, this model is a poor predictor of violent families, and in any event, it assumes that a malevolent patriarch is the rightful family leader.

Sociological theorists helped both in identifying those families with a potential to commit violence and in suggesting which factors can be changed to prevent future violence—or at least to keep the violence from being duplicated by the next generation. Therefore, before we discuss these theories in detail, we will note that sociological research in families tends to be based more on surveys and less on the experimental designs often used by psychologists. This is natural given that ethical and legal issues surround a nonpunitive, rehabilitation-oriented intervention before the eruption of violence occurs.

In addition, as the unit of analysis being examined grows larger, the potential for confounding variables grows exponentially whether it is sociobiologists studying brain patterns and chemistry, psychologists studying individual behavior, or family theorists studying family units.

Family-oriented research, often conducted by sociologists, uses many individual variables to explain why a particular family unit might explode into violent behavior. Although most sociologists are highly cognizant of psychological insights in explaining domestic violence, they believe this is not the sole, or even the primary, factor in predicting domestic violence. Gelles (1993a) stated that only 10% of abusive incidents might be labeled as primarily caused by mental illness, whereas 90% were not amenable to psychopathological explanations (Steele, 1976; Straus, 1980).

Part of the argument might be definition. Many personality dysfunctions, such as low impulse control, are not considered pathological as they do not always lead to a negative outcome but to a personality disorder in which an individual with such a trait is considered at greater risk for violent behavior with certainly family structures. For this reason, many sociologists believe that psychologists, by concentrating on certain psychologically disturbed individuals, are significantly underestimating the importance of family and other social structures.

Gelles (1993b) argued that by broadening the framework to encompass social and family structures, the sociologist or family theorist should be holistic and neither exclude nor minimize the contributions of psychological or social psychological variables; instead, one should place these variables within a wider explanatory framework that considers the impact of social institutions and social structures on what is defined as socially unacceptable violent behavior.

Social Control—Exchange of Violence

Sociologists also provide insight into when and where admittedly aggressive tendencies are likely to be expressed as unacceptable violence rather than being directed into socially acceptable activities such as sports or being a great trial attorney (apologies to one of our co-authors). Few individuals are "walking time bombs," potentially exploding at any passerby. The exchange/social control theory first promulgated by Richard Gelles in 1983 posits that most individuals, even if prone to violence, carry out their aggression in settings where they are likely to escape serious repercussions for violence.

Gelles observed that violence and abuse tend to occur when the largely psychologically driven rewards are greater than the perceived costs, including the potential offender's fear of social approbation or the prospect for social sanctions. In this theory, domestic violence is a low-risk way for people to express violent tendencies as it is viewed as a private crime not subject to social intervention. Also, even those highly susceptible to violent tendencies because of psychological makeup simply never need to commit acts of physical violence if they have the economic or political resources to impose their will without such action. Following this perspective, those without economic, social, or personal resources (e.g., the poor and especially the poor from disadvantaged minority groups) would predictably be more likely to carry out violence than those who have the same tendencies but can express them in more socially acceptable ways. Those with a stake in society are more likely to conform and be deterred from acts of violence.

Family-Based Theories

Family-oriented theorists and sociologists place their primary research focus on the determination of characteristics of the family structure that most predictably lead to high levels of domestic violence. In this regard, the family is viewed as a unique social grouping with a high potential for frustration and, hence, violence (Farrington, 1980; Straus & Hotaling, 1980).

These researchers often comment on the irony of a family model that tends to generate conflict and violence while being, at least theoretically, designed to maximize nurturing love and support. This might be a result of the assignment of family responsibilities and obligations based on age and gender rather than on competency or interest. Researchers also have cited societal trends of family structure as contributing to increasing levels of domestic violence. For example, the increased social isolation of families in modern society is said to neutralize those inhibitive and supportive agents like close extended families, strong ties to a neighborhood, and membership in churches, which might otherwise inhibit someone with violent tendencies. Therefore, those families that most lack close personal friendships, typifying a stable relationship, are considered at greater risk of domestic violence (Steinmetz, 1980).

The Violent Family

We are uncomfortable with an overarching acceptance of a violent household as it might easily be misused to foster social acceptance of violence in certain households and, hence, to diminish social support for protecting these individuals. However, ideology aside, we recognize that additional research on violence by other family members is needed. For example, one study has shown that if the husband had not previously assaulted the wife but she had assaulted him (however mild the assault), there was a 15% probability that he would seriously assault her the next year—far higher than normal. Furthermore, increases in recidivism among male offenders have been correlated to the actions of their spouses. A recidivism rate of 6% has been reported when the female partner abstained from violence compared with a rate of 23% when the wife used minor violence and 42% when the wife engaged in severe violence (Feld & Straus, 1989).

Research by Michael Johnson (1995, 2000) proposes a typology of violent relationships that accounts at least partially for the impact of a violent family structure on subsequent acts of domestic violence. He believes that there are distinct causes, developmental dynamics, and probable requirements for different types of interventions. His typology of domestic violence is based on the dimensions of physical aggression and coercive control.

Intimate terrorism (which he labeled *patriarchal terrorism*) is perpetrated by a partner who is the generally violent offender described previously. In contrast, *common couple violence* is committed by both partners, either or both of whom might be individually violent but neither of whom is controlling. The violence might be a product of the couple's behavioral relationship. Hence, the same offender might not be abusive in a different relationship.

Johnson is careful to separate this category from *violent resistance,* in which a victim's violent behavior is committed by a "victim" against a partner who is both violent and controlling. In his research, Johnson (2000) found that only 11% of violence fit the "terrorism" category. Although we might not agree with the relative importance of a mutually combative family structure, it is clear that at least in some cases, the dynamics of the family unit might be the chief cause of the violence.

In an examination of Johnson's typologies, Felson and Outlaw (2007) provided empirical data that did not totally agree with these typologies. However, Johnson's description of intimate terrorists as highly controlling has been questioned by both Stets and Hammons (2002) as well as Felson and Outlaw (2007), who did not find an increased likelihood for controlling husbands to engage in more serious forms of violence, as well as unprovoked, frequent, and injurious violence. Instead, they found that more serious violence was associated with motivate, regardless of gender.

Learning Theory

Childhood socialization also has been studied as a predictor of future domestic violence. Children growing up in violent homes learn that specific types of abusive behavior, including attitudes and belief systems justifying the use of violence, are acceptable. A basic premise of this theory is *modeling*—children learn their behavior from those around them.

Straus (1973) and Giles-Sims (1983) examined how particular family structures recurrently lead to suppressed or alternatively increased levels of violence. The extent of familial violence within a family is typically measured by well-designed, neutrally applied conflict tactics scales designed to rate empirically the conditions under which family violence was likely.

Families in which violence is taught at a young age are likely to have children who model this behavior. Indeed, one study reported that 45% of male batterers had witnessed their father beating their mother (Finkelhor, Hotaling, & Yllö, 1988; Sonkin et al., 1985). From this perspective, family violence should become the chief focus of research, as it would best predict how violence will occur and how severe it will be in particular families. We should note that learning theory is gender neutral and encompasses violence against women by their intimates and violence by women against men.

Is Domestic Violence an Intergenerational Problem?

Sociological theorists have long reported that there are groups within most societies that develop a "subculture of violence" with reinforcing values and norms that make violence much more likely. This insight could be applied to explain why domestic violence might be concentrated in some communities and why different subcultures within a particular society have different overall rates of violence (Wolfgang & Ferracuti, 1967, 1982). It also serves as a basis for exploring why family violence seems to be transmitted across generations.

Consequently, the experience of violence in childhood and children's witnessing of violence both within and outside the family have been explored as factors in predicting both subsequent violence and victimization in later adult intimate relationships, and it is referred to as the intergenerational transmission of family violence. Learning theorists suggest that the process of learning a power abusive interactional style where the only strategy for handling negative feelings and anger is for the more powerful to act aggressively toward the less powerful might be the direct link to why violence travels between generations. Children "learn" that relationships consist of two roles: victimizer and victim. As a result, these children tend to view other, more nuanced and socially acceptable relationships as frightening, undependable, and insecure. Several studies have reported a powerful association between childhood observations of violence, particularly parental violence, and the child's subsequent potential to become a batterer. Some even maintain that witnessing violence better predicts future violence than direct victimization.[2]

As we have discussed previously in examining the sociobiological bases of abuse in the development of children's brains, sociological findings also have raised questions about whether children who witness domestic violence are themselves in need of protection (Jaffe, Wilson, & Wolfe, 1986a).

A considerable body of research addresses the long-term consequences confronting these children. They often experience many of the emotional problems that affect victims, including psychosomatic complaints, depression, and anxiety. Children who witness violence are also at greater risk for adult victimization, mental health problems, educational difficulties, substance abuse problems, and employment problems.[3]

The "cycle of violence" or intergenerational transmission of violence thesis has been advanced in many policy arguments for effective intervention in domestic violence. Interventions that limit or curtail domestic violence also will have indirect consequences, limiting the exposure of children to violent role models.

Why is this true? One theory is that childhood acceptance of aggression as "normal" within a family interacts with common childhood personality traits among boys (impulsive and immature behavior, self-esteem doubts, a tendency to take offense easily, and anger control issues) to increase a tendency toward battering (Hotaling & Sugarman, 1986; Riggs & O'Leary, 1989, 1992; Straus, 1980). Straus observed that batterers seem to have developed a long-term association between "love" and violence, perhaps caused by physical punishment from caregivers or others in the family starting in infancy (Straus, 1980). In this manner, parental violence seems to be related closely to repetitive spousal aggression (Simons, Wu, & Conger, 1995).

Nonetheless, although there are clearly adverse effects to witnessing violence, the strength of relationship across all types of batterers is not clearly established. Many children witness violence in the family; of those children, only a minority actually become abusive themselves, whether to their children or to their intimate partners. We do know that most people placed in the same situation seek and achieve nonviolent relationships throughout their lives.

---

[2]cf. Barnett et al., 1991; Hotaling & Sugarman, 1986; Caesar & Hamberger, 1989; Widom, 1989, 1992; Widom & Maxfield, 2001.

[3]See especially Buzawa et al., 1999; Finkelhor et al., 2009; Gilbert et al., 2009; Hotaling & Sugarman, 1986; Hurt, Malmud, Brodsky, & Giannetta, 2001; Short, 2000; and Widom, 1992.

Also, since existing research models have not been experimental, they tend to lead to messy data sets. For example, when studying the effects of a child who comes from a violent family, what constitutes exposure to abuse? Should it not be measured in terms of frequency and severity? It would seem intuitively reasonable in terms of long-term consequences, to assume that one-time exposure to one parent slapping another might differ from witnessing regular severe beatings.

Second, children are exposed to violence from a variety of sources. Therefore, identifying the role of exposure to violence in the family compared with witnessing violence in the community, or being a direct victim of violence, is difficult to determine. The National Survey of Children's Exposure to Violence conducted in 2008 reported that "more than 60% of children age 17 and younger were exposed to violence either directly or indirectly during the past year."[4] However, slightly less than 10% of these incidents involved witnessing violence in the family (Finkelhor, Turner, Ormrod, Hamby, & Kracke, 2009). Their overall exposure was broken down as follows:

Figure 4.1   Children's Exposure to Violence

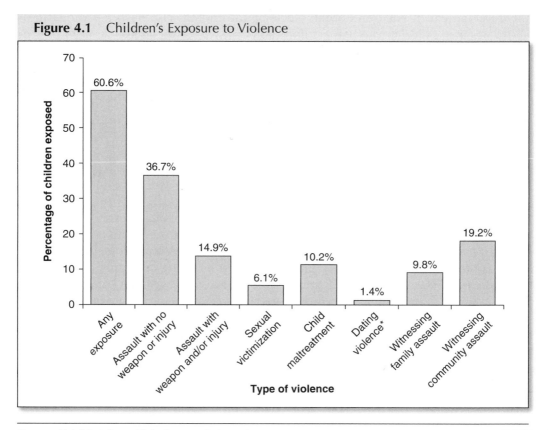

Source: Exhibit 1 from Finkelhor et al. (2009).

* Figures for dating violence are only for children and adolescents age 12 and older.

---

[4]Exposure for the purposes of the survey included children who (a) were witnesses to a violent act; (b) learned of a violent act against a family member, neighbor, or close friend; or (c) received a threat against their homes or schools.

Third, how are these events affected by the specific characteristics of the child, such as age, personality, and other risk factors in their life such as poverty, parental substance abuse, or exposure to violence in other settings? These interactions are frequent and likely to be complex. For example, children exposed to parental violence also are far more likely themselves to be physically abused and neglected—estimates as high as 15 times the national average (Osofsky, 1999). They also are more likely to be at greater risk for exposure to sibling violence, violence in the schools, and street violence (Finkelhor, Ormrod, & Turner, 2007; Finkelhor et al., 2009; Osofsky, 1999).

Finally, other aspects of maladaptive family structure also have been implicated, including separation and loss events (Corvo, 1992), aggressive parental "shaming" and guilt inducement (Dutton, 1998), and socialization into accepting male entitlement to power and the use of physical dominance to achieve control (DeKeseredy, Saunders, Schwartz, & Alvi, 1997).

Sociodemographic Correlates of Violence and Underserved Populations

Poverty and Unemployment

Many battered women's activists and organizations, naturally seeking to develop consensus for aggressive domestic violence policies, have noted that domestic violence crosses all economic boundaries (Moore, 1997; Swanberg, Logan, & Macke, 2005; Swanberg, Macke, & Logan, 2007). The observation that victims are drawn from all socioeconomic classes and ethnic groups has been based on ideological beliefs and the desire to push universal policy changes rather than on empirical research rigorously examining the correlates of abuse.

Unfortunately, such studies often have relied on unrepresentative samples of a few highly vocal middle- and upper-middle-class suburban White women. Many of these women have become spokespersons for battered women or were the focus of the press, perhaps because the media find their plight more newsworthy or shocking than that of more representative abused women (i.e., those who are poor, minority, and/economically or socially disempowered).

In contrast, most empirically based survey research in the United States consistently reports that domestic violence is disproportionately concentrated in poor populations and in certain ethnic subgroups. Violence is not only more prevalent among those who are economically disadvantaged, but also it helps trap them into a life of continued poverty (Kaufman Kantor & Jasinski, 1997; Moore, 1997; Renzetti, 2009; Straus & Smith, 1990; Yllö & Straus, 1990).

The lack of family income increases the potential for violence. Many intuitively believe that financial stress and feelings of powerlessness negatively affect behavior. It also is impacted by the increase in alcoholism, separation, and divorce, which are more prevalent within families undergoing economic stress (Benson & Fox, 2004; Romero, Chavkin, Wise, & Smith, 2003).

One can examine the evidence supporting this argument in four ways. However, the empirical data collected seems only to examine male rates of domestic violence against female partners.

First, we are aware that the ongoing recession has increased poverty worldwide, which should correlate with increases in domestic violence if the two phenomena are related. In its most direct form, domestic violence homicide rates have a staggering correlation with unemployment. Although national data for 2009 have not yet been published, cities are beginning to report dramatic increases in domestic homicides. For example, in Philadelphia, nondomestic homicides decreased by 9% from 2008 to 2009. In contrast, domestic violence homicides increased from 35 to 60 in the same year.

Second, recent evidence strongly suggests that nonfatal domestic violence rates also increase with high male unemployment. The results of a 5-year study reported that rates of domestic violence in cases where the male is always employed is 4.7% compared with 7.5% in cases where the male experiences one period of unemployment and up to 12.3% for males with two or more periods of unemployment. Therefore, women with male partners who experienced two or more periods of unemployment were almost three times as likely to be victims of domestic violence compared with women with partners who remained employed (Benson & Fox, 2004; National Network to End Domestic Violence, 2009).

Third, evidence suggests that victim requests for assistance have increased dramatically. This can be measured by calls to the National Domestic Violence Hotline, which dramatically increased as the economy deteriorated in 2009. In addition, the Mary Kay Ash Charitable Foundation reported in May 2009 that 75% of the nation's domestic violence shelters reported an increase in women seeking help since December 2008. Their study attributed this increase to financial issues.

Clearly, financial strain seems to be associated with higher rates of domestic violence. One study reported rates that were approximately 3-1/2 times higher than those with low levels of financial strain (2.7% of couples reporting low levels of financial strain compared with 9.5% for couples reporting high subjective perceptions of financial strain). They also report more than twice the rate for repeat violence (less than 2% compared with a little more than 5% (Benson & Fox, 2004).

One obvious factor is the greater stress of making ends meet without the financial safety net that most have. Minor emergencies, medical bills, or other mishaps can create a strong feeling of being powerless to control their destiny. Loss of a job or an increase in mortgage or rental payments might make the risk of homelessness a reality. Therefore, stress clearly increases with a lack of money and familial problems, and it is a strong predictor of subsequent domestic violence.

In addition, domestic violence can produce the conditions that breed subsequent violence. Domestic violence often is a barrier to employment (Moe & Bell, 2004). Batterers actively interfere with a victim at her place of employment; attempt to disable her vehicle or take money used for public transportation; use threats against her, her children, or pets if she goes to her place of employment; inflict facial cuts and bruises; or even physically restrain or incapacitate her so that she cannot leave her residence. Therefore, victims are at far greater risk for frequent periods of unemployment and welfare dependence than nonvictims (Renzetti, 2009; Walker, Logan, Jordan, & Campbell, 2004).

The theory behind financial strain and increased domestic abuse seems to be well established. Recent research focused on domestic violence in the case of sudden natural disasters graphically shows that domestic violence as well as violence in general increases after any major disequilibrium. The "pressure and release" model posed by Wisner, Blaikie, Cannon, and Davis (2004) demonstrates how root causes in the political and social system (such as a patriarchal society) can interact with existing poverty and result in acts of antisocial behavior in cases where disequilibrium occurs. This model has been applied to domestic violence by many studies that show that service demands for victims of domestic violence dramatically increase after natural disasters such as Hurricane Katrina (Jenkins & Phillips, 2008) and various earthquakes (Wilson, Phillips, & Neal, 1998) that have affected the families' income and resources.

In the previous statement, we are not indicating that affluent women are not subject to battering. As we discussed previously in this chapter, some batterers have deep-rooted biological or psychological predispositions toward aggression and violence. Those types of batterers increase in all kinds of social strata, and as incidents have demonstrated, they can become violent under a variety of circumstances without any financial strain.

In fact, for these types of batterers, the relationship between family income and the potential for abuse might be minimal. In some cases, the potential for violence might increase as family income increases, especially if that increased income is from earnings of the potential victim. For these batterers, the victim's participation in the labor force, even though it increases total family income and ostensibly removes the family from the lowest economic strata, might actually increase risks for abuse by symbolically threatening her partner's position of economic power (Kaukinen, 2004).

It might be that for this subclass of batterers, the total level of family income is not as important as the batterer's perception that his income and social status is lower than the victim's. If the victim earns more or has a higher status position than her spouse, then violence might be more likely to occur because some men are highly threatened by female partners who "outrank" them in social measurements (Melzer, 2002).

Victims who live with such psychologically impaired batterers might, of course, be empowered by creating the means and support networks needed for her ultimate independence (Gibson-Davis, Edin, & McLahanan, 2005; Kaukinen, 2004).

Ethnicity and Domestic Violence

As discussed in Chapter 3, domestic violence differentially impacts women in the United States. Coker (2000) discussed how research has tended to simplify the diverse experience of women in this country. She observed that many studies purporting to examine "women of color" have relied primarily on African American women and that, in contrast, research on White women became the de facto surrogate for all women. Even when such studies tried to expand their scope, results are sometimes difficult to interpret. For example, Coker noted that in perhaps the largest study examining domestic violence rates among Latino women, the study included only women who spoke English (Coker, 2000).

The following sections attempt to highlight what we know about some of the additional risk markers that each of these groups face. In the following discussion, we need to emphasize that higher rates of domestic violence in any racial or ethnic group are not inevitable. Rather, race might be a risk marker, increasing the likelihood of violence, compared with the population as a whole.

Domestic Violence in the African American Community

As discussed in Chapter 1, many minority groups, including African Americans, seem to be at an increased risk for abuse. It would be overly simplistic to state that this is because of some inherent features of the African American family structure. Instead, to some extent, the higher observed rates of domestic violence between some ethnic and racial minority groups is simply attributable to higher rates of poverty.

It seems that both environmental stress and family pathologies—including poverty, social dislocation, unemployment, and population density—all play a role in increasing the rate of violence in this community (Bent-Goodley, 2001). The effects of poverty as well as other related factors are highlighted by the fact that these differences diminish (but are not totally absent) when other sociodemographic and relationship variables are controlled (Tjaden & Thoennes, 2000). Therefore, by itself, differential data in rates of domestic violence between African Americans and others support a race-based explanation for crime (e.g., a "Black subculture of violence"). Instead, it is more consistent with arguments supporting an association between violence with populations characterized by economic and social isolation, which is a life situation found more typically in the Black community (Sampson & Wilson, 1995).

For example, M. P. Johnson (2000) found that unemployment was a significant predictor of violence. She suggested that some men might perceive employment as a critical component of their masculine identity and resort to violence in an effort to regain lost status. In addition, urban poverty differentially affects African American women who are more likely than White women to live in neighborhoods with high rates of poverty overall. This is likely to have a disproportionate impact on the availability of services for African American victims of domestic violence (Coker, 2000).

The effects of differences in social structure also might encourage more domestic violence among African Americans. The fact is that middle-class African American women also are more likely to experience domestic violence than White middle-class women. It has been suggested that the lifestyle behaviors or traditional cultural values that govern relationships are maintained (at least for one generation) even when social class changes (Bell & Mathis, 2000; Bent-Goodley, 2001). Employment might still be a factor in middle-class African American households. In addition, as noted previously, some men feel extremely threatened when their domestic partners earn more or have a more prestigious career. They might feel psychologically threatened and use violence to reassert power in their relationships (Yllö & Straus, 1990). This might partially account for the higher rates of domestic violence among middle-class African American women since African American women have higher rates of college education and often better (or at least steadier) job prospects than their partners. A rationale for why domestic violence might have increased in the African American community in the 1960s and 1970s might be that minority women began to challenge the position of African American men economically and politically (West, 1999).

To some extent, relatively higher rates of domestic violence in the African American community also can be viewed simply as maladaptive behavior in response to continued actual or perceived societal oppression, racism, and discrimination (Oliver, 1999; Williams, 1999). It also has been argued that slavery created the expectation of strong African American women as they were expected to perform the same work as men (Weisz, 2005).

The experience of powerlessness, anger, and distrust of a dominant community might be responsible for increasing the potential for abuse between intimates of color (Bent-Goodley, 2001). One author posed the intriguing hypothesis that American society has "allowed" African American men to become the "head of the household and given him physical control over African American women in tacit exchange for the men's avoidance of confrontations with the White power structure" (Franklin, 2000, p. 61). The development of a strong African American political culture in the 1980s and 1990s meant that minority women—even those who knew of extensive domestic violence problems in their community—remained silent for a far longer period than their White counterparts to support their community as a whole and together challenge the negative stereotypes of African American society (Bent-Goodley, 2001; Weisz, 2005).

It has been questioned whether there is an ecological disparity between races. Middle-class African American women are still far more likely to experience domestic violence than their White counterparts (Hampton, Carrillo, & Kim, 1998). At this point, no one can be sure why this is true. It might simply be a result of the transition in social class from the lower socioeconomic classes to the middle class. It also has been suggested that former lifestyle behaviors or traditional cultural values and norms encourage women to maintain even a fatally flawed relationship (Bell & Mattis, 2000; Bent-Goodley, 2001).

It also might be possible that poverty differentially affects African American women. African Americans are far more likely than White women to live in neighborhoods with high rates of poverty and overall violence (Coker, 2000). Research in New York City suggested that 70% of poor Blacks compared with only 30% of poor Whites living in New York City resided in predominantly poverty-stricken and crime-prone neighborhoods (Sampson & Wilson, 1995). This is likely to have a disproportionate impact on the availability of services for Black victims of domestic violence (Coker, 2000). In addition, the stress of living in a neighborhood with an omnipresent threat of drugs, gang violence, and other social pathologies might increase family levels of stress dramatically. Furthermore, the well-studied mutual antipathy between much of the African American population and the police might mean that, realistically, police are only going to be called after more severe violence has occurred, making arrest in today's environment nearly inevitable.

Cultural norms implicit in many recently arrived immigrant groups often define the "appropriate treatment" accorded women by male intimates. Although a true definition of culture is ambiguous, referring to a group's social doctrines varying by gender, class, religion, race, ethnicity, and other variables, we do know that the cultural norms among immigrant groups often clash with the behavior demanded by our legal system.

As is generally known, many ideologies from immigrant cultures marginalize and intentionally limit, if not totally marginalize, women's economic and social power in a relationship. That factor alone places them at an increased risk for victimization (Raj & Silverman, 2002). In one direct example, the use of physical force to control or discipline women is acceptable or encouraged in some South Asian and Northern African Muslim immigrant communities (Kulwicki & Miller, 1999; Raj & Silverman, 2002a and 2002b).

Schwartz and DeKeseredy (1997) examined the significance of a male peer-support model as a factor that might coexist in the context of traditionally male-dominated environments (e.g., ethnically centered bars as well as cultural and athletic events) with cultural norms that support male control of women. This model suggests that the link between alcohol and violence is a result of perceptions of masculinity that link heavy drinking and violence to control of a woman and/or children. This equates to a masculine or "macho" self-image in some immigrant communities.

Furthermore, Bowker (1983) suggested that male peers in many subpopulations still feel justified in violence against partners and accept, if not outwardly approve of, such conduct. He found that the frequency of contact and interaction with male peers was related to both the frequency and the seriousness of domestic assault.

Many such cultural differences and ideologies can place women at greater risk of intimate partner violence. For example, in Asian and Middle Eastern immigrant communities, role expectations for women often are far more rigid, and the right of men to "discipline" their wives physically often is explicitly accepted (Raj & Silverman, 2002b).

It is interesting that women in these communities often are acculturated more easily to new societal norms than their male partners and are more willing (if not eager) to adopt American expectations for their behavior (Bui & Morash, 1999; Kulwicki & Miller, 1999; Raj & Silverman, 2002b). The result of this conflict in role expectations increases the woman's risk of violence. Their partners will prefer to maintain the type of control their past culture granted to males. Numerous studies indeed report that intimate partner violence is more likely in relationships in which the male partner holds more culturally traditional role expectations for women (Bui & Morash, 1999; Morash, Bui, & Santiago, 2000).

Finally, in a somewhat different situation, many recent immigrant victims of domestic violence might be socially isolated. They often do not have the traditional family supports available in their home country, and they might effectively be isolated from outside contacts by the offender (Abraham, 2000; Raj & Silverman, 2002b). As such, these victims might be less likely to receive available support because of cultural expectations (Raj & Silverman, 2002b).

These women often are deterred by their lack of familiarity with the legal system and, if they are here illegally, fear that they will be deported if they report abuse. Research on Latina victims of domestic violence has reported the high levels of fear of abuse by undocumented women. These victims often are afraid that police involvement will lead to their deportation and to possible separation from children (Coker, 2000).

Some abusers are known to take advantage of this situation. It has been reported that many batterers deliberately fail to file the necessary immigration papers to legalize the victim's immigration status (Teran, 1999).

Finally, as described in Chapter 2, the greater impact of traditional conservative religious beliefs in recent immigrant families might make husbands more likely to assert their control and their victimized wives to tolerate abuse without leaving or contacting authorities.

Native Americans

Given the long and ignominious history of White–Native American relations, it is not surprising that social problems that are closely associated with widespread social disorganization emerged shortly after tribal relocations. Many Native Americans live on reservations in miserable conditions. The numbers and statistics pertaining to poverty levels, unemployment, and infant mortality—to name but a few of the social problems Native Americans on reservations face—clearly demonstrate dire living circumstances. This is compounded by relatively high rates of substance abuse, which is a strong correlate with domestic violence, as discussed earlier in this chapter. For these reasons, it is not surprising that American Indian and Alaska Native women report far higher rates of intimate partner violence than women of any other racial background (Tjaden & Thoennes, 2000).

SUMMARY

Why is sociobiology and the study of personality traits important? Simply put, if such correlative factors can be identified in an offender, then the subsequent potential for establishing a successful therapeutic resolution is increased greatly. We, of course, recognize that some biologically or psychologically based pathologies are far beyond society's current treatment capabilities. If it were possible to address a hormonal influence successfully and to intervene effectively with individualized psychological treatment, then we might accommodate society's goals for rehabilitation. However, currently, we must face the fact that our ability to address a particular abuser's needs far exceeds the goals and capabilities of court-sanctioned batterer intervention programs. These programs often rely on group treatment with far more generic program content and, therefore, might not be successful for offenders with the specific biologically or psychologically based problems noted previously or for offenders who display patterns of more generalized violence rather than intimate-only violence.

In addition, the identification and analysis of various family pathologies regardless of type seems to be predictive of patterns of abuse and seems equally likely to continue for generations. Such patterns are complex and are not likely to be amenable to the "quick fix"—the desire to identify, arrest, and punish rapidly the obviously guilty. This solution is typically offered by the criminal justice system.

However, the existence and extent of the role of family risk markers might facilitate and assist society with future development of a more effective, individualistic response to batterers. We might witness a decline in recidivism if sentencing dispositions could consider pathologies and provide for individualized medical or psychological interventions rather than (or as an adjunct to) a more generic, behaviorally based offender treatment program.

DISCUSSION QUESTIONS

1. What types of policies or policy changes would a psychologist concerned with batterer personalities advocate compared with a feminist who believes that society is basically supportive of male violence?

2. How should biology affect our policies and intervention strategies toward batterers?

3. Consider Johnson's typologies or the Holtzworth-Munroe typology discussed in the chapter. Should we be intervening in common couple violence? Should we intervene differently in these types of incidents than in cases of "terrorist" violence?

4. How can resources best be used to prevent revictimization?

Selective Screening 5

Barriers to Intervention

She sits upon the floor
Curled up in a ball
Remembering the fight
Her body smashed into the wall
Knowing she must go
Somehow she must leave
But she thinks it's futile
After all, who'll even believe?
So through the years she waits
Trembling, beaten, alone
Needing help but doubting anyone will believe her crying moans
Yearning to tell the police
To all them on the phone
Wanting to tell them all the things he has done,
that by their ignoring they have condoned.
Once sure, determined, and proud
She is now a shadow compared to the past
Now timid, shy, and unsure of how much longer she will last
So she sits upon the floor
Curled up in a ball
Trying to get help
But doubting anyone will care at all
Beaten, bruised, but undefeated
She waits for that one day
When it won't be unsafe to go
And even worse to stay.

—Laura Buzawa

Chapter Overview

Domestic violence, in its extreme form, clearly should be addressed by criminal statutes. After all, the victim knows she (or, on occasion, he), has been attacked, the crime if reported to the police is relatively straightforward, and no detective work is needed to determine the "suspect." In most cases, the offender remains on the scene, or if not, the victim can easily assist police to his probable location, or the police can wait a short time until he returns.

Despite this potential for intervention, until fairly recently, most victims did not seek police assistance, and when it occurred, it often was perfunctory and designed to divert the case from the criminal justice system. Many victims have misgivings about calling the police and, correctly or incorrectly, perceive their complaints will be dismissed or the police will be unable to prevent future violence. To the extent these perceptions exist and deter calls for assistance, they are reality.

To a large extent, the police antipathy toward domestic violence calls discussed in this chapter has changed over time as a new generation of officers and police administrators have matured. However, remnants of the "traditional pattern" of nonintervention linger. They typically are not present as official policy but are in the form of standard operating procedures that effectively limit intervention and/or officer cynicism that diminishes their willingness to intervene aggressively or to change dramatically "street-level" behavior.

Victim Case Screening

The Failure to Report Crime

The process of systematic reduction of agency involvement in domestic violence starts with substantial "screening" by victims who fail to file reports. This has been a long known phenomenon to sociologists who ascribe "relational distance" as a reason for lower domestic assault reporting rates compared with other assaults (Black, 1976). Relational distance refers to the relationship between the victim and the offender, with intimate partners. We also now know that many victims of domestic violence, as a result of societal norms, fear of retaliation, or economic or psychological dependence do not report domestic violence. These cases, for whatever reason, are therefore self-screened out of the criminal justice system without ever being known or recorded.

Estimates prior to the enactment of new domestic violence legislation were that only an insignificant number of victims (2%) ever called the police (Dobash & Dobash, 1979). Then, 14 years after passage of the first of the universal state statutes targeting domestic violence, a large-scale survey stated that only 7% of cases were reported to the police (Kaufman Kantor & Straus, 1990).

This is a key area of controversy when examining statistics regarding domestic violence, which has major implications. Currently the extent of victim reporting of such crimes depends markedly on the instrument used to measure "nonreporting." Ongoing discrepancies might be partially explainable based on the different definitions of domestic violence and data collection we covered in Chapter 1. Official statistics might have a built-in bias and not "notice" unreported domestic violence incidents. This can artificially increase the percentage of potential victims who might call the police and for whom conclusions might be drawn. Other studies might use more culturally appropriate, if more difficult to aggregate, data and, in some cases, add extreme coercive control to their definitions of abuse. These studies consistently show higher rates of nonreporting. For this reason, we will discuss both official and nonofficial data.

Official statistics that are based on the National Crime Victimization Survey (NCVS) are collected by the Bureau of Justice Statistics and report a growing willingness to call the police. Until its revision in 1992, selected respondents were contacted by telephone and screened for interview by simply asking whether they had been the victim of a crime within the last year. If they answered "no," the interview ended. Many domestic violence victims might have not viewed themselves as the victim of a "crime" and/or could not easily talk because the offender was present.

Data from the revised telephone survey during the period from 1993 to 1999 showed that approximately half of women reported they had notified the police of an incident during the period between 1992 and 1996. This figure increased to 54% in 1998 (Greenfeld et al., 1998; Rennison, 2001). Finally, in a very surprising development, the most recently published NCVS data indicate that 62% of female victims and 64% of male victims reported intimate partner violence in 2004–2005 (Catalano, 2007). Researchers using these "official" data sets have examined longitudinal trends of reporting from the 1980s through the 1990s. They have concluded that there was no significant increase in reporting during the 1980s but that a significant increase in victim reporting occurred during the 1990s. However, the increase in reporting was not greater than for other assaults, which suggests that this increase may be part of an overall trend of victims to now report crime, rather than a reflection of the impact of specific policy changes in the response to domestic violence (Felson & Paré, 2005).

If correct, this should be regarded as a profound change, regardless of the reason. In the past, the criminal justice system was clearly known to serve less than half of domestic violence victims with unofficial data showing strikingly little criminal justice involvement. These data suggest that victims are increasingly likely to consider the criminal justice system as a primary resource, at least for immediate assistance. As we will discuss in later chapters, these data do not mean that the criminal justice system is necessarily effective or is the preferred responder, but they do mean that it has become the primary mechanism for cases to receive societal intervention. Furthermore, the data show that a new metric system needs to be adopted. We need a greater ability to integrate the criminal justice system response into more effective *long-term* solutions that might be offered by others, including health care and social service providers.

Unfortunately, despite evidence that suggests a substantial increase in reporting since the 2% rate reported by Dobash and Dobash in 1979, we really cannot be certain that self-reporting has increased as dramatically as official statistics seem to suggest.

Unofficial, but well-executed, studies consistently show much higher rates of underreporting. In one of the largest such studies, a 1985 sample of more than 6,000 households, the National Family Violence Survey (NFVS) stated that only 6.7% of incidents were reported to the police overall and that only 14% of those experiencing serious violence reported the assault (Kantor & Straus, 1987; see also Dutton, 1988). This figure, although dated, is typical of the more than 100 studies examining reports to the police of "conflicts." In these studies, the percentage of victims reporting a domestic assault is almost always less than 20% (Straus, 2000; also Hutchison & Hirschel, 1998; Kaukinen, 2002).

There naturally are limitations to official data sources. First, there are funding constraints. The primary problem of the current official survey source for victimization data, the NCVS, is that it costs too much to conduct in current economic times (Groves & Cork, 2008). Second, even with the 2010 revision, and into the foreseeable future, the survey relies on contacting participants via landline telephone numbers only. However, a high percentage of the population now uses cell phones, many exclusively, especially younger individuals who are at greater risk for all forms of victimization. In addition, people in the lower socioeconomic strata might not have any phones or be living in a shelter or on the street. Third, as mentioned, there is always the risk that a respondent denies victimization because the offender is present when the survey call is made.

Finally, many smaller studies such as those in specific communities reveal striking dissimilarities among people who are victimized, including recent immigrants who state that they fail to report because of language difficulties or for cultural reasons, including disapproval within their community and fear of deportation of the abuser. When these data are not shown on official surveys, we are unclear the extent to which substantial underreporting exists.

In other words, individual definitions of an assault might be dependent on whether the behavior is considered part of a study on how people resolve conflict, such as the "unofficial" but widely followed NFVS, as opposed to an individual's experiences with self-defined crime, as in the officially sponsored NCVS. The discrepancy between official estimates showing more than half of cases being reported and private studies showing only a small percentage of reports might at first seem trivial, but actually it is highly significant. If the police truly receive calls from less than 20% of abused women, then these cases are the exception, and the criminal justice system, although an important element of societal control, might realistically be relegated to the periphery of measures of social control.

Who Reports and Who Does Not

Studies analyzing official data have now released the demographics of "reporters." One analysis of the Violence Against Women Survey reported the following information:

- Women were more likely to report than men, but this was largely confined to the Black community.
- Victims who were drinking or using drugs were less likely to report.
- Older victims were more likely to report.
- Black female victims reported more frequently (70%), whereas Black males were least likely to report (47%), and White victims both female and males were almost equally likely to report (58%), whereas reporting rates for Hispanics were unusually high, 86% for males and 66% for females.
- Victims where the offender used a weapon had higher rates of reporting.
- If the victim was injured, she or he was more likely to report.
- Neither education or income was related to the likelihood of reporting (Felson & Paré, 2005).

It is known that the Black subculture historically disapproves of law enforcement involvement because of cultural norms and expectations and their dislike for police intervention (Bent-Goodley, 2001). Furthermore, studies report similar biases against reporting crimes among other subpopulations, including Hispanics.

For different reasons, including distrust of the motives of the police, community pressure not to involve outsiders, and fear of gaining the attention of immigration authorities, the number of calls might be depressed in groups ranging from Appalachian Whites to recent immigrants.

Why Has Victim Reporting Increased?

We know that in the past many victims feared physical or economic reprisal if they reported domestic abuse (Dobash & Dobash, 1992; Frieze & Browne, 1989; Hanmer, Radford, & Stanko, 1989b). These might involve additional beatings, stalkings, and threats of loss of income or even of losing children because of retaliatory reporting of child neglect or substance abuse.

That sense of innervating fear might be dissipating, and it has been argued that women's fear for their safety is more likely now to motivate them to contact the police rather than to deter them (Felson, Messner, Hoskin, & Deane, 2002). This coincides with the NCVS finding that only approximately 12% of females and 5% of males gave this explanation for nonreporting (Catalano, 2007).

As we will describe in later chapters, most jurisdictions now aggressively enforce domestic violence statutes. Paradoxically, such aggressive enforcement might deter some remaining victims from reporting. We know that women often omit information about abuse in discussions with relatives and friends for fear of them taking action that the victim cannot later control (Dunham & Senn, 2000).

It would seem logical to infer that many victims would be even more reticent to contact police when their control over agency action is far more limited. A key to recent reforms is that police now often provide an aggressive response to domestic violence assaults by arresting offenders. Although this addresses the immediate risk to the victim, it also effectively removes her control. As we explore in depth later, this trend toward mandatory arrest policies, especially when coupled with a highly publicized policy of aggressive case processing by prosecutors and the judiciary, might deter some victims.

This is evidenced by responses to the NCVS survey where the most common reason given for not reporting domestic violence is the belief that it is a "private or personal matter" (Catalano, 2007). It is interesting that almost twice as many men as women gave this as the reason. Furthermore, many victims are concerned with protecting the offender. The most recent NCVS data reported that 14% of females and 16% of males cited this as their rationale for not reporting (Catalano, 2007).

Victim characteristics also differentially affect their reaction to criminal justice intervention. Although their past experiences with the criminal justice system might provide a "rational" basis for future reporting behavior, other life experiences might affect their likelihood to report new violence. These include prior history of victimization both as a child and as an adult.

Victims who experienced violence as a routine part of their lifestyle might be prone to accept violence and, hence, are less likely to report abuse. Some, especially those raised in families where domestic violence was an ever present reality, might not perceive physical violence as a crime or even as "abusive." A domestic assault in that context might not even be thought of as a crime or threat to personal safety (Straus, 1999). Hence, although acts such as "slapping," "kicking," "pushing," or "shoving" are obviously legally termed an assault, it might remain problematic for many victims to consider this worth reporting to the police (Ferraro, 1989a; Langan & Innes, 1986; Straus, 1999).

Even if victims recognize that domestic violence is unacceptable, many might still believe it is purely a personal or family problem. This also helps to explain why much higher rates of assaults by *former* partners are reported to police compared with assaults by current partners. In one study, the NCVS found former partners reported 25 times more assaults in the previous year compared with current partners (Bachman & Saltzman, 1995). Although some differences are to be expected as victims disproportionately leave abusive relationships, the extent of the disparity suggests some suppression of victim reporting in cases of ongoing relationships.

It also is possible that many victims might seek help from sources other than the police, including medical professionals, social welfare agencies. and religious institutions. Invoking the law is the most formalistic type of help-seeking behavior. As researchers and advocates, we might consider this the preferred victim strategy. However, many victims might desire informal approaches, or at least those that do not involve the police. Indeed, despite widely adopted reforms, many victims are still unwilling to report their victimization to the police and seek assistance from family, relatives, and friends (Hutchison & Hirschel, 1998; Kaukinen, 2002).

Victims also might take into consideration the various costs—economic and emotional—of legal intervention. They might believe their complaint will not be taken seriously; family, friends, or relatives might blame them for their victimization; or they might lose custody of their children—a fear that is not irrational given increasingly aggressive intervention by child service agencies into "troubled families." There are personal costs to victims in terms of time, emotional energy, and stress that are associated with the criminal justice process. In addition, victims might believe reporting to the police jeopardizes their ability to work on improving an obviously already troubled relationship.

Does Social Class Affect the Decision to Report?

There might be a different economic profile of reporting compared with nonreporting victims. It has long been theorized that social factors cause a far greater percentage of unreported violent crimes among intimates to exist among the middle and upper classes. For this reason, the police disproportionately saw domestic violence in lower socioeconomic groups. Although the extent of underreporting has reduced markedly over time, studies have reported that poor women were more than twice as likely to report abuse to the police as their higher income or white counterparts (Bowker, 1982; Hamberger & Hastings, 1993).

Researchers have advanced many explanations for past nonreporting by the middle and upper classes. Black (1976, 1980) more fully attributed this to the then prevalent model of a single-income family resulting in the economic dependency of middle-class women. Black (1980) stated this succinctly:

> [A m]iddle class white woman is more likely than a lower class black woman to live in a condition of dependency. . . . She is more likely to live on the earnings of her husband, in a dwelling financed by him . . . "a housewife." . . . Such a woman is not readily able to leave her situation one day and replace it with an equivalent the next. . . . Frederick Engels long ago pointed to the relationship between "male supremacy" and the control of wealth by men: "In the great majority of cases today, at least in the possessing classes, the husband is obliged to earn a living and support his family, and that in itself gives him a position of supremacy without any need for special legal titles and privileges. Within the family he is the bourgeois, and the wife represents the proletariat (1884, p. 137)." (Black, 1980, p. 125)

From this perspective, Black (1980) concluded:

> It is therefore almost inconceivable that a totally dependent woman would ask the police to remove her husband from his own house. If he beats her, she is unlikely to invoke the law . . . middle class people are unlikely to call the police about their domestic problems. (p. 125)

An alternative to Black's (1980) hypothesis was suggested decades ago in terms of social status rather than economic chains of dependency. Although domestic violence seemingly existed in all classes, violence in the middle to upper classes was more likely to be diverted to doctors, the clergy, or other family members (Parnas, 1967; Westley, 1970). They theorized that these victims preferred to bring their problems to "social equals" rather than to the police, who were presumed to be from a lower working class.

This dynamic, although an interesting theory, might again be a relic of past times. There has been a tremendous growth in the amount and range of services available at no cost to victims. Furthermore, Black's (1980) observation at the time was a powerful predictor of reporting. However, modern empirical research both conducted "officially" and by private research has failed to substantiate this theory. It is entirely possible that the advent of dual-career families and the realistic possibility of getting child support and enforceable restraining orders has eliminated any such class distinctions.

Moreover, this trend has occurred in other countries at the same time. A recently published study using Canadian national data found that income, education, and income status did not seem to impact a victim's decision to report (Akers & Kaukinen, 2009). Instead, they found that women living in a cohabiting relationship, women with children, and women who experienced severe injuries were the key factors affecting reporting.

By understanding that the overall pattern of social class distinctions might no longer be valid, it also might be true that aggregate data could mask some important predictors of who calls the police. Among poor victims, some victims who lack an extended family structure or close ties to community organizations might find their only realistic source of immediate help is to call the police. However, a subset of poor women that might be least likely to report are poor women who have had prior experiences with the criminal justice system for their own criminal behavior, including substance abuse. Furthermore, substance abuse is far more prevalent among poor victims of domestic violence and often starts *after* the abuse begins (James, Johnson, Raghavanm & Woolis, 2004; Renzetti, 2009).

Bystander Screening

As a result of victim screening, calls from nonparticipants, including neighbors, friends, relatives, and bystanders have become one of the primary methods by which social agencies are made aware of domestic violence. Such calls might, however, provide their own differential screening. They are not necessarily motivated by the seriousness of the assault but by the disruption to the reporter's activities as a result of noise or property damage, morbid curiosity about the incident, to see how the police would react, or because as relatives of the victim, they really care.

Bystanders also implicitly screen cases by ethnic group and class and might explicitly screen them on the basis of marital status, often implicitly allowing married couples to settle such issues privately regardless of overheard violence. When outsiders observe disputes, these couples often become known as the neighborhood "problem family" and the disputes as a simple "family disturbance" or as an expected neighborhood occurrence. Such incidents were far less likely to elicit calls to the police than those perceived to be threats to the public order.

In contrast, cases involving girlfriends and boyfriends or former cohabitants more likely involve incidents outside a residence that are more likely to be observed and reported than those involving married or currently cohabiting adults. The significance of witnesses and bystanders in reporting acts of domestic assault also might increase the conception of the problem as being almost exclusively found among the lower socioeconomic classes. Because of urban congestion in poor neighborhoods, such cases are more visible to neighbors, are more likely to receive attention, and therefore might be the source of a subsequent call to the police.

The net effects of victim and bystander call screening are threefold. First, for whatever reason, criminal justice agencies disproportionately see indigents, especially in certain minority groups and urban neighborhoods. As a result, both they and the public tend to view domestic violence primarily as a problem for these groups. This conception makes it easier to ignore, as is done with many social pathologies of the poor. If the public realized the extent to which all social classes are affected, to at least some degree, a more effective response might be demanded.

Second, the most severe cases of domestic assault might not necessarily be the ones to reach the criminal justice system. Instead, those most disruptive to public order and thereby known to others outside the family are disproportionately reported. For this reason, disclosure rates do not seem to be closely related to incident severity—at least as measured by injury to the victim. Although Kaufman Kantor and Straus (1990) reported that 14.4% of incidents involving major violence were reported to police compared with 3.2% of minor violence, Pierce and Spaar (1992), basing their study on comparative police and emergency room data, reported that the most severe cases of violence resulted in calls for medical services rather than for police referrals. Few of these were subsequently reported to the police as victims refused to cooperate or the physicians did not recognize the underlying problem.

Third, regardless of the study or the statistical techniques used, it seems that a substantial unfilled potential demand exists for community services.

The Police Response

There are two primary characteristics to the classic police response to domestic violence. First, the police did not desire intervention in domestic violence incidents. Second, there was a strong, and often overwhelming, bias against the use of arrest in cases of domestic violence.

Police Screening

In addition to the failure of victims and bystanders to report domestic violence, police departments as organizations have historically limited reported domestic violence cases. One primary method used to reduce the number of police responses to domestic violence was "call screening." To maximize allocation of scarce resources and to avoid responding to low-priority calls in times of high demand, many police departments make call screening a routine practice. Call screening is an essential practice in many departments allowing them to assign priorities to all incoming calls requesting police services. Those with low priorities, usually including simple assaults, do not receive authorization to dispatch a police unit until a unit becomes available, if it ever does.

The importance of call screening is that it operates as a filter, effectively determining what the criminal justice system views as a problem. In an organizational sense, those citizen problems that are screened out simply do not exist. This action, although seeming unbiased, poses a severe challenge to the historic treatment of domestic calls.

Why has this supposedly "neutral" standard operating procedure disfavored victims of domestic violence? Call screening in most urban departments occurs only during peak periods of demand for service—typically weekends and nights. These periods are an exact overlap to when domestic violence calls are most likely to occur.

In a more covert manner, call screening has had the effect of discouraging certain callers from demanding a police response because during the busy night hours, such callers often have been referred to social service agencies, which are typically closed during the weekends. If police intervention was still requested, dispatch would occur only when time permitted, often after the offender had left, preventing any real chance of an arrest.

Call screening might simply be considered an adaptive organizational response to help overworked organizations limit environmental demands, which is functionally similar to triage in a medical setting. Decisions concerning the immediate dispatch of a unit are primarily predicated on the dispatcher's long-distance determination that commission of a felony is imminent. Although such an explanation seems both rational and unbiased, in practice, it is neither (Manning, 1988). When responding to typically ambiguous and volatile domestic violence calls, there is always the possibility of a negative interaction that prevents an effective response.

Regardless of the reason, studies in the 1980s suggested that call screening greatly limited police intervention in cases of domestic violence. Pierce, Spaar, and Briggs (1988) observed that 50% of the 3.2 million calls for police assistance in Boston were for service calls, including approximately 80,000 for "family troubles." Police dispatchers, however, reported an additional 24,400 calls that could have been included in that category but were reclassified by the police dispatch to a "no response" status.

One study in Great Britain reported a variant on this theme. Officers would be actually dispatched, but if they heard nothing from outside the residence, they would exit the premises and report "all quiet on arrival" or "no call for police action," thereby effectively screening the case from the system with virtually no police commitment of resources. The author of this study reported that fully 60% of all domestic calls were never processed past this point (Sheptycki, 1991).

The negative effect of call screening also has been cited in many other studies during the 1980s. For example, Ford (1983) reported that in Marian County, Indiana, between two thirds and three quarters of all domestic violence calls were "solved" without officer dispatch. The reasons for such a high rate of case disposal might be related to the known tendency of police personnel to denigrate domestic offenses. Consequently, a call that seemed to be a serious felony assault with a dangerous weapon could merely be termed a "family trouble" call, afforded very low priority and often effectively was screened out.

Clearly, call screening in the past presented serious ramifications. An ostensibly unbiased method of allocating resources effectively eliminated many domestic violence calls. The department's failure to respond or the delay of an officer's dispatch could be so lengthy that the call's emergent nature became lost, the threatened violence had already occurred, or the offender had left the scene (Ford, 1983). Victims often received no attention from police officers who might have prevented new injuries or have officially documented past criminal activity. The failure to respond to complaints denied the victim's status, discouraging her from reporting further abuse, and perhaps encouraging an assailant to believe abusive conduct was tacitly condoned.

When police intervention occurred, it was criticized as inappropriate. In the context of domestic violence, police response had long been viewed as being perfunctory in nature, dominated by the officer's overriding goal—to extricate him or her from dangerous and unpleasant duties with as little cost as possible and to reinvolve himself or herself quickly in "real" police work.

Why Police Did Not Historically Consider Domestic Abuse "Real" Policing

To understand how police responded when a call was screened "in," it is imperative to know how officers perceived their own role and mission as well as their organizational culture. The police culture clearly prefers law enforcement functions in which prospects for action and resulting arrest are higher. In contrast, they almost uniformly dislike non–law enforcement tasks. Officers perceive their job in the legalistic sense: as law enforcers. As a result, although laws and department policies have historically provided the officer with extensive guidance concerning the technical basis for deciding to make an arrest, they generally did not formally address "order maintenance." The fact, of course, is that police officers have always had a variety of non–law enforcement tasks in which an arrest clearly would be inappropriate or at least highly unlikely. These duties include traffic control, performing rescues, providing transportation to hospitals, and delivering subpoenas and warrants. Police officers also performed a variety of tasks in low-level dispute resolution such as "toning down" loud parties, taking care of the drunk and homeless, and intervening in most family disputes. In these tasks, regardless of whether an assault has been alleged, arrest powers were only infrequently used—a tool of last resort. The dichotomy between the reality of the police experience and the mythology of the police officer as "crime fighter" and "law enforcer" created by the occupational culture has been repeatedly cited. Researchers long have noted that arrests for any crime are rare for officers even though symbolically important in an occupation in which the daily activities tend to be dull and repetitive (Berk & Loseke, 1980–1981; Reiss, 1971; Van Maanen, 1974).

Regardless of reality, it has been a truism that police were socialized from their earliest training into a culture that did not highly value "social work." A new recruit, to be an accepted member of the police or as "one of the boys," was required to adopt this occupational code. Key elements of this cultural norm included the protection of other officers, admiration of a "good pinch" or a "good collar" by a fellow officer, and explicit acceptance of the same normative framework as other officers as to what constitutes "serious crime." The bias against social work still existed among law enforcement as recently as the late 1990s (Gaines, Kappeler, & Vaughn, 1999; Kappeler, Blumberg, & Potter, 2000; Manning, 1997).

The importance of police self-image, therefore, lies less in reality than in the efforts made by many police officers to conduct themselves consistent with this self-image. As a corollary, most officers judge each other's competence on the basis of performing crime-fighting tasks, such as the apprehension of criminals. They simply do not value highly or even see as positive those instances of successful intervention in "private" disputes (Stanko, 1989). The impact of this occupational code is important to understanding police practices. Obtaining and keeping informal prestige or status with peers was, and still is, imperative to most officers. As stated in the following manner: "His most meaningful standards of performance are the ideals of his *occupational culture*. The policeman judges himself against the ideal policeman as described in police occupational lore and imagery. What a 'good policeman' does is an omnipresent standard" (Manning, 1978, p. 12).

This attitude is reinforced in many departments where rank-and-file officers have maintained a closed, internal culture with strong antipathy toward the public at large, toward politicians, and often even toward their own command (Manning, 1978; Punch, 1985; Radford, 1989). Using this frame of reference, responding to domestic violence calls had until recently little occupational value to an officer. Many officers trivialized such offenses, and arrests were typically infrequent. Because the offender was known and domestic violence was a "minor" misdemeanor offense, any arrest that resulted would be considered a "garbage arrest," not worthy of recognition (Stanko, 1989).

However, this did not adequately explain why most police still considered responding to domestic violence calls among their worst duties. Instead, it is necessary to examine additional factors that have reinforced negative police attitudes.

Organizational Disincentives

Police departments historically have provided few formal organizational incentives for good officer performance in responding to domestic violence assaults. To the extent that civil service and not the whim of superior officers affected an officer's chances for promotion, typical practices measured easily quantifiable skills, including arrest rates and subsequent clearances or convictions. Similarly, written tests for promotion still heavily emphasized textbook knowledge of law enforcement tasks such as substantive criminal law, criminal procedure, and departmental policies regarding arrests and case documentation. Meanwhile, at a minimum, officers were expected to incur no blemishes on their record by exposing themselves or the police department to civil suits or citizen complaints.

Perhaps inadvertently, these evaluation criteria provided a major disincentive for performing domestic violence and sexual assault tasks. If an officer spent the necessary time handling a domestic assault case, assisting a victim with referrals to shelters, and making follow-up calls, he or she decreased the chance for responding to a call involving a major felony arrest. From an organizational perspective, the officer used his or her time "unproductively."

Even worse, by taking an activist approach, the officer further increased the likelihood that the offender, or at times even the victim, might file a complaint based on claims of overzealous or overbearing police conduct.

Are Domestic Violence Calls Extraordinarily Dangerous to the Police?

Officers still overwhelmingly cite their extreme danger when responding to domestic violence calls. They often are vaguely aware of statistics that "demonstrate" that officers responding to disturbance and assault calls often are killed or injured. Of more impact are the frequently heard "war stories" circulating in most departments recounting incidents in which a victim, whom officers have sought to help, has turned on and bit, slapped, hit, stabbed, or even shot the officers as they tried to arrest the attacker.

Until the mid-1980s, the Federal Bureau of Investigation (FBI) actively reinforced such fears by publishing statistics reporting the category of "responding to disturbance calls" as responsible for most officer deaths (Garner & Clemmer, 1986). Not surprisingly, then, both police and family violence researchers have emphasized the potential danger to officers in handling domestic cases (Bard, 1970; Parnas, 1967; Straus, Gelles, & Steinmetz, 1980). Similarly, police training has certainly emphasized the prospects of danger. With few exceptions, training programs have emphasized the inherent danger of the call to the police. They also make frequent exhortations to the effect that if an officer does not follow standard procedures, he or she dramatically increases the chance of injury or death. Police training placed its first priority on office safety, rather than on the protection of battered women (Buzawa, 1988; Eigenberg, 2001).

However, the methodology first used in the composition of the Uniform Crime Reports (UCR)/FBI statistics was flawed and overstated the real rate of police injuries and deaths related to domestic violence efforts by approximately three times. This is because the category used for "disturbances" included gang calls, bar fights, and any other general public disturbances, as well as responding to domestic disturbances. Although the FBI reported data now separate fatalities resulting from domestic homicides, they continue to include the broader category of disturbances when reporting injuries. Therefore, although data for 2005 indicate that 30.5% of assaulted officers were assaulted in a disturbance call, we still do not know what percentage of these calls were domestic in nature.

The figures on deaths of officers do demonstrate that handling domestic violence might be dangerous, even if not as dangerous as initially thought. The FBI/UCR reports of the causes of officer deaths are probably far more accurate than those for injury. Deaths of sworn personnel during the course of duty are obviously going to be very well screened. The last available statistics provided by the FBI are for calendar year 2005. During that year, 5 of the 55 officer deaths were in response to domestic incidents. Although individual annual statistics varied, in the 10-year period between 1996 and 2005, there were 59 domestic-related officer homicides out of the 575 total slain officers. Significantly, the overall fatality trend did not seem to be affected either by the growing police willingness to make domestic violence arrests or by the greatly improved domestic violence training now provided to officers.

There seems to be a consistent trend of approximately 10% of overall officer deaths in recent years related to responding to domestic calls. However, unlike homicides, data on injuries resulting from domestic violence incidents are not separated out from general disturbances such as bar fights. Part of the reason for the high numbers of domestic violence–related officer injuries is that there is simply a high number of domestic violence calls, especially when full enforcement has become the norm. Consequently, a high percentage of officer time is spent in responding to domestic calls. It is not surprisingly, then, that such activities *do* constitute one of the highest sources of officer injuries.

Given the disproportionate amount of time that officers spend responding to domestic violence calls compared with other incidents in the disturbance category, responding to domestic violence calls might not be as intrinsically dangerous as other police activities. Nevertheless, many officers have perceived physical risks dramatically increasing when they abandon "neutrality" to make an arrest. Therefore, regardless of reality, the effect of such perceptions is clear: Continued fear of death or injury has reinforced officer dislike of handling domestic calls. When officers respond to a domestic violence call, not surprisingly, many emphasize a defensive-reactive strategy, with a foremost priority on protecting their own safety. Under such circumstances, it is not surprising that innovations in police responses or a more activist approach were discouraged unless mandated by law or an actively enforced and monitored policy.

Structural Impediments to Police Action

Traditionally, there were several structural impediments to an aggressive police response. One severe handicap had been long-term statutory restrictions that gave officers the authority to make arrests for misdemeanors only with prior issuance of an arrest warrant. In effect, this required a prior action by a magistrate or justice of the peace or allowed action only in those relatively few cases in which a misdemeanor was committed in the officer's presence. This contrasted with statutory authorization of warrantless arrests in felonies, for which an officer needed only probable cause to believe that the suspect had already committed the crime. Domestic violence until recently was almost inevitably characterized as simple assault, which is a misdemeanor.

Until domestic violence statutes were first enacted in the 1980s, police officers were legally unable to make warrantless arrests unless the violence continued in their presence or a previously existing warrant had been issued. Officers could rarely rely on warrants because, at that time, police information systems were usually nonexistent or at best rudimentary, meaning that officers did not typically know whether there was an outstanding warrant when they responded to a violent family. Information systems and record keeping for dispositions short of a conviction frequently did not exist in any acceptable, readily accessible form. Therefore, when there were new convictions, incidents of family violence or disturbances were not systematically recorded by police departments so that they could track repeat offenders or victims (Pierce & Deutsch, 1990; Reed, Fischer, Kantor, & Karales, 1983).

Second, a department's priorities might have effectively discouraged arrests for a low-status misdemeanor with relatively poor chances of conviction (Buzawa & Buzawa, 1990). In this context, officers often believed that victims of domestic assault are inherently unreliable and unpredictable and, as a generality, do not make arrests based merely on complaints of assault. Although Stanko (1985) believed the "unreliability" of victims was simply a self-serving, if pervasive myth, Sanders (1988) argued that such claims do in fact have legitimacy. The evidence of discrimination is not clear, or is at least inconsistent, because at least some early studies of police practice demonstrated that police did not differentiate domestic violence victims from equally problematic complainants for other types of crime (Sanders, 1988; Sheptycki, 1993).

Third, some have argued that failure to make domestic arrests simply validated the observation that the police culture does not care about victim rights—especially when the victim is a disenfranchised woman, a woman of color, or when she complains of domestic abuse (Ferraro, 1989a; Stanko, 1985).

Clearly after the initial "reforms" were enacted, police behavior did not automatically change. Early studies after initial "reforms" favoring arrests, where appropriate, demonstrated that even if departmental policy officially required officers to adopt presumptive arrest policies, officers circumvented such a policy, even to the extent of implicitly defying the orders of their police chief (Ferraro, 1989a). From a less critical perspective, many officers whom we have interviewed over the years seem to believe sincerely that arrest is not always the appropriate solution and that violence could increase if they made an unnecessary arrest—even if that was the policy favored by their department.

Finally, the sheer volume of domestic violence cases has been cited as creating an organizational challenge to understaffed and overworked departments. As noted earlier, disputes and disturbance calls as a class are the largest category of calls that police receive. They tend to occur at night or on weekends when criminal activity and traffic responsibilities simultaneously invoke their greatest organizational demands. Apart from other factors we have noted here, it is not surprising that recurrent spouse abuse calls received lower response priority, at least absent of knowledge of past violence or imminent threats to a potential victim's life.

The Classical Bias Against Arrest

The foregoing factors contributed to the perception that police disproportionately discriminated against domestic violence victims by failing to arrest. Indeed until the later 1990s, literature reporting data from many locations seemed to document that relatively few domestic violence incidents resulted in arrest, especially if not accompanied by serious injuries (e.g., a nonaggravated assault).

To understand the impact of this, we need to recognize that the primary coercive sanction available to police is to make an arrest, and this power is predicated on the officer's belief that there is probable cause to support that a suspect has committed a crime. Therefore, it might be assumed that legal variables, such as the strength of the case, should predominate in the arrest decision. In domestic violence cases (as in all cases of misdemeanor assault), instead, there was, and in some departments remains, a persistent, if now unwritten, bias against arrest. Within this context, the decision to arrest remains problematic, dependent on victim and offender characteristics, situational determinants, and patterns of decision making that are not consistent among individual officers or police organizations.

Legal variables, such as finding probable cause that all elements of a crime have occurred, are prerequisite to all but abusive use of arrest powers. Domestic violence crimes, however, lack common barriers to charging a defendant. Unlike many other offenses, the perpetrator and location of a domestic assault is known, injuries or potential danger are often obvious, and at least one witness—the victim—is usually available. Therefore, if we were to view this solely as whether the officer were to find probable cause, a high arrest rate in domestic cases should be expected. However, historically, the closer the relationship between offender and victim, the less likely an arrest.

Empirical measurements of arrest rates have varied depending on the crime's definition and the officer's estimates of probable cause. Regardless of measurement techniques and the definitions of the crime chosen, arrests in incidents of domestic violence were infrequent until the 1990s, with estimates varying from 3% (Langley & Levy, 1977), to 4% (Lawrenz, Lembo, & Schade, 1988), to 7.5% (Holmes & Bibel, 1988), to 10% (Roy, 1977), and to 13.9% (Bayley, 1986).

The bias against arrest crossed national boundaries. Although most empirical research analyzed U.S. arrest practices, other studies confirmed this practice. For example, in one Canadian city, London, Ontario, prior to a new mandatory arrest policy, the police charged domestic violence assailants with the crime of "assault" in only 3% of the cases that they encountered. This was despite the fact that in 20% of the cases, victim injuries were sufficient to have police advise the victim to seek medical attention (Burris & Jaffe, 1983). Similarly, studies in Great Britain (Freeman, 1980; Hanmer et al., 1989a), the Netherlands (Zoomer, 1989), Australia (Hatty, 1989), and Northern Ireland (Boyle, 1980) consistently have observed and criticized police refusal to make arrests in domestic violence cases.

Prosecutorial Screening Prior to Adjudication

Once a victim's case enters the judicial system, barriers to further prosecution continue. We discuss this not only for its historical significance, but also because this is still the response in many jurisdictions.

Traditional Patterns of Nonintervention by Prosecutors

Evidence suggests that although the responsiveness of prosecutors has been growing, there remains a bias to drop cases in many jurisdictions. Unlike the national surveys on reporting domestic violence to police, there is a lack of research examining overall prosecution rates. A recent review of research conducted in 26 jurisdictions addresses prosecution rates. These researchers reported a rate as low as 4.6% in Milwaukee in 1992 and as high as 94% in Ontario, Canada in 2005 (Garner & Maxwell, 2008).

Prosecutorial and judicial screening might occur because of the rapid changes in law enforcement. As discussed earlier, there has been a massive and steady increase since the mid-1980s. If not carefully managed, the interplay between a police department's new pro-arrest—and especially, mandatory—arrest policy might have unanticipated consequences. Domestic violence statutes with mandatory and presumptive arrest requirements have caused a rapid reform in police practices and have markedly increased the number of cases forwarded for prosecution. The prosecutor's office, however, has always had far more legislative discretion than police and has always had fewer constraints on their decisions (Miller, 2005).

Furthermore, they do not receive increased funding when specific policies or mandates change. Hence, they typically do not receive the additional resources needed to prosecute a growing caseload. The net result is that the additional workload of domestic violence cases has competed for basically the same limited amount of judicial and prosecutorial time. Since prosecutors often have far less constraints on their decision-making ability, they retain discretion as to how to respond to their increasing workload.

The historic response of prosecutors to cases of domestic violence has been similar in behavior to that of the police—using allegedly impartial "screening" techniques to dismiss the majority of cases brought to them prior to adjudication. Prosecutors did this both by outright case dismissal and by dramatically limited charges after police filed initial charges. The effect of this prosecutorial screening has been severely criticized as subverting potentially more aggressive police responses. It is easy to assume that at least in the past, prosecutors might not have taken domestic violence cases seriously when multiple charges of felony battery and specific domestic violence offenses were reduced to generic, simple assaults, which in turn became quite amenable to a judicial dismissal. When police were motivated to make domestic violence arrests a priority, their efforts—and ultimately their commitment—could easily be undermined by prosecutorial inaction. To understand contacts between the prosecutor's office and the victim, it might be important to review the features of prosecutorial organization. We believe several key aspects are of significance.

Prosecutorial Autonomy

Prosecutor offices are organizationally committed to maintaining decision-making autonomy. When a victim enters a prosecutor's office, she often is confronted with an organization that has its own bureaucratic goals and operational norms. Victims might not realize that the self-declared primary purpose of the prosecutor is to enforce society's rights to sanction activities harmful to the public order by punishing offenders and deterring future misconduct. Because its primary mission addresses societal goals, victims have no right to insist on prosecution. Furthermore, the decision of which charges to advance and which charges to dismiss or settle do not require victim consent.

This might seem intuitively obvious, as prosecutorial discretion—the ability of the state's officer to choose to charge, prosecute, or settle criminal cases—is a key feature of American jurisprudence. It is doubtful, however, that most victims understand this fully, and they erroneously tend to expect that the prosecutor's staff operate primarily to redress their particular crime(s). This creates potential barriers between the victim and her nominal allies. Their differing interests, unless carefully managed, provide an environment in which distrust and victim disparagement inevitably lead to high rates of voluntary dismissals.

One British study reported that the entire experience was extraordinarily frustrating to victims who could not understand what was happening or why some cases were dropped, others prosecuted, and still others "continued" without a concrete resolution. This has contributed to extremely high rates of voluntary case dismissal (Cretney & Davis, 1997).

The Reality of Budgetary Pressures

In the third edition of this book, we assumed that prosecutorial screening had become less of an issue over time. We no longer are certain this is the case. Based on anecdotal, but we believe real, evidence, budgetary pressures have caused many officers to increase the proportion of cases screened.

As with virtually all public service agencies, prosecutors typically operate with fiscal constraints and limited budget flexibility. They also are unlikely to be able to add resources in response to any crisis or new unfunded mandate. This has, of course, been compounded by the virtual collapse in 2008 and 2009 of many states' financing. Agencies whose funding was primarily based on individual and corporate income taxes has declined along with net incomes, sometimes by 20% to 30%, in a remarkably short period of time. The cumulative effect of budgetary pressures is to force the lead prosecutor to allocate his or her scarce resources selectively. Special attention is always reserved for homicides of crimes of a "heinous nature," drug, and other high-profile cases such as official corruption, cases involving public figures, and more recently terrorist offenses. Other crimes might then be prosecuted to the extent the prosecutor believes discretion is appropriate if the cases cannot be plea-bargained or otherwise rapidly disposed.

In this context, responding to a rapid influx of domestic violence prosecutions has proven especially problematic. Reformed police practices undoubtedly have increased the number of cases forwarded for prosecution. The prosecutor's office often has been given no additional staffing and is already straining to respond to massive numbers of drug offenses, gang violence, and other violent crimes. The net results compete with the same limited amount of prosecutorial time. This has created a tremendous increase in a prosecutor's workload.

Prioritizing Prosecutorial Efforts to Targeted Offenses

By this mechanism, the magnitude of drug cases has, in turn, been compounded by the longer sentences imposed by courts and by federal and state sentencing guidelines, removing discretion in judicial sentencing—incidentally leaving almost 1 in 100 adults in the United States in prisons or jails, which is the highest incarceration rate in the world (Pew Center on the States, 2008; Sabol & Couture, 2007). An unexpected, but predictable, consequence of such legislation has been that many drug defendants have little incentive to plea-bargain because their sentences cannot be substantively reduced. Whatever their other merits, such constraints have diminished the ability of an assembly-line process that previously had rapidly disposed of more than 90% of criminal offenses. In 1989, a report of the Conference of Chief Judges of the nine most populous states commented that lawmakers and officials who had adopted such policies failed to consider the impact of the huge flood of cases on the courts. This report warned of either an imminent or existing caseload crisis or of a possible "breakdown of the systems" if solutions were not found (Labaton, 1989).

Unfortunately, in the 21 years since that report, the "drug" caseload has grown even larger, now impacting family courts as well as traditional criminal courtrooms. Since the September 11, 2001, terrorist attacks, we now have many new crimes, including breaches of security or other terrorism-related crimes, as well as computer and Internet-based crimes, which also are adding to the prosecutorial workload.

The Impact of These Constraints on the Prosecutorial Response

A critical problem for prosecution of domestic violence crimes is that until recently, many prosecutors have not perceived that their practices might have screened out legitimate domestic violence cases (Belknap, Fleury, Melton, Sullivan, & Leisenring, 2001; Weisz, 1999). Under these circumstances, fiscal crises from an organizational perspective became a justifiable reason not to respond aggressively to domestic violence.

Under this kind of pressure, it is most surprising that prosecutors and their staffs have attempted informal strategies to reduce domestic caseloads by outright dismissal or other diversions from the criminal justice docket. Domestic violence cases are typically characterized as being in the category of less favored misdemeanors, or when felonies are first offenses are not usually covered by sentencing guidelines. It is, therefore, not surprising that they disproportionately become subject to pressure for settlement or dismissal. Perhaps this can be best summarized by the comments of a West Virginia assistant prosecuting attorney: "As a one woman, part-time domestic violence 'unit' that maintains a 'no drop' policy of sorts, I am without the resources to back it up. Many if not most prosecutors share this impediment to which little attention is given inside or outside the domestic violence community. It takes time to properly prosecute a domestic violence case, more time than those who fund and manage prosecutor offices and law enforcement agencies are willing to pay for" (Hartman, 1999, p. 174).

Unique Factors Limiting Prosecutorial Effectiveness

The unique characteristics of prosecuting domestic violence and sexual assaults also have increased the probability that such crimes would not be treated as seriously as they might otherwise warrant. Although a common problem in a civil setting, the complexity of intimate partner relationships often negates the simplistic dichotomy needed for criminal conviction. It also might be denigrated because it often involves offenses committed out of public view thereby being perceived as "less threat to the public order" and perhaps seeming to be a personal problem belonging in civil court.

With sufficient resources, the general bias against relationship cases, in particular, would be interesting by not particularly significant. Unfortunately, as explained earlier, the system operates without sufficient resources and forces many disfavored cases to be dropped. In addition, the prosecutor's bias against handling "relationship cases" might be in direct conflict with victim expectations.

We believe it is fair to state that women are more likely than men to operate from a "culture of relationships." The significance of maintaining personal relationships (i.e., performing obligations within the family structure) often leads many women to make decisions based on compromise or even a known subordination of her own needs to those of her partner, children, elderly relatives, and others. In sharp contrast, prosecutors expect victims to behave more like the stereotypical man, acting autonomously from the offender and the rest of her family, responding "rationally" by maximizing her own gains and concentrating solely on legally germane facts. This conflict and organizational perspective creates enormous potential for misunderstandings that can fatally effect the interaction between the victim and those agencies (Weisz, 1999).

Screening as a Result of Organizational Incentives

The organizational imperative in most prosecutors' offices is to achieve high rates of felony convictions. The number and percentage of cases successfully processed to a guilty plea or conviction are measures for evaluating prosecutors' performance and the efficiency of their offices. In times of budgetary crisis, such measures might prove critical in sustaining or even increasing allocated resources in a zero-sum budgetary game between fiscally strapped agencies. Domestic violence cases still fail this "real life" test in most jurisdictions despite widespread statutory reforms.

Organizationally, criminal justice institutions maintain a marked distinction between misdemeanor and felony offenses. Most domestic violence cases continue to be classified as misdemeanors, although as described later, they are now denominated as domestic violence–specific misdemeanors. This distinction seems to be another product of the relatively low significance attributed to domestic cases, not a reflection of the degree of injury or potential threat to the victim posed by the incident.

The misdemeanor/felony distinction remains important. In most other contexts, an assault by an intimate might be termed a felony. For example, in one national crime survey, it was reported that more than one third of misdemeanor domestic violence cases, if committed by strangers, would have been termed "rape," "robbery," or "aggravated assault"—all felonies. In 42% of the remaining misdemeanor cases, an injury occurred. This rate of injury for domestic misdemeanor crime was higher than the combined injury rate of all of the foregoing felonies (Langan & Innes, 1986).

These surprising statistics occurred partially because in U.S. jurisprudence, mere injury is not typically determinative of the severity of the crime charged. Unless a homicide occurs, evidence of premeditation and use of a weapon are far more important in the charging decision. Further, except as described later, in certain jurisdictions, domestic violence offenses are treated in isolation and out of context of a persistent pattern of battering or abuse. Even a violation of a temporary restraining order—a fairly obvious intentional crime—remains by statute a misdemeanor in most states, merely a cause for civil contempt in many other states, and at the discretion of the court as being either civil or criminal in still others. As such, even the creation of new remedies has done little to effectively change organizational incentives to relegate such cases to a lower priority.

Some critics have also argued that crimes are downplayed simply because they are crimes against women, historically a disfavored group. We cannot find sufficient evidence to strongly support this conclusion in most jurisdictions; however, regardless of the reason, the effect of the dichotomy is to lessen the willingness of a prosecutor or court to waste its scarce resources to process domestic violence cases (Langan & Innes, 1986).

Case Attrition by Victims: Self-Doubts and the Complexity of Motivation

Earlier in this chapter we discussed why many victims never call the police. Now because of mandatory or presumptive arrest policies, many more cases reach the prosecutor's office. What is the result? Perhaps inevitably, in domestic violence cases, victim or attrition dismissal rates are extraordinarily high. This might occur either because the victim drops charges or because she refuses to appear as a witness.

Certainly victim "led" attrition has remained a concern. A series of studies in different jurisdictions conducted during the early years of reforms demonstrated that, absent unusually aggressive measures, attrition rates for victim-initiated cases hovered between 60% and 80% (Cannavale & Falcon, 1986; Field & Field, 1973; Ford, 1983; Lerman, 1981; Parnas, 1970; Rebovich, 1996; Ursel, 1995; Vera Institute of Justice, 1977; Williams, 1976).

Despite increased societal attention to domestic violence, the rate of prosecution is still limited by the unwillingness of victims to cooperate (Belknap et al., 2001; Hirschel & Hutchison, 2001). In fact, one study that controlled for type of evidence, witnesses, and relationship reported that when domestic victims cooperated, prosecutors were seven times more likely to press charges (Dawson & Dinovitzer, 2001). Commentators note that prosecutors still believed that they were hindered by extraordinary rates of victim noncooperation (Guzik, 2007).

Why should such high rates of victim-initiated case attrition persist? Once an arrest has occurred, we strongly believe that victims should not be considered irrational decision makers, and instead their instrumental and rational reasons should be examined rather than their emotional attachments in their decision to cooperate with prosecutors. Victims might be far less concerned with deterrence as an esoteric concept than with using the criminal justice system to accomplish primarily personal goals. Hence, to understand this better, we need to examine what might motivate victims to support prosecution, as well as how the process of prosecution might weaken these desires.

We start with a belief that there are six predominant motives for a victim to support prosecution: (1) curiosity about what alternatives are available to help her and her family; (2) confirmation of her status as an empowered person but who has been victimized (a sort of "coming out"); (3) a matter of principle (i.e., a crime has been committed, and it should be reported); (4) to facilitate the assailant's entry into an effective batterer treatment program; (5) increasing her legitimacy as a victim in subsequent police encounters both to enhance her future safety or to maintain economic independence should separation occur; and (6) revenge.

None of these factors is, of course, mutually exclusive, nor do they motivate all victims equally. The problem is that these motives, with the exception of the last two, seeking future leverage and revenge, might rapidly diminish or be satisfied once the victim observes the prosecution process.

For example, the first of these motivators, the desire for more information, might be resolved very early in the process of prosecution. Information about prosecution and alternatives are now widely disseminated. Given the known desire of the criminal justice bureaucracy to dispose of as many cases as possible, one might cynically observe that information given on alternatives to prosecution are provided because the alternative adds to a burgeoning caseload rather than attempts to determine the most appropriate disposition.

Similarly, the second motivation of "empowerment" might be satisfied quickly. Initiating prosecution might be the only initial alternative for a victim to gain control in an abusive relationship. Actual, continued prosecution would then be of only secondary importance to the control gained as a "power resource" through the threat of continued prosecution. Thus, the victim might use the criminal justice system as a strategic, but very limited, tool in a purely rational manner rather than seeking to prosecute a case through to conviction (Ford, 1991).

If we are not to become advocates of prosecution for its own sake, or for societal goals that might be of limited relevance to any particular victim, we need to understand that some domestic violence victims might not be as deeply committed to continued prosecution as are other victims. In addition, their reasons are rational from their personal perspectives.

Also, although inappropriate, many victims tend to blame their own behavior for a violent incident. Self-doubt and guilt in relationship cases, in general, and intimate partner violence, in particular, is far more significant than for other victims of violent crime (Buchbinder & Eiskovits, 2003). Victim self-doubts might uneasily coexist with the desire to pursue the arrest and prosecution of an offender. Many victim advocates would observe that such a result is predictable given the process of socialization that is reinforced by constant societal pressure. Regardless of reasons, victim self-doubts might result in prosecutor attitudes that "high dropout" cases are not worth the expenditure of scarce resources (Guzik, 2007).

Part of the reason for the high rate of victim attrition initiated might be a result of the lack of the victim's belief that she is supported by society. The fact is that many victims do not broadcast to friends or work colleagues that they were abused for a variety of reasons, including "shame" and acute helplessness. Similarly, those victims who do not perceive institutional or formal support from victim advocates, dedicated prosecutors, or other officials within the criminal justice system often will be more likely to drop a case. This aspect of social isolation can become a critical pathway that weakens a victim's commitment to prosecute a case (Belknap, Melton, Denney, Fleury-Steiner, & Sullivan, 2009; Bennett, Goodman, & Dutton, 1999).

This aspect of social isolation might be extremely important in cases of domestic violence prosecution. One of the primary control tactics of abusers is social isolation. Often, through the course of previous incidents, the victim might have lost her network of friends and relatives who could potentially support her actions. If the prosecutors, victim advocates, or other parties that might be expected to support prosecution do not fill this void, this social isolation is likely to persist, and a victim would be predictably far less likely to prosecute (Stark, 2007).

The attitudes of the prosecution and members of the office staff in many jurisdictions might contribute to a victim's sense of isolation, thereby influencing her to drop charges (Belknap et al., 2001; Dawson & Dinovitzer, 2001; Erez & Belknap, 1998). As noted earlier, virtually all criminal justice agencies from their earliest history have had a bias against intervention for cases involving private relationships. Although statutes and rules theoretically now have eliminated such discrimination, court personnel in domestic violence and similar cases often have made victims feel personally responsible for case outcome.

This occurs because in many cases that are prosecuted through conviction, public order was also affected, although the victim suffered the most direct harm. For this reason, prosecutors often encourage or, even require by a subpoena, victims in nonrelationship cases to support prosecution. In domestic violence incidents, the violation to the public order is not as evident to the prosecutorial staff, although they have been ambivalent about intervention. Not unexpectedly, they might subtly, or even at times overtly, encourage a victim to drop charges.

Another factor affecting victims and their desire to continue prosecution is that a victim's attitude toward the crime and her abuser might alter over time. Memories of a crime often recede. Those victims who are in a continued relationship with a cyclical batterer often experience a prolonged "honeymoon," in which the offender seeks to please the victim out of atonement or fear of prosecution. He might even cease battering altogether. In time, continued prosecution of the criminal case might become the only event that reminds her (and the offender) of the battering incident and threaten to end a current harmonious period. Other victims might have successfully left the batterer and negotiated acceptable financial support or terms of custody. These victims might now justifiably fear that prosecution would simply anger the batterer, jeopardizing this hard-won status.

Victim Costs in Prosecution

The fact is that prosecution of domestic abuse cases might inflict major and unanticipated costs for a victim. One such "cost" is retaliation. Available empirical evidence suggests that many victims might be subject to subsequent retaliation or offender intimidation. Whatever the potential for retaliation that might be suggested by statistics, no one can provide certainty to a frightened victim, particularly if she is with a high-risk offender. Such victims' fears, as we have discussed, actually often are valid.

One well-documented, if somewhat dated, study reported that nearly half of the victims reported that their assailants had physically threatened them if they proceeded further with the judicial process or if they sought a temporary restraining order. This was not an idle threat. The batterers as a group were demonstrably dangerous. Victims were aware of prior criminal records for 55% of batterers; still others, of course, had criminal records unknown to the victims, 2% of assailants had firearms of which the victim was aware, and two thirds of those with weapons had already threatened or assaulted the victim with these weapons (Klein, 1994b).

Similarly, victims correctly feared retaliation against their children. Klein (1994b) noted that 25% of offenders directly threatened kidnapping the couple's children if legal action was pursued. Abusers also often threatened to lie or exaggerate the victim's personal problems as a parental caregiver to child protective services. Thus, victims with their own substance abuse problems, or who had perhaps neglected or abused their children as a consequence rather than as a precedent to their own abuse, were threatened with child custody loss (Stark, 1997)

Although Stark's study focused on incentives for a victim's decision to drop a restraining order, there is every reason to believe that such acts of intimidation would occur more frequently when a criminal prosecution was pending. The stakes for the offender in an active criminal case far exceed those of a prospectively applied court order. In many judicial systems, there has been an utter failure to give victims information about methods to protect themselves via temporary or permanent restraining orders—and how to get these orders enforced.

Although less dramatic, there also is the real possibility that indirect economic harm of continued prosecution might deter victims from prosecution. If the victim continues to cohabitate with the offender for financial reasons, she might fear direct economic loss if the offender loses his job. In other cases, reducing alimony or child support might be a real risk. Actual out-of-pocket monetary losses often occur in the event of a conviction or if extensive court time is required (Bent-Goodley, 2001; Coker, 2000; Mills, 1999). Direct economic harm to the victim might occur if she is required to take time off from her job or to arrange for child care to allow her to appear in court. In many cases, the seemingly arbitrary scheduling of criminal cases might force a victim to wait for hours in order to provide a few minutes of testimony or, as often happens, lead to a complete waste of her time if a defendant's counsel is successful in continuing the case to a later date.

The batterer often fans such fears of economic retaliation. Klein (1994b) reported that monetary threats were made by 42% of abusers in his study, which is an especially difficult prospect since in his study 31% of the victims were unemployed and 67% earned less than a poverty wage. A couple's minor children might present significant issues for those who want to be sure they are protected but still wish to maintain an intact family structure. Financial ties (intensified by welfare reforms) might make some victims critically dependent on an abuser's financial support for minor children, which is a factor at odds with strict punishment models. A simple threat to have a person arrested or to initiate prosecution might terminate an abusive relationship. Pursuing prosecution past that point might not be in the interests of the victim because it might increase the risks of retaliation while forcing her commitment to a process with little direct benefit.

As a result of these factors, although the goal of assisting and empowering victims via prosecution might be understood in the abstract, it often is lost in practice. This is especially true if prosecution serves mainly to attain larger societal goals of punishing an offender or deterring other potential batterers. Several studies have shown that victim preferences were rarely solicited, and when known, they were rarely honored if they contravened policies designed to punish and deter offenders (Buzawa & Buzawa, 1996). Because victim choices normally influence the criminal justice system to some degree (and the quest for restorative justice is pushing this to the forefront), policies that remove or limit victim input into decision making are unusual.

In short, the general assumption that prosecution is in the victim's interests might not be accurate. In fact, at times there might be an irreconcilable dilemma: to assist and empower a victim might not involve the offender's subsequent case prosecution.

The Impact of Victim-Initiated Attrition

Although victims might not desire arrest, let alone subsequent prosecution through conviction, we recognize that they might truly need a strong team of law enforcement personnel and prosecutors. In the more traditional society of past decades, the family, church, and/or friends might have provided victims with support. In the highly mobile 21st century, such assistance is much more problematic, making victim reliance on formal agencies more acute. Despite the growing presence of social service and nonprofit agencies, domestic violence victims often do not have real-time access to such assistance at critical moments without criminal justice support. For this reason, criminal justice agencies, especially law enforcement personnel and the prosecutor's staff, do not just enforce their own mandates but also serve as critical gatekeepers to the provision of services of other essential actors.

A Judicial Annoyance: Handling Battling Families

Although virtually every state has passed domestic violence statutes, until recently, the judicial response to sexual and family violence has neither been as comprehensive nor as advanced as the police, or now even that of the prosecutor's offices, in many jurisdictions. Why? The police, however grudgingly, are fully expected to follow the laws as written. Although prosecutors have the power to exercise discretion, their discretion has begun to be limited by active oversight or even by the initiation of the no-drop policies discussed earlier.

In contrast, judges have the express responsibility to adjudicate criminal responsibility and the conduct of offenders. Although many, if not most, are willing to experiment with innovative approaches, others are largely unsympathetic with the goals and methods espoused in domestic violence legislation and often are disturbed by potential impingement of a defendant's rights. Because of their unique position, they can effectively refuse to enforce statutes, and the ability of most victims to contest judicial decisions in misdemeanor cases is, in practice, virtually nonexistent.

Research on the study of what works in the judiciary is less advanced (or at least less disseminated) than in the case of the police or even prosecutors. Although many policy analyses have been published by victim rights advocates, feminist attorneys, and law reviews that strongly advocate further change, issues of judicial operational performance have not been widely circulated. Nonetheless, the national consensus needed to force systemic change has begun to coalesce, imparting a current degree of uncertainty exceeding that of the police.

As a result, judicial management of domestic violence cases has only recently gained saliency as a public issue. Initial attention was the result of occasional newspaper series exploring the extent to which the system does not work or sporadic outcries to an especially outrageous unguarded public comment by a trial court judge who, at a minimum, was unaware of the political necessity to refrain from critiquing abuse victims. Such attitudes are not atypical. Although unspoken, they are endemic and systematized. The degree to which these attitudes still prevail is unclear. Clearly, there are still many judges who hold victims largely responsible for their victimization and do not consider such cases appropriate for judicial intervention (Hemmens, Strom, & Schlegel, 1998).

Similarly, because most commentaries on the judicial response have been published in law journals or advocacy publications and are based on nonquantitative measures, there has not been a research catalyst for change equivalent to the Minneapolis Domestic Violence Experiment (MDVE). Therefore, changes in the orientation and training of individual administrators is more a product of the impact of professional groups such as the National Council of Juvenile and Family Court Judges, the American Bar Association, the State Justice Institute, and the National Judicial College coupled with the push for federal funding from the Violence Against Women Act (see Valente, Hart, Zeya, & Malefyt, 2001).

As a result of such factors, the current performance of judges is even more inconsistent than that of the police. Davis Adams, director of EMERGE, the country's oldest treatment program for batterers (located in Massachusetts) with intimate experience with the system in that state, has argued that everyone in Massachusetts knows the rhetoric, but when dealing with individual cases, the consistency breaks down (Polochanin, 1994). A report published by the *Boston Globe* (Adams, 1994) used the Massachusetts database on the history and disposal of restraining orders, which is a good indicator of the commitment of judges to these crimes; this database showed startling variations in enforcement between different counties. In some counties, including Suffolk County (Boston), more than 60% of such claims of violation were dismissed. In other jurisdictions, as few as 18% of cases were dismissed. Similarly, sentencing of the offenders to jail time for restraining order violation ranged from 0% to 26%, with even the high estimates well below expectations considering that the applicable domestic violence statute clearly favored stiff punishment for violating restraining orders.

The reasons for the discrepancy seem to reflect the operations and attitudes of courts. Adams (1994) faults many judges in whom he now sees a backlash because they are tired of hearings regarding battered women. This was partially confirmed by detailed analysis of individual court statistics demonstrating that some judges would rarely dismiss cases, whereas others might dismiss up to 75% under certain circumstances. Regardless of the reasons, it seems that there is a virtual patchwork approach toward handling domestic cases, sometimes even within the same jurisdiction.

Case Disposition by the Judiciary

Historically, cases that are not filtered out of the system by action or inaction of the police or by victims or prosecutors often received summary dispositions by the judiciary. Although it would be easy to overgeneralize, judges, at least in the past, shared the consensus of prosecutors that most domestic violence cases could not readily be helped by the full prosecution of an offender (Dobash & Dobash, 1979; Field & Field, 1973). Given the organizational context of extreme time pressures and limited resources, it is not surprising that in the past it was repeatedly noted that judges minimized domestic violence cases and disproportionately dismissed them.

Similarly, until the full effect of the ongoing recent reforms, the sentencing of convicted domestic violence offenders has been quite lenient, with few offenders sentenced to serve any time in jail (Sherman, 1993). One study was made in Ohio of all misdemeanor domestic violence assault charges in the state during 1980. This research was conducted after Ohio passed a new domestic violence statute designed to sensitize the criminal justice system to the problems of battered women. Although termed "misdemeanors," many of these cases involved injuries and potentially serious conduct that in another context would have been termed felonies (Quarm & Schwartz, 1983).

The sentences imposed graphically illustrate how the crimes were trivialized. Of 1,408 cases, 1,142 (81%) were dismissed. Of the 1,142 dismissed cases, 1,062 (93%) were dismissed because the victim requested this action (for the vast variety of reasons described in this chapter) or failed to appear. Of the remaining 256 cases, 166 guilty verdicts or pleas were received. Despite being in a jurisdiction otherwise noted for harsh sentencing, only 60 miscreants (36%) spent any time in jail, with one third (20) spending between 1 and 15 days (including time spent in jail awaiting trial), one third (20) between 16 and 30 days, and only one third (20 out of the original 48 cases) more than 20 days. Similarly, only 12% of the miscreants were fined more than $100. Simple probation, instead of imprisonment or fines, was the sentence in almost two thirds of the cases (Quarm & Schwartz, 1983).

The same results were reported in several other studies even when, in the rare occasion, domestic violence cases were treated as felonies. Another study, also conducted in Ohio, reported that even in the rare circumstance that a domestic violence defendant was convicted and received a prison sentence, sentence terms were shorter than they were for other types of offenders (Erez & Tontodonato, 1990). Similarly, in one study conducted in Alaska, the overall result of court actions (after taking into account "voluntary dismissals") was that domestic violence offenders were less likely to be convicted, and if convicted, they were less likely to be sentenced to jail (Miethe, 1987). Why did such results occur, even in the face of blunt statutory directives to enhance the response to domestic violence? Few empirical studies have surveyed judicial attitudes to explain behavior. We can, however, surmise that several key factors are involved. First, trial criminal court judges are attorneys, primarily recruited directly from the ranks of prosecutors or indirectly after a prosecutor has become a successful defense attorney. For the reasons we described earlier, prosecutors have long had a troubled history in responding to these offenses. Becoming a defense attorney would be unlikely to change their attitudes toward aggressive enforcement.

Second, judges are in a unique position to impose their own will on a case. Since this crime has never received the mandatory minimum sentences meted out in certain drug and other offenses, they can, if they choose, ignore statutory directions. Because of "separation of powers," such decisions cannot be overturned by the legislature. Moreover, as judges, they do not have to justify sentencing and other case dispositions to victims, prosecutors, or defense attorneys. As most domestic violence cases are treated by the system as misdemeanors, the operating reality is that there is no appeal from their decisions.

For the last decade, the study of so-called gender bias in the courts received significant research attention, especially from feminist writers and their political allies. As a result of claims of gender bias, the National Organization for Women (NOW) Legal

Defense and Education Fund worked with the National Association of Women Judges to study systemic gender bias in the courts (Schafran, 1990). By 1989, 30 states had such gender bias task forces. Interestingly, it has long been assumed that gender bias is not simply, or even at this time, primarily a case of intentional ill will against women. Instead, it is more likely to be differential treatment in situations in which gender should not be considered as a result of stereotypical beliefs about the gender's temperament, expectations, and proper roles (California Gender Bias Task Force, 1996).

Such attitudes were found to exist by the judges and by their staff. For example, the California 1996 task force reported that 53% of male court personnel thought that women exaggerated domestic violence complaints. Not surprisingly only about one quarter of female court personnel shared these beliefs. Similarly, whereas 40% of the male court personnel believed that domestic violence cases should be diverted or that counseling should be used rather than prosecution, only 21% of female court staff agreed with this (Hemmens et al., 1998).

Hemmens and colleagues (1998) summarized the findings of the state reports and found that gender bias was most prevalent in domestic violence cases. Although a significant part of their findings related to the actions of prosecutors and defense attorneys, many reports commented on inappropriate attitudes and actions by the judiciary. For example, Utah in 1990 reported that cases of domestic violence were minimized compared with nondomestic assaults (Utah Gender Bias Task Force, 1990). The Maryland report stated that "51% of male attorneys and 68% of the female attorneys believed that judges sometimes failed to view domestic violence as a crime" (Hemmens et al., 1998). Hemmens and colleagues quoted several particularly egregious examples cited in the state-sponsored gender bias studies.

For example, one state trial court judge commented, "I have difficulty finding where this defendant's (the husband) done anything wrong, other than slapping her (his wife). Maybe that was 'justified'" (Utah Gender Bias Task Force, 1990, p. 44). A study in Massachusetts revealed that some victims report improper or irrelevant questions during court proceedings. Over three fourths of the responding attorneys said judges sometimes allow questions as to what the victim did to provoke the battering. Comments made by judges included, "Why don't you get a divorce" and "Why are you bothering the court with this problem?" (Hemmens et al., 1998, p. 24).

Third, even the more enlightened judges who have sought to provide an adequate answer to such crimes have faced real issues. They are aware that the evidence of which party was at fault can be quite tangled in many cases, creating relatively weak cases when presented at trial. Even when guilt is clear, many have long acted on the assumption that their goal was primarily to "rehabilitate" the domestic violence offender, not primarily to punish him. This has been perceived by many as being responsive to victims who want rehabilitation, not punitive results. Not surprisingly, it was noted that in most courts the likelihood and duration of jail sentences has simply not been increased as a result of reforms, although this did not prove true in an in-depth study of case dispositions in New York City (Peterson, 2001).

We recognize that judicial decisions toward leniency, when prompted by evidentiary challenges or respect for genuine victim preferences, are, on balance, positive. We have certainly met many judges whose commitment to the resolution of domestic violence cases cannot be questioned, and their actions in these difficult cases can be open to interpretation. We are, however, less sanguine that the result of judicial action in many, if not most, courtrooms truly reflects victim preferences and not preexisting judicial attitudes to dispose rapidly of this part of a judge's overwhelming caseload. Unfortunately, the effect of judicial attitudes and practices that negate the importance of this crime, like those of prosecutors before them, cascades throughout the criminal justice system.

Frankly, the judiciary has always retained the potential to lead the criminal justice system by example or direction. They are the ultimate authority, with the power to ratify or negate the actions of the police and prosecutors, as well as to define the parameters and seriousness of a particular crime. They might use such power to compel effective action or, as in the past, strongly imply that domestic violence is not a "real" crime.

The cost of judicial action that is not conducted properly is high. In many cases, victims have essentially been deprived of legal protection, and offenders might have perceived that the whole matter was "no big deal." Additionally, police with policies that emphasized the role of arrest or that even made arrest mandatory undermined such cases, resulting in their being routinely dismissed or in the sentencing trivializing the inherent serious nature of an assault.

Only recently have there been widespread systemic efforts to coordinate the actions of the judiciary. To date, although individual judiciary actions are being examined, no one has really attempted to force consistency in actions among the thousands of judges nationwide. In this manner, the response of the judiciary, compared with those of the police or prosecutors, is even more problematic. Many judges lead their communities in the fight against domestic violence. Others, sometimes even in the same jurisdiction, treat such cases lightly or either resent or lack the resources to respond to the flooding of their court dockets with misdemeanor cases that often are dismissed.

The federal Violence Against Women Act (1994), reauthorized in 2000 and 2005, has greatly facilitated judicial efforts by establishing standards, providing technical assistance, and funding improvements to those courts not yet increasing efforts toward a proactive response. Although not being at all coercive toward the courts, it has provided guidance by highlighting achievements of innovative efforts by designating model courts such as the Quincy District Court. Databases and evaluations also have begun to develop in an effort to confirm the relative performance of particular courts. Also, by establishing new federal crimes and enforcement responsibilities, there is increased pressure for courts to take these crimes more seriously. In the absence of any judicial uniformity, the following is a discussion of several major changes now being evaluated and adopted, specifically the move to divert appropriate cases systematically at an early stage out of the criminal system through mediation and court-mandated counseling as well as the development of specialized courts. Furthermore, an integrated approach to handling domestic violence cases is explored later in this treatise. As will be discussed more fully in Chapter 11, considerable progress has been made.

SUMMARY

Victim advocates have long been concerned about victims not known to the criminal justice system. This chapter discussed two different sets of reasons for this. First, there is a wide range of reasons why victims fail to report. Often, these reasons are valid from the victim's perspective as there is a fear of retaliation or other consequences that might result. However, these preferences might be diametrically opposed to society's interests in identifying and intervening with offenders. Nonetheless, evidence does suggest that there has been an increase in reporting in recent years.

Second, there have been long-standing concerns with agency screening of calls for reasons that might be less than ideal. Often they are not based on "official" policies, but instead they are idiosyncratic because of individual or organizational factors not relevant to the situation.

Hopefully, the growing trend of victims to report victimization will be met with an improved ability to protect and serve them. This should result in a greater congruence between what is in the victim's interests as well as that of society as a whole.

DISCUSSION QUESTIONS

1. You read about the concerns with call screening—by both the victims and the police. It also addressed the need to consider the *totality* of the police job rather than take any given crime problem and give disproportionate attention to it (often driven by political or perhaps liability considerations). What policy recommendations would you suggest and why?

2. As you hopefully noticed when reading the MDVE and the Replication Studies, the policy implications remain unclear. First, for those of you interested in the validity (and usefulness) of research, what variables *should* the researchers have examined rather than unemployment and racial status and why?

3. Based on your readings of the research to date, what policy recommendations do you recommend to improve victim reporting? Who should we be encouraging them to report to?

The Impetus 6
for Change

Chapter Overview

This chapter will discuss the modern movement for change in the police response to domestic violence. Change originated from an unusual confluence of political and legal pressure from women's rights and battered women advocates, research, and organizational concerns over the possibility of liability if the police continued past practices of neglecting domestic violence victims. The interaction of all these sources of influence is worthy of examination as it helps us understand our current concepts of belief systems and "best practices."

Political Pressure

Political pressure began to mount in the late 1960s and early 1970s over observed inadequacies of criminal justice responses to issues of interest to women. The growing women's rights and "feminist" movements that emerged raised consciousness about societal neglect toward the unique problems confronting women. Initially, the inability of the criminal justice system to respond to violence against women focused on stranger rape and assaults. However, it soon broadened as activists recognized the severity of the problem of intimate violence.

One source of the pressure was the professionals who assisted battered women through shelters and legal services networks. These networks were, at first, largely decentralized, assisting battered women through hundreds, if not thousands, of local community-based volunteer efforts. Later, such groups were assisted by statewide "coalitions" to prevent violence against women. Whether on their own or through the assistance of umbrella groups, shelters acquired the services of volunteer and paid attorneys, victim advocates, and social workers. These trained professionals soon realized that the needs of domestic violence victims were not being met by criminal justice agencies.

A pattern variously described as "patriarchal" or "cavalier" began to be used to describe the attitudes and, even more important, the practices of male-dominated police agencies and prosecutors. Concerns grew rapidly when advocates came to believe that police arrested everyone *but* domestic violence assailants (Berk & Loseke, 1980–1981). As a result, advocating more aggressive use of arrest became the natural consensus position among domestic violence activists (Coker, 2000; Ferraro, 1989b; Mills, 1999). This group provided the driving leadership needed to promote enactment of domestic violence legislation. This occurred first at the local and state levels and much later at the national level.

As discussed, the reasons for the differences in perspective were explainable, if not adequate. Advocates for battered women were faced with policing that traditionally had emphasized public order and authority without official intervention in "private matters," that is, an organizational commitment to intervene in the family using only informal strategies for resolution. This also was amply reinforced, as Sanders (1988) noted, by police ideology in which protection of the "public order" was paramount, individual rights of secondary importance, and the safety of a particular victim was typically relegated to minimal importance.

The contribution of victim advocates was to argue that, regardless of the reason, police would not or could not adequately respond to the concerns of women. It was simply factual that women were more likely to be raped, murdered, and assaulted by someone they knew in private rather than in public places. Conversely, men were more likely to be the victims of public disorder. Criminal justice agencies were, regardless of any inherent sexism, far more likely to respond to crimes in public places.

Societal pressures emphasizing a legalistic intervention to long-standing social issues also became significant. To understand better the impetus for the changing role of law enforcement in domestic violence, it is essential to acknowledge that political climate. Since the widespread riots in the mid-1960s and the proliferation of drug usage at the same time, the "war on crime" became (and still is) a reliable vote winner. This strategy was first used successfully by presidential candidate Richard Nixon in 1968 and was reinforced during the 1980 presidential campaign, when candidate Ronald Reagan argued that a "new morning in America" was at least partially dependent on being much "tougher" on criminals. A "tough-on-crime" or "war-on-crime" approach has become a consistent and successful political theme both among Republican candidates and, partially as a reaction, among "centrist" Democratic aspirants to higher office.

In short, recent decades have experienced a marked increase in the societal propensity to use its coercive police powers to "solve" social problems and a relative unwillingness to invest in efforts to attempt to reform miscreants. Not surprisingly, criminal justice agencies have been increasing in budget, size of staff, and numbers of cases processed (Garland, 2001). It can be argued that the increasing role of law to maintain social control indicates the perceived weakness of informal controls. Pressure to criminalize domestic conflict—such as prohibition, Mothers Against Drunk Driving, and Students Against Drunk Driving—was more in the nature of a reform movement. Policing disorder and emphasizing misdemeanor arrests were part of, and an extension of, this trend (Manning, 1993).

As might be expected, threats of random street violence and drug abuse were generally viewed as a law enforcement issue justifying a greater punitive response. Placed in this context, it is not surprising that the previously lax treatment of domestic violence became a political issue.

There are certainly parallels with this period to the earlier reform era of the late 1880s. Key distinctions between the current and earlier reform periods have made the challenges to the system far more powerful. Today's mass media, and the growing ability of special interests to influence legislation, have made the movement to increase law enforcement in this area into a national phenomenon. Similarly the existence of support services to assist women with shelter and legal advocacy, even when not well funded, has given increased national visibility to the tremendous numbers of women injured by intimates. Finally, tantalizing stories of celebrity spouse abuse or death have been regularly reported, giving national feminist and battered women's groups enormous media attention and focusing public opinion even more on domestic violence.

Even after the start of domestic violence reforms, national attention to domestic violence was periodically stoked by instances of nationally televised domestic violence. For example, In 1990, the media were captivated by Carol Stuart's murder in Boston. Her husband, Charles Stuart, had frantically reported the crime using a cell phone to call 911 from their vehicle.

He described in graphic detail how a Black man had shot both of them in an attempted robbery of their vehicle. This account was nationally broadcast both because of its inherent drama and because it played to White suburban fears about random minority street crime in urban areas. Many in the Boston Police Department placed responsibility on an innocent Black man and tried to obtain his confession. These efforts were derailed by Charles Stuart's suicide, as others within the police department, as well as members of the press, developed leads that indicated Stuart was the killer. This incident was ultimately recognized as reflecting both society's tendency to blame street crime committed by minorities for most violence and police departments' inability to recognize domestic violence.

In 1994, the public allegations about domestic violence among celebrities—for example, Roseanne and Tom Arnold as well as Axel Rose—was rapidly followed by the national media circus attendant to the domestic violence and stalking involved in the O. J. Simpson–Nicole Simpson case. Not surprisingly, such media attention, including gavel-to-gavel coverage of the O. J. Simpson trial and repeated cover stories in newspapers and national newsmagazines, led to dramatic increases in calls for service to domestic violence hotlines, shelters, the police, and the courts.

"Stone Cold" Steve Austin

WWE Professional wrestler "Stone Cold" Steve Austin, whose real name is Steve Williams, turned himself in to police on charges of assaulting his wife, fellow WWE performer Debra Williams. In June 2002, Debra Williams called police to the couple's house in San Antonio, and police saw a "large noticeable welt" beneath her right eye, as reported by the TV show *Entertainment Weekly*. Austin was not at the house when police arrived, and he was not arrested. In August 2002, Austin turned himself in, posted $5,000 bond, and was released pending future legal action.

(Continued)

(Continued)

Riddick Bowe

In February 2001, former heavyweight boxing champion Riddick Bowe was arrested and charged with third-degree assault for a fight with his wife, Terri Bowe. Police arrived at the Bowe house on Long Island and found Terri Bowe suffering from cuts and bruises, according to an Associated Press (AP) report ("Bowe Let Go – Sort of," 2001). Riddick Bowe pleaded innocent to charges of assaulting his wife and was released from jail on $2,500 bail. The AP reported that the couple was "splitting up after a 'very brief marriage.'" Bowe was arrested again in March 2003 on a domestic violence charge of second-degree assault, less than 1 week before he was scheduled to begin serving a prison sentence for abducting his first wife, Judy, and their five children. Bowe was arrested after Prince George's County police responded to a domestic disturbance call. Bowe's current wife, Terri, was taken to the hospital, but her injuries were not believed to be serious, according to a *Washington Post* article ("Bowe Files for Chapter 11 Bankruptcy," 2005). Bowe served an 18-month prison sentence for the 1998 abduction of his first wife.

Jim Brown

Former National Football League star Jim Brown was released from prison in July 2002 after serving time for vandalizing his wife's car. Brown received a 6-month sentence after he refused to undergo court-ordered domestic violence counseling and community service. Brown was convicted in 1999 of vandalism for defacing Monique Brown's car. He was acquitted of the charge of making a terrorist threat against Monique Brown after threatening to kill her during an argument. Brown served 4 months of his 6-month sentence.

James Brown

In February 2004, singer James Brown was arrested and charged with criminal domestic violence for allegedly shoving his wife, Tomi Rae Brown, to the ground and threatening her with a chair. Tomi Rae Brown suffered scratches and bruises and was taken to a hospital in Augusta, Georgia, for treatment. Brown denied the charges and was released from jail. If convicted, he faced a maximum penalty of 30 days in jail and a $500 fine, reported the AP (Grace, 2004). In November 2003, some advocates for victims of violence spoke out against the decision by leaders at the John F. Kennedy Center for the Performing Arts to give James Brown a lifetime achievement award. Brown was honored anyway for his contribution to the arts at the Kennedy Center Honors in December 2003. In 1988, Brown was charged with assaulting his then-wife Adrienne, but the charges were dropped when she refused to testify against him. He also settled several lawsuits filed against him that alleged sexual harassment. Kay Mixon, President of the Comby Center for Battered Women, a shelter that served Adrienne Brown, told the *New York Post*, "It's a disgrace that the Kennedy Center is giving him this award. . . . He is a batterer. He didn't batter her just once, but over and over again" (Celebrities Violence, 2008).

The Role of Research in Promoting Change

Early Research

Research linking the criminal justice system to domestic violence also had a dramatic effect alerting the policy elite to the existence of the problems of domestic violence and legitimizing support for pro-arrest policies. In this regard, the research itself became a factor independent of the adequacy of its design, accuracy of conclusions, or the utility of the particular policy nostrums being promulgated.

Academic interest in family violence first emerged with concerns about child abuse. The seminal article "The Battered Child Syndrome" by Kemp, Silverman, Steele, Droegenmuller, and Silver (1962) focused on the necessity that physicians and other primary caregivers such as social workers recognize and intervene in such cases. This article and subsequent publications, however, focused less on criminal law implications and more on the etiology of the problem and treatment of the victim and offender.

Several years after the Kemp et al. (1962) article, Parnas (1967) published "The Police Response to the Domestic Disturbance." This was followed in 1971 by Morton Bard's "Police Discretion and Diversion of Incidents of Intra-Family Violence" (Bard, 1967, 1973). This study analyzed the effect of a demonstration project on family crisis intervention, funded by the Law Enforcement Assistance Administration (LEAA). This project, in turn, became the theoretical foundation for many other family crisis intervention projects (Liebman & Schwartz, 1973).

Although the specific tenets and a critique of family crisis intervention as a technique will be addressed later, the impact of the Bard study (1973) was that it reinforced the concept that changing the police response could dramatically reduce the impact of domestic violence.

Although the domestic assault policy at that time was for police to do as little as possible and then leave the situation, Bard convinced LEAA that crisis intervention techniques had significant potential. As a result, the Office for Law Enforcement Assistance funded a feasibility study for a special unit of crisis intervention officers. As the following section demonstrates, the impact of highly publicized research sponsored by the federal government can be at a scale disproportionate to the relative merits of the research itself.

Garner and Maxwell (2000) noted that the political impact of the research was far greater than warranted, based on empirical findings: Despite the weak design and results that indicated that the program had negative results on officers and victims, Bard's research was, in its day, quite influential. In addition to the visibility in the *New York Times,* between 1971 and 1976, the demonstration and testing divisions of the National Institute of Justice (NIJ) spent millions of dollars paying officers overtime to attend training that encouraged the use of Bard's intervention program in more than a dozen police departments across the United States. Elements of the program were promoted by the International Association of Chiefs of Police and discussed positively in the widely distributed *Law Enforcement Bulletin* (Mohr & Steblein, 1976). Police Family Crisis Intervention had become a major, if not the dominant, law enforcement approach to addressing domestic violence. Despite the evaluation's negative program findings, the evaluators advocated their own untested version of police family violence intervention training

(Wylie et al., 1976). *"The clear lesson is that the strength of federal financial support for a social intervention does not necessarily mean there is an extensive body of knowledge supporting the efficacy of that approach"* (Garner & Maxwell, 2000, p. 87; emphasis added).

The next important study, *Domestic Violence and the Police*, was provided by Marie Wilt and James Bannon (1977). They demonstrated that domestic violence was directly related to homicide; that in 85% of incidents, the police had been called at least once before; and that in 50% of incidents, police had been called five or more times. Although it was concluded that an ineffective police response contributed to the excessive rates of death and injury to victims as well as to the high cost of intervention for police departments, no suggestions were given for exactly how the police could intervene effectively.

This body of domestic violence research was supported by other research criticizing the efficacy of rehabilitation efforts for violent offenders. The famous research of Lipton, Martinson, and Wilks (1975) on the impact of rehabilitation and their conclusion that "nothing worked" contributed to the temporary eclipse of the influence of researchers. After all, if researchers acknowledged that known approaches to date had been a failure, then clearly more drastic measures were needed. Whereas societal reactions to intervention failures had been to question the quality of the intervention or the resources allocated to its implementation, the current political climate was far less tolerant of such "benevolent" explanations.

The cumulative impact of this research, as well as subsequent studies, contributed to developing a consensus among researchers and policymakers regarding the then-current police policies of noninterference. There was widespread agreement that passive police responses further contributed to societal tolerance and to high rates of domestic violence and that alternative police strategies could reverse this trend.

The Evolution of Research Supporting the Primacy of Arrest

By the 1970s, there was widespread disillusionment among practitioners, researchers, and some police administrators regarding then-current domestic violence policies and practices. In part, this was a reflection of the general societal movement away from what Garland (2001) referred to as "penal welfares." Among criminologists, major philosophical differences began to emerge, whereas previously the discipline had demonstrated a far more consistent posture.

Debates regarding the control of domestic violence as a possible exception to policies of tough enforcement continued to persist, however. One side argued that the dichotomy between aggressive enforcement against street crime and lax enforcement of crimes against intimates was justified in that domestic incidents involved "families" and intimate partners. Still others believed such incidents were more trivial and less likely to incur injury, that victims were less likely to desire police intervention and prosecution, and that, therefore, an arrest would not result in conviction, negating the value of such efforts (Myers & Hagan, 1979). Many writers successfully challenged these assumptions and instead maintained that criminal justice institutions were demonstrating sexist behavior by presenting such rationales (Dobash & Dobash, 1979; Matoesian, 1993; Smart, 1986). Over time, there was a growing concern that the use of formal social controls needed to be increased with an emphasis on legal remedies.

These sentiments were highlighted by a National Academy of Sciences report addressing the role of criminal justice sanctions as an effective crime control strategy (Blumstein, Cohen, & Nagin, 1978).

Such concerns gradually permeated the general attitudes of practitioners, policymakers, and the public (Garland, 2001). This represented substantial change. Although reliance on the law often is believed to be a result of the failure of informal social controls (Black, 1976), many sociologists initially doubted the ability of laws to effect levels of domestic violence (Straus, 1977). Nonetheless, primary emphasis began shifting to increased police use of arrests as a deterrent to domestic violence. It has long been known that arresting certain domestic violence offenders was both proper and essential, at least in some situations. After all, making an arrest was the only method by which police could ensure separation of the couple and the prevention of violence, at least until the offender was released. Similarly, despite a strong past bias against arrest, arrests for non-domestic-violence–specific charges, such as drunk and disorderly conduct or public intoxication, often were used. Also, arrests were an acknowledged method for the police to regain control from a disrespectful or otherwise threatening assailant and to maintain the officer's situational dominance (Bittner, 1967, 1974).

By the early 1980s, consensus was reached on the historically limited role of arrest. It had been replaced by an expanding debate among policymakers, researchers, practitioners, and advocates about arrest as a mechanism to deter violence and as a means to strengthen other traditional criminal justice measures that were clearly inadequate.

Deterrence as a Rationale for Police Action

The concept of deterrence as a general preference for crime control became a dominant perspective in mainstream academic literature and in policy circles. Theories that now shape official thinking and action are control theories of various kinds. They posit that offenses are not the result of specific unmet individual needs, such as inadequate socialization or deprivations, but inadequate societal controls (Garland, 2001).

Not surprisingly, the two trends were linked; many researchers and activists increasingly advocated deterrence as a justification for use of arrest (see especially Dobash & Dobash, 1979; Martin, 1976). It is in this context that research favoring use of arrests flourished.

Beginning in the 1970s, a series of experiments, involving some of the country's most prominent researchers, were conducted to try to determine whether police actions specifically deterred offenders and to develop the most effective police response to domestic violence. These are worth exploring in depth because of their key importance in stimulating change and the resultant ongoing debates over both the reliability and the validity of their findings, as well as their impact on current policies.

The Minneapolis Domestic Violence Experiment

Sherman and Berk (1984a, 1984b) conducted the Minneapolis Domestic Violence Experiment (MDVE), which was reported as "The Specific Deterrent Effects of Arrest for

Domestic Assault," in the early 1980s. This report had a virtually unprecedented impact in changing then-current police practices. The research was initially funded by the NIJ to study application of deterrence theory and originated from a National Academy of Sciences Report titled *Deterrence and Incapacitation: Estimating the Effects of Criminal Sanctions on Crime Rates,* which was edited by Blumstein et al. (1978).

The MDVE asked 51 volunteer patrol officers in two precincts to adopt one of three possible responses to situations in which there was probable cause to believe that domestic violence had occurred. Officers were randomly assigned one of three choices: (1) to separate the parties by ordering one of them to leave, (2) to advise them of alternatives (possibly including mediating disputes), or (3) simply to arrest the abuser. During a period of approximately 17 months, 330 cases were generated. The authors then evaluated the possible success of these various "treatments" in deterring recidivism. Recidivism was measured both by official arrest statistics, such as arrest reports and, when available, by victim interviews. The researchers later reported that 10% of those arrested, 19% of those advised of alternatives, and 24% of those merely removed repeated violence (Sherman & Berk, 1984a). From this, they concluded that arrest provided the strongest deterrent to future violence and consequently was the preferred police response.

It is important to realize that the MDVE was a limited experimental design that did not purport to answer definitively or even necessarily to address the question of the "proper" police response to domestic violence.

Methodological Concerns of the MDVE

In fact, the Minneapolis study was strongly critiqued both for its methodology and for its conclusions. Severe criticism was raised in several areas. Responding officers apparently had advance knowledge of the response they were to make. As such, they had opportunity to reclassify offenses to fall outside the parameters of the experiment (Mederer & Gelles, 1989). They might do so if an arrest was assigned despite the officers not desiring to do so—either because of police traditions or possibly to avoid extra paperwork. Even in official statistics of the experiment, several cases (17) were dropped from the experiment, and in fully 56 of 330 cases (17%), the officers gave a treatment different than that required.

Unionized, rank-and-file police officers have never been committed to honoring an experiment by academic outsiders (not exactly their favorite group). There is, in fact, considerable evidence that the MDVE experiment did not control the officers.

Three of the fifty-one officers assigned to participate in the study made most of the arrests, which suggests that the other officers assigned to participate might have actively or passively subverted randomization techniques.

Furthermore, the study only used volunteer officers. This, plus anecdotal evidence, strongly suggests that most officers simply acted the way they thought the situation demanded, indirectly sabotaging the project's validity. Similarly, 5% (16) of the 314 cases were excluded (Sherman & Berk, 1984a).

The victim measurements also were questionable. Only 49% responded in the 6 months after interviews, leaving conclusions based on the database innately suspect.

Binder and Meeker (1988) as well as Lempert (1987, 1989) provided a thorough critique of the MDVE, including these as well as additional concerns. Gartin (1991) attempted to address many of the methodological concerns by a reanalysis of the archived data from the MDVE and found that statistical significance depended on which data sources were used and how the data were analyzed. Gartin concluded that arrest did not have as great a specific deterrent effect as the original research had suggested.

The external validity or generalizability of the conclusions in this study also was suspect. The actions of the officers were, by the nature of the experiment, treated in a vacuum largely independent of the downstream effect of other criminal justice actors. In our view, it is difficult to determine the effect of any police action without explaining how domestic violence prosecutors, courts, probation officers, or social service agencies subsequently handle the cases.

Despite initial disclaimers to the contrary, the Sherman and Berk study immediately became the most cited study in the field. Findings were reported in the *New York Times* (Boffey, 1983), in a Police Foundation report (Sherman & Berk, 1984a), and in numerous academic journals (Berk & Sherman, 1988; Sherman & Berk, 1984b), and they were widely publicized across the country as a whole. Hundreds of newspapers and nationally syndicated columnists discussed these findings, and several major television networks provided prime-time news coverage, often with special documentaries (Fagan, 1988; Sherman & Cohn, 1989). The 1984 Attorney General's Task Force on Family Violence even cited the MDVE findings as a basis for recommending that all law enforcement agencies should develop policies requiring arrest as the preferred response for domestic violence incidents (U.S. Attorney General's Task Force on Family Violence, 1984).

In their summary of the significance of the 1989 MDVE, Maxwell, Garner, and Fagan (2001) stated that "a 1989 survey of local police departments concluded that the published results of MDVE may have substantially influenced over one-third of the police departments responding to their survey to adopt a proarrest policy" (p. 4).

The Role of Publicity in Promoting Research

Part of the reason for the profound impact of the MDVE was the promotional campaign that followed. At least one of the authors, Professor Sherman, stated that he believed it was the "obligation" of social scientists to solicit publicity (Sherman & Cohn, 1989). He recounted how he and his colleagues made decisions about how to manage the story, including persuading local television stations to feature documentaries or "action" tapes for national news shows (even before the results of the experiment were known). Efforts to continue to manage the press continued even to the extent of releasing the final results on the Sunday before Memorial Day, assuming that there would be less competition on a slow news day (Sherman & Cohn, 1989) and notifying the *MacNeil/Lehrer NewsHour* of the study's release well in advance.

Such publicity efforts, which were extraordinary for social science research, were justified as an attempt to "get the attention of key audiences effecting police department policies" (Sherman & Cohn, 1989, p. 121). As Sherman remarked, he also "wanted the audiences to be influenced by the recommendations and be more willing to control replications and random experiments in general" (p. 122).

The NIJ did not release any publications on the study, hold any meetings or conferences, nor fund any demonstration programs testing the use of arrest, however. The massive publicity generated by this research was almost entirely due to the efforts of individuals (Garner & Maxwell, 2000).

The impact of the Minneapolis study was certainly a result, in part, of the extreme publicity it received and the impression that its conclusions, however tentative, were federally funded and supported. Under such conditions, administrative debates on the relative merits of arrest compared with other potential avenues of reform became nearly irrelevant. In fact, despite its acknowledged limitations, by the mid-1980s, the study reinforced to the point of orthodoxy the view among feminists that police should arrest and a mandatory arrest policy should be instituted when possible.

For this reason, the research and policy implications of the MDVE and the attendant publicity campaign clearly deserve extensive study. An interesting dialogue between proponents and opponents of such research was published in several articles (Binder & Meeker, 1988; Sherman & Cohn, 1989) and became the topic of a widely attended debate at the 1990 Academy of Criminal Justice Sciences Annual Meeting in Denver, Colorado. Echoes of these debates have continued over the years as reanalyses and discussions of the findings continue to be conducted (Maxwell et al., 2001).

All parties have acknowledged that widely reported research, although preliminary in nature, might dramatically affect social policy. As might be expected, the differences among the participants are in the perception of the duty of researchers. Binder and Meeker (1988) found it more responsible to wait until final research was available before publicizing preliminary findings. In contrast, Sherman and Cohn (1989) stated that researchers had a duty to try to effect change in response to a critical problem. They believed this duty existed despite their knowledge of research limitations and the concern of others that prematurely basing policy on a preliminary study that is extensively publicized might cause adoption of a policy that would do more harm than good (Lempert, 1987).

Although we commend Sherman and Cohn's (1989) sense of public responsibility, we believe the concerns expressed by Binder and Meeker (1992) greatly outweigh claims of civic duty. Premature publication and reliance on preliminary research might lead to the adoption of faulty policies, which could scarcely be imagined in the context of experiments on new drugs or proposed medical interventions. Certainly, it is unrealistic to assume that agencies will simply change their methods of operation when future research provides different conclusions or finds unanticipated consequences (cf. Mastrofski & Uchida, 1993).

Finally, there are practical dilemmas to this approach. Stated succinctly, "Sherman's take the-best-evidence-and-run-with-it approach to policy making . . . will inevitably generate a policy zigzagging that requires of police departments and policymakers a much greater flexibility than is evident in most communities" (p. 265). It also implies a willingness to subject social policies to the uncertainties of preliminary social science. We believe this is inherently arrogant and potentially harmful.

When policies about the application of criminal sanctions change, they do so principally because they respond to substantial potential shifts in the degree of moral outrage or tolerance toward a given crime and the prospects of a particular reform to address that crime. Ultimately, the risk is that police might become less likely to respond to accurate scientific evidence about the impact of proposed policies, which is a major defeat for social science research in general. This perhaps has contributed to the decline in the influence of social science research recently noted by Garland (2001).

The extensive publicity given to this study—and to many of the subsequent "policy-oriented" studies that followed—should be placed in context. Could this be considered the inevitable result of the growing predominance of "professional" experts and researchers who now move freely from "think tanks" to semiautonomous university centers, depending on which administration is in charge? For these researchers, the sponsorship of their research and, in some cases, even for the bulk of their compensation, was primarily dependent not on excellence in teaching but on successfully appealing for federal funds from "activist" government agencies.

Logically, to continue to attract funding, the inherent bias of such research would be to show that "reforms" positively affected policy. The result might arguably have been better, more policy-specific research; undoubtedly, it did result in a huge increase in the influence of preliminary "research" into the development of national policies in many areas, including domestic violence.

The Impact of the MDVE

Although the Minneapolis experiment might best be referred to as being merely a "pilot study," few now deny its great policy impact. This occurred directly via policymakers and indirectly via researchers. Often, other researchers or the policy-making elite unrealistically assumed that the study demonstrated that arrest was always the best policy (Humphreys & Humphreys, 1985).

Similarly, as we review later in this chapter, federally funded research on the proper role of the criminal justice response to domestic violence was dominated by the six replications of the Minneapolis experiment. As a result of funding limitations, virtually no alternatives to arrests were explored in federally funded research projects.

In any event, within 1 year of the study's first publication, almost two thirds of major police departments had heard of the Minneapolis experiment, and three quarters of the departments correctly remembered its general conclusion that arrest was the preferable police response. Similarly, the number of police departments encouraging arrests for domestic violence tripled in 1 year from only 10% to 31%—a figure that increased again to 46% by 1986 (with more than 30% of all such departments stating they had changed their position at least partially because of the Minneapolis study). This impact was immense. The fact that it generated wide-scale abandonment of police doctrine that had remained static for decades is still probably an understatement of its importance in changing policy.

The study served as a catalyst for ongoing politically based efforts at change, being favorably cited by other influential researchers and policymakers who were then considering implementing state domestic violence laws (Cohn & Sherman, 1987).

Deterrence Theory and the MDVE

Apart from concerted efforts to publicize the findings, why did the MDVE so resonate with policymakers? In part, it resulted from the emergence of the predominance of the theory of deterrence. As indicated, advocates and battered women's support groups seized Sherman and Berk's (1984a, 1984b) conclusions. For years, their advocacy and lit-igation had little visible effect on convincing police departments of the seriousness of domestic violence and the need for greater victim respect. Therefore, the attention placed on the study was fortuitous, supporting an agenda favored by a significant policy elite. Under such conditions, research disclaimers were predictably ignored.

In addition, the belief that arrest would actually stop domestic violence offenders from reoffending had a great deal of intuitive appeal. Arrest or the potential for arrest would provide a deterrent to potential offenders. At that point in time, consideration was not given to the criminal justice response once an arrest had been made. As we dis-cuss in Chapter 11, the likelihood of a case continuing in the criminal justice system was highly unlikely; however, at the time, arrest itself was thought to provide an end point in the cycle of victimization for women.

Indeed, this could be perceived as part of a trend among "crime control" propo-nents to advocate deterrence as a mechanism to prevent future criminal behavior. Von Hirsch (1985) noted the radical shift from a "treatment model" favoring offender rehabilitation predominant during the 1960s and early 1970s to one that implicitly conceded that rehabilitation had little effect. The increased challenge to the treatment model left a void that deterrence theorists happily filled. Economists began to apply their disciplines to criminal justice policy development, an area that had been the province of sociologists, psychologists, and political scientists. They theorized that "crime could effectively be reduced . . . through sentencing policies aimed at *intimi-dating* potential offenders" (p. 7).

The Replication Studies

Part of the reason for the extensive publicity campaign discussed earlier was to pres-sure the NIJ to replicate the study in additional cities instead of using its scarce resources to focus research on victims or other aspects of the response to domestic violence. Certainly Sherman and Berk (1984a, 1984b) encouraged replication. In addi-tion, questions, criticisms, and concerns were escalating in the research community, and support for replications became widespread. In deciding to replicate the MDVE, the researchers probably realized that it was not in the political interests of the NIJ to support replication studies because their earlier findings were in accordance with the political preferences and ideologies of the federal government at that time (Garner & Maxwell, 2000).

In any event, the NIJ decided to expend most of its limited research funds on domes-tic violence on six experimental replications of the MDVE study. It is interesting that a concern among other researchers was the huge expenditure of funds to employ essen-tially the same type of research methodology. Their concerns, which were not addressed by the NIJ, focused more on victims' needs and on employing designs that encompassed more qualitative components, seeking input from victims directly. This became a source of controversy among other researchers, although according to Joel Garner (who was at that point an NIJ program manager), arguments against funding experimental research designs were not persuasive (Garner, 1990).

In any event, the NIJ subsequently funded six additional experiments. These experiments were collectively known as the "Replication Studies," and their results were revealing.

Omaha, Nebraska

Dunford, Huizinga, and Elliott (1989) conducted the first replication study in Omaha, Nebraska. When both victim and offender were present (330 cases), the officers were explicitly instructed at the time of their initial response as to which of the three options they should use, that is, to arrest, to separate the parties by removing the offender from the household, or to use mediation.

Compared with the MDVE, greatly improved methodology, including matching ethnic backgrounds of the victims to female interviewers, was used to attain victim cooperation and to categorize resultant input. Not surprisingly, far more victims cooperated (73% at 6 months).

Dunford and his colleagues (1989) reported that arrested offenders were more likely to reoffend based on official police data but less likely to reoffend based on victim interviews. These findings were not statistically significant, however, leading the researchers to conclude that the relative impact of arrest versus other treatments was not profound because arrest by itself did not seem to deter future assaults any more than separation or mediation. Although this did not seem to provide any rationale for making arrests—the preferred plan—the study also did not find that using arrests increased subsequent assaults. From this, Dunford et al. concluded the following: "It is clear, however, that arrest, by itself, was not effective in reducing or preventing continuing domestic conflict in Omaha, and that a dependence on arrest to reduce such conflict is unwarranted, perhaps erroneous and even counterproductive" (p. 67).

A second component (247 cases) involved offenders who had already vacated the premises. Offenders in this group were randomly assigned to issuance of a warrant or to no further police action. This data set provided the surprising result that more than 40% of the officers were not present when the police arrived. This was significant because little attention had been paid to the fact that a large percentage of offenders left before police arrived, and it led future researchers to question whether, in fact, there were differences between offenders who remained and those who stayed (Buzawa, Hotaling, Klein, & Byrne, 1999; Dunford, 1990; Dunford, Huizinga, & Elliott, 1989, 1990).

There also were clear differences based on the treatment chosen when the offender was absent. Absent offenders who were the subject of an arrest warrant were less than half as likely to recidivate than others—5.4% versus 11.9% (Dunford et al., 1989). Therefore, this experiment provided tentative evidence that the issuance of a pending arrest warrant seemed to deter prospective offenses. In addition to the more structured experimental approach, the researchers also reviewed police records for 45 months after the survey began. They found that although victims were at most risk for repeat violence immediately after the first incident, almost 25% were significantly reabused after the first anniversary of their prior contact with the criminal justice system. This finding presented interesting policy implications about whether contact with the criminal justice system does, in fact, deter offenders and whether as a routine basis probationary supervision of assailants should be extended.

RESPONDING TO DOMESTIC VIOLENCE

Milwaukee, Wisconsin

A second replication study by Sherman, Schmidt, et al. (1992) was conducted in Milwaukee, Wisconsin. Many of the earlier methodological problems of the MDVE were expressly addressed by this research design. These researchers chose to study four police districts containing high concentrations of minorities and to compare the results of offenders who were merely warned by the police with those who were arrested and held for a short period of time (3 hours) and those arrested and held for a longer period of time (12 hours). The duration of holding was tested to see whether a "short arrest and hold" might merely provoke an offender.

It was true that when repeat violence was measured after 6 months, arrest deterred more than by the mere issuance of a warning, whereas the duration of the hold period did not significantly affect outcome. This result, however, did not continue. Outcomes of arrest versus warning groups became roughly equal up to 11 months. After that time period, the arrested group showed even higher levels of recidivism. The report concluded that arrests seemed to deter the employed offender but not the unemployed (Sherman, Smith, Schmidt, & Rogan, 1992). Perhaps this result should not have been surprising. Less self-promoted research such as that of Dutton (1987) had long reported that being arrested seemed only to have an effect for 6 months, which is a relatively short period. Within 30 months, there was a 40% recidivism rate despite arrest. In short, Dutton had already concluded that any contact with the criminal justice system, unless reinforced by long-term counseling or other activities, might simply cause a relatively short-term behavioral change. Hirschel, Hutchison, and Dean (1992) reported that offenders might not be concerned about the impact of arrest because many have a long history or arrests or are aware of the fact that arrest seldom leads to prosecution.

In addition, the research strongly suggested that deterrence occurred among many of those arrested. Specifically, arrest seemed to deter White offenders with a reduction rate of approximately 39% over those offenders who were merely warned—versus a modest increase among Black offenders. Unemployed offenders, both Black and White, seemed to be least deterred by arrest, being the group most likely to recidivate in general and most likely, statistically, to show a long-term negative effect after arrest.

These results have received considerable, if perhaps unwarranted, speculation as to their meaning and importance. It is not surprising that Blacks who might have a history of negative experiences with many police departments, including that of Milwaukee, might react adversely to arrest, especially if the arrest is not sensitively carried out or if the victim is not supplied with information as to how she can obtain support services. Although difficult to quantify in the context of a mass experiment, it might be the result of the behavioral interaction between the officer and Black citizens that partially or even primarily accounts for part of the variance between racial groups not explained by disparate employment status.

The results of the unemployed offenders are even more intriguing. Logically, if an offender has had significant past experience with the police, he might not be as deterred as someone who has not, and thus, the experience with police intervention is a shock. This might not necessarily mean, however, that arrest was the wrong strategy to pursue with this group. Instead, it might signify that police and courts should implement complementary actions after an arrest. Unfortunately, because of the somewhat artificial strictures of this experimental design, this thesis could not be tested.

Charlotte, North Carolina

Hirschel, Hutchison, Dean, Kelley, and Pesackis (1991) conducted the third replication study in Charlotte, North Carolina. Charlotte has a relatively high crime rate and high unemployment. In addition, at the time of the study, the city had an approximately 70% minority population, allowing the researchers to address the police response to this subpopulation.

The Charlotte experiment focused on misdemeanor-level violence committed in that city during a 23-month period (August 1987 to June 1989). Cases were randomly assigned to three categories of responses: (1) advising on separation of couples, (2) issuing a citation for the offender to appear in court, and (3) arresting the offender at the scene. In addition, all officers were instructed to advise each victim of the availability of shelters and victim assistance programs.

According to official statistics, arrest was associated with increased reoffending. This contrasted with the findings from victim interviews in which arrest was associated with reduced reoffending. Neither finding was statistically significant, however, and the researchers concluded that the data did not support arrest as being more effective in deterring subsequent assaults. Subsequently Garner and Maxwell (2000) suggested that the research designs used might not have been capable of detecting differences that could have existed because of the number of interviews (338) in this case.

The group and jurisdiction selected in Charlotte might have contributed to an especially "tough" test of the effects of arrest. Almost 70% of the offenders had previous criminal histories. It had been hypothesized that this group is among the least likely to be deterred by yet another arrest (Sherman, Schmidt, et al., 1992). Of even greater importance, only 35.5% of those arrested or who had received a citation were ever prosecuted, and less than 1% ever spent time in jail beyond the initial arrest. Simply put, arrest used in an administrative vacuum seemed unlikely to be a significant deterrent to a group of offenders already inured by past experiences with the criminal justice system.

Colorado Springs, Colorado

Berk, Campbell, Klap, and Western (1992) conducted the fourth replication study for a 2-year period in Colorado Springs, Colorado. They drew a large sample—1,658 incidents of misdemeanor violence. The study was unusual in several ways. It involved a highly unrepresentative proportion of military personnel (more than 24% of the offenders and 7% of the victims). Also, only 38% of the cases involved an assault, whereas others were claims of "harassment," "menacing," and other related offenses.

This study assigned respondents to one of four options: (1) an emergency order of protection alone, (2) the protective order coupled with arrest, (3) the protective order coupled with crisis counseling, and (4) the officer's response limited to merely restoring order (Berk et al., 1992). Although victim interviews found a deterrent effect, this was not reflected by the official data.

Of equal or greater importance, the study seemed to show only a limited effect of a case being assigned to the Safe Streets Unit; 18.8% of those who received their services reported continued violence compared with 22.4% of those who had not. This 3.6% difference was not statistically significant nor was the frequency of reported abuse markedly different.

Miami, Florida

Pate and Hamilton (1992) conducted a fifth replication from August 1987 to July 1989 in the Metro-Dade Police Department, Miami, Florida. The study involved 907 cases in which the officers had arrest discretion. The sample was somewhat unusual in that it only involved male offenders as a result of then-current Florida law.

Two interventions were tested—arrest versus nonarrest as an initial action and whether there was a follow-up assignment to the Safe Streets Unit. This specialized unit consisted of a number of detectives, supervisors, and support staff, all of whom had received an intensive 150-hour training course in handling domestic violence. The unit established case histories and interviewed the couple.

They tried to assist parties to reach acceptable solutions to their problems. Referrals to appropriate agencies and outside resources also were made. Although updated in its approach, this unit shared the same orientation that the Family Crisis Intervention Teams first used in New York City, which we will discuss later in this chapter. Based on victim interviews and police records, this study reported significant differences between those offenders who were arrested and those who were not. Using the common 6-month follow-up, 14.6% of arrested abusers had reabused their victims compared with 26.9% of those who were not arrested. In addition, the frequency of violence was greater among those who had not been arrested. Victim's reports, however, indicated that there was no significant effect of treatment chosen on the 29% that were unemployed offenders (Pate & Hamilton, 1992).

A second experiment with these data involved the provision of follow-up police services. The authors reported that there were no significant differences in revictimization rates for those victims receiving follow-up services based both on official police data and on victim interviews (Pate, Hamilton, & Annan, 1991).

Atlanta, Georgia

The Atlanta, Georgia, Police Department was intended to be the seventh site of a replication study, but the researchers never submitted a report to the NIJ nor did they ever publish the findings.

A New Analysis of the Data

Maxwell et al. (2001) recently reported a new analysis of the data from the replication studies with the exception of Omaha and, of course, Atlanta. Their analysis attempted to address the concern that none of the replication studies employed the same outcome measures, measurement strategies, or methodologies as the MDVE. They determined that the only analyses possible were based on prevalence, frequency, and time to failure in official records as well as on prevalence and frequency of reoffending in victim interviews. Although they did report that overall arrest decreased the likelihood of reoffending, the findings were not statistically significant when using official data but were significant when analyzing victim report data.

It can be argued that victims only report a small percentage of reoffending, however, and that those who are willing to be interviewed or could be located might be those who were most likely *not* to be revictimized. In research involving several data sets, Buzawa and Hotaling found that victims only reported about half of new offenses. Those dissatisfied with the police response and who believed that the police either overreacted or increased the danger of the situation were unwilling—and, in fact, feared—disclosing new assaults (Buzawa et al., 1999; Buzawa & Hotaling, 2000; Hotaling & Buzawa, 2001). Also, the research protocol in how follow-up interviews were conducted in the replication studies might easily have affected the willingness of victims to disclose an unreported assault to a researcher out of fear that the offender would be arrested.

In addition, we now have research suggesting that many offenders find new victims once a victim is unwilling to tolerate violence or reports it to the police (Buzawa et al., 1999). Therefore, although it is possible for revictimization to be reduced, reoffending rates might remain stable.

The Reaction to the Replication Studies

Reaction to the replication studies and their failure to confirm the earlier MDVE findings were predictable. Feminists and battered women advocates severely criticized their methodology, their sensitivity to policy implications, and their conclusions (Bowman, 1992; Zorza, 1994; Zorza & Woods, 1994).

Bowman (1992) wrote the following:

Quantitative research has often elicited a good deal of criticism from feminists. Quantitative methods are considered suspect because they place a greater value on "objective" and quantifiable information than on other sources of knowledge. Relying solely on such data assumes a separation—indeed, a distance—between the researcher and the object of study since they isolate the factors under study from their socio-economic and historical context. Further, there is a failure to hear directly from the victim herself and include data as to how *she* interprets the situation. In the domestic violence field, moreover, survey research is greeted with particular mistrust because of early studies, which were perceived as both insensitive in their design and biased in their results. (p. 201)

An especially telling critique has been leveled at the heart of the experimental approach—isolating one individual variable (in this case, arrest) from all other factors and then assuming that this factor might truly be studied independent of its organizational and societal milieu. Zorza and Wood's (1994) overall analysis of the replication studies best summarizes this position:

The problem inherent in police replication studies is that they isolate the initial police response from any other possible responses to domestic abuse and fail to realize that the effect of arrest on domestic abuse is only one of potentially dozens of issues, which should be studied. Although the experimenters occasionally reported the rarity of conviction and especially imprisonment, they failed to evaluate what steps prosecutors and the courts took and why, what sentences the offenders received, what type of batterer treatment programs were utilized and for how long, how batterers were monitored for attendance . . . were orders of protection issued, or what assistance was provided to the victims. . . . In the absence of answers to all these questions, one cannot properly assess whether some other part of the system supported or completely undermined police efforts. (p. 972)

Deterrence theorists might simply treat these studies as a failure to confirm the deterrence hypothesis without providing any exceptionally insightful views of the necessary role of the police and the rest of the criminal justice system on the control of domestic violence. Sherman, Smith, et al. (1992) state it in following manner: "A policy of nonarrest may erode the general deterrent effect of arrest on potential spouse abusers. Yet a policy of arresting all offenders may simply produce more violence among suspects who have a low stake in conformity" (p. 688).

We believe that there is a middle ground. Regardless of their individual and collective methodological shortcomings, the replication studies collectively suggest that the role of arrest as a monolithic response for responding to all cases of domestic violence is problematic. Deterrence might exist for some but not all offenders. Furthermore, although not addressed by the replication studies, what is of at least equal significance is the differential impact of arrest on victims. Nonetheless, arrest clearly is an essential tool even if it does not deter certain types of offenders. As we have seen with the MDVE, extensively published research does not guarantee that the results will remain constant in other settings and at other times. Although some offenders might not be deterred, others (both those arrested and those who might otherwise batter in the future) might be so dissuaded.

In any event, such a conclusion would place a wholly inappropriate emphasis on the concept of deterrence. Arrest historically has not been used because of its capacity to deter offenders but to serve as the primary vehicle by which offenders are brought into the criminal justice system. In addition, it is an important reminder to the victim, the offender, and society at large that a particular conduct will not be permitted. These issues are discussed in more detail in Chapter 8.

We believe that the replication studies should be considered along with other evidence suggesting the necessity of providing a coordinated criminal justice response. Arrest could then be a useful tool that is part of a coordinated response rather than an end by itself.

Dunford et al. (1989) perhaps best stated this conclusion when discussing the implications of the Omaha replication study:

> Since arresting suspects is expensive and conflicts/assaults do not appear to increase when arrests are not made, one response to these data might be a recommendation to effect informal dispositions (separate or mediate) in cases of misdemeanor domestic assaults in Omaha. A significant problem with this approach, however, is that it seems ethically inappropriate, it violates the recommendations of the Attorney General's Task Force . . . and it may be illegal . . . to patently ignore the rights of victims. (p. 204)

A policy that encourages, but does not mandate arrest may be useful from several points of view. First, it would allow officers . . . to respond to the wishes of victims who do not want, for a variety of reasons, suspects arrested. . . . Second, when an arrest is seen as an entry point into a coordinated criminal justice system rather than an end point, it may shift the burden of deterrence from a single official police intervention (arrest) to a sequence of other interventions, each of which may have some salutary effect. This view recognizes that suspects chronically involved in domestic violence most frequently do not admit to having a problem in this regard . . . are not easily treated . . . and do not seek help voluntarily . . . to deal with such problems and thus might require sustained long-term interventions to change their ways. It supports arrest in domestic assault instances in which probable cause for an arrest is present and when victims support the arrest of suspects, not because arrest is a panacea for deterring domestic violence, but because of penalties and the leverage that an arrest implicitly facilitates. (pp. 61–77)

Legal Liability as an Agent for Change

The final major force impacting the police response to domestic violence was that individual officers, as well as entire police departments as organizations, were exposed to substantial risks of liability awards, fines, and injunctions if they failed to make an arrest for domestic assault. This concern dramatically restricted their freedom to continue with previous practices and contributed to the development of written domestic violence policies and training.

Several lawsuits in the late 1970s claimed that the Oakland, California, and New York City police departments failed to protect battered women (*Bruno v. Codd*, 1977; *Scott v. Hart*, 1976). In both of these cases, trial courts ordered the police to provide better protection to the victims of domestic violence. These cases were important because the courts clearly recognized that the police had not served the class of victims of battered women, resulting in damages. In these early cases, the remedies requested were largely prospective, for example, to force police to treat victims of domestic assault the same as other victims of crimes. Remedies typically were to force the police to adopt more aggressive and proactive policies.

Although these cases laid the legal groundwork to establish that poor police policy and practices could result in a court order, it has generally been recognized that the seminal case forcing police change was *Thurman v. City of Torrington* (1984). Because this case is a graphic portrayal of police indifference and had a profound impact on police procedures, it is worthwhile to discuss it in detail.

In this case, Ms. Thurman and other relatives had repeatedly called the police, pleading for help to protect her from her estranged husband, but they had received virtually no assistance, even after he was convicted and placed on probation for damage to her property. When she asked the police to arrest him for continuing to make threats to shoot her and her son even while still on probation, they told her, without any legal basis, to return 3 weeks later and to get a restraining order in the interim.

In any event, she did obtain the court order, but the police then refused to arrest her husband, citing a holiday weekend. After the weekend, police continued to refuse to assist based on the fact that the only officer who could arrest him was "on vacation."

In one final rampage by her husband after a delayed response to her call for emergency police assistance, Ms. Thurman was attacked and suffered multiple stab wounds to the chest and neck, resulting in paralysis below her neck and permanent disfigurement. The responding officer stated that he was at the other side of the house "relieving himself" and thought the screams he heard were from a wounded animal.

Her attorneys argued two major theories for police liability: negligence and breach of constitutional rights. Simply stated, the negligence theory claimed that police, being sworn to protect citizenry, had a duty to take reasonable action when requested to prevent victim injury from a known offender.

The second theory was that the police, as agents of the state, violated her fourteenth Amendment constitutional rights by failing to provide equal protection under the law. This claim was based on differential treatment accorded by police to largely male victims of non-domestic assault compared with primarily female victims of domestic assault. This was considered sex discrimination because most victims of serious injuries in cases of intimate partner abuse were women.

The court found a clear hidden agenda of the Torrington Police Department. Police actions were found to constitute deliberate indifference to complaints of married women in general and of Ms. Thurman in particular. This was negligent and violated the equal protection of the law guaranteed Ms. Thurman. A $2.3 million verdict was awarded to Ms. Thurman and her son. An excellent description of the legal rationale of the judgment is contained in Eppler (1986). The *Thurman* case was widely reported in the popular press, police publications, and research journals, and it was addressed in a variety of legal seminars nationwide. It graphically confirmed to all parties, including prospective legal counsel, that financial penalties could be imposed on municipalities that abjectly fail to perform their duties.

The impact of *Thurman* and similar cases was twofold. Fear of liability became a prime factor motivating departmental administration, the least out of self-protection, to require more justification if arrests were not made. In some cases, this actually nudged departments to adopt pro-arrest policies.

Fear of liability awards was even more important for those departments located in jurisdictions that had adopted, by statute or department policy, mandatory or presumptive arrest. Such statutes could easily be used by plaintiffs' attorneys to establish the standard of care that police owed to victims of domestic violence. In this context, it is noteworthy that one state's mandatory arrest law was cited in a legal advocacy journal as providing a "sound basis" for asserting a legally enforceable right of action to victims hurt by police failure to make arrests (Gundle, 1986; restated by the Victim Services Agency, 1988).

As a result of a number of cases both before and after *Thurman*, there was a proliferation of consent decrees resulting from negotiated settlements of class action lawsuits to stop tacit "no arrest" policies. As a result, several police departments operated under consent decrees for many years requiring them to treat domestic violence as a crime, to make arrests when appropriate without consideration of marital status, and to advise victims of their legal rights.

The importance of having these orders in place is twofold: If the order is violated, a clear standard of care has been set—and not met—making liability relatively easy to determine. In addition, if the violation was intentional, the police administrators and the officers in question risk contempt of court, possibly risking personal fines or incarceration. (For a summary of the early cases, see Ferraro, 1989a; Victim Services Agency, 1988; and Woods, 1978. For a discussion of the full breadth of civil litigation and its impact, we recommend Kappeler, 1997.)

Unfortunately, although such consent decrees have been imposed in a number of jurisdictions, including Oakland in *Scott v. Hart* (1992), New York City as a result of *Bruno v. Codd* (1977), and many other locations, there is a lack of empirical research examining the extent to which actual operational practices were changed after such orders were in effect. We can, however, hypothesize that the prospects of paying substantial attorneys' fees (even if ultimately successful), of the drain on management attention, and of the potential for a public relations and financial debacle each applied pressure on police departments to adopt policies that were easy to explain and defend. Such policies, if written clearly and, presumably, applied and enforced, would have the effect of insulating police departments from organizational liability and shifting that risk to the individual officer.

This book does not, of course, purport to describe the latest legal findings on police liability, or lack thereof, but only to describe the influence of litigation as a factor in changing the police response to domestic violence. In that vein, there has been little, if any, rollback of policies simply because the U.S. Supreme Court in *DeShaney v. Winnebago County Dept of Social Services* (1989) made it far more difficult to sue police departments. In this case against a social service agency, the Supreme Court disallowed the action even though the county had seemingly negligently sent a minor child back to his father, who then brutally murdered him. The county was held not liable for damages caused by the private violence of one party against another. This can be contrasted with *Canton v. Harris* (1989), which the Supreme Court decided 6 days after *DeShaney*. In that case, the Supreme Court found liability against a police department after it determined that the department had not adequately trained an officer on its own policies, resulting in injury to people who should have been protected. Similarly, liability under state law for negligence or even intentional liability might continue to pose potential problems for police departments that fail to deal with domestic assaults in a systematic fashion.

The collective impact of these suits was that, by the early 1980s, there was a highly unusual blend of research, pressure from advocates, and legally based administrative need for change. These factors all operated in one direction—to force the police to increase arrest rates in domestic violence cases.

SUMMARY

The irony is that as of the writing of this edition, two of the three reasons for the change in practices have been severely eroded, with research no longer consistently reporting that arrests are the best method for handling domestic assaults. Similarly, legal liability against the police has been minimal—at least at the federal level and for many states. Nonetheless, there is no apparent relaxation in the push for mandatory arrest, as we discuss in the next several chapters. Arguments are still made about the need to protect departments from liability and lawsuits, and early research is still cited to support its effectiveness despite contradictory evidence.

DISCUSSION QUESTIONS

1. What factors do you think most accounted for change in the community where you live? If you think more change is needed, what would most facilitate it?

2. Why do you think there is such variation in how communities have changed their response?

3. What role do you believe liability should play in effecting change? Do you believe cities should "pay" for negligence on the part of those who respond to domestic violence victims?

4. Who should be held responsible for failure to respond properly to a victim—the individual or the agency/organization for whom they work? Why?

5. Do mandatory arrest policies rely on faulty assumptions regarding the "deterrence"?

6. Do mandatory arrest policies adequately differentiate among the vast range of incidents and relationships that fall under domestic violence statutes?

The Evolution of Arrest Preferences 7

Criminalizing the Societal Response

Chapter Overview

By the early 1980s, there was widespread disillusionment with the classic police response to domestic violence (as described in Chapter 4). In part, this was a reflection of the general U.S. attitudes favoring the increased use of formal social controls to "deter crime." Policies favoring punitive rather than rehabilitative responses gradually permeated practitioner, policymaker, and general public attitudes (Garland, 2001).

Regardless of the reason, an expanded debate began as to the proper course of action to follow. The dialogue was joined by policymakers, practitioners, advocates for battered women, and researchers. A new pro-arrest consensus emerged when the traditional policy of nonintervention lost credibility and after the first reform of "crisis intervention" lost credibility. The concept of deterrence as a general preference for crime control became the dominant perspective in mainstream academic literature and policy circles.

Not surprisingly, the two trends were linked; deterrence as a justification for the use of arrest came to be regarded widely as the *only* true reform. The line between researchers and activists began to blur, with both vehemently advocating arrest even though research on the deterrent impact of arrest remained inconclusive.

As explained in Chapter 6, these changes were the result of the unusual congruence of an acknowledged failure of past approaches combined with political pressures, potential legal liability for nonresponding agencies, and highly publicized research. Such pressures were reflected in, and then reinforced by, a wave of state and federal legislation. The result was a clear bias in policy toward the use of arrests as the primary focus for criminal justice intervention.

In this context, a critical question needs to be posed as to whether police actions should really be viewed in isolation rather than as part of an overall systemic response to the problem of domestic violence. The key to that question, and one that we will explore more fully in this chapter, might be whether a positive outcome is likely to occur if the police make an arrest but no prosecution occurs or a case is dropped without a conviction.

Conversely, as a weapon in the arsenal of domestic violence prevention, is arrest effective only if it leads to an aggressive overall criminal justice response that relegates arrest to an intake system? The discrete police action of making an arrest must, however, be viewed as part of a mosaic of possible interventions. The certainty of apprehension, subsequent arrest, aggressive prosecution, forced attendance in batterer treatment programs, and even "target hardening" via issuance of restraining orders might be different phases of handling the case within a unified criminal justice system. In this context, an arrest should be reframed as "successful" only if it serves as the typical, and in most cases the only, entry point or "gateway" for subsequent intervention. The answer to these questions, as well as the impact of arrest on the offender, potential offenders, victims, police agencies, and society in general, begins with the study of deterrence.

Deterrence Theory

To understand the pivotal role of arrests in domestic violence, we need to understand the concept of deterrence, since this theory, for better or worse, has largely shaped modern criminal justice policy in this area. The centrality of arrest as a deterrent is somewhat exceptional for police since, in most offenses, an arrest without commitment to subsequent prosecution and conviction or plea bargain would be regarded as a singular failure.

For example, we never define the mere apprehension and arrest of a burglar without prosecution as a success. However, when the goal becomes deterrence of future misconduct rather than actual conviction for a past criminal offense, there might be a change in how we define success. Regardless of merit, this theory deserves a full explanation. The deterrent effect of arrest, which was first popularized in the context research conducted by Sherman and Berk (1984a, 1984b), is now widely followed by the criminal justice establishment even if many researchers might now question wholesale applicability to domestic violence.

Specific Deterrence

The theory of specific deterrence is grounded in core economic principles regarding the rationality of decision making. It presumes that individuals, even violent offenders, rationally consider the benefits of a particular behavior against its potential consequences. Therefore, when an offender is punished by means of an arrest or other criminal justice sanction, the threats of punishment become more credible and deter future misconduct.

Over the years, many researchers argued that domestic violence was an ideal setting for the application of deterrence theory. Williams and Hawkins (1989) noted that although classic deterrence theory focused on formal punishments as actual consequences of committing a crime (see also Gibbs, 1985), this analysis was inadequate. Instead, in domestic violence cases, it was the act of being labeled publicly as a "wife beater" and attendant fear of social scorn and ostracism that deters possible recidivism. The shock of an arrest, especially to a man who often does not confront the police, would then deter future violence.

Deterrence theory, although rooted on economics, also is consistent with the more psychologically based learning theory, positing that the best time to attempt to correct deviant behavior is immediately after such conduct occurs. Learning theory predicts that immediate punishment need not be very severe to prevent reinforcement of deviant behavior. In contrast, aberrant behavior might otherwise recur if the deviant act, in this case spousal abuse, went unnoticed and unpunished. The premise to the application of deterrence theory to domestic violence is that arrest can itself serve as sufficient punishment to prompt changed behavior (Williams & Hawkins, 1989).

In contrast, most lay people, to the extent that they give any thought to the matter, assume that "punishment" only can commence after a person has been convicted of a crime. This ignores the reality faced by the criminal justice system. The public simply does not understand that conviction in a contested case requires a considerable commitment to use sorely stressed public assets, whether the police, public defenders, prosecutors, judiciary, and after conviction, probation and penal departments of the state. Furthermore, formal criminal justice system case processing does not typically gain momentum for several months after an initial arrest is made. Delays of several months to more than 1 year are common, if not the norm in many jurisdictions. Although such delays are rarely advantageous for any of the involved parties, delays in these cases can be critical to the safety and well-being of victims and their children. Evidence suggests that most reoffending occurs prior to their court appearance (Buzawa, Hotaling, Klein, & Byrne, 1999; Wilson & Klein, 2006).

General Deterrence

Specific deterrence of current offenders is not the only goal of making highly visible domestic violence arrests. In addition to deterring current offenders, arrest has been claimed to be an effective deterrent for potential offenders. This is based on the "logical," if unproven, assumption that potential offenders weigh the benefits and costs of their possible actions before committing an offense. Hence, "general deterrence" might occur in addition to "specific deterrence" of past offenders (Nagin, 1998).

This theory is plausible. The general public assumes that if arrested, there will be serious consequences (Carmody & Williams, 1987; Dutton, 1988; Williams & Hawkins, 1989). The concept of general deterrence has been applied to arrests in the context of domestic violence. In one early study of anticipated indirect effects of an arrest for domestic violence, 63% of men stated they would lose self-respect if arrested. Most men also feared family stigma and social disapproval after arrest. In contrast, although the possible ultimate costs of a conviction, time in jail, or loss of a job were far more severe, they perceived correctly these outcomes as highly unlikely, and hence not very effective, as a general deterrent against domestic violence (Williams & Hawkins, 1989).

Deterrence theorists believe this is predictable because although conviction and sentencing for a domestic violence–related offense would be far more serious than simple arrest, the chances of conviction have historically been so low that the threat lacked any real credibility. In contrast, public perception of the likelihood of an arrest might serve as an effective deterrent. A variety of factors impacts perceptions of the threat posed by a specific sanction (Carmichael & Piquero, 2006).

Can Arrest Be an Effective Deterrent?

Although the police now use arrest as a deterrent against domestic violence, the theory that an arrest will have a key impact on such actual and prospective offenders is somewhat inconsistent with other studies on deterrence and lacks overwhelming evidentiary support. Subsequent tests of arrests since the Minneapolis Domestic Violence Experiment were largely inconclusive (Garner & Maxwell, 2000). Realistically, deterrence depends on an offender consciously weighing the prospects of a negative response by society to a particular act. The behavior can then be calculated rationally in light of the long-term risk of arrest compared with the shorter term "gain" from committing physical abuse. Unfortunately, reality, as usual, is somewhat more complicated than theory.

One trend, although extreme, can illustrate the problem. As this chapter was being written in late 2009, there were a well-documented spate of incidents throughout the United States in which the domestic violence offender first killed his victim, their children, and even often her family and friends. Either because of remorse or more likely because he knows that arrest, followed by conviction and lengthy incarceration, is virtually inevitable, the offender then commits suicide. Is it logical to assume that the deterrent value of a mere arrest will control such irrational rage?

As we will explore more fully, exposure to the criminal justice system will affect many offenders in differential ways—some anticipated and beneficial, and others far less so. Therefore, it is important to improve our understanding of when arrests might realistically deter crime.

Can Arrests Deter the Hard-Core Offender?

Deterrence-based principles seem to be overly simplistic if applied to all offenders. Although overall rates of domestic violence might have decreased partly because those offenders who are less likely to be generally violent offenders were deterred from committing acts of violence, in the past, police rarely, if ever, arrested domestic violence offenders. Currently, with the well-publicized emphasis on arrest, it is plausible that many, if not most, of the remaining offenders are not easily deterred. The relatively low-risk offenders such as the occasional "domestic violence–only" offenders might indeed be capable of controlling their behavior if there is a credible deterrent. Such offenders might have battered because they perceived they could get away with it, were under significant stress, or had recently consumed excessive alcohol or drugs. However, research has demonstrated that this group overall is less likely to reoffend, regardless of whether an arrest is made, as long as there is some effective police response. *Consequently, arrest as a deterrent seems to have the most value in the group needing it the least.* For many of these offenders, basically their entire criminal career is a result of the criminalization of domestic violence, and their need for societal conformity will itself be a deterrent.

In short, many batterers are not generally violent but are occasionally violent during the course of a relationship—often in the context of substance abuse. These offenders seem to be more likely to desist after an arrest without requiring subsequent criminal justice action. A more modest achievement of arrest might be that it helps identify offenders and their families likely to need future intervention and/or treatment services.

For most offenders, a certainty in consequences might increase the probability of compliance with rehabilitation, especially if substance abuse is the immediate trigger for the violent behavior. If this is the limited and indirect deterrent value of an arrest, however, perhaps the goal could be accomplished with fewer resources by aggressively prosecuting and highly publicizing fewer but more severe cases of domestic violence.

In contrast, as discussed in Chapter 4, the "generally violent" offenders typically require a more comprehensive criminal justice intervention, not simply an arrest to address a single misdemeanor act of domestic abuse. Hard-core deviants and those who have already been arrested for domestic violence or other charges are unlikely to be truly deterred by yet another arrest. Their behavior might simply be part of a life course of serious, often violent, crime. In other words, these individuals might simply diversify their prior criminal career as the result of entering a domestic relationship.

For these high-risk offenders, we question the underlying goal of a mechanistic application of deterrence theory. Arrests cannot be shown to deter these offenders. Even if it somehow did deter these criminals from committing more domestic assaults, a mere arrest that does not address the underlying tendency of an assailant toward violent outbursts might serve to displace these tendencies. The offender might perceive that he can abuse others—perhaps children, aged relatives, or people in barroom brawls—with less police interference.

Because domestic violence researchers typically have focused on reoffending against the same victim, they might view this as a victory; however, if the potential for displacement also is considered, then it is entirely possible that the offender might simply target a new victim. This outcome is not unlikely for an offender who does not change his attitudes toward using an assault to gain power or uses violence in response to anger. For these offenders, police intervention might reduce revictimization of one particular victim and redirect victimization to another target (Reiss, 1986, cited in Elliott, 1989). Should the substitution of one victim for another be considered to be a societal gain?

Evidence supports this displacement of violence. For example, it has been found that offenders with the greatest criminal history and greatest number of restraining orders are those most likely to find new victims rather than to reoffend against the same victim (Buzawa et al., 1999; Buzawa & Hotaling, 2007). Alternatively, let us assume that if the victim finds that arrest does not deter subsequent assault, then she might leave. This creates a strong possibility that an offender, whose attitudes and behavior remain largely unchanged by a simple arrest, will simply abuse a different victim (Elliott, 1989). Under either of these scenarios, where an abusive relationship ends but an active abuser remains "at large" and his behavior unchanged, the deterrent value of an arrest might not justify the cost of increased arrests.

From the previous discussion, we conclude that the primary problem with relying on arrest as a deterrent to domestic violence is the limitation inherent in the practical application of deterrence theory to the hard-core offenders. An established theory supports this outcome. Crimes that are economically motivated or require careful planning would intuitively seem to be more amenable to the economic concept of deterrence than offenses that are spontaneous or originate in the context of serious mental health pathology or substance abuse. Indeed, noneconomic crimes in general and impulsive explosive violence in particular, especially if coupled with substance abuse or other mental health concerns, are the least apt to be deterred. In this regard, domestic violence usually is an impulsive act by offenders with a limited repertoire of responses to stress, attacks on self-esteem, or frustration by those who have few inhibitions against using violence (Ford, 1988). For an offender with these attributes, it is difficult to argue that violence will be deterred unless underlying issues are addressed by an effective rehabilitation program.

In stating this, we recognize that well-respected researchers believe many violent men *can* control their aggression. They argue that such men use violence as a weapon to establish dominance in settings where they are least likely to be punished—typically the home—and can control the degree of violence used. Therefore, most men who beat their partners and children while in an alcoholic rage somehow manage to desist when the police arrive or when they are in public.

This might indeed be true for some assailants, but we believe this theory is overly simplistic to generalize among all batterers. In fact, Buzawa et al. (1999), Wilson and Klein (2006), Klein and Tobin (2008), and the Minneapolis Domestic Violence Experiment replication studies have all reported consistently that the most violent domestic abusers are the most violent criminals in general, arguing fairly persuasively that no level of deterrence can be assumed with these generally violent offenders based simply on arrest or even conviction, especially if not coupled with continued monitoring and/or treatment.

Additional empirical research further documents this key distinction and reports that hard-core abusers account for the most numerous and severe acts of domestic violence. Offenders now viewed by the police often are serious repetitive criminals—those who are regarded widely as being the most likely to pose serious, long-term risk to victims regardless of a mere arrest (Buzawa et al., 1999; Buzawa & Hotaling, 2007; Pierce, Spaar, & Briggs, 1988; Piquero, Fagan, Mulvey, Steinberg, & Odgers, 2005; Sherman, 1992; Straus, 1996; Wilson & Klein, 2006).

In one study conducted in Quincy, Massachusetts, researchers reported findings from a 10-year follow-up of batterers (Wilson & Klein, 2006). At the initial time of the arrest, 86% had a prior criminal history. Of those with a criminal history, 41% were for domestic violence only offenses, whereas 59% were for other offenses as well as domestic abuse. Eighteen percent of batters were rearrested for domestic violence offenses, 22% for other offenses only, and 60% for both domestic and other offenses. After arraignment, 71% of these offenders were arrested in the following 9-year period, 38% were for domestic violence only, and 62% were arrested for other offenses. For those offenders who initially committed domestic violence-only offenses, 20% reoffended, compared with an 84% reoffense rate if they had committed other offenses. Similarly, Hirschel, Buzawa, Pattavina, Faggiani, and Reuland (2007) reported a reoffending rate of 29% for offenders with no criminal history, compared with a 71% rearrest rate for offenders with a prior nonviolent criminal history, and 79% for offenders with a prior violent criminal history.

Therefore, the argument that Williams and Hawkins (1989) advanced that the "humiliation" of an arrest serves as a deterrent might apply only to certain offenders who are generally less violent and do not have a criminal record. For them, the fear of arrest and its indirect effects might indeed serve as an effective deterrent as the social stigma of an arrest could result in job loss or other negative consequences.

Even if accompanied by a night in jail, the minimal incremental costs of arrest alone to a hard-core offender might be so minimal as to reinforce the crime's benefits.

In jurisdictions without a comprehensive strategy for arrest, offenders might simply conclude that the "cost" of a possible arrest is acceptable (Dutton, 1987; Fagan, 1988; Maxwell, Garner, & Fagan, 2001). This is especially true for offenders who have experience with the criminal justice system and find that a misdemeanor domestic assault is treated less seriously than other offenses, for example, a felony larceny (Buzawa et al., 1999).

Offenders might know that in most jurisdictions, batterer treatment and/or probation is the typical sentence for a misdemeanor assault, and in rare cases where jail sentences are imposed, they tend to be of a short duration. This practice creates profound risk for victims. Using interview data, Ford (1992) found that more than 95% of those arrested had previously battered the same victim and that 94% had done so in the previous 6 months. Therefore, repeat offenders are likely to be driven by factors that are not easily controlled or changed. Klein (1994a) confirmed this, finding that such offenders fit profiles similar to other serious violent offenders.

Arrests as Punishment: A Peculiar Use of Deterrence Theory

We also admit to a philosophical concern regarding the use of an arrest as a punishment. Arrest used for its deterrent value seems to be a subversion of the legitimate, but limited, arrest powers constitutionally given to police. Police never have been given constitutional power to inflict pain and humiliation to obtain social goals, no matter how laudable. Instead, it is recognized that no agency, especially the police, has this authority, independent of established legal procedures, to adjudicate guilt.

We recognize that it would be simplistic to ignore the daily informality inherent in dispensing street-level justice and the lingering impact of previous police inaction in cases involving domestic violence. However, making an arrest for its deterrent value, without an attendant commitment to prosecute those arrested, establishes a very dangerous precedent. We recognize that the goal of deterrence of spousal assaults is sound; however, we are concerned that if a policy of automatic or mandatory arrest is used to deter crime, than any remaining checks on police abuse of power are largely absent.

This concern is realistic as exemplified by the Exclusionary Rule. The Exclusionary Rule forbids the introduction of illegally obtained evidence. Judges, including those on the Supreme Court who continually enforce the Exclusionary Rule in cases of police misconduct, believe that it is a primary restraint that limits improper police conduct in performing searches and seizures, making arrests, or obtaining confessions. What would restrain improper police conduct if the act of an arrest itself is simply a tool to punish an offender? If the police have the organizational mandate to punish via arrest, should they not also have the right to "rough up" the offender while they are at it? After all, would this not strengthen deterrent value by giving the abuser a "taste" of what he dished out? Such police violence would provide a particularly strong societal message that such acts are crimes that will not be tolerated. We are not advocating such behavior. The fact is that our society has never trusted police with such unchecked power. The theory of deterrence as punishment to justify an arrest might push society toward outcomes that we do not wish to observe.

How Do Police Decide Which Actions to Take?

We need to move beyond the admittedly highly charged debate of using arrests as a deterrent. Assuming that arrests are not "mandated," or even if mandated, such mandates are not actually enforced in practice, the police can take a variety of actions in cases of domestic violence, which include making an arrest. We know that arrest has not historically been the typical outcome in either non-domestic or domestic assaults; arrest has traditionally been infrequent and often considered a last resort. To understand how police act, we must examine what they confront when they reach the scene of a possible crime. Police act situationally; that is, they tend to treat all cases that share the same characteristics in a similar manner (Elliott, 1989; Faragher, 1985; Sanders, 1988; Sherman, 1992). Although they might seem to always act the same over time, these decisions as an aggregate become highly influenced by legislative mandates, policies, and training.

Despite legislative and policy mandates that seek to encourage officers to make more frequent arrests, the decision to arrest remains a highly variable outcome in many jurisdictions. Researchers, therefore, have tried to identify factors or variables that predict the arrest decision. Situational, offender, victim, and organizational variables, and more recently, community characteristics, have all been the major focus of efforts for researchers to understand the extent to which arrests can be predicted, provide insight regarding the role of extralegal variables that affect the arrest decision, and identify the circumstances under which pro-arrest policies might encounter resistance.

Arrest as a Situational Construct

It is not a new concept that police base arrest decisions on the situational characteristics of an incident and on their interactions with the parties involved. It is well known that police determine their course of action in response to many factors that might be related to the crime only tangentially. This, of course, leads to several critical questions for this text: What are the situational characteristics of the police–citizen encounter that are most likely to lead to arrest? Perhaps equally important, how does the use of "legal" factors (e.g., incident characteristics) and "extralegal" factors (e.g., victim and offender characteristics) interact with police performance in domestic violence cases, and how might these and other policy preferences affect the decision to arrest assailants?

First, in the context of professionally accepted roles and missions, most police officers believe that arrest priority should be given to cases in which public order and authority have been challenged, attaching only secondary importance to the protection of an individual victim. Because most domestic violence cases are not public in nature, they would normally be expected to be of less importance.

It is only in recent years that pro-arrest policies might, in many departments, have skewed arrest decisions in domestic assaults versus non-domestic assaults. Despite these laws and official policies, arrest remains nonroutine and somewhat problematic in many jurisdictions. This is not surprising and might not indicate any effort to subvert arrest statutes or policies. In cases of verbal altercations, police might be called proactively before any violence or threat of violence, and in keeping with the problem-oriented approach to policing, a variety of alternatives should be considered. In other cases, the true status of the "victim" and "offender" cannot be determined reasonably or probable cause to arrest is insufficient. In still other cases, for which arrest is not mandated, officers might follow a victim preference not to arrest. Even within a particular police department, a variety of organizational, attitudinal, situational, and sociodemographic variables affect the decision to arrest.

It is difficult to understand fully what factors account for domestic violence arrest decisions. Researchers typically cannot obtain retrospectively all the needed data on the incident, victim, and offender. Furthermore, police decision making involves a web of factors that often are not well understood. Statutory requirements and departmental policies clearly influence the probability of arrest (Hirschel et al., 2007). These include community norms and expectations, organizational culture, and officers' individual characteristics and belief systems. In addition to these relatively constant sources of variability are the "true" situational variables that occur in each encounter (e.g., the characteristics of the incident, victim, and offender). Complicating the matter even more are the unique twists of responding to intimate partner violence in which common strategies are pursued by one or both parties to negotiate the meaning of the situation to counter expected police reactions (i.e., "he/she initiated it," "we both got physical," "it's a one-time thing," "we're both under a lot of stress," etc.). Perhaps the most important question to ask is what are the proper discriminators of the decision to arrest and to what extent do police follow them?

We recognize that most police officers now believe they should, and do, arrest when the incident indicates a high degree of potential danger or that a serious criminal assault has already occurred. Police need to focus on cases in which there is potential for violence or a history of assaults (or both). In fact, legal requirements or rules are now thought to be the best predictor of the arrest decision (Klinger, 1995; Kruttschnitt, McLaughlin, & Petrie, 2004; Mastrofski, 1999; Mastrofski, Worden, & Snipes, 1995). In a recent examination of 577,862 incidents of assault and intimidation for the year 2000, offense seriousness was the most important predictor of arrest among mandatory, presumptive, and discretionary arrest jurisdictions (Hirschel et al., 2007).

The decision to arrest becomes critical in cases where the police have discretion. Although this discussion is generalized in nature and, hence, might not properly reflect many less common variables, three major factors seem to determine when the police decide to make an arrest: (1) situational or incident characteristics, (2) victim traits and attitudes toward the police, and (3) assailant behavior and demeanor.

Situational and Incident Characteristics

Most police officers seem to attach primary significance to several incident characteristics, specifically (a) offender presence; (b) initial characterization of a crime as a misdemeanor or a felony; (c) who called the police; (d) the presence of weapons; (e) serious victim injury; (f) the presence of children; (g) victim–offender relationship; (h) perceived mitigating circumstances; (i) hostility, intimidation, or violence toward the police; as well as (j) criminal history and officer perception of the likelihood of future violence or offender dangerousness.

Offender Absent When Police Arrive

A key situational or incident-related factor in the decision to arrest is whether the suspect leaves the scene of the offense (Buzawa & Hotaling, 2000; Eigenberg, Scarborough, & Kappeler, 1996; Feder, 1996; Robinson, 2000). In fact, some researchers have found it to be the most significant predictor of arrest (Robinson, 2000). Clearly, in stranger assaults, this is understandable. A misdemeanor arrest is more difficult when the offender has left the scene and might be unknown to the victim or witnesses. Police might simply lack the needed resources or inclination to identify and/or locate the offender. However, typically, police do not have difficulty identifying domestic violence offenders. They also should be able to locate most domestic assault offenders easily by questioning victims and witnesses, thereby making this less of an appropriate discriminator for these offenders.

Why is this important? Estimates are that more than 50% of intimate abusers leave before police arrive (Berk & Loseke, 1980–1981; Buzawa et al., 1999; Dunford, 1990; Feder, 1996; Hirschel & Hutchison, 1992; Robinson, 2000). Any distinction in treatment of these offenders is, therefore, not only unwarranted in terms of police inability to locate perpetrators, but also it perversely impacts first-time offenders. In the limited studies of offenders who left the scene before police arrived, Dunford (1990) reported that, on average, their victims were far more fearful than those whose offenders remained. In another study, offenders who left the scene were twice as likely to reoffend within the next year as those who stayed (Buzawa et al., 1999).

Even though typically those who flee the scene are more violent than those who stay, most police agencies do not aggressively pursue, or even issue, warrants for domestic violence offenders who have left. Robinson (2000) reported that 55% of offenders at the scene were subsequently arrested compared with only 2% when the suspect was absent. In a multijurisdictional study, Hirschel et al. (2007), reported that 59.7% of the offenders remained at the scene. These offenders were far more likely to be arrested (74.4%) than those who left prior to police arrival (42.4%). These differences might be a result of the lingering police perception that domestic violence does not warrant real policing, at least if additional time was required to locate and apprehend offenders. Officers might assume erroneously that once an offender is no longer in the presence of a victim, she is safe.

Given the high percentage of cases in which offenders are absent when police arrive, it would be helpful for police to understand better the great risk these offenders pose to victims and encourage departments to develop formal policies for enforcing outstanding warrants for arrest.

Characterization of a Crime as a Misdemeanor or a Felony

In many departments, organizational priorities and limited resources force departments to prioritize attempts to arrest a felony suspect by establishing priorities that limit follow-up on misdemeanor offenses. Although this policy might seem reasonable on the surface, the classification of a single domestic incident as a misdemeanor versus a felony offense might be subject to inaccurate or at least incomplete police analysis. As discussed previously, many domestic violence crimes are labeled as misdemeanors inappropriately when the level of injury and apparent intent would justify a felony charge. Also, often a single incident is part of an ongoing battering relationship that would in its totality be considered extremely serious (Stark, 2007). If these are properly linked, then the distinction between the assumed "less severe" domestic violence misdemeanor and the serious felony incidents might prove illusory.

Who Called the Police?

As a group, police seem to differentiate domestic violence cases based on who initiated the call for service. In the abstract, we would expect police to be more responsive if the victim initiated the call. After all, this indicates victim commitment to the intervention, and with a possibly willing witness, it increases the likelihood of successful case prosecution. Historically, however, research suggests the reverse occurs (Berk & Newton, 1985; Buzawa & Hotaling, 2000). Research continues to find lower percentages of arrests in intimate partner incidents. Even in a recent study, arrests occurred in 56.9% of cases when the victim initiated the call compared with 71.3% when someone else contacted the police (Hirschel et al., 2007).

This surprising distinction might relate to the self-perceived mission of the police to protect public order rather than intervene in private disputes. From this perspective, when a bystander has become involved to the extent of calling the police, the conflict is no longer confined to its principals but becomes a matter affecting the public order. Therefore, when a bystander calls, the initial police characterization of the call would be as a "disorderly conduct" or as a public "disturbance," which is a classic mission for police concerned with public order maintenance.

The involvement of an external complainant might, therefore, be viewed to increase officers' perceived need to do something to resolve the threat to public order. In addition, in cases where the third party is a witness, officers might perceive that they have a stronger case against the offender.

This finding is important because bystander reporting might be increasing more rapidly than victim reporting. Growing public awareness of domestic violence, campaigns to stop violence in the home, and concern for domestic assault as expressed in the popular press, news accounts, and in television docudramas have increased reporting by neighbors and bystanders (Cassidy, Nicholl, Ross, & Lonsway, 2004; Robinson & Chandek, 2000a, 2000b). For example, Klein (2005) reported that most calls to the police for domestic assault in Rhode Island did not come from the victim but from witnesses or people overhearing the incident.

Presence of Weapons

As expected, when incidents seem to have greater potential for serious consequences, the likelihood of arrest increases. Several authors have reported that if an assailant uses or threatens to use a weapon or threatens to kill, then the odds of arrest increase dramatically (Kane, 1999; Loving, 1980). The use of weapons impacts the officer's assessment of a victim's risk. Clearly, this factor is important in decisions to arrest. Kane (1999) reported that officer perceptions of the situation's overall risk to the victim was the most important factor in the police decision to arrest.

We agree that the presence or use of a weapon should impact considerations of perceived danger. However, the officer's determination of risk is itself the product of an interaction of a variety of factors, including not only the incident, victim, and offender, but also the officer's attitudes, training, socialization, as well as departmental policies and practices. Hence, an officer's predictive construct of an offender—that is, officer perception of whether a given offender is dangerous—might not be consistent with reality.

For example, a police officer, based on past experience or simple prejudice, might believe a young male of color is far more likely to be at risk than an older White male who committed the same offense. Similarly, seemingly obvious decisions, such as determining a victim's safety, might be affected by underlying beliefs of which neither the police nor either party can agree, or even articulate at times. Even relatively straightforward analyses such as the presence or use of a weapon to determine the degree of potential injury involve a surprising amount of subjectivity. For example, would a young male of color with a knife in his car intrinsically constitute a greater potential threat than an elderly White male that "happened" to have invested in a gun safe that included weapons and ammunition? Kane (1999) reported that just such subgroup differences among offenders interacted with officer's predictive constructs to determine how police assess risk.

Incident Injuries

Research suggests that from 40% to 50% of domestic violence incidents involve victim injury (Dunrose et al., 2005, p. 33; Rennison & Welchans, 2003). However, the impact of victim injury on the arrest decision is unclear. Most early research prior to the passage of pro-arrest legislation consistently concluded that the degree of violence or threat of violence was of only minimal significance in the arrest decision (Berk & Loseke, 1980–1981; Eigenberg et al., 1996; Feder, 1998; Jones & Belknap, 1999; Klinger, 1995; Worden & Pollitz, 1984). Even when victims were in danger and requested an arrest, numerous studies report that most officers consistently refused to make arrests unless other factors favoring arrest were present (Berk & Loseke, 1980–1981; Black, 1980; Brown, 1984; Davis, 1983).

Recent research from the last two decades clearly shows a dramatic change in police behavior in this area, reporting that victim injuries are related positively to making arrests (Buzawa & Austin, 1993; Buzawa & Hotaling, 2000, 2006; Eigenberg, 2001; Feder, 1996, 2007; Hirschel et al., 2007; Hotaling & Buzawa, 2001).

Police have become more attentive to public needs in this area. Surely, the degree of victim injury should be considered by police, as well as by prosecutors and judges in deciding whether to prosecute and in the sentencing phase of a criminal proceeding. Taken to the extreme, the punishment for attempted murder is far less than that of murder, even if the motive, intent, and method of attack are the same. Similarly, the distinction between felonious larceny and a misdemeanor level of the same crime is based primarily on the property stolen, not on the similar larcenous intent.

Presence of Children

Most researchers now report a greater likelihood of arrest if an offense is committed in the presence of children or children seem to be at risk of abuse or neglect, either from the commission of the crime itself or from situational factors at the home (Buzawa & Austin, 1993; Eigenberg et al., 1996; Hirschel et al., 2007).

We acknowledge that a study of misdemeanor domestic assaults by Kane (1999) found an inverse correlation between the presence of children and the probability of arrest. However, we suspect this anomalous result is an exception because Kane's study was expressly limited to incidents with no explicit risk to the victim and with no violation of a restraining order. In those circumstances, police might decide that there is less potential for a long-term negative impact to the child and that an arrest might conversely present a disruption and potential economic burden to the family.

Existence of a Marital Relationship

Early research reported that offenders who were married to the victim were less likely to be arrested (Bachman & Coker, 1995; Dobash & Dobash, 1979; Ferraro, 1989b; Martin, 1976; Worden & Pollitz, 1984). The consensus was that in traditional models of police behavior, the relational distance between the offender and the victim inversely affected the probability of arrest. One rationale for this pattern of behavior was that the police perceived a continuing relationship between the victim and the offender, which would decrease the likelihood of victim cooperation and make a conviction far less likely. Police would then, however inappropriately, conclude that their efforts were of little value if the victim would end her relationship with the abuser.

Finally, in the past, it was certainly possible that some police, then reflective of society in general, considered that some degree of violence was a legitimate "self-help" response to marital strife or infidelity (Saunders & Size, 1986). However, even if police adopted this regressive perspective, this assumption would never extend to include violence to punish infidelity with boyfriends or casual acquaintances.

On a more optimistic note, more recent research generally found that marital status is unrelated to arrest (Buzawa & Austin, 1993; Feder, 1997, Hirschel et al., 2007). Many researchers believe that domestic violence legislation and proactive arrest policies have minimized, if not eliminated, this factor.

Perceived Mitigating Circumstances

Some evidence suggests that arrest practices are influenced by normative ambiguities in family and relationship issues (Buzawa & Hotaling, 2000, 2006). Research on several Massachusetts communities has suggested that the likelihood of arrest for domestic assaults involving the use of force is low for those parties who can provide the police with a plausible rationale for the incident. The police seemed to accept an explanation involving the offender experiencing of a major life event.

Violence "explained" by a crisis such as an impending divorce or separation, the birth or impending birth of a child, a child about to be removed from the household, or a serious mental health problem of the offender resulted in arrest in only 1 of 5 instances, which is far below other groups of offenders. For example, the presence of a single factor, the prospect of imminent divorce, had a profound effect. The authors reported that the single claim of a recent or impending divorce reduced the likelihood of arrest to less than half of other offenders (Buzawa & Hotaling, 2006).

In contrast, offenders who offered the police more pedestrian excuses for violence citing "everyday conflicts" (e.g., problems with drinking, fights over money and sexual jealousy, time spent at work, and child custody issues) as the reason for their violent behavior were three to five times more likely (depending on the police department) to be arrested than those with a major life crisis (Buzawa & Hotaling, 2000, 2006).

We are, of course, concerned that, in some departments, police might simply be content with such an explanation and, therefore, are less willing to protect victims when offenders simply provide a facile rationale for their conduct. A significant question is why such distinctions are important. For reasons that we will address in the following discussion, if such distinctions relate to victim preferences, then they might be appropriate; however, if they reflect officers' personal beliefs or their identification with the offender's personal circumstances, then there is the potential for a serious impact to fair, impartial enforcement of the law.

Criminal History

A history of offenses reported to the police usually is a key determinant of the decision to arrest an offender (Buzawa & Hotaling, 2000; Gondolf, Fisher, & McFerron, 1988; Hotaling & Buzawa, 2001; Klinger, 1995; Smith & Klein, 1984; Waaland & Keeley, 1985; Worden & Shepard, 1996). The validity of determining the offender's criminal history, for domestic violence, as well as overall criminal history, is emphasized when determining whether an arrest should be made. Police in general view past criminality as a legitimate criterion in the arrest decision (Buzawa & Hotaling, 2006; Kingsnorth, 2006; Klein, 2005; Klinger, 1995; Worden & Shepard, 1996).

Unfortunately, although we agree with this factor, a growing number of departments can access outstanding restraining orders and warrants, and many departments still lack the technology for easy access or do not use the resources to obtain information on a real-time basis. Another source of data, criminal history, is even less likely to be immediately available to the responding officer until long after the arrest decision is made. Furthermore, many police agencies that do provide such information only consider prior *domestic violence* history rather than overall criminal history. As discussed previously, this might underestimate the risk posed by chronic, generally violent offenders (Wilson & Klein, 2006).

The Role of the Victim in the Arrest Decision

Victim Preferences

Commentators have long asserted that victim preference should be an important determinant of arrest (Black, 1980; Eigenberg et al., 1996; Feder, 1996; Sheptycki, 1993). In many jurisdictions, an informal operational requirement for a domestic assault arrest might be the victim's desire for the arrest. Without victim concurrence, most jurisdictions had policies or at the least standard operating procedures actively discouraging arrest (Bell, 1984). Some studies during the 1980s confirmed that the probability of an arrest increased by 25% to 30% if the woman agreed to sign a complaint and decreased by a similar amount if she refused. Berk and Loseke (1980–1981) as well as Worden and Pollitz (1984) reported that victim preferences accounted for the largest variance in arrest rates in every study examined.

Other studies, however, have reported that victim preferences or injuries were only of limited importance in the decision to arrest. In these studies, decisions instead were influenced by other factors. For example, Bayley (1986) reported that assailant arrest was not even correlated with victim wishes. In another study sampling certain Massachusetts police departments, the police could not have been strongly affected by victim preferences as evidenced by their inability to report the victim's arrest preferences in more than 75% of the cases (Buzawa & Austin, 1993).

Another study suggested that mandatory arrest practices might, in some departments, drastically limit "deference" to victim desires. Hotaling and Buzawa (2001) compared domestic versus non-domestic assaults in two communities with mandatory arrest policies but only for domestic violence assaults. As is discussed more extensively in Chapter 15, the result was apparent—an overall arrest rate of 77% for domestic assaults compared with 36% for non-domestic assaults.

Although differences in arrest practices in the departments studied apparently reflected officer compliance with mandatory arrest policies, it is possible that the ability to make a warrantless misdemeanor arrest in cases of domestic assault (available in all 50 states) was the reason for differences between domestic and non-domestic assault cases.

Victim Behavior and Demeanor

The interaction between the police officer and the behavior of the victim is more complicated. Police often apply strongly moralistic beliefs of proper and improper behavior, which is perhaps the reason that they chose careers in law enforcement in the first place. Such judgments might affect their response to a victim when responding to a domestic violence incident.

Often, police do not find either party to be "guilt free," especially if the offender justifies his actions in the context of victim "misbehavior." In this context, the victim's demeanor toward the officer might be as significant as her degree of injury. If she is rational, undemanding, and deferential toward the police, then her story might evoke more sympathy and attention, probably because it is assumed that within the context of the relationship, the woman had retained those same characteristics (Ford, 1983). Buzawa and Hotaling (2000, 2006) found strong correlations between the victim appearing "upset" and "trembling" and the likelihood of arrest. In fact, they reported that "victim trembling" was related more strongly to arrest than injury.

Women who are angry, aggressive, hostile to police intervention, and/or under the influence of alcohol or drugs might be viewed as less credible than other victims. Such victims might be recognized as unreliable and prone to deception.

Other victim actions at the scene clearly influence the police. For example, victim "cooperation" with the officer influences the likelihood of arrest (Belknap, 1995; Buzawa & Austin, 1993; Ferraro, 1989a; Smith, 1987). This might be a result of the lingering effect of police stereotyping domestic violence victims as providing little support or dropping complaints, ostensibly because they reconciled with their abusers. In police parlance, they are "fickle." Officers also know that there is an increased likelihood for case dismissal without victim cooperation or acquittal at trial because of lack of evidence.

They also might believe that if the victim is unwilling to extend the effort to initiate a complaint, then the seriousness of the injury might not warrant disrupting their own schedules. Research on victim cooperation has, until recently, largely measured victim cooperation solely by their preference for arrest. More appropriate measures for determining cooperation might include victim willingness to speak with a domestic violence advocate, avail herself of shelters, and/or explore the possibility of a restraining order.

There is considerable concern regarding how police observations might be a reflection of an officer's—or organization's—belief systems that result in a bias and/or differential treatment of specific subpopulations of victims. This result is complicated even more by whether the police behavior can be defined as a bias unsubstantiated by any empirical facts or as the result of an objectively increased likelihood of future violence that, nonetheless, disproportionately impacts specific groups.

Officers, like much of the general population, react to the traits and conduct of a victim. If, for example, the officer judges the victim to have a "deviant" lifestyle, then arrests are less likely. To some extent, this can be viewed as a reflection of society's norms, biases, and expectations regarding the behavior of victims and offenders. Of particular significance is the failure to identify women as victims who do not behave according to expected societal norms (Chesney-Lind & Irwin, 2008; Chesney-Lind & Pasko, 2004) that differ substantially from acceptable male behavior.

The category of victim apparently also has an impact on the decision to arrest. Research finds that those victims who conform to societal expectations (such as in cases we will discuss subsequently involving female victims compared with male victims) are more likely to have their assailant arrested (Buzawa & Hotaling, 2000, 2006; Chesney-Lind, 2006). In fact, police officers inevitably view the conduct of any party through the prism of their own beliefs. We assume that if an officer is biased against helping certain domestic violence victims, then arrest is less likely. Some research has found that biased officer attitudes toward certain types of victims disproportionately influence their response to domestic violence compared with other types of assaults in which arrest is more predictable (Feder, 1998).

This behavior is expected. A necessary aspect of police decision making is to make rapid value judgments in situations where the reality is unclear. In the face of ambiguous facts, research has indicated that officers make judgments based on their inherent assumptions regarding the propriety of a victim's conduct (Manning, 1978; Skolnick, 1975).

In such cases, the nature of the relationship between the parties, as well as their behavior and demeanor, might be considered by police as valid factors in evaluating the criminal behavior of either party. Officers scrutinize the victim's behavior as well as that of the assailant, which might affect who is identified as "victim" and as "offender."

We admit that data on the effects of police "judging" victims are inconsistent. In a detailed study of the interaction between officer expectations, victim actions at the scene of the incident and police reactions to what an officer might perceive as a deviant lifestyle, Robinson (2000) asked officers to report a "global rating" of victim cooperativeness. She reported that victim cooperation globally defined in this manner did not have a significant impact on the arrest decision; however, she also reported four variables that significantly predicted an officer's rating of victim cooperativeness: (1) whether the officer believed the victim had a substance use problem, (2) whether drugs or alcohol were present at the scene, (3) whether the suspect was present at the scene, and (4) the officer's length of service. In contrast, if the woman is abusive, disorderly, or drunk, then officers rarely make arrests or, at least, fail to follow victim preferences.

Another study reporting on extensive field observations in Detroit noted that when officers did not follow preferences of a female victim, it often was because she was not "liked" by the responding officers who would label her as being too "aggressive," "obnoxious," or otherwise causing problems for the officer (Buzawa & Austin, 1993).

Male victims provide a different dimension of the officer's reaction to a victim who did not conform to societal norms. The special case of male victims of female violence, although not a primary subject of this book, is instructive. It has been well documented that male victims are less likely to report a domestic assault (Langley & Levy, 1977; McLeod, 1984; Steinmetz, 1980; Straus, 1977–1978). A contributing factor to their reluctance to report assaults is a realistic expectation of limited police empathy or subsequent inaction. In the early 1990s, male victims asserted that even when severely injured, the police did not respect their desire for arrest of a female abuser. For example, one man required hospitalization for treatment of a stab wound that just missed puncturing his lungs. Despite his request to have the offending woman removed (not even arrested), the officers simply called an ambulance and refused formal sanctions against the woman, including her removal. Indeed, all the male victims who were interviewed consistently reported having the incident trivialized and being belittled by officers (Buzawa & Austin, 1993).

Officers might assume incorrectly that a male victim should be capable of preventing violence by his partner or that he initiated the violence. If not, he no longer conforms to accepted standards, perhaps rendering his account of events suspect. In any event, a female intimate partner is less likely to be arrested.

Unfortunately, readers will note that most of the research showing the disparate treatment of male victims of domestic abuse is dated between the 1980s and early 1990s. Frankly, we have reason to doubt this dichotomy still exists. Although significant research attention has been focused on the impact of traditional male views on the police treatment of female victims, similar research has not yet been extended to encompass how traditional views of "proper conduct" affect police response to male victims.

We know that in one analysis of data from the National Violence Against Women Survey, Felson and Paré (2007) did not find differences in the likelihood of arrest for crimes committed against men or women with deviant lifestyles including substance use or victim precipitation (conduct promoting the offender physically retaliating).

They did note, however, that women as a group were less likely to be arrested for an assault against a male partner, suggesting this is an area where gender stereotypes of victims and offenders might remain.

We hope that in time we will have a better understanding of what this observation signifies. It is possible that officers perceive male offenders as potentially more dangerous to their victims or are aware of a criminal history—both more likely overall. These additional factors might affect police arrest decisions.

It also is possible that with the passage of more aggressive domestic violence intervention statutes, police behavior toward male and female perpetrators of abuse will or has already changed. For example, several studies performed during the last decade report that female against male intimate partner assault was more likely to result in the arrest of the female than the converse (Felson & Paré, 2007; Hotaling & Buzawa, 2001).

In another report, a detailed analysis of approximately 600,000 intimate partner, domestic, and non-domestic assaults, Hirschel et al. (2007) reported that *no* statistical differences were found in the likelihood of arrest for either males or females controlling for incident characteristics. This finding might be a result of the samples and time frames used by the researchers. The early studies showing a bias against male victims were reporting police behavior in the 1970s and 1980s (probably exhibiting more of the traditional police response), whereas Hotaling & Buzawa (2001) used data from several small Massachusetts police departments collected for the year 2000. Felson and Paré (2007) relied on Violence Against Women Act data collected in 1994–1995, and Hirschel et al. (2007) used National Incident Based Reporting System data from the year 2000.

Police Perceptions of Violence as Part of Victim's Lifestyle

Another arrest criterion is the officer's subjective perception that violence might be a "normal" way of life for a particular victim and offender (Black, 1980; i.e., "battling spouses"). As discussed by Ferraro (1989b), when officers observe a regularly recurring pattern of violence, they might believe it normative for the relationship. Consequently, they are less likely to believe that any police response, including arrest, will be successful in deterring future violence. Many officers might dichotomize between "normal citizens," similar to themselves, and "deviants," perhaps viewed to use excessive alcohol, not able to speak fluent English, or belong to minority groups. For these groups, some officers, however inappropriately, might perceive battering as merely a part of an overall family pathology and, therefore, not amenable to any effective intervention. We cannot defend this practice, as this obviously presents an insidious attack on equality in the provision of services for all citizenry. However, to some extent, it does seem likely that it still impacts police behavior.

Current research broadens the focus from examining the individual's norms to those of the community. As a result, key issues are emerging, which are creating considerable controversy. There is a question of whether certain communities or neighborhoods might be allowed to have differential norms regarding police suppression of violence.

For example, in a school situated in certain neighborhoods, an act of aggression by a student might be expected by the victim's parents (and possibly by community norms) to result in a physically aggressive response by the victim. Regardless of efforts by school officials, a victim's failure to respond in kind would result in increased long-term risk to the victim because of his/her inability to "take care of himself/herself." However, in an affluent, suburban setting, the social reality, parental expectations, and the police response are likely to differ considerably.

Of course, it is possible that assuming officers react directly to community, race, and ethnicity is an insufficient and stereotypical analysis of a complex phenomenon. In this regard, Ferraro (1989b) reported that the key variable really reverted back to the previously described typology of the victim as a member of a "deviant" population, which might in turn be based partially on race or other problematic criteria. Although this differential might exist in certain departments, it is clearly not found in others. For example, in the

Buzawa and Austin (1993) study of Massachusetts departments, no arrest disparity based on race of the victim or offender was found. Similarly, a study using a large, national data set reported that although 31.2% of incidents involved Black offenders, only 29.9% were actually arrested, suggesting little real difference (Hirschel et al., 2007).

It seems that patterns of differential enforcement for different racial groups might have diminished as the cultural diversity and training in departments have increased in the last decade. For example, Buzawa and Buzawa (1990) examined attitudes within the Detroit Police Department and reported that Black and female officers present markedly different operational arrest patterns than their White male counterparts, who are the subjects of traditional analysis of police behavior. As officer diversity has increased, the previous patterns of predominantly White male departments might no longer hold true.

Assailant Behavior and Demeanor

Research has found consistently that officers' arrest decisions often are influenced by their reaction to the offender's behavior and demeanor (Black & Reiss, 1967; Buzawa & Hotaling, 2000; Hirschel et al., 2007; Mastrofski et al., 1995; Terrill & Paoline, 2007; Worden & Shepard, 1996). Hence, if the offender seems argumentative, behaves aggressively toward the victim, or otherwise challenges police authority, then an arrest is likely to be made, as much to establish control of the situation as to respond to the incident. Most police administrators would view this as a fair discriminator since such insubordination increases the likelihood of an assault on the responding officer or an offender who, by his conduct, demonstrates that he is truly "out of control."

Similarly, domestic violence research suggests that an offender's demeanor dramatically affects the probability of arrest. Assailant demeanor, especially lack of offender civility toward the police, dramatically increases the rates of arrest (Bayley, 1996; Dolon, Hendricks, & Meagher, 1986; Smith & Klein, 1984; Worden & Pollitz, 1984).

For example, an arrest nearly always occurs if an assailant remains violent in the officer's presence (Ferraro, 1989a). Perhaps because of the implied threat to the officer's authority or a lack of respect, an arrest is likely if the offender is perceived to constitute a direct threat to the officer even independent of the strength of the case (Black, 1980). Similarly, when police respond to gang locations or other places where they feel threatened, they tend to act more aggressively and use their powers far more frequently (Ferraro, 1989a).

It also has been observed that arrests are likely when the suspected abuser was belligerent or drunk. In one study, Bayley (1986) found that in a jurisdiction allowing officer discretion, two thirds of offenders who were hostile were arrested, whereas none who were civil toward the police were arrested. Buzawa and Austin (1993) attempted to improve their understanding of the relative importance of offender demeanor in the arrest decision. They noted that in a situation where officers were presumed to make arrests, but in reality had nearly unfettered discretion over the arrest decision, even victim injury was not as predictive of arrest as offender demeanor. In one case, an uninjured victim who had called the police cut the assailant with a butcher knife near his eye, requiring several stitches. No arrest was made because the assailant was drunk; in fact, the officers were not sure if he could have been potentially dangerous to the victim.

It is important to distinguish between a person perceived to be "under the influence" and the important, but not necessary, interaction with demeanor.

Earlier studies suggested that being under the influence of alcohol or drugs positively affected the likelihood of arrest (Berk, Fenstermaker, & Newton, 1990; Jones & Belknap, 1999; Smith & Klein, 1984; Worden & Pollitz, 1984). Now, however, more recent studies attempt to "tease out" closely related variables and often reach markedly different conclusions. For example, when simply examining the likelihood of arrest if drugs or alcohol are involved in the incident, Hirschel et al. (2007) reported a decreased likelihood of arrest. However, when such impaired offenders displayed anger, their likelihood of an arrest was far greater than nonimpaired offenders.

Variations Within Police Departments

Officer characteristics constitute a critical set of variables affecting the arrest decision. Not surprisingly, different officers have far different propensities to make arrests. For this reason, many studies have concluded that the police–citizen encounter is profoundly unpredictable from the viewpoint of the victim and offender. The response depends heavily on the officer's orientation toward domestic violence, skill level, and time constraints. Although difficult to quantify or predict, these factors are evident.

Some studies relate to legally irrelevant but organizationally significant facts. For example, earlier authors in the 1980s noted that police might be less likely to make a domestic violence arrest late in his/her shift, as it is not considered of sufficient significance to justify potentially staying late (Berk & Loseke, 1980–1981; Ferraro, 1989b; Stanko, 1989; Worden & Pollitz, 1984). Alternatively, because many departments now require supplemental paperwork for cases of domestic assault, charges might be downgraded to "simplify" the booking.

Research suggests that both attitudinal factors and demographic variables add to variance in arrests among different officers. Certainly, in the absence of specific enforced mandatory arrest domestic violence policies, individual attitudes of officers toward domestic violence cases seem to affect arrest preferences dramatically. When confronted with a report of serious injury to a victim, one study found that approximately 50% of the officers would regularly arrest, whereas the remaining 50% would not do so on any consistent basis (Waaland & Keeley, 1985).

The reasons for this difference are not clear. Officers often have different role expectations. Some view their primary mission as being a crime fighter or maintaining public order; others are more service oriented, concerned with assisting victims. From this, one might expect that those oriented toward a service approach would make arrests at a higher rate than those viewing their mission as crime fighting.

Gender Differences

Differences in the use of arrest powers also have been attributed to officer demographic characteristics. Male–female distinctions have been examined most frequently. The preponderance of research suggests that female officers are not necessarily more likely to arrest but are reported by victims as being more understanding, showing more concern, and providing more information about legal rights and shelters for victims. In one somewhat dated survey by Homant and Kennedy (1984), 40% of a male and female officer sample stated that the two groups handled domestic violence situations differently. Male officers perceived female officers as "softer," "more uncertain," "weaker," "more passive," "slower," and "lazier," whereas female officers saw themselves as more concerned with domestic violence than male officers, "feminine," and "nonviolent," but they agreed that they were more "passive." The extent of a male–female dichotomy in practice was in turn questioned by several authors (Ferraro, 1989a; Radford, 1989; Stanko, 1989) who believed that to work in a male-dominated organization, some female officers behave similarly to men because of occupational socialization or the desire to fit in. This theory is generally unproven by empirical research.

Research from the last two decades reports that female officers do make fewer domestic violence arrests than their male counterparts (Martin, 1993; Robinson, 2000). Although perhaps unexpected, the decreased rate of arrests by female officers is not indicative of indifference. Instead, female officers are reportedly more likely to follow victim preferences not to arrest despite any official policy to the contrary (Robinson, 2000). Therefore, female officers simply might not be as likely to exercise their authority, or even to follow department's proactive or mandatory arrest policies, if they believe it does not serve the interests of the victim and her family.

Officer Age and Arrest

Other officer demographic features have been considered to affect arrest rate and the overall officer response. Buzawa and Buzawa (1990) found variations on the basis of officer age. This result held even when controlling for exposure to domestic violence training. Older officers clearly were more likely to be exposed to departmental socialization, training, policies, and practices that in the past were less supportive of an aggressive police response to domestic assaults. Not surprisingly, older and "more experienced" officers made fewer arrests than their younger peers (Bittner, 1990; Stalans & Finn, 1995).

It also might be important to put these findings in the context of the overall likelihood of older officers making arrests because research examining police socialization argues that older officers are simply less aggressive and less likely to make arrests in general compared with younger, more motivated (or perhaps using a different frame of reference, more confrontational) officers (Van Maanen, 1978).

Of course, it might be that the generational differences will gradually reduce over time. Large numbers of officers have been hired since the 1990s who were provided initially with a pro-arrest orientation. As a result, several studies have failed to find great variation among officers by age cohort despite that older officers still have attitudes less supportive of victims than younger compatriots (Robinson, 2000; Worden, 1993).

Officer Race

Officer's race also has been examined. On the one hand, White officers have been viewed in some contexts, such as street crime, to be more coercive and likely to arrest

Black suspects. Alternatively, they might be more biased about "endemic" violence in Black communities and, therefore, less likely to want to intervene. Black officers might not share these stereotypes regarding normal behavior in Black families.

The results are not definitive. In one classic study, Black (1980) noted that the arrest practices of Black officers in some contexts were more coercive toward Black citizenry, compared with their White cohorts who sought to enforce the law impartially. In any event, to date, research provides no consistent empirical support for major racial differences in arrest decisions (Walker, Spohn, & DeLeone, 1996).

In some way, the entire dynamic of officer race, arrest practices, and community preferences all interact. Typically, an aggressive arrest policy by White officers in policing a minority neighborhood is perceived by many as being harsh and discriminatory. Indeed, from this perspective, police arrests can be viewed as targeted since there is a disproportionate impact on low-income neighborhoods and specific racial and ethnic minorities. Alternatively, these same practices in the context of domestic violence also can be perceived as "for the community," as they often are initiated by a victim or people trying to help her. This emphasizes the need for examining organizational variations within a jurisdiction to understand how the officer characteristics like race and, for that matter, sex and ethnicity truly interact with discrete neighborhood needs and preferences (Hassel, 2007; National Research Council, 2004).

Organizational Variations

The physical attributes of a police jurisdiction obviously vary by such factors as land area, population, and resulting population density. The characteristics of a department's service community have been shown to affect police practices. In one study of suburban departments in the 1980s, suburban police departments recorded higher rates of domestic violence, which were less likely a result of a real crime wave in these communities than because suburban residents reported their complaints to police as a matter of course. Nonetheless, the suburban police departments initiated criminal complaints at lower rates than rural and urban departments (Bell, 1984). Bell concluded that the three types of departments—urban, rural, and suburban—had markedly different policy orientations toward domestic violence. In addition to such generalized variation, specific features of a department and its organizational milieu have been shown to have a dramatic impact on arrests and other behavior in cases involving domestic assault.

Consider the impact of domestic violence policies in a rural community compared with an urban community. With large and sparsely populated areas to cover, rural law enforcement agencies deploy a service model that differs considerably from that used in urban areas. In an urban area, several police officers might be responsible for patrolling a small area of a city and/or might be devoted to one area of specialization, including a domestic violence unit. In contrast, in a rural area, one deputy sheriff might be responsible for covering a large geographic area.

This model presents obvious challenges for rural departments, such as increased response time (Gallup-Black, 2005; Logan, Walker, & Leukefeld, 2001; Weisheit, Wells, & Falcone, 1995). This factor might impact arrest outcome significantly, as a delay in response time is likely to increase the probability that an offender will leave the scene, which is a factor known to decrease the likelihood of arrest dramatically. Delayed response time also might decrease the likelihood that an officer will have probable cause to make an arrest in a misdemeanor assault.

Officers in urban jurisdictions also have been described as adopting a more legalistic and less service-oriented style of policing compared with other departments (e.g., favoring arrests if provided for by statute) (Crank, 1990; Liederbach, 2005). Conversely, rural and small-town police agencies have been reported widely to present a more service-oriented approach to policing and to engage in far more informal citizen interactions (Liederbach & Frank, 2003; Weisheit, Falcone, & Wells, 1996). As a result, there would seem to be a greater likelihood for a more diverse response to arrest mandates. Police officers in these rural and small-town agencies also are more likely to respond to community norms and expectations, whereas in more urbanized jurisdictions, organizational characteristics are more likely to dominate arrest practices (Crank, 1990; Liederbach, 2005; Wilson, 1968).

Although these considerations suggest that the overall arrest rates should be lower in rural jurisdictions, the higher crime rates in the more densely populated urban areas seem to offset this factor. However, because of the current fiscal crises, large departments might now lack the resources to respond to incidents and/or make arrests (Liederbach, 2005).

Similarly, a recent study examined the impact of urban versus rural jurisdictions on domestic violence arrest rates. Researchers reported higher arrest rates in rural jurisdictions independent of the domestic violence legislative framework. However, they could not measure the impact of actual workload of officers or arrest for incidents other than intimidation, simple assault, and aggravated assault (Pattavina, Hirschel, Buzawa, & Faggiani, 2007).

Organizational Imperatives

To understand fully the reality of modern policing is to understand that virtually all departments are facing incessant and debilitating battles for funding and for trying to prove their effectiveness and efficiency. In turn, individual officers often have become responsible for their own "metrics" as the perceived efficacy of individual officers are measured by such discrete measures. The classic police metric is an arrest or "collar" leading to a conviction. Realistically, this mandate drives officers to spend time on cases that are likely to lead to such convictions. The effectiveness of police officers, which is a key aspect of promotion, is determined partially by their number of major felony arrests. Similarly, police departments seek to justify to the community their share of scarce resources by focusing on major crimes and emphasizing the number of felony arrests and the percentage of convictions.

Because most domestic violence cases are misdemeanors, the time spent might not be considered as justified and, therefore, is considered a "waste of time" by officers trying to advance their careers and departments trying to justify budget requests and maintain high performance ratings.

Of course, we must emphasize that many police departments have contributed to this dilemma because their officers regularly downgrade domestics to misdemeanor assaults even though these cases would otherwise fit the textbook definition of a felonious assault (Buzawa & Buzawa, 1990). Other studies have focused on attributes of the criminal justice system that are not related directly to the police, to determine whether they affect arrest rates. For example, at least one study reported that extraneous conditions such as overcrowded jails or lockups seem to reduce domestic violence arrest rates (Dolon et al., 1986), as do inconvenient court hours or court locations (Ford, 1990).

SUMMARY

This chapter addressed why arrest came to be viewed as the preferred intervention for domestic violence. Although considerable variations existed in the police response, these differences did not seem to coincide with legal variables. Instead, they often were the result of officer sociodemographic characteristics and belief systems; characteristics of the victim, offender, and incident; and organizational incentives including policies, supervision, and training. These factors often would impact the likelihood of victims receiving assistance and/or of offenders being arrested. As realization grew that domestic violence cases were less likely to result in arrest compared with non-domestic cases, emphasis began to be placed on showing the same level of formal intervention in domestic violence cases compared with non-domestic cases.

We now have a better understanding of what factors impact the arrest decision, as well as how practices need to be changed. As a result, in recent years, considerable emphasis has been placed on developing pro-arrest or mandatory arrest policies in response to legislation. The time spent training officers in both preservice and in-service training has grown, and now most police academies include at least some training on the need for arrest in cases of domestic violence. Nonetheless, as will be explored in Chapter 5, variations still exist within and between departments.

DISCUSSION QUESTIONS

1. How does the criminalization of domestic assault fit into an overall societal trend toward crime?

2. Are there logical, less intrusive, alternatives to arrest for many situations?

3. How has deterrence theory been applied to domestic violence interventions? How well do you think it has worked?

4. Should the characteristics of a victim impact the police response to a domestic violence incident? Why or why not?

5. Should we expect that organizations vary in how they handle domestic violence calls? Is that appropriate?

Variations in Arrest Practices 8

Chapter Overview

All states now have passed statutes demonstrating their commitment to an aggressively pro-arrest response to domestic abuse. As we noted previously, these statutes and corresponding police policies vary considerably. The two types of "pro-arrest" policies are mandatory policies and preferred (or presumptive) arrest policies. This categorical distinction is highly significant as this theoretical difference might impact actual police behavior both in intended and in unintended ways. A mandatory policy directs action and, in theory, limits discretion, whereas a presumptive arrest policy simply serves to guide, albeit strongly, officers' use of discretion in the direction of making an arrest. In a presumptive arrest jurisdiction, whereas the policy often will explain the advantages of making an arrest, the actual decision of whether to "arrest," "separate," or merely "warn" parties is made by the officer on the scene.

As the use of mandatory arrest is viewed by many as the "model" and has been growing in prominence, this chapter will present an in-depth analysis of the rationale and impact of this policy.

The Rationale for Mandatory Arrest

Mandatory arrest policies have been primarily based on the belief that mere policy pronouncements in favor of the police arresting offenders might be insufficient to change street-level justice. The key becomes the elimination of or at least strong limits on officer discretion. Some proponents, especially in the early years of police reforms, felt police needed to be "coerced" into doing the right thing—making arrests of obviously guilty batterers. Their issue was plainly the abuse of police discretion.

More recently, as the process of change has become ingrained in police culture far more deeply and considerable evidence has shown an increase in the rate of arrests for this crime, the primary rationale for mandatory arrest has changed. Proponents of these policies now do not necessarily believe that abuse of discretion is the only, or even the primary, problem with normal police practices. Instead, they might believe that the basic problem is the inherent situational ambiguity of the police–citizen encounter in the context of domestic violence. Thus, many advocates for mandatory arrest do not critique the integrity of police officers nor necessarily even question their desire to assist domestic violence victims when they fail to arrest.

Proponents believe that giving police substantial discretion in a domestic violence case forces an officer under intense time pressure and a highly charged situation to make a series of critically important decisions. Broken into its components, the officer must interpret often highly ambiguous facts rapidly, usually while hearing several wildly different explanations, make an initial determination of the legal requirements needed to invoke a variety of possible criminal statutes, and then analyze all the potential consequences of these various alternatives. Only then can discretion be applied appropriately.

Furthermore, they realize that although theoretically there should be an independent decision for each specific domestic violence intervention, inevitably police will be influenced and often bound by their officer background in such cases, whether the officer views such cases as capable of resolution by police actions. Consequently, supporters of mandatory arrest believe that the inherent problems of applying discretion itself, not its intentional abuse, justify a policy mandatory arrest.

Many proponents of mandatory legislation and administrative policies also recognize that officers might lack sufficient domestic violence training to respond effectively, or might actively disapprove of their loss of customary discretion. Implementing mandatory or pro-arrest policies, therefore, tries to force change in officer behavior without first having to change police attitudes. Attitudinal change, although apparently considered of less immediate importance, would then occur at some later point, if at all, by training officers on the rationale of the policy and by conversion resulting from their immersion into the procedure, and over time, recognition that police intervention actually works.

It also is hoped that implementation of an arrest policy would collaterally increase the likelihood that the arrested offenders will be prosecuted. An arrest signifies to the other key actors in the criminal justice system, including prosecutors and judges, that an officer believes there is probable cause that a crime has been perpetrated by the defendant. In contrast, prosecutors and judges in general, and in domestic violence cases in particular, disfavor victim-initiated criminal complaints.

The Advantages of Mandatory Arrest for Victims

Mandatory arrests have been justified primarily by a theoretical model that explains how arresting offenders might benefit domestic assault victims by confirming their status as victims. Consider how this contrasts with past practices. Often, when called to the scene of a "domestic disturbance," officers simply admonished everyone to "keep the peace." At most, an assailant was arrested for being drunk, for "disorderly conduct," or for "disturbing the peace." This arrest charge gave no recognition that he had actually committed an assault against a victim. The label of being a "victim" rather than a brawling "combatant" might increase the victim's confidence in her ability to access legal rights. In addition, in many jurisdictions, police intervention might be the primary, if not the sole, mechanism for a victim to gain access to non-criminal-justice-agency support services (Stark, 1993).

In addition, by placing the burden of an arrest fully on police, the theory was that less hardship would be placed on already-traumatized victims. After all, these victims might have suffered from situational stress reactions and often exhibit classic symptoms of posttraumatic stress disorder (PTSD), sometimes known as "battered woman syndrome." PTSD can occur as a cluster of symptoms including panic attacks, depression, and high levels of anxiety. When the police respond aggressively by arresting an offender, the victim can be greatly relieved, because both the immediate source of her terror has been removed and the responsibility for subsequent coercive actions taken could not be viewed as her responsibility.

Finally, such a policy might fulfill perceived victim needs for retribution. The underlying rationale of retribution is that, given similar factors, victims of interpersonal violence deserve the same societal reaction as victims of stranger violence. Although many researchers might discredit the legitimacy of retribution as an element for the establishment of criminal justice policies, retribution is a well-recognized goal of criminal justice intervention as it institutionalizes retribution and obviates the need for vigilantism. We are not as ready to dismiss the importance of retribution as a legitimate goal. Recent social science research in the field of applied psychology demonstrates that most humans have a deeply ingrained goal to feel that there are negative consequences for misbehavior. The failure to do so weakens their own commitment to maintaining public order and following societal rules (Sachdeva, Iliev, & Medin, 2009).

Societal Reasons Favoring Mandatory Arrest Practices

A policy favoring arrest might have an additional indirect societal impact. As indicated previously, some victim advocates and feminist authors believe that society has classically used the implicit threat of violence against women (if committed by males) as a strategy to reinforce societal domination by the more powerful male group. Current examples of official tolerance of violence in most societies are difficult to find. However, one does not have to peruse international news long before seeing stories of "honor killings" to preserve the family's "honor" against a young lady's "sins," and of beatings or even of killings by vigilantes or even state-supported "morals police" in many countries to realize that this might not be a great exaggeration.

In the larger context, domestic violence might simply be an exemplar of the more powerful putting the weaker group "in its place" by using or threatening to use violence as a means of social control. From this perspective, the failure to arrest batterers in each instance tacitly condones such conduct, thereby impinging on the social equality of women. In contrast, a policy mandating domestic violence arrest has the potential of finally undermining one of the pillars of sexism in society—the past rights of men to dominate women and children physically within a patriarchal family unit without fear of government intervention.

We need not fully subscribe to this view to realize that the increased role of arrest, even mandating it in certain circumstances, might be of potential benefit to society. In a more "value-neutral" version of the previously stated theory of societal sexism, arrests might simply serve as an aggressive boundary-maintenance function, thereby indicating clearly that such abuse will no longer be considered a private family matter. If police always enforce existing laws against domestic violence, then societal tolerance for abusive behavior might rapidly diminish as the behavior and actually treat it as a crime.

The direct analogy is to the increased enforcement of drunk driving laws in the past several decades. By most accounts, this movement first resulted in less toleration of drunk drivers by the public and, over time, in an actual reduction in the number of drunk drivers and resultant accidents.

Unfortunately, because of the limitations of research and the inability of sociologists to secure sufficient research grants for testing such hypotheses, the role of arrest in indirect potential for societal change has not been explored in mainstream criminal justice literature and might, at least at this time, be more of a hope than a reality. Until the enactment of the Violence Against Women Act of 1994, little funding was available to enable practitioners to gather data to test such hypotheses. This consequence of the early focus of funding agencies on deterrence and experimental research was unintended. Feminist research is becoming more widely publicized and supported as its representation in academe continues to grow.

The Controversy Regarding Mandatory Arrest

We know now that the passage of domestic violence reform legislation has resulted in an increase in arrests for both intimate partner violence as well as other relationships included under such statutes. Also, we understand better its claimed benefits and previously theorized consequences. If we assume that resources in a jurisdiction are made available and a policy of mandatory arrest is implemented at the street level, the merits of such a policy and its costs and drawbacks, therefore, need to be considered carefully. To start, we need to consider critically the supposed major benefits and its costs to all concerned.

The next section of this chapter will examine whether the increase in the role of arrests has achieved its primary goal of a reduction in violent assaults, and then it will explore the validity of concerns that continue to be voiced regarding the impact of removing police arrest discretion inherent in the adoption of mandatory arrest statutes and policies.

Have Increased Arrests Suppressed Domestic Violence?

Many studies have examined the impact of mandatory arrest on subsequent offender behavior (see, e.g., Berk, Campbell, Klap, & Warren, 1992; Dunford, Huizinga, & Elliott, 1989; Garner, Fagan, & Maxwell, 1995; Garner & Maxwell, 2000; Hirschel & Hutchison, 1992; Maxwell, Garner, & Fagan, 2001; Pate & Hamilton, 1992; Sherman, Schmidt, et al., 1992). As an aggregate, it seems that mandatory arrest has not had the desired effect on either offenders or victims. In terms of offenders, it was anticipated that the use of mandatory arrest strategies would act as a deterrent to subsequent violence by offenders. This has not proven to be the case.

It might be that the greatest impact on domestic violence offenses can be achieved by focusing mandatory arrests only on those offenders who are chronic and then only with the acknowledgment that if arrested, they will be prosecuted and an adequate sentence will be achieved. This conclusion might be surprising in light of statistical indicators reporting a decrease in domestic violence assaults.

Decreases in domestic violence (up until the recent recession) have coincided largely with the increased emphasis on arrest. On the surface, this might suggest a strong causal relationship. However, despite the success of domestic violence legislation in increasing rates of arrest, the actual impact on the rate of intimate partner violence is not as certain. It is probable that the increased likelihood of arrest has deterred many former or potential "casual" offenders who generally could control violent tendencies if they were presented with an effective deterrent. However, as we have already discussed, although these might be most offenders by number, this group does not commit the bulk of serious violence.

We also need to acknowledge the overall societal context in which crime trends are analyzed. Data indicate that the overall rates for serious domestic violence offenses seem to have decreased between 1990 and 2005 but not at a faster rate than for other violent crime. According to recent National Crime Victimization Survey (NCVS) data, violence overall, including non-domestic assault, has decreased at greater rates than domestic violence. Data for domestic homicides and the impact of criminal justice intervention are inconsistent at best, suggesting that the impact of the increased use of sanctions has been of limited impact (Catalano, 2007; Dugan, Nagin, & Rosenfeld, 2001).

How can rates for domestic violence be decreasing without attributing at least a major part of the decline to the change in agency behavior? It can be argued that observed declines in assaults are at least partially a function of current societal demographics. We have long known that violence is committed largely by younger individuals typically prior to the age of 30 years. The high-violence age cohorts younger than this age are decreasing as a percentage of the overall population.

In addition, until the recent financial crisis, increased numbers of police and increased rates and length of incarceration, particularly for young minorities, undoubtedly had, to some extent, an effect on violent crime rates.

Although this might not seem relevant, this point is of great importance. Recent research suggests that those offenders reaching the criminal justice system who continue to reoffend despite increased sanctions tend to be "generally violent" (Wilson & Klein, 2006). If increasingly severe jail and prison terms incapacitate such people for lengthy periods of time, the overall societal problem of domestic violence might diminish, regardless of whether arrest itself, or any other technique employed by the police, is effective.

In the context of these changing demographics, the Bureau of Justice Statistics reports that the decline in intimate partner violence between the period 1994 and 2005 was no greater than the decline of violence against other relatives, friends, and acquaintances, as well as nonstrangers, and significantly less than the drop in violence for stranger violence (Catalano, 2006; Rennison & Planty, 2006). Obviously, this finding is troubling to those with theoretical expectations regarding the impact of mandatory arrests since this is the only crime that has a mandatory arrest component. We are not aware of any jurisdiction where there is a mandatory arrest policy for non-domestic assaults. Clearly, additional research is needed to determine whether higher arrest rates are associated with increased victim safety and/or reduced reoffending.

In any event, as we discussed previously, researchers need to typologize offenders and acknowledge that these variations have an impact on the effect of any type of intervention. It is known that arrest by itself does not stop chronic violent offenders. Unfortunately, it would be legally indefensible to try to arrest only the "occasionally violent" on the theory that deterrence will only work with this group. In fact, merely articulating a policy favoring arrest for a first-time offender but to ignore the "hard-core" abuser graphically demonstrates its folly. Instead, such a policy can be implemented only as part of an overall framework that heavily favors arrests while providing alternative intervention strategies for an occasional batterer committing a minor assault.

The Costs and Unintended Consequences of Arrest

In addition to questioning the overall positive impact of mandatory arrest practices, there also are some major concerns with its application in practice; the 5 primary concerns are (1) the widening of the scope of mandatory domestic violence laws to capture assaults not originally anticipated to be covered, (2) the unexpected costs to victims of mandating arrests despite victim preferences to the contrary, (3) the growth in the phenomenon of arrests of female "offenders" and "dual arrests" in general, (4) the individual and societal costs of disempowering victims who might not want an arrest, and (5) the possibility of misallocation of extremely limited agency resources.

The "Widening Net" of Domestic Violence Arrest Practices

Recent domestic violence legislation has expanded considerably the scope of relationships covered. Although initial domestic violence statutes typically addressed only violence between married couples, political pressure was applied by advocates for groups not covered by the original statutes. As a result, definitions have been subsequently expanded in virtually all states to encompass a broader range of domestic relationships. We now know that the passage of domestic violence reform legislation has resulted in an increase in arrests not only for intimate partner violence but also for other relationships that are included under such statutes (see, e.g., Chaney & Saltzstein, 1998; Hirschel, Buzawa, Pattavina, Faggiani, & Reuland, 2007; Municipality of Anchorage, 2000, pp. 8–9; Office of the Attorney General, State of California, 1999; Wanless, 1996, pp. 558–559; Zorza & Woods, 1994, p. 12).

A growing body of empirical evidence finds that girls, being both of minor status and female, are at an increased risk for arrest than either boys or adults (Chesney-Lind, 2002). In a recently released report by the Girls Study Group, it was reported that although the arrest rate for juvenile females between 1980 and 2003 increased much more than for male juveniles, juvenile males were still five times more likely to be arrested for aggravated assault. This finding is exacerbated even more by the fact that the greatest increase in police arrests has been in the area of simple assaults, and as in the case of adult women, a far greater proportion of simple assaults is committed by juvenile females than by males (Zahn et al., 2008).

A recent study by Buzawa and Hirschel (2010) examined differences by both age and gender. They found that the differences in arrest rates were primarily attributable to age, not gender, and that juveniles were far more likely to be arrested for assaulting adults, whereas adults were far less likely to be arrested for assaulting a juvenile, with adult females having the lowest arrest rate regardless of whether the adult assaulted was male or female.

Collectively, these studies suggest that an unintended effect of domestic violence statutes is that the acts of many juveniles have been criminalized. This effect probably would not have occurred absent these statutes.

Second, any mandatory policy, by definition, cannot take into consideration victim preferences or their perspectives, concerns, and possibly their prior experiences. We also cannot address the impact an arrest will have on the offender, along with real concerns regarding safety, financial resources, and children discussed earlier.

Although a plethora of studies have examined whether the intended outcomes of policy mandates have been achieved in terms of arrests, there has been a lack of research on the costs and unintended consequences of such policies. Over the years, we have suggested a variety of known costs and unanticipated consequences of arrest. Initially, we should examine how an arrest not initially desired by the victim is likely to impact her willingness to report future acts of violence. Most studies suggest that most calls for domestic violence are primarily initiated by victims; NCVS data reported that 72% of the reassaults were reported by the victim (Felson, Ackerman, & Gallagher, 2005), and National Incident Based Reporting System (NIBRS) data found that 66.1% of domestic calls to the police were made by victims (Hirschel et al., 2007). However, this finding indicates clearly that a large number of incidents are initiated by other parties. The failure to report can be explained in several ways. If one assumes that the nonreporting of domestic violence incidents is similar to the nonreporting of crime in general, then there are at least four separate reasons for nonreporting. First, many victims simply might not want intervention by the criminal justice system or prefer some other form of assistance. A large number of victims did not initiate the previous call leading to criminal justice intervention. Nationally, research has found that victim-initiated calls ranged from one third to two thirds (Felson, Messner, Hoskin, & Deane, 2002; Hirschel & Buzawa, 2002). These victims might not have wanted any intervention or, alternatively, might have wanted assistance (and actually would have or did engage in alternative help-seeking behavior).

Third, victims might not view the particular offense as serious enough to warrant criminal justice system intervention. For example, victims might be more likely to report subsequent assaults but less likely to report restraining order violations. Alternatively, victims might believe an assault must involve an injury to justify police involvement. This would seem to be supported by recent research finding that women with severe physical or psychological violence or injury were more likely to call police than other abused women (Bonomi, Holt, Martin, & Thompson, 2006). Specifically, there were 96% more calls when a weapon was involved, 58% more calls if they were severely sexually abused, and 50% more calls if they were severely physically abused. Of interest is that women with children at home made 32% more calls to the police (Bonomi et al., 2006).

Fourth, victims might be skeptical about the effectiveness of criminal justice involvement for their situation. Like other crime victims who do not report law violations, victims who had previously reported a domestic violence assault might believe that since they had already been involved with the criminal justice system, it was unsuccessful at providing a remedy for the situation. Some victims might have felt that criminal justice intervention previously had, or might now exacerbate, an already bad situation.

Fifth, the criminal justice system might not have followed victim preferences and, therefore, this group of victims might have sought alternative sources of help or simply not seek any additional assistance.

Although the nonreporting of revictimization can be explained in many possible ways, a significant number of women do report subsequent incidents of victimization to the police. In these cases, a victim's need for immediate assistance and the seriousness of the situation might subsume any other considerations in the mind of the victim. She might prefer alternative sources of help and/or fear the consequences of intervention but call the police because she needs their assistance to ensure her safety and/or the safety of her children. The research question is obvious: Can the differential response to revictimization be examined in cases of domestic violence?

Why might a victim of a domestic assault not desire an arrest of her abuser? Are there rational reasons or should society assume that it knows what is best and act accordingly by always arresting an offender? To answer this question fully we need to explore why a victim of abuse might not desire involvement of the authorities. To understand this seemingly paradoxical behavior more fully, we need to have an insight into a victim's goals and motivations.

Victim goals are similarly diverse. Some might wish to salvage a flawed relationship in which aggressive behavior is now customary, whereas other victims might have already terminated contact with the offender. Victims might believe that an arrest will make a bad situation worse, or as described previously, they might have had negative experiences with police interventions in the past. Victims also vary in their perceptions of the level of danger, threat, and harm that is presented by an offender. Obviously, not all offenders present the same degree of danger; some victims are threatened or assaulted by a first-time offender, and others find themselves the target of a serial batterer.

Jurisdictions with mandatory arrest policies cannot incorporate the complexity of these victim needs and preferences into policies and practices. Victim situations are not all alike; yet such policies treat a victim as if they were. It might even be said that many criminal justice practitioners consider victim preferences largely irrelevant because the overarching goal of the system is to punish offender misbehavior rather than to accumulate victim preferences and needs. Still others might acknowledge that victims have legitimate preferences but believe that having been victimized, they cannot judge what is in their best interests. Following this, "professionals" should make these decisions.

Unanticipated Costs of Arrest to the Victim

To understand the impact of mandatory arrest on victims, it is important to realize that victims as well as offenders are not a monolithic group but are a highly diverse population (Hirschel, Hutchison, & Dean, 1992). Many victims are trapped by dependency on the offender, believing that they must remain in an abusive situation for economic, physical, or even emotional survival (Barnett, 2000).

A victim might be affected adversely by the arrest of an offender in a variety of ways. The most problematic reason for this might be fear. She might justifiably fear physical or economic retaliation or other acts committed by the assailant or by his family, relatives, or friends.

Sometimes the motivation for reabuse, subsequent to arrest, is strictly revenge. At other times retaliation, or threats thereof, are designed to intimidate and prevent a victim from pressing charges. If already severely physically or emotionally traumatized by abuse, she might find the additional demands attendant to supporting arrest realistically beyond her capabilities.

We understand that on the surface, such fear should not prevent the police from using an otherwise effective tool such as arrest. Indeed, the police, prosecutors, and courts should exercise their strongest possible efforts to prevent witness intimidation, which is a threat to the entire criminal justice system as well as to the victim herself. However, victims might have additional concerns, and primary among them are the financial costs resulting from an arrest. Although the arrest alone might not have a serious financial impact on the family, it might affect an offender's current or future employment, thereby limiting the offender's ability to maintain child support or other payments. Furthermore, the offender might threaten or actually stop child support, leaving the victim scrambling for assistance from an overburdened family court system.

Many victims might be deterred from reporting abuse if arrest is likely. Findings from the Chicago Women's Health Study report that fear of consequences for the offender was the primary reason provided by more than 50% of victims not contacting the police for a domestic assault (Fugate, Landis, Riordan, Naureckas, & Engel, 2005).

In addition to the obvious direct costs of time and effort to the victim that result from the arrest of a family member, it also is likely to traumatize other family members. Children, who are already affected by the abuse, might suffer from the arrest itself or from the stigma associated with the incident.

We understand that long term, it is developmentally better for children to witness parental arrest. However, in many, if not most, cases, a child identifies closely with his or her parent and typically would not benefit, at least in the short term, from watching him or her being led out of the house in handcuffs. Unfortunately, all too often, children align their loyalties with the offender and blame the victim for disrupting the family. This does not mean arrest should not be used when indicated, merely that all collateral ramifications should be considered.

Ambivalence, as discussed in detail in the chapters regarding prosecution, often translates into a victim's failure to support criminal cases after an arrest is made. Domestic violence victims are far more likely than other victims to be motivated by self-protection and less on vengeance in calling police and pursuing prosecution. Many domestic violence victims might simply want "restoration" or redress, not vengeance or absolute punishment. They might be far less concerned with the abusers' punishment than with using the criminal justice system to achieve these purposes (R. C. Davis & Smith, 1995; Lerman, 1992). Although many people who are victimized by someone with whom their relationship has ended might want aggressive prosecution, others simply seek an immediate end to abuse.

Susan Still

Susan Still appeared on *20/20* with Diane Sawyer and later on *The Oprah Winfrey Show* to share her story of 24 years of emotional and physical abuse by her former husband. The abuser, Ulner Still, received a 36-year prison sentence in December 2004, which was the longest sentence given to the crime of domestic violence that did not result in the death of the victim. Ulner Still would instruct his two sons and one daughter to call their mother a "white slut" and would order his 12-year-old son to videotape him beating her. He would then play these tapes again later, in front of his children as well as friends. He would mock her, and her children would as well. He continually manipulated the children to join him in his abusive behavior toward her.

With the encouragement of her supervisor, Susan and her two sons sought protection from the police in May 2003 and reported her husband for domestic abuse. Although Susan took custody of her two sons, then 13 and 8, they blamed her for the abuse and for breaking up their family. Their daughter (21 years old at the time) not only sided with the father, but also she testified on his behalf.

Since that time, Susan began speaking publicly to groups about her experience, and her sons gradually began to realize that they had been "brainwashed." This was a very difficult and slow process. However, in 2007, when her sons appeared with her on *The Oprah Winfrey Show*, one son described his mother's abuse as analogous to waking up and brushing your teeth—a typical part of the day. Life at that time was "survival of the fittest." He now believes what happened to his mother was wrong and that he has changed. Susan Still said that she was proud of her boys because they now better understand their experiences growing up in that environment.

Sources: New York City Domestic Violence Court Open House, Center for Court Innovation, March 24–25, 2009; Winfrey, 2007.

Arrests and Minority Populations: A Special Case?

Mandatory arrest policies seem to affect minority populations disproportionately. Ciraco (2001) found that after the passage of mandatory arrest laws in New Jersey, there was a statewide increase in reported offenses of 51% during the previous decade. However, this increase was observed most in counties with the greatest proportions of persons below the poverty line. In poor, urban areas where minorities are overrepresented, neighbors or bystanders are more likely to report a domestic violence simply because they hear a disturbance. The unanswered question is who initiated the call to the police and whether victim's interests were served by an arrest. Currently, empirical data are lacking that provide an understanding of how the calls that reach police attention by victim reporting compared with others among specific subpopulations.

There is, after all, little doubt that domestic violence is a major problem in African American society since such violence is the highest among racial and ethnic minorities and the poor in general (Fagan, 1996). Nevertheless, for many racial and ethnic minority victims, the risks of involvement of the criminal justice system might outweigh its potential benefits. Many African Americans have, with good cause, protested that they were disproportionately subject to arrest and police brutality.

Research has consistently found minorities to be less likely to trust the criminal justice system (Bent-Goodley, 2001; Black, 1980; Coker, 2000; Robinson & Chandek, 2000b). An integral part of their community, African American women are more likely to have witnessed or even to have experienced police mistreatment. It is possible that many African American women currently believe racism is more serious than sexism, even when the latter involves personal risk (Bent-Goodley, 2001).

We need to recognize that at least in the past, in the African American community, the label of being either the victim or the offender of intimate abuse created an unwanted stigma for both parties. Some African American women have gone so far as to reject the entire concept of domestic violence as a concept of "white feminism and male bashing" (Bent-Goodley, 2001, p. 321).

Specific characteristics of regressive policing domestic cases might play on such fears. Many African American women might have greater fear than other victims that their children might be taken away from them, especially in states mandating full investigation of cases in which children were present (Bent-Goodley, 2001).

In addition, there might be a realistic fear of being arrested themselves, especially if the police uncover other criminal activities in the family such as drug addiction or even alleged child neglect or abuse when responding to a domestic assault. The fact is that for a host of reasons, the likelihood of victim arrest among minorities increases with proactive or mandatory arrest policies against domestic violence (Coker, 2000).

Not surprisingly, victim behavior is affected by these factors. One study reported that African American women were 1.5 times less likely to call the police compared with White women (Joseph, 1997). This finding is extremely significant because domestic violence is more likely to be known by police among urban, lower socioeconomic classes, in general, and minority communities, in particular.

It is likely that the increased use of arrest among minority communities, especially with the adoption of mandatory arrest policies, will strengthen the number (and validity) of claims of disproportionate use of arrest and physical force on minority men (Forrell, 1990–1991; Zorza & Woods, 1994). It also is likely that the increased use of arrest will strengthen the number (and validity) of claims of disproportionate use of arrests and physical force on Black men (Forrell, 1990–1991; Zorza & Woods, 1994). Therefore, it is necessary to determine whether other less-intrusive measures would be of similar effectiveness with far fewer negative consequences.

As noted, virtually any police intervention in domestic violence, even if flawed, has some deterrent effect for many batterers (Carmody & Williams, 1987; Feld & Straus, 1989; Ford, 1988; Pierce & Deutsch, 1990). If this is true, should this affect the "default position" of arrests within a minority community that has been, as a group, subjected to police abusive practices? Is not arrest the police action most likely to increase tensions and dissatisfaction within the minority community?

The Role of Victim Satisfaction With Police Response in Reporting Revictimization

So far, we have stated that a uniform policy might not meet the needs of a diverse set of victims. The question might be posed as follows: To what impact does the failure to meet these needs have on subsequent victim behavior? The answer might at least partially lie in the extent to which victims decide to report revictimization based on their prior experiences with the police.

As described in Chapter 5, it has been known that a relatively large percentage of victims of domestic violence never report such incidents to police. This observed reluctance to call the police has continued through studies performed during the last decade (Buzawa & Buzawa, 2003; Felson, Messner, Hoskin, & Deane, 2002; Felson & Paré, 2005; Kruttschnitt, McLaughlin, & Petrie, 2004). In the past, as demonstrated graphically in Chapter 5, many victims realistically feared that the police would simply fail to act appropriately and, at best, respond perfunctorily or even exacerbate the situation by demonstrating that the offender's conduct was tacitly condoned when no police action was taken.

This dynamic, however, clearly should have changed as the police have become increasingly committed to more proactive intervention, including, in many jurisdictions, mandatory arrests of batterers. It is now recognized, even by the general public, that the police response to reported domestic violence has undergone a major transformation in many, if not most, jurisdictions (Buzawa & Buzawa, 2003; Felson & Paré, 2005).

Today, it simply cannot be said that police as a group trivialize domestic violence. In fact, currently the primary critique of police action today is that it is too uniform in some jurisdictions with regard to mandatory arrests, and that arrests are made regardless of whether appropriate for the situation because of overly rigid policies or statutes mandating arrest. As a result, some have surmised that many victims might be prospectively deterred from calling the police because of fear of further losing control of the situation (Buzawa, Hotaling, Klein, & Byrne, 1999; Mills, 1998, 1999, 2006).

For this reason, reporting subsequent abuse or revictimization to the police becomes an extremely interesting subset of the interaction between police and victims. In such cases, by definition, the victims have already encountered the aggressive actions of the police. For this reason, an analysis of victim rereporting behavior would either reinforce (if victims are not deterred from further reporting of violence) or undermine (if they are deterred) the impact of an aggressive, system-wide intervention.

Proponents of mandatory arrest have assumed that the initiation of aggressive intervention strategies would result in increased victim willingness to participate in the criminal justice process should a reoffense occur. Specifically, victims would be empowered through intervention and, therefore, more likely to report subsequent problems with the offender. Most research simply did not address the factors that might predict when victims report revictimization from those victims that do not, nor did it disentangle the effects of other criminal justice components (e.g., prosecution, sentencing, or corrections) on the subsequent behavior of victims.

Logically, and supported by research, victims often become frustrated with the criminal justice system if it is unsuccessful at preventing reabuse and, therefore, might not report it (Buzawa & Hotaling, 2006). Revictimized individuals were far more likely to have taken out prior restraining orders and had the offender arrested. Despite their intervention, the victim was revictimized. It is certainly understandable that many of these victims become discouraged with the efficacy of current intervention strategies and decide not to report subsequent victimizations to the police.

Moreover, it is possible that victim frustration resulting in "nonreporting" of current abusers is related not only to the criminal justice system's response to this incident but also to a series of prior victimizations. Revictimized women who failed to report their revictimization to the police were far more likely to have endured childhood sexual abuse and have been subjected to serial victimizations throughout their lives.

One avenue of research on criminal behavior that has been particularly informational during the past decade is the discussion and an exploration of crimes through a life course. Equally compelling is the notion of how victims react throughout their life course. Although we have given considerable attention to offender careers in crime, less attention has been spent on studying victimization careers, not only in terms of individual victimization but also in terms of family victimization through the life course.

The Increase in Female Arrests

The traditional image of intimate partner violence is of a male offender and a female victim. As discussed in Chapter 2, the extent to which there is gender symmetry in intimate partner violence continues to be hotly debated. After all, acknowledging that the weaker partner might resort to violence in intimate relationships does not mean that he or she is an abuser. It is important to understand the context in which violence is used and whether such behavior was offensive or defensive in nature. Police reports indicating role reversals between victim and offender in a series of incidents might therefore be the result of a failure to understand defensive behavior or to identify a primary aggressor, rather than a reflection of reality (Chesney-Lind, 2006; Hirschel et al., 2007).

The police are legally required to rely on criminal codes as the basis for arrest decisions. Criminal codes focus on an individual act, usually physical harm or threat of physical harm. As a result, applying "legalistic definitions" that emphasize violence rather than a continuing pattern of psychological and physical abuse might force a diverse range of incidents into one of a fixed set of formal categories, preventing police from dealing with the complexities and unique aspects of each case. This is then reinforced by police training that teaches them to focus on the evidence presented in the current incident rather than to consider the incident in the context of prior events (Manning, 1996; Rice, 2007).

For example, a woman who has been the victim in an ongoing pattern of violence might find that the police arrive only to misinterpret an act of self-defense on her part out of context, resulting in her arrest. The inability or refusal of police to distinguish victims from offenders is one possible explanation for the existence of high dual-arrest rates.

Of course, some might explain this growing rate of female arrests for domestic assaults as evidence of a growing propensity for women to engage in violence, or at least a greater willingness of police to respond to such behavior. As noted in Chapter 2, many family violence theorists have written about female violence as being fairly common.

The preponderance of the evidence suggests that women commit a considerable number of violent acts in intimate relationships. Many such acts are not self-defense, even if women's rates of violence are considerably lower, and their acts are less severe, than those perpetrated by males.

Steffensmeier, Zhong, Ackerman, Schwartz, and Agha (2006) empirically addressed the issue of the possibility of increasing rates of female violence by contrasting the trends reported in the NCVS and Uniform Crime Reports (UCR) program for female-against-male intimate partner violence during the period 1980 to 2003. Despite the significant increase in arrests, the UCR reported no change in the relative rate of offenses committed by women for homicide and sexual assault, and the NCVS reported little or no change in female rates of assault. Furthermore, the gender gap has remained fairly stable during this period as well. This finding has been further substantiated by other researchers who report that female violence seems to be overall less severe than that of males (Hirschel et al., 2007; Moffitt, Caspi, Rutter, & Silva, 2001).

It also has been substantiated that a consequence of the nationwide efforts to enforce mandatory arrest policies in intimate partner cases has been a distinct and disproportionate increase in the number of women arrested for intimate partner violence, both as sole offenders and as part of a "dual arrest" discussed immediately afterward (De Leon-Grandos, Wells, & Binsbacher, 2006; Hirschel et al., 2007; Miller, 2005). Recently, Meda Chesney-Lind (2006) has observed that although the FBI (in 2004) reports that the male arrest rate for assault decreased by approximately 5.8% between 1994 and 2003, the female arrest rate increased by 30.8%. Likewise, Greenfeld and Snell (1999) have noted an increase in female convictions for aggravated assault, which they believe can be attributed at least partially to the increase in arrests for domestic assault. The overall rate of women arrested specifically for domestic violence differs by jurisdiction and time. Several studies have examined the specific rate of female arrests as a percentage of total domestic violence arrests. These results vary widely from 30.8% (Connecticut State Police, 2000), to 17.4% (Domestic Violence Training and Monitoring Unit, 2001), to 28% (Governor's Division for Prevention of Family Violence, 2001).

The Increase in Dual Arrests

Much of the increase in female arrests is the result of the increase in cases where the police have arrested both parties (e.g., a dual arrest in which both the male and the female partners are arrested) (see, e.g., Epstein, 1987; Haviland, Frye, Rajah, Thukral, & Trinity, 2001; Martin, 1997; Saunders, 1995; Victim Services Agency, 1988; Zorza & Woods, 1994).

In the first detailed study of dual arrests, Martin (1997) examined the disposition of domestic violence cases handled by the criminal courts in Connecticut just after implementation of a mandatory arrest policy in 1988 and found the dual-arrest rate in adult intimate family violence cases to be 33%. Research has shown wide variations in dual-arrest rates. Where statewide data are available for domestic violence cases, dual-arrest rates are as high as 23% in Connecticut (Y. Peng, personal communication, July 10, 2002) and as low as 4.9% in neighboring Rhode Island (Domestic Violence Training and Monitoring Unit, 2001); furthermore, dual-arrest rates are 8% in Arizona (Governor's Division for Prevention of Family Violence, 2001).

Current arrest data might mask even higher rates of dual arrest. One study in Massachusetts reported that in cases of domestic violence where both parties were injured, it was common practice to arrest one party and "summons" the other to court. As a result, dual-arrest rates including summons were higher than originally reported and were at 16% (Rice, 2007).

Many researchers and advocates believe that dual arrest typically discriminates against women who are primarily victims of domestic assault, as indicated in most research findings. This belief is bolstered by research clearly showing that offenders are viewed by the criminal justice system as likely to represent the more serious of the batterers (who are predominantly male) and that women's physical violence is likely to neither cause injury nor be motivated by attempts to terrorize her partner (Kaufman Kantor & Straus, 1990; Stets & Straus, 1990). Although women do engage in acts of violence, as an aggregate, women's violence might be an act of self-defense because the cases police witness are less likely to reflect the (usually) minor cases involving mutually violent relationships.

Primary Aggressor Statutes

In some cases, dual arrests might simply be the result of practices that fail to require and/or train officers to identify the primary aggressor. We do note that most states have tried to address this by enacting "predominant" or "primary" aggressor language in domestic violence statutes (Ham, 2005).

Primary aggressor statutes have attempted to reduce dual arrests by specifying that in cases where both parties are violent, arrest should be limited to the primary aggressor or to the person who initiated violence. Such statutes codify common law exception to the crime of "assault" and "battery" by recognizing that people can legitimately commit violence in self-defense.

However, even when such provisions are present, application of a "primary aggressor" provision relies on the police use of discretion. Police use of discretion, as we should remember, was denigrated largely by proponents of mandatory arrest policies. Furthermore, these difficulties can be exacerbated by the use of primary aggressor statutes when they do not provide clear guidelines for determining a primary aggressor in cases of domestic violence. There also might be a lack of sufficient police training and/or a lack of unequivocal information needed at a crime scene to identify the primary aggressor. As a result, mandatory arrest jurisdictions are more likely to have higher dual arrest rates (Hirschel et al., 2007). Even when statutes are present, only two states prohibit the arrest of the nonpredominant aggressor (Erwin, 2004).

In some cases, dual arrests might be a result of insufficient police training in identifying the primary aggressor. Alternatively, some advocates argue that such arrests might constitute a tacit mechanism to punish women who burden the police with domestic "problems." There are, however, additional explanations for high dual-arrest rates.

This situation might be compounded by the observation that batterers have become increasingly adept at manipulating the criminal justice system in an effort to control or retaliate against their victims and might make efforts to "preempt" victims from notifying police by calling in their own claims of having been abused (Buzawa &

Buzawa, 2003; Chesney-Lind, 2006; Chesney-Lind & Pasko, 2004; Klein, Wilson, Crowe, & DeMichele, 2005).

Another different problem occurs when the woman really is the primary aggressor. Many officers will assume adult male-against-female violence involves a male primary aggressor. However, they might find that they are in a situation in which the female (according to both parties' admissions and to evidence on arrival) is primarily at fault. Assumptions of male guilt as well as of political and/or organizational pressure might discourage officers from arresting the woman as aggressor, and being uncertain, the officers simply arrest both. Thus, it is possible that men as well as women might be the unintended victims of a mandatory arrest policy.

This observation is supported by some research. Jones and Belknap (1999, pp. 265–266) found in their Boulder, Colorado, study that "those identified as male victims were more than three times as likely to be part of a dual arrest couple than those individuals identified as female victims." Similar findings were reported by Buzawa and Hotaling in their study of three Massachusetts towns that when a male was a victim, the female was five times less likely to be arrested than was a male (Buzawa & Hotaling, 2000, 2006). The results of a multisite study of men's batterer intervention programs reported that the female victims initiated violence in 40% of the cases during a treatment follow-up period. Hence, the batterer's crime was more of an overreaction rather than a first initiation of violence (Gondolf, 2005).

Furthermore, primary aggressor statutes have a key weakness in that they rarely address the phenomenon of long-term patters of abuse adequately. The true aggressor might not have struck a physical blow at the particular time that the police were called. As discussed previously, the criminal justice system implicitly requires the identification of a crime with a defined victim and offender. For this reason, long-term abuse resulting in a victim's retaliatory violence might be treated perversely as a domestic assault by the victim.

The Violent Family

A different problem exists when police are confronted with families in which violence is a normal part of dispute resolution. We discussed previously how violence in some families might be mutual, forcing police to judge who initiated a particular violent incident, rather than who is generally the primary aggressor. Even when it is clear that one party is at fault, this victim–offender dichotomy attendant to criminal law precludes one from viewing domestic assault as a type of interaction that, in some cases, might be a response to conflict. A person's status might not only be difficult to identify but also not remain constant across incidents. We know that in some violent relationships, both partners might be violent and victimized at various points in their lives (H. Johnson, 2001; Straus, 1999). M. P. Johnson (1995) reported that in situations with "common couple violence"—so-called battling couples—minor but recurrent acts of violence are initiated by either party, but the type of violence generally viewed by the police (and in shelter and clinical samples) is more likely to involve serious and frequent beatings, as well as the terrorizing of women.

Unfortunately, police typically do not (or are not allowed to) consider these factors when determining which party is a victim. They are forced to identify a "victim" and an "offender." Although this process might involve identifying the person with the most serious injury as the victim, research by Buzawa and Hotaling (2000) indicates that this is not always true. More insidious factors such as police evaluation of social norms and family structure enter into the arrest decision. This study reported that women were most likely to be seriously injured, but they also were less subject proportionate to their offenses to arrest, being the "preferred" victims, regardless of the extent of their injuries. This discrepancy might seem to be explainable simply because men commit more serious acts of interpersonal violence than women.

However, the same study reported another context in which police arrest practice did not seem to follow statutory guidelines neutrally. It reported that minors were six times more likely to be arrested under domestic assault statutes compared with either adult men or women. Despite child abuse laws that protect juveniles until the age of 18 years, an arrest is far less likely to be made when a minor is the victim of domestic assault by a parent than if the parent were assaulted by the child (Buzawa & Hotaling, 2000, 2006).

In addition, an analysis of a large-scale national data set found that adult females were least likely to be arrested, followed by adult males, and then juvenile males. Juvenile females were the most likely to be arrested of all groups, respectively, for non-intimate-partner domestic assaults (e.g., other family members and relatives) (Buzawa & Hirschel, 2008).

> Some jurisdictions have avoided high rates of dual arrest. In these jurisdictions, again for organizational or political reasons, officers might be discouraged both from arresting women and from making dual arrests. For example, if a woman initiated violence by throwing an object at her partner, resulting in a bruise or cut, and the man retaliated violently, causing similar bruising, many officers were found to make no arrest or simply to arrest the man.
>
> Furthermore, the likelihood of prosecution in such cases is likely to affect officer behavior, with both formal and informal knowledge of the prospects of prosecution affecting their actions (Manning, 1997). Research conducted in three Massachusetts towns found that only 3 (less than 1%) of 319 domestic assault cases produced dual arrests and that none of these dual arrests involved a female committing violence against a male intimate partner. Although these towns did not have high dual-arrest rates, many domestic assaults that could have been defined as mutually violent seemed to be redefined so as not to merit even a single arrest. This occurred even though in 18.8% of nonarrest cases, in which both parties acted violently, one of the parties was injured (Buzawa & Hotaling, 2000).

A fundamental question is, when, if ever, is dual arrest appropriate? There is no easy answer to this question, particularly because there is no empirical data quantifying the extent to which some families have two violent partners, and sometimes violent children (M. Johnson, 1995, 2000; Straus, 1999). In 2007, findings from a large-scale national study on dual arrest were released.

The researchers reported that dual-arrest rates are higher in mandatory arrest states compared with preferred or presumptive arrest rates and that "discretionary arrest" states have the lowest dual arrest rates. In addition, there were no significant differences in dual-arrest practices between males and females in heterosexual intimate partner violence. The significant differences in dual-arrest rates for same-sex intimate partner relationships were surprising, where the odds of a dual arrest were ten times greater than in a heterosexual intimate partner relationship (Hirschel et al., 2007).

Is a Uniform Arrest Policy Justified in the Context of the Diversity of Victim Needs?

It is clear that the primary goal of all domestic violence legislation is to prevent subsequent violence. Will the implementation of mandatory arrest practices, however, disempower victims and possibly work against their best interests? In many cases, the goals of assisting and empowering domestic violence victims is not as straightforward as in other criminal contexts. Even among violent crimes, victims of domestic violence might differ from other victims if only based on their intimate knowledge of the offender and the relationship.

Victim Preferences

The previous discussion did not intend to suggest that victims do not want police intervention; most victims do. Victims might want police intervention without necessarily wanting an arrest. One study found that victims consistently wanted the police to respond to incidents, even if arrest was not always desired. More than 84% of all assault victims wanted a police response, with no real difference between domestic assaults (83%) compared with non-domestic assaults (88%). A follow-up question asking the victim's first choice for who should handle the incident (e.g., the police, themselves, medical or counseling personnel, family neighbors, or family members) found that, for both domestic and non-domestic assault cases, more than two thirds (67% and 68%, respectively) wanted the police to handle assaults (Hotaling & Buzawa, 2001).

Interesting data were uncovered in terms of the primary action that the victim wanted the police to take. Choices given were "arrest," "control the offender," "do nothing," or "do not know." The overall result showed that 47% wanted an arrest, 39% wanted control, 9% wanted to do nothing, and 5% did not know; however, this result conceals data that reveal a major difference in the two populations. In domestic assault cases, only 33% wanted an arrest made compared with 52% who wanted the offender controlled but not arrested. In non–domestic assault cases, 76% wanted the offender arrested and only 12% wanted the offender controlled.

These data show, as reported in many other jurisdictions, that most victims of domestic assault do not prefer arrest as their first option. Given the current policy preferences for domestic violence arrests, data also show that police refuse to follow the victim's request more frequently in domestic assault cases (25%) than in non–domestic assault cases (4%).

Not surprisingly, the victim disagreed with arrests made in 60% of domestic assaults compared with only 12% of non-domestic assaults; situations in which the suspect was not arrested but the victim disagreed occurred in 4% of domestic assaults and in 44% in non-domestic assaults. Clearly, the police in the jurisdictions studied determined the need for arrest independently of victim preferences in cases of domestic assault.

In contrast, the areas of agreement in which the suspect was arrested and the victim agreed with the arrest were less (29%) for domestic and more (36%) for non-domestic assaults or when the suspect was not arrested and the victim agreed (8% in both domestic and non-domestic assaults).

Mandatory arrest statutes or policies might, therefore, lead to adverse consequences in which victims are, at least, disempowered and, at worst, deterred from calling the police in the future because unwanted arrests are made. These data strongly suggest there might be significant numbers of domestic assault cases in which the offender was arrested and the victim disagreed, dramatically increasing the potential of adverse impact on the victim.

Does Failure to Follow Victim Arrest Preferences Deter Future Reporting?

In the previously reported study, 62% of victims said they would report future crimes, 12% said they would probably call the police, and 27% said they definitely would not report future crimes.

Findings about the willingness of victims to report a subsequent incident also were observed by Apsler, Cummins, and Carl (2003), who reported that 80% of victims interviewed in a Boston suburb would report a future incident, regardless of whether their initial preference for arrest was followed. Similarly, a study in Toronto reported that 76% of women surveyed would report a future incident (Lanthier, 2008).

An analysis of NCVS data from 1992 to 2002 was less optimistic in its findings of actual victim reporting. Felson, Ackerman, and Gallagher (2005) reported that although 17% of victims were reassaulted, only 56.5% were reported to police, and these cases included incidents reported by witnesses as well as by victims.

More recent research suggests that the dismissal of victim preferences might be to discourage the future use of the system both by victims who wanted the system to do *more* (those who wanted more severe criminal charges brought against the offender) as well as by those who wanted it to do *less* (those who felt taking the case forward would decrease their safety) (Buzawa et al., 2006). Based on official records, only 22.1% of victims in this sample were revictimized. By comparison, the results of victim interviews indicated that more than 49.2% were revictimized. If prevention of revictimization is the goal of policymakers, then this finding suggests that new strategies must be developed simultaneously in two areas: (1) New methods need to be used to persuade victims to report subsequent victimizations to police, and (2) new strategies need to be developed that make the identification of subsequent revictimization a community concern rather than a problem of victim notification. In terms of this latter point, it certainly seems possible that the strategies employed vis-à-vis the federal government's reentry partnership initiatives (see, e.g., Taxman, Young, & Byrne, 2003) could be applied directly to the problem of domestic violence. Specifically, one avenue to explore is the use of local community police agents, in conjunction with the courts and corrections system, as part of a proactive, system-wide revictimization detection strategy. This strategy would allow the police to respond proactively to the problem of potential revictimization by identifying offenders of domestic violence, talking directly with offenders about the implications of reoffending on their liberty and lifestyle prior to sentencing, and then directly monitoring offender behavior toward the victim in particular and the community in general. By redefining domestic violence as a *community* problem, the new domestic violence partnership would effectively take the primary responsibility to detect and report revictimization out of the hands of the victim, thereby reducing the potential control of the offender over the victim.

Given the empirical evidence regarding prior substance abuse and/or criminal histories of these offenders (including the serial domestic abuser subgroup members who seem to continue their abuse with new partners), it certainly makes sense to view this group of offenders as a potential continued threat to the community.

The Limitations of Police Response to Stalking

Antistalking legislation, beginning with the 1990 California antistalking statute, has now been enacted in every state. The proper police response to stalking is, however, even more difficult to determine than in cases of domestic assault. The issue posed here is typically not simply whether to make an arrest but what constitutes an offense for which an arrest might be made. The actual effect of an arrest on a stalker's propensity to continue stalking as opposed to other possible law enforcement actions has not, to the best of our knowledge, been examined empirically to date. Unless stalking occurs as part of an overall mixed pattern of violence, harassment, and threats, stalking might simply be a precursor offense to other, more traditional criminal activity. As such, although there are now criminal statutes on the books, realistically it is difficult to expect police to arrest someone for what might initially be perceived as random or relatively minor occurrences. In some states, it might be impossible to make arrests because of statutory restrictions that allow arrest only for cases of actual threats. Unfortunately, we know that subsequent violence cannot be predicted easily based on the specific harassment activity.

In such cases, the only realistic police intervention strategy might be to support stalking victims by helping them seek and enforce restraining orders, the violation of which can justify an arrest. The responding officer should assist a stalking victim in developing sustainable evidence of such behavior. For example, the victim's first impulse might be to remove or destroy obscene messages from the stalker. As stated by J. Reid Meloy (1997), who is a noted forensic psychologist,

> [i]n all cases of relational intrusion, both before and after the behavior has passed the threshold of criminal stalking, the victim should thoroughly document each incident (date, time, place, and event) in a daily log, and keep any tangible proof of its occurrence. This may include but is not limited to, photos, audio tapes, videotapes, letters, notes, facsimile transmissions, printing of e-mail messages, unwanted gifts, and suspicious, inappropriate, or frightening items (one perpetrator scratched the name of his victim on a

bullet cartridge and mailed it to her). Evidence such as this establishes a course of conduct in stalking cases and may be central to convincing the trier of fact that the victim was in reasonable fear. (pp. 176–177)

Activity of this nature would need to be coordinated closely between a specific police officer knowledgeable about the circumstances (who has investigated the prior criminal activity of the alleged perpetrator) and a prosecutor willing to maintain a case despite lack of physical violence. In addition, either that officer or other crime prevention officers should assist the victim in target hardening as well as in documenting any incident. The types of such evidence might be extremely varied.

Variations Between Police Departments

We can safely state that research on the actual response of the criminal justice system to domestic assault shows highly inconsistent results; this is illustrated dramatically by Hirschel et al. (2007) when examining arrest patterns among jurisdictions in 19 states using NIBRS data. It does seem that the implementation of mandatory domestic violence arrest statutes has resulted in the highest overall arrest rates for both domestic and non-domestic assaults. "Preferred arrest" states have had the next highest arrest rate, followed by discretionary arrest rates. Thus, it seems that legislation *has* had an impact.

However, what is puzzling is the extreme range of arrests within these states. Diverse findings among studies regarding factors affecting the decision to arrest are to be expected. The conclusion to be drawn might simply be that these observed variations are real; no one set of variables works as a constant among all departments (Buzawa & Hotaling, 2003; Buzawa et al., 1999, 2006; Hirschel et al., 2007).

How Police Street-Level Behavior Has Changed as a Result of Pro-Arrest Legislation

The reality of how police organizations actually respond to pro-arrest statutes and policy directives remains problematic and, at times, unpredictable. We will explore the extent to which actual change has occurred in arrest practices in street-level behavior of law enforcement. The process of implementing organizational change rarely received adequate attention from policymakers. As a result, a pattern of state-mandated changes in law enforcement practices has been decoupled from the administrative detail sufficient to ensure actual change. A failure to focus critically on strategies to implement change effectively results in inadequate or even simplistic solutions. The result might be that policies fail to change actual practices or street-level behavior.

Alternatively, policies might become so transformed in practice that the problem not only remains but also creates new problems (e.g., the phenomenon of "dual arrests" described subsequently in this chapter). Because administrative or legal pronouncements and statutory changes do not automatically translate into effective operational behavior, this section concentrates not only on the mandate of changes but also on an assessment, even if preliminary, of the impact of such mandates on actual service delivery. What do we know about implementation issues in this area? Researchers have long been aware of the difficulties in successfully implementing politically mandated changes on "independent" agencies (Bardach, 1977). Since the 1970s, concerns have been raised that bureaucratic institutions might transform policy mandates with their own standard operating procedures and their own mechanisms for rewarding and punishing behavior (Salamon & Wamsley, 1975). There is a recognition that bureaucratic discretion coexists with the exercise of political control (Ringquist, 1995) and even a frank admission that we often do not know about the determinants of political control, or even at times the causal mechanisms of control (Wood & Waterman 1991, 1994). As a result, there is a wide variety of responsiveness depending on the type of agency and the type of directive involved (Gruber, 1987; Moe, 1987).

Such issues are, in turn, compounded by the structure and traditions of the criminal justice system. Police departments, despite their reputation as paramilitary "command and control" bureaucracies, are known to be remarkably resistant to change. This is partially because of the inability of command officers to observe officer behavior directly, the ingrained "respect" and deference for officer discretion from commanders who were former line officers, and the training systems for which formal academic instruction is limited and in-service training often nonexistent. Rookie officers and more experienced officers who often are resistant to change coupled with strong police unions contribute to difficulties in implementing change. Such structural bases for resistance to change often are supplemented and reinforced by a widely recognized feature of the police culture: a highly insular and self-reinforcing organization in which both civilians in general and civilian control over police practices in particular are regarded suspiciously and perhaps with cynicism or simply are dismissed with outright derision (Crank, 1998; Manning, 1997).

Most police departments we have studied over recent years now have adopted detailed policies about handling a maze of subjects; now, these policies typically include domestic violence (sometimes to an excruciating level). They "read well" in that they express institutional commitment to politically correct policies and administrative control. To some extent, the reality of policing is different than these policies suggest. After all, policies might be written in part to insulate the department from legal liability rather than to express a genuine concern for policy adherence. At times, absolute compliance might not be expected or even desired by department leadership. This makes street-level implementation of any legislation or policy directives problematic at best and, to us, focuses attention on the methods used to facilitate actual behavioral changes.

Do Organizational Policies Mediate the Impact of Mandatory and Presumptive Arrest Statutes?

Policy manuals: Don't bother. If they're general, they're useless. If they're specific, they're how to manuals expensive to prepare and revise. . . . The only people who read policy manuals are goldbricks and martinets. The goldbricks memorize them so they can say (1) "That's not in this department," or (2) "Its against company policy." The martinets use policy manuals to confine, frustrate, punish and eventually drive out of the organization every imaginative, creative, adventuresome woman and man. If you have *to have a policy manual, publish the* Ten Commandments.

Source: Townsend & Bennis, 2007, p. 98.

Although sometimes we are equally frustrated by rigid policies, we do recognize that in practice they are invaluable, both to exert organizational control and to demonstrate what issues are most salient to command officials. In the case of policing domestic violence, policies can be a barometer of the organizational commitment to statutory requirements. They represent a formalization of the organization's expected conduct and reduce variability among individuals by limiting their discretion and proscribing a uniform organizational response (Hall, 1991). In fact, the National Research Council emphasized the significance of policies to formalize restrictions on officer discretion. They also observed that there was evidence to support the importance and efficacy of policies to affect line behavior (Skogan & Frydl, 2004).

No one expects that domestic violence can, or even should be, equal. The reality is that more than 16,000 local and state law enforcement agencies exist in the United States and that approximately half employ less than 10 officers (Reaves, 2007). For example, a policy in New York City requiring a two-officer response and/or immediate access to victims' services is likely to be unrealistic in a rural area. Many states have included model policies as part of their legislation that all jurisdictions are expected to follow. It is likely that agencies need to tailor these policies for the reasons stated previously even though it is broadly expected that policies are developed in accordance with existing or new statutory mandates. In general, it would be anticipated that departments in states with mandatory arrest statutes provide less discretion in their policies compared with departments in states with presumptive or discretionary arrest statutes.

Nonetheless, police administrators retain considerable discretion in their decisions regarding the development of domestic violence policies. Although many police administrators try to respond aggressively in preparing detailed policies, others display lower levels of commitment at monitoring their implementation. Consequently, administrators might provide an unstated message regarding the relative importance of statutory mandates, which might serve to provide tacit approval for the continued use of officer discretion and practices for nonarrest in cases of domestic assault.

Once a domestic violence policy is developed, several factors determine their impact. First, there is a need for regular policy revisions and updates in response to continuous statutory changes. This change is not driven simply by new improved methods of policing now being advocated by administrators. A review of state domestic violence statutes reveals that the volume of new statutes and statutory revisions continues to grow. Miller (2005) reported that more than 1,500 new domestic violence statutes have been passed since 1994. The extent to which police policies promptly reflect these changes is unknown.

Second, departments need to develop effective strategies for their dissemination (Buzawa, 1982; Buzawa & Austin, 1988; Miller, 2005). The significance of their dissemination might be enhanced or, alternatively, minimized and marginalized through both preservice and in-service training programs (Buzawa, 1982).

Third, supervision seems to be a critical variable in identifying the failure of police to comply with policy mandates (Rothwell & Baldwin, 2007). Street-level practices historically demonstrate a pattern of line officers subverting policies that are not supported by the rank and file. These practices include call screening and officer downgrading or redefining calls to not require immediate assistance in the hope that such delays would allow the situation to "resolve itself" (Buzawa, 1982; Manning, 1997). In fact, supervision practices (e.g., management reinforcing abstract policies) have been reported as the only significant predictor related to the frequency of reporting for minor conduct violations by police officers (Rothwell & Baldwin, 2007).

Fourth, patrol officers often consider policies to be abstract and unrealistic and unable to solve the types of concrete problems they confront (Dixon, 1997; Manning, 1997). Therefore, it is important that policies focus on responses at the patrol officer level. In this case, policies often are written by attorneys and are not really targeted to the audience for which they are ostensibly written. It can be argued that their primary purpose might be to protect the jurisdiction from liability. In the case of domestic violence policies, they are typically written by the City Attorney or State Attorney General's Office. It has sometimes been argued, perhaps somewhat facetiously, that policies are written "by attorneys, for attorneys."

Research suggests that a large percentage of, if not most, jurisdictions have some type of domestic violence policy in place that conforms with statutory mandates (Hirschel et al., 2007). In addition, the trend in jurisdictions in states with discretionary arrest statutes seems to be the implementation of more restrictive policies than otherwise mandated by state statute.

Impact of Policies

These policies matter. One study examining domestic violence policies for the year 2000 reported that only 28% of jurisdictions in discretionary arrest states reported a policy allowing an officer's discretion in their arrest decision (Hirschel et al., 2007).

Eitle (2005) examined the impact of mandatory arrest policies on the probability of arrest across 115 cities and reported that cities with mandatory arrest policies even in the absence of statutory requirements experienced higher arrest rates in domestic violence incidents than those without mandatory arrest. This finding was true even when organizational variables (i.e., formalization of policies, organizational size, and education level) and incident characteristics were controlled (Eitle, 2005).

Little attention has been focused on organizational commitment to change and what structural changes are made to ensure compliance.

Unfortunately, many police departments still have minimal domestic violence policies, despite state legislative requirements. Although many police administrators try to respond aggressively to this problem, others display varying levels of commitment to domestic violence through their efforts at monitoring policy implementation.

Some administrators simply file these policies in their office. Others distribute the policies at rapid-fire roll calls. Still others discuss them in detail at roll call. Finally, there are departments that mandate a strong effort to ensure that all officers receive in-service training both on the new policy and on their role in intervention.

The impact of policies also depends on what happens to them after they are published. For example, researchers worked with several departments to develop a common domestic violence incident report form. One department was successful in having all officers complete these reports, another was somewhat successful, and a third was totally unsuccessful. The difference is that the department that succeeded in gaining compliance simply designated a sergeant to review all officer reports and ensure that the supplementary form for every domestic assault was included. The sergeant took the needed time to provide constructive feedback to officers and to require officers to provide additional needed information where needed and where appropriate, including the rationale for failure to arrest (Buzawa & Hotaling, 2003).

Differences in observed arrest practices might largely reflect different implementation strategies. From these data, we can conclude that although changes might occur after initiation of new policies, these might be inconsistent among departments and do not always comply with the "ideal" contemplated arrest profile.

Such factors lead us to dismiss, or at least seriously question, the "global" conclusions of researchers either who try to generalize results from a limited number of departments or who rely on aggregate data from many departments—or national data—that mask major departmental variations. Obviously, many departments have recently instituted pro-arrest policies, which have the potential to predict officer behavior more accurately; however, past circumstances suggest that new policies might not override an organization's past practices and culture. These departmental differences might be based on organizational attributes or possibly on the general orientation of the department toward calls for assistance and the community in which it operates. Although little empirical research is available in the context of departmental responses to domestic violence, several researchers have differentiated between "service" and law enforcement–oriented agencies.

The Importance of Training

Training is a primary vehicle for reinforcing existing and planned practices reflective of the goals of an organization's leadership. In the context of policing, training becomes decisive because the methods and practices of police training have historically been instrumental in either implementing change or, conversely, thwarting implementation of new progressive policies. Manning and Van Maanen (1978) discussed the overriding importance of the academy in the police socialization process in which police occupational perspectives are transferred to new recruits and the course content is presented in such a way as to ensure its continuance.

Before conferring arrest powers, police departments rely on an extensive routinized training program of at least 8 weeks to impart basic knowledge of substantive criminal law, criminal procedure, and departmental regulations to recruits. Even after the formal training program, officers maintain "rookie" or probationary status. In most departments, rookies are assigned to experienced patrol officers until they are considered sufficiently familiar with required tasks and departmental practices. The failure to provide police training might greatly contribute to the likelihood of diverse practices that either enforce or even sabotage policies that ostensibly favor arrest. Often, especially in smaller or more rural jurisdictions, this is simply a function of resources, either for the agencies to develop and provide their own training, or to spare the time needed for personnel to attend outside training. Whatever the reason, the lack of training increases the likelihood of a more varied response to legislative or policy mandates for arrest (Sudderth, 2006; Van Hightower & Gorton, 2002).

Before we explore the impact of more current policies, we need to understand how training affected past practices. For a variety of reasons, classic police training programs made the response to domestic violence less effective. In the past, every component of the training process—time allocation, instructor selection, content, and in-service traineeship—tended to reinforce existing negative stereotypes against domestic violence cases. Harris (1973) observed that in classic police academies, great emphasis was placed on the "ethic of masculinity" and on the development of the officer's identity as "first and foremost . . . a man" (p. 291).

Before the 1960s, typically there was little or no specific training on domestic violence. In the 1960s and, in some departments for years thereafter, officers were instructed simply to quiet tense situations, advise on social welfare agencies that might provide assistance, and quickly extricate themselves (Bard, 1970; Berk & Loseke, 1980–1981; Loving, 1980).

In the late 1970s, when assisting the Detroit Police Department in the development of a new training program, one author of this book (Buzawa, 1978) conducted a nationwide review of existing domestic violence programs. At that time, in virtually all police training programs, the training component related to domestic violence was perfunctory and typically composed of a single, 4- to 8-hour lecture segment under the general rubric of handling "disturbed persons." The content was not restricted to, nor did it even necessarily address, the topic of domestic assault. Instead, it included proper techniques for handling hostage situations, potential suicides, mentally disturbed individuals, violent alcoholics and addicts, as well as child abuse, with brief mention of domestic disturbance calls. To the extent that they were addressed as a separate topic, domestic calls were explained to the recruits as a largely unproductive use of time, ineffective in resolving a family problem, and potentially dangerous for the responding officer. Recruits were told that the desired outcome was to restore peace and maintain control as a vehicle of restoring the public order and self-protection. Arrests were actively discouraged as a waste of time. The only exception was if disrespect or threats by an offender or victim indicated that the officer might lose situational control. Recruits were trained that arrest, therefore, was primarily to assert authority rather than to respond to prior criminal action.

In the past, departmental choice of training staff did not usually result in interested or qualified instructors in the field of domestic violence. Except for those relatively few larger departments with dedicated permanent training sections, police academies traditionally used senior line personnel. Frequently, the basis for their selection was "temporary disability" or other special duty restrictions, such as having been involved in a prior shooting or other incident requiring a departmental investigation prior to being placed back on active duty. These instructors had little interest in training itself, generally lacked instructional background, and had little substantive expertise or affinity for the topic of domestic violence.

As a result, it is not surprising that the primary mode of instruction was an explanation of official policies of nonintervention accompanied by colorful (if not totally accurate) stories about their own personal experiences. Few, if any, training materials or multimedia aids were available or used, and outside expertise was rarely sought. Formal in-service training in this area was rare before the early 1980s. During the initial entry period, a recruit relied on the perceptions of relevant teachers such as experienced officers to develop his or her own views toward proper organizational practices and objectives. The trainee, after all, had few relevant experiences to guide his or her behavior during the often-frightening immersion into the reality of policing (Van Maanen, 1975). The field training process, in which the rookie was assigned to learn under the direction of an experienced officer, usually reinforced prejudices against domestic violence cases. In fact, this experience often served to undermine an academy's instruction in those few cases in which the academy might have attempted to promote a more activist police response (Van Maanen, 1973). For these reasons, it was acknowledged by both senior police officials (Bannon, 1974) and researchers (Loving & Quirk, 1982) that traditional police training failed to provide police officers with any rudimentary skills required for successful domestic violence intervention. In one study based on research conducted in the mid-1980s, 50% of the officers in a department were not even aware of the elements of probable cause for domestic violence assault (Ford, 1987). As Bannon (1974) observed, "the real reason that police avoid domestic violence situations to the greatest extent possible is because they do not know how to cope with them" (p. 4).

Until recently, police training programs have reinforced prevailing occupational ideology toward domestic violence. The net effect of such a training process was to enhance the likelihood that officers would attempt either to avoid a response or to complete domestic violence calls as quickly as possible to devote energy to the more "appropriate" police work. In summary, the training process in the 1970s and the 1980s was a largely unrecognized factor that impeded the implementation of actual change even when "officially" desired by departmental leadership.

Domestic violence legislation has provided a major impetus for many states to improve their police preservice and in-service domestic violence training. As of December 2005, 32 states and the District of Columbia mandated preservice training, and 21 of these states defined the minimum required content to be included (Miller, 2005). However, only 8 states mandate in-service police training as a component that has been attributed to the failure to stipulate in-service police training requirements in general (Miller, 2005).

Current Training

As noted by Miller in 2005, legislation has greatly changed the landscape of police training. Many departments, either through their own initiative or following training curricula recommended by organizations such as the International Association of Chiefs of Police (IACP), have transformed training from a factor blocking arrests to one that supports stated pro-arrest objectives. In this regard, these organizations have been leaders in trying to institute change. Their most recent policy on domestic violence written in 2006 is exceptionally detailed, describing issues such as the proper role of police, making referrals to appropriate agencies, promoting officer safety, and providing for extra training for command officials. As such, the IACP assumes that departments will commit considerable department resources.

Aspects of this type of comprehensive training include emphasizing the role of domestic violence intervention by police, arrests in the context of domestic violence strategy, and training that focuses not only on the law but also on attitudinal change. Innovative teaching methods such as role playing, especially of instances in which the officer is placed in an unusual position (acting as the victim or the offender), also might prove beneficial (Malefyt, Little, & Walker, 1998).

It would be wrong, however, to assume that training has been transformed uniformly to support aggressive police intervention.

In most departments, basic training time has not increased. Officer candidates still spend an overwhelming, perhaps inordinate, amount of time on physical fitness and firearms techniques (Eigenberg, 2001). In sharp contrast, the amount of time devoted to domestic violence varies considerably from 2 to 30 hours, with an average of 10 hours. Similarly, the ability of training to be relevant to specific organizations and their communities and the trainer's skill at influencing officer attitudes and behavior through such training has a critical impact.

Nonetheless, progress is occurring and 29 states now mandate extensive domestic violence training, with 21 of these actually setting forth minimum training standards that simply could not be covered in the allocated time (N. Miller, 1997). Therefore, a critical question to be addressed is whether the training content of the program is determined by statute or departmental policies, and who delivers the training.

In addition to mandating the quality of domestic violence training to get maximum impact, all officers need to be aware of and trained on their agency policy as well as state statute. In some jurisdictions, in-service domestic violence training, which provides updates to police officers on best practices and legislative updates, are provided only to those officers in a specialized domestic violence unit. As a result, much of the relevant information is not provided to patrol officers that might critically impact the initial police response and how the incident report is written. On a somewhat anecdotal basis, as part of a class project for one of the authors, a police officer gathered information on the domestic violence training provided to his unit and the prosecutor's office. He reported how helpful the class assignment was because neither he, nor his peers, had received any information on how to identify a primary aggressor, despite the existence of a primary aggressor statute intended to limit dual arrests. Thus, although a simple statement in their policy mandated this, officers simply did not know how this was done.

The impact of inadequate training for the rank and file resonates throughout the entire system. Typically, only reports for those incidents identified as domestic violence must be reported to the domestic violence unit. According to one study based on observations of reports in several Massachusetts police agencies, between 40% and 50% of reported domestic incidents involved domestic assaults but were never characterized as an assault and, therefore, never were processed further within the entire criminal justice system (Buzawa & Hotaling, 2007). What is included in those cases not forwarded might be situations in which the officer did not or could not identify a primary aggressor, lacked probable cause, or simply preferred the "old" way of setting such incidents informally.

Equally problematic is the continuing reliance on "unofficial training" that rookies have with experienced officers. To date, we are not aware of any official training programs in the country that rotate new officers to specific tours of duty with experience in handling domestic crises. Instead, the typical pattern is a rotation with an experienced patrol officer who might be a good role model in general but might or might not be particularly responsive to domestic violence incidents or be trained to import such skills to new recruits.

In-service police training is equally problematic. In-service domestic violence training is now routine in many departments and in fact is mandated under some state domestic violence statutes; however, the extent and quality of such training varies enormously from a brief roll call or video (not effective) to a much more formal, and far more likely to be effective, departmental or offsite training program (Gaines, Kappeler, & Vaughn, 1999).

Because such programs cost considerable funds in the form of overtime for other officers to replace those receiving training, there are strong organizational disincentives for departments to allocate resources for these purposes (see Eigenberg, 2001, pp. 277–281, for a review of why training continues to have a problematic impact). As a result, the uneven status of training might explain a great deal of the variation in arrest practices among departments, despite the fact that approximately 30 years have passed since pro-arrest policies were widely adopted and publicized.

SUMMARY

A dramatic increase in the number of states mandating arrest in cases of domestic violence has occurred, and still more departments require it by policy. However, mandating arrest remains controversial, and despite its intent to ensure consistent application of laws, as can be observed by the foregoing discussion, there is still considerable variation in the arrest decision. A variety of victim, offender, incident, and organizational factors still play a major role; however, the relative importance played by each set of variables varies within and between jurisdictions. This suggests that differences are not simply the result of legislative variations between the states. We know that departmental policies, training, and supervision all play critical roles in determining the police response to domestic violence.

In addition, we now realize that there is no "right" answer. What might be in a victim's interests might not coincide with societal interests. A victim who leaves an abuser might find that an arrest results in unnecessary costs, including potential financial support from the abuser. Conversely, it is in society's interests to identify an offender so that he or she is known to the criminal justice system and potential new victims. Thus, when these interests are in conflict, the dilemma remains. As we will discuss in Chapter 13, new initiatives including restorative justice approaches, are attempting to address this for some victims.

DISCUSSION QUESTIONS

1. What is your opinion of the following case in light of mandatory arrest statutes? Could this case have been handled better under such statutes, or is this the inevitable consequences of mandating arrest?

   In the *Shelbyville Times-Gazette* on June 24, 2009, a story by Brian Mosely described the arrest of a couple in that community for domestic assault with the alleged weapon being Cheetos.

James Earl Taylor, 40, and Mary S. Childers, 44, allegedly were involved in an argument, and according to Cpl. Kevin Roddy's report, the pair became "involved in a verbal altercation" with each other "at which time Cheetos potato chips were used in the assault."

"There was evidence of the assault," the report read, "however no physical marks on either party and the primary aggressor was unable to be determined."

Both parties were charged with domestic assault.

Source: Mosely, 2009, para. 3 & 4.

Are there logical, less intrusive alternatives to arrest for many situations?

2. Does the willingness of victims to report incidents and cooperate in subsequent activities crucially depend on police responding to their "real" preferences and needs? In other words, are victims going to be less likely to call for help and are police going to become increasingly frustrated with "uncooperative" or "ungrateful" victims?

3. Will police actually respond in the mandated manner?

4. Are agency costs for arrest in jurisdictions where it has actually been implemented and the implicit reallocation of existing resources ever truly subjected to any sort of rigorous cost/benefit analysis?

5. Whose interests should the criminal justice system consider in the decision to arrest if societal goals for intervention conflict with victim preferences and/or needs?

The Role of State and Federal Legislation 9

Chapter Overview

Waves of unprecedented statutory changes that began in the 1970s have altered the official response to domestic violence. This chapter will explore how such legislation has markedly changed the official approach toward intervention.

Although there is considerable variation in the scope and limitations of domestic violence statutes, they strive to make profound structural change in the response of government agencies. Such changes have primarily been concentrated in three areas: (1) the police response to domestic violence, (2) the handling of cases by prosecutors and the judiciary, and (3) the increased availability and enforcement of civil restraining orders. Statutory mandates, both at the state level and through the enactment and reauthorizations of the federal Violence Against Women Act, also have made distinct contributions and have led to dramatically increased funding for shelters and other assistance for victims.

Domestic Violence–Related Laws

Early Changes in Laws

As we noted in our summary of the history of intervention, there were few legislative mandates addressing domestic violence until the last quarter of the 20th century. Nearly unprecedented change commenced with the 1977 enactment of Pennsylvania's landmark Protection from Abuse Act. Since then, every state has adopted reforms.

These statutes, especially in their earliest forms, were not uniform and often contained significant exceptions or limitations. Furthermore, they rarely allocated funding or other resources needed to ensure that organizational change really occurred. Despite such limitations, these statutes collectively began to provide the first comprehensive legislative framework to build reforms.

A complete review of all of the substantive provisions of reform legislation would be far beyond the scope of this effort. For those interested, in December 2005, Neil Miller of the Institute for Law and Justice wrote an excellent compilation of such provisions enacted as of that time. His compendium, which has been updated at 5-year intervals, demonstrates the diversity of statutes current at that time along with cogent suggestions for continued reform.

This chapter will focus on several key reforms: the removal of warrantless arrest barriers, the expansion of substantive grounds for arrest, the enactment of comprehensive domestic violence criminal codes, and the limits on official discretion.

Statutory Removal of Procedural Barriers to Arrest

Procedural impediments to the use of arrests have been largely eliminated. As discussed in Chapter 3, before the late 1970s, most states followed English common law that required an officer to witness a misdemeanor before making a warrantless arrest. Because most acts of domestic violence are classified as simple assault and battery, which is a misdemeanor, this posed a key limitation. If the act was not repeated in the presence of the officer, no arrest could be made, and thus, a victim had to initiate and sign a criminal complaint separately—an action rarely undertaken by domestic violence victims or enforced by arrest. Alternatively, the police might be forced to arrest for a general purpose, non–domestic violence charge such as disorderly conduct or public intoxication. These charges, however, rarely connoted the existence of a serious assault. Consequently, they would usually be "flushed" from the system with regularity.

This practice was in sharp contrast to the ability of an officer to arrest without a warrant on finding probable cause that a felony had occurred. Furthermore, in cases of non-domestic assaults, witnesses would more typically provide police with the standard of probable cause required for police to make an arrest.

By the mid-1980s, the first wave of statutory enactments had eliminated most of these statutory restrictions. In fact, even by 1992, 47 states and the District of Columbia had already enacted statutes authorizing arrest in such cases. Now every state does. Thus, enacting this provision alone was initially expected to result in a significant increase in arrests for domestic assault.

Expansion of the Grounds for Arrest to Include Violations of Protective Orders

At the same time that the procedural restrictions were swept away, the first domestic violence statutes often incorporated other changes to allow greater use of arrests. Civil protective and temporary restraining orders were soon authorized in all 50 states for prior restraint on possible assailants.

Of particular importance to the police, such statutes either initially or through later amendment expressly provide for enforcement of a protective order by warrantless arrest. In effect, their enforcement was thereby "criminalized" even if no substantive crime was recognized. This was in sharp departure to the older style "peace bonds," in which conduct might have been prohibited by a magistrate but enforcement was via simple civil forfeiture of the bond—a rather cumbersome and rarely used process.

This reform had considerable potential importance. Police previously operated with extraordinary caution, often refusing to find probable cause for an arrest for a misdemeanor assault. In contrast, the temporary restraining order, or more permanent "protective order," typically restrained any contact between the suspect and the person under protection, giving police a far more flexible vehicle to find probable cause to make warrantless arrests. The existence and violation of the orders also was much easier to prove in court. Finally, police failures to enforce a known protective order led to numerous lawsuits on a variety of constitutional grounds contesting previously passive police responses.

The Creation of Domestic Violence–Specific Crimes

Another major change has been enactment of substantive changes to states' criminal laws. Currently, all states have enacted statutes creating a separate criminal offense for domestic or family violence. At first glance, explicit domestic violence laws may appear superfluous. After all, every state has a lengthy legal history prohibiting assault and battery since their adoption of English common law.

There are, however, several key advantages to a statute specific to domestic violence. These statutes direct law enforcement to types of crimes more common with domestic violence, not the specific requirements of common law assault and battery. Through various amendments during the past 15 years, coercive behavior such as harassment, intentional infliction of emotional distress, or threats other than the threat of assault that were not technically either assaults or batteries could be prosecuted.

Also the existence of one centralized statute that addressed most types of domestic abuse as well as traditional violent assaults could in theory focus law enforcement attention. This happened both because police officers had an enhanced knowledge of the new domestic violence legislation and, somewhat cynically, because they now recognized increased exposure to civil liability for a knowing failure to enforce a specific criminal statute.

Fourth, the earlier statutes that had simply allowed warrantless misdemeanor arrests often contained major procedural limitations. For example, often there were strict limits on the time between the event and the arrest, requirements of visible injury, or both. The creation of express domestic violence statutes freed the police from such unnecessary restrictions. Similarly, because a domestic violence assault violation was more specific, it was assumed that the legislative intent to mete out punishment appropriate to the crime would influence courts as they imposed sentences. Although difficult to monitor, it was certainly hoped that innovative sentences such as including injunction-type conditions, threatening deferred prosecution, and forcing assignment of a batterer to counseling programs would become the norm. Although these sentences were available in the past and might be undertaken at the initiative of an individual judge, they were not always intuitively obvious because sentencing judges typically only rapidly reviewed a plea bargain on a generalized assault charge.

Finally, most such state statutes now require their agencies to retain accurate records of the occurrence of domestic violence and resultant case dispositions. When such cases were aggregated into the generic category of "assault and battery," it was difficult to determine accurately whether domestic abuse cases were prosecuted with the same vigor as other assaults.

Although such statutes clearly have great potential for widespread impact, evidence of the extent of inspired change is more problematic. Initially, this was a result of a series of constitutional challenges to such sweeping new laws. The U.S. Commission on Civil Rights (1978) stated, at that time, that many judges were questioning the constitutionality of such statutes on the grounds that they created unwarranted and major protected classes largely based on claimed impermissible distinctions of gender or marital status.

In addition, the efficacy of these earlier statutes was limited because they were initially a patchwork of widely dissimilar laws, contained major gaps, and lacked coherence. In 1991, after reviewing the new statutes in all 50 states, one commentator concluded that their impact had been severely eroded primarily because "elements of a well thought out program are missing (perhaps) due to haste in drafting, lack of adequate resources for legislative research, or perhaps out of legislative reluctance" (Zalman, 1991).

More Recent Statutory Amendments

The initial enactment of domestic violence legislation to a jurisdiction's criminal code was not the final product. In all states, the first spousal abuse or domestic violence act merely initiated a subsequent wave of related legislation designed to correct inadequacies of past laws or, as in the case of stalking legislation, address a previously unknown problem.

The impulse to pass new statutes has not abated. In our second edition (1996), we believed many, if not most, issues were already addressed. We discussed how many new innovations led to growing police, prosecutorial, as well as judicial powers and mandates.

What has continued to surprise us, and perhaps others, is that the volume of new statutes has not diminished, but increased, as of the writing of this fourth edition. Miller (2000) reported that 100 new laws had been passed regarding domestic violence in 2000, 160 in 1999, 64 in 1998, and 83 in 1997. In his December 2005 report, he noted the continued adoption of statutory amendments. Even after Miller's second compendium we continue to hear each year of new refinements to existing domestic violence laws.

Although research of such statutes would evidently be dated as of the publication of this book, broad trends of these later enactments can be identified. Typical measures are designed to amend the earlier reform statutes to make them more of a cornerstone for state intervention as opposed to simply one disjointed measure.

For example, new "gap limiting" statutes have eliminated (or severely limited) the "marital exemption" defense to charges of spousal rape. The issue of sexual assault of married parties had never been widely addressed in the past. Now there is a plethora of statutory amendments designed to allow evidence of a sexual crime against a wife under certain narrowly defined circumstances. Typically, the use of these statutes is still somewhat limited. There are strict reporting time limits for the prosecution of sexual assaults in a marital setting. Usually, they mandate evidence of the victim's past efforts to stop sexual relations, and/or the cessation of cohabitation. In another book, we will explain how such requirements may still be too restrictive.

These amendments also showed an awareness that the earlier domestic violence statutes often were poorly drafted and not well enforced. Thus, many legislatures tried to limit the ability of police, prosecutors, and magistrates from turning severe assaults against intimates into simple misdemeanors by providing various "aggravating" or "enhancing" aspects of an assault that would make such an assault a felony.

The list of these is broad but often states now include one or more of the following factors: use of a weapon in an attack, a certain degree of injury to the victim, the presence of children witnessing the crime, a second or third act of domestic violence, and another assault occurring within a certain time period like 72 hours of the first resulting in an enhanced prison sentence (Miller, 2005).

At this time, statutes mandating particular police practices have continued to be reenacted in many states. These continue to reflect continued concern over the actual services delivered to victims as opposed to merely being promised. Matters formerly left to officer discretion are increasingly becoming matters of statutory mandate. For example, many states have greatly increased reliance on mandatory arrests, at least for certain incidents, which we discussed in the previous chapter.

Also, mandated police behavior was by statute no longer confined to simply making an arrest. Instead, specific conduct of the officer often is addressed. This includes imposing requirements such as the following:

- Determining whether there is an existing restraining or protective order

- Providing transportation for the victim and her children and attention to any children present (this is now routine in most states)

- Arranging for social services

- So-called victim's rights laws requiring that police inform a victim of the right to demand an arrest and to obtain court protective orders and often to have shelters available to her

- Mandating not to release offenders prematurely who had been arrested for violation of a restraining order

- Developing and implementing written incident report forms identifying the alleged occurrence, the police response, and reasons for their actions if an arrest was not made (under the impetus of Violence Against Women Act [VAWA], requiring that such incident reports be filed and, even more significantly, mandating that if no arrest is made or if a dual arrest has occurred, reasons be stated explicitly)

- Requiring police to remove any dangerous weapons from the scene of a domestic assault

- Perhaps in the ultimate recognition of the inability to protect victims, a South Carolina statute now "authorizes" officers to take victims of domestic violence into protective custody if the officer believes the victim is in a life-threatening situation (SC S. 1287, 1994)

Legislative amendments now change the operation of courts and prosecutors' offices but have tended to be somewhat less coercive than laws directed toward the police, perhaps displaying greater deference to prosecutors and the separation of powers. Such changes include the following:

- Granting more authority for prosecutors to charge a domestic assault as a "felony" rather than as a misdemeanor

- Allowing courts to sanction uncooperative victims such as those who refuse to testify at subsequent trials. (For example, although limiting the grounds, California recognized the court's capability to find a victim in contempt of court for refusing to testify [CA A. 363, 1991]. Note, in response to an outcry by some battered women advocates, several years later, a less punitive provision was adopted, allowing the introduction of a victim's videotaped testimony at a preliminary hearing to be admitted into a trial, if otherwise admissible, thereby obviating the need for her further testimony [CA S. 178, 1993].)

- Prohibiting "mutual orders of protection"

- Giving the presumably more capable and sympathetic family court exclusive jurisdiction over cases involving any violations of domestic abuse orders [HI H. 2712, 1992]

- Adding provisions in the "victim rights" statutes mandating that prosecutors offer to meet with victims to discuss offender sentencing or before they are allowed to accept reduced charges

- Requiring prosecutors to have written policies on handling domestic violence cases

- Adopting compulsory "no-drop" statutes (discussed extensively in Chapter 8)

- Allowing judges to grant probation to a convicted abuser upon an express condition that requires their participation in a batterer treatment program

Many states have broadened the original scope and duration of ex parte and other protective orders. Some have extended their duration from the original 10-day "norm" up to a 1-year ex parte order if the respondent fails to appear at a hearing after notice is attempted. Similarly, enforcement of violations of court orders has been significantly boosted by enhancement of penalties associated with violation of these orders. In fact, as early as 2000 in 48 states, violation of an existing court order constituted a separate offense, which therefore means no underlying crime of domestic abuse need be proven (Miller, 2000). Adding teeth to this measure, a growing trend has been to make repeat violations of such restraining orders a felony.

Sentences for batterers also have been addressed in this round of legislative amendments. Not surprisingly, the measures have generally been designed to punish more severely rather than to accelerate rehabilitation. Some states now limit a batterer's access to diversionary programs. For example, California requires that defendants charged with misdemeanor domestic violence offenses not be eligible for existing diversionary programs unless the defendant has no conviction for any violent offense and has not been diverted under similar statutes within 10 years (CA A. 226, 1993). Michigan does not specify an express date, but limits by number the instances in which an alleged offender can have domestic charges dropped (MI H. 4308, 1994).

Non-criminal-code statutes affecting batterers also have been enacted. At times, these include preventing batterers from obtaining firearms or at least handgun licenses (which is consistent with VAWA, as we will discuss later).

In response to complaints of inadequate police training, the types and levels of training of agency personnel and comprehensive standards of conduct have been increasingly specified. Most states by statute now require some level of police training on domestic violence. In addition, a small minority now require in-service domestic violence training.

Finally, most states by statute now require local written policies and procedures. The impact of such policies may be great. They may force higher level administrators to prioritize resources and set forth the standards that they expect of their officers. Also such policies, if communicated widely, hopefully act to standardize police responses far more than when unfettered discretion was the norm. Finally, by providing a standard of care should a victim be injured or killed because the policy was not followed, there is a virtual "roadmap" for litigation against the police department or the responsible officer.

The diversity of the foregoing statutory changes prevents any easy generalization as to their cause and probable effect. In fact, as we more fully detail in the discussion on stalking statutes, the inability of states to establish a fixed legislative set of requirements regarding domestic violence may actually impede effective responses to crimes, at least in the short term, until some consistency between new rules, funding for new mandates, and new training requirements have been widely adopted within the states.

During the long term, we would expect this cascade of new legislation to diminish, and, after time has passed, it is hoped it will lead to greater organizational adherence to "best practices" regarding the control of domestic violence. Whether such behavioral changes occur because of actual attitudinal change as opposed to concerns with liability caused by failure to perform an explicit legislative function is subject to ongoing debate.

State Antistalking Legislation

Until he rapes me or kills me, the police can't do anything. When I'm a statistic of some kind, they'll put every man they have on it.

—From a victim of stalking

Initial Statutes

In many ways the sudden enactment of antistalking statutes in the 1990s has mirrored the rapid rise of domestic violence laws in the late 1970s to the 1980s. Before 1990, no state had explicit antistalking legislation. Instead, statutes generally addressed "criminal trespass" and "terrorist threats" and were very specific requiring a particular pattern of behavior. Hence, they were only occasionally used for domestic violence situations.

Common "harassment" statutes, of the type now on the books in virtually all states, considered stalking-type behaviors to be low-level misdemeanors. Such omnibus statutes were designed to curtail offensive physical contact, insults, false reports, and other relatively petty offenses. Harassment laws, which are general in nature, also were severely limited in application by numerous judicial decisions that had held that unless "fighting words" or other speech not protected by the First Amendment were involved, such laws might be unconstitutional. As such, these laws did not prove useful in combating stalking related to domestic violence or other serious predatory behavior.

Similarly, although many local jurisdictions had separable antistalking ordinances, such efforts were scattered, could be circumvented if the victim or offender left the jurisdiction, and provided for minimal enforcement or punishment. In this regard, the criminal code for stalking situations largely paralleled the classic frustrations of policing domestic violence. Here, the police were stymied in that typically no crime was committed before a violent assault.

The nation's first statewide antistalking statute was enacted in California in 1990. This statute was passed largely as a response to the stalking and subsequent July 1989 murder of actress Rebecca Schaeffer, who starred on the television show *My Sister Sam*. In addition, five murders the year before had taken place in Orange County, California, in which the victims had actually obtained restraining orders and had reported to authorities that the restraining order "did not work."

The California statute defined stalking in a manner that was explicit (California Penal Code, 1992, section 646.9). A stalker "willfully, maliciously and repeatedly follows or harasses another person and who makes a credible threat with the intent to place that person in fear of death or great bodily injury." By its terms, the statute required concurrent findings of the following elements: willful malice, repetitive following or harassing, a "credible threat," and "intent" to place the recipient in "reasonable fear of death or great bodily injury."

This statute was obviously limited in that it required finding both behavior and intent, leaving its application severely constrained, in particular because an overt threat and proof of intent to cause fear of the threat were required. In addition, it did not provide for warrantless arrests, increasing penalties for a violating court order, nor for conviction in subsequent offenses. It also had less than adequate provisions for victims of domestic violence–related stalking in which the incidents might individually seem trivial (such as repeatedly going into the same stores right after the victim entered). In an effort to respond to such criticisms, California revised its stalking statute in 1992 to increase the grounds allowed and to increase the attendant penalty for violation.

During the next several years, increasing, although largely anecdotal, evidence of a rise in stalking in most states led to the recognition of obvious statutory gaps. There ensued a virtual deluge of new statutes. For example, unusually tough legislation (potentially imposing up to 4 years in prison for stalking) passed in Illinois. In hearings, lawmakers were told that stalkers had killed five victims in Illinois in the past year; most related to domestic violence were husbands or boyfriends who were removed from their residences, stalked, and then killed their former intimates. In addition, victims of domestic violence–related stalking in what is now a familiar pattern recounted to the legislature how they were terrorized even after the newly issued restraining orders were imposed and how they continued to receive harassing mail and calls even after the attacker was incarcerated.

Subsequent laws became extraordinarily varied in both their terms and level of enforcement. Specific provisions of such statutes now typically include the following prohibitions: pursuing or following, harassing, nonconsensual communications, surveillance or lying in wait, trespassing, approaching or continued presence, disregard of warnings (to leave), and intimidation. In addition, some states that did not expressly state the acts that were proscribed now implicitly leave the courts to create a common law for this crime.

The Model Code Provisions and the Second Wave of Antistalking Statutes

Later statutes began to adhere to the following tenets of the 1993 Model Anti-Stalking Code for the States (National Criminal Justice Association, 1993), proposed by the National Institute of Justice:

Section 1. For purposes of this code, (a) "Course of conduct" means repeatedly maintaining a visual or physical proximity to a person or repeatedly conveying verbal or written threats or threats implied by conduct or a combination thereof directed at or toward a person (note electronic harassment was not covered); (b) "Repeatedly" means on two or more occasions, and (c) "Immediate family" means a spouse, parent, child, sibling, or any other person who regularly resides in the household or who, within the prior six months, regularly resided in the household.

Section 2. Any person who (a) Purposefully engages in a course of conduct directed at a specific person that would cause a reasonable person to fear bodily injury to himself or herself or a member of his or her immediate family or to fear the death of himself or herself or a member of his or her immediate family; and (b) Has knowledge or should have knowledge that the specific person will be placed in reasonable fear of bodily injury to himself or herself or a member of his or her immediate family or will be placed in reasonable fear of the death of himself or herself or a member of his or her immediate family; and (c) Whose acts induce fear in the specific person of bodily injury to himself or herself or a member of his or her immediate family or induce fear in the specific person of the death of himself or herself or a member of his or her immediate family is guilty of stalking.

The key components of this code were that (a) an explicit threat would not be required (the Code recognized that conduct, even absent a threat, may be just as serious a predictor of future violence); (b) a course of conduct that would cause a reasonable person to have fear was covered, even if the intent to actually cause fear was not present (because many stalkers, especially domestic violence stalkers, may be under a delusion that their victims want to reunite with them); and (c) states were encouraged to make violation of the stalking code a felony (to allow greater flexibility in sentencing and to impress on potential offenders and the criminal justice system the seriousness of the crime).

Despite the promulgation of the 1993 Model Code, statutory coverage was varied. For example, a threshold issue is what level of threat is required to sustain a conviction. Threat requirements for conviction seemed broken into several groups. The majority followed the Model Code and merely required a threat, or even conduct without an expressed threat, that would make a reasonable person fearful. This was the easiest standard for prosecutors to meet because it allowed them to introduce circumstantial and cumulative evidence in place of a "smoking-gun"–type of expressed threat.

In contrast, the remaining states required that an expressed threat be made and that the threatening person have the apparent ability to carry out the threat or have commenced actions. The weakness in such statutes is evident. Stalkers may seek to operate (barely) out of its statutory confines by not making overt threats even while terrifying victims. This is a potent threat, especially when some observers have commented to the authors that at many batterer treatment groups, conversations take place about "how to get even with the ***** by making her life miserable" yet circumventing the wording of domestic violence and stalking laws.

Thus, a significant limitation existed if proof that the defendant intended to cause and actually did cause a reasonable fear on the part of the person being stalked was required. Although it could theoretically be argued that intentionally frightening behavior should be the only conduct that is criminalized, such intent is customarily denied by the defendant and is in practice very difficult to prove.

As a result, many states began experimenting with a more flexible statute structure by providing for an "aggravated" or "enhanced" offense on the presence of certain types of stalking. For example, some states have made it a felony to possess or show a weapon in aid of stalking, whereas other states treat the use of a weapon, the confinement or restraint of the victim, or the subjection of the victim to bodily harm as an aggravating offense, justifying substantially increased penalties.

Not surprisingly, penalties for violation also were extraordinarily varied. In most states, on the one hand, the basic penalty is a misdemeanor—subjecting those convicted to not more than 1 year in jail (or less) plus a fine. On the other hand, even these states have allowed enhancement of the penalties to a felony level in cases involving the violation of court orders, prior felonies, possession of weapons, creating a "credible threat," or causing bodily harm. By December 2005, Miller reported that such stalking statutes loosely coalesced around three punishment models. Fourteen made any conviction for stalking a felony, 23 made the first act of stalking a felony or misdemeanor depending on the behavior, and some of these had explicit guidelines on what circumstances should cause a felony prosecution, threat posed, and motivation of the stalking. In the 12 other states, 9 provided for conviction for a felony after a second offense and 3 only upon a third conviction (similar to the "three strikes and you are out" laws). No state restricted punishments for even first-time stalkers to misdemeanor status (Miller, 2005)

Although the statutory directives to law enforcement remain somewhat limited, some states have paralleled their treatment of domestic violence to states that have given the police the power to make warrantless arrests of stalking subjects on determination of probable cause, even absent witnessing the incidents (similar to domestic violence cases). In addition, some states expressly require law enforcement to provide victim assistance or notification that a defendant has been released before trial. In other states, that duty may be implicitly assumed.

Recent Trends in Stalking Laws

States have been adopting ever more comprehensive statutes. For example, a growing trend is to recognize explicitly the interjurisdictional nature of stalking by allowing "enhancement" (increased sanctions) in a stalking offense based not only on conduct committed in their state but also on previous violations in other states. In addition, there is no requirement that the second offense justifying sentencing enhancement be against the same victim, demonstrating knowledge that it is not only the behavioral interaction between the offender and a particular victim, but the innate behavior of the offender, that accounts for the crime's importance to society. Finally, in some states, a "presumption of ineligibility for bail" exists in the event of a third stalking offense.

The level and volume of statutory changes make it impossible for a volume of this type to keep current with the restrictions now being set forth in statutes. Indeed, in the second edition of this book, published in 1996, we were able to state that, after passage of the California law in 1990, virtually all states (48 and the District of Columbia) had antistalking statutes, often having already been amended to cover apparent loopholes. Since then, the statutory basis has continued to change at an almost dizzying rate. In a March 2001 report, the U.S. Department of Justice reported 11 amended antistalking statutes; in 1999, there were 26 new state statutes related to stalking; and by August 2000, there were 27 new amendments to stalking laws (U.S. Department of Justice, 2001, p. 20). As recently as December 2005, a compendium of changes in the law made it clear that such statutes were still in flux.

The most recent directions of stalking amendments have been eclectic because there is no unifying authority. New measures have tended to mirror societal trends and include the following:

- Adding cyber-threats to the definition of stalking
- Allowing the courts to compel psychological evaluations
- Expanding the coverage of stalking laws to differentiate between "normal" stalking and "aggravated" felony stalking, based on a prior court injunction or restraining order
- Compelling statewide data gathering on stalking behaviors
- Authorizing "antiharassment" protective orders
- Prohibiting the purchase or transportation of a firearm or explosives for any person subject to a stalking order of protection
- Requiring employers to provide leave for crime victims (including victims of stalking) to attend court hearings and receive medical or psychological treatment
- Requiring police officer certification training to include instruction on stalking
- Authorizing preventive detention or electronic monitoring if danger to the victim is demonstrated
- Allowing employers to seek an injunctive order against harassment of employees at the workplace
- Allowing the crime of stalking even if the alleged perpetrator is already incarcerated
- Creating address confidentiality programs for victims of stalking
- Assessing court fees against the harasser rather than the complainant in successful civil harassment order proceedings

What does this frenzy of state laws indicate? We believe several factors are evident. First, in common with the early statutory experience with domestic violence, the initial statutes did not prevent stalking. If they did, it is doubtful that the majority of states would be changing them on such an ongoing basis. Such change indicates a high degree of continued legislative frustration.

Second, state statutes are not being amended in any consistent manner. The actions are instead somewhat disjointed and idiosyncratic, indicating perhaps a response to specific failures (e.g., cases in which a stalker has injured or killed a victim despite an existing statute when the statutory structure was perceived to contain an unacceptable loophole).

Third, our concerns regarding the constitutionality of some of these laws is still germane. When legislation is passed quickly and without consistency, it greatly increases the chance that certain provisions will be held unconstitutional.

Fourth, this degree of legislative "churn" makes it difficult for police officers as well as prosecutors and court officials to know the current status of the relevant statutes. Although advocates and researchers will be able to uncover this information, it is nearly impossible to train agency workers when laws change continually.

Fifth, until laws standardize and become stable, research on the efficacy of such statutes will be difficult, will become "dated" very quickly, and will not be able to guide policy effectively, as opposed to reacting to anecdotal events or pressure from interest groups.

Are Antistalking Statutes Constitutional?

In the second edition of this text written 14 years ago, we predicted that there would be extensive litigation regarding constitutionality and application of antistalking statutes. This has indeed proven true. The May 2001 U.S. Department of Justice publication, *Stalking and Domestic Violence: Report to Congress*, chronicled 464 state and 17 federal stalking and related cases in which challenges to antistalking and related laws were addressed. Of these cases, 157 directly challenged the express stalking statutes (124 largely on constitutional grounds; U.S. Department of Justice, 2001). Defense attorneys have raised constitutional challenges using a multitude of grounds including First Amendment rights and "freedom of expression" as incorporated in the Fourteenth Amendment prohibiting unwarranted state (and local) curtailment of such liberties. They also argued as a factual matter that "stalkers" were merely "expressing their feelings" toward the recipient.

The significance of that argument was that simply because such expressions might place an individual in fear, however reasonable, society should not curtail a citizen's rights to self-expression. They also argued that because the definitions of improper conduct were not clear, they might have a "chilling effect" on permissible communications and hence be challenged as being impermissibly "overly broad" because of their natural tendency to inhibit otherwise protected free speech or, by being too vague, to be unconstitutional for being "void for vagueness."

Court challenges aside, the reality is that courts have always recognized that the right to free speech has never been considered absolute. Limits have long been set on unprotected speech, such as obscenity, defamation, and imminent threats of illegal activity (see *Miller v. California*, 1973). Similarly, the time, place, and manner of making comments, even if not expressly falling under one of the recognized exceptions to free speech, have long been held to justify reasonable limits (see *Paris Adult Theatres v. Slaton*, 1973). Thus, a balancing of interests was required.

The key to the successful resolution and enforcement of these statutes, as briefly summarized by the Department of Justice, were as follows:

1. Statutes need not (and typically did not) require any proof that the defendant was going to carry out his threats.

2. An intent to knowingly cause a victim's fear must be included in a case, thus giving the trier of fact (ultimately the jury) the ability to decide whether the conduct might be unintentional.

3. Statutes must use careful wording. Terms such as "to annoy" or "to alarm" are too loose and need limiting definitions to prevent challenges for being too vague.

As a result of litigation and after a series of amendments, most stalking statutes now require a trier of fact to determine that a defendant willfully and intentionally instilled fear in the recipient. The courts have even allowed statutes that sanctioned "reckless behavior" by the offender to be used as proof of intent to cause reasonable fear. After all, it is rare that a perpetrator with knowledge of the existence of an antistalking law would say, "Sure, I intended to cause her to fear me." An evasive response is far more typical, citing the repetitions of "coincidence" and "misinterpretation" by the victim.

Gaps in Current Laws

The issue remaining is that some stalking behavior can be so amorphous that, over the years, potential stalkers find ever-changing, repetitive, novel behaviors and, hence, at least at first, are difficult to define as illegal even under the most liberal stalking statutes. The U.S. Department of Justice report best states this as follows: Unfortunately, at least two major gaps remain in states' legislative initiatives against stalking and their interpretations by the courts. State legislatures and courts frequently fail to recognize implied or conditional threats in their construction of the stalking crime. Stalkers who follow, repeatedly contact, and otherwise terrorize their victims in a persistent and even obsessive manner may slip through the cracks of the criminal justice system if they refrain from spelling out threats. Such legislative loopholes need to be addressed (U.S. Department of Justice, 2001, p. 39).

Similarly, new technologies have led to new behavior. For example, the explosive growth of e-mail has inevitably led to cyberstalking, which is rapidly becoming a primary method to stalk victims—and is now starting to be addressed by "cyber-bullying legislation." The U.S. Department of Justice report stated that prosecution of such offenses may require specific statutory language prohibiting the use of these media to harass: By and large, courts are not interpreting older stalking legislation to cover recently developed communications technologies. Such narrow interpretation of antistalking codes does not cover cyberstalking and other modes of high-tech terrorization. Thus, many states may need to enact specific legislative bans on the use of such media for stalking purposes or at least as part of an anti–"cyber bullying" statute.

Similarly, no existing statute can adequately cover the full range of activities a stalker might pursue. The hope is that the risk of serious sanctions imposed by stalking legislation deters conduct close to the purposes of the statute. The dilemma for stalking legislation is that any particular act may not, by itself, comply with narrow categories contained in any statute. As amply demonstrated, however, no one can deny that the failure to restrain stalking places people at risk, especially past victims of domestic violence; in which case, the offender's propensity for violence and choice of target are clear. As a matter of practice, judges hearing stalking charges should be fully aware at the bail hearing of the circumstances of the stalking, presumably including all past instances of domestic violence. Conditions for release should specifically include propensity for future violence and targeting of a particular victim.

The Federal Legislative Response

In our first edition, we observed that there was only an aborted federal response to domestic violence. In our second edition, we discussed the then recently enacted VAWA of 1994 sponsored by then Senator Joe Biden. This was reauthorized in 2000, and later in 2005, in each case increasing the scope and content of the law.

Initial Efforts

The initial strategy of those advocating change to the federal response to domestic violence was to publicize the failures of the state-based criminal justice system and thereby to obtain a federal commitment to force structural change. Indeed, sympathetic congressmen in the late 1970s and early 1980s held numerous hearings on proposed federal legislation. These focused primarily on shelter funding as well as on mass education and training for affected agencies.

These hearings uniformly heard witnesses explaining the widespread nature of the problem, decrying the inability of law enforcement and the judiciary to take effective action and emphasizing the necessity of federal funds to assist in upgrading and standardizing shelters and other victim resources. The U.S. Commission on Civil Rights (1982) ultimately issued a widely cited report. In this report, domestic violence is described as a civil rights problem of overwhelming magnitude. Ironically, before this report was even published, virtually all of the federally funded programs that were positively cited in this report had already been eliminated because of the new Reagan Administration's changes in federal priorities.

Indeed, strong conservative opposition kept federal funding of shelters and research on domestic violence prevention and treatment to a minimum. In an example of such a reaction, Senator Jesse Helms then critiqued the provision of any federal support to domestic violence shelters because they constituted "social engineering," challenging the husband's place as the "head of the family" (Congressional Record, 1980).

Despite such resistance by social conservatives, several federal agencies including the Attorney General's Office, the National Institute of Justice, the Bureau of Justice Statistics, and the National Institute of Health remained active in funding much needed research and demonstration projects; these federally funded projects in turn became springboards for evaluation and policy recommendations.

Although promising individual projects have been funded, little long-term sustaining effort was in place until the federal government in 1994 passed VAWA.

The Violence Against Women Act of 1994 (VAWA)

The VAWA was sponsored by then Senator Biden and enacted as Title IV of the Omnibus Crime Control and Law Enforcement Act of 1994. This legislation promised a significant change in the level of federal commitment to the control of violent crimes against women and children. Among other provisions designed to deter sex and hate crimes against women were measures expressly targeting control of domestic violence.

Several key provisions in VAWA dramatically affected the federal government's role. First, $120 million was made available from fiscal year (FY) 1996 to FY 1998 for grants to state and local government as well as to Native American tribes to implement mandatory or pro-arrest policies; improve tracking of domestic violence victims; increase the coordination among police, prosecution, and the judiciary; strengthen local advocacy and service programs for victims of domestic violence; and educate judges about domestic violence. Similarly, VAWA authorized $30 million in grants to rural states, localities, and Native American tribes to improve prosecution of domestic violence and child abuse.

Applicants for assistance (state and local agencies) first had to certify that their laws encouraged or mandated arrests for domestic violence offenders and those violating restraining orders; demonstrate that their laws, policies, and practices discouraged dual arrests of offenders and victims; and demonstrate that the abused person need not pay costs for filing criminal charges or to secure a protection order.

Second, VAWA funded the National Domestic Violence Hotline (NDVH), which became operational in February 1996. A nonprofit private organization, the Texas Council on Family Violence was selected to establish and operate this toll-free service, including maintenance of a national database of local providers of services as well as those providing local and state hotline services. According to the NDVH Web site (http://www.thehotline.org), it now contains a database of more than 4,000 shelters and service providers throughout the United States and its territories. Since its inception, more than 700,000 telephone calls have been received from victims, family members, and others. Currently, the associated Web site is comprehensive, allowing victims and service providers to get answers to frequently asked questions, gain access to resource materials, and find assistance in each state. It also provides specialized materials on domestic violence in the workplace, teens and dating violence, as well as community and outreach programs.

Moreover, there is a distinct difference between the service population of people who seek help from the hotline versus those who seek help from police. According to NDVH data, for approximately 60% of callers, contacting the hotline was the first step taken; many callers stated that they were unaware of existing community resources or were afraid to ask for help at local agencies where they might be recognized. This is important because, as described earlier, no matter which measurement is adopted, close to 50% of victims of domestic violence never contact the police.

The real area of the NDVH's impact may be on the "hard-core offender," given the inability of the locally based criminal justice system to protect against a truly determined assailant. As its Web site states, the hotline

receives more than 21,000 calls per month from victims, survivors, friends, and family members, law enforcement personnel, domestic violence advocates and the general public. (http://www.ndvh.Org/get-help)

The NDVH has been exceptionally successful. From 1996 through 2009, the NDVH answered more than 2 million calls. Currently it receives approximately 21,000 calls per month and provides access to translators in more than 170 languages (http://www.thehotline.org/about-support).

Third, VAWA created federal criminal penalties for anyone who traveled across state lines with the intent to injure a spouse or intimate partner or to violate the terms of a protective order and then intentionally committed a violent crime that caused injury or violated a protective order. In effect, this provision federalized interstate domestic violence–related stalking laws and may be a useful adjunct to them.

Fourth, federal court proceedings increased their victim orientation by expressly allowing victims of interstate crimes the right to appear in court to speak about the danger of pretrial release of the defendant. At the same time, state courts were required to enforce protection orders issued by the courts of another state. This made it markedly easier for women forced to vacate their homes to evade violence without having to reapply for court protection in a new location (or to reveal their new address to the offender).

Fifth, various provisions of VAWA increased funding for community-based agencies that target domestic violence and stalking. One provision allocated $325 million to be provided to states and Native American tribes. State coalitions against domestic violence and various research centers were to disseminate funds for construction and operational costs for battered women's shelters and other projects designed to "prevent family violence and to provide immediate shelter and related assistance for victims of domestic violence and their defendants" (VAWA, 1994). Finally, development of a number of model programs were funded to teach youth about domestic violence and violence among intimate partners; $10 million was given to nonprofit organizations to set up community programs in domestic violence intervention and prevention.

When VAWA was enacted, it was not universally popular. Conservatives attacked it as being an unnecessary and overly intrusive invasion on states' rights and, as noted earlier, an invasion on a husband's right to rule his family. Of equal concern, even major organizations such as the ACLU expressed concern about VAWA stating that the increased penalties it added were rash, that the expressed desire to achieve pretrial detention in the form of pro-arrest policy was repugnant to the U.S. Constitution, and that the mandatory HIV testing of those only charged but not convicted of a crime was an infringement of a citizen's right to privacy (ACLU, 1994).

Nevertheless, we note that in its letter of 2005, the ACLU supported the reauthorization of VAWA and stated that

> VAWA is one of the most effective pieces of legislation to end domestic violence, dating violence, sexual assault, and stalking. It has dramatically improved the law enforcement response to violence against women and has provided critical services necessary to support women and children in their struggle to overcome abusive situations. (ACLU, 2005)

We also note that some provisions that required state action as opposed to providing funding for state initiatives were struck down by the U.S. Supreme Court in 2000 for violating states' rights on federalism grounds (*United States v. Morrison*, 2000). Only the civil rights remedy of VAWA was struck down. Program funding was upheld, as were demonstration grants, as well as the overall intent of the program.

VAWA was originally supposed to have a "sunset "after the provisions were adopted widely by the states and Native American tribes. This has not occurred, and the federal role in domestic violence prevention has grown over time.

The VAWA Reauthorization Act of 2000

The original VAWA provisions were set to expire in 2000. Extension of the act became the subject of heated congressional debate not only regarding the amount of money expended but also because the philosophical issue of whether the federal government should lead in intervention had never been settled. Despite this doubt and a significant delay to achieve bipartisan support, the legislation passed, and the total amount of money authorized during 5 years was $3.3 billion. Major initiatives included "Services Training Officers Prosecutors" or STOP Grants, with $925 million for distribution to police, prosecutors, courts, as well as state and local victim service agencies; $875 million to fund communities to develop shelters; and $200 million to fund civil legal assistance to help women obtain civil protective orders. In addition to these relatively highly funded items, there were additional areas that were not well funded, including $25 million transitional housing for victims and their families and $30 million for supervised visitation centers.

It is clear from the type and extent of funding that high priority was given to criminal justice and legal service agency efforts that were, in effect, of indirect benefit to victims, with less money directly channeled to victims themselves. If we were more cynical, we could surmise that this was a result of a bureaucratic compromise in which funding for such agencies was the chief goal of the federal government—or at least that the lobbying by state and local agencies was more effective than that of the national women's groups who also supported the law.

Nonetheless, when federal money was not an issue and simple policy declarations could demonstrate legislative concerns for victims, the legislation clearly broke new ground. Included were requirements that states give full faith and credit to each other's protective orders; that immigrant women subjected to threats of domestic violence, even those illegally in the country, would be protected and might even get permanent legal status; and that studies would be conducted to determine whether victims of domestic violence had equal access to insurance and unemployment compensation, as well as whether employers were adequately dealing with the problem.

In addition to providing increased funding, the VAWA Reauthorization Act of 2000 added a much needed legal assistance program for victims of domestic violence and sexual assault, promoted the reform of structured supervised visitation programs for families experiencing domestic violence, and further protected immigrants experiencing domestic violence, dating violence, sexual assault, or stalking by establishing specialized U and T visas and by focusing on the trafficking of persons.

Originally in 1994 VAWA was considered by many to be a product of victim advocates that was supported by a minority of the population. However, by 2005, despite the election of a Republican Congress and a Republican President (George W. Bush Jr.), and despite opposition by conservative talk show hosts like Rush Limbaugh, VAWA became a mainstream position and was reauthorized.

In addition to past funding streams that were largely continued, it now contained provisions that exclusively served to protect immigrant victims of domestic violence, as previous efforts even including that of the 2000 reauthorization of VAWA were considered inadequate. Federal recognition was given to the provision of culturally sensitive and linguistically specific services for certain target communities. Also, enhancements were made to programs and services for victims with disabilities and VAWA service provisions now expressly included violence against teenagers. Although the crime of rape is not exclusively, nor even primarily, specific to domestic violence, it certainly occurs in the context of marital rape. Thus, the first federal funding stream to support rape crisis centers as authorized by this act also was significant to victims of domestic violence.

Funds were given to grantees to develop prevention strategies to stop violence before it occurred. A provision was added to protect individuals from being evicted from public housing because of their status as victims of either domestic violence or stalking.

Over time, the reauthorization of funding for VAWA in 2000 and 2005 has had an enormous impact. In September 2009, on the occurrence of the 15th anniversary of the initial funding of VAWA, the Department of Justice reported on subgrantees receiving funds from the various states and Native American tribes reported during the year 2007. They noted that 505,000 separate victims were served in one capacity or another, more than 1,200,000 services were made (some victims obviously requiring multiple interventions), and more than 4,700 individuals were arrested for violations of protective orders (U.S. Department of Justice, 2009).

Sixth, specific powers were given to federal institutions. For example, the U.S. Post Office was directed to protect the confidentiality of domestic violence shelters and abused persons' addresses. Similarly, other various federal agencies were required to collect data and conduct research on domestic violence. Overall responsibility for the development of a research agenda was given to the National Institute of Justice. The Office of the Attorney General was delegated the role of determining how states might collect centralized databases. Federal crime databases were to be made available by state civil and criminal courts to assist in responding to domestic violence and stalking cases. At the same time, $6 million was provided to assist states and local governments to improve data collection. At the same time, the Centers for Disease Control and Prevention was directed to study the costs to health care facilities for victims of domestic violence and related issues.

Federal Efforts to Combat Stalking

The federal response to stalking has been unusually swift. In 1993, the U.S. Department of Justice Bureau of Justice Assistance first mandated federal assistance to state and local law enforcement, only 3 years after passage of the first state statute. One result was that the National Institute of Justice funded a proposal to develop the model state antistalking statute described earlier. In 1996, a federal interstate stalking law (18 U.S.C., §2261A) was enacted, prohibiting as a federal offense the crossing of state lines (or in U.S. maritime jurisdiction) with the intent to injure or harass another person (provided that) this caused reasonable fear of death or serious bodily injury to that person or to a member of that person's immediate family. Although the original law covered only the intent to injure or harass, as stated earlier, the VAWA Reauthorization Act of 2000 expanded the definition to cover interstate travel with the intent to kill, injure, harass, or intimidate another person, the person's family, or the person's former or current intimate partner (Federal Interstate Stalking Law of 2000). Similarly, the law now federalizes the use of mail or cyberstalking via the Internet.

Federal crimes, of course, invoke federal criminal sanctions and federal sentencing. Guidelines dramatically limit the authority of federal judges to change sentences. Of these sentences, penalties range from 13 months and supervised release to life imprisonment. Restitution also has been granted. Finally, because of the existence of this relatively new federal statute, extensive federal resources at the U.S. Department of Justice have been committed. These funds have been used to develop antistalking task forces with state and local law enforcement and the development of multijurisdictional training programs for law enforcement, prosecutors, judges, and victim advocates.

Although potentially the most sweeping of all antiharassment statutes, this federal response is limited and, per the U.S. Department of Justice, is not meant to "supplant" state efforts. There simply are not the federal resources to prosecute significant numbers of cases, especially after the terrorist attacks on September 11, 2001, which have tied up virtually all available resources. Hence, this effort should best be considered as an adjunct when the interstate nature of harassment effectively prevents state prosecution.

Since enactment of the new antistalking statutes from 1996 through October 2000, the U.S. Department of Justice had prosecuted 35 cases against 39 stalkers and had won convictions against 39 stalkers (U.S. Department of Justice, 2001) and 25 defendants in 23 years (11 cases were still pending) by 2001. This extraordinarily high conviction rate shows that the statute can be effective but remains selectively used. This is perhaps because of the lack of knowledge of the underlying incidents, because prosecutorial discretion has limited the number of cases brought, or possibly because state and local law enforcement agencies were prosecuting these cases.

Future Legislation

It is by no means the case that legislative initiatives at any level of government have been completed. We are aware of numerous efforts to amend state laws and increasing efforts to involve the federal government in the control of domestic violence. For example, earlier this year, in February 2010, landmark bipartisan legislation was introduced, called the International Violence Against Women Act (S. 2982). This bill was introduced by Senators Carey and Boxer, Democrats from the Senate Foreign Relations Committee, and was joined by Republican Senators Collins and Snow. Similar legislation (H.R. 4594) was introduced by Representatives Delahunt and Schakowsky, Democrats, and Poe, Republican. If enacted, this bill would be the first time that the U.S. foreign policy establishment addresses violence against women as a diplomatic priority. This would then directly impact foreign policy through assistance to international grant programs. The bill, although still in Committee, has been endorsed by Amnesty International USA, The Family Violence Prevention Fund, as well as 40 international and 150 U.S.-based groups. The primary goal is to have the U.S. government expressly support nongovernmental organizations that combat violence against women, bolster education-oriented programs for women, strengthen health services for victims of violence against women, and require that foreign government participants bring perpetrators of violence against women to justice. At the time of writing (spring 2010), this act had not been passed; however, it had received 21 co-sponsors in the Senate and, as noted earlier, has bipartisan support. If passed by Congress, we would anticipate a rapid signing by President Obama.

SUMMARY

This chapter provides an overview of the development and growth of state and federal legislation addressing violence against women. Although state statutes were initially limited and narrowly circumscribed, they have evolved into far more comprehensive and powerful tools in the battle against domestic violence. Similarly, the federal Violence Against Women Act has now become institutionalized and has undergone several reauthorizations. Support for this type of legislation is clearly becoming accepted as necessary by increasing numbers of the general population.

DISCUSSION QUESTIONS

1. What do you think should be the scope of domestic violence legislation in terms of relationships and acts covered?

2. What do you think is missing from your state statute? How does it compare with statutes in other jurisdictions?

3. Unlike the federal legislation, state statutes and their revisions are not given funding appropriations. How can funding for state statutes be ensured?

4. Do you think VAWA should address male victims of domestic violence and sexual assault?

5. What do you think is missing from state and federal legislation?

Case Prosecution

The Journey From a Roadblock to a Change Agent

10

Chapter Overview

In Chapter 5, we discussed why many victims never call the police. Now because of mandatory or presumptive arrest policies, many more cases reach the prosecutor's office. What is the result? Perhaps inevitably, in domestic violence cases, victim or attrition dismissal rates are extraordinarily high. This might occur either because the victim drops charges or because she refuses to appear as a witness.

Much has been written about the lack of assistance and support that have historically been provided by prosecutors and the courts to victims of domestic violence. We describe briefly the victim's experiences and how victims' access to the justice system in the past has been hindered by her interactions with prosecutors. We study this now not only—or even primarily—for historical significance but also because victims still receive this response in many jurisdictions.

After this discussion, we will cover extensively how prosecutors' offices interact with victims, and finally, we will describe the development and implications of various forms of mandatory prosecution or no-drop policies.

The Varied Reasons for Case Attrition

Case Attrition by Victims

A series of studies in different jurisdictions conducted during the early years of criminal justice reforms demonstrated that, absent unusually aggressive measures, attrition rates hovered between 60% and 80% (Cannavale & Falcon, 1986; Field & Field, 1973; Ford, 1983; Lerman, 1981; Parnas, 1970; Rebovich, 1996; Ursel, 1995). Despite increased societal attention to domestic violence, the rate of prosecution is still limited by the unwillingness of victims to cooperate (Belknap, Fleury, Melton, Sullivan, & Leisenring, 2001; Hirschel &

Hutchison, 2001). In fact, one study that controlled for the type of evidence, witnesses, and relationship reported that when domestic victims cooperated, prosecutors were seven times more likely to press charges (Dawson & Dinovitzer, 2001). Why should such high rates of victim-initiated case attrition persist?

Variations in Victims' Reasons for Prosecution

Once an arrest has occurred, Ford (1991) found that victims were, contrary to the beliefs of many prosecutors, not emotionally driven or irrational decision makers. Instead, when victims were asked to explain their reasons to support or reject prosecution, they cited instrumental and rational reasons rather than emotional attachments in their decision of whether to cooperate. For example, victims are logically far less concerned with general deterrence as an esoteric concept than with using the criminal justice system as a whole to accomplish their personal goals of enhancing safety, maintaining economic viability, protecting children, or having an opportunity to force participation in batterers' counseling programs (Ford, 1991).

For example, the existence of a victim's minor children might present significant issues for those who want to be sure that they are protected but still wish to maintain an intact family structure. Financial ties (intensified by recent welfare reforms) might make some victims critically dependent on an abuser's financial support for minor children, which is a factor at odds with strict punishment models. For example, in July 2009, California Governor Arnold Schwarzenegger cut all state funding for the 94 agencies who provide services for domestic violence victims (Castelan, 2009, citing an Associated Press report). Furthermore, a simple threat to have a person arrested or to initiate prosecution might terminate immediate abuse. Therefore, pursuing prosecution past that point might not be in the interests of the victim because it might increase the risks of retaliation of family breakup while forcing her commitment to a process with little tangible benefit, at least from her perspective.

As a result of these factors, although the goal of assisting and empowering victims might be understood in the abstract, it is generally lost in practice when a prosecutor's primary agenda is to obtain convictions. This is especially true when the office is seeking to support a larger societal goal of punishing an offender and/or deterring other potential batterers (Lerman, 1992). In short, the generalized assumption that mandatory prosecution is always in the victim's interests might not be accurate. In fact, at times there might be an irreconcilable dilemma: To assist and empower a victim might not involve the offender's subsequent case processing (Mills, 1997, 1998, 1999).

Several studies have shown the extent of disconnect between the victim's desires and those of the prosecutor. In one study conducted by several of the authors (Buzawa & Buzawa, 1996), it was apparent that prosecutors did not listen to victim desires. We found that victim preferences were rarely solicited and, when known, were rarely honored if they contravened the official policy to prosecute most cases for the societal goals of punishing the immediate offender and of deterring potential future offenders (Buzawa & Buzawa, 1996; cf. Lempert, 1989). Because victim choices normally influence the actions of the criminal justice system to some degree (and the quest for restorative justice is pushing this to the forefront), such explicit policies that remove or limit victim input into decision making are unusual.

Although victims might not desire arrest, let alone subsequent conviction, we recognize that in reality, they might truly need law enforcement and court involvement. In the more traditional society of past decades, the family, church, or friends might have provided support to victims. In the highly mobile 21st century, such assistance is more problematic, making victim reliance on formal agencies more acute. Despite the growing presence of social service and nonprofit agencies, the reality is that victims of domestic abuse often do not find or use these agencies at critical moments without encouragement and support from criminal justice agencies. For this reason, criminal justice agencies, especially law enforcement, not only enforce their own mandates by making an arrest but also serve as critical gatekeepers to the provision of services of other essential actors. In the context of mandatory arrest policies, such "referrals" are far more likely to go to the prosecutor's office—despite whether they are desired by a victim.

Self-Doubts and the Complexity of Motivation: Changes in Victim Attitudes During the Life Course of a Violent Relationship

It is not surprising that the complexity of victim motives predicts high dropout rates. We will discuss the following six predominant motives for the initiation of prosecution by a victim: (1) curiosity over how the criminal justice system might be of assistance to her specific needs, (2) confirmation of her status as a victim reporting a crime and getting control over an abusive partner in an ongoing relationship (a sort of "coming out" as a battered woman), (3) a promised increase in her own legitimacy as a victim in subsequent police encounters, (4) a desire for restorative justice (e.g., being compensated for her victimization), (5) a matter of principle (i.e., a crime against her has been committed and should be reported, and punishment for the offender should be meted out), as well as (6) fear for her safety if there is no prosecution.

Let us examine how each one of these rationales might weaken over time. Such an analysis is important because if we do not wish merely to become advocates of prosecution for its own sake, we must understand that there are varied reasons for a particular victim. Some might be easily settled at early stages of prosecution, and others might require conviction of an offender. What we can see, however, is that there might be a logical basis for explaining the fact bemoaned by a generation of prosecutors that domestic violence victims simply are not as deeply committed to continued prosecution as are victims of other forms of criminal behavior.

As to the first motive, although an effort to determine how courts might assist a victim might seem to be an unusual motive for the decision to pursue a criminal charge until recent passage of victim right's laws, the legal system, commencing with the initial police intervention, typically provided little substantive help to victims. Given the known desire of the criminal justice bureaucracy to get rid of these undesirable cases, one might cynically observe that information on alternatives to prosecution is provided not with the intent to best handle the offender, but because the victim's demands have become a nuisance.

The second goal, confirmation of her status as a victim, is probably attained after her report resulted in the offender being arrested. Certainly if it is made clear that she, as the aggrieved party, can press charges, this goal might be satisfied relatively early and actual conviction might not be necessary. Ford (1984, 1991) suggested that initiating prosecution might be the only available alternative for many women to gain control in a relationship. The actual course of the prosecution would then really be of only secondary importance to the control gained as a "power resource" through the threat of prosecution. In this manner, the victim is primarily using the criminal justice system as a strategic tool rather than to achieve conviction. In any event, the goal of learning about and using available resources is quickly satisfied either by the police or by initial contact with victim advocates or other personnel in the prosecutor's office.

The third goal, which is an implicit recognition of her legitimacy as a victim in future encounters with the police, might, from the victim's perspective, be satisfied by the police making the initial arrest. In addition, most courts now rapidly grant ex parte temporary restraining orders and might expeditiously grant permanent injunctions. Actual case prosecution is not needed to achieve this objective.

The victim's fourth possible goal of finding out whether the courts may assist her might not be satisfied by the case proceeding to trial and conviction. In the better judicial systems, she might find that court personnel, especially victim advocates, provide vital assistance both in stopping future abuse and in providing pathways for her to receive significant and needed resources, including links to shelters and short-term financial support for her and her dependents.

Moreover, as Labriola, Bradley, O'Sullivan, Rempel, and Moore (2009) noted, the actual incidence of prosecution and courts providing such victim-oriented assistance, even in the context of highly specialized criminal domestic violence courts, remains a "hit or miss" proposition.

In more traditional courts, it is even less likely to occur. As we will report in Chapter 12, a victim's desire for restorative justice, or being compensated for her victimization, is not something that prosecutors and courts do particularly well. Their process is largely mechanistic and "offender centered" in the context that punishment of the offender for his crime against the state is paramount—not providing compensation to the victim.

To be fair, the failure to attempt restorative justice in a court setting is difficult. After all, if a couple continues to cohabitate, can money taken from the offender and given to the victim realistically provide meaningful recompense? Indeed, the entire premise of the restorative justice movement described in Chapter 12 derives a large part of its legitimacy from the recognition that traditional modalities of court sanctions are ineffective at providing victim-centered restorative justice. If a victim seeks such recourse, then typically she will learn that the prosecutor and courts do not view this as their primary (or, in most cases, ancillary) mission in case processing. When this is "learned" by the victim, its value for her to seek continued prosecution essentially disappears.

Fifth, many victims seek prosecution for the potential to obtain retribution or punishment for the crime committed against their person. Reasons for this vary. Some simply want to punish and teach the offender a lesson. This goal might not be satisfied until a final guilty verdict is achieved; however, for some, simply having the offender arrested and thereby publicly "shamed" accomplishes this goal. Also shear desire for punishment can weaken over time as many victims simply want to forget about the incident and move on with their lives. In this context, the typically extended period between arrest and any trial works, perhaps unconsciously, toward weakening the resolve of victims.

In regard to the sixth goal, many are scared of future abuse and hope that the involvement of the prosecutor and the courts will prevent the offender from committing further

violence. Many also are aware of concomitant substance abuse or anger control issues with
a person that they still love and want to remain as their partner. For these victims, having
the offender sentenced to a batterer intervention, anger control, and/or a substance abuse
program presents the key possibility of rehabilitation and the prospect of "reforming" a
bad but still desired relationship. Still others fear for their safety and hope that the courts,
through either punishment or incarceration, can protect her and her family. These desires
might support further prosecution through conviction. If the victim believes that criminal history indicates a low chance that the offender will be rehabilitated, she might enthu-
siastically seek conviction and a sentence of extended incarceration. Others might be
satisfied by an early willingness of an offender to attend a court-monitored batterer intervention program and have little inclination to press for a conviction.

In addition to the diversity of victim goals in initially supporting prosecution, in
many cases, a victim's attitude toward the crime and the offender alter over time.
Memories of the crime and the perpetrated harm recede after an extended period. Those
victims who are in a continued relationship with a cyclical batterer often experience a
prolonged "honeymoon" after a particularly violent episode. In these situations, the
offender seeks reconciliation with the victim because of atonement or fear of prosecution. Alternatively, he might have ceased battering altogether. In time, continued prosecution might become the only event that reminds her (and the offender) of the battering
incident and threatens to end the current harmonious period. Finally, the victim might
have successfully left the batterer and negotiated acceptable financial support or terms
of custody. She might now justifiably fear that prosecution would simply anger the batterer, jeopardizing this often hard-won status.

Also, although largely inappropriate, many victims tend, at least partially, to blame
their own behavior for a violent incident. Self-doubt and guilt in relationship cases in
general and where intimate violence has occurred is far more significant than for other
victims of violent crime. Such doubts might coexist uneasily with the victim's desires for
retribution, deterrence, and perhaps rehabilitation that had led the victim initially to
help in charging the offender. Many victim advocates would, of course, know that such
a result is predictable given the socialization process reinforced by constant societal pressure. Regardless of reasons, victim self-doubts might result in prosecutor attitudes that
"high-dropout" cases are not worth spending scarce financial resources.

Traditional Agency Attitudes Toward Prosecution and Case Screening

The problem of widespread agency personnel indifference to domestic violence
offenses still exists, even in far more subtle forms than in the past. The skepticism of
many prosecutors and members of their staff in many cases still tends to influence victims to drop charges (Belknap et al., 2001; Dawson & Dinovitzer, 2001; Erez & Belknap,
1998). We noted previously that prosecutors in general disfavor relationship cases.
Unlike most other prosecutions, court personnel in domestic violence and similar cases
generally make victims feel personally responsible for case outcome. This occurs
because, in other contexts, although the victim is considered to have suffered the most
direct harm, the public order also has been affected. For this reason, prosecutors often
encourage, or even require by subpoena, victims in nonrelationship cases such as
stranger assaults to support resultant prosecutions.

In domestic violence incidents, the violation to the public order is apparently not as evident to the prosecutorial staff, leading, at least in the past, to profound agency ambivalence about intervention. Not unexpectedly, these officers of the court subtly, or even at times overtly, encourage victims to drop charges. Hence, prosecutorial attitudes and behaviors might contribute to high rates of victim attrition.

The prosecutor's office often does not facilitate victim cooperation. For example, research (conducted in Denver, CO; Boulder County, CO; and Lansing, MI) has reported that 20% of victims who did not go to court on the scheduled date did not appear because they had not been informed of the court date (Belknap et al., 2001). This study also noted that women reported numerous other obstacles that, if considered by the prosecutor's office, could dramatically increase the likelihood of their appearance in court, including the provision of childcare and/or transportation difficulties and addressing safety needs. As described more fully in Chapter 12, even the most innovative courts often do not take the most rudimentary steps to help victims. In domestic violence criminal courts, only a small proportion—25%—provide childcare services or transportation, and relatively few provide structural safeguards such as separate waiting areas or separate facilities in courtrooms (Labriola et al., 2009).

Regardless of the reasons for the high attrition rate sought by domestic violence victims, these victims have served to reinforce frustration and cynicism among agency personnel. Prosecutors' offices typically lack sufficient trained personnel and simply lack the time, background, or inclination to understand why victims drop charges. They often express cynical thoughts to the authors in interviews, such as "no real harm must have occurred," "the victim was never serious about the charges," "the victim is a 'masochist' for continuing to live with the man," or "the victim had lied earlier to the police to obtain revenge on an unrelated dispute" or "to influence a pending divorce, custody, or child-support proceeding" and was now "scared she would be caught in a lie." Some personnel were sympathetic to victims and believed that the victim might be "trapped" in an unsafe relationship. They generally believed that "the criminal justice system cannot help" when a victim maintains that the continuation of a relationship is the primary concern.

In the context of an overwhelming lack of prosecutorial resources, a high victim-dropout rate clearly reinforces prosecutorial decisions to exercise discretion by refusing to bring charges or to dismiss charges. One result has been that both victims and offenders are faced with a prosecutorial office and judicial system that seems to have little predictability. Cases that would be continued in another context or a different jurisdiction (even against the express wishes of the victim) are dropped, despite clear evidence that would sustain successful prosecution.

The Role of Victim Behavior and Motivation in the Decision to Prosecute

The tendency of prosecution to use several extralegal variables to screen cases differentially has been noted (Ellis, 1984; Hirschel & Hutchison, 2001; Schmidt & Steury, 1989; Stanko, 1982). Perhaps of greatest significance are those prosecutors who believe they have the right to evaluate a victim's motivation and thereby assess her commitment to continued prosecution. This is considered a legitimate case discriminator independent of the inherent strength of the case. As a result of many prosecutors' attitudes, one study found that the victim's continuing relationship with the offender was a key factor in decisions about whether to continue prosecution (Schmidt & Steury, 1989).

Schmidt and Steury reported that charges were far more likely to be filed if the victim claimed to have no continuing sexual intimacy with the offender. Hirschel and Hutchison (2001) confirmed this finding in Charlotte, North Carolina, and reported that previously married or cohabiting couples were more likely than those currently married or cohabiting to have their cases prosecuted. Although these studies contradicted other research by finding little effect of marital status per se, they found a significant negative correlation between prosecution and continued victim–offender cohabitation. This result could be attributed to organizational concerns regarding a victim's commitment to prosecution or, more charitably, to a victim-oriented concern that maintaining a prosecution in this context might prove to increase her risk of future abuse.

In a position to increasing commitment to domestic violence cases, the National District Attorneys Association (NDAA) stated in 1980 that, in deciding whether to prosecute, a district attorney should consider whether it is likely that a victim will cooperate, whether the victim agreed to live apart from the defendant, and in general to consider "the relationship of the parties" (National District Attorneys Association, 1980). We hasten to add that the NDAA position has been explicitly changed to understand that the victim might be subject to pressures not to continue prosecution. Although this position was subsequently reversed, at least publicly in the face of stringent criticism by researchers and victim advocates, we suspect that, as a matter of practice, it still guides many prosecutorial charging decisions.

Inherent in such a position is the assumption that a victim's unshakable commitment to continue prosecution is a valid case discriminator. We believe this is profoundly incorrect as a basis for the exercise of prosecutorial discretion. If a primary concern is for injuries suffered by the victim and the prevention of future violence, then the bureaucratic goals of achieving high conviction rates should be subordinated.

Nevertheless, the reality is that in the past, concern for the victim's misfortune has not been prosecutors' prime motivation. Instead, the critical factors have been whether the injury was of a type and quality that could not be ignored—for example, death or an overwhelmingly vicious and publicized attack—or if the victim stubbornly refused to drop charges. The prosecutor's office was then forced to confront a complaint. If the charge was filed and abandoned, then measurements of their capability to obtain high conviction rates were adversely affected. The possibility that the victim might have achieved her goals in the interim would, of course, be irrelevant in this context.

Prosecutorial Assessment of Offender Characteristics

Another important factor in deciding to prosecute is whether the prosecutor perceived that the offender is truly recalcitrant or, conversely, unlikely to recidivate. One study found that a history of abuse was related strongly to future charging decisions. Of perhaps greater surprise was that the prior record seemed to influence the prosecutor even more than the evidentiary strength of the case (Schmidt & Steury, 1989).

For many offenses, use of drugs or alcohol has been taken by officials to mitigate the intent and, therefore, the nature of a crime. In domestic violence cases, the reverse seems to be true (Schmidt & Steury, 1989). Although this might be a result of a generalized phenomenon of tougher law enforcement against substance abusers, it also might be a result of the prosecutor's recognition that drug-induced violence is likely to reoccur at higher rates among addicts than nonaddicts.

Organizational Factors Within Prosecutor's Offices That Affect Responses

Finally, organizational imperatives beyond the knowledge or control of most victims have, at least in the past, affected the decision to initiate or continue prosecution. Perhaps the most significant of these is the tendency of prosecutors to treat police-initiated arrests more seriously than a victim's complaint. This is understandable. Both agencies employ people that have an inclination to use criminal law to punish wrongdoers.

Police and prosecutors require each other's mutual support. In this context, subsequent prosecution legitimizes an officer's arrests, and the police reciprocate by providing prosecutors with the needed evidence to sustain high conviction rates. If a police officer arrests a suspect and the prosecutor declines to pursue a charge, then the police officer might interpret this decision as questioning his or her competency or authority.

Also, the prosecutor might view police-initiated charges as somehow having been screened for content. Whatever the reason, police-initiated charges are organizationally considered to be more legitimate (Cole, 1984; Jacoby, 1980; Schmidt & Steury, 1989). In contrast, citizen-initiated complaints by victims are treated as having no organizational "sponsor" and no designated bureaucrat having responsibility or accountability for any decisions. Ford, Reichard, Goldsmith, and Regoli (1996) noted, however, that this factor might not necessarily be as significant in the decision-making process as the increased commitment and cooperation in victim-initiated cases.

Imposing Procedural Barriers: Why the System "Encouraged Victims to Abandon Prosecution"

Even if the prosecutor's office does not formally dismiss charges, requiring the victim to take responsibility for dropping a case, a variety of procedural barriers often has been imposed, either formally or through a process of accretion, to prevent charges from being filed, or if filed, subsequently pursued. For example, Ford (1993) reported that at one point in Marion County, Indiana, several time-consuming procedures needed to be followed before a domestic violence–related arrest warrant could be issued on a victim's behalf. In non-domestic cases involving violent activity, an arrest warrant was issued within 1 to 2 days of the victim filing a complaint.

This rapid response did, in fact, happen in domestic violence complaints when the victim was accompanied by a police officer, thereby showing the prosecutor that the officer had a personal attachment to the matter and demonstrating the officer's appraisal of the case's legitimacy. However, when the complaint was initiated solely by the victim, it took 2 weeks or longer to issue a warrant. Also, after this 2-week period, an arrest warrant often would not be issued at all. Instead, a summons to appear in court later would be mailed to an offender. As a result, in only one third of the cases was any arrest made within 1 month after a victim initiated a complaint; and incredibly, in only 62% of cases was an arrest made after 6 months (Ford, 1983). Obviously, the prosecutor's office was not trying to process these complaints and the police were not eager to serve warrants.

Other procedural hurdles have been used to screen out undesirable or frivolous cases. In the Indianapolis study, a mandatory 3-day waiting period existed before the court would receive a domestic violence complaint. This forced a second victim-initiated action before any organizational evaluation of the merits of the case took place (Ford, 1983). This particular procedural hurdle is virtually unheard of outside of domestic violence complaint processing. The net effect was to force the victim to reaffirm what might have been a traumatic initial decision to prosecute before there was evidence that the prosecutor's office would help.

Not surprisingly, this served as an effective mechanism for discarding domestic violence complaints. In the Indianapolis study, Ford noted that 33% of married women filing domestic violence complaints had these placed on hold and 78% of them failed to return. This result compared with corresponding figures of 60% and 52%, respectively, for those who had filed for divorce and 46% and 59%, respectively, for those who actually divorced. In this case, the screening device ostensibly used for organizational reasons to eliminate frivolous domestic violence complaints might have frustrated approximately two thirds of the small minority of women victims who had already called the police and then taken the further initiative of filing a criminal complaint.

How Did Prosecutor Offices Respond to New Pro-Arrest Policies?

Initially, pro-arrest domestic assault policies might have dramatically increased the number of domestic violence cases referred to prosecution; however, because of the factors cited earlier in this chapter, large increases in arrests were, to a certain extent, offset by corresponding increases in dismissals. Thus, in many prosecutor offices, there was, and in many case still is, no difference in the number of cases resulting in conviction than prior to the change in arrest practices. Prosecutorial actions then created a "funnel effect" in which domestic violence cases were channeled out of the criminal justice system by nullifying police charging behavior and, ultimately, undermining pro-arrest policies.

According to one study in the 1990s, the major effect of the institution of mandatory arrest policies was simply to move discretion from the time of arrest to the time when prosecutors screen cases (Davis & Smith, 1995). This same study, which was conducted in Milwaukee, Wisconsin, after mandatory arrest policies for domestic violence were implemented, presents data that support such concerns. These researchers reported case rejection rates of 80% at the prosecutors' initial screening. They speculated that the underlying reason for this high rejection rate was to avoid the enormous burden that a high number of domestic violence cases would bring to bear on existing resources. Prosecutors, in effect, simply developed adaptive responses to pro-arrest laws that effectively screened out large numbers of cases. Although such practices have long been suspected, empirical evidence of their existence was not provided until the mid-1990s by Davis and Smith (1995).

Case screening by prosecutors was accomplished through the use of relatively obscure and typically unpublished collateral procedures. For example, in the study by Davis and Smith (1995), the Milwaukee Prosecutor's Office had a policy in which misdemeanor domestic violence offenders were charged only when the victim came to a charging conference the day after arrest. This resulted in merely 20% of cases being prosecuted and the remaining 80% of cases screened out. In 1995, when the Milwaukee prosecutor changed this policy to stop requiring victims to attend charging conferences, the rate of accepting cases tripled overnight from 20% to 60% of cases. The authors of this report strongly suggested that the analysis of criminal justice impact on the handling of domestic violence should change focus: "Whether this same displacement of discretion from the decision to arrest to the decision to prosecute has occurred elsewhere as a result of mandatory arrest laws is unknown, but it is certainly an important subject for investigation" (Davis & Smith, 1995, p. 546).

What happened when the policy in Milwaukee changed? Did this event increase everyone's satisfaction? Unfortunately, it did not. This research also found that after the new charging policies were implemented, case backlog increased greatly; time to case disposition doubled, convictions declined, pretrial crime increased, and victim satisfaction with case outcomes and the prosecutor's handling of the case actually decreased (Davis, Smith, & Nickles, 1998). Hence, the failure to add sufficient resources in effect unintentionally sabotaged the prosecution's well-intentioned efforts.

The degree to which prosecutors expressly face this dilemma is uncertain. Certainly, prosecutor's offices are now aware of the heavy new emphasis on aggressive handling of domestic violence. Often, no-drop policies (which will be described subsequently in this chapter), which mandate prosecution, are instituted typically with great fanfare. The actual effect is less clear. One researcher reported that although two thirds of the prosecutors' offices now had official no-drop policies regarding the handling of domestic violence cases, fewer than 20% of these offices admitted that their decision-making policies and plea-bargaining negotiations had actually been affected (Rebovich, 1996).

It is apparent that, at least in the past, a complex interaction evolved between the motives and the actions of the domestic violence victim and prosecutor's office. Each profoundly misunderstood the other's individual and organizational motives and needs.

Victims of most crimes assume that once criminal justice processing is commenced, the procedure is straightforward. Few realize at the outset the inherent complexities created by the need for their continued involvement or the uncertainty caused by the requirements of protecting the offender's constitutional rights. Unfulfilled expectations, which are normal to most victims of criminal conduct, are coupled with the domestic violence victim's often ambiguous or conflicting motives for prosecution and the apathy and, at times, even hostility of a bureaucracy nominally dedicated to protecting her interests.

Under such circumstances, it would be unrealistic to assume anything other than high rates of victim attrition. Similarly, the prosecutor and his or her staff often cannot understand why victims refuse to leave abusive partners or fail to assist rigorously the prosecution of their abusers. This misunderstanding, in turn, changes their behavior in a manner that implicitly reinforces these misperceptions—that is, even more women drop charges or fail to appear because of the indifference or cynicism of prosecutors and judges or the erection of Byzantine barriers that "test" their commitment to prosecute. Although, for the reasons we described previously, some victim-initiated drops might be unrelated to prosecutorial or court behavior, the experiences of the victim with agency personnel influence the rates of the victim's "voluntary" decision to exit the criminal justice system.

Subsequent victim actions to drop a case "voluntarily" reinforce negative staff attitudes, which affect the whole criminal justice system by greatly increasing the deleterious effect of the "prosecutorial funnel" noted earlier. Furthermore, low rates of prosecution and conviction reinforce and justify often persistent reluctance of police officers to become involved in "no win, no outcome" domestic violence cases. Thus, two negative feedback loops are strengthened by the initial victim–prosecutor misperceptions.

The Changing Prosecutorial Response

Have Prosecution Rates Actually Increased?

Evidence of the extent of the change by prosecutors is mixed. One study reported only modest change. Evidence suggests also that the increase in arrests has not been met with a similar increase in cases prosecuted. An analysis of a large-scale national data set reported that mandatory arrest jurisdictions had *lower* rates of prosecution than preferred arrest jurisdictions (Hirschel, Buzawa, Pattavina, & Faggiani, 2007; Hirschel, Buzawa, Pattavina, Faggiani, & Reuland, 2007). However, what is interesting is that mandatory arrest jurisdictions had a greater proportion of simple assault cases compared with preferred arrest jurisdictions. This finding is currently being examined to understand more completely the reason and extent of such variations.

Another study reported that it was now far less likely than in the 1990s that prosecutors will routinely drop domestic violence cases (Klein, 2008). A recent report reviewed 120 research studies conducted on prosecution rates between 1973 and 2006. An average prosecution rate of 64% was found, and the reported prosecution rates were steadily increasing for this crime.

Similarly, a Special Report issued by the Bureau of Justice Statistics in 2009 summarized the findings from an examination of state courts contained in 15 large, urban counties. It found that, overall, domestic violence cases were likely to have more serious outcomes than non–domestic violence cases. They reported that domestic violence offenders who committed aggravated assault were less likely to have their cases dropped compared with non–domestic violence offenders. These offenders also were more likely to be convicted for their offenses (87% domestic violence offenders versus 78% non-domestic offenders). Similarly, they were less likely to be diverted out of the system (12% versus 20%, respectively).

How can we reconcile such different survey results? Perhaps the best answer is that these studies suggest that cases are not being dropped as frequently as in the past when most cases were dismissed by the prosecutor. However, when the prosecutor's office is flooded with marginal cases, which is more likely in a mandatory arrest jurisdiction, the system "adapts." More cases are dismissed early in the process to preserve the limited resources of the rest of the criminal justice system, thereby largely negating (or at least limiting the effect of) mandatory arrest policies. In theory, mandatory arrest is intended to ensure that cases are prosecuted and that a judicial disposition is imposed. Those researchers who are familiar with how organizations respond to new demands without additional resources will not be surprised by such an outcome.

Victim Advocates

Many prosecutors, especially in larger jurisdictions, have added victim advocates to their staff or as staff to the court system. Typically, victim advocates are not attorneys but are highly trained and motivated professionals in the field of the control of domestic violence. In addition, many jurisdictions that have a comprehensive response to domestic violence provide victim advocacy via a protocol that assigns such services to affiliated agencies such as family shelter service agencies, general social welfare programs, or other non–criminal justice agencies.

Although we recognize that such programs might have their own agenda separate from the prosecutor's office, in this context we treat their contribution in the same light as if the advocates are formally retained by the prosecutor's office. Another caveat is that although literally hundreds of advocacy programs are available, there is a lack of agreement on what advocacy actually is (Edleson, 1993).

The growing use of advocates was supported by the recommendations issued in 1992 by the National Council of Juvenile and Family Court Judges. These recommendations included providing victim assistance in initiation and management of cases and a commitment to pursue prosecution in all instances in which a criminal case could be proven, including, when necessary, proceeding without the active involvement of the victim.

The primary purpose of victim advocates is to assist the victim in coping with the unfamiliar and often threatening process of the criminal justice system. To understand the unique importance of such advocates in the case of domestic (or child abuse) cases, we must understand that being battered by a close intimate often inflicts significant concurrent psychological abuse (Gondolf, 1998; Tolman, 1992). In turn, this pattern of abuse has the residual effect of encouraging self-doubt among survivors (Barnett, Martinez, & Keyson, 1996). As a result, levels of posttraumatic stress disorder (PTSD) frequently are severe (Dutton-Douglas, 1992). As noted in Chapter 4, it is common for survivors to be disengaged, have difficulty with concentration, and display a basic inability to make decisions.

As noted previously, the suffering incurred by many victims often is reinforced by lack of knowledge of the criminal justice system, making it difficult for them to know how to access the police, the prosecutor, and the courts. In one study, Jaffe, Hastings, Reitzel, and Austin (1993) reported that the most common suggestion of survivors for improvements to the criminal justice system was to obtain more information on available court proceedings and community services (compare with L. V. Davis & Srinivasan, 1995, which reported that one of the most important factors in having women sever abusive relationships was giving them knowledge of the available resources to help them do so).

In an excellent article summarizing legal advocacy for domestic violence survivors, Weisz (1999) reviewed how female victims used advocacy services to fill in basic gaps in knowledge of the operations of the police and the courts and to obtain economic and legal assistance and other services.

A concerted program using victim advocates also has the advantage of sensitizing prosecutors to the problems of prosecuting domestic assaults. The concept of a knowledgeable victim advocate might provide critically needed support to a woman who, with relatively few resources, has to confront an indifferent bureaucracy. Finally, such advocates are expected to explain to the victim the availability of shelters, prior restraints, and the services of other social welfare agencies. A lack of knowledge of such services undoubtedly led to many victim-initiated dismissals in the past.

We do note that a tension exists between advocacy to provide information and support to a victim who, out of preference or necessity, remains within a relationship that has in the past been abusive (Cahn, 1992; Lyon & Goth Mace, 1991) and advocacy (as will be described subsequently in this chapter) that promotes victim participation and support of the criminal justice process (Hart, 1993).

Often, those advocacy agencies housed within the prosecutor's office are perceived to act in the overriding interests of ensuring efficient case processing for their employer, the prosecutor, whereas victim advocates whose agencies act autonomously are more likely to prioritize victim needs. This difference in outlooks was observed by a comprehensive study of domestic violence courts, which reported in 2009 that victim advocates associated with prosecutors' offices were more likely to push for victim support of prosecution compared with victim advocates associated with private agencies that supported victims regardless of whether the victim supported criminal prosecution (Labriola et al., 2009).

The Impact of Victim Advocates

A series of articles during the past several decades has described how advocacy helps victims learn about their legal options (Hart, 1993). Advocates help a victim obtain a better understanding of the context of their abuse, as well as provide a better ability to communicate with support agencies (Finn, 1991). The ultimate result is that battered women who receive advocacy services, according to one source, are more likely than others to continue processing their case through to conviction (Weisz, 1999).

Victim advocates can graphically demonstrate the system's sensitivity to a victim's needs and provide needed coordination of services both within and apart from the actual prosecution of offenders. In addition, victim advocates can assist victims in gaining a better understanding of the criminal justice process and its capabilities in providing assistance.

Empirical evidence supports the finding that such approaches will, at a minimum, increase victim satisfaction. Whetstone (2001), who reported on the impact of a specialized domestic violence unit (which included a victim advocate), found that most victims were "overwhelmingly positive about their experience with the unit" (p. 390). Victims described being satisfied with services received, their understanding of the process, and the belief that their safety was improved by their experiences with the police and victim advocates. Jolin and Moose (1997) reported victim satisfaction and increased feelings of empowerment even if reoffending occasionally reoccurred.

It is even possible that a critical component of growing levels of victim satisfaction with the criminal justice system might be the movement in many jurisdictions to use effective victim advocates. Although victim advocates can provide assistance and support throughout the process, they also provide victims from the beginning with more realistic expectations of the likely outcomes and information about how to maximize safety and well-being.

This is a possible explanation for why some studies report satisfaction with intervention, regardless of its impact on reoffense rates (Jolin & Moose, 1997), whereas others only report satisfaction if there is a subsequent impact on their safety (Whetstone, 2001). In general, women who are assisted by victim advocates might believe that they are more likely to achieve their goals than they would be if services had not been provided (Sullivan, Tan, Basta, Rumptz, & Davidson, 1992). In the Quincy District Court of Massachusetts (QDC) study, Buzawa, Hotaling, Klein, and Byrne (1999) reported that a well-developed victim advocacy program engendered high levels of victim satisfaction. Eighty-one percent of recipients of such services were either very satisfied or quite satisfied with the services; 77% said they would use such services again if confronted with a similar problem. Similar findings were found in the Orange District Court (Massachusetts). More than 77% of the victim advocates reported being "very" or "somewhat" satisfied with the victim advocates (Hotaling & Buzawa, 2001).

Potential Limits of Victim Advocates

Despite the potential of these programs, they might produce undesirable effects for particular victims. Currently, in a climate of budget austerity for public agencies, virtually every institution must compete with each other for available funds to justify its actions with some "empirical" measures of success. If a victim advocate program is judged by simplistic "empirical" evaluation criteria (as we have at times observed), it might merely measure the success of a program through the undiminished lens of lowered levels of case attrition as opposed to more appropriate holistic, victim-centered measurements. We are concerned that the use of more important goals such as cessation of battering and victim satisfaction with the criminal justice process can easily be subverted to serve organizational goals that can justify budgets in the face of austerity measures such as increasing the rate of convictions regardless of victim needs or desires.

For this reason, prosecution-based programs have the potential to be counterproductive when agencies try to measure success by their abilities to commit victims to the prosecution process, thereafter defining success solely by their own vested interests (Ford & Burke, 1987; Labriola et al., 2009). This is not only a theoretical concern. Prosecutorial organizations, which are faced with high caseloads and increasing backlogs, might find their interest best served by having fewer total cases but with a larger percentage of convictions. This, of course, directly conflicts with the legitimate expectation of victims to have easy access to a judicial system staffed with helpful, but not domineering, personnel.

This role conflict might perpetuate misunderstanding between victim advocates and victims, which is reflected in complaints we have heard from many committed personnel, such as "Look what we've tried to do without any success or gratitude," which are met with victim responses, such as "They don't understand me and my family and are trying to run my life." Ultimately, we believe that a system that largely measures success by the reduction of case attrition might actually diminish victims' access to justice by deterring them from pursuing otherwise available alternatives. Subsequent research should be conducted to determine whether this concern is widespread or only of limited scope.

It has indeed been shown that victim advocacy services provided outside a prosecutor's office (or a court) were less likely to result in a negative interaction (Labriola et al., 2009). At its best, the victim advocacy is supportive, helping the woman learn about her legal options. If the legal advocates are not necessarily bound by organizational imperatives to achieve high levels of conviction, then it is certainly possible that advocacy might be tailored more to the needs of the particular victim, which might or might not involve prosecution through conviction. Of course, if such victim services are funded privately, then it might be the case that there is less control over the quality of services. Some advocates might be exceptional in terms of their commitment to victims and their knowledge of the system. Others, especially if they are part-time volunteers, simply might not have the level of training or the detailed knowledge of how the prosecutor's office and the courts work to assist victims in the best possible way.

The Impact of No-Drop Policies

Description of No-Drop Policies

Advocates for domestic violence victims have long pointed out the lack of efficacy of traditional prosecution policies dependent on victim support. Even in the most supportive courts, victims of domestic assault do not prefer prosecution. In one "activist court," domestic assault victims were more than nine times more likely than nondomestic assault victims to report that they wanted the prosecutor to drop their cases, thereby frustrating court personnel (Hotaling & Buzawa, 2001).

Concern over "excessive" case attrition has led many jurisdictions to promote measures that limit the freedom of both victims and prosecutors to drop prosecution. Such policies have many variations, but all seek to limit unfettered discretion to drop cases. At the mildest and by far the easiest to justify and embrace, prosecutors might be told to follow victim preferences for prosecution unless there is a compelling state interest to the contrary. Other models far more problematically restrict the victim's role in charging and case disposition decisions while retaining the prosecutor's discretion in deciding which cases to pursue.

Some policies also expressly target prosecutors' past practices by imposing strict limitations on their discretion to file or later drop charges. This can extend to a "mandatory filing policy" in which prosecutors are instructed to file charges in every case regardless of victim desires or the prosecutor's assessment of the evidentiary strength of the case as a whole (Peterson & Dixon, 2005).

By far the most controversial policies have been to impose both a mandatory filing policy as well as restrictions on subsequent dropping of charges—that is, a no-drop policy. At its most coercive, this policy might even compel a victim to serve as a witness. When carried to its logical conclusion, she might be subpoenaed and, if recalcitrant, held for contempt of court.

It is important to recognize that such policies vary considerably in different jurisdictions. "Hard" no-drop policies profess never to follow victim preferences insisting on case dismissals, whereas "soft" no-drop policies permit prosecutors and victims to collaborate and drop charges under certain limited circumstances, such as if the victim has left the batterer.

Current Use of No-Drop Policies

Before we give statistics regarding the use of no-drop policies, we need readers to understand that the terminology used might not reflect reality. For example, a study of no-drop policies in four jurisdictions (San Diego, CA, the first jurisdiction with such policies; Omaha, NE; Everett, WA; and Klamath Falls, OR) suggested that "no drop" really did not mean "no drop" per se. Instead, it was more of a "philosophy" rather than a strict policy—at least in these cities—with none of the jurisdictions prosecuting every case filed. What did they do to put teeth in the policy? The jurisdictions each required a coordinated intake process to determine which cases should be screened out before the imposition of a no-drop policy; provided for coordination with the judges, who would then relax the rules of evidence; and, perhaps equally important, made available additional resources to make the policy feasible (Smith, Davis, Nickles, & Davies, 2001).

Officially at least, no-drop policies have been widely instituted in many large jurisdictions. Rebovich (1996) noted that 66% of a sample of local prosecutors in jurisdictions with populations of more than 250,000 officially had no-drop policies, with 83% stating it made no difference whether the police or the victim initiated the complaint. Of these, however, 90% reported "some flexibility" in the application of these policies.

The widespread nature of such official policies was partially a result of the initial federally funded demonstration programs in Cleveland, Los Angeles, Miami, Santa Barbara, Seattle, and Westchester County, New York (Lerman, 1981), followed by a consensus among policymakers that this was the way to proceed.

Rationale for a No-Drop Policy

Although obviously rarely stated as a justification for a no-drop policy from an organizational perspective, such policies have the potential to be "productive." At an organizational, more than at a societal, level, no-drop policies limit unproductive dropped cases, thereby increasing clearance rates through convictions.

The more appropriate theoretical underpinnings of no-drop policies derive from the belief that unless abusers are adequately prosecuted, their violence will continue, causing additional physical and emotional damage to victims, their children, or perhaps even other victims (Cahn & Lerman, 1991; Waits, 1985; Wills, 1997). At its root, the state interest is said to center on the theory that even if victims successfully terminate being battered, an overriding state interest in aggressive enforcement remains.

As such, these policies rely implicitly on the concept that domestic violence is primarily a crime against the public order of the state, not against the individual victim whose interests could in theory be "purely" protected by civil action, protective order, or a victim's decision of whether to self-initiate prosecution. Like the mandatory arrest policies that they are patterned after, no-drop polices are meant to encourage a higher level of specific and general deterrence as the perceptions and reality of a conviction after a domestic violence arrest is increased—a fact that will presumably rapidly become known to current and potential batterers, thereby preventing future abuse.

Based on our discussions with many prosecutors, many of whom are well intentioned and dedicated, believe that a goal of consistent prosecution transcends and, hence, supersedes the victim's interests. As one prosecutor noted,

[t]he prosecutor's "client" is the State, not the victim. Accordingly, prosecutorial agencies that have opted for aggressive prosecution have concluded that their client's interest in protecting the safety and well-being of all its citizens overrides the individual victim's desire to dictate whether and when criminal charges are filed. Aggressive prosecution is the appropriate response to domestic violence cases for several reasons. First, domestic violence affects more than just the individual victim; it is a public safety issue that affects all of society. Second, prosecutors cannot rely upon domestic violence victims to appropriately vindicate the State's interests in holding batterers responsible for the crime they commit because victims often decline to press charges. (Wills, 1997, pp. 173–174)

In addition to state-oriented goals, advocates for no-drop policies assert that victims might benefit even if they do not currently appreciate the efforts for prosecution.

Several reasons support this statement. First, limiting discretion alleviates the problems of victims with uncooperative agencies relying on often unsympathetic court personnel by forcing these officials to justify dismissals only by insufficiency of available evidence.

This "benevolent" attitude assumes that the implicit advantage of a no-drop policy is that batterers will be identified and then "treated" or at least punished by the criminal justice system. The "system" is implicitly trusted over the opinion of the victim when determining whether offenders should be incarcerated or placed into batterer intervention programs. This would implicitly reduce the likelihood of future battering incidents, providing potential victims with the knowledge that they are consorting with a batterer and increasing the likelihood for heavier sentencing for reoffending.

Although we might not agree entirely with this policy, supporters of such no-drop polices have a solid understanding of the limits of trying to change batterer behavior. Batterers clearly have historically subverted the normal operation of the criminal justice system. As a group, batterers are, after all, master manipulators. Many can be expected to do just about anything to convince their victims to get the prosecution to drop charges. Many call from jails threatening retaliation. Others cajole their victim with promises of reform. Some will stress (perhaps truthfully) that they might lose their jobs, and hence, the family income will plummet as a result of a conviction. They often send love letters, pledging future bliss and happiness.

They also can terrorize victims from jail by having their family members engage in such behaviors as turning off her utilities, harassing her at work, or threatening to retaliate physically. Some even pay for the victim to leave town so that she will not be issued a subpoena. Many prey on the victim's personal weaknesses, especially drug and alcohol abuse, physical and mental disabilities, and her love for their children. They negotiate financial and property incentives that cause acute memories of terror and pain to fade dramatically. Prosecutors not inclined to take a case through to trial might inadvertently allow these vulnerable victims to succumb to their batterers' intimidation and manipulation tactics. In contrast, no-drop prosecutors will hold the batterers responsible regardless of the victims' lack of cooperation.

Supporters of no-drop domestic violence policies thereby claim that the alternative we might prefer, that is, empowering victims by giving them the discretion to prosecute or even to threaten to prosecute a case, in actuality, empowers batterers to manipulate and endanger their victims' lives, their children's lives, and the safety and well-being of the entire community. They note that by proceeding with the prosecution with or without victim cooperation, the prosecutor minimizes the victim's value to the batterers as a potentially unwitting, or at least intimidated, ally to defeat criminal prosecution. A no-drop policy is, therefore, said to be preferred as it does not allow batterers to control the system of justice through the manipulation of their victims (Wills, 1997, pp. 179–180).

Protection of Children as a Justification for No-Drop Policies

Finally, although the interests of the state might seem somewhat esoteric compared with the concrete needs of the victim, we need to recognize that there are other clear victims of violence, such as children, whose interests might not be adequately protected by the victim without forced prosecution of an abuser. Again, as stated by Wills (1997):

> Most notably, children are secondary victims of violence in the home. The link between domestic violence and child abuse, both emotional and physical, cannot be ignored. Each year, between three and ten million children are forced to witness the emotional devastation of one parent abusing or killing the other. Many are injured in the "crossfire" while trying to protect the assaulted parent, or are used as pawns or shields and are harmed by blows intended for someone else. Some are born with birth defects because their mothers were battered during pregnancy. Children of domestic violence are silent victims who suffer without the options available to adults. Thus, aggressive prosecution furthers the State's goal of protecting not only the victim, but also the children in homes where domestic violence occurs. (p. 175)

As we noted in previous chapters, the exposure to ongoing domestic violence threatens the mental health of children severely and impacts greatly on their thought processes. It also can increase the risk of an intergenerational cycle of abuse.

Evidence That No-Drop Policies Might Be Effective

Some evidence indicates that the institution of no-drop policies can markedly improve poor past practices. In San Diego, under the older discretionary policy, it was reported that abusers were not deterred by the criminal justice system as they understood the system simply did not enforce its own stated rules. Officials found that, under the old policy, when abusers learned that a case would be dismissed if the victim refused to cooperate, levels of violence increased.

In 1985, however, the city implemented a no-drop policy. Domestic homicides fell from 30 per year in 1985 to 20 in 1990 and to 7 in 1994. Thus, it has been claimed that no-drop policies both decrease recidivism and strengthen the message that intimate abuse will not be tolerated (Epstein, 1999, p. 15).

Deborah Epstein, director of the Domestic Violence Clinic at the Georgetown University Law Center and codirector of the Superior Court's Intake Center, noted a similar type of improvement in Washington, D.C. She stated that in 1989, the prosecutor's office tried fewer than 40 misdemeanor cases out of 19,000 emergency calls reporting family abuse. By 1995, the rates had not changed markedly. The charging rate for prosecutors was approximately 15% of those arrested, and few of those cases ever proceeded to a plea or trial. She attributed the low numbers of successful prosecutions to "special" policies of applicability only to domestic violence. Chief among those was a policy by which charges would be dropped at the victim's request at any time with no questions asked.

In 1996, Washington, D.C., instituted a no-drop policy with a domestic violence unit. That unit filed approximately 6,000 misdemeanor cases in the first year and 8,000 the next year. Even more interesting was the case disposition. Fully two thirds of those arrested faced prosecution. According to Epstein (1999), this is exactly the same rate as for stranger violence. In addition, the rates of convictions in domestic cases—69%—closely approximated those for other misdemeanor, nonjury trials. Clearly, a no-drop policy in this court with these committed prosecutors resulted in an overwhelming change from an ineffective previous regime.

Limitations of No-Drop Policies

As stated previously, we have concerns with the implementation of no-drop prosecution policies. These policies are the functional parallel of police mandatory arrest policies. Although a policy of limited victim and prosecutor discretion certainly has some obvious merits in the context of the pressures placed on domestic violence victims to dismiss cases, we believe they might be operationally impractical in many settings and might impose serious costs to both victims and agencies alike. This poses several relevant policy questions. Is the state interest actually served by such policies? Second, what is the impact on the victim? Is it best in actual practice for societal interests to triumph over victim interests?

The state interests in no-drop polices are not nearly as clear as advocates would believe. For example, there is a need to address the reality of limited available prosecutorial resources. We believe it safe to assume that given perilous, long-term conditions of state and municipal finances, actual resources will not increase merely because a new policy mandates prosecution of one specific class of crimes. Therefore, any increase in agency time demands from this type of crime must be offset by a diminished capacity of that same organization to perform other tasks related either to domestic violence or other issues.

Using this type of global implementation analysis, placing limits on prosecutorial discretion indeed might be justifiable given the past tendencies of many prosecutorial bureaucracies to downplay the importance of domestic cases. It is difficult, however, to argue persuasively that a district attorney should not have the resources to prosecute and that a court should subsequently be unable to try, other contested criminal cases (perhaps even felonies) merely because prosecutors are mandated to try all misdemeanor domestic violence cases, especially when a victim does not want the case to be prosecuted.

Therefore, we believe that as part of an integral justification for this position, advocates of no-drop policies should expressly analyze the displacement of limited resources attendant to such a policy, and as part of their argument, they should be required to state explicitly what tasks being performed by these prosecutors (with limited, if any, ability to increase resources) should now be foregone to implement a true no-drop policy.

If this is not done, then real-life difficult choices of harried administrators are simply dismissed, and the true impact of a policy is not being debated fairly. That glib statement might or might not be true in the long term. Currently, empirical evidence on this is

lacking. However, it is clearly not a response to the real question: Which domestic violence cases can advocates of a no-drop policy tell the prosecutor to dismiss? If none are
presented or the suggestion is wholly impractical politically (similar to advising them to
stop enforcing drug crimes), then we must recognize that an "advocate" has not truly
faced up to the difficult choices inherent in developing realistic policies at a state and
local level.

Let us look at what happens in actual practice. In a study conducted in Milwaukee, an
analysis was performed of an aggressive policy of having prosecutors charge virtually all
domestic violence crimes without a corresponding increase in resources. After implementing an aggressive, no-drop policy, the following was found:

- Case backlog increased greatly.

- Cases filed with the court contained a larger proportion of victims who did not
  want their cases prosecuted.

- The time to disposition doubled.

- Convictions declined.

- Pretrial crime increased.

- Victim satisfaction with case outcomes and with the prosecutor's handling of the
  case declined. (Davis et al., 1998, p. 71)

From this, the following overall conclusion of the researchers toward no-drop policies
was negative:

> The district attorney's policy to prosecute a larger proportion of domestic violence arrests
> had several effects, none of them positive, which may have been due in part to insufficient
> allocation of resources. One effect of the new policy was to bring into the court system a
> larger proportion of cases with victims who were not interested in seeing the defendant
> prosecuted. Victim satisfaction with prosecutors and with court outcomes declined after the
> new screening policy. As the special court became overwhelmed with cases, case-processing
> time increased back to the level that had existed prior to the start of the specialized court
> [thus, in effect, sabotaging the effect of a different reform, a dedicated domestic violence
> court]. (Davis et al., 1998, pp. 71–72)

Alternatively, in other jurisdictions, it might be the case that as a result of the lack of
a planned implementation strategy that explicitly takes resources away from the prosecution of other offenses, no-drop policies revert to discretionary policies in reality and
become "paper-only" policies. Several prosecutors have noted that even those offices
widely publicized as being "no drop" develop procedures that, in effect, screen cases.

For example, an analysis of the practices of the San Diego City Attorney's Office noted
that it refused to prosecute one third of all domestic violence cases; essentially, they did
not prosecute if independent corroborating evidence was lacking when the victim
declined to cooperate.

It is easy to understand why even the most committed office would develop such
screening techniques. As one prosecutor explained, if the victim recants, then the proper
prosecution for domestic abuse cases is similar to a homicide in that independent corroborating evidence has to be used in place of the victim's testimony (Hartman, 1999).

However, except for the relatively rare occurrence of a federal grant, no additional resources are typically received. The reality is that misdemeanor cases are typically tried by the most over-worked and least experienced district attorneys. If they must try cases of such complexity without additional resources, the burden may be overwhelming. Taking iffy misdemeanors to trial in my jurisdiction is seen as wasteful, not unethical. *As long as I do my trial preparation on the weekends at home, so far, I am allowed my idiosyncrasy. However, if I want the help of another prosecutor for misdemeanors, I am shown the door not only by my own prosecutorial kind, but also by legislative bodies that persist in passing statutes which amount to unfounded mandates* (making the prosecution of most domestic crimes more time-consuming and intricate). . . . *We've gotten tough enough already; the only real solution . . . is putting our money where our mandates are.* So long as the domestic violence equivalent of MADD [Mothers Against Drunk Driving] encourages their elected representatives to add more "politically correct" but fiscally ignored burdens on those of us who try to prosecute these cases, we're never going to get there. (p. 74; emphasis added)

By some official measures, societal interest is achieved only if high conviction rates result. Indeed, some jurisdictions, such as the county of Los Angeles, have high conviction rates (Wills, 1997); however, the actual impact on conviction rates of no-drop policies in other jurisdictions is unclear.

Several studies have attempted to understand more clearly the reasons why. One research report stated that when victims do not support prosecution or are unconvincing witnesses, the result is far lower conviction rates despite the increase in committed resources (Davis et al., 1998). This concern is not hypothetical. Consider the following:

The problem is that the policies backfire. When we force arrest and prosecution on battered women, they often recant and lie. One prosecutor in Los Angeles, who will remain anonymous, estimated that most battered women are reluctant witnesses who are willing to perjure themselves when they are put on the stand against their will. (Wills, 1997, p. 190)

One researcher who interviewed a state's attorney's office (the local prosecutor) in a no-drop jurisdiction was told by these court officers that between 80% and 90% of victims were uncooperative (Guzik, 2007).

Indeed, we believe the extent of this problem is difficult to overstate. Despite being an advocate for mandatory prosecution, Wills (1997), the head deputy of the Family Violence Unit of the Los Angeles County District Attorney's Office, noted that victims in Los Angeles County recanted in more than 50% of cases. Another study using Canadian data found that, according to prosecutors, almost 60% of all decisions not to prosecute were because of the victim's total noncooperation, including refusal to testify, recanting, or retracting testimony or failing to appear in court (Dawson & Dinovitzer, 2001; Ursel, 1995).

As such, even an advocate for mandatory prosecution had to recognize obvious practical problems with implementation of such a policy, and Wills (1997) acknowledged the real conflict between prosecutors and victims was that:

[p]rosecutors and the courts have taken a long time to accept that a domestic violence victim's "refusal to press charges" is the norm in domestic violence prosecutions. Indeed, prosecutors traditionally are reluctant to charge batterers because victims frequently change their minds and later drop the charges. Faced with having to testify in court, domestic violence victims, especially battered women, routinely recant, minimize the abuse, or fail to appear. (p. 177)

Thus, it is evident why, for reasons of practicality, such a policy is almost never used for other misdemeanor offenses. Society's interest in a no-drop policy implicitly depends on no reaction by victims to the behavior of the criminal justice system. This is paradoxical in that to have any real long-term impact on rates of abuse, domestic violence advocates tacitly, or even at times explicitly, assume that batterers will desist from battering as a reaction to the threat of future prosecution.

We have a great deal of difficulty advocating a policy that implicitly forces a victim to lie and align with her batterer against society. Can this be what advocates of no-drop policies really want? Moreover, most victims are forced into prosecuting cases against their will, and advocates do not seem to expect the victim to react otherwise. We believe this to be highly simplistic and somewhat patronizing. It is probable that if a victim rationally (in her own mind) does not agree with prosecution, then a no-drop policy might deter victims from reporting future crimes. In these jurisdictions, if implementation actually occurs, victims will be faced with the realization that once a case enters the court process, they lose control to what seems to them an impersonal and overbearing bureaucracy.

After all, disempowering victims is the antithesis of the goal of most abused women and advocates. Those supporting this type of control are probably unaware that they might often be further reinforcing the belief that the "helpless" or "fickle" victim is the primary reason for the system's lack of responsiveness, rather than the system's inability to flexibly address individual victim needs.

Data in a study of a model court in Quincy, Massachusetts (the QDC), gave support for this concern (Buzawa et al., 1999), reporting that a latent outcome of aggressive policies dismissing victim preferences seemed to discourage the future use of the system by those victims who feared for their safety. Victim interviews found that these women were more than 2.5 times less likely than other victims to report revictimization in a 1-year period after the initial study incident (Buzawa et al., 1999):

> Implicit in many of the arguments raised in favor of "no-drop" policies, such as victim intimidation by batterers, batterers as master manipulators, and prosecutors as "guardians" of the rights of victims, is that the victims are, as a class, incapable of assessing their peril. This lacks empirical support. In fact, the QDC study found that the victims' preferences and perceptions of dangerousness were generally very good predictors of subsequent revictimization. Women who did not experience revictimization within a 12-month period were more than twice as likely as those who were revictimized to have preferred no criminal justice involvement. A greater number of women who felt that going to court would decrease their safety were accurate in their assessment. Women who were "forced" to prosecute and who felt that going to court reduced their ability to bargain with the offender were also more likely to be revictimized. (p. 116)

Proponents of no-drop policies argued that despite the failure of victims to cooperate, police can provide sufficient evidence for these cases to move forward, including victim statements, photographs, and medical reports. However, as we have discussed, despite improved responses by the police, prosecutors still face crucial evidentiary problems in obtaining the needed documentation from police. For example, one district attorney noted that in his county, only one police department regularly provided their office with taped victim statements (Guzik, 2007).

Therefore, in many jurisdictions, prosecutors are faced with a theoretical mandate to prosecute all cases but without any additional resources and the real prospect of unco-operative key witnesses. As a result, prosecutors develop a variety of informal strategies to help resolve their dilemma.

First, prosecutors often will overcharge offenders by increasing the severity of the charge relative to the actual offense or, alternatively, by charging them with multiple offenses (Guzik, 2007). In fact, some victim advocates encourage this practice as part of a strategy for prosecutors to facilitate the prosecution of these cases.

A second strategy prosecutors use in no-drop jurisdictions is to allow offenders to avoid bail for a felony offense in response to a guilty plea to a misdemeanor offense, which typically does not require bail. Alternatively, if the offender is out on bail, then they look for a reason to reverse the decision by arresting the offender, typically for vio-lation of a restraining order. Offenders often violate specific conditions of these orders by contacting the victim or her children, or the use of alcohol or drugs (Guzik, 2007).

Courts also might be forced to become even more coercive. Restraining orders might then become routinely ordered by the courts, rather than at the request of the victim, in the somewhat manipulative hope that the conditions will be violated providing an eas-ier crime to prosecute (Guzik, 2007). As a result, not only do victims not have control over the initial decision to prosecute, but also a restraining order might be taken out without her specific request and conditions might be set that might not be in accordance with her wishes. For example, because of dependent children or a lack of other assets, a "no-contact" restraining order might not be in the family's interest.

Although guilty pleas might increase as a result of such strategies, we believe the process itself becomes extremely coercive and the types of cases and dispositions that are rendered might not mirror the profile of a court with less restrictive charging policies.

Although our primary concern might not be with an offender's rights, such practices also might be regarded as an effort by the system to trap offenders into more serious charges. Defense attorneys might feel pressured into urging offenders to accept a plea out of concern for the judge's reaction at his lack of cooperation for a "reasonable" plea (Guzik, 2007):

> [T]hese tactics and powers shape the suspects' behavior, decision making, and relation to himself and his partner in different, sometimes contradictory ways. The no-contact order and aggressive charges apply leverage intended to have him plead guilty by making the process more punishing. These tactics are buoyed by the silencing, warnings, admonish-ments, and accusations placed against him in pretrial proceedings. (pp. 66–67)

Can No-Drop Policies Be Justified Based on Superior Results?

What has empirical evidence shown about the impact of prosecution on deterring reoffending behavior? The classic study of mandatory prosecution was conducted in Indianapolis, Indiana (Ford & Regoli, 1992). This study was an experimental assignment of 480 men charged with misdemeanor assaults on their domestic partners. They were assigned to one of three tracks: diversion, prosecution with a recommendation of coun-seling, or prosecution with a presumptive sentence. The study found that the prosecu-tion policy adopted affected batterer behavior. Although they found that victims who chose not to prosecute were at greatest risk of reabuse, they did not find the lowest levels of reabuse in the no-drop prosecution category. Instead, they concluded that victim complainants were at the best advantage when they were permitted to drop charges but, in fact, were persuaded to follow-up with them. In fact, they reported that this was the only policy with a preventive impact; it was significantly more effective than traditional processing (Ford & Regoli, 1992).

In short, enhancing the empowerment of the victim, rather than the actual prosecution, might be a key factor, despite the ideal situation in which the victim and prosecutor cooperate with each other to convict the abuser. Ford and Regoli's (1992) conclusion is instructive:

> The Indianapolis experiment, however, offers the surprising finding that, contrary to popular advocacy, permitting victims to drop charges significantly reduces their risk of further violence after a suspect has been arrested on a victim-initiated warrant, when compared with usual policies. We believe that under a drop-permitted policy, women are empowered to take control of events in their relationship. Some are empowered through prosecution such that they can use the possibility of abandoning prosecution as a power resource in bargaining for their security. . . . Others are empowered by the alliance they form with more powerful others, such as police, prosecutors, and judges. (p. 206)

In addition, a study of abusers prosecuted in the Specialized Felony Domestic Violence Court in Brooklyn, New York, reported that within 18 months of disposition, 41% of the defendants charged with a domestic violence felony were rearrested, with 8% for a violent felony and 11% for violation of a protective order. The rearrest rate for violators of protective orders (a felony) was 53%, with 4% for a violent felony and 33% for another order violation (Newmark, Rempel, Diffily, & Kane, 2001).

Clearly, no-drop policies are preferable to a past system of prosecutorial indifference or judicial abuse of their vast discretion. However, to some extent, that is an unfair comparison. A fairer comparison might be to review results between two jurisdictions with the same statutory requirements, one with a no-drop mandate and one that uses current preferred practices but not a no-drop mandate. Fortunately, such a comparison was conducted and the results are interesting. Brooklyn, New York, has a universal filing policy. The Bronx, although equally committed to stopping domestic violence, does not have such coercive methods and largely follows victim preferences in the decision to file or not file a case (O'Sullivan, Davis, Farole, & Rempel, 2007).

O'Sullivan et al. (2007) studied 272 cases that were declined for prosecution in the Bronx. In Brooklyn, cases filed without victim support typically were dismissed after 3 months. A 6-month follow-up revealed no significant difference in rearrest rates under each policy, although new arrests were more likely to be charged as felonies in Brooklyn. The Brooklyn policy also was more costly and required that the prosecutor be given more resources compared with the Bronx. These additional resources were needed for victim outreach, staff court appearances, case investigation, and efforts to collect evidence. From this perspective, Brooklyn's policy, although progressive and well intentioned, was not as viable as the Bronx. It required far greater use of scarce agency assets, undoubtedly displeased some victims (and possibly deterred their future reports of offenses), ultimately resulted in unproductive numbers of cases that were not pursued to conviction as the burden on prosecutors to prove a case in the face of victim noncooperation made such efforts untenable.

Finally, in rearrest rates, the only other real outcome measurement, there seemed to be no difference. Based on this evidence alone, especially if duplicated in other settings, universal prosecution does not seem justified. This type of result also has been shown in outcome measures of serious violence.

Some evidence has indicated that prosecution of domestic violence cases might not help as many victims as we would like, especially in cases where the assailant is an exceptionally violent perpetrator. A study of homicide data in 48 states sponsored by the National Institute of Justice (NIJ) reported that increased prosecution rates for domestic assault (even when controlling for several variables) were associated with increased levels of homicides among White married couples, Black unmarried intimates, and White unmarried women—hardly the positive result anticipated (Dugan, Nagin, & Rosenfeld, 2001).

Does a No-Drop Policy Adversely Affect Victims?

A no-drop policy that forces prosecution restricts victim autonomy. This concern is not insignificant. Even an advocate of no-drop policies such as Professor Epstein (1999) observed the following:

> As police and prosecutors escalate their response to domestic violence cases, survivors increasingly confront a criminal justice system that can perpetuate the kinds of power and control dynamics that exist in the battering relationship itself. In many cases, prosecutors take complete control over the case, functioning as the sole decision maker and ignoring the victim's voice. *If a victim changes her mind mid-way through the litigation and seeks to drop charges so that the father of her children can continue to work and provide financial support, a prosecutor may refuse to do so, on the ground that this would not serve the interests of the state in punishing violations of the social contract. Such re-victimization can thwart the survivor's efforts to regain control over her life and move past the abusive experience.* Thus, where the bulk of control was ceded to the perpetrator under the old automatic drop system, it is now ceded to the prosecutor. Although battered women have a far greater influence over the criminal justice process today than ever before, the system's responsiveness to their individual needs remains limited. (pp. 16–17; emphasis added)

The extent of conflicts between victims (who do not want a case to be filed or, if filed, to proceed) and prosecutors driven to prosecute without victim support should not be underestimated. Prosecutors certainly are aware of the reality of this problem as conflicts with victims occur frequently when no-drop policies are adopted. Rebovich (1996) confirmed Wills's previously cited observation that more than 50% of victims refused to testify. He reported that many of the larger prosecutors' offices had considerable problems with uncooperative victims. For example, 33% of the prosecutors who responded claimed that more than 55% of their cases involved uncooperative witnesses; 16% claimed the number to be between 41% and 55%; and 27% estimated that it was between 26% and 40%. Only 27% reported a 0% to 25% lack of cooperation (Rebovich, 1996).

Not surprisingly, to accomplish their own organizational goals, Rebovich (1996) reported that prosecutors often became coercive with victims; 92% of such officials used their subpoena power to require victim testimony. Surprisingly, the least coercive methods to overcome a lack of victim cooperation—use of victim advocate testimony and videotapes of initial victim interviews—were used the least (10% and 6%, respectively), and relatively few used expert witnesses who could testify on such issues as why victims often refuse to cooperate (Rebovich, 1996).

No-drop policies that are coupled with a strong victim advocacy program also might have an additional adverse impact. Victim advocates housed within the prosecutor's office are one of the great innovations of modern reforms and might not be perceived as true "victim" advocates. There is the potential for a clear conflict of interest between the victim, who might not want to pursue a charge, and the victim advocate, whose task as defined by the prosecutor's office is to ensure victim cooperation.

Unfortunately, this might cause the victim to lose trust and be less communicative with the advocate, her nominal ally. She might even find her legitimate fears of adverse consequences minimized by her nominal "advocate" as her case is "pushed" through the system.

The promotion of simplistic views of victim needs ignores the complex nature of a victim's decision to desist prosecution. Many advocates for battered women are now better understanding that there are, in fact, unanticipated consequences to such policies. Linda Mills (1997), who was an early advocate for victim empowerment, might have best stated this concern:

> A small but growing number of feminists are beginning to worry that universally applied strategies, such as mandatory prosecution, cannot take into account the reasons women stay in abusive relationships or the reasons for their denial. These feminists fear that the State's indifference to this contingent of battered women is harmful, even violent. . . . By violent, I refer to the institutional violence inflicted through the competitive dynamic that dominates the relationships between the State, the survivor, and the batterer. The State, in its obsession to punish the batterer, often uses the battered woman as a pawn for winning the competition. This destructive dynamic is abusive in itself to the woman. (p. 188)

Not surprisingly, Mills (1998) argued persuasively for what she described as a "tailored service" for victims rather than mandatory policies that fixate on offender conviction. As noted previously, a victim might prefer dropping charges after she has been successful in achieving her primary goals. The failure to allow her to use this power seems foolish and is common. One study of cases prosecuted in several jurisdictions in Massachusetts found that of those victims not wanting the case to go forward, 27% reported they had already obtained what they wanted from the offender or worked things out, and an additional 23% had already ended the relationship with the offender and felt no further need to prosecute (Hotaling & Buzawa, 2001).

A victim's safety also might be theoretical. As noted previously, homicide rates do not seem to be affected positively by prosecution. Professor Ford of Indiana University noted that a victim might be safest if she retains the power to drop charges at her discretion. This gives her the ability to use the system to work toward her ends with the threat of continued prosecution as a "victim power resource" (Ford & Regoli, 1993; cf. Hotaling & Buzawa, 2001). In sharp contrast, the reality of the process of prosecution is that most victims wait 6 to 9 months from the time of complaint to the time of trial. During this period, significant changes might occur. Many victims, often with the support of family, friends, acquaintances, service agencies, or formal and informal mediators, can successfully negotiate a satisfactory outcome. They legitimately might fear that prosecution would jeopardize such arrangements. This fear often is real. As a trial date approaches, many batterers begin to harass the victim, create obstacles with visitation, and jeopardize the negotiated arrangements she has already achieved.

Under these circumstances, it is not always in a victim's interest to continue prosecution. In this regard, our perspective directly challenges the assumption of other writers (Cahn & Lerman, 1991; Waits, 1985), who have maintained that prosecution must be completed to achieve long-term cessation of violence. Perhaps the dilemma might be resolved by understanding that many women might be safer if they can drop actions freely but ultimately might be less safe if they do. The implication of this insight might be that victims need to be treated as full partners in the prosecution of the case, which necessitates that the victim be given full disclosure of the long-term trends of familial violence, including the tendency to escalate attacks, the potential of effective prosecution to end such a cycle, and a realistic assessment of the costs and delays that she will likely incur if the case is prosecuted fully.

Furthermore, we must be sensitive to the realities of U.S. culture. The negative effects of enforced prosecution might disproportionately impact racial and ethnic minority victims—those who might most need the assistance of the criminal justice system. It has become increasingly clear that the impact of prosecutorial and judicial intervention might be affected by race, socioeconomic status, ethnicity, and cultural norms (Dobash & Dobash, 2000; Thistlewaite, Wooldredge, & Gibbs, 1998). For example, immigrants, especially those whose partners are in the country illegally, might strongly wish to avoid prosecution for fear that it might lead to job loss or even deportation of the family's sole source of financial support. This fear is not uncommon.

Recent reforms in U.S. immigration statutes mandate that even lawfully registered permanent resident immigrants convicted of virtually any major crimes, including domestic violence and stalking, might be deported. Conviction for a domestic assault might, therefore, be totally devastating in situations in which a woman needs the batterer's financial assistance. Even without a legal "sword of Damocles" hanging over a family's head, many victims of domestic violence in immigrant communities might be somewhat insular, and women held responsible for deportation of a fellow immigrant by the community might find themselves and their families subjected to severe ostracism, or perhaps even violent retaliation, within their own communities (Epstein, 1999).

Some evidence indicates that this fear is widespread. Bui and Morash (1999) reported that Vietnamese immigrant women who were victims of batterers feared that new laws would lead to the deportation of their husbands after arrest and conviction of a domestic violence offense. This fear has resulted in decreased levels of reporting abuse—which is directly contrary to the goals of most domestic violence advocates.

Many additional minority group members, even if native born, belong to races or ethnic groups that have had a long, uneasy relationship with police characterized by harsh treatment of suspects and the widespread scapegoating of their community. Not surprisingly, many minority women might not want to draw the attention of these agencies, let alone be told how and when their cases will be prosecuted. They also are aware that many minority community leaders feel that convictions for such "minor" offenses perpetuate the stereotype of criminal behavior. Prosecutors and courts also need to be aware of the fact that certain subpopulations of women, including minority women and those of lower socioeconomic status, are at greater risk of revictimization or retaliation and might therefore be more reticent.

Victims Charged With Child Endangerment

Perhaps the most difficult dilemma is what happens to victims with dependent children. Pro-prosecution reforms are exposing latent tensions between the needs of two seemingly aligned groups—(1) victims of domestic violence as well as (2) their children and their respective advocates. All too often, female victims of domestic violence are aware, or perhaps more accurately, should be aware of physical or sexual abuse of minor children. Unfortunately, abused women who bring their assailants to the attention of the police might be subject to claims that they have "failed to protect" their children. Many have had their children removed from their custody for such reasons or have even been prosecuted.

Of course, the problem is that few advocates for child welfare consider the precarious nature of the female victim of domestic violence—a person traumatized by an intimate partner and by physical violence who, for financial, emotional, and communal reasons or because of immigration status, often cannot realistically leave her abuser. In turn, domestic violence victim advocates often fail to comprehend the ongoing damage to children caused by the exposure to relentless acts of violence in the family, despite whether those acts are committed against children directly. The fact of the matter is that many women, perhaps because of their own psychological issues including anger displacement or profound substance abuse, might neglect or physically mistreat their children.

One commentator noted that in New York State, the legal system has become a source of implicit danger to battered mothers rather than a source of assistance. This came from a recent trend to hold mothers strictly accountable for their actions and the actions of their spouse toward their children (e.g., it was common for mothers filing for a civil protective order to face a criminal charge of child neglect for "exposing their children to domestic violence; Lemon, 2000). In other words, even if the child had not been victimized, the mere exposure of violence toward the mother allegedly constituted a crime committed by the mother. A report from the NIJ (Whitcomb, 2002) described how prosecutors nationwide have been responding to changing statutes designed to protect children from the effects of violence in the family.

Whitcomb (2002) conducted a survey of 128 prosecutors who worked in 93 offices in 49 states. They had jurisdiction over both felony and misdemeanor cases involving family violence and/or child maltreatment cases. She described a pattern in which children who witnessed acts of domestic violence were used as a power resource by many prosecutors to increase victim cooperation and the offender's willingness to plead guilty to lesser charges by a threatened felony charge of child endangerment.

Three scenarios prototypically were involved when the interests of the mother might not coincide with that of her children: (1) An abused mother is alleged to have abused her children, (2) both mother and children are abused by the same male perpetrator, and (3) children are exposed to domestic violence but are not abused themselves. For each scenario, respondents answered these questions: Would your office report the mother to the child protection agency? Would your office prosecute the mother in the first scenario for the abuse of her children? Would your office report or prosecute the mother in scenarios 2 and 3 for failure to protect her children from abuse or exposure to domestic violence? Table 12.1 shows prosecutors' responses to these questions.

We know that many women who are victims of domestic violence have minor children in the household. Currently, we are expecting women to report all acts of abuse; however, the results of such reporting might expose her to loss of custody of the children (nearly automatic in some jurisdictions when a report of child endangerment is being investigated) and even in extreme cases might subject her to threats of prosecution for child abuse or child endangerment either because of her own activity or because of her inability to resolve her own battering. We can expect that, as this dilemma becomes more widely publicized, many women will simply refuse to seek needed assistance despite long-term risk to the safety and well-being of themselves and their children. It is not surprising that litigation on this point has already begun. In fact, a class action was filed in federal court against the Child Services Administration and the New York City Police Department, claiming that both had a practice of taking children from victims of domestic violence and putting them in foster care, regardless of whether the child was in danger (Lemon, 2000).

In addition, in many instances, continued maternal drug or alcohol abuse really does result in severe impact on her ability to care for minor children—a fact often cited by abusive fathers in custody hearings. Although one might argue that is in the ultimate interests of the children to be out of a home where either parent abuses substances or neglects their welfare, the impact of child services intervention on domestic violence case handling, however, is clear: If victims calling the police for assistance become themselves subject to prosecution for child abuse or neglect charges or are at serious risk or losing child custody, then many will simply not call the police. The problem of victim deterrence from reporting is likely to worsen as child custody policies harden, and in our view, this is likely a typical example of the "law of unintended consequences."

The Likelihood of Conviction

We assume that the goal for bringing criminal charges is to secure a conviction of a crime that is at least somewhat related to the offense that occurred. This is often simply not the case if a victim is uncooperative with case prosecution. One assistant state attorney named Matt described the real life dilemma to a researcher as follows:

> "I got in all the evidence that I wanted to, the 911 tape got in. (The defendant) even said he put his hands on her out of anger . . . and I'm going against a defense attorney who is saying things like, 'If this is a crime, then we have to open up prisons all over the state,' 'when you go home at night, don't you dare touch your wife.' Stuff that is completely inappropriate. And anyways, not guilty within a half an hour. I mean BOOM, not guilty in a half hour." Reflecting on why he lost what he felt was a strong case, Matt shared what the judge told him following the decision: "It was a jury trial, but there weren't any injuries, so you know how these cases go" in Centralia County. Nancy, the victim's advocate, echoed this point, "in this county, with our juries, you will not get a conviction if a victim is uncooperative." (Guzik, 2007, p. 49)

Therefore, unless we are to subscribe to the somewhat controversial theory that the process absent conviction should be the punishment (e.g., being ensnared as a criminal defendant is sufficient punishment for a crime), there might not be any real punishment if the victim does not agree with the prosecution strategies employed. To the extent that advocates of no-drop policies cite the punishment factor of having a defendant go through a trial and be acquitted, they should be aware that this is exactly the theory that was used by police officers in the early 19th century that condoned beating up offenders to extract street justice. After all, no one has given any right or legitimacy to prosecutors or court personnel to extract punishment independent of either a trial or a guilty plea.

Alternatives to Mandatory Prosecution

We believe that it is incumbent on proponents of extreme measures, such as prosecutorial no-drop policies or the coercion of victims to achieve convictions, to determine whether less disruptive measures would accomplish the same goals. Initially, we need to stop counting rates of victim-led case withdrawal as a defeat for criminal justice agencies. True, in many cases, the victim might need encouragement to continue. However, the line between encouragement and outright coercion is, in practice, obviously being crossed in many jurisdictions. We suggest that prosecutors and victim advocates be trained to more accurately distinguish between a victim who is being subjected to a manipulative offender and a victim whose reasons for case attrition are benign, as a result of achieving her goals before the conclusion of the case. If they seem to not be motivated by overt fear of offender retaliation, then they should decide simply to follow her preferences.

We also believe that prosecutorial concerns over undue case withdrawals could be addressed through several less coercive practices. Implicit in this statement is the belief that victim cooperation with prosecution might depend on factors beyond the purview of the criminal justice system. Many such procedural improvements can be made. All of these options are well within the control of the police and prosecutor, who can then influence (but not coerce) the victim to continue prosecution—if such actions are in her own best interests. Otherwise, we believe that victims should be allowed to participate in the key decision of whether to prosecute a batterer. Some of the following less coercive measures are obvious.

First, for many years, some police departments have used vastly improved incident report forms that require detailed information on domestic assaults. Electronically preserved photographs of bruises and or easily made contemporaneous videotapes can be attached to reports economically and easily, and time spent on interviews with parties at the time of the incident can make the officer an effective witness to a prosecution and make later extensive victim testimony unnecessary.

Second, prosecutors can make additional efforts to address victim's needs more satisfactorily and to provide greater support. Legitimate fears of offender intimidation might be partially addressed by making the victim's reasons for discontinuance more visible and, therefore, more appropriate for resolution. Simply forcing defendants to appear in court at arraignment accomplishes some level of "offender intimidation," providing an opportunity for the prosecutor to determine whether there are issues of victim intimidation. At such hearings, prosecutors might insist that the defendant abide by certain restrictions, such as no contact with the victim and no subsequent battery as a condition of release. When such restrictions are imposed, a violation can be used to justify incarceration before trial and to signal which cases require aggressive action by the system. When properly administered and not abused, certain pretrial diversions—a succession of battering and attendance at treatment programs—might accomplish the same result as actual conviction, with few costs to the system or to the victim. Ignoring the efficacy of such processing in favor of no-drop policies would seem to dissipate scarce resources unnecessarily.

Third, a long-term training program to sensitize court personnel, of the provision of a well-staffed advocacy program, with the ability to help victims to understand and navigate through the judicial process might serve the purpose of reducing case attrition without imposing a no-drop policy. Simple measures might accomplish alignment of prosecution and victim goals. It has been noted that prosecutors, being trained as aggressive lawyers, typically lack the innate ability to handle social problems or even to be comfortable addressing victims' feelings. This makes it difficult for them to speak to victims in a nurturing, rather than an overbearing, manner (Mills, 1997).

Relatively modest changes in the prosecution of cases, such as inviting women to file complaints in informal and confidential settings at locations other than the prosecutor's office (emergency rooms, female-run facilities, etc.), might start the process of committing the victim to prosecution. Similarly, prosecutor's offices could offer to provide victims with transportation to court, pay for day care if necessary, and provide private waiting rooms so no victim intimidation might occur prior to a proceeding. An approach that recognizes barriers to victim support of prosecution and actively seeks prosecution would demonstrate that the system does not prejudge her as being either hopeless or helpless but instead demonstrates a willingness to nurture and empower her (Mills, 1997).

Fourth, a relatively modest change in court procedures could accomplish many of the perceived goals for a no-drop policy. Specifically, it could become the policy that cases without actual serious injury might be freely dropped at the request of the victim. Alternatively, coercion should be used in a targeted manner. In cases in which an injury did occur and is documented by irrefutable electronic evidence or sworn statements of officers or other witnesses, the victim could be told to cooperate with the prosecution unless she appears in open court and explains on the record why she wants the charges to be dropped. Along with her testimony, the criminal history of the offender would greatly assist the court in determining the likelihood of intimidation compared with the victim's genuine belief that the case does not warrant prosecution. This would help a court identify cases of victim intimidation and expose the reasons for the victim's decisions.

If adopted, this practice also addresses the fact that in many cases, alleged victim non-cooperation might be more a function of the failure of the prosecutor and court to communicate effectively with the victim. Having a mandated but informal appearance by a victim before allowing her to drop a case would make certain that cases were not being dropped because of miscommunications among the prosecutor, court, and victim, and it would give an opportunity for the victim to be heard in court (Belknap et al., 2001). A sympathetic judge would then be able to explain if, in his or her opinion, continued prosecution could expand the victim's interests without coercion.

Fifth, in large jurisdictions, specialized domestic violence units in prosecutors' offices might provide more informed and efficient prosecution of cases. In most jurisdictions, younger, less-experienced prosecutors handle a variety of misdemeanor cases on an assembly-line basis. A group of dedicated prosecutors with specialized training might allow for improved efficiency in operations, thereby enhancing conviction rates. Even in smaller jurisdictions, having a designated prosecutor handle all such cases could accomplish similar results. In either case, "vertical prosecution"—having one prosecutor handle a given case from intake to final disposition—greatly increases the likelihood of involvement of the prosecutor and victim.

Sixth, there is persuasive evidence that increased contact of prosecutors with victims can enhance the prospects of guilty verdicts dramatically, regardless of whether coercive policies toward victims are in place. In one study, Belknap et al. (1999) analyzed 2,670 case dispositions in a midwestern court and reported that 44% resulted in a guilty verdict, 51% were dismissed, and 5% resulted in a not-guilty verdict. Not surprisingly, prosecutors blamed the victims for the high dismissal rate. They said it was because of the victims' failure to appear in court.

Belknap and colleagues noted that in reality, victims often were not responsible for poor case outcomes. In many instances, the victim was not even told of relevant court dates; in other cases, there seemed to be little positive feedback from the prosecutor to encourage victim cooperation. Belknap et al. (1999) reported that

> [t]he best predictor of court outcome is how many times the prosecutor met with the victim. The more often the prosecutor met with the victim, the greater the likelihood that the defendant was found guilty, was fined more, and received a greater number of days sentenced to both probation and incarceration. (p. 9)

She also observed that victims were at times more afraid of the courts and the law than they were of the danger posed by the offender. As a result, her recommendation of making the court system more user-friendly for victims and with more informal contacts with prosecutors could reduce the concerns of the woman, making her more likely to voluntarily testify and enhance the probability of convictions without coercion. Other research also has emphasized that within the prosecutor's office, the frequency and quality of meeting with victims and victim advocates within the prosecutors' offices (or similar advocates) are critical to sustaining a victim's desire to prosecute a case (Weisz, 1999).

Seventh, no-drop policies might be needed, but reserved for repeat batterers, especially those who have either previously attacked the same victim or who have a chronic unrelated history of violence—"the generally violent" or " serial batterers" are a subset of offenders described in an earlier chapter. Our growing knowledge base shows that they account for many, if not most, incidents and account for the vast bulk of serious injuries. Therefore, the test of a more limited policy might provide most of the societal benefits advanced in support of general no-drop policies while targeting seriously limited resources toward those that clearly deserve such attention.

In contrast, those offenders who have the greatest likelihood to respond to more rehabilitative approaches would then have the resources needed to access these less-coercive services to achieve lasting change.

It might be that these less-intrusive measures might accomplish the bulk of the intent of no-drop policies. After all, the basic reason for such policies has been the understanding that most cases are dropped at victim request; yet it is functionally difficult to determine whether the victim does so of her own volition or as a result of intimidation or discouragement by rigid practices in the prosecutor's office.

Eighth, jurisdictions with specialized domestic violence prosecution units generally have higher prosecution rates. A study of San Diego's City Attorney's Office reported a prosecution rate of 70% of cases brought by police, whereas in Omaha, Nebraska, the prosecution rate was 88% of all cases. In addition, dismissal rates dropped considerably in other jurisdictions, for example, from 79% to 29% in Everett, Washington, and from 47% to 14% in Klamuth Falls, Oregon (Klein, 2008; Smith, Davis, Nickles, & Davies, 2001).

SUMMARY

This chapter began by discussing the reasons why victims might choose to prosecute offenders or, alternatively, their reasons for wanting charges dropped. In addition, preferences might change over time as the result of ongoing changes in the course of case processing or in the victim's personal life.

Next, we reviewed changes in the prosecutorial response, including factors impacting their decision. Clearly, the growing role of victim advocates has provided additional support for victims who choose to move forward with case prosecution. However, the goal of victim advocates who are part of the prosecutor's office might be focused primarily on obtaining a conviction and only secondarily on following victim preferences if they want charges dropped. Victim advocates who are not part of the criminal justice system are more likely to be victim focused and provide victims with more options.

Finally, we can observe that the implementation of no-drop polices by prosecutors has been met with mixed results. From an agency perspective, there might be practical reasons why this is difficult, including lacking the needed resources and the failure of victims to cooperate. From the victim perspective, she might determine that her interests are better served if she is allowed to drop charges. Perhaps the real question is whether victims' preferences should be a factor in the decision-making process. We do know that if we mandate prosecution when victims fear for their safety or the safety of their children, then we have a responsibility to ensure their protection.

DISCUSSION QUESTIONS

1. To what extent are victim decisions to move forward with case prosecution based on valid criteria? How often is their decision motivated instead by fear?

2. Should prosecutors be able to prosecute cases without victim cooperation? If so, how? Should they force victims to testify and penalize those who refuse? Can sufficient evidence be obtained to ensure victim cooperation is not needed?

3. Is it worth the financial cost of prosecuting all cases of domestic violence? How do they handle growing caseloads without an increase (and, in these times, a potential decrease) in budget?

4. What is the value of prosecuting all cases?

5. If pleas are more likely to save time, is this preferred overprosecuting fewer cases with more serious charges?

Civil Courts and the Role of Restraining Orders

11

Chapter Overview

Civil courts, where a party can seek private redress for wrongs committed against them, might be expected to be a key venue for victims of domestic violence. This chapter will discuss how avenues of civil law were problematic for victims of such crimes until the last 30 years. On its face, this was surprising because we have long known that the criminal justice system and attendant courts see relatively few cases of domestic violence committed within the middle and professional social classes. Although such violence occurs, it is typically unreported to police or prosecutors or, until recently, even recognized by doctors and others who might otherwise be expected to demand intervention.

This chapter will then discuss the significant role civil courts can play in responding to domestic assault by the issuance of orders seeking to prevent future violence. These orders can be called restraining orders, protective orders, injunctive decrees, or simply court orders. Although civil courts primarily litigate suits between private parties, they have long had the power to issue injunctive decrees prohibiting improper conduct. However, court orders in the context of domestic assault were infrequent until specific domestic violence statutes were passed. In fact, prior to the 1970s, women typically had to begin divorce proceedings even to be eligible for any meaningful judicial relief (Chaudhuri & Daly, 1992).

Tort Liability, a Possible Judicial Remedy?

Under the English common law doctrine of "coverture," a wife was considered the "covert femme" to be treated legally "as one" with her husband. The husband, as the "dominant partner," was legally responsible for his wife's acts. Furthermore, she was stripped of her legal right to enter into any contracts, acquire or dispose of property, could not be an executor of an estate, and even had a subordinate position as the potential guardian of her children. More specifically, he had the right to sue on her behalf and no suit could be brought under her name without his express consent. Naturally, lawsuits by a wife against her husband were simply not allowed, regardless of the grounds. The Married Women's Property Acts were passed by states in the United States in the 1890s to early 1900s. They initially provided the rights for a married woman to own property and, more germane to this chapter, the right to sue under her name without obtaining the express permission of her husband. Such statutes, however, did not typically grant the wife the right to sue her husband, even if they were separated.

As a result, in most jurisdictions there were a series of inconsistent legal decisions that had the effect of preventing an effective civil remedy. The U.S. Supreme Court in *Thompson v. Thompson* (1910) seemingly chose to ignore the expressed language of a federal statute for the District of Columbia and dismissed a wife's lawsuit against her husband, finding that Congress simply could not have intended such a major change to existing practices.

In contrast, during that same year, the New York Supreme Court in *Schultz v. Schultz* (1882) rejected such a limited reading of its statute and authorized a lawsuit. The language is still valid more than a century later:

> Without pursuing this matter further, it is considered quite sufficient to say that the language of the statute is . . . quite comprehensive enough to include the husband as one of the persons against whom the wife may bring an action for assault and battery . . . (the effect of allowing such a suit) would be to promote greater harmony by enlarging the rights of married women and increasing the obligations of husbands by affording greater protection to the former, and by enforcing greater restraint on the latter in the indulgence of their evil passions. The declaration of such a right is not against the policy of the law. It is in harmony with it, and calculated to preserve peace, and in a great measure prevent barbarous acts, acts of cruelty regarded by mankind as inexcusable, contemptible, detestable. It is neither too early nor too late to promulgate the doctrine that if a husband commits an assault and battery upon his wife he may be held responsible civilly and criminally for the act, which is not only committed in violation of the laws of God and man, but in direct antagonism to the contract of marriage, its obligations, duties, responsibilities, and the very basis on which it rests. (*Schultz v. Schultz* [1882], paraphrased from Quester, 2007, footnote 169)

Over time, the reasoning of the *Schultz* court won, and limitations on suits with regard to a spousal assault are now infrequent. As a result, wives can now sue their husbands in virtually all states for such torts as an assault.

Currently, private suits might easily include recompense for assaults, physical injuries as a result of a battery, or intentional infliction of emotional distress. Damages can be awarded on the basis of pain and suffering, out-of-pocket costs of new shelter, moving expenses, medical care, and child support, as well as more speculatively for punitive damages designed to "send a message" to the defendant or other potential batterers. In addition, several states such as California, Florida, and Iowa have enacted specific statutes allowing civil lawsuits against spouses for domestic violence. Not surprisingly, some attorneys have specialized (or at least have agreed to take) civil cases for assault and battery or intentional infliction of emotional distress against victims. In several, well-publicized incidents in Massachusetts, defendants, including the head judge of a major city in the state, were found responsible to their victims for civil damages. Not surprisingly, virtually all such cases were settled out of court under sealed court orders but supposedly for relatively high monetary amounts (English, 1992). For a comparatively small group of victims whose offenders were financially well off, assistance might be received from civil lawsuits for damages, as well as from protective orders. In these cases, the defendant typically has assets and a job from which wages might be garnished to support a judgment. The theoretical basis for an award is now easy to establish because civil courts have allowed private recovery for claims of the intentional infliction of personal injury (Zoeller & Schmiedt, 2004).

Naturally, such private lawsuits are currently only a marginal resource to stop battering resulting from the problem of court backlogs and the need for a defendant to possess discrete, sizable assets—not typical for most batterers reaching judicial attention. In addition, because civil suits for damages punish past abuse rather than enjoin potentially harmful future conduct, they might have only a limited value as a direct weapon to stop future violence.

Another more indirect role for tort law might, however, exist: Several states have expressly allowed a suit for tort liability against a treating doctor that failed to report domestic violence (Miller, 2005). It could be argued that such third-party liability should be inferred under domestic violence tort statutes even without such statutes having an explicit statutory mention of such legal liability. Since most health care providers have assets and malpractice insurance, third-party liability suits might well proliferate in the future. Furthermore, such a lawsuit might be warranted if there was any third party who could arguably have had knowledge of such abuse; for instance, he or she had a duty to warn (such as health care providers, social workers, members of the clergy, etc.), failed to take action, and injuries subsequently occurred (Hart & Sussman, 2004).

The Role of Domestic Violence Restraining Orders

Instead, the primary use of civil courts has been the gradual, but inconsistent, growth in issuance of civil protective orders. Why has such a potent resource for victims not assumed a primary role in the control of domestic violence? As we will explain, the reality is that the latent strength of such a proceeding often has been outweighed by the limitations posed by court attitudes and legal precedents.

Together with the concerns described, the power to issue this type of injunctive order was historically considered ancillary, or secondary, to the court's substantive power to decide matters of law and try issues of fact. Since the issuance of a protective order was not the court's primary purpose, judges have historically used injunctive orders sparingly. They were primarily initiated at the request of a prosecutor or by claimants in civil court to limit otherwise uncontrollable threats. Restraining order use also was limited because, as with lawyers, judges and prosecutors tend to be process oriented. They were acutely aware of their limited authority to issue prior restraints on conduct without notice and were aware of the danger of infringing on a respondent's constitutional rights. As a result, courts routinely required high standards of proof that the respondent posed a threat to the complainant, often to the degree of "beyond a reasonable doubt."

One of the recent significant innovations in judicial responses to domestic violence has been the widespread adoption of statutes and policies encouraging judges to grant injunctive orders to stop abuse immediately. There is virtually no disagreement that domestic violence victims need protective orders in cases of the threat of repeat violence.

In one recent study, 68% of women seeking a restraining order had been victimized by prior violence (Carlson, Harris, & Holden, 1999). Another study reported that more than 50% of women applying for restraining orders had been injured during the incident that led to the issuance of the order (Harrell & Smith, 1996).

Research in two Colorado counties reported that women filing for temporary restraining orders experienced an average of 13 violent acts in the year before filing. Similar findings were reported in Dane County, Wisconsin, where approximately one third of women filing for ex parte orders were assaulted at least 10 times in the 3 months before filing (M. P. Johnson & Elliott, 1997).

The Process of Obtaining Protective Orders

Protective orders differ from a criminal prosecution in that they might be heard in general-purpose or family courts and rely on the civil powers of the court to judge disputes or a specialized family court's authority to resolve marital and familial matters. Because the issuance of a restraining order is not typically a criminal case, civil rules of procedure and evidence apply. The proceedings are explicitly designed to prevent future unlawful conduct rather than to punish past criminal behavior (Finn, 1989). Hence, in most states, the evidentiary standard is "preponderance of the evidence" rather than the more rigorous criminal standard of "beyond a reasonable doubt" (Miller, 2005).

Courts typically attempt representation of both parties at a hearing prior to issuance of any permanent or even most preliminary injunctions. If the matter is urgent, however, such as the threat of immediate violence, courts might temporarily authorize ex parte orders to remain in effect for a short time without the alleged offender being present or even represented by counsel (hence, "ex parte"). Orders of a short duration often are called temporary restraining orders (TROs). Civil restraining orders were, in fact, developed expressly as a technique by advocates of battered women to circumvent the reluctance of police, prosecutors, and criminal courts to handle domestic violence cases properly (Klein, 1996; Schechter, 1982).

In addition, although not directly related to their customary mission, several jurisdictions have given criminal courts the power to issue permanent and preliminary injunctions as well as TROs apart from an ongoing criminal case. For example, as early as 1977, New York State gave both criminal and county courts concurrent jurisdiction over domestic violence with equal powers to issue TROs and permanent injunctions. This enhanced the ability of criminal courts to divert appropriate cases from the criminal justice system without relying on another court to assume jurisdiction. Although, as discussed, protective orders are customarily issued by civil courts, they are directly relevant to the criminal justice system. Violation in the context of domestic violence is now punishable not only by a contempt of court finding, but also it constitutes independent grounds for justifying, or in many states mandating, a warrantless arrest. In Massachusetts, a fairly typical state, violation of a civil order is a misdemeanor punishable by incarceration for up to 30 months in the County House of Corrections. In other states, violation remains punishable by contempt of court, which is the traditional mechanism for enforcement. This process might be slow and cumbersome, but it does allow for severe punishment.

Several types of domestic violence–related protective orders have become common. In addition to general civil protection orders or TROs, which have been specifically adopted for domestic violence cases in all states and the District of Columbia, most states have enacted protection orders ancillary to a divorce or other marital proceedings. Although specific statutes vary, divorce-related orders require evidence of the likelihood of improper conduct before issuing an order, typically for past physical abuse to the plaintiff-divorcee or the children. The broad scope of marital orders parallels that of the generalized protective order statutes. In addition, because these are coupled with interim custody and support orders, their immediate impact might be considerable.

The Explosive Growth of Restraining Orders

Beginning with Pennsylvania in 1976, all 50 states and the District of Columbia have enacted laws providing victims of domestic violence direct access to courts via protective orders by the early 1990s (Keilitz, 1994). Before these statutes, women typically had to initiate divorce proceedings to be eligible for a protective order in the context of a divorce or family court (Chaudhuri & Daly, 1992).

Since the passage of the Violence Against Women Act (VAWA) in 1994, there has been an increased emphasis on courts granting such orders and on the criminal justice system enforcing them. Pursuant to VAWA, the Federal Bureau of Investigation (FBI) now operates a national registry for restraining orders as part of its National Crime Information Center (NCIC). FBI official data show that between 600,000 and 700,000 permanent orders are entered annually. It is well known that this number substantially understates the actual number of restraining orders since eight states do not participate in the NCIC registry, and many states have incomplete coverage. Furthermore, temporary orders of protection are not counted. Although some might be superseded by a permanent order, some of them are simply not counted (Miller, 2005). Sorenson and Shen (2005) estimate that there are more than a million such orders granted nationally.

Because of several key limitations that we will discuss in the subsequent discussion, the initial somewhat narrow statutes that allowed domestic violence restraining orders have been amended almost constantly, leaving a patchwork of statutes with very inconsistent provisions and limitations in different states. The actual availability of protective orders in any particular case might be greatly limited by statute or, even more frequently, by arcane and often unpublished court administrative rules. Such restrictions are constantly in flux as statutes and administrative policies are revised. A list of some representative restrictions is useful, however:

- Lifestyle factors of the victim and offender often curtail the ability of granting an order. Several states do not allow orders to be issued to former spouses, and some do not allow orders to be issued to people who have never been formally married, even if they are intimates.

- Administrative limitations have been placed on the type of past conduct that might be used to justify imposition of a restraint. Some states have required proof of actual physical abuse and refuse to grant protective orders in cases of threats or intimidation.

- Limitations have been administratively placed on ex parte TROs—arguably the most important form of protective order given the strong potential for immediate violence. These continue to reflect the judiciary's ambivalence toward using what they consider an extraordinary remedy.

- Numerous procedural limitations exist in many states, including filing fees (which might be waived) or an inability of a victim to obtain an emergency order at night-time or on weekends—precisely the time when she is most at risk (Finn, 1989; Finn & Colson, 1998).

Neal Miller reported in as late as December 2005 that an incredible complexity of differing statutory schemes remained for protective orders. Furthermore, these schemes do not stay the same. In any given year, many states might amend these statutes, typically to remove procedural roadblocks to their issuance or enforcement. For example, after VAWA was reauthorized in 2000, 36 states added dating violence (removing restrictions requiring a marriage). Still, as Miller noted, widespread inconsistencies remain among states as well as notable coverage gaps.

Recent studies suggest that the use of restraining orders also varies considerably among different jurisdictions. One study published in 2006 reviewed statutes allowing restraining orders in all jurisdictions within the United States (DeJong & Burgess-Proctor, 2006). The purpose of the study was to determine what statutory rights were provided for victims, and then the authors rated the progressiveness of the statutory provisions. Factors included whether,

- pursuant to VAWA, were orders from other jurisdictions given full faith and credit;

- were weapon restrictions allowed as part of the restraining order (the 1994 VAWA prohibited the purchase and possession of a firearm by persons under a domestic violence restraining order);

- did the statute prohibit mutual restraining orders where a judge simply issued orders against each party without seeking to determine whether both parties posed potential risks to the other;

- whether the statute was broad enough to allow for same-sex and dating relationships as opposed to simply orders between married parties;

- were there provisions for waiving filing fees as well as a provision for assistance when victims needed it;

- could a victim file for a restraining order independent of filing for criminal charges;

- would the address of the complainant be kept confidential;

- would violation of a restraining order be considered to be a felony or merely another misdemeanor; and

- were there provisions for treatment or mandatory counseling as part of the order?

DeJong and Burgess-Proctor (2006) reported that although most states were in full compliance with VAWA, there was tremendous variation in other provisions. Specifically, they reported that some states were "victim friendly." In these states, statutes contained most of the provisions listed. Overall, they found that midwestern states received the highest scores (with Missouri at the top) and that northeastern states such as Massachusetts had the second highest. Not surprisingly, the southeastern states had the lowest scores, which the researchers attributed to their more conservative attitudes. In another example, despite VAWA, fewer than half of the states enacted legislation prohibiting firearms purchase and possession while under a restraining order (Vigdor & Mercy, 2003, 2006), whereas 13 states did not automate their restraining order database to provide access for background checks for purchases of firearms and ammunition (Sorenson & Shen, 2005). In another area of importance, as of late 2006, at least 35 states and territories made enforcement of restraining orders mandatory on the part of law enforcement as compared with only 13 that made enforcement "discretionary." This trend toward mandatory enforcement has increased sharply in recent years as restraining order statutes are amended to enact tougher penalties (Roederer, 2006).

Not surprisingly, given deep statutory discrepancies, states vary considerably in their rates for issuance of restraining orders. In the 29 states that had complete data for the NCIC survey, they reported an average of 342 per 100,000 restraining orders annually. This figure disguises considerable variations in different locations. The rate in Florida was 504 orders per 100,000, whereas the rate in Tennessee was 115 per 100,000.

The Growing Role of Restraining Orders: The Massachusetts Experience

One state, Massachusetts, has had several studies published examining the use of restraining orders over an extended period of time. Although certain factors are unique, it might be representative of the experience in other states. Originally, the use of protective orders in this state was restrictive even though the statute provided for 10-day TROs to be granted ex parte if necessary and full restraining orders after a hearing with notice to the restrained party.

Eve Buzawa participated in developing and analyzing a research program conducted by the Massachusetts Committee on Criminal Justice funded by the U.S. Bureau of Justice Statistics. This program examined domestic violence practices in eight randomly selected police agencies in the state from October 1986 to December 1986. Despite fairly comprehensive statutes offering general civil- and divorce-related injunctions and official policies to use such orders when needed, police rarely reported having encountered victims protected by injunctive decrees. In fact, out of the 86 domestic violence cases that the officers reported, only 15 protective orders were found to be in effect (Holmes & Bibel, 1988).

Even when an officer reported that a victim was protected by a TRO and a warrantless arrest could be made if terms were violated, arrests were made in only 3 of the 15 cases, or 20% of the potential offenders. This finding was compared with 11 arrests in the 171 incidents or 7% in which a TRO had not been issued. Because TROs were present in less than 10% of the cases and because even in their presence an anemic 20% arrest rate occurred, the role of such orders was very modest. Not surprisingly, of attorneys surveyed, 53% reported that judges rarely or never imposed sanctions against violators; however, 40% of judges stated that they often used sanctions (Gender Bias Commission of the Supreme Court, 1989, cited in Klein, 1994a).

Evidence suggests that this was not atypical during this period. In 1987, in all of New York State, only 25,000 protective orders were issued, compared with 2,000 orders issued in 1990 in a more activist court (The Quincy District Court of Massachusetts [QDC]) with a jurisdiction of only 250,000 people.

This number of orders issued began increasing in the 1990s as advocates and courts began using the statutes. By 1993, in Massachusetts, more than 50,000 TROs were granted, a number that had increased at the rate of 10,000 per year during the early 1990s (Klein, 1994a). Why the increase? The number of protective orders sought and granted seems directly related to then-current events—such as spectacular instances of celebrity murders or stalking—as it was to the steady need for such orders. Ptacek (1999) suggested that media attention played a critical role in forcing the judiciary to be more responsive to domestic violence victims:

> More than anything else, it seems, judges fear public humiliation in the news media. They don't fear feminists or other advocacy groups: indeed, refusing to bend to the pressure of such groups is a mark of judicial pride, perhaps, especially in a state where judges are appointed rather than elected. One judge who trains other judges on domestic violence said that when she encounters antipathy for battered women or resistance to issuing restraining orders in her trainings, she responds with the question: "Why do you want your name on the front page of the *Boston Globe?*" (p. 61)

Nevertheless, one study confirmed that restraining orders still were not widely enforced in the state of Massachusetts in the late 1990s. Kane (1999) reported the effects of breaking the terms of restraining orders in two Boston police precincts. His report was unequivocal: The violation of a restraining order by itself did not automatically lead to an arrest despite its being required under Massachusetts's law (Kane, 1999).

Since the late 1990s, the number of restraining orders has actually declined, 45,000 in 1996 (Commonwealth of Massachusetts, Executive Department, 1997) and 35,000 in 2000 (Massachusetts Office of the Department of Probation, 2001). The reason for the decline is somewhat speculative; however, it seems from a recently published study that judicial decision making does not tend to be as structured as we might wish (Ballou et al., 2007). Ballou et al. examined the 70% of the initial TROs that ultimately resulted in a continuance hearing, which is a hearing where both parties are represented as part of the process for seeking to obtain a permanent restraining order. They found that judicial decision making was abbreviated, with the judge's behavioral observations of the petitioners and the respondents weighing heavily. Unfortunately, they concluded that such observations might be relatively weak indicators of actual credibility as many victims of domestic violence are highly traumatized. They might seem to the judge to be overwrought and, perhaps, even irrational. The perpetrator, in contrast, might seem to be calm and controlled during the court proceeding (Ballou et al., 2007).

Not surprisingly, the judges' reliance on behaviors and attitudes of the involved parties can introduce substantial room for error and the ultimate possibility of inaccurate decision making. Several judges who have extensive experience in family and probate courts noted that their caseload necessitated quick decisions regarding restraining orders, often within 5 to 15 minutes. They were concerned that their lack of information and "a misleading surface presentation of victim and/or abuser, or by one party's lack of legal representation" might lead to wrong decisions (Ballou et al., 2007, p. 274).

Some courts, even quite recently, do not understand that violation of restraining orders should be treated seriously as required by statutes.

A Michigan woman who complained that her husband violated a protective order against her was ordered to be handcuffed to him by the judge who is handling the couple's divorce.

When Sabrena and Kirk Smith's stories contradicted each other during a Jan. 25 hearing, Muskegon County Judge Gregory Pittman ordered them to be shackled to a holding cell bench "until somebody decides that they're going to not lie to the court," The Associated Press reported.

The two weren't released until Sabrena Smith dropped her complaint. Sabrena Smith said she had been telling the truth and only withdrew to be released from jail.

Her attorney, Jenny McNeill, said she "didn't see any other way to get her out of there."

The judge said he was sure neither spouse posed a threat to the other or he wouldn't have issued the order.

"In hindsight, I probably wouldn't do it again," Pittman said, "but in no way would I ever put a person who has been assaulted in that situation."

Sabrena Smith plans to file a grievance against Pittman and seek a new judge. She added said she didn't feel endangered while she was cuffed to her husband, "just angry."

Kirk Smith's lawyer, Harold Closz, said the judge's handcuffing order was "unusual," but not necessarily inappropriate.

Source: "Divorcing Couple Shackled Together by Judge," 2002.

The Advantages of Obtaining Protective Orders

For several reasons, civil protective orders have the potential to assume a central role in society's response to domestic violence. Perhaps first and most importantly, courts have far wider discretion to fashion injunctive relief, unlike strict sentencing restraints that are typically imposed on criminal proceedings. Most states have expressly provided judges the authority to grant any relief available under their state constitution. Courts now often issue the following protective orders in domestic violence cases:

- Prohibiting continued contact with the victim either in person, by telephone, or through the mail
- Mandating the offender enter counseling
- Limiting visitation rights to minor children
- Vacating a home, even if owned only in the name of the restrained party
- Allowing the victim the exclusive use of certain personal property, such as a car, regardless of title
- Preventing stalking at or near work, school, or frequent shopping areas

This list should not be viewed as exhaustive in that this is a court's equity power to fashion suitable relief. To accomplish this, a court might restrain any type of improper conduct and will not be limited to granting any particular remedy. Instead, the provisions of an order are meant to be tailor-made for the specific situation.

Second, protective orders give the judicial system an opportunity for prospective intervention to prevent likely abuse. This avoids the necessity of requiring proof of past criminal conduct beyond a reasonable doubt. This is particularly useful for cases in which threats, intimidation, or prior misdemeanor activity suggest that the potential for serious abuse is high, yet the serious violence is only threatened and has not yet occurred. Hence, protective orders might be the best and, at times, the only timely remedy to prevent abuse from escalating by intervening before commission of an actual assault. This, plus the existence of flexible terms, has the potential for far better intervention strategies than the blunt instrument of criminal law.

Third, because violation of an order is now a criminal offense in all states, the existence of the order itself provides a potent mechanism for police to stop abuse—that is, the right to arrest and subsequently convict for violation of its terms. When made aware of a no-contact order, a well-trained officer can easily prove a prima facie case of its violation (usually just making contact) compared with the more difficult task of determining probable cause of commission of substantive crimes. As discussed, federal and state initiatives now mandate that police departments keep records of such orders so that an officer can retrieve the information from a dispatcher or by computer at the same time the suspect is checked for warrants. Nevertheless, our own research has repeatedly found that many officers simply had no idea whether an order existed. However, the use of protective orders makes it more likely that police will act decisively by giving officers an independent method for verifying recidivism and providing evidence that a victim is willing to pursue legal redress.

Fourth, at least until the *Gonzales v. City of Castle Rock* (2005) decision that we will discuss subsequently, when the police respond to a protective order, they might be inclined to take action to limit their own legal liability. Otherwise, the victim's counsel might later present such an order to establish that an officer failed to "carry out required duties." Although as we will see this doctrine has been cut back by recent court cases, in the eyes of the officer, breach of the duty owed to victims might make the officer and the police department potentially liable if an injury occurs when an order is not enforced. Even if legal liability does not occur, as under *Gonzales,* the officer's actions might be "second guessed" and judged a failure by his or her police superiors as well as at times by the press or politicians, thereby embarrassing the department.

Fifth, obtaining a protective order from a court might have the effect of empowering the victim. Specifically, an order will usually give her unfettered control over her home and other essential assets. Knowledge that the local police can enforce such an order should make the victim more secure and most offenders less likely to resume abuse. Such empowerment might be dramatic in that the victim, if assisted by a knowledgeable advocate, has the potential for far more control of the proceedings than in a prosecution. After obtaining a protective order, she can overcome indifference or even hostility among prosecution and court personnel. She also can retain more control by using or withholding the injunction or, paradoxically, choosing whether to alert police of a violation. Although it might seem to be illogical to obtain and then not actually use an injunction in a state that has adopted mandatory arrest and prosecution policies, this might be the only method for the victim to prevent the system from inexorably gaining total control over both the victim and the offender.

Sixth, in many dimensions, civil protective orders incur far fewer victim costs than criminal prosecution. Specifically, the mere issuance of a protective order does not jeopardize the job of an offender as might arrest, conviction, or even possible incarceration. Although this might not seem important to an outsider, incarceration often interferes with alimony or child-care payments. Hearings themselves are far less likely to require a significant time commitment from the victim.

Fear of offender retaliation also should significantly lessen in that harm from violating a protective order is prospective in nature. The victim might constantly remind the offender of what could happen if he violates the order rather than angrily remembering a punishment that has already been inflicted.

Seventh, divorce-related injunctive orders play a unique role. Counselors familiar with obtaining injunctive orders typically represent divorcing women. Family court or domestic relations judges and court personnel also are frequently knowledgeable about the scope of, and protection against, domestic violence. Even in no-fault divorce states, family court judges make property allocations in the absence of the parties' agreement and decide contested custody cases. Under such circumstances, obtaining a protective order might deter future contact, thereby modifying the offender's previously uncontrollable behavior.

Eighth, civil relief can be far timelier than in criminal cases. Because civil protective orders are meant to deter future abuse rather than to sanction past criminal activities, there are far fewer delays from the time relief is sought until granted. In a civil court, a preliminary hearing can usually be scheduled within 1 to 2 days after the complaint is filed. In contrast, criminal hearings often are delayed excessively because of failure to serve the defendant, an overwhelmingly crowded court docket, or continuances—often at the behest of the defendant whose attorney uses delaying tactics. Even in some progressive courts committed to handling domestic violence cases aggressively, the average period of delay between case intakes to disposition can stretch from 6 to 8 months (Buzawa, Hotaling, Klein, & Byrne, 1999).

Ninth, protective orders can be useful if criminal case prosecution would be problematic. Examples include situations where the evidence of actual assault is unclear, if the victim would be a poor or reluctant witness, or when, because of alcoholism or drug abuse, she might be unable to get a conviction (Finn & Colson, 1990). Frankly, although we believe the needs of the criminal justice system should take a distant second place to those of the victim, the reality is that overloaded dockets might cause less serious or more problematic cases to be dropped unless aggressively pushed by a victim or her advocate. In these cases, protective orders might be the most realistic protection for victims, however imperfect.

The Limitations of Protective Orders

Despite statutory provisions to use protective orders in domestic violence cases, several factors have limited their use. At first the primary obstacle was that the actual issuance of an order relied on judicial discretion, and enforcement was problematic at best.

For reasons discussed earlier, many judges remained reluctant to issue decrees. Although the legislative intent might be to grant such orders freely when needed, courts have always considered prejudgment injunctive relief to be a significant restriction on personal liberty and, at the least, ancillary to their primary mission of adjudicating contested facts (Quinn, 1985; Waits, 1985). They were never issued as a matter of course, and judges, in fact, required past commission of serious domestic violence before issuing an order even when not expressly required by statute. Such reticence is naturally increased when an ex parte order of the type common in a TRO is considered and a respondent's constitutionally protected liberty and property rights are curtailed without effective due process (initially the target might not even be told about its issuance).

In fact, the primary legal critique has been that they deprived defendants of constitutional rights. For example, although the reference is dated, judicial concerns were clear in the following passage where, in 1985, the administrative judge of the New York City Family Court circulated this memorandum to all family court judges in New York City (Golden, 1987):

> The propriety of issuing such an order without . . . notice to petitioners raises I believe due process questions because this practice denies petitioners timely notice of respondent's allegations and an opportunity to prepare an adequate defense. . . . Although this issue is certainly within the discretion of each judge, I urge that you discuss the above . . . [to] be aware of the consequences of their issuing . . . orders of protection. (p. 324)

Constitutional arguments were at first aired in a series of U.S. Supreme Court cases wherein ex parte prejudgment orders were subject to due process restrictions. Without exploring these in depth, the U.S. Supreme Court has long mandated that ex parte actions balance private rights being abridged with the governmental reasons for action, the intrinsic fairness of the existing proceedings, and the probable value of providing additional safeguards (*Mathews v. Eldridge,* 1976, citing *Fuentes v. Shevin,* 1972; *Mitchell v. W. T. Grant,* 1974).

A 1994 report by Gondolf, McWilliams, Hart, and Stuehling suggests that such difficulties persisted. Gondolf et al. did find that most petitioners (96%) who appeared at the hearing were granted some protective orders. Despite statutory encouragement of granting broad orders, however, petitioners found their requests for relief were significantly cut back.

The importance of this is that when the courts significantly cut back requested relief, effective protection for victims often was dramatically curtailed. For example, a "no-contact" order is nearly universally requested, because its violation is far easier to prove, and contact typically precedes active harassment or violence. The report found that almost 50% of victims requesting such actions were refused. Similarly, depending on location, requested financial support was denied for 40% to 88% of the requesters. This might be crucial for many economically dependent women. Even requests for weapons confiscation were denied in 88% of the cases despite an obvious correlation to the possibility of more serious future violence. Gondolf et al. noted that this could lead many advocates for battered women to conclude that the purpose of the law enabling issuance of protective orders was not being fulfilled.

In short, although the application of these laws might be upheld when taken to an appellate or supreme court, this has little practical relevance for many victims. They might confront a hostile judge who knows that a denial of a preliminary injunction or a

TRO is unlikely to ever be appealed. Under such circumstances, judges have ignored the availability of TROs—at least in the past—and in one state they even have actively lobbied to have the law repealed (Lerman, 1984). Similarly, this less than ringing endorsement of such orders by senior judges demonstrates that victims and their advocates might continue to encounter difficulty in having these orders routinely issued.

Despite the favorable judicial resolution of claims of constitutional restraints on protective orders, studies have continued to confirm that many judges do not issue or dramatically curtail restraining orders (Solender, 1998). Such judicial restrictions often are the result of overly zealous interpretations of procedural requirements made especially difficult for inexperienced advocates (Zorza & Klemperer, 1999). Therefore, at least one commentator has termed the issuance of protective orders as "useless" (Barnett, 2000, p. 358).

Another difficulty is that, as a practical matter, the process of obtaining an injunctive order must be both initiated and pursued by the victim. Despite often being handicapped by a posttraumatic stress reaction and the necessity to take legal actions against a spouse, she also might face seemingly arcane procedural requirements and indifference— or sometimes even hostility of court personnel or the judiciary (Goolkasian, 1986; Waits, 1985). Similarly, victims often hesitate to file restraining orders because of fear of retaliation by the victim, fear of disbelief, and even fear of unfamiliar and unfriendly courtroom rituals (Ptacek, 1999).

As we noted earlier, to be truly effective and enforced, police departments must have obtained copies or at least have a readily available reliable source of the terms of the order. Although the victim might receive a copy, it might not be readily available, and the police might legitimately worry that they are exceeding terms of the order or it might have expired, thereby exposing them to charges of false arrest. For this reason, best practices should require court clerks to notify police departments. In fact, such computerized databases often exist, but they might not be available or kept current because they suffer from budgetary pressures and overall neglect. Significant information gaps still exist as a result of these systemic failures. Although the VAWA Reauthorization Act of 2000 began to assess and improve such systems, truly effective databases are not universal.

We also should mention that there is at least some evidence that the statutes allowing restraining orders are not evenly applied. *The Journal of Family Violence* published the results of one small-scale study of the issuance of restraining orders in a rural district court in Massachusetts (Basile, 2005). The study found that injury rates for males applying for restraining orders were equal to the injury rates for females (58% and 67%, respectively). Nevertheless, they were granted a lower percentage of restraining orders, which the researcher from the Fatherhood Coalition of Milford, Massachusetts, found to be statistically significant. Basile believed the numbers of males seeking such orders were themselves suppressed because of expectations of not being adequately served by the court system. The most significant differences were in the awards of custody. As cited by many fathers' advocates, female plaintiffs were far more likely to be granted custody of children. Male plaintiffs only received a custody award 8% of the time compared with 31% of females. They also were approximately one third less likely to have the judge order the surrender of firearms. The author posited that his study demonstrated that courts were not immune to social norms and that despite the gender-neutral language of the statute, they would exhibit different tendencies when responding to male compared with female requests for protection:

> The present study finds that in this one court setting, male victims of domestic violence were not afforded the same protections as their female counterparts. This inequality in court response occurred even though male and female plaintiffs were similarly victimized by their opposite gender defendants. . . .
> Of particular concern, is an inequity in custody awards of minor children. None of the males in the study population were able to secure custody of their minor children for more than a few days. (Basile, 2005, p. 178)

Unfortunately, because this study only consisted of 38 males and 231 females, we must cite this as a tentative result worthy of continued exploration. It might, however, be worth studying since the issuance of restraining orders is continuing to grow (Basile, 2005).

Similarly divorce-specific protective orders have not been effectively used to prevent violence. By their inherent nature, marital orders are limited to cases involving formal marriage, not alternative lifestyles, where violence statistically is more apt to occur. Even in marriages, many courts require an aggrieved spouse to initiate divorce proceedings to retain jurisdiction. In addition, the entire no-fault divorce movement and the pressure of high caseloads encourage court personnel and the judiciary to try to limit clearly adversarial actions. Finally, despite lack of any empirical evidence, some of the judiciary (along with many divorce attorneys representing men in divorce cases) has expressed concern that women in a divorce might be motivated to allege domestic violence falsely in an attempt to influence custody or property allocation. Because of such fears, divorce-related restraining orders often are not immediately granted or are granted ex parte for only a very short period. Although these limits might be legally and even practically justifiable, this does set significant roadblocks to their use.

The following news report from Channel 4, KNBC TV, Los Angeles, which aired on July 22, 2006, suggests why immigrants may not always seek restraining orders:

A judge who threatened deportation to Mexico for an illegal immigrant seeking a restraining order against her husband has been dropped from the roster of part-time judges used by the Los Angeles County Superior Court.

Judge Pro Tem Bruce R. Fink, a family law attorney from Orange, was removed from the list of about 1,200 attorneys who are used as substitute judges for the county court spokesman Allan Parachini said Friday.

"A lot of people run from controversy," Fink said. "It doesn't bother me. Remember, I was doing this as a volunteer."

During the July 14 hearing in Pomona, Fink asked Aurora Gonzalez if she was an illegal immigrant.

Gonzalez, who accused her husband of verbal abuse and threatening to report her to immigration authorities, acknowledged being in the country illegally.

"I hate the immigration laws that we have, but I think the bailiff could take you to the immigration services and send you to Mexico," the judge responded, according to a court transcript. "Is that what you guys want?"

Fink later warned Gonzalez that he was going to count to 20 and expected her to disappear by the time he was finished.

"One, Two, Three, Four, Fix, Six. When I get to 20, she gets arrested and goes to Mexico," Fink said, according to the transcript.

Gonzalez left the courtroom and Fink dismissed the case.

She moved into a domestic violence shelter last month, and could not be reached for comment.

Gonzalez has since resubmitted her request for a restraining order and had it granted, Parachini said.

Experts said that Fink as a state judge had no authority to order an arrest for violation of a federal immigration law.

"I did not want this woman deported," Fink said. "Now I understand that the court does not get involved in immigration status as long as it is not thrust upon it."

Source: Reprinted with permission of the *Los Angeles Times,* http://articles.latimes.com/2006/jul/22/local/me-judge22

Should Violations of Restraining Orders Be Judged by Criminal Courts?

An argument can be made that criminalizing the violation of a civil restraining order might limit its ability to protect victims. Criminalizing the violation of a civil protective order, if enforced, would act to protect the victim by providing a relatively easy method to arrest an offender that is unable to control conduct demanded by a court. The individual does not need to hire her own lawyer and have that lawyer fight a crowded civil court docket to obtain enforcement. However, her individual needs might be overlooked because of an increasing trend toward retribution inherent in the criminal process. In many cases, although the victim has a restraining order, she might not want the order enforced because the violation might be technical, or she might have reason to believe that she or her children are not at risk. She might even be in the process of seeking its termination. These factors could worsen in certain populations such as illegal immigrants or those seeking citizenship where a conviction might threaten automatic deportation. A mandatory arrest during breach of a restraining order might thereby limit her autonomy, much the same way that mandatory arrest has been believed to limit the victim's ability to determine the outcome (Hitchings, 2005). Conversely, prosecutorial discretion and the existence of ever increasing criminal caseloads might simply mean that the victim really has no advocate in the system that will ensure priority for the enforcement of a breached order.

Since most courts of limited jurisdiction within a state are created by statutory authority, perhaps the best outcome would be to allow enforcement of a restraining order to be judged by *either* criminal courts or a civil judge in the jurisdiction where the court order was actually initiated. This would allow states to continue criminalizing the violation of a protective order, but add the possibility that an advocate for a battered woman has the additional recourse of seeking redress through a battered woman's advocate or her own personal counsel. In stating this, we recognize that statutes would have to be changed, probably in the context of granting enhanced powers to civil judges to allow for arrest and remand for contempt of court. This power could, of course, be limited in duration if the state reasonably thought that it wanted heavier sanctions imposed by criminal court judges.

The California Case

Because of VAWA, most states now have started to compile comprehensive records of restraining orders issued. One detailed survey of the use of such restraining orders was conducted in the state of California. Researchers at UCLA School of Public Health worked with the California Department of Justice and the California Wellness Foundation to develop and publish a comprehensive data set. This data set is a statewide restraining order system that became operational in 1991. Known as the Domestic Violence Restraining Order System (DVROS), it now includes additional types of restraining orders to prohibit all such people from obtaining a firearm. It is a central repository for restraining order information that allows rapid retrieval by law enforcement agencies and prevents easy access to the Department of Justice to prevent legal purchases. It can be accessed by law enforcement officers through a 24-hour/7-day-a-week telecommunications system to assist them in determining whether a person of inquiry might be the subject of a restraining order. The system is supposed to be updated by law enforcement and criminal justice agencies in real time. Since December 1999, DVROS has been linked to the NCIC for national files when the background check is conducted for the purchase of a firearm. The only weakness in the system is that in most counties, the protected person must deliver the information to a law enforcement agency that will enter the information into DVROS, whereas the preferred practice, used in some counties, is for the courts to take a more proactive approach, and fax the information to the police. In three other counties, the courts enter the data in DVORS themselves. As a snapshot in time, they found that there were 227,941 active restraining orders against adults in California as of June 6, 2003. This figure is actually greater than the number of marriages recorded in the state in a 1-year period and the 80,000–87,000 new orders annually represent approximately 8% of the roughly 1 million total restraining orders issued in the United States. As expected, most of these were for domestic violence (Sorenson & Shen, 2005).

Figures 11.1 and 11.2 show that rates for restraining orders were highest for African Americans and for 24- to 35-year-olds.

As Figure 11.1 illustrates, there is an extraordinarily high use of restraining orders against black males between 18 and 54 years of age, which far dwarfs their actual percentage of the general population. This figure, of course, is partially a reflection of the higher rate of domestic violence among African Americans, as cited in Chapter 3. However, it might be that the disparity is partially a reflection of the higher willingness of African American victims to seek court assistance, or for African American offenders to have orders entered against them. Furthermore, it is certainly possible that the relatively lower rates of reporting among Hispanic Americans might be a result of concern over immigration status.

Figure 11.1   Restraining Orders per 100,000 Men in California, by Age Group and Ethnicity

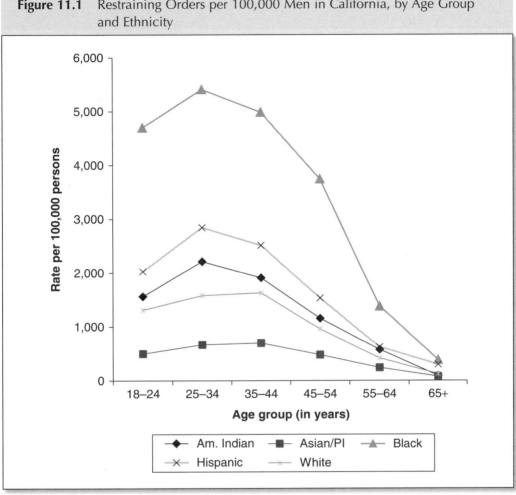

Source: Sorenson and Shen, 2005.

Figure 11.2 demonstrates that far fewer restraining orders are entered against women, typically in a proportion of approximately a quarter the rate of their demographic male equivalents.

The DVROS file contains information about the restraining order, the person protected, and of course, the person restrained. Although there are no data as to the reason for the restraining order (which might be a best practice if such information categorized properly), it does include identifying characteristics of the restrained person, including sex, date of birth, race, ethnicity, fingerprints, hair color, and body marks. Thus, it is precisely tailored for law enforcement, if not for subsequent research. As noted by Sorenson and Shen (2005), possible enhancements would include nature and length of the relationship, number of times and time period of violence, injuries sustained, and whether children were witnessed or harmed. Most restraining orders had a fairly rapid expiration

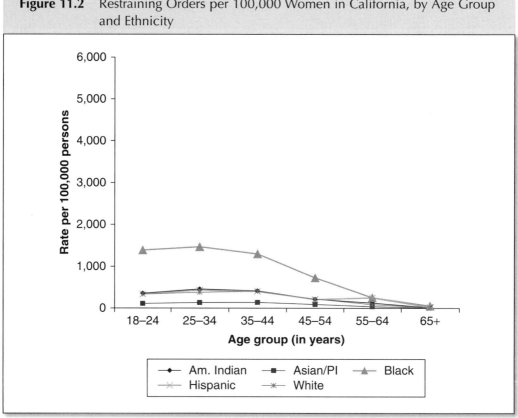

Figure 11.2 Restraining Orders per 100,000 Women in California, by Age Group and Ethnicity

Source: Sorenson and Shen, 2005.

period. Almost half (48%) of the orders expired within 18 months, and approximately 3% of the orders were permanent for the lifetime of the party.

Restrained persons were, on average, 35 years old, and most (63%) were ethnic minorities. Eighty-four percent of those restrained were males and 16% were females. That figure is broken down even more as follows: Seventy-two percent of the restraining orders involved a restrained male and protected females, 19% were same sex (11% male on male, and 8% female on female), and 8.5% were for a restrained female and a protected male (Sorenson & Shen, 2005).

It was somewhat unusual that half of all restraining orders were issued in criminal courts as an ancillary order to a criminal proceeding, with Blacks and Hispanics far more likely to be involved in criminal proceedings (57% and 55%, respectively), compared with 45% for Asians, 42% for American Indians, and 40% for Whites. Data in other states do not suggest such a high preponderance of restraining orders issued in active criminal cases.

One study of North Carolina's Homicide Prevention Act suggested the role of restraining orders was not highly significant. The Act was designed to prevent people with protective orders from owning or possessing firearms or ammunition and required them to surrender all firearms, ammunition, and firearms purchase permits to their local sheriff within 24 hours of receipt of the order. The study found that less than half of the plaintiffs seeking a restraining order were asked by the judge about the defendant having access to a restraining order. This proportion did not change after enactment of the Homicide Prevention Act even though this legislation required "that the court shall inquire of the plaintiff, at the ex parte or emergency hearing, the presence of ownership of, or otherwise access to firearms by the defendant" (cited in Moracco, Clark, Espersen, & Bowling, 2006, pp. 51–52). The only impact was that the courts far more frequently checked firearms restrictions as part of the restraining order.

It is certainly possible that the lack of enforcement of restraining order prohibitions on firearms is an artifact of the court's collective unwillingness to confiscate firearms. Even in California, which has a far more aggressive use of restraining orders, Sorenson and Shen (2005) reported that less than half of the restrained parties were provided with information on their possession of firearms and ammunition. In fact, one tenth did not receive firearm restrictions at all (Sorenson & Shen, 2005).

Within states, there is also tremendous variation between jurisdictions. For example, Logan, Shannon, and Walker (2005) reported that even in the same state, Kentucky, there was considerable variation, both in eligibility criteria and in procedural difficulty in obtaining restraining orders. They reviewed three rural counties and compared them with an urban county, including data from state police, court dockets, key informants, and qualitative data from abused women. Although the statute demanded that law enforcement and the courts have a "fair, consistent, and accessible" process to victims needing restraining orders, the actual process of obtaining these orders depended greatly on the community context. The key variables were whether women could and did obtain protective orders, whether they varied by officials applying different eligibility criteria, and whether institutions had de facto different levels of difficulties in obtaining such orders based on their affordability, availability, accessibility, and acceptability among court and law enforcement personnel (Logan, Shannon, Walker, & Faragher, 2006). They found considerable variation in victim experiences obtaining protective orders, stipulations in such protective orders, and the willingness of local agencies to enforce such orders. Although the sample was relatively small, consisting of only four jurisdictions, they were able to conclude that there were more obstacles in rural jurisdictions rather than in the urban county studied (Logan et al., 2005). As we will discuss in the *Gonzales* case, this finding might not be uncommon.

When Will Women Use Restraining Orders?

There has been research on the conditions under which battered women will be able to use the court system effectively to obtain restraining orders. Women who are economically dependent on their abusers obviously are at greater financial risk than those that are financially independent. Not surprisingly, economic dependence has been found to have a great impact on the victim's perseverance in obtaining a permanent restraining order (Muscat & Iwamoto, 1993; Tolman & Rosen, 2001).

Similarly, the extent and frequency of abuse could so terrify women that the most severely impacted victims might paradoxically be the most likely to fail to obtain a permanent order.

There also is a predictable interaction between the demands of court procedures and the crisis attendant to being a victim of battering. It has long been known that to use the courts effectively, as with most criminal justice agencies, it is best to present an appearance of a calm demeanor, remembering exactly what has occurred and the expectations that the person has of the agency. In contrast, battered women as a corollary of abuse, often develop symptoms of posttraumatic stress disorder (PTSD). They might act forgetful, confused, and indecisive—conditions that directly contribute to being marginalized by many court personnel (Jones, Hughes, & Unterstaller, 2001). Similarly, the unwillingness of many victims to discuss the details of abuse in front of an audience might, along with the time-consuming steps needed to obtain a restraining order, account for attrition by many victims (Fiedler, Briar, & Pierce, 1984; cf. Ptacek, 1995, who reported that embarrassment for many victims was combined with overall fear of appearing in front of unknown and intimidating judges and other court personnel).

Are Restraining Orders Effective?

There have been considerable anecdotal accounts published where some women and their attorneys and advocates state that in effect, "The order was not worth the paper it was printed on" (for an example, see Goodmark, 2004, footnote 21). Still others are convinced that the issuance—and subsequent enforcement of the order, if necessary—literally might have saved their lives. It is of course possible that both outcomes might be occurring for different victims. Certainly what we now know of the differences among abusers would strongly suggest that many abusive people, perhaps most family-only offenders, would not risk jail or their careers by violating such an order. For victims of these people, the order can be invaluable. Others, such as sociopaths, might simply become engrossed on the means to avoid the scope of an order while continuing to stalk or harass their victims. Finally, psychopaths might be infuriated that the women have defied them by seeking such orders; therefore, violence might escalate into a rage where the offenders literally feel they have "one shot" to terminate their victims before turning the gun on themselves.

Several studies have tried to report empirically on the actual efficacy of protective orders in preventing abuse. In an early study conducted before the enhanced enforcement typical of modern statutes, Grau, Fagan, and Wexler (1985) suggested that TROs, when used in isolation and without the full commitment by the prosecutors, courts, and police, were basically ineffective. The researchers interviewed 270 recipients of TROs and found that the orders were generally ineffective in reducing either the rate or the severity of abuse by serious abusers. Indeed, 60% of the victims studied were abused again regardless of the presence or absence of restraining orders. A second comprehensive study by the Urban Institute also demonstrated that restraining orders did deter some battering but not completely. In a comprehensive study (Harrell, Smith, & Newmark, 1993) of the impact of 779 protective orders issued in 1991, researchers interviewed both victims and batterers in Denver and Boulder, Colorado. Not surprisingly, the interviews disclosed that TROs were sought by 56% of those that had previously been injured, not those merely worried about future attacks. These injuries typically were not trivial, with approximately 40% of those injured needing medical care. The order did seem to have an impact among most offenders. Although many offenders tried to "work things out" or "talk their way out of the order," only 4% contested its terms. More important, according to both victims and batterers, 85% of the offenders subsequently did obey all conditions of the protective order (Harrell et al., 1993). The impact was not uniform for all provisions of the order. Instead, compliance was best at its core—the cessation of violence. In contrast, offenders as a group largely ignored provisions requiring economic support.

In short, although abuse might have largely ceased, it is clear that the mere issuance of a protective order does little to stimulate the respondent to support his family. In common with most divorce or separation statistics, 88% of victims with permanent orders and 81% of those with TROs stated that they had not received any money for support despite protective orders to the contrary. In addition, a clear majority of men refused to honor child-support provisions (Harrell et al., 1993).

Furthermore, respondents contacted 75% of the victims with permanent no-contact orders. This noncompliance was statistically similar to the 80% of victims who were contacted when they were without any permanent orders. Finally, collateral effects were observed. Although physical abuse might stop, other behaviors that we might generically call "stalking" began: 52% of victims reported unwanted phone calls, 21% said they were actually tracked or stalked, and 21% stated that the respondent entered her residence in violation of the order (Harrell et al., 1993). Since the time of these studies, all states have implemented antistalking statutes that allow restraining orders for stalking behavior against intimates or former intimates. Their impact seems similarly discouraging, however. When women obtained restraining orders for the specific purpose of stopping an offender from stalking, the vast majority reported that the orders were violated (Tjaden & Thoennes, 1998). Such behavior occurred across the board with few readily apparent victim-relationship characteristics predictive of success or failure. Although women with children were more likely to be assaulted, the severity of past incidents and the relative duration of abuse were not closely related. Fully 93% of the batterers believed that the police or the courts would intervene if they did not comply—a clear requirement for deterrence. The real correlates seemed to be the man's behavior toward the issuance of the court order. When permanent orders were resisted in court by the abuser or when he attempted in court to obtain child custody or to remain in the house, recurrent abuse was far more likely (Harrell et al., 1993).

Although the Urban Institute study lent some credence to the potential for TROs, it was less sanguine about the actual prospects for obtaining a permanent injunction. Only 60% of those who had obtained a TRO sought a permanent order (Harrell et al., 1993). It is unclear why the remainder did not. Some presumably achieved all that they required through the TRO. Other victims, however, might have been discouraged by difficulties in court (restrictive court hours, limited court locations, high fees, and other judicial impediments to action) or feared retaliation.

The latter is a real concern because despite actual cessation of abuse, the study reported that most female victims (68%) would be hesitant to return to court if their partners violated the restraining order. This was largely in response to their fear of revenge by the offender. In addition, 58% said it "wouldn't help," and 57% said it "would worsen the problem." Also, the TRO might not be served to the respondent, which is a necessary precondition to issuance of a permanent order (Harrell et al., 1993).

Mears, Carlson, Holden, and Harris (2001) reported that the positive effects of restraining orders were not apparent despite the fact that seeking and obtaining a protective order represented active victim efforts to seek outside support in preventing revictimization. The researchers reported that there was virtually no additional protection from revictimization because of the issuance of a protective order if protection was measured as the number of days from original to second victimization. Instead, they found that there was no statistically significant difference between those receiving a protective order, those simply arrested, and those who had a protective order coupled with arrest for violation of a protective order. If anything, they found that women from low-income communities who obtained protective orders were at increased risk for revictimization (Mears et al., 2001).

In contrast, a study sponsored by the National Center for State Courts seemed to cast the outcome of protective orders in a more favorable light, reporting that victims of domestic violence who were interviewed 1 and 6 months after obtaining a protective order generally perceived that well-being was positively enhanced by issuance of protection orders. Furthermore, this impact increased over time. Incidents of reabuse were low, and 95% said they would obtain a protective order again (Keilitz, Hannaford, & Efkeman, 1997). Another study published in 2003 reported that victims who sought and received protective orders were safer than those that did not for at least a 9-month period (Holt et al., 2003).

Similarly, several studies of victim attitudes toward restraining orders said they felt more "empowered" by the restraining order process, but only if they were able to have an effective restraining order issued (Fischer & Rose, 1995; Ptacek, 1999). The role of victim empowerment as a defined positive outcome might be important. We can understand that empirical studies might focus on easily measured rates of reabuse or official reports of restraining order violations, but in some cases, a broader measurement of "success" is needed.

If we examine "effectiveness" on the basis of preventing further acts of violence, little positive impact is consistently shown by studies; some show a positive result, whereas others show very little. However, this does not mean that when reabuse occurs that police will ignore the subsequent event. In fact, the police and official reaction to the issuance of the protective order itself might affect future abuse. In any event, studies now clearly show that women feel "empowered" or "protected" by such orders and that the lifting of fear is itself extremely valuable.

Are There Inherent Limits to Restraining Orders?

Because of the persisting phenomenon of recurrent abuse even when protective orders are granted, we might need to conclude that there are real intrinsic limits to their efficacy. After all, research has amply demonstrated that hard-core recidivists are not deterred by prospects of the social stigma associated with an arrest or even incarceration (Buzawa et al., 1999). Such offenders are unlikely to stop merely because of another piece of paper. The only effective method of stopping these chronic abusers is for a district attorney to determine that a felony prosecution is warranted, followed by conviction and incarceration, often for an extended period. Although protective orders stop many potential offenders, the use of protective orders for "hard-core" offenders might prove an illusory remedy, allowing many people to think they have solved the problem without, in fact, having handled the worst offenders. In this context there is a real danger of the availability of restraining orders being inappropriately cited by non-sympathetic parties to undermine domestic violence enforcement by claiming that society "has done all we can do" to help its victims and, therefore, that no other law enforcement or judicial actions need be taken.

In addition, as described earlier in the discussion on the Massachusetts experience, actual decision making by judges in hearings on the continuance of restraining orders tends to be rapid and highly subject to the possibility of an erroneous result. In many cases, because of psychological or physical trauma, the victim might simply not be capable of articulating her needs. In contrast, many batterers, especially those whose psychological profile fits a borderline or sociopathic personality disorder, might be articulate and fully capable of minimizing or justifying aberrant behavior. As a result, the granting of a permanent order and the attached conditions might fail to reflect adequately the potential danger to a victim and her children (Ballou et al., 2007). Unless a jurisdiction commits to the resources necessary for a model system to review restraining order requests, as we will discuss in the subsequent section, the prospect of incomplete protection is a very real and persisting danger.

Can Restraining Orders Be Misused?

Some men's rights groups have argued that restraining orders might be sought deliberately as a tactic in the context of divorce cases to influence judges in marital disputes and in childhood custody fights. Other than anecdotal reports, often from parties in such a suit, we are not aware of any studies that have demonstrated that this is a widespread realistic concern. Most studies have continued to demonstrate that people seeking such orders do so only as a result of existing severe abuse or as a credible threat of the same occurring. Nonetheless the concern has been expressed, and it is of course theoretically possible.

In fact the greater problem might be that some courts will allow abuse of the process of obtaining a restraining order. The reality is that in many cases of domestic violence, an abused person will strike back in self-defense. There might be little violence involved and no injury claimed. However, the system, unless monitored carefully, might allow perpetrators of abuse to misuse the system by filing a complaint against the original party. Some judges might be tempted to dismiss BOTH requests rather than to spend the time needed to determine the primary aggressor and thereby ruling as to which request is valid. This becomes even more of a risk in jurisdictions where the existence of other protective orders in other locales is not centralized and there can be dueling petitions in different courts (Sack, 2004).

In 1994, VAWA specifically addressed this issue. The law, in general, provides that each state should give full faith and credit to the restraining orders of another state. However, there is a special "carve out" of mutual restraining orders that is not enforceable in other jurisdictions unless the judge makes specific findings of fact. However, most divorce proceedings and criminal actions never cross state lines so the applicability of VAWA's finding is somewhat limited in actual practice, if not in guidance.

A more difficult problem can develop when manipulative batterers with resources misuse the protective order system. Batterers often have considerable knowledge regarding statutory provisions for protective orders. Therefore, the phenomenon of a "race to the courthouse" by the batterer and his victim has become increasingly prevalent (Goodmark, 2004, footnote 95). It often is difficult for a court to determine which petition is real as the batterer's petition might merely mirror that of the victim. When there is little physical evidence, the victim might find herself having sought legal protection but becoming instead subject to a civil protection order (Goodmark, 2004).

Judges also might misuse protective orders to find the victims to be in contempt of court. In Kentucky, one judge, Meaghan Lake Thornton, fines victims who initiate contacts with batterers, even though this might be necessary for her to obtain child support, coordinate child activities, and other similar reasons (Goodmark, 2004). Finally, there is a very problematic interaction between the theoretically voluntary process of a victim obtaining protective orders and the interests of the state in protecting children from observing acts of domestic violence. An increasing number of jurisdictions are holding that simply observing one parent abusing the other constitutes child abuse or child neglect unless the abused parent takes actions to prevent future abuse, including filing for a restraining order. Furthermore, child protective services might order victims to seek a restraining order. If a victim fails to do so, she might risk having a family court judge, at the instigation of a social worker, make a finding that she herself has committed child abuse or child neglect by continuing to allow her children to witness continued abuse. Conversely, a judge might be the party that reports children who witness violence to Family Services. In one recent case in Pennsylvania, the judge denied a mother's request for protection from an abuse order on behalf of her children and instead removed her children and immediately placed them in foster care (*Gall v. Gall*, [2002], cited in Goodmark, 2004, footnote 113).

Coercing a victim to obtain a theoretically voluntary order on her behalf is, at the least, highly problematic. Some protective orders might require full-blown evidentiary hearings that might threaten a woman's livelihood. Similarly, the woman might be aware that obtaining a restraining order might increase her risk for future violence. Therefore, she might legitimately prefer not to seek an order (Goodmark, 2004).

The Complex Problem of Restraining Order Violation

In all but one state, the violation of a protective order is punishable either as a separate criminal offense or as criminal contempt of court or both (Miller, 2005, p. 77). Some states specify a minimum automatic jail term—even if of a relatively short duration.

Several studies have documented the extent of the problem of reabuse even in the face of protective orders. This warrants continued study as to when and why such reabuse occurs. One study found that more than 15% of all restraining-order defendants were arrested for violating the orders within 6 months of their issuance (Isaac, 1994). Still other offenders presumably violate protective orders, but these are not reported because of victim fears of retaliation or loss of control in a jurisdiction with mandatory arrest or no-drop prosecution policies.

Grau et al.'s (1985) initial research suggested that aggregating offenders might mask two markedly different offender subpopulations. Although it is reasonably clear that the hard-core offenders ("cobras" in Jacobson and Gottman's [1998] terms) would never be deterred, a different result occurs when analyzing the behavioral impact on the family-only, "situationally violent" offenders. For those with less serious histories of family violence or in which the abuser was less violent, future acts of domestic violence did decline significantly.

A second study conducted in a model court tends to reinforce Grau et al.'s (1985) analysis. A comprehensive study of the QDC reported that in 1990, almost 50% of 663 male restraining-order defendants reabused the same victim within 2 years, 34% were arrested for violations of restraining orders, and 95% became subjects of new orders reflecting new incidents. Such substantial reoffending behavior seemed heavily correlated to age and criminal history with younger men and those with a criminal history most likely to reoffend (Klein, 1996).

In all of Massachusetts in 1992, more than 6,000 individuals were arrested for violating restraining orders. Of these offenders, almost 1,000 were placed on probation. In short, these studies graphically demonstrate that although our operating assumption is that court restraining orders should dramatically affect the cycle of abuse, unfortunately, to date, there is little empirical evidence that such an impact occurs for all types of batterers. Several other studies have found that revictimization is a serious problem, ranging from 23% to 50% of women who have sought protective orders (Carlson et al., 1999; Chaudhuri & Daly, 1992; Harrell & Smith, 1996; Klein, 1996). In addition, the 1997 Keilitz et al. study, although generally finding that protective orders were effective (72% were not battered within 1 month and 65% were not battered at the follow-up), also reported that the criminal history of the offender in a protective order was strongly correlated with both future violence in general and the severity of the subsequent violence in particular (Keilitz et al., 1997).

Our discussion of the deterrent effect of restraining orders assumes that prosecutors and courts will actively enforce protective orders once issued; however, recently published accounts of excessive rates of dismissals of such cases suggest that such an assumption must undergo more testing. If it is found that the prosecutorial and judicial organizations fail to enforce such orders within a relatively short period, batterers, victims, and the community at large will know this is reality. Under such circumstances, deterrence will inevitably become less effective, and protective orders might begin to atrophy into a useless, even cynical, vehicle to quell public demands for effective, but resource-intensive, actions.

There is not yet a consensus as to which factors predict when restraining orders will be violated and reabuse will occur; however, several tentative hypotheses have been advanced. For example, Harrell and Smith (1996) observed that victimization despite protective orders was higher among those having dependant, minor children. This to us is logical because the presence of minor children typically means that the offender still wants continued close contact with the family—and it is in such potentially highly stressful contacts that abuse is far more likely. Even if a no-contact order is in place, a batterer might take extraordinary legal risks to ensure continued visitation if there are children involved. Carlson et al. (1999) also unsurprisingly observed that revictimization occurred more frequently in lower socioeconomic and minority groups. Financial issues, especially court-ordered support, often exacerbate the offender's feelings of being wronged (especially if he is being forced to pay support without any visitation rights).

In addition, a consistent body of research relates violation of protective orders to criminal history. Harrell and Smith (1996) found that prior offenders were likely to reoffend.

Similarly, in his review of the QDC, Klein (1996) reported this relationship. Buzawa et al.'s 1999 research, also on the QDC, reinforced the findings of the earlier Klein research. They found that offenders who had restraining orders had the most violent and abusive criminal histories and the highest rates of substance abuse, as well as the highest rate of reoffending. Although that study was, by definition, one that examined cases of reabuse, it clearly reinforced the perception that restraining orders might be effective for the overall population, but for the subpopulation of offenders with an extensive criminal history (the "cobras"), it had little or no positive impact (Buzawa et al., 1999).

However, we need to understand that research that seemingly suggests that protective orders are ineffective should not be taken out of context. Women tend to take out restraining orders disproportionately when offenders already have criminal histories of violent behavior (Waul, 2000). Keilitz et al. (1997) reported that 80% of those seeking protective orders had an offender who had criminal histories; Klein (1996) found that 65% had criminal arrest histories. Waul reported that women whose partners had a criminal record with at least one domestic violence offense were significantly more likely to obtain a protective order than women whose partners did not have prior domestic violence charges.

Similarly, Buzawa et al. (1999) reported that victims seeking restraining orders sought them against offenders who averaged twice the criminal history of the offenders whose victims did not seek restraining orders. A simple comparison of reoffending rates for those who did and did not seek restraining orders would therefore not provide a valid comparison, at least at an aggregate level. Instead, this could simply represent an artifact of the differential population seeking restraining orders compared with those victims who did not. We hope that future research will clarify the role of criminal history by isolating this crucial variable to measure its seemingly overwhelming significance. In any event, at this stage, it seems premature to conclude that restraining orders "do not work."

The fact is that it is extraordinarily difficult to determine generally the efficacy of restraining orders. We know that a substantial number of domestic violence victims who seek restraining orders will be subject to reabuse. We also know that there are some factors, such as the presence of minor children, lower levels of income, and, perhaps most important, criminal history, that seem to predict the likelihood of reabuse and, hence, in the broadest sense, make a restraining order "ineffective." We believe it premature to marginalize the role of restraining orders, especially because, as noted, most victims believe that the issuance of protective orders does have merit. We also are aware that most research, at least until the QDC study, did not control for criminal history in determining whether restraining orders were effective at preventing reabuse. Hence, any conclusion of the "failure" or intrinsic limits of protective orders is, to our minds, premature.

Judicial Enforcement of Restraining Orders

Actual enforcement of restraining orders is extremely important. If they are not enforced, it is obvious that their value is limited. Furthermore, batterers might interpret enforcement failure as a continued lack of societal concern for their abusive behavior. There is a fundamental principle of law that "deprivations of law require remedies."

Professor Tracy Thomas noted that the right to a remedy is a basic right protected by the Due Process Clause of the Fourteenth Amendment. As she put it, "without remedies, rights are mere ideals, promises, or pronouncements that might or might not be followed" (Thomas, 2004, p. 1639). Commentators have for decades realized the implicit power of lawsuits to force police actions where they do not want to perform their statutory duties. As we have discussed in previous chapters, not so benign neglect was the norm. That behavior has receded under the impact of public scrutiny, statutes mandating action, and the widespread adoption of more activist department policies. However, in many jurisdictions and certainly among many officers around the country, there remains a deep reluctance to intervene, bordering on active antipathy. In that case, the only remedy, albeit not for the unfortunate victim who has typically been killed, is a heavily publicized lawsuit demonstrating that when police are derelict in their duties, there will be severe consequences.

Judicial Enforcement of Restraining Orders in the Face of Police Misconduct

In the past, and even, as graphically illustrated in several cases we will cite extensively, a few police officers and sometimes police departments have failed to enforce restraining orders effectively. In those cases, victims or their representatives have had several methods to get legal recourse. Clearly, if state law permits, they could file a civil lawsuit in a state court for the tort of negligence or some other charge permitted against state officials derelict in their duties.

Federal courts were, until relatively recently, the preferred venue for cases. State case law, at least until the 2005 *Gonzales* case, did not have as predictable results as in federal court. Also, for the simple reason that victory in a case often required considerable resources and actual monetary damages awarded could be small, federal forums were preferred because the United States Attorney's Fees Act of 1976 gives victims, who win their case alleging malfeasance of officials, the ability to recover attorneys' fees (del Carmen & Walker, 2003).

Liability under federal law is primarily based on Title 42 of U.S. Code Section 1983. Most victims who file such lawsuits use either the Due Process or the Equal Protection clauses of the Fourteenth Amendment of the U.S. Constitution—extending protection to citizens for the violation of rights by the actions or inactions of state and local officials. With respect to due process, victims of domestic abuse might allege both substantive and procedural due process violations, although each type of violation is subject to different legal analytical standards. The U.S. Supreme Court has held that procedural due process rights can originate from state statutes that purportedly create benefits for private parties. The court also has held that the Constitution does not grant individuals an absolute entitlement to such rights; rather, they should be created by state law. Therefore, to have a legitimate claim of entitlement, a victim must have "more than a unilateral expectation of it" (*Board of Regents of State Colleges v. Roth*, 1972).

In the few domestic violence cases alleging police misconduct that have actually gone to court, victims generally allege that they are entitled to police protection from abuse, especially if a state court has granted them a protective order and/or a restraining order detailing the extent to which an alleged batterer can come into contact with the victim.

A victim who files a Section 1983 lawsuit claims that an officer or police department violated a constitutional right or right given by federal or state law.

In most trials where this has been asserted, the relevant state law provided for mandatory enforcement of legally issued restraining orders. Furthermore, to prevail, the plaintiff must prove that the law was clearly established, meaning that reasonable officers would agree that the law on that issue was clear to them. If reasonable officers would differ as to whether the law was clearly established, then the officer who is sued is entitled to qualified immunity or protection from suit (del Carmen et al., 2003). Effectively, this means that to have a good chance to prevail, plaintiffs' attorneys will only go to a federal court if they believe police misconduct in not enforcing a restraining order was egregious.

A 2005 Supreme Court case, *Gonzales v. City of Castle Rock*, cast significant doubt on the federal judiciary's willingness to mandate enforcement of restraining orders in the context of violating the victim's due process rights. The facts of the *Gonzales* case suggest that the Castle Rock Police Department (Castle Rock, CO) did a poor job of enforcing an existing restraining order. In 1999, three girls, ages 7, 8, and 10, were shot to death by their father. Their mother, Ms. Gonzales, was getting a divorce from the father, Simon Gonzales, and had obtained a restraining order after he had frightened the family, by acting erratically, including putting a noose around his neck and attempting to hang himself in front of his young daughters. There were repeated calls to the police, even after separation with numerous accusations of stalking as well as breaking and entering. As a result, Ms. Gonzales obtained a restraining order to keep him away from the rest of the family. The restraining order stipulated that he could only be with his daughters on alternate weekends. One month after the restraining order was issued, when he was not supposed to have any contact, he took them in his pickup truck and drove off. Before 6 p.m., Ms. Gonzales called the police officers and advised them of the restraining order. Colorado law *mandates* arrest for the violation of a restraining order. During an interview on the news program *60 Minutes* in March 2005, she stated that their first reaction was, "Well he's their father; it's OK for them to be with them." To which she replied, "No, it's not OK. There was no arranged visit for him to have them" (Leung, 2005, para. 14).

By 10 p.m., she had learned that he had taken them out of the city of Castle Rock to an amusement park in nearby Denver. She asked the Castle Rock Police Department to inform the Denver Police Department of the restraining order violation where the police could have easily intercepted them as there was only one way in and out of the amusement park. The Castle Rock Police Department refused, stating that she should call them back in several more hours. Although some facts are disputed by the Castle Rock Police Department, Ms. Gonzales stated that, "she read them the part of the restraining order that instructs police, 'to use every reasonable effort to protect the. . . . children to prevent . . . violence'" (Leung, 2005, para. 23). Furthermore, as she told *60 Minutes*, she had begged and pleaded with the police to go and get her girls.

When her husband did not return after 10 p.m., she called the police a third time and was told to wait until after midnight before calling again. At midnight, she went to his apartment and, when he was not there, made her fourth call to the police and drove to their station where she told another officer about the restraining order. Around 3:20 a.m., Simon Gonzales drove to the police station where he emerged from his truck, shooting at the building with a semiautomatic gun he had purchased that evening. The police returned fire, killing him (a fairly common "suicide-by-police" scenario). When they looked in his truck, they found the bodies of the three girls. An autopsy concluded that he had shot each of them in the head after leaving the amusement park.

Ms. Gonzales sued the police department for $30 million. Her express purpose was to force police departments throughout the country to improve training regarding the enforcement of restraining orders. She claimed that she was deprived of her right for procedural due process by the police department's implicit dismissal of the protective order, in clear violation of the Colorado State statute that required them to use "every reasonable means to enforce."

The U.S. District Court granted Castle Rock's motion to dismiss findings that Ms. Gonzales had failed to state a claim for which relief could be granted (*Gonzales v. City of Castle Rock,* 2001). The District Court found that even though the Colorado law was on its face mandatory and required the police to use all reasonable effort, it conferred no "property right" on behalf of the plaintiff. Therefore, she had no right to sue, even though it was undisputed that the Castle Rock Police Department did not even place a phone call to another police department when they knew the location of the person violating a known restraining order—and three minors had been taken out of the jurisdiction in violation of the restraining order.

On appeal, the 10th Circuit Court of Appeals, reversed the decision of the District Court and found that based on the explicit *mandatory* language of the Colorado statute and its legislative history, the statute clearly created a protected property interest falling under the Due Process Clause. The Court of Appeals stated that, "Colorado courts have stated unambiguously that in Colorado statutes, 'shall' does in fact mean 'shall'" (ID. At 1265). See *People v. Guenther* (1994). ("The word 'shall, when used in a statute, involves a 'mandatory connotation' and hence is the antithesis of discretion or choice'") (*Gonzales v. City of Castle Rock,* 2005).

The decision of the Court of Appeals to overturn the District Court decision was consistent with the U.S. constitutional doctrine of Procedural Due Process. This doctrine relies on the principle that when the state chooses to establish a benefit or right for citizens (such as free education, public housing, providing a test for drivers licenses, etc.), it may not deny such benefits in an arbitrary or unfair way. In this case, Colorado statutorily established a benefit to potential victims of recurring violence to grant statutory authority for domestic violence restraining orders but also to mandate police enforcement of such orders. By doing so they specifically eliminated traditional police discretion, limiting discretion solely to a determination as to whether the violation of an order had occurred. In this particular case, it seems fairly obvious that the Castle Rock Police Department had facts demonstrating a known violation, and not too much of a stretch to understand that this particular violation might put three minor children at risk. Nevertheless, they took no effective action, in our mind, clearly acting arbitrarily.

Unfortunately, after the Court of Appeals decision, many municipalities became extremely worried that this case could open considerable liability for nonenforcement. The Castle Rock Police Department was joined by the National League of Cities, the National Sheriffs Association, and the U.S. Department of Justice in amicus or "friend of the court" briefs, stating that the police could not have predicted the terrible outcome of what was, at the time, a mere "domestic dispute." Interestingly enough, four police associations signed a brief opposing the actions of the Castle Rock Police Department and the International Association of Chiefs of Police (IACP), normally highly supportive of police discretion, refused to support the town's position (Meier, 2005).

Then the U.S. Supreme Court in *Gonzales v. City of Castle Rock* (2005) reversed the Court of Appeals and dismissed the lawsuit. While typically the Supreme Court defers issues of the state law to state courts, the Court chose to interpret a Colorado statute, without obtaining an advisory opinion of the Colorado supreme court. In a 7–2 decision written by Justice Scalia, they found that a person "protected" by a restraining order has no "property right" in the enforcement of that order. Therefore, they have no right to sue when a police department refuses to enforce it. In doing so, it is our opinion that the Court ignored the intent of the state legislature when it created mandatory action on the part of the police.

Enforcement of Restraining Orders After Gonzales

It is still too early to determine the ultimate effect of the *Gonzales* case on either police or judicial enforcement of restraining orders. There remains the potential of a devastating impact on the role of restraining orders in protecting victims, at least in some jurisdictions. The U.S. Supreme Court is, of course, the final arbiter in interpreting due process under the U.S. Constitution. Clearly such Due Process claims cannot be heard unless, and until, the Supreme Court reverses or limits *Gonzales*.

Police officials now know that there is no federal court recourse if they ignore victim requests for restraining order enforcement. Victim advocates should therefore advise victims in some locales that they might be at the mercy of their local police department's priorities and should now work with elected representatives to make these priorities consistent with state statutes and more enlightened practices.

Conversely, potential abusers might be advised by their attorneys that local police departments might or might not choose to enforce restraining orders; hopefully most will be told that their police departments rigorously enforce such orders. However, some undoubtedly will be told that their particular departments assign little weight to enforcement.

Despite this decision, we suspect that few police departments will act as cavalierly as the Castle Rock Police Department. The fact that the IACP chose not to support their actions is a good sign that other departments have higher standards then those displayed in the *Gonzales* case.

In addition, as mentioned, the Fourteenth Amendment also includes protections granted under the Equal Protection Clause. The Equal Protection Clause has been used by victims of domestic violence who allege disparate police response and treatment. For example, the Thurman case, *Thurman v. City of Torrington* (1984), one of the first cases involving an equal protection violation, the victim alleged that police "provided less protection to women abused by their male partners than to persons abused by someone with whom the victim has no domestic relationship" (Blackwell & Vaughn, 2003, p. 132). The police were held liable because they could not justify their different response to victims in intimate relationships as opposed to those who were not in such relationships. This potential liability for police inaction still exists and might well mean that police departments will not lightly shirk their responsibilities.

Also, a different line of due process cases also might fairly quickly develop in some states. A state supreme court can interpret state laws and constitutions far differently than a federal court. Hence, although the U.S. Supreme Court has made it abundantly clear that it will not demand enforcement of such orders in federal courts, this decision need not be followed by the various state supreme courts.

In interpreting their own constitution and laws, a state supreme court might find that police conduct takes away a victim's "property" or otherwise allows a suit to continue. If given the opportunity, juries might well conclude that a police department that chose not to enforce "mandatory" restraining orders constitutes sufficient negligence for a victim or her estate to recover. Specifically, when state courts are asked to consider enforcing a state law that mandates arrest upon a violation of a restraining order, they probably now will be confronted with claims of violations of due process of their state constitution as well as with claims of violation of the particular state law.

One early such state case was decided only months after *Gonzales*. In *Moore v. Green* (2006), the Illinois supreme court followed a long line of cases and continued to interpret a 1986 Illinois statute (the Illinois Domestic Violence Act) as requiring mandatory enforcement of restraining orders. The court found that two Chicago police officers could be held civilly liable for the death of a woman who had a protective order against her husband. The facts of the case clearly demonstrated cavalier conduct. Ms. Ronyale White had recently obtained an emergency protective order against her estranged husband, Louis Drexel. He defied the order and entered her home unlawfully. She called 911 four times to report that he had illegally entered her home and to plead for immediate police assistance. During the course of the 911 calls, the police department was aware of the severity of the incident as the recorded dispatch tapes revealed a threatening male voice in the background (Litchman, 2007, footnote 3). These facts also were recorded on a cassette tape that she had placed in her pocket as he threatened her with a loaded gun. The two officers that were dispatched to her home took 15 minutes to respond to the scene. Police supervisors testified that the response should have taken closer to 3 minutes (Ciokajlo, 2006). After their arrival at the residence, officers never entered the home. Instead, they apparently inspected their patrol vehicle and made personal calls while Drexel attacked and killed White.

After the Illinois Supreme Court decision, the city of Chicago agreed to settle the case for $4.25 million and the officers were suspended without pay. One can imagine that as a result of this settlement, the Chicago Police Department will more closely adhere to the Illinois statutory requirements for mandatory enforcement of restraining orders. It is, however, disturbing that such police conduct, and the need for monetary penalties, persists decades after the problem of police inaction was addressed by statute, department policies, and even the threat of personal lawsuits that the Illinois courts have allowed on numerous occasions.

Similarly, a few states have, by statute, expressly addressed the issue of police liability for failure to enforce protective orders. These states might allow such suits but only under more narrow circumstances, making recourse to the courts far more problematic. Litchman (2007) analyzed statutes in Washington (where a lack of good faith on the part of the police must be shown), California (where the police to be held liable must be found to have increased the risk of the plaintiff, by example, creating false reliance on their promise to assist), and New York (where an existing protective order can help establish that a special duty is owed by the police to the victim of violence, but reliance on such a duty has to be shown).

Finally, given the wide spectrum of negligence theories that are available under state tort law, it is likely that plaintiffs might now be more likely to prevail against sloppy police procedure in state courts, although compensation might be limited and, as noted, there is no reasonable likelihood of recovering attorneys' fees. State cases based on negligence will likely be based on a judge finding that there is at least some reasonable basis for a jury to conclude that the police had opportunity to prevent a future crime by enforcing the terms of a protective order, for example, removing firearms used later to kill a victim or other very clear violations of their responsibilities to enforce a state statute.

Is There a "Best Practice" for Obtaining and Enforcing Restraining Orders?

More Potential Enhancements to Restraining Orders

Several researchers have posited that the process of obtaining and enforcing restraining orders can be vastly improved from the widely variant practices currently in use. The following suggested enhancements seem to be worth consideration. First, during the course of issuing a permanent restraining order, judges can be required to consult with trained consultants that are capable of developing a psychological profile of the party to be restrained. Ballou et al. (2007) referred to this as the development of a psychological model for judicial decision making. The psychological model would include history and indicators of violence, the attitude of the alleged perpetrator, the relationship dynamic between the parties, as well as other psychological, social, and behavioral factors (Ballou et al., 2007).

The model described in Table 11.1 is still under development and will be refined over time. However, the idea of a well-defined set of criteria for judicial decision making in the context of relatively short hearings holds promise as a best practice.

In addition to the development of a risk assessment instrument for judges and their staff, we believe that other reforms should be considered. There certainly is no lack of innovative approaches that are being tried—even if they have not yet been empirically verified as being effective. For example, the state of Maine allows the issuance of a protection order without any finding of abuse as long as both parties consent to the order. This might have an advantage in that no findings of fact need to be made by a judge. Since such findings can later be used as evidence in custody decisions and have other long-term implications, this provision might increase the ability of orders to be issued as well as the willingness of parties to seek such orders (Miller, 2005).

Second, the continued violation of a restraining order should subject an offender to increasingly severe penalties. For example, in Minnesota, a single violation of a restraining order is subject to a minimum term of incarceration of 3 days. However, if there is a prior domestic violence conviction, the minimum becomes 10 days. If there are two priors within 5 years, a felony charge is added and a minimum stay of 30 days is mandated (Miller, 2005). It is indeed possible that the prospect of a certain minimum jail sentence might deter some offenders.

Third, several states, including Florida and Massachusetts, provide assistance for victims who claim that restraining orders have been violated. In Florida, once a violation of an order is claimed, the state takes over its enforcement—the matter then truly loses

Table 11.1 Psychological Model: Significant Psychosocial Factors for Consideration in Continuance of Restraining Orders

Is there a history of domestic abuse, assault, or other criminal behavior?

Are there other restraining orders or criminal cases on his record?

Are there other credible reports of child abuse and/or former partner abuse?

Have there been threats or violent incidents at work/school/in social situations?

Have there been threats or violent incidents at home?

Are there reports of aggressive behavior (property damage, abuse of pets, ripping phone out of the wall, etc.)?

Is there an underlying lack of empathy or concern for others or a general attitude of entitlement (despite favorable presentation)?

Is he logical, responsive to questions, and convincing?

Is he primarily thinking or concerned about himself?

Does he blame circumstances, alcohol, or the victim?

Does he deny or minimize his battering?

Does he claim good intentions or self-protection?

Is there a failure to take responsibility for his behavior?

Does he seem overly or covertly full of rage about the restraining order or her behavior?

What are the psychological reactions of the victim?

Are there signs of trauma such as fear, anger, or illogical or confused thinking?

Are there reports of behavior indicating trauma such as heightened startle response, weight loss, or sleeplessness?

What are the behaviors of the batterer in the relationship? Are domestic violence risk factors present?

Is there a history of alcohol or other drug abuse?

Are there indications of jealousy or possessiveness?

Are there attempts to control her behavior, her interactions with friends and family, or her finances?

Are there any reports or indications of threats or stalking?

Does he answer or interrupt her?

Are there indications that he has witnessed or experienced violence in his childhood?

Does he own guns, knives, or other weapons?

Does behavior in other relationships (work, etc.) suggest an attitude of entitlement or lack of empathy?

Are there indications of behavior indicating domination (imposed sex, intimidation, or controlling her activities such as phone use, transportation, choice of friends, and ability to work)?

Source: Ballou et al., 2007, Table 1, p. 283.

its "civil" nature and becomes far more like a criminal case. Courts might require the state prosecutor to file a contempt of court motion, or they might notify the prosecutor that they will proceed on their own initiative to punish contempt of court (Miller, 2005).

SUMMARY

This chapter provided an overview on the role and use of restraining orders, as well as on the strengths and limitations of their use. What has been more difficult to determine is their effectiveness. To some extent, this depends on the criteria used to measure victim success. Although some report increased victim satisfaction, the question is whether this might put victims at even greater risk if, in fact, they do not increase their safety. Does the presence of a restraining order mean that victims are less vigilant in taking steps to ensure their own safety? Alternatively, can restraining orders be better implemented in ways that can be coupled with strategies to better protect victims?

DISCUSSION QUESTIONS

1. How can we improve the effectiveness of restraining orders?

2. Can restraining orders better ensure victim safety by the conditions imposed?

3. Should temporary restraining orders be part of an offender's criminal history?

4. What should be the process by which a victim can obtain a restraining order?

5. Is using "victim satisfaction" an adequate reason for the use of restraining orders?

Models for Judicial Intervention 12

Chapter Overview

Previously, we discussed how the adoption of more aggressive prosecutorial policies, including widespread use of no-drop policies, has increased the number of domestic violence cases reaching the judiciary. Coupled with growing statutory directives and police enforcement of these offenses, a marked increase in judicial caseloads has occurred. Courts, meanwhile, historically were viewed as the final component of the criminal justice system that was able to resist change. Given the inherent separation of powers among the legislative, executive, and judicial branches of power in all jurisdictions, a legislative directive need not necessarily transfer quickly, if ever, into changed judicial action.

More than 15 years ago, however, the judiciary began to recognize the need to increase the attention paid to domestic violence and violent families. In 1994, the National Council of Juvenile and Family Court Judges first published the *Model State Code on Domestic and Family Violence* through the Advisory Committee of the Conrad N. Hilton Foundation Model Code Project of the Family Violence Project, placing enhanced attention on the role of the judiciary in responding to domestic violence, spurring a reanalysis of past approaches, and suggesting many innovative approaches. This effort also advanced a suggested "model code" for processing domestic violence with early intervention, supporting enhanced police arrest practices and even mandatory arrest for violation of protective orders and certain domestic-related crimes. Furthermore, it established standards for prosecution and victim assistance by prosecutors. Perhaps because of the background of its membership, which is primarily family court judges, it also focused on the problems of child protection and custody in domestic violence cases, which is an area often ignored in other courts.

Since then, many judicial conferences and training sessions have addressed improving court response to domestic violence. Organizations such as the National Center for Juvenile and Family Court Judges, the Center for Court Innovation, the Institute for Law and Justice, and the American Prosecutorial Research Institute have greatly contributed to these efforts, both through their direct work with prosecutors and the judiciary as well as through their research.

This chapter will continue this discussion by providing a review of how change has transpired in the area of sentences imposed. We will then address the development of specialized domestic violence courts over the last two decades, as well as other structural innovations that hold considerable promise at better addressing victim needs.

The Process of Measuring Judicial Change

Measuring the breadth of any judicial change is difficult. To a large extent, we must rely on aggregate data that might mask major variations between and within jurisdictions. As a result, a particular victim or offender's experience in one courtroom might bear little resemblance to what would occur in another court—even one within the same jurisdiction. Even so, such aggregate data can help define national trends. Furthermore, since the Department of Justice prides itself on the use of comprehensive aggregate data sets, this information tends to be published and disseminated widely, thereby exerting considerable influence on policymakers who, in turn, might perceive that an issue has been resolved.

Recent research has focused mostly on case processing and sentencing used in specialized domestic violence courts, which is a distinct minority of courts, although growing in number. General aggregate data by definition do not distinguish between what happens in these specialized courts from traditional court settings. Thus, these studies, with whatever limitations, should be where we begin to examine how domestic violence cases are processed when they enter the judicial system.

What happens to cases before a trial is conducted? As discussed previously, the conviction rates for domestic violence crimes have extraordinary variability—exceeding, for example, variance in convictions for other violent crimes that typically are prosecuted to a guilty plea or trial. In most jurisdictions, the judiciary still allows prosecutors largely unfettered freedom to drop most abuse cases without a finding or admission of criminality—the traditional model of court behavior. This happens because there is no method or role for the judiciary to oversee most prosecutors' offices. Hence, such informal bargaining with the prosecution might, in effect, become the de facto "sentence" for committing a crime of domestic violence. One judge noted that this increased the difficulty of her job because "deals" were often agreed on before she was presented with the case. She found that the agreement often distorted the reality of what happened considerably and impeded her ability to impose her preferred disposition. We discuss such informal case dispositions in Chapter 10; however, we need to note that in the context of formal criminal cases, much of the discretionary activity occurs behind the scene, subject to minimal judicial control in many jurisdictions.

After determining what cases are screened out before reaching judicial attention, the key question becomes what characterizes case disposition for domestic violence offenders who reach the stage of a final adjudicated plea and what are the resultant sentences? The following other key questions also emerge: First, what happens during the course of a judicial proceeding; and second, is there consistency of sentencing for convicted domestic violence offenders?

In measuring the efficacy of the judiciary, one unique factor for domestic violence is the speed of the process itself. Unlike many other criminal cases where the risk of an offender reoffending against the same victim is low, during the period that a court retains jurisdiction of a domestic case, there is an enhanced risk of continued victimization. Research has shown that offenders are most likely to reoffend during the first month after the initial incident (Klein & Tobin, 2008).

Unfortunately, this is precisely when cases in most criminal dockets are just in their initial stages. In addition to actual reinjury, offenders are most likely to violate restraining orders that were imposed in the initial court appearance or to intimidate victims to prevent them from assisting in prosecution. There are multiple reasons domestic offenders pose such risks. Abusers are typically charged with misdemeanor offenses (Klein, 2009). This means that offenders are rarely kept in custody before trial. The initial arrest is most likely to be either overnight or, if committed during the weekend, only for several days while waiting for arraignment.

Because misdemeanors are not viewed as "serious" crimes, few jurisdictions provide meaningful supervision of such defendants prior to trial. Although many jurisdictions prohibit offenders from having contact with victims while cases are pending, "no-contact" bond conditions often are violated. Even violation of no-contact orders often will go unpunished because of extended periods between court appearances (Visher, Harrell, & Newmark, 2007).

As a result, research has begun to identify this period as a critical time for judicial oversight in making a difference in outcomes. Whereas in the past, most judges did not feel responsible for offender conduct prior to adjudication, many courts are now experimenting with pretrial innovations to determine whether courts can control offender conduct prior to an official determination of guilt.

The Impact of Judicial Activism: Analysis of a Case Study

Perhaps the best demonstration of these techniques is the procedures developed for, and the lessons learned from, the Judicial Oversight Demonstration (JOD) Project. The JOD was started in 1999 to determine whether quickly coordinated responses by the community and the judiciary could keep the victim safe. Three courts were selected, Dorchester County, Massachusetts; Milwaukee, Wisconsin; and Washtenaw County, Michigan. The results were to be studied 10 years later in a project evaluated by researchers at the Urban Institute on behalf of the National Institute of Justice (Visher, Harrell, Newmark, & Yahner, 2009).

The courts in this field test were committed to taking a more active role in managing domestic violence cases before trial. The key to this change was that the entire criminal justice system was involved. Although the prior state of each court was different, the following strategies were adopted in all three courts:

- A full-time project director was appointed to organize meeting and planning sessions.

- Procedures for obtaining a protection order were expedited.

- Judges regularly reviewed batterers' compliance with the terms of their probation.

- Planning sessions efficiently helped to modify the court system and to coordinate community responses to domestic violence.

- Courts maintained a wide network of partnerships with community organizations and treatment facilities.

- Judges, attorneys, and law enforcement officers attended special training sessions with experts in domestic violence.

- Staff worked exclusively on domestic violence cases and became specialists in handling these kinds of cases.

By taking such actions, all jurisdictions committed to reinforce pro-arrest policies procedurally and to provide coordinated victim advocacy and services, and the court system took the lead responsibility from the prosecutor's office to supervise defendants. Judges oversaw all aspects of the case from the hearings to sanctions for pretrial misbehavior. They oversaw enhanced victim services, created specialized courtroom procedures to assist victims, and ensured that personnel were well trained. Key personnel such as court clerks and others were trained in both case processing and in recognizing and enforcing protective orders. Judges were asked to expedite procedures for protective order hearings.

The key reform focused on centralizing, to the extent possible, cases of domestic violence. In the urban areas of Dorchester and Milwaukee, a dedicated judge or judges were assigned. In the case of Dorchester, six separate general jurisdiction judges who previously handled domestic violence cases were consolidated into a single courtroom. This court used a vertical adjudication model, where one prosecutor took the case all the way through the system and one domestic violence court handled all criminal court proceedings, as well as restraining orders and preindictment hearings. In Milwaukee, which is a larger jurisdiction than Dorchester, four specialized courts were created for domestic violence cases. Whereas in the past, all courts had heard misdemeanor cases, a specialized domestic offense court was created an all district courts.

In Washtenaw County, Michigan, which was more spread out and less densely populated than Dorchester, it was deemed necessary to maintain a domestic violence court at each of the four district courts; however, each court established a "domestic violence docket day" each week to get judges and their staff to focus on this issue.

The courts developed procedures either to supervise defendants directly prior to trial or to monitor their behavior. Victims were assisted by enhanced services from nongovernmental service agencies funded by the JOD project. These services were provided at the courthouse in Dorchester and Milwaukee.

It seems that judicial involvement and willingness to coordinate cases eliminates inconsistency, leads to better coordination among agencies, provides the capability of a quick court response to the violation of restraining orders, and connects services to victims.

Also, although critical data on actual reoffending are not yet available, it seems that victims felt far more satisfied with the police, prosecutors, and the courts; felt that the project would help stop future violence; and reported stronger feelings of safety and well-being. Furthermore, offenders had more conditions of probation placed on them than comparison offenders, complied at a higher rate with court orders to attend batterer intervention programs, and were given harsher penalties for failure to comply with court ordered compliance programs.

Not surprisingly, the impact of such interventions varied among different groups of offenders. Younger offenders (ages 18–29 years) were more likely to be positively affected as were those where the victim and offender were not as engaged in a long-term relationship (did not have children together or had been in a relationship for less than 3 years). Somewhat surprisingly, it also was found to be more effective when there had been a higher number of prior arrests (seven or more), possibly because judges were more willing to react strongly to abuse.

Although the results are not final, comparison groups were studied in two of the three jurisdictions. In the case of Dorchester, they matched similar cases in a comparable city in Massachusetts—Lowell, Massachusetts. Washtenaw County compared these cases with those in Ingham County. Since there was no comparable jurisdiction to Milwaukee in the state of Wisconsin, the researchers used a quasi-experimental design.

Case Disposition at Trial: Variability in Judicial Sentencing Patterns

Once a case is set for a plea or trial, the issue is not whether defendants are inappropriately acquitted. Once a case actually goes to trial, available evidence clearly establishes that most trials result in conviction, and not-guilty findings are rare. A comparison of studies reported that total not-guilty findings at trial ranged from a high of only 5% to a low of 1.6% (Klein, 2009). That rate seems to be appropriate and acceptable for trials as, in some cases, guilt simply cannot be proven beyond a reasonable doubt, perhaps because of conflicting accounts of witnesses or the refusal of a key witness (such as the injured party) to testify.

For this reason, our focus is on those who actually are convicted and thereby sentenced. Primarily, these crimes are misdemeanors because virtually all jurisdictions treat domestic violence as a misdemeanor, absent aggravating factors. Given the far greater discretion granted to judges in sentencing miscreants rather than felons, the key factor is what percent of convicted offenders are actually incarcerated after a finding of guilt. Also, because of the potential impact on recidivism, we want to know how often courts impose requirements to complete a batterer intervention program or have intensive supervision, also called "judicial monitoring," as part of the sentence.

There is currently no uniformity in sentencing offenders to jail time. Disparity toward ordering prison sentences occurs independent of whether a court is reputed to be proactive in handling domestic violence cases. For example, in one study of a progressive court in Quincy, Massachusetts, three quarters of the domestic violence suspects (74%) were charged with some form of assault and/or battery, a quarter of the defendants were diverted after a plea to sufficient facts, a quarter were placed on probation, and only 14 percent were imprisoned (Buzawa, Hotaling, Klein, & Byrne, 1999). This finding was insignificantly different from the Massachusetts average of 12.6% (Bass et al., 1994, as cited in Klein, 2009) even though from the authors' experiences, many other jurisdictions in the state of Massachusetts do not have nearly the reputation for aggressive treatment of domestic violence as does the Quincy court.

A similar pattern was found in a study of Cook County's (Chicago) practices where a misdemeanor court sentenced only 23% of convicted offenders to jail (Hartley & Frohmann, 2003; Maxwell, Robinson, & Klein, 2009). In contrast, other studies show markedly different ranges of incarceration. In one Ohio jurisdiction, 70% of those found guilty of misdemeanors were incarcerated, and almost 20% were sentenced for more than 150 days (Belknap, Fleury, Melton, Sullivan, & Leisenring, 2001).

In New York City, a study of Brooklyn reported that in 35% of the misdemeanor cases, guilt was established and resulted in incarceration. In other states, results varied widely independent of whether dedicated domestic violence prosecutorial units existed that were presumably supportive of efforts to achieve meaningful sentences for proven violations (Cissner & Puffet, 2006).

One study of four jurisdictions with such dedicated units reported sentences for incarceration that ranged from 20% to 76% (Smith, Davis, Nickles, & Davies, 2001). Although one would expect some differences based on different statutory frameworks, this extreme variation suggests that there is no consistent pattern in sentencing.

Why is there such variation reported in these studies? Partially this might be because of the age of the study. Some evidence suggests that sentences involving at least some incarceration might be increasing. For example, in Ohio, the number of domestic violence offenders sent to prison increased ninefold between 1991 and 2005 (Klein, 2009; Wooldredge, 2007).

In addition, subsequent variability in sentencing occurs based on court sentencing practice. Some courts review a domestic violence offender's criminal history before determining whether incarceration is warranted. For most offenses, it is typical and appropriate for judges to consider whether there is a pattern of previous criminality to determine whether jail should be imposed. In fact, in many states, commission of multiple misdemeanors (typically three) automatically results in reclassification of subsequent offenses to felonies. Consideration of criminal history is not used to discriminate between habitual offenders and a one-time miscreant.

In contrast, many other courts do not seem to consider criminal history in sentencing domestic violence offenders. For example, in Ohio, researchers found no relationship between offender's criminal history and sentence severity (Maxwell et al., 2009; Wooldredge, 2007). However, in Massachusetts, we found a pattern in which criminal history justified enhanced sentences.

This aspect of sentencing variability should be addressed clearly. As we have discussed in previous chapters, in the case of domestic abuse, a criminal record in felony prosecutions is critical in predicting reoffending. In addition, research has repeatedly demonstrated that past decisions on whether to charge a domestic offender with the commission of a misdemeanor or a felony is both arbitrary and typically downgraded in the charge compared with other types of offenses. We can understand where the "assembly-line," no-incarceration disposition of misdemeanor offenders might normally be justified by the relatively less severe charges compared with convicted felons. However, prior to such actions, judges should understand that their decision to charge an offender with a misdemeanor compared with a felony often has little to do with the severity of the crime itself or the propensity of the offender to reoffend. Only a careful examination of the offender's criminal history will allow imposition of the correct sentence, whether that involves jail for a repeat offender, deferred prosecution for a first-time offender, or attendance at targeted batterer intervention programs.

In addition to disparity in sentencing convicted offenders to jail, extreme variability exists in the judicial use of batterer invention programs or "enhanced" court-ordered supervision as a condition of probation. As might be expected, a study of domestic violence courts with specialized prosecutors in three different states found that conditions of probation were much broader than in comparable jurisdictions without domestic violence specialization. Such conditions typically included testing for drugs and alcohol, lengthier batterer intervention programs, increased numbers of no-contact orders, increased mental health evaluations, mandatory employment, and weapon restrictions (Harrell, Newmark, &Visher, 2007; Maxwell et al., 2009)

Patterns for Domestic Compared With Non–Domestic Violence Offenders

One critical question is whether courts treat domestic violence cases as seriously as they would those of an equivalent non-domestic assault. As discussed previously, courts historically treated domestic violence assaults far more leniently than non-domestic assaults. The question is the extent to which prior practices have changed.

The latest federal report published by the Bureau of Justice Statistics (BJS), *State Court Processing of Domestic Violence Cases* (Durose, Langan, & Smith, 2008), originally dated February 2008 (revised March 12, 2008), purports to show dramatic changes. This research consisted of aggregate data from 15 large urban counties responding to a request made to 40 of the 75 largest urban counties in the country. The researchers provided a comprehensive review of 2,629 violent felony cases of which approximately one third were categorized as being "domestic violence" and the remainder "nondomestic violence." Subsequent data were divided between sexual assaults and aggravated assaults. Their reported findings show dramatic improvement.

In 7 of the 11 measures of conviction and sentencing outcomes, no differences were found between domestic violence and non–domestic violence sexual assault cases. In the other four case processing measures, domestic violence and sexual assault offenders had a higher prosecution rate (89% versus 73%), higher overall conviction rate (98% versus 87%), higher felony sexual assault conviction rate (80% versus 63%), and a longer average incarceration sentence (6 years versus 3 1/4 years) compared with non-domestic cases.

Similar to sexual assaults, 7 of the 11 outcome measures for aggravated assaults found no difference between domestic and non-domestic defendants. Again, the domestic violence defendants had higher conviction rates (87% versus 78%), higher violent felony conviction rates (61% versus 52%), higher aggravated assault conviction rates (54% versus 45%), and higher misdemeanor conviction rates (22% versus 16%) (Durose et al., 2008).

The overall conclusion of the researchers was that "the study found that case processing outcomes for domestic violence cases were the same as, or more serious, than the outcomes for non-domestic violence cases" (Durose et al., 2008, p. 1). On the surface, this extensive data set and sophisticated data analysis would seem to end any concern that the judiciary currently fails to provide equal attention to domestic violence cases. Unfortunately, the data set has serious limitations, and we believe at this time that it should not be used to make any definitive conclusions.

Although the report is titled *State Court Processing of Domestic Violence Cases* and implies that their conclusions apply to all state courts, in fact the data set only deals with felony cases in 15 large urban counties. We already know that most domestic violence cases are initially categorized by police, and subsequently by prosecutors, as misdemeanors.

It is this disproportionate nature of the charging system that renders an easy comparison between domestic and non-domestic assaults problematic. If, for example, a higher rate of the domestic violence cases were being misclassified as misdemeanors, whereas few non-domestic ones were, any implied similarity in case disposition would have little external validity.

In addition, being aggregate data, the study does not differentiate among jurisdictions. A cursory review of the 15 jurisdictions presented suggest that many of them already have adopted a reformed judicial model for the specific purpose of addressing serious domestic violence cases (Pima County, Alameda County, Riverside County, San Diego County, and Dade County). It is certainly possible that consistent with the data presented subsequently in this chapter, these jurisdictions have a considerably different profile than other counties. Without separating them, the use of aggregate data to advance a conclusion is troubling.

In fact, only 16 counties (of which 15 were selected) responded to this voluntary request for data. It is possible, perhaps even likely, that the counties that responded knew that they had a better record for handling domestic violence cases and/or maintained appropriate data. Certainly the fact that many of these counties already had specialized domestic violence dockets would suggest they had developed a more aggressive approach to domestic violence than many other jurisdictions. For this reason, this study might not be generalizable to the overall experience of domestic violence offenders in state courts.

The data set also contains a fundamental limitation in its significance for intimate partner violence as the researchers adopt a definition of domestic violence that includes all violence among family members, intimate partners, and household cohabitants (such as roommates). We noted previously that approximately one third of domestic violence cases involve relationships other than intimate partner. It is easy to understand that such a data set can dramatically change findings. For example, we would logically expect that within the sexual offense category, the crime of incest might be punished far more seriously than any other sexual assault—either in a non-domestic context or in the context of a marital rape.

There is evidence that a conflation of such data occurred in this report. Specifically, for sexual assaults, no physical force was used in 26% of the cases. Although these were labeled as a "domestic" sexual assault, it is highly unlikely that any case, with the exception of incest on a minor, would ever be prosecuted in the absence of physical violence. As we would expect incest cases to be prosecuted rigorously and convicted defendants to be sentenced to long terms, including these data in a comparative outcomes measure might easily have skewed overall findings.

Third, we found it interesting that although the study's conclusion is that there is little differentiation between domestic violence and non–domestic violence cases, two key variables were not considered. First, the authors noted as an aside that of the domestic sexual and aggravated assault cases not prosecuted, 78% were dismissed or declined for prosecution because the victims would not cooperate. No comparable data were available for non–domestic violence cases. Based on past domestic violence data, especially in courts where mandatory prosecution has been adopted as a de facto standard for domestic violence, we continue to have a high expectation that victim preferences increased total case attrition in domestic violence cases.

Fourth, although the authors noted that incarceration rates were not lower in felony domestic violence cases and sentence durations were similar, they did not correlate this finding with the fact that a greater percentage (26%) of domestic assault offenders had a criminal history at the time of arrest compared with only 18% of non-domestic cases. One would naturally expect a heavier sentence in the case of those that have been previously sentenced, making the lack of any difference surprising.

Finally, the researchers did not address variations among statutory sentencing schemes between domestic violence and non–domestic violence cases. As discussed previously, the statutes use of restraining orders has come about in the context of domestic violence. How many of the convicted defendants in the domestic violence cases have violated existing restraining orders? Many state statutes now provide for multiple charges for both the underlying assault and the statutory offense of domestic violence. One would expect that multiple charges would be levied and possibly an additional sentence imposed for restraining orders. No evidence of this was reported.

For all of the reasons stated previously, we do not believe that the thesis that courts act uniformly toward domestic violence cases and non–domestic violence cases has been definitely answered as of the time of final review of this edition.

A more comprehensive study might in the future answer this unresolved public policy question. It would need to include an analysis of the police department's initial description of incidents (cross-correlated if possible with victim reports), tracking initial charges through the prosecutor's offices, and then into the courts. This examination could ascertain whether many domestic violence offenders were being diverted out of the criminal justice system into batterer treatment programs. This systematic diversion is in contrast unlikely to occur in the same numbers for stranger assaults as there are no mechanisms to do so (e.g., there is no state-certified program for diverting offenders committing non-domestic assaults).

When these factors are considered, past studies have found major differences in judicial handling of domestic violence cases. In one in-depth study comparing the processing of domestic and non-domestic assault cases in the state of Arizona, the researchers concluded that there were, in fact, disparities in handling such cases. Domestic violence conviction rates were lower than for non–domestic violence offenders, and both misdemeanor and felony domestic violence offenders were less likely to be incarcerated than men arrested for non–domestic violence offenses (Maxwell et al., 2009). This result is consistent with our own impressions.

Domestic Violence Courts: The Focus on Victim Needs and Offender Accountability

Clearly, a primary reason for the creation of domestic violence courts was the recognition that traditional models of handling such cases were lacking in providing safety and services to the victim, in punishing and perhaps rehabilitating offenders, and in educating the public of the problems of domestic violence and deterring the commission of similar crimes in the future. In essence, the same factors that led to pressures on the police in the 1980s and 1990s, and more recently on the offices of the prosecutors, became the impetus for change in the judicial response to domestic violence. Although overt political pressure was perhaps less important of a factor to a largely independent judiciary, the willingness of politicians at the local, state, and federal levels to fund an enhanced response became a primary instigation for the initiation of these new courts.

In addition to abuse-specific factors, we also need to place the growth of domestic violence courts in the context of other major judicial reforms adopted recently. Since the first edition in the early 1990s, a variety of "problem-solving" or "collaborative justice" courts have emerged. One estimate is that there have been more than 3,000 established nationwide, including courts dealing with drugs, mental health issues, community courts, and of course, domestic violence (Huddleston, Marlowe, & Casebolt, 2008). Although each court tackles a different set of issues, all try to improve outcomes for defendants, victims, and communities by addressing the underlying offender problems that cause the specific offense (Berman & Feinblatt, 2005; Casey & Rottman, 2005). Many of these make referrals to community-based programs and adopt innovations with community partners and compliance monitoring (Wolf, 2007).

Specialized courts are not a new innovation. It has long been recognized that "problem-solving" courts needed to be created in response to specialized needs of drug offenders, crimes committed by juveniles, and poor decisions made by those legally incompetent to handle their own affairs. Typically, these courts focus on the rehabilitation or reintegration of an offender into society rather than on punishment for prior behavior. Therefore, problem-solving courts such as drug courts focus primarily on the needs of the offender. In these types of courts, the treatment team usually is part of the judicial system and, thus, works closely with judges in determining the appropriate disposition and ensuring changes in the offender's future behavior. The treatment team also provides intense supervision coupled with treatment to address the underlying issues.

Domestic violence courts, while specialized and emerging from the same effort to separate out "intractable" crimes from the general court systems, differ from other "problem-solving courts" whose emphasis is on rehabilitation. Drug and mental health courts, after all, deal primarily with victimless crimes and, therefore, should focus primarily on the defendant. Domestic violence courts need to focus on ensuring victim safety as well as on addressing the offender's crimes.

In the case of a conflict between the defendant's needs and those of the victim, domestic violence courts will place priority on the needs of the victim and her children. Although they certainly could, and should, seek rehabilitation of an offender and might not be as focused on punishment per se, the needs of the offender are considered secondary to those of the victim's interests and society's interest in stopping these types of prevalent crimes. These courts, therefore, seek to ensure the accountability for any offenses committed, in addition to the deterrence of future misbehavior.

Perhaps the most articulate explanation of the difference between the average "problem-solving" court and the domestic violence court was stated by Labriola, Bradley, O'Sullivan, Rempel, and Moore (2009):

> Perhaps more critically, most problem solving court models operate under the assumption that the defendant's criminal behavior stems from underlying problems that treatment or services can resolve. While many domestic violence courts subscribe to this analysis as well, the premise is more controversial. Many agencies that work with victims

of domestic violence argue that the underlying problem is not an aberration of individual offenders but of social norms. Furthermore, . . . there is considerable doubt over whether court mandated programs can attain success at rehabilitation in this area. (p. 3)

As will be discussed in Chapter 13, the initial efforts to provide a nonjudgmental approach included mediation and offender treatment focused on rehabilitation. Their primary focus now, however, is to ensure offender accountability (Shelton, 2007). Most courts state that increased offender accountability and the provision of coordinated victim services is part of their primary mission (Berman, Rempel, & Wolf, 2007; Gavin & Puffett, 2005).

In the broader context of problem-solving courts and specialized domestic violence courts, the first domestic violence court was established in 1991 in Philadelphia. In what might have been the first of its type in the nation, a specific Philadelphia courtroom was dedicated to serving the 5,000 people each year who sought emergency restraining orders after normal business hours (e.g., from 5:00 p.m. to 8:30 a.m.). Victim advocates were quoted as saying that this single innovation reduced the time spent getting an order from 3 hours to 30 minutes ("Special Court," 1991).

Of even greater importance, for the first time, these cases were heard by specially trained masters, not by police commissioners, who concurrently heard all bail hearings and preliminary criminal arraignments, as well as issued general bench warrants. Victim support was provided by volunteers from Women Against Abuse (a local advocacy and shelter group), who staffed the courtroom from 5:00 p.m. to 2:00 a.m. on a regular basis, helped victims fill out lengthy forms, and secured legal assistance for indigents ("Special Court," 1991).

After the Philadelphia court success, and even more importantly the passage of the Violence Against Women Act (VAWA) in 1994, innovations followed in many disparate jurisdictions with elements of what would later be termed a "domestic violence court." The initial steps were, of course, limited often with general-purpose courts providing some personnel to assist domestic violence victims during "off hours" and authorizing senior clerks and clerk magistrates working night hours to issue restraining orders without the necessity of a judicial signature.

In late 1994, Milwaukee became another early adapter, featuring an innovative approach. A specialized court was set up to maintain a highly structured, 90-day schedule decreasing case disposition time. The express rationale was to make victims less likely to change their minds, be pressured by offenders, or fail to cooperate. In addition, victims were considered to be in less danger from batterers if case processing time was reduced, especially when the court imposed severe sanctions for reabuse during sentencing of a case (Davis, Smith, & Nickles, 1997).

Thereafter, Dade County's (Miami) Domestic Violence Court Experiment focused on implementing dual treatment for both battering and substance abuse (Goldkamp, 1996). Unlike other domestic violence courts, the focus of this court was primarily on targeting treatment of violent behavior attributed to substance abuse rather than on the integration of civil and criminal cases or on providing additional social services.

Although each such innovation has different origins and features, there has been a rapid growth in the number of these specialized courts or specialized processes within general courts that focus on domestic violence. From the initial start in Philadelphia in 1991 to 2000, more than 300 domestic violence courts were established nationwide

(Keilitz, 2000). By 2007, at least an additional 51 courts were added to the list compiled in 2000 (Shelton, 2007). By 2009, the five states with the highest number of domestic violence courts had a well-established infrastructure with many separate domestic violence courts. New York State had more than 60 domestic violence courts, California more than 20, and Michigan and Florida more than 15 each (Labriola et al., 2009). The growth rate of such courts has been phenomenal. One recent study of one single type of domestic violence court (those that only handle criminal domestic violence issues) found that of the 129 such courts now in existence, only 2 were founded in the 1980s, almost a third in the 1990s, and almost two thirds in the last 10 years (Labriola et al., 2009).

In addition, it has been noted that outside the United States, more than 50 domestic violence courts are in operation in Canada (Quann, 2007) and nearly 100 in England (Crown Prosecution Service, 2008, as quoted by Labriola et al., 2009, and by Moore, 2009). Although it is clear that the number of these specialized courts has markedly increased over the past decade, no one is certain of the number of such courts, as definitional distinctions can expand or contract the number reported. For example, a recent study was more restricted than we might have expected, specifying that they had to be "criminal" courts as opposed to "family courts." Using these criteria, the study identified 129 domestic violence courts in the United States (Labriola et al., 2009).

A View From the Bench

Libby Hines

Judge Elizabeth "Libby" Pollard Hines presides over a specialized docket dedicated to domestic violence (DV) cases in the 15th District Court in Ann Arbor, Michigan (Washtenaw County). The district courts in Washtenaw County were one of three sites selected by the U.S. Department of Justice, Office on Violence Against Women (OVW) for the *Judicial Oversight Demonstration Initiative* (JODI) from 1999 to 2004 to determine what works best in cases of domestic violence.

As a district court judge in Ann Arbor, Michigan, I am privileged to preside over a dedicated docket of misdemeanor DV cases. I know that if I do my job well, it is homicide prevention. How many times have you turned on the TV or picked up a newspaper to read of a woman murdered by her husband, former husband, or boyfriend? Too often, without intervention, domestic violence escalates and victims are seriously injured or killed. In my community, we decided to intervene early, before the misdemeanor assault became a murder, before the case made headlines. Using a problem-solving approach and always respecting our different roles and ethical constraints, we judges work with prosecutors, the defense bar, police, victim advocates, batterer intervention programs (BIPs), probation, and others to hold people convicted of DV accountable and maximize victim safety. Cities in which this coordinated community response has been used report dramatic drops in domestic homicides.

Victim advocates from our local DV shelter are called by the police to the scene of a DV arrest to offer information and support. DV cases are given priority in court. An attorney is appointed for the accused unless he or she has retained counsel. That way, the defendant's rights are protected, a delay is avoided, and another layer of protection is offered for the alleged victim as there is now another person to reexplain any "no-contact" or other conditions of release set. Advocates can staff our courtrooms because of our coordinated dockets. Specially trained probation officers monitor convicted defendants on a more intensive basis and offer safety planning, information, and other services to victims. The victim can make a more informed decision as to how best to keep safe. Probation officers work closely with the BIP and victim advocates. There is on-going risk assessment. We judges do our best to make sure our orders are appropriate and enforced. Defendants are required to appear at frequent judicial review hearings to *prove* they are complying. There is zero tolerance for reassault. In an accountable but respectful way, we offer offenders an opportunity to change by completing a long-term BIP.

I know that my decision in a DV case affects not only the adults before me but also any children in the home. Even if children do not see or hear the assault, they see the aftermath. The harm to children exposed to domestic violence is well documented.

When I sign the order of discharge from probation, defendants are given the opportunity to say anything they want. The same defendants who complained about going to a BIP at the time of sentencing now say the program has changed their lives for the better. They wish it were offered in the schools. If it had been, offenders tell me, they would never have been in court.

While we do not pretend to have all the answers in Washtenaw County, I know we have improved lives. I believe we have saved some, too.

The Variety of Domestic Violence Courts

Types of Domestic Violence Courts

Unlike general civil and criminal courts that have been in operation for hundreds of years, the organizational structure for domestic violence courts is not consistent. For example, they might be established as a special division of a civil court, a criminal court, or a family or probate court. The key differentiation is the degree and nature of their specialization in handling abuse cases and their interaction between agencies including prosecutors, probation, and parole, as well as social service agencies, mental health agencies, victim advocacy groups, domestic violence shelters, and batterer intervention programs. Such courts typically must establish protocols and procedures to ensure coordination of services and interventions.

To simplify the typology of domestic violence courts now being established, one author (Sack, 2002) characterized three different models of courts with variations within them. The first is a dedicated civil protection order docket. Sack believes that as of 2002, the dedicated civil protection order docket was the most common model where petitions and hearings claiming a violation of a protection order comprise much of the docket. These cases were typically assigned to one judge who only handled orders of protection, even if the judge also might retain a more general caseload in smaller jurisdictions. The second model is the *criminal model* that allows specific criminal courts to focus on domestic violence cases. This has been made possible because legislation in many states has defined domestic violence as a separate criminal offense. The judges in these courts are specifically trained in both components of that state's law as well as (hopefully) strategies for case processing and sentencing. As noted previously, a recent survey published in December 2009 found 129 such criminal domestic violence courts within the United States.

Finally, there is the domestic violence court with related caseload or integrated domestic violence court, where one judge will handle a case where there are criminal elements and accompanying civil matters. These civil matters might include issuance of restraining orders, child custody, and matrimonial matters. The key to this type of court is that repeated civil proceedings such as divorce or issuance of protective orders are handled by specialists, along with jurisdiction over criminal matters such as a trial for a prior domestic assault.

Of the three models, the integrated domestic violence court is the most inclusive in that one judge ultimately hears all aspects of the particular case, regardless of whether it falls under the rubric of commission of a crime or addresses ancillary but still highly important matters involving the future relationship of the parties and their families.

There are obviously extreme variations on this theme, depending on jurisdictions and legislative mandates. In any event, such integrated courts should provide an integrated system that can handle both civil protective orders (and their violations) and criminal cases, thereby providing for integrated adjudication of all aspects of the victim–offender relationship, regardless of which case first reached juridical attention.

No consensus has developed as to which model is the best. Given the variety of domestic violence court models, it is not surprising that judges have expressed a wide range of opinions on the preferred model. For example, at a meeting at the Center for Court Innovation in 2009, one judge noted that he preferred the separation of criminal from civil cases as he observed that victims often act differently in civil compared with criminal hearings. In the criminal context, a victim might be protective of the offender's behavior and might say she intends to remain with the offender since she, often for a variety of reasons, does not want him actually convicted. However, in child protection and custody hearings, that same victim might fear loss of child custody to that same offender, and thus sometimes, she might take a different position regarding the offender's conduct. This particular judge thought it helpful to view the victim's demeanor in both contexts when attempting to make an overall decision on a past conduct and future outcomes (personal communication, Center for Court Innovation meeting, March 2009).

To our knowledge, no research comparing the impact of structure on the efficiency or outcome measurements as a function of organizational structure into one of the foregoing categories has been completed. These innovations have developed only recently, and as of yet, no one model has been identified as ideal. Since these courts have been characterized by decentralization and adapting to their specific community (Berman et al., 2007), such diversity in implementation might be the preferred approach.

By definition, regardless of where it is organizationally housed, we consider a domestic violence court to be a special-purpose judicial unit designed primarily to handle violence against intimates. Its physical location or organizational structure should not limit the inclusion of such a court. However, as we will observe on occasion, the structure apparently affects the orientation of the court and its capabilities or at least its willingness to provide services to victims.

The Goals of Domestic Violence Courts

We would assume that the goals of these types of courts would be fairly reasonable and consistent: Punish past acts of physical abuse, protect victims from further abuse, and rehabilitate offenders. Such clarity of goals has not been reported, however. For example, in the recent comprehensive study of one type of court, domestic violence criminal courts, there was extensive variety in what goals were considered extremely important.

Table 12.1 Domestic Violence Court Goals: Percentage of Court Survey Respondents Rating Each Goal as "Extremely Important" ($N = 129$)

	Number identified	Number that responded	Survey response rate	% of Respondents that are associated with DV courts
Northeast	**79**	**27**	**34%**	**25%**
New York	57	17	30%	100%
Connecticut	8	5	63%	100%
Maine	4	0	0%	0%
Pennsylvania	4	3	75%	0%
New Hampshire	2	1	50%	0%
Massachusetts	2	1	50%	0%
Rhode Island	1	0	0%	0%
Vermont	1	0	0%	0%
South	**73**	**29**	**40%**	**44%**
Florida	17	7	41%	57%
North Carolina	15	8	53%	63%
Alabama	13	3	23%	0%
Texas	9	4	44%	100%
Delaware	4	1	25%	0%

(Continued)

Table 12.1 (Continued)

	Number identified	Number that responded	Survey response rate	% of Respondents that are associated with DV courts
Oklahoma	5	1	20%	0%
Virginia	3	1	33%	100%
West Virginia	1	0	0%	0%
Kentucky	1	1	100%	100%
Maryland	1	1	100%	100%
South Carolina	1	1	100%	100%
Tennessee	1	1	100%	0%
Georgia	1	0	0%	0%
Washington, D.C.	1	0	0%	0%
Midwest	**42**	**20**	**48%**	**57%**
Michigan	14	7	50%	100%
Illinois	12	8	67%	100%
Iowa	7	3	43%	0%
Indiana	5	1	20%	100%
Ohio	1	1	100%	100%
Minnesota	2	0	0%	0%
South Dakota	1	0	0%	0%
West	**85**	**45**	**53%**	**50%**
California	18	15	83%	60%
Washington	23	9	39%	22%
New Mexico	11	4	36%	0%
Arizona	4	2	50%	100%
Utah	6	2	33%	50%
Nevada	5	4	80%	0%
Kansas	4	1	25%	100%
Hawaii	4	1	25%	100%
Colorado	2	2	100%	0%
Oregon	3	3	100%	66%

	Number identified	Number that responded	Survey response rate	% of Respondents that are associated with DV courts
Idaho	2	1	50%	100%
Wisconsin	1	1	100%	0%
Alaska	0	0	–	0%
Wyoming	1	0	0%	0%
Other	**1**	**1**	**100%**	**100%**
Guam	1	1	100%	100%
Total	**275**	**122**	**44%**	**61%**

Source: Labriola et al., 2009, Table 4.1, p. 27.

We predicted, of course, that increasing victims' safety would be an extremely important goal as reported by 83% of respondents. We did not, however, predict that rehabilitation of offenders would be so low on a priority list (39% of respondents) or that the
two other likely measures of increasing victim satisfaction also would be far less important; facilitating victims' access to services was cited by 50% as an extremely important
goal, and improving the victims' perceptions of court fairness was cited by only 29% as
extremely important.

It might be the case that personnel in criminal courts, regardless of their commitment
to domestic violence, will revert in stated goals to those of a general criminal court—we
need to determine whether personnel in other types of courts, such as family courts, are
as focused on "traditional" criminal court concerns or whether they have a wider set of
goals that might more accommodate the needs of victims for services and the rehabilitation of offenders—as opposed primarily to securing their punishment for past acts.

Surprisingly, there was an extraordinary difference among these criminal courts on
what might be considered to be another potentially vital matter, that of rehabilitating
offenders. Only 27% of the respondents (judges, prosecutors, victim advocates, and
court staff) viewed rehabilitating offenders as extremely important. Moreover, there
were vast differences in different jurisdictions. In this national sample, there was a heavy
overweighting of New York court respondents. Only 19% of the New York respondents
thought rehabilitating offenders was extremely important compared with 53% of personnel outside of New York State (Labriola et al., 2009).

We note that other courts, especially family courts, take a more holistic approach to
their goals. Typical stated goals in a family court might include the following:

- Enabling close coordination with, or even leadership of, the coordinated efforts of
  prosecutors, batterer intervention programs, victim service, and other social service agencies for the family in crisis.

- Providing risk assessments for future violence within a family. When that assessment is completed, it is then incorporated into judicial decision making. The key distinction is that such evidence of future violence is decided in a civil context allowing far less of a burden of proof than in a criminal court.

- Issuing orders to respond to victim needs for offenders released on bail, typically by maintaining court oversight of either the family through frequent appearances or systematic use of probation and/or victim services through the police and/or prosecutor's office.

- Leading strategies to ensure public awareness of domestic violence and the consequences to batterers that are brought to justice.

The Structure and Content of Domestic Violence Courts

Since their initial implementation, domestic violence courts have always displayed considerable variation in the powers that they have, the issues they are prepared to deal with, and their standard operating procedure when confronted with similar types of domestic abuse. Although not mandated by statute, they were established with their existing legislative frameworks in response to their unique communities. As a result, they incorporate many different procedural and substantive variations. Therefore, next we will discuss what we believe to be the essential elements of such a court.

As numerous national studies have shown, no one particular model can be labeled as the archetypal domestic violence court. Instead, they include some or all of the following elements: specialized calendars, intake units, case screenings, specialized judicial assignments, and court-ordered and -monitored batterer intervention programs. As one author pointed out, unlike traditional courts, "most of the courts have some of these processes and components, but few of the courts have all of them. Moreover, the combinations and configurations of these processes and structures vary substantially across the courts, and no clear patterns are evident" (Keilitz, 2004, p. III–9–6). The key is that typically formal arrangements are made to integrate the court with counseling, treatment, substance abuse programs, and marshalling of available resources for victims and, at times, their children. Specialized court personnel are trained in coordinating case management, linking the current case to any related pending cases or to those that are subsequently filed (Winick, 2000).

Survey results have shown the marked diversity of these courts. In a telephone survey published in 2004, Keilitz reported findings from several of these courts. Of the 106 studies, 67 reported having a special calendar, some for protective orders, some for domestic violence misdemeanor offenses, and of less frequency, some for domestic violence felonies. Intake management and services were provided by 66, or less than two thirds, of these courts. Typically, they assisted with protective order petitions and screening for other cases. However, she reported that few courts assisted them with legal and other economic matters, including divorce, child support, paternity, and so on. This could be viewed as an appropriate limitation on their mission and role, or conversely, as an inability of the court to deal with the full range of a victim's needs (Keilitz, 2004, p. III–9–7).

Case screening and coordination were provided by 68 or two thirds of the courts. Although most of these seemed to coordinate case management, far fewer seemed to use case screening techniques for the express purpose of protecting the victim; for example, if there were many such incidents involving the defendant, then a judge should perhaps consider this when making bail and sentencing decisions or when developing civil protection (or restraining) orders and safety plans. Keilitz (2004) reported that only 19 of the 106 courts used case screening for those purposes. Judicial assignment and training also varied considerably.

For example, in New York State, an "integrated domestic violence court" is considered to include at least two different types of cases, for example, a domestic violence criminal charge coupled with either a child custody and/or matrimonial issue. Each jurisdiction within the state handles such cases assigned according to the judge's preferences. Some judges, such as those in Brooklyn, separate out their domestic violence criminal dockets from related civil issues by hearing each type of case on different days. This is to ensure that both victims and offenders recognize that these cases are treated differently, as the standard of proof is different, as well as the interests of society.

Alternatively, in the Bronx, the approach is, "one family, one day," whereby a single judge hears all relevant issues involving the same family unit or couple at the same time (e.g., past criminal acts, requests for restraining orders, or child protection orders). This approach seeks to minimize hardship on the victim by avoiding multiple trips to the court for different hearings. Interestingly enough, often multiple attorneys and parties will be involved in each case—an attorney representing a child's interests, separate attorneys representing both the victim and the offender for the civil matters, a victim advocate, and of course, an attorney for the offender for the criminal charges.

The designation of a judge exclusively to handle domestic violence cases might not be feasible in smaller jurisdictions, or in larger municipalities that resist all "single-purpose" courts. Less than one quarter of the 106 courts studied assigned judges exclusively to domestic violence, whereas almost half the courts had a mixed docket that included a dedicated domestic violence calendar, as well as many other cases (Keilitz, 2004). It is somewhat disturbing that she reported that relatively few of the courts required extensive domestic violence training. Judges received such training as a result of their own initiative; however, only six courts required their formal participation in domestic violence training prior to their appointment (Keilitz, 2004).

The need for additional training also would seem warranted given the need for judges to be "cross-trained" in handling civil and criminal cases. Criminal courts are focused on the rights and obligations of offenders, whereas civil cases are equally focused on both parties.

One recent study of one type of domestic violence court, specialized criminal domestic violence courts, illustrates the extent of variety in procedures used. The variety is especially pronounced when examining services provided to victims. Seventy-nine percent of domestic violence criminal courts did provide victim advocates. The survey reported certain defined services provided by these victim advocates to victims, including 80% who accompanied victims to court, 79% who assisted with safety planning, 79% who explained the criminal justice process, 73% who provided housing referrals, 64% who facilitated prosecution, and 56% who counseled the victim. However, data did show that those victim advocates who were affiliated with prosecutor offices were far more likely to place higher priorities on having the victim facilitate prosecution compared with those employed by private agencies. Not surprisingly, the latter group emphasized prosecution less often and were more concerned about the victim achieving her own goals, which might or might not include prosecution (Labriola et al., 2009).

However, despite best intentions, court structures seem to miss some major opportunities to assist victims. For example, most surveyed considered that the physical safety of the victim attending court was a major concern. Nevertheless, only 40% provided separate seating areas in the court, 50% provided escorts in the court house, 40% lacked separate waiting areas (where victims might be particularly vulnerable), and 76% do not provide child care. From a victim's perspective, addressing these primary concerns would seem far preferable than more coercive strategies such as the issuance of subpoenas for prosecution or the implementation or enforcement of mandatory prosecution policies.

To date, no national professional association or a source for sharing information regarding best practices exists, although the Center for Court Innovation in New York City has been active in its efforts to provide technical assistance and information to judges throughout the country. It also has established a judicial Web site for judges to share information regarding their experience.

We hope that research conducted with these courts will begin providing us with empirical results of relative levels of victim safety and victim satisfaction, as well as more conventional outcome measures, before further assessing the various models.

These courts typically expedite the handling of requests for protective orders and their enforcement. Personnel are aware of unique issues in intimate violence cases and typically receive direct training to handle these. Many specialized courts also have become agents for change, both within their own jurisdictions and as a result of affiliation with national groups.

What Factors Contribute to a Successful Domestic Violence Court?

Perceptions of Judicial Empathy and Fairness

To the extent that domestic abuse judges are not political opportunities but are selected instead because of their knowledge of the applicable laws and their judicial temperament, most agree to handle these difficult and emotionally draining cases because of their personal commitment to end the cycle of domestic violence offenses in their jurisdiction. The paradox is that while being engaged and committed to ending abuse, these judges also must not be perceived as unduly biased toward victims. If not, the legitimacy of their subsequent orders might be questioned. Some defense attorneys, always in the context of "nonattribution," have commented to us that they believe domestic violence judges are too "pro-victim." They believe the imposed standards of proof often are less rigorous for her than for other victims.

However, although anecdotal tales are common in the defense bar, this might not prove to be a realistic concern. Research has reported that these courts do not focus on retribution in sentencing (Crowell & Burgess, 1996; Peterson, 2001). Perhaps it might simply be that a goal to have formalized procedural safeguards attendant to any criminal proceeding and the fact that most judges understand that strict impartiality of judges must be maintained to assure the public that the necessary neutrality of the court will be maintained.

In addition to necessary perceptions of fairness, an effective judge in a domestic violence court must be trained to understand the dynamics of domestic violence at levels far beyond that of simply knowing legal issues. Success or failure is not dependent on conviction of the offender given that the parties and the violent behaviors typically are well known. As we described previously, almost all cases that reach trial result in conviction. Success instead depends on the development of a therapeutic jurisprudence in which the judge not only dispenses "justice" but also develops and supervises a sentencing structure that effectively rehabilitates an offender.

This often is complicated by the fact that offenders and victims have an ongoing relationship, occasionally still being intimates, or have common children, impacting a victim's commitment to criminal case prosecution. Furthermore, a victim might act in ways that an outsider might dispassionately perceive are clearly adverse to her long-term interests. For this reason, the full range of judicial options that might ideally be available are lacking or constrained by their limited capacity. Although a judge typically would dispense justice through sentencing, therapeutic justice entails the additional task of addressing the long-term needs of the victim and her family as well as of the offender.

Problems can easily develop. A judicial error in failure to impose a prison sentence might severely compromise a victim's safety and that of her children. There also is a high risk of judicial "burnout" from being forced to decide cases rapidly that are nominally misdemeanors but where the emotional content is high, injuries can be severe, and the price of a judicial mistake can literally be deadly.

Resource Availability

To be effective in this area, it is essential that domestic violence courts maintain some form of extended hours or, in smaller communities where this is impractical, close coordination with police departments who can and will respond aggressively to domestic violence incidents. Not surprisingly, a primary barrier to establishing specialized courts is that additional resources are initially required to ensure their success. This was demonstrated by the experiences of the Milwaukee Domestic Violence Court (Davis, Smith, & Nickles, 1998). Despite early successes with one of the nation's first domestic violence courts, after a time, sufficient resources were not allocated and maintained, and such courts began to develop procedures that informally "limited" demand by setting barriers to entry that made sense "administratively" but effectively eliminated much of the cases where the court should have retained jurisdiction for the safety of the victim, her children, and society in general.

We note that the key cost driver usually is not an increased number of judges needed but the high level of support resources that must be allocated to assist in case prosecution, victim assistance, and offender monitoring. These people are necessary to coordinate the complicated legal, financial, and treatment aspects of such cases.

For example, although traditional courts typically handle many misdemeanor cases on an "assembly line" basis, to handle a misdemeanor domestic violence case effectively, initial research on most violent behavior of the claimed assailant should be presented to the judge before he or she hears the case (if convictions resulted, then such evidence is admissible).

This evidence is essential, as offenders with a "generally violent" or criminal background are far more likely to continue battering, and in many cases, they are subject to enhanced penalties, including being transferred to courts handling felony cases.

In stating this, we recognize that without such resources to cope with an "assembly line" of similarly sounding offenses, a normal judge after rapid handling of a typical misdemeanor case will enter a verdict and then rapidly proceed with hearing the next case in their docket.

In most domestic violence cases, this process would pose a serious risk. As demonstrated in our chapter on extended probation, perhaps the single factor associated most closely with subsequent "success" in preventing future battering is continued court supervision and monitoring of offenders' attendance, completion of batterer treatment programs, and attendant conditions of their orders. As might be expected, this requires resources far beyond that given to most "minor" criminal cases.

From this, we concede that if traditional measures of "cost per case" or "cases handled per judge" are used alone, then special-purpose courts will never be as "efficient" as general-purpose courts. After all, the latter needs the flexibility with their workload to balance their caseload between sporadic, crisis-driven work and the more prosaic and predictable motion-and-trial practice that constitutes the bulk of their normal workload. We reject such metrics for domestic violence courts since they are far too easy to distort the fundamental purposes of this court. Besides, by not having multiple cases in the system and by decreasing the rates of reoffending, the long-term savings of domestic violence courts are significant.

Although perhaps counterintuitive, the ability of well-funded specialized courts to process cases rapidly also becomes a major cost benefit to the system. We know the question is usually presented from the viewpoint of those who argue that given the inherent budgetary pressures in courts today, why should these cases receive additional resources to expedite case disposition?

To understand these systematic cost advantages more fully, we must explore the burdens placed on general-purpose courts handling a typical domestic violence case. One of the primary cost drivers are cases that have overlapping jurisdiction. This problem can be compounded by the fact that multiple civil and criminal cases might be present in different jurisdictions within a state or even in different states. Judicial databases typically lack the integration needed to obtain and link all the needed information relevant to all cases involving one offender. As a result, victims and their advocates often do not have ready access to proof of prior restraining or other court orders, and batterers in one situation can escape attention as a serial offender. Creating a specialized court, the mandate of which is to coordinate all civil and criminal actions related to a particular couple, inevitably reduces the likelihood of overlapping, inconsistent, and inadequate judicial reaction to chronic battering, thereby reducing the total resources needed to address the problem.

The answer to the legitimate question, "Are domestic violence courts efficient?" requires knowledge of the ongoing dynamics of many assault cases. An extensive body of research has documented strong tendencies for such assaults to escalate over time. Research also has shown that repeat acts of violence occur quickly, usually within a month of the previous incident (Buzawa et al., 1999). Even if court personnel did not primarily seek to improve the victim's safety but instead wanted to escape the mountain of disjointed cases involving problem offenders and their victims, the rapid case processing tends to prevent multiple offenses, often later including felonies, from clogging their system needlessly.

Similarly, the training of court personnel and judges to support victims might prevent the phenomena of massive numbers of cases being dropped "voluntarily" by victims without resolution of any underlying issue. Although the most immediate benefit to the victim, this also prevents the offender from engaging (and being held liable) in additional criminal offenses and helps prevent concurrent child abuse and other related problems that will inevitably come back to increase judicial dockets. For these reasons, the initial investment in such specialized courts will not only better serve victims, offenders, and their families, but also it might actually save the judiciary system as a whole.

Monitoring Batterer Compliance

Judicial supervision seems to be a key mechanism for the current control and future moderation of batterer behavior. Unfortunately, this is not always done. We consider a good risk assessment of past batterer behavior an essential component in lethality assessment. This is true because unlike criminals who commit crimes for economic reasons, the future actions of batterers might best be predicted by the occurrence of other "lifestyle" risk factors, such as substance abuse or violent criminal history.

In the Keilitz (2004) survey, of the 82 courts surveyed on this point, only 70 monitored batterer compliance and only 43% of those reported any type of hearings to review offender compliance. Instead, it was merely raised during regular status hearings (Keilitz, 2004). We note that even in the context of criminal domestic violence courts, only a minority of courts actively assess the offender's prospects for future violence or their past conduct when making decisions on continued pretrial release or in case dispositions (Labriola et al., 2009).

Both the 2004 and 2009 studies report that although many domestic violence courts initiated significant organizational, procedural, and staffing changes, relatively few had done so comprehensively. Furthermore, there was little consistency in their efforts. The extensive diversity among domestic violence courts limited the ability of the research to generalize factors influencing success or failure, as the authors could not assume that the models examined had similar goals, structure, level of funding, and/or available outside resources to draw on.

Advantages to Domestic Violence Courts

Although we will admit there is little published rigorous outcome research on domestic violence courts, there are several theoretical advantages.

First, as we noted, the alternative traditional court system might ultimately cost the entire system far more in terms of resource expenditure with inferior results to all the parties involved. When there is no specialized court, domestic violence cases can result in a series of uncoordinated, overlapping, and even contradictory case law. For example, just two acts of violence might cause concurrent actions in a civil court for issuance of a restraining order, a second civil courtroom for violation of an existing restraining order, criminal courts (either misdemeanor or felony level) for prosecution of each separate offense (as the original assault and each additional action are, after all, separate offenses), a court to hear issues of custody for minors, and finally, a court for property and other marital disputes in connection with divorce proceedings.

Typically, each of these courts has its own highly structured and often arcane intake procedures and operating rules. Hearings are held in different courts, often in different buildings, and they might result in differing, sometimes even conflicting, decisions. Differences in procedural requirements, case knowledge, and even the temperaments of individual judges might confuse even the most motivated and knowledgeable attorney—and be confusing to clients. Technology and communication issues often are problematic as databases might not be compatible and/or personnel might be unwilling or unmotivated to share needed information.

Duplicative court systems might increase the costs and emotional trauma for the victim, the family, and even the offender. The numbers of such appearances and their emotional costs for victims and their children can be staggering. The certainty of outcome in multiple court cases is less likely to result in the best-coordinated outcome for the parties involved.

The lack of interaction both within and between courts as well as relevant agencies is truly staggering. It can test the persistence of a victim and her family, and as discussed later, even the batterer and the courts. Therefore, the greater consistency and coordination of approach to the problems of the victim and her family and the necessity to bring to bear multiple interventions toward the offender are a key advantage of domestic violence courts.

One commentator noted a particularly egregious case involving a Kentucky couple that occurred during 1995–1996. The physical violence used by Robert Graves against his wife, Karen, resulted in 16 hearings involving 10 different judges in civil and criminal courts. In addition, three family law cases, including one for divorce, were heard by three judges and involved eight hearings. Robert, as the batterer, was enrolled in three court-ordered anger control and substance abuse programs, and advocates from at least four agencies tried to help Karen and her children. The author noted there was no evidence that any of the agencies or courts communicated with each other, despite Karen's recorded pleas that they do so. Ultimately, after 2 years of this, Robert killed Karen with a shotgun and then committed suicide. The courts subsequently issued a self-critical report (Epstein, 1999).

Second, as discussed previously, an explosion of criminal cases has been confronting our courts. Nationwide, street crime increased in the 1980s and 1990s, and there began an exploding volume of drug-related arrests and arrests for gang violence. During the first decade of 2000, concern about prospects of terrorism also consumed scarce law enforcement resources. Therefore, misdemeanor domestic violence offenses have been frequently relegated to a low priority and have resulted in pressure for efficiency of outcomes, case dismissal, and/or inordinate delays.

Despite efforts to "limit" the impact of domestic violence cases on the judiciary, domestic violence cases have rapidly increased their proportion of judicial caseloads. Mandates for arrest and prosecution have resulted in growing numbers of additional domestic violence cases. Ostrom and Kauder (1999) noted that whereas "official" Bureau of Justice Statistics showed a decline of 21% in the rate of reported domestic violence between 1993 and 1998, claims of domestic violence filed with the courts increased by 178% between 1989 and 1998. Although there is not a perfect correlation of dates and "official" statistics are themselves suspect, it seems irrefutable that there is a growing volume of domestic violence cases, which is a trend not likely to end soon. Therefore, issues of court processing time are of increased concern in virtually all courts (Epstein, 1999).

Even in the Quincy District Court in Massachusetts, which was previously described as a model for processing domestic violence cases but within a general jurisdiction court, the average processing time for domestic violence cases includes a 6-month delay from intake to disposition. This time lapse is highly significant as findings from this court demonstrated that most victims who were revictimized were found to be at greatest risk during the first month after the first incident (Buzawa et al., 1999). Domestic violence courts, hence, present a realistic prospect of delivering comprehensive relief for victims at an earlier stage of the judicial proceeding (Keilitz, 2004).

Third, many victim advocates still maintain that many key court personnel in most general jurisdiction courts, including docking clerks as well as the judiciary, maintain strong antivictim biases. Many overworked judges and their staff fail to understand the psychological, social, and economic reasons that some victims stay with batterers, might not follow procedural guidelines, and might not cooperate fully with efforts to prosecute a case through to conviction. Thus, concerns persist that in general jurisdiction courts, the procedures for processing domestic assault cases are inefficient. Educating and providing experience to court personnel in handling domestic violence is essential. In reality, however, personnel in a general jurisdiction court rarely are familiar with every type of offense they handle. Specialized domestic violence courts effectively limit such problems by concentrating educational and training resources on a small cadre of more committed personnel. This greater knowledge and empathy of domestic court judges toward victims and children has been cited as one key advantage of domestic violence courts (Keilitz, 2004).

Fourth, as amply shown previously, domestic violence courts tend to be "trend setters," developing new mechanisms for enforcing batterer compliance with treatment programs, demanding long-term rehabilitation in such areas as substance abuse control, and maintaining time needed to monitor offenders using dedicated probation officers and other court professionals. This provides these courts with a far greater opportunity for long-term intervention and supervision, a factor that by itself is now starting to be recognized as a key discriminator in the likelihood of successful outcomes, including increased victim satisfaction with the judicial process and a reduction in repeat victimization and reoffending.

Finally, by decreasing the scope of the court's jurisdiction, there will be a greater ability for the courts, and if necessary, advocacy groups and researchers, eventually to gather empirical data and then evaluate the success of specific components of their service model. As such, it can facilitate efforts to promulgate "best practices" within the judiciary.

Can a Family Court Be Effective as a Domestic Violence Court?

We noted previously that there were three models of domestic violence courts. One method, giving such cases to a smaller group of family courts, might be the key in certain jurisdictions. Keilitz (2004) noted that approximately three quarters of the domestic violence courts she surveyed had no assigned full-time judge. This might be in response to the size of the jurisdiction, which might be too small or subject to fiscal constraints. However, alternative frameworks within their current structure allow the jurisdiction to provide many functions of domestic violence courts whose primary mission is to judge criminal culpability. Most jurisdictions now have family courts or surrogate courts. These courts might be specialized to a greater or lesser degree in family problems or at least do not have a comprehensive docket of civil and criminal cases. A typical family court would, however, have comprehensive jurisdiction over all aspects of a family (e.g., divorce; child abuse, welfare, and custody; support orders; and sometimes jurisdiction over crimes committed against or by juveniles). By their nature, family court judges might be far more trained in the complexity of domestic issues and might, therefore, be logical guardians of family rights. Many courts already address domestic violence issues as they pertain to ongoing divorce or child custody. It would seem to be a logical extension to give judges official jurisdiction to handle civil and criminal aspects of domestic violence.

In a report titled *Unified Family Courts: A Progress Report*, the American Bar Association (ABA) addressed this limitation by recommending that family court jurisdiction be broadened to include intrafamily criminal offenses, including all forms of domestic violence, rather than limiting these courts to civil matters, their traditional mandate (ABA, 1998). The National Council of Juvenile and Family Court Judges (1999) also supports expanding the jurisdiction of such courts.

Several states have implemented such "unified" family courts tailored to fit the orientation, needs, resources, and capabilities of the particular jurisdiction and state. The state of Oregon, for example, allows courts to bundle cases where there are different levels of coordination of services. The first, level 1, groups together related cases that concern one family, and the court administrator assigns the judge who has been most involved in all open cases. The second, level 2, provides for a permanent assignment to one judge, and the third, nonmandatory level 3, provides for a comprehensive plan and an integration of services (Schwarz, 2004).

The state of Hawaii also administers the State of Hawaii Family Court, which has jurisdiction over "abusive family and household members," restraining orders between family members, and traditional aspects of divorce, paternity, mental health, juvenile delinquency, and child abuse, and neglect (Schwarz, 2004).

In many ways, the advantages of this type of court parallel those of other domestic violence courts—but might be essential in smaller jurisdictions without the capability to field a court wholly dedicated to domestic violence. A family court with sufficient jurisdiction would allow one judge to hear all aspects of the problems of a troubled family. The key advantage to the victim would be to obviate the need to work with different courts prosecuting an assault case, obtaining a restraining order, or settling child custody and other related issues. The likelihood of inconsistent results and excessive costs for both the victim and the judicial system in general would be greatly reduced. In addition, because the judge understands the complexity of the family's issues, he or she might be far more comfortable with issuing decrees and could mandate more appropriate case dispositions. Alternatives to contentious proceedings, similar to the somewhat dated model of "family mediation," might be requested more frequently if both parties understood that the family court with extensive knowledge of prior issues was ready to reassume jurisdiction if there were continued violence.

Despite these advantages, there are some limitations and potential difficulties with relying on a family court to become a jurisdiction's de facto domestic violence court.

The model clearly relies on the assumption that family court judges have jurisdiction, have been trained, and are willing to handle criminal issues, at least with respect to the breach of restraining orders. As such, attention must be paid to the provision of consistent outcomes. For example, in Hawaii, where an explicit effort to reinforce a unified family court was undertaken, the experience has been that family court judges being given the mandate and trained to examine persistent and repetitive patterns of abuse were found to impose harsher sanctions than general criminal courts (Schwarz, 2004).

We believe that neither the prosecutor nor the defense attorneys should have an advantage as the result of a defendant brought before a family court judge compared with a general criminal court. Otherwise, unless prosecutors were jurisdictionally restricted, they would almost inevitably seek the courts with tougher sentencing policies. Such forum shopping is fundamentally unfair to both the accused abuser and the many victims. We are concerned that if left uncontrolled, this could destroy much of the benefit from having such courts and might lead to representatives of abused victims believing they are getting "second-class" or diluted justice. Conversely, this practice might foster the belief among defendants and their counsel that the courts are biased against them.

Overlapping jurisdictions of family and general-purpose courts also means that someone in the system needs to provide extensive training for advocates, as well as for the judiciary. In New York State, one author observed that despite concurrent jurisdiction of family courts and criminal courts for the issuance of protective orders, attorneys for domestic violence victims often had difficulty with advising victims as to which would be the preferred venue. To add to the confusion, New York State police are now required to inform domestic violence victims that they have the right to proceed concurrently in both family court and criminal court (Schwarz, 2004). Although it is hard to argue that more knowledge is worse than less, a typical victim simply lacks the understanding to determine which court best serves her needs. When this occurs, there is an obvious potential for victims to be swayed toward a particular court depending on the officer's orientation.

We also recognize that family court personnel and attorneys typically have focused on civil case dispositions. By their historical use and even their definition, family courts have traditionally been oriented toward achieving a mutually beneficial "win–win" outcome. If a family court has been focused on preserving a family, then it must change its orientation dramatically in the face of prior criminal conduct. Preserving societal and victim-specific goals of preventing abuse should obviously trump the desire to keep a family intact unless the victim strongly articulates a contrary desire (Dunford-Jackson, Frederick, Hart, & Hofford, 1998).

Although additional training might address this shortcoming, there could be a natural predisposition of court personnel and attorneys to focus on the civil aspects of a case and less on the goal of punishing past criminal conduct. This could be compounded because a family court judge would need to be well versed in the different evidentiary standards for civil and criminal cases, and a prosecutor who was prosecuting a crime in such a court might be exposed to unfamiliar civil law standards and procedural requirements. As a result, in giving family courts jurisdiction over criminal cases, implementation issues might be more complicated than is initially apparent.

Assignment to a family court also might perpetuate a batterer's perception that there is some degree of mutual responsibility (e.g., "blame shifting"—a psychologically comforting thought to someone who has committed a crime). Therefore, in some ways, simply handling a case in family court does not convey the same societal message that happens when a specific batterer is being tried for a specific criminal offense in either a general criminal or a domestic violence–specific criminal court. Hence, to the extent that structural change is intended to convey a societal message, the assignment of domestic violence cases to a noncriminal family court might be less effective in promoting deterrence.

Finally, by their name and nature, family courts are more appropriate for traditional families. It is far more difficult to obtain jurisdiction in nontraditional relationships where the involved parties are unmarried. As we know from the political debates raging throughout the United States, in virtually all states, nontraditional couples, including same-sex couples and many short-term cohabiting relationships, are barely recognized legally. These victims would not be helped by a family court because there is no legally recognized relationship. Although there is nothing intrinsically preventing family courts from handling "civil unions" or other long-term relationships, in many states, their jurisdiction might not be allowed to expand to all varieties of cohabiting relationships. Also, this venue would not be the best in cases where the victim desires to sever a relationship and no children are involved to complicate such a decision.

This suggests that despite a desire to have one forum, a family court is unlikely to have by itself the ability to handle violence within all the relationships included under current domestic violence statutes. Therefore, even if a jurisdiction has a well-developed and fully empowered family court, a formal strategy needs to be put in place to ensure consistency between criminal and family courts for these nontraditional relationships.

Innovations in New York State

We believe it would be illustrative to provide an in-depth examination of the system established in several counties in New York State. These studies collectively are well done methodologically and provide insight into the efficacy and limits of special-purpose domestic violence courts.

In the past, in all counties, a victim could have his/her case heard simultaneously in family court, criminal court, and the state supreme court. These courts each had their own judges, prosecuting attorneys, and referral agencies. Authorities in Kings County, New York (Brooklyn), implemented a different approach, a specialized Felony Domestic Violence Court (FDVC) in June 1996. It was designed to handle approximately 5% of the most serious domestic violence cases that should be considered as felonies rather than the far more numerous (95%) misdemeanor cases. Officials mandated a coordinated response to domestic violence felonies between criminal justice and social service agencies through a model felony court responsible for all aspects of domestic violence. The key components were as follows: (a) identifying key criminal justice and social service agencies, (b) setting caseloads that only included domestic violence felonies, (c) staffing with specially trained and dedicated personnel from each criminal justice agency, (d) providing a network of social service agencies, (e) working with the local district attorney to assure vertical prosecution (e.g., assignment of a single prosecutor), (f) assigning victim advocates and an assigned judge, (g) standardizing interventions including regular use of protection or other court orders to protect victims and court-mandated interventions such as batterer treatment for offenders, (h) ensuring offender compliance by monitoring and controlling defendants both preadjudication and postsentencing including requiring frequent court appearances and tracking offenders during probation and parole, and (i) providing services and protection for victims by partnering with advocates from Safe Horizon and the District Attorney's Counseling Services Unit (Newmark, Rempel, Diffily, & Mallik-Kane, 2004).

After its implementation, as expected, the caseload of the FDVC expanded rapidly as unmet service demands were finally being addressed. This increase resulted from a variety of factors including the increased willingness of the District Attorney's Office to indict and prosecute domestic violence offenders, as well as an increase in statutory criteria mandating arrest as well as upgrading violation of most protection orders from misdemeanor offenses to felonies (Newmark et al., 2004). Therefore, the total proportion as well as the number of cases falling under the jurisdiction of a felony domestic violence court rose considerably.

Newmark et al. (2004) noted that the FDVS caseload began to decrease after 1999. The National Institute of Justice (NIJ)–funded evaluation of the court could not determine the reason for the decline in the FDVC caseload. The researchers suggest that it might be the result of a decrease in arrests that occurred because of decreased reporting or alternatively (and frankly less likely) an actual decrease in felony-level domestic violence offenses (Newmark et al., 2004).

In response to the success of this court, as well as of similar courts throughout the country, in 2001, Judge Jonathan Lippman, who was New York State's chief administrative judge, initiated additional experiments in 4 more of the 62 counties of the state (the Bronx [Queens], Westchester, Monroe [Rochester], and Rensselear counties). He proposed special-purpose domestic violence courts using trial judges from the existing state supreme court (New York State's trial-level judges). Families referred to such courts were assigned to these judges and were offered social services, such as victim counseling, in addition to traditional case processing.

A factor influencing this successful initiative was that the court administrators knew that the New York courts previously had highly successful experiences with special-purpose drug courts for nonviolent drug offenders. These courts diverted many offenders from developing a long record for drug-related felonies. Judge Lippman also realized that because of factors unique to New York's fractured court systems, domestic violence cases were, at the time, organized into a multiplicity of courts, including the state supreme courts, "surrogate" or family courts, and many other tribunals (Mansnerus, 2001).

Judge Lippman expected that the number of total domestic violence cases would decline dramatically when the system moved from its pilot phase to include all state courts. When the pilot effort was initiated, there were 80,000 domestic violence cases, 20,000 contested divorces, and approximately 200,000 family court cases involving custody that had elements of "family offenses," including assaults, sexual abuse, abuse or neglect of children, and stalking. Judge Lippman estimated that combining cases could reduce the total number of separate court cases by approximately 50,000 per year. In addition, although unstated, was the expectation that, over the long term, the effectiveness of these courts would reduce caseloads by limiting instances of reoffending (Mansnerus, 2001).

Central to establishing these specialized courts was developing a cadre of knowledgeable court personnel empowered to provide a comprehensive, coordinated response starting at a court-unified intake center. Knowledgeable clerks at that center acted as "gatekeepers" for various agencies and private advocates. Case assignment was made to one judge, who became responsible for all subsequent progress. This was considered necessary to decrease time spent on understanding the family and to minimize the offenses involved; to prevent inconsistent rulings, limiting case-processing time was to be achieved by preventing the courts from being subject to other, higher profile non–domestic violence cases.

Implications of the New York State Innovations

Unlike most court reforms, some studies now evaluate their impact and potentially show key areas that might be adapted by other jurisdictions.

Kings County Felony Court—The first major study evaluated the Kings County Domestic Violence (Felony) Court in Brooklyn, New York, described previously. As stated, this court's mission was to handle the approximately 5% of domestic violence cases in the county that were considered severe enough to be treated as felonies rather than the much more common misdemeanors. They found that this court made a major positive substantive difference in case processing (Newmark, Rempel, Diffily, & Kane, 2001).

Specifically, the District Attorney's Office was more likely to indict minor cases of domestic violence to increase its ability to monitor defendants and allow victims access to services. Furthermore, dismissal rates were relatively low, ranging from 5% to 10% of indicted cases at least during the 1998–2000 time frame. Thus, the researchers concluded that many cases that in the past would have been improperly disposed of as misdemeanors were now categorized properly as felonies and were tried in the felony domestic violence court. Victim services were expanded in this specialized court, which was primarily attributable to the assignment of a victim-services advocate who helped obtain a protective order. During the study period, conviction rates did not change, although conviction by guilty pleas increased and the number of trials decreased, representing a savings to the judicial system. Case processing time, a negative given the costs involved, did increase, however—and is perhaps an unavoidable feature of a court that treated its cases as the serious incidents that they represented.

This initial study is on balance positive, but we have some reservations about its certainty for long-term change. The researchers noted that it was extremely important that there was cooperation and agreement as to the goals and objectives among all the participating agencies.

The reason we temper our confidence in the ability of these reforms to last is that the Newmark et al. (2004) study was based on data from the first 6 months in 1997, although the report was republished by NIJ in 2004. Newmark et al. (2004) noted that although their largely positive findings were based on 136 cases in the first half of 1997, the caseload of the felony court had diminished since early 1999, hopefully because of the long-term rehabilitation of many offenders.

This conclusion is questionable, however, since the transience of many offenders and the continuing life cycle of new offenders entering the system should have provided a relatively steady stream of new cases. The alternative rival hypothesis is more troublesome, that perhaps the system has degraded over time because of growing caseloads, budgetary pressures, agency burnout, or even offenders and their counsel learning how to manipulate this court. Hence, subsequent information from police, prosecutors, the judiciary, and court personnel is needed before any conclusion is possible.

New York Misdemeanor Court Reforms—Although case processing of felonies is important as these offenses are the most egregious, the reality is that these cases are only a small percent of the total caseload and, hence, an almost insignificant part of the court time devoted to domestic violence.

A recent study compared processing of the 95% of the cases that are misdemeanor with the felony case processing in Brooklyn (Kings County) to the Bronx (Queens County). This study illustrated how one procedural decision, "mandatory" case filing versus "nonmandatory," could have a major impact on the judicial system, victims, and batterers (Peterson & Dixon, 2005). Specifically, they compared prosecution outcomes in Brooklyn where domestic violence prosecution policy is mandated, even for misdemeanors, with that of Queens County (the Bronx), which does not mandate case processing for miscreants.

The researchers used 2001 data to analyze outcomes and determine the impact of this policy difference on important outcomes. This study is highly significant. Although there are some demographic differences between the Bronx and Brooklyn, these differences are not that extreme, both being boroughs of New York City. Both are also subject to the same state domestic violence statutes. The key difference is that the Bronx courts decide whether to prosecute misdemeanor cases largely on the basis of victim preference, primarily pursuing cases where the victim signed the complaint, indicating her commitment to case prosecution. As a result, fewer cases were prosecuted in the Bronx. In contrast, in Brooklyn, the District Attorney's Office adopted a mandatory domestic violence policy, filing charges for almost all misdemeanor cases regardless of victim wishes. In both jurisdictions, although victims were encouraged to proceed with case processing, in the Bronx where victims refused to sign complaints or meet with the District Attorney, the complaints ultimately were dismissed.

Several key differences in outcomes were noted. Not surprisingly, in Brooklyn, almost all cases (99%) were filed for additional processing, proving that the mandatory policy was being implemented. In the Bronx, despite the nonmandatory nature, 83% were actually filed. One effect was immediately observable. In Brooklyn, cases took an average of 12.7 weeks to reach disposition compared with 9.6 weeks in the Bronx, which represents an approximately 30% increase in time.

Whereas Peterson and Dixon advanced the argument that this added court processing time in Brooklyn was good in that it provided an increased period of court oversight over arrestees, "oversight" absent conviction is not typically an acknowledged role of the criminal justice system. Instead, it can be considered more properly as an indicator of inefficiency. In addition, the authors' conclusion asserting a beneficial impact as a result of extended court oversight prior to disposition has been contradicted by other researchers who report that most reoffending occurs during the period prior to case disposition (Buzawa et al., 1999; Klein, 2009), which suggests that this period of increased oversight as a result of increased time to process a case is not an effective feature.

In addition, and perhaps of even greater significance, there is a lower conviction rate in Brooklyn. Even though only 17% of the cases were not filed in the Bronx (compared with 1% of cases in Brooklyn), 50% of the filed cases in the Bronx resulted in conviction compared with only 21% in Brooklyn, which is the mandatory filing jurisdiction. The researchers noted that this distinction was highly statistically significant. It meant that even with a drop of 16% of cases not filed, there was still a smaller percentage of the total cases (whether or not prosecuted to conviction) that were successfully filed in the non-mandatory jurisdiction of the Bronx.

In the Bronx, 83% of cases filed times a 50%-conviction rate equaled 41.5% (convictions divided by case filings). In Kings County, 99% of cases were filed times a 21%-conviction rate, which resulted in only a 20%-conviction rate of total cases reaching the attention of the District Attorney (e.g., including those not filed along with processed cases). Hence, from a common measure of determining case efficiency, conviction rates within the Bronx system were actually more than twice as efficient as that of Brooklyn.

Therefore, unless the outcome of prosecutorial oversight resulted in lower reoffending, current data suggest that the Brooklyn mandatory case-filing system is not warranted. Our conclusion is based on several factors. First, it is imperative to note that prosecutorial and judicial resources are not unlimited. To the extent that mandatory case processing results in an inherently inefficient process represented by cases that are brought but later discontinued with a finding, it is incumbent for those advocating this process to demonstrate why this process is justified. Furthermore, supporters should explain what other criminal cases the finite number of prosecutors and courts should not handle in order for them to have time to focus on the domestic violence cases not successfully processed to conviction.

Second, as we have noted elsewhere, most reoffending occurs during the period prior to judicial decision making; therefore, an extended period of inaction by the court system often is not to the victim's advantage.

Third, we believe that disempowering victims by removing their inability to make decisions is a negative outcome. In this case, only 17% of victims decided they were opposed to prosecution in the Bronx. Should all the negative impact of victim disempowerment be imposed on everyone simply to facilitate prosecution of the small percentage of cases that have a vanishingly low probability of remaining in the system until conviction? This is especially true since some victims might be endangered by case prosecution. These victims typically are aware of their danger and, thus, might have valid reasons for declining prosecution.

SUMMARY

Although domestic violence cases can be, and are still, prosecuted in traditional criminal courts, there have been increasing efforts to develop innovative approaches that are more responsive to victim needs and that maintain offender accountability. Many believe that criminal courts are the preferred option for all cases of domestic violence offenses to ensure that there is a clearly identifiable offender and victim, and to highlight that domestic violence is a crime.

Others prefer a more focused approach in which domestic violence cases are treated in a separate court to facilitate a more rapid disposition. Those who advocate this approach believe that offenders are more likely to be held accountable and processed through disposition. Some domestic violence courts have separate criminal dockets in which criminal offenses are heard separately from civil matters. Integrated domestic violence courts attempt to streamline this approach by having all matters pertaining to a given victim and offender heard simultaneously.

All these approaches have advantages and disadvantages. There are no clear answers as to the preferred approach. To a large extent, this depends on the criteria used to measure success—victim safety, offender accountability, offender punishment, and/or offender treatment.

DISCUSSION QUESTIONS

1. Integrated domestic violence courts attempt to save victims multiple trips to court by hearing all related matters including child custody hearings and restraining orders on the same day. However, it has been argued that since civil matters look at victims and offenders "equally" rather than assuming a victim/offender dichotomy, this strategy is disadvantageous to victims. What are your thoughts?

2. Similarly, integrating all matters in one day means that each matter has its own set of attorneys. Thus, the victim and the offender each have attorneys (and possibly a victim advocate) for the criminal charge and a different set of attorneys for the civil matters. Does this inhibit the processing of criminal charges?

3. Can criminal courts be improved by offering many of the same advantages in terms of expeditious case handling and ensuring offender accountability that are offered (at least in theory) by domestic violence courts?

Community-Based and Court-Sponsored Diversions **13**

Chapter Overview

Many members of the judiciary have recognized that a primary reason the criminal justice system has been ineffective is the relative inflexibility of intervention strategies and treatment modalities. This chapter will address the rise and limitations of several alternatives.

Two models of diverting domestic violence cases from the criminal justice system were developed during the last 20 years. First, we will discuss restorative justice approaches as an alternative to formal criminal justice case processing. These approaches broaden earlier informal strategies designed to address victim, offender, and community needs. We will focus on the practice most used historically—victim–offender mediation—and discuss several different variants on restorative justice (e.g., family group conferencing and peacemaking circles). Although restorative justice has been somewhat eclipsed by batterer treatment programs, this method has at times been widely adopted and might return to favor given the ever-changing political climate toward criminal justice involvement and the existence of real financial constraints on agency time and resources.

Next, this chapter will discuss batterer intervention programs (BIPs) or batterer counseling by court mandate as a condition for pretrial diversion or as a part of sentencing subsequent to guilty plea or trial verdict. We will discuss in depth the key components of such programs, how they might differ, and what we now know about their use, effectiveness, and limitations.

Restorative Justice Approaches

Restorative justice in cases of domestic violence encompasses a wide variety of informal strategies intended to meet the needs of victims, offenders, and communities alike. It recognizes the fact that most victims of domestic violence do not call the police. So, regardless of the relative merit of criminal justice versus informal methods of handling such cases, the traumas and specialized needs of many victims, will never be brought to the attention of courts.

The basic intent of restorative justice is to expand the available options for victims while maintaining a measure of offender accountability. It also makes an effort to create a focus on the needs of the victim and the community, unlike the criminal justice system that is really designed to focus on the direct consequences to the offender of committing crimes in the past.

In the context of the criminal justice system, the needs and expectations of the victim often are of only ancillary interest to the main actors—the police, prosecutors, defense bar, and court. These issues are real. Feminists have long argued that, in the past and currently, the victims have not been well represented in formal criminal justice proceedings (Goodman & Epstein, 2008; Sokoloff & Pratt, 2005). Even in the minority of courts with victim advocates who are, after all, expressly hired to resolve these issues, they often are retained by prosecutors' offices and, as a result, have a competing goal to have the victim cooperate with prosecution at times despite her wishes (Labriola, Bradley, O'Sullivan, Rempel, & Moore, 2009).

Restorative justice tries to address these victim-centered needs and originates out of a long-standing desire to develop viable alternatives to the criminal-justice system. These methods were developed initially to handle antisocial behavior by juveniles or breaches of the peace that might have originated out of relatively low-level conflicts. The key concept is to draw the victim into the resolution of an incident, have the offender truly understand the degree to which he or she has violated the rights of the victim and or the community, and finally to have the offender participate in some effort that will remediate the harm caused and lessen the possibility of the antisocial action reoccurring.

A variety of different means has been used to draw the interests of the victim and community into the process of limiting inappropriate behavior by an offender.

Although the methods of restorative justice differ, they share the following traits:

1. A primary goal is to repair the harm done to the victim (and often the community).

2. A forum is provided to give the victim a chance to address to the offender and the community the impact of the offense.

3. The organizers demonstrate a desire to decrease the official role of the state while increasing the involvement of the families and the community.

4. The proponents might be as concerned with the community impact of violence as they are with the punishment of a particular offender.

A wide variety of types of activities now commonly referred to as "restorative justice" has been developed. These include court-sponsored mediation or victim–offender "reconciliation" or "dialogue" that we will cover in depth; family group counseling, also called "community conferencing"; and the "peacemaking circle," which we will mention briefly.

As noted previously, these efforts began in the context of society in the 1990s trying to answer in a nonpunitive sense a wave of crimes committed by juveniles. These approaches had been attempted with juvenile offenders in many contexts internationally or used as part of traditional approaches to achieve justice among Native Americans

(McCold, 2006). One study in 2005 stated that more than 1,200 such programs had been developed worldwide (primarily for youthful offenses) (VOMA, 2005, quoted in Ptacek & Frederick, 2009). Another study using different criteria for inclusion stated that although these alternative programs are relatively common in the United States, they are even more common in the United Kingdom, Germany, France, China, and India (Braithwaite, 2006).

Studies of the effects of restorative justice models in the original target population of juvenile offenders have been positive (see Ptacek & Frederick, 2009, for an extended discussion). However, the results on the application of such techniques to cases of intimate abuse are not common.

The application of techniques of restorative justice to domestic violence has not been without controversy. In response to the demands of battered women advocates, many jurisdictions have banned such techniques in domestic violence out of concern that they will be used inappropriately in practice to shuttle criminal behavior from the purview of the courts that would punish actual crimes (Daly & Stubbs, 2007). Nevertheless, several methods of restorative justice, such as family group counseling and peacemaking circles, have been used in some contexts in the area of domestic violence, and the techniques are still being taught (see especially Nixon, Burford, Quinn, & Edelbaum [2005] and Goel [2000], as discussed in Ptacek & Frederick, 2009).

We will cover mediation in the most detail, as in the past it was the de facto standard alternative to criminal case prosecution, and by far the most has been written about this area, including evaluations of its strengths and limitations.

Court-Sponsored Mediation Programs

Mediation first began in the 1970s in both the United States and Canada. In one community survey, respondents preferred court-sponsored mediation to conviction for abuse followed by jail or even probation (Stalans, 1996; Stalans & Lurigio, 1995). Similarly, a 1992 public poll favored "counseling," not arrest (Klein, Campbell, Soler, & Ghez, 1997). Only if the female victim was punched or "hit hard" did the percent favoring arrest increase to between 50% and 90%, depending on the degree of injury inflicted (Klein et al., 1997). Clearly, both mediation and counseling have a legitimate, although bounded, scope of support by the public, as well as by many courts.

In contrast to public support, the extent to which victims favor such approaches is far less certain. Hotaling and Buzawa (2001) reported in this study of cases where criminal charges were filed, only 13% of victims would have preferred mediation as an alternative to court prosecution, and less than one third preferred "informal meetings" with a court official to work out a judicially enforced solution. Often, this was not for punitive reasons, however, because more than two thirds of victims believed psychological counseling for offenders, such as batterer treatment, offered the greatest potential for preventing reoffending, and fewer believed traditional criminal justice sanctions would be effective.

In contrast to informal efforts by police to settle a domestic assault at the scene, formal mediation uses the services of a skilled intermediary. Parties are shown how to resolve serious differences without resorting to violent or otherwise inappropriate behavior. Mediation has several significant advantages. The theory behind the use of mediation as a diversionary program is that the abuser, and even at times the abused party, usually denies the criminality of spouse abuse. Mediation avoids the need for such a determination (or, from a different perspective, improperly refuses to make such a finding). The process and techniques for settling conflicts without violence are taught to both the offender and the victim. Some have favored this as a method of circumventing an impersonal court system that discriminates against the needs of individual women. It serves also as a method of educating both parties about their legal rights and respon-sibilities. Of even more significance, it addresses the apparent desires of many victims who have indicated repeatedly that they do not want the offender's continued prosecu-tion through conviction.

Even more significant, previous chapters in this book have demonstrated amply that many, if not most, victims prefer alternatives to the "command and control" orientation of the criminal justice system. Currently, many such victims are dissatisfied with the decisions or at least the processes of the criminal justice system. We predict that such discomfort might increase as prosecutors place more aggressive attention on claims of "child endangerment," especially since such advocates for the children might not even retain the pretext that the victims' interests are of their paramount concern.

In mediation cases, the parties, facilitated by the mediator, customize decisions that might be best for them and, as they perceive, for their children. Despite intensive time commitments for counselors and mediators, most cases do not require much of the far scarcer and costlier prosecution and judicial resources. Consequently, mediation might be considered expedient to an overburdened system facing gridlock in trial courts. Perhaps in comparison with traditional prosecution, studies have shown that partici-pants of effective programs view the process as being fair and generally rate it favorably, at least in comparison with the vagaries of the traditional, overworked, and somewhat cynical court system (Smith, 1983). If the mediators are prepared for the possibility of domestic violence and are correspondingly careful to equalize power relationships and maintain mechanisms to intervene actively if it seems that violence is likely to recur, some authors have stated that mediation might prove beneficial even in the context of domestic violence (Johnston & Campbell, 1993; Yellot, 1990).

Based on an assumption of cooperation among discordant parties, mediation is largely a "self-help" process by which the impartial mediator facilitates conflict resolu-tion. The focus is on addressing the emotional and informational needs of victims. The mediator does not have the authority to mandate any particular settlement but instead typically seeks to develop a process for solving disputes nonviolently. Marital conflict mediation in the 1990s experienced phenomenal growth as a means of having a client-controlled, less-expensive system of settling disputes (including divorces) among spouses (Hilton, 1993). In fact, during the 1990s, it was observed that courts used medi-ation as the "first avenue" of trying to affect an interpersonal dispute (Umbreit, 1995). This was true even though the best estimates were that between 50% and 80% of all marriages referred by the courts to mediators involved family violence (Maxwell & Bricker, 1999; Newmark, Harrell, & Salem, 1995).

Mediation efforts to contain domestic violence have several precedents. Crisis inter-vention centers nationwide were set up across the country in the 1990s to diffuse many kinds of interpersonal disputes, sometimes including domestic violence. The mediation programs of more direct relevance to this book have been the use of pretrial mediation sponsored by prosecutors' offices and structured mediation in divorce cases in which past abuse has made the threat of criminal prosecution real. These programs might be run by prosecutorial or judicial staff or might be contracted out using the services of local crisis-management agencies.

Whether or not it is officially acknowledged, court-sponsored, divorce-related mediation has been widely used in cases of domestic violence. Virtually all studies of divorce mediation suggest that domestic violence is prevalent in divorce mediations, with estimates of the co-occurrence at 50% to 80% of all mediated divorce cases (Kurz, 1996; Maxwell, 1999; Pearson, 1997). Nevertheless, where such court-sponsored programs exist, mediation generally resolves 50% to 70% of referrals without subsequent judicial input. Although typically divorce mediators have the responsibility of advising parties that they can "opt out" and pursue criminal conduct if domestic violence has occurred, Pearson (1997) as well as Thoennes, Salem, and Pearson (1995) each noted that less than 5% of such cases were excluded from mediation because of domestic violence.

Mediation programs are extraordinarily varied; however, they all entail a meeting with the offender, the victim, and a trained mediator. Typically, they are initiated by a referral of the case either by a prosecutor, victim advocate, or the attorney for one of the parties. Some programs use a structured framework seeking to teach long-term dispute resolution in a nonviolent context or to negotiate key aspects of legal separation through divorce-related mediation. Some have even included initial direct sessions with a mediator and a surrogate or advocate for the "adversary." A typical mediation session involving intimates is designed to use a neutral trained facilitator or mediator to provide both parties with a safe and structured forum in which they can express their needs and aspirations in a relationship and hear those of the other party. Stated succinctly, "the mediator is an advocate of a fair process" (C. W. Moore, 1986). This is true whether the parties' shared goal is to "reform" the relationship or to end it with a minimum of rancor and collateral damage to the parties or their children.

The mediator attempts to facilitate negotiations by making each side understand reasonable requests from the other party and appeal to both parties' desires to achieve a "fair result." The process of mediation is, thus, designed to be "self-empowering" to each of the participants, giving both a degree of "buy in," hence making them responsible for the decisions that are reached. To the extent achieved, the result might be accepted more readily than those "mandated" by a court.

Mediating a relationship involving domestic violence creates numerous problems, some insurmountable in cases of serious violence. First, such cases should never be the subject of the "mandatory" mediation divorce statutes that many states developed during the 1950s. Also, during the course of the mediation, both parties should be informed that any future violence will not be tolerated and that constructive techniques for expressing anger must be developed. In the unlikely case where there is a high potential for continued violence, the victim should be given guidance about her legal rights, including prosecution and available support systems for victims of battering. This practice was widely adopted; virtually all modern divorce-related mediation services have protocols on how to handle cases of domestic violence (Thoennes et al., 1995).

In other programs, individual counseling of both the accused offender and the victim precedes joint sessions between the spouses. This decreases the immediate trauma of past incidents, allows a careful evaluation of the parties' commitment to mediation, begins teaching each party his or her rights and responsibilities, and might provide a pathway to requisite psychological counseling. To memorialize the process and reinforce the commitment to change, a formal signed mediation agreement usually is prepared that sets forth mutually agreed-on goals.

Does Mediation Reduce Violence?

Although few empirical studies have been performed, especially since batterer intervention programs began to eclipse mediation in the late 1990s, some findings have suggested that in appropriate cases, mediation might provide approximately equal reductions in the rate of violent recidivism, at least as compared with traditional sentencing. One early study found the District of Columbia's mediation service to be effective in reducing future violence, and mediation was considered fair by both parties (Davis, Tichane, & Grayson, 1980). Of course, it might be inappropriate to compare recidivism rates with rates in the 1980s, which was a time when domestic violence cases were far more likely to be handled poorly. Despite the merit of this critique—we should aim for the best response possible—comparisons between real-world alternatives are among the best indicators of useful social policy. Thus, it is essential to consider carefully the comparative advantages and limitations of mediation.

Limits of Mediation

Mediation shares some of the basic tenets, and hence limitations, of the "conciliatory" style of policing. Specifically, mediators as a profession and mediation as a process are not inclined to fix blame on either party, and typically mediators do not insert their value judgments regarding their actions. As a result, mediation often will fail to identify explicitly either a "victim" or an "aggressor."

Implicit in mediation is the assumption that the parties should be able to compromise disparate interests to maintain a previously dysfunctional violent relationship. Precedence should be given to violence abatement as opposed to the implied primary goal of mediation and maintenance of the family unit. From that perspective, mediation simply might be an attempt to address family maintenance concerns without changing the underlying neglect of women's legitimate interests for protection and for violent acts committed against them.

This effect might be subtle. In the zeal to reach a mutually satisfactory accommodation, victims might be "pressured" into abstaining from aggressive or "provocative behavior," thus achieving the abuser's goal of dominating a relationship without even the necessity of resorting to violence. For example, we assume a mediator would not react well to claims of such "provocative behavior" as failing to perform household chores adequately; however, are we certain the mediator might not tell an abused woman not to protest if her partner does not do any household chores or perhaps stays out all night, leaving his wife to care for minor children?

We know that it is precisely these types of conflicts over behavior that often precipitate acts of intimate violence. In short, should the mediator counsel a woman to agree with her partner to avoid abuse? In this context, what should be addressed is the inability of the aggressor to resolve inevitable familial conflicts without resorting to violence rather than a "conflict" to be mediated. Without overstating the point, it is critical that mediation should not be allowed if there is evidence of serious, repetitive violence. Otherwise, the guise of keeping a family together will restrict a woman's autonomy, as well as the ability of the criminal court to intervene. Not surprisingly, a critique of divorce-court-sponsored mediation has developed, arguing that the common practice of "mandatory" mediation in divorce cases, regardless of domestic violence, deprives women of their right to be recognized as victims of a crime and might even decrease their safety while the case is being "mediated" compared with aggressive prosecution of domestic violence (Gagnon, 1992; Hart, 1990). Recent statutory amendments typically prohibit the use of mandatory mediation if domestic violence is present; however, if both parties deny violence, then it is unlikely to serve as a limitation.

Mediation as a strategy might, therefore, allow a batterer to avoid the criminal justice process, despite having committed clear criminal acts of domestic violence. Some of these offenders will psychologically be better able to continue denying the reality of their criminal actions. In fact, it is possible that by implying that neither party is solely responsible, an assailant might be encouraged to view his conduct as not being expressly wrong but merely the result of a problematic relationship in which his actions are at least partially attributable to victim "provocations."

The basic concern with mediation is that in these circumstances, if used inappropriately, the result might be continued victim subjugation, with clear criminal acts treated as a by-product of a "dysfunctional" relationship between "involved parties." At worst, mediators might facilitate domestic abuse inadvertently by ignoring the criminal nature of an assault and assuming that there is mutual responsibility for the physical aggression of one party, by explicitly assigning a higher value to facilitating agreement than addressing violent behavior, and by trivializing past and potential future assaults in the mediation "contracts" or "agreements" (Ellis, 1993; Hilton, 1991, 1993).

Such negative outcomes are a real risk. By analyzing transcripts of mediations, Cobb (1992) described how mediators of that time ignored or trivialized past violence in their effort to reach a "therapeutic" mediation. From this, she concluded (but without presenting any empirical data) that mediation likely increased the risk of subsequent injury to the abused party (Cobb, 1992). This ignorance might not be intentional because, as we noted earlier, virtually all mediation services have established protocols on handling domestic violence mediation. Despite such policies, it has been observed that, often, the mediator fails to uncover many instances of violence because of their inability to draw out the information or because they are reluctant to ask probing questions that might seem to compromise the mediator's "neutrality" (Pearson, 1997).

Other times, the process of mediation itself cannot be considered a serious intervention in an ongoing violent relationship. Although there is the potential for long-term mediation or counseling to address issues, a "single shot" or short time-limited period of abuse, the mediator often will not recognize unfolding patterns of abuse, particularly if the victim is affected by posttraumatic stress and is either intimidated by the offender or is perceived by the mediator as "overly demanding" (Maxwell, 1999).

An ineffective mediation might have unfortunate results even beyond the missed opportunity to intervene effectively by prosecuting to conviction (Pirro, 1982). After all, even if ineffective at stopping violence, mediation does increase the likelihood of the family unit staying together, at least during the period of the mediation. It is apparent that intimacy and frequency of contact increases the potential for conflict. If the mediation is unsuccessful at stopping a prior assailant from committing repeat acts of violence, then there is a real probability that more harm will result than if the case had not been diverted.

Most authors critique mediation because cases of repeat assault should be treated as a crime rather than subject to mediation as part of a conflict situation. If not, the opportunity for identifying, sanctioning, and deterring future violent behavior might be lost, and the process simply "mediates violence."

Dated research by Smith (1983) suggested that violence even after mediation is no idle concern, with 36% of victims reporting more violence after mediation and 41% having increased fears of revenge. Of course, this study did not answer what percentage of these women would have had such a poor result without mediation because they were already a population at risk. Similarly, by the nature of the study (one program), it could not reflect the potential for conflict management of all the various forms of mediation. Ellis (1993) noted the lack of any empirical evidence to support claims of a harmful effect. His review of mediation efforts, in fact, noted a small number of studies and did not find such a negative pattern. Not surprisingly, most mediators also vehemently deny allegations that they were simply "mediating violence."

For this reason, we need to synthesize these findings. We believe there is a role for mediation, but it is limited, best reserved for less serious cases of violence where there is no criminal history. One example, in a case of a single assault, where no weapon was involved, there was no injury or any likelihood of serious injury, and mediation rather than prosecution was preferred by the victim. A similar case might be made for mediation where the specific act of violence seems to be more in the context of an ongoing "mutual conflict" than of one disempowered party (typically the woman) having been continually victimized by an intimate partner.

We recognize that these limitations might create serious intake or selection problems, given the lack of agreement over the definition of severe abuse or whether an imbalance of power prevents a woman from effectively being able to "mediate." Using these criteria to disqualify a couple might, for example, include even one incident that involves major injury, intent to cause such an injury, or use of a weapon. The key would be that participation by a couple with a high potential for serious abuse should not be allowed in a program designed to address relatively minor abuse. This would be consistent with the increased trend in many statutes to recategorize repeat misdemeanor domestic assault as a felony, subjecting the assailant to the potential for more severe sentencing.

Mediation in this context also should contain the following structural safeguards:

1. The mediator should have the assailant admit unconditionally that he or she did assault the victim and develop a consistently applied and carefully preserved record of any prior violence that might have precipitated the mediation, perhaps in the form of mutually signed agreements in which the violent episodes are described in detail. If this structural safeguard is adopted, then in the case of a subsequent assault, the prosecutor will be able to introduce such an agreement as evidence and possibly invoke laws for habitual offenders or at least commit to have his or her office react to past offenses.

2. Structured mediation should be developed that begins to resemble a conditional sentencing that is fundamentally different than the typical nonjudgmental emphasis in common divorce mediations. Ultimately, the result is a "contract" or "agreement" containing "teeth" that establishes conflict-resolution strategies and behavioral modifications to which both parties agree.

3. Any such sanctioned agreement must include "no-abuse" covenants and, if needed, commitments for either or both parties to attend substance abuse or anger control therapy.

4. If a trained mediator believes one party (typically a victim suffering posttraumatic stress) cannot adequately represent his or her interests, then mediation should not be allowed. Similarly, if the proposed mediator believes that inappropriate temperament or strongly ingrained belief in a master–subordinate relationship is present, then an adversarial process with a victim advocate would be superior to a mediated court diversion program.

5. The prosecutor's office should be involved to the extent that it is willing to "enforce" the nonviolence provisions of mediation agreements either through careful case monitoring if mediation is conducted under court order or through an announced willingness to pounce on any subsequent violence. For example, the prosecutor's office should consider an express statement by the parties where mediation is sought so that it will prosecute both the initial crime (whose prosecution may have been suspended) and any subsequent offense to the full extent of the law if additional violence occurs.

Even if mediation is desired by both victim and offender, they must be made to understand and expressly acknowledge in a document that would be admissible in court that participation in court-ordered mediation carries with it an enhanced risk of future penalties in the event of future violence and a prosecutorial commitment to reinstate a suspended prosecution for both the original act of violence and any new offenses.

Such requirements would obviously limit inappropriate use of mediation. Because a mediation program requires the participation of both parties, it is not appropriate for separated parties where neither party seeks reconciliation. These concerns also have contributed to legislation in most states that explicitly exempts domestic violence victims from otherwise required mediation in divorce cases.

In some jurisdictions, the use of divorce-related mediation in the presence of an active domestic violence restraining order has been hotly contested. Some mediation agencies such as the Court Mediation Service of Maine refuse to take any such cases because they believe mediation between parties with obviously unequal bargaining power is inappropriate (Pearson, 1997). Similarly, even the American Bar Association's Family Law Section Task Force, the Academy of Family Mediators, and the Association of Family and Conciliation Courts have called for formal restrictions on mediation in the presence of violence. In most instances, however, mediation remains available, although not mandated, even if past instances of domestic abuse have occurred.

Mediation programs also require a continued commitment of state and local funding. Too often, such mediation and other "demonstration projects," which are announced with great fanfare by federal and state funding agencies, begin, are proven initially effective in some cases, and are continued for a time. In subsequent periods of budgetary austerity, however, the push for "efficiency" in terms that are easily quantifiable becomes overwhelming. Mediation programs might be uniquely vulnerable to such dilution because they are highly dependent on the qualifications and time commitments of all parties including the mediator. Degradation of results might easily occur if quantifiable metrics of efficiency, such as cases per mediator, become the measure of efficacy. Unfortunately, the accountability of mediation is low because of the necessary secrecy of most mediation. Therefore, systemic decay caused by insufficient funding or a decline in organizational commitment might not be recognized immediately.

Has Mediation Reduced Domestic Violence?

In the context of domestic violence case disposition, mediation might have some public support; it has been widely used and is less expensive to the system than traditional processing through conviction. What is less clear is whether empirical research has demonstrated the actual positive impact of mediation on participants. Although limitations to court-sponsored mediations to date are real, empirical research has not found that divorce-court-related mediations, which is the most typical form, have increased the disempowerment of women or increased the likelihood of violence during or after participation in the mediation process. One study following a series of cases reported a steady and relatively sharp decrease in abuse during the year after termination of the mediation (Ellis & Stuckless, 1996).

A second comprehensive study used a variety of data techniques to explore how domestic violence issues impact divorce-related mediation (Pearson, 1997). Pearson reported that through training of mediators, the presence of criminal court alternatives, and other safeguards, the chance of negative impacts on victims did not seem significant. As a result, satisfaction with the entire mediation process was not negatively correlated with a history of domestic violence (Ellis, 1993; Ellis & Stuckless, 1996; Pearson, 1997, quoting Davies, Ralph, Hawton, & Craig, 1995; Newmark et al., 1995).

Family Group Conferencing

Family group conferencing, which also might be referred to as community conferencing, involves a trained facilitator meeting with family members, friends, criminal justice personnel, and service providers (Ptacek & Frederick, 2009). Unlike mediation, community members play an important role and "settlements" cannot be reached until representatives of the community at large agree with the result.

Many of the same advantages and disadvantages of mediation are present with family group counseling. Clearly, this practice has a place in the use of community resources to understand and control what might otherwise be private abuse within a family. In fact, community involvement in the process has several distinct advantages over largely private mediation. First, it signals to both the existing abuser and any potential abuser who finds out about the public aspect of family group counseling that the community itself will not tolerate the actions of those who continue to abuse. Several authors reasoned that this method could sharpen the community's focus on the problems of victims of intimate violence (Pennell & Buford, 1994).

Second, the victim can develop powerful alliances within the community, helping to rebalance an existing imbalance of power that occurs whenever violence is adopted as a means of one person controlling the actions of a second person.

Third, it is implicit to us that if the community representatives recognize the existence of an underlying issue such as substance abuse, then they will make certain that the resources are given to resolve these issues concurrently.

Finally, as pointed out by Koss (2000) and by Koss, Bachar, Hopkins, and Carlson (2004), the existence of such alternatives might mitigate either actual or perceived racism that might now be preventing victims of color from seeking adequate levels of assistance from the criminal judicial system.

Unfortunately, community conferencing shares many of the problems of private mediation discussed previously. If a victim is pressured to participate, then she may publicly be perceived as simply part of a "battling couple," who is more or less as responsible as her abuser. A continuing cycle of abuse does not necessarily mean that the results will be "superior" in any objective sense in the form of stopping future violence. Little research has been performed to examine the efficacy of this approach, and it is certainly possible that the results could be worse than with the mediator alone. For example, we have mentioned that in many recent immigrant communities, as well as certain other more insular religious groups, a woman, in the interests of preserving the family unit, might find herself under more pressure to acquiesce to the demands of her husband.

As we have discussed previously, many such communities put the burden of family stability squarely on the shoulders of the woman, whether abuse has occurred or not. Such pressure would not occur in a modern court or even with a competent mediator. However, there can be no assurance that cohesion of the family unit will not become the overriding goal of the family or "community" participants. In addition, on the one hand, we recognize that many battered women's advocates remain deeply concerned that such approaches simply have too great a potential to devolve into an invisible "fix" of the problem of domestic violence by assigning it not to courts with suitably coercive powers but to nonjudicial dispute resolution that might erode the hard-fought gains of past years (Coward, 2000; Daly & Stubbs, 2006; Frederick & Lizdas, 2003). On the other hand, literally no one is arguing that such innovations should supplant criminal justice agencies. If they are viewed as an adjunct, then this might add a degree of flexibility to the handling of domestic violence cases that unfortunately is sorely lacking in a time of mandatory arrest and prosecution policies.

We believe that the entire concept of restorative justice is real, has some role to play in cases of domestic violence, and in certain cases, is the preferred method of handling violence. However, we do believe that more careful, empirically based research needs to be done before we could recommend widespread use of group counseling as the preferred method of handling domestic violence. Until such research is conducted and favorable results are published (and replicated), we advocate that such measures should have a limited role where they might run parallel to traditional court-based systems and with strict guidelines and procedures for their use.

Peacemaking Circles

Peacemaking circles originated with the indigenous cultures. This practice shares the same goals as both mediation and conferencing. As with conferencing, it includes members of the community, criminal justice personnel, and service providers. However, the distinction is that there can be multiple circles, or meetings, with different parties on different aspects of the case (Ptacek & Frederick, 2009). Therefore, the victim might be in a circle with service providers while the offender is in a circle with social service providers.

Restorative Justice: Circles of Peace

Circles of Peace is a program that began in 2004 and uses a restorative justice circle approach. It was founded by a Santa Cruz County Justice Judge, Mary Helen Maley, and Linda Mills, a professor at New York University. Their intent was to establish a culturally sensitive domestic violence prevention and treatment program. Their program consists of 26–52 weeks of meetings known as Circles that include the batterer, the family, and the victim, if desired. Trained professional facilitators and community volunteers facilitate these meetings, and a person close to the family is identified to ensure victim safety during the treatment period.

The Circles of Peace program shares many of the comparative advantages and disadvantages as with family group counseling. Clearly, in some cases, the community is oriented toward such approaches as they are a "traditional" method of solving relatively minor disputes. See especially the discussions about the use of such traditional methods among Native American populations in the United States and Canada in Stuart (1997) and in Ptacek and Frederick (2009).

In the case of such communities and in smaller jurisdictions composed of relatively homogenous ethnic and social groups, we can observe that these might prove valuable as an adjunct to traditional methods of criminal court determinations. One empirical study of the results of peacemaking in a Native American context (a Navaho reservation) reported that many preferred this to the regular justice system, which was viewed as far too hierarchical, with a win/lose mentality, and not doing enough to improve the actual living conditions of victims of domestic violence (Coker, 1999).

Even in these contexts, we note that some authors have expressed concern that inherent pressures to settle short of a criminal conviction might force abused women in such communities to lose the benefits of new legislation in protecting their safety through convictions and other coercive measures taken against batterers (Aboriginal Women's Action Network [AWAN], 2001; Incite, 2003; and the extensive discussion presented in Ptacek & Frederick, 2009). Furthermore, even Coker's (1999) largely favorable study of this in the Navaho context found that pressure was placed on some victims to participate and that agreements, even when reached, were difficult to enforce as some peacemakers felt it their responsibility to promote family unity, and these agreements lacked the legal standing to bring courts in to prevent future abuse by a past offender.

Regardless of potential merit, we find peacekeeping circles as an institution difficult to implement in a large and diverse metropolitan area where the innate inefficiencies of seeking consensus might become overwhelming and the knowledge gained from any particular circle of peace might be difficult for the community at large to know about or absorb as a "boundary-maintaining" mechanism. In other words, it would be unlikely to have a realistic chance at influencing others the way it might in a small insular community. Without such an external effect, the additional costs of seeking a consensus among a wide variety of people might be difficult to justify compared with straightforward mediation or even the use of criminal courts where actions tend to be publicized more widely.

Batterer Intervention Programs

The Role of Batterer Intervention Programs in a Divergent Offender Group

It is clear that any attempt to address domestic violence systematically must include some effort to reform the behavior of offenders that have already committed domestic violence offenses. If not, significantly increased rates of recidivism will occur. Therefore, even authors firmly committed to assisting victims of domestic violence recognize that the development of effective batterer intervention is an essential part of how the community must respond to domestic violence (Jackson, Feder, Forde, Davis, Maxwell, & Taylor, 2003).

Although batterer intervention programs and mediation share the distinction of being programs to divert offenders from the criminal justice system, they present some real distinctions with batterer intervention programs, having one key advantage over mediation for more serious cases of abuse. The focus of batterer intervention is firmly on inappropriate actions of the offender and the necessity of modifying this behavior. As a result, it should lead offenders more predictably to realize that they have acted inappropriately and need to change their behavior in contrast with the conflict-resolution model implied by mediation.

By now, many judges, especially those with extensive experience in handling a domestic violence caseload, realize that traditional sentencing—fines or incarceration—has had only a limited and indirect effect on batterers, in which violence is typically unpredictable and irrational. Instead, a growing realization has been that, to be effective, sentencing must contain elements of an effective judicial monitoring of offender behavior post assault. Prosecution and courts have handled this, although by no means uniformly, by diverting offenders into treatment programs before the trial, or, more recently, by delivering a split sentence after conviction that includes a batterer intervention component in lieu of incarceration, pending no subsequent abuse occurs.

Recently, a proliferation of these programs has occurred throughout the country. The most recent estimate identified 2,265 batterer programs nationwide in 2007, and the researchers believed this to be much lower than the actual number (Labriola, Rempel, O'Sullivan, Frank, McDowell, & Finkelstein, 2007; Rempel, 2009).

Programs for clinical assistance to domestic violence batterers have been in existence for decades. One trend has been the direct involvement of the criminal justice system in increasing the flow of client referrals from judicial proceedings. Even as early as the mid-1980s, it was estimated that one third of offenders being treated by counselors came from court referrals (Goolkasian, 1986).

The increasing relative importance of court referrals has changed the direction of many programs. Initially, mental health practitioners maintained that the profound personality changes needed to eliminate deeply ingrained violent tendencies would occur most likely when the client chose counseling by voluntarily identifying behavior as problematic.

Although this might indeed be true, many batterers are not sufficiently determined to take or at least complete independent corrective action. This is especially true of batterers who, as a group, have been described often as denying the essential deviance of their acts. Such people will seek treatment voluntarily. Instead, they seem to need the threat of court sanctions to enroll in and complete counseling programs. Court involvement might be accomplished through the initial diversion of the suspect before trial or as part of the court's oversight (through probation) of his sentence. Diversion to counseling before trial also has been informally handled by prosecutors, formally through administrative procedures (as in the federally funded demonstration projects noted previously), or even by some state statutes. In addition, court-mandated counseling is growing rapidly as a part of sentencing or as a condition of a plea bargain. In fact, Rebovich's (1996) study of large prosecutors' offices found that 50% relied on postcharge diversion options suspending case processing while the offender is treated. Eighty percent of prosecutors using such programs believed that they were effective. It was interesting that 63% of the programs were pretrial diversions even though 66% of the offices described how they had instituted no-drop policies. Pretrial diversion often was incorporated into no-drop policies; 93% of the prosecutors reported that successful completion resulted in all charges being dropped compared with only 7% demanding conviction, albeit on lesser charges (Rebovich, 1996).

Most individuals participate within the program as part of a court mandate. It has been estimated that court orders account for approximately 80% of program participants (Bennett & Williams, 2001).

There is good reason to link counseling with court-ordered batterer intervention programs. Research suggests that criminal justice interventions are more likely, or perhaps only likely, to be effective when combined with judicial monitoring of offenders (Andrews & Bonta, 1994; Dutton, 1998; Gendreau, Cullen, & Bonta, 1994).

Some batterers wrongly perceive that society tolerates (or has tolerated) domestic violence as part of an overall patriarchal society. Criminal justice intervention in itself, regardless of type of independent rehabilitation efforts, might signify to this group that domestic violence is no longer acceptable. For many of these offenders, a continuing relationship with the victim or minor dependent children increases the importance to them of stopping unacceptable conduct even without formal therapeutic intervention.

As discussed previously, we recognize now that offenders are a diverse group with a wide range of attitudes, personality characteristics, and behaviors. Despite their dissimilarities, research has clearly disclosed that for many of the most severe batterers, the act of domestic assault is merely one manifestation of a pattern of violent behavior reflected by numerous arrests and convictions for violence against family members, relatives, intimates, acquaintances, and strangers. For this group, requiring batterer treatment with its focus on intimate partner violence might be of limited effect, given the overall problem of violent tendencies. Currently, virtually all programs have ignored such distinctions and, in fact, address batterer violence only in the context of intimate relationships.

These offenders might have deeply rooted personality disorders and are closely related to substance abuse or dysfunctional expressions of emotions. For these offenders, it is necessary to address a much broader range of issues than typically encompassed in state-certified batterer treatment programs. Incapacitation as well as supplemental or alternative rehabilitation interventions might be the only methods that can prevent recidivism. It is unlikely that any intervention (short of lengthy incarceration) without effective rehabilitation will be effective (Klein, 2009).

Without effective treatment, even when repeat violence is prevented, unexpected consequences might result. For example, it is likely that offenders will adopt alternative and potentially equally harmful, yet less legally liable, behaviors, such as sexual assault, verbal aggression, threats, and stalking. Alternatively, they might simply alter targets to other family members or a different partner. The point is that increasing the fear of arrest and ultimate incarceration is unlikely to stop all forms of violence on the part of batterers without interventions targeted toward the underlying problems.

Characteristics of Batterer Intervention Programs

Typically, judges now mandate that a batterer attend batterer intervention programs (sometime rather derisively called BIPs). These programs generally operate on the implicit assumption that batterers change behavior only after altering their attitudes, perceptions, and interpersonal skills, with the use of appropriate programs.

Whether such a program can be effective under a court order has not been documented fully. After all, treatment programs rely on a series of assumptions, some of which have not yet been proven empirically across the diverse range of batterers. They generally assume that character traits or inappropriate learned behavior patterns favoring violence lead to recurrent violent explosions. Most programs implicitly assume that these patterns are consistent among batterers, by assuming that batterers will respond to a standardized intervention. From this, it is assumed that batterers can change their behavior but only after altering such attitudes, perceptions, and interpersonal skills through intervention of skilled counselors.

It also is assumed that the offender wants to be rehabilitated. If not, rehabilitation as a process might be difficult, and compliance might evolve into an offender's learning what to say and when, knowing what the treatment program administrator or therapist wants to hear, not into real attitudinal change. Paradoxically, early writers noted that some offenders had retrograde misogynist comments routinely made in groups of batterers, which were actually reinforced by other batterers (Harrell, 1991).

Proper intervention begins with an understanding that the classification of batterers and the availability of appropriate programs for different types of offenders is critical. For example, it has been argued that batterers found to be generally antisocial and suffering from serious psychopathology should not be included in "standardized" batterer treatment programs because they are unlikely to respond appropriately. When included in such programs, their victims might be in increased danger. Many victims might believe that the offender is "improving" and therefore remain with the individual during the treatment period (Goolkasian, 1988). Instead, this type of offender might require long-term, extensive court supervision, coupled with more individually based treatment, and distance from those he might harm.

Therefore, effective programs should reflect the diversity among batterers (National Research Council, 1998; Saunders, 1993). In a later study, Gondolf and White (2000) argued that such offenders were the exception, not the rule. They reported that 60% of "repeat reassaulters," which constituted 20% of program participants, showed no serious personality dysfunction or psychopathology. They argued that batterer counseling might be appropriate for many of these seemingly high-risk offenders.

Previously, we demonstrated the covariance between domestic violence and a variety of factors such as poverty, substance abuse, personality disorders, and employment. Although the need for an individualized response to batterer psychopathology might be argued, few would disagree with the premise that additional treatment should be given for those whose battering coincides with severe substance abuse. Simply treating someone with power-control theory or even anger-control management is unlikely to succeed when the critical trigger is the loss of inhibitions caused by severe alcoholic binges.

This might be significant because apart from batterer programs housed within correctional facilities, program access to counseling as a diversion from the criminal justice system is part of a court-ordered diversionary process.

We note that the judiciary has historically been reluctant to categorize batterers or otherwise recognize different types to try to determine the likelihood of program success. Some programs use formal contracts to match offender commitments to change their behavior and attend counseling sessions with an agreement from the prosecution regarding future behavior.

Within limits, such agreements might be tailor-made to the offender's individual behaviors or needs (Chalk & King, 1998). For example, given the strong correlation between substance abuse and domestic violence, they might contain intermediate goals such as cessation of substance abuse or prevention of any subsequent contact with the victim until counseling has been completed. Naturally, the long-term goal of all such programs is to rehabilitate the offender, ending his propensity for violence. The prosecutor's office might handle case screening with assistance from domestic violence specialists or in an integrated treatment model coordinated through probation.

Similarly, even the timing of treatment programs has a significant impact on their success. Counseling, or batterer treatment following the concept of a "teachable moment" in learning theory, ideally should begin almost immediately after a violent episode, when the offender feels most remorseful, most frightened of the criminal justice system, and most receptive to demands for change. There is a sound therapeutic basis for such early intervention. It is well known that the defendant might be most amenable to behavioral change within the period immediately after the battering incident.

Avoiding long court proceedings typically lasting more than 6 months from incident to conviction (and then longer for sentencing) might increase the impact of counseling and its ultimate chance of success. Consequently, most intervention programs now hold the offender accountable by forcing him to acknowledge criminal conduct, even if in the context of a "no-contest" plea to a charge of assault before addressing the violent behavior via an intervention program.

Program Characteristics and Conditions for Participation

In the previous editions of this book, we noted that treatment standards varied considerably in duration, modality, and emphasis. It was, therefore, difficult to describe a model program, or even to evaluate batterer treatment programs in general since one batterer treatment program bore little resemblance to those in another jurisdiction, even in the same state. Now, as part of the increased attention to domestic violence, most states have developed standards for batterer intervention treatment. As of 2008, 45 states plus the District of Columbia now have such standards and regulations, whereas in 1999 there were only 25, and often of far less detail (Maiuro & Eberle, 2008, as compared with Austin & Dankwort, 1999).

Program Duration

The standards that states have developed might vary, but directives by definition include what constitutes a batterer intervention program. An excellent review by Maiuro and Eberle (2008) describes the status of state standards. The standards imposed typically include minimum duration, prescribed content, modality of treatment, and victim involvement. They note that the recommended duration of treatment varies among the states from a minimum of 12 weeks in Utah to a year or more, with most (62%) requiring a minimum of 6 months, and approximately 50% using a 90-minute session once or twice a week. California mandates programs for all domestic violence offenders that seem to be of the greatest duration—a 52-week batterer program supervised by local probation departments (Rempel, 2009).

Program Content

Maiuro and Eberle (2008) posited an interesting analysis of program content standards. Many states have adopted what we might call a "feminist perspective" on domestic violence. In these states, a program seeking certification would need to focus on "power and control dynamics." This approach is interesting in that it assumes that various other emphases either would be misplaced or would detract from the overall treatment of a batterer. For example, although many researchers believe that several individual variables affect the likelihood of domestic violence, these are not emphasized.

Although psychological and psychopathology factors are recognized as possible contributing influences in some standards, many states forbid the primary use of treatments based on mental health or "disease" models, psychodynamic theory, impulse control disorders, codependency, family systems, or addiction models (35%). The common rationales for limiting the use of such approaches have to do with minimizing the perpetrator's sense of responsibility or potential endangerment of the victim (Maiuro & Eberle, 2008, pp. 136–137).

We find this limitation on program orientation too restrictive. As discussed previously, the reasons for domestic violence and likelihood of reoffending vary considerably among batterers. The implicit assumption of relatively rigid standards primarily is framed by a perspective that violence relates to issues of power and control dynamics.

Although this orientation might be appropriate for many batterers, its emphasis mini-mizes the role of mental health issues, anger-management skills, and substance abuse. These factors might limit the efficacy of treatment if not adequately addressed. An illus-tration is an offender who might never believe in feminist theory on "power and control dynamics." His upbringing, psychodynamics, socialization, and/or religious training might result in a belief system supporting the man as the patriarch of his family. For example, a religious leader might say any theory to the contrary defies "God's law." Are we to state that batterer treatment programs will supersede strong religious beliefs?

If not, an alternate approach needs to exist to stop these offenders from continuing violence against women. However, it would be a mistake to assume that just because a program geared solely to "power and control" issues leaves him utterly cold that a dif-ferent program focusing on anger control would necessarily fail.

Similarly, many acts of domestic violence occur or are comorbid with substance abuse. Many domestic violence–treatment programs state that substance abuse issues "have to be controlled" prior to entry into batterer programs. That sounds appealing in theory, but in practice, most reoffending occurs long before substance abuse can be totally resolved. Although this is not a treatise on the control of substance abuse issues, we know that eradication or least control of a substance abuse issue is neither quick to achieve nor easy to maintain. Most substance abuse issues need continuous reinforce-ment. Finally, there is a serious disconnect between such programs and the various state statutes defining domestic violence. As stated previously, one third of incidents captured under domestic violence statutes and, hence, whose offenders are subject to these stan-dardized treatment modalities, are not there because of violence in an intimate rela-tionship. For example, should a 15-year-old juvenile who assaults his or her parent be mandated to attend a program with a focus on "power and control"?

For these reasons, the use of ideologically driven standards to control content rigidly and omit key individual variables effectively seems problematic at best. Hence, although the standards might be good in setting a minimum requirement in terms of duration and the necessary background and training of care providers, they also might set undue restraints on therapies that might have significant utility.

Group Therapy as the Treatment Norm

It is interesting that the guidelines used now emphasize group therapy as the primary source of intervention. Two states, Georgia and Maine, have standards that prohibit the use of individual therapy (Maiuro & Eberle, 2008). Since previous studies have demon-strated that there is no recognized superior modality of treatment (see especially Norlander & Eckhardt, 2005), we suspect that the real reason is that individual therapy might be too expensive for a state to sanction.

We find such guidelines once again to be too restrictive to the extent that if indi-vidual, psychological issues dominate an offender's behavior, these might be addressed only tangentially in a group setting with other individuals who have a broad range of issues. Similarly, it is well known to psychologists that some individuals are resistant to group therapy treatment. These people, who might need help the most, tend to be nonverbal and are only willing to confide in one person, the therapist, and not in a group of peers.

It is interesting that it has been proposed that the lack of a person's ability to handle conflict verbally rather than physically is predictive of future violence, making the mandating of group therapy even more puzzling. Finally, some might argue that group therapy risks a reinforcement of batterer behavior. Some batterers will get to know each other and, being resistant to the "power and control ideology" espoused, might informally discuss alternative methods of tormenting their victim. In short, the facile assumption that group therapy is the ideal approach for all offenders does not seem justified.

Victim Participation

Unlike counseling programs discussed previously in this chapter, virtually all programs prohibit required mandatory or otherwise coerced victim participation in the treatment (Maiuro & Eberle, 2008). Most will, however, notify victims of the status of the offender in the program, and some will allow her participation or the participation of other family members on an as-needed basis. We believe this is appropriate as mandatory participation of the victim might victimize her even more, especially if she has chosen to terminate the relationship.

Continued Involvement of the Judicial System

Suspension of prosecution is a critical element to diversionary use of batterer treatment programs. In such instances, the criminal case is not heard or the sentence is suspended if the offender agrees to and attends required counseling sessions. If a counseling program is deemed successful for a particular offender, then after an established time—typically 6 months to 1 year—the original suspended prosecution is dropped and records of the original offense are destroyed or "filed."

Counseling or batterer intervention programs used for pretrial diversion should be considered different from counseling imposed as a form of sentence. In the former case, prosecutors must be cognizant of the responsibility to protect defendants' constitutional rights; this includes making certain defendants are aware that charges will be reinstated if they quit the counseling program. In summary, batterer treatment programs cannot be viewed in isolation from a strong criminal justice presence enforced by the prosecution and courts. In a National Institute of Justice sponsored analysis of batterer intervention programs, Healey, Smith, and O'Sullivan (1998) listed, among other things, the following relationships between such programs and the criminal justice system that they thought would increase the likelihood of program success:

- Expedited disposition of domestic violence cases by the system, so that if the offender does not remain in treatment, the alternative is stark and credible
- Specialized domestic violence courts with centralized dockets, again to reinforce the credibility of the system
- Rapid collection of relevant offender data to ensure similarity for diversion and that the type of program used is best matched to the offender
- Coordination of batterer intervention with substance abuse treatment with the periodic monitoring by probation officers of the offender's substance abuse status

Therefore, if the offender leaves counseling or recidivates, the prosecutor ideally should be committed to prosecuting both the original and any subsequent offenses. Whereas the counseling itself would typically be handled by community-based mental health professionals rather than by probation officers, subsequent case tracking to monitor for new offenses, violation of terms of probation, or other court orders would be handled by probation officers that have relatively easy access to judges and prosecutors.

The fact is that the act of battering indicates the existence of a potential for continued violence, even when batterer intervention programs are instituted. As such, it might be critical to distinguish risks for future violence by offenders based on a host of factors and risk markers such as criminal history and age at first offense (Buzawa, Hotaling, Klein, & Byrne, 1999), heavy substance use and psychopathology (Gondolf, 1997), victim input (Buzawa et al., 1999; Hotaling & Buzawa, 2001; Weisz, 1999), and even batterers' self-assessments.

Despite efforts to develop a valid predictive instrument that would best assess when treatment programs could be a safe substitute for incarceration, no such categorization is available and is one that is unlikely to appear in the near future, given the vast array of factors involved (e.g., situational variables such as access to the victim, further substance abuse, and offender compliance) that might prove to be intervening variables (Gondolf, 1997).

Advantages of Batterer Intervention Programs

There are several distinct advantages of court-sponsoring and mentoring batterer intervention programs. These finesse the two greatest weaknesses of the current response to domestic violence: the inability of the criminal justice system to prevent victims or prosecutors from dismissing charges and the inability to tell how likely a given offender is to reoffend or engage in future violence.

By selective use of these programs as a diversion, the finite resources available in the criminal justice system also might be focused more effectively on recidivist batterers or on cases in which the potential for serious continued violence seems greatest based on past or current attitudes and behaviors.

Most of our attention will be placed on court-mandated batterer treatment programs, since as we will discuss, they have a higher rate of program completion and seemingly correlate highly with a future successful outcome.

However, we also are aware that in certain cases, perhaps of first-time offenders with a relatively minor offense, a pretrial diversion into "treatment"—be it anger control, other mental health concerns, and/or substance abuse—might be appropriate in the instances where the judicial sentence would undoubtedly provide only a monetary fine, probation, or counseling. In these cases, the ideal option for these relatively low-risk offenders is to accomplish behavioral change quickly without incurring the heavy transactional costs to the judicial system or the necessity of labeling the offender as a convicted miscreant, risking secondary deviance or costing the victim and her family.

Because assignment to a batterer intervention program is considered less "punitive" than an adjudicated sentence and conviction for a domestic violence offense, this type of therapeutic intervention can start literally months before treatment is imposed as a condition of sentence. As noted previously, early intervention tends to be far more effective at facilitating long-term behavioral change.

Finally, we should note that an advantage of batterer treatment programs might be the effect on people other than the batterer. Research has shown that most victims are more satisfied with case outcomes if their batterer is forced to attend a batterer intervention program. That is not surprising given that it demonstrates that the system has recognized that a crime has been committed and is actually attempting to prevent future victimization. As we will discuss, the imposition of a batterer intervention program might collaterally help the victim because if the batterer cannot complete the program (even if the program itself is not of much use), if the risk of future violence is high, and if prosecutors and the court can come to realize that fact, they will target considerable resources toward those who do not complete the programs.

There also are tertiary benefits to batterer treatment programs for other members of the family; for example, children might be even more likely than their parents not to understand the Byzantine machinations of the criminal justice system. They can presumably understand more easily that their father (or mother) has a serious problem that is being addressed. This might make the child more likely to recognize that battering itself is abnormal and is not condoned far more than simply imposing a prison sentence where the family is inextricably broken up by "external forces."

Impact of Batterer Intervention Programs

Even though many states now mandate treatment for men convicted of domestic assault or require treatment as a condition of deterred sentencing, the effectiveness of such programs has been severely questioned. An initial 1998 meta-analysis of seven studies examining the impact of batterer intervention reported no profound effect for treatment, with a recidivism rate of 32% for the treated offenders and 34% for the control group. A subsequent analysis of research relying on police and court data for rates of reoffending found only a modest effect—14% for treated offenders compared with 22% for the control group (Levesque, 1998). A National Institute of Justice analysis perhaps best summarized current concerns.

Although numerous evaluations of batterer interventions have been conducted, most of these studies were inconclusive because of methodological problems, such as small samples, a lack of random assignment or control groups, high attrition rates, short or unrepresentative program curriculums, short follow-up periods, or unreliable or inadequate sources of follow-up data (e.g., only arrest data, only self-reported data, or only data from the original victim) (Babcock, Green, & Robie, 2004). Among evaluations considered methodologically sound, most have found modest but statistically significant reductions in recidivism among men participating in batterer interventions (Healey et al., 1998).

The most recent NIJ-sponsored study by Klein (2009) summarizes the current perspective on the value of most programs as they are currently used (e.g., not necessarily "ideal programs" but those that have actually been implemented):

> During this time, there have been more than 35 evaluations of batterer intervention programs, but they have yielded inconsistent results. Two meta-analyses of the more rigorous studies find the programs have, at best, a "modest" treatment effect, producing a minimal

reduction in rearrests for domestic violence. In one of the meta-analyses, the treatment effect translated to a 5-percent improvement rate in cessation of reassaults due to the treatment. In the other, it ranged from none to 0.26, roughly representing a reduction in recidivism from 13 to 20 percent.

On the other hand, a few studies have found that batterer intervention programs make abusers more likely to reabuse or have found no reduction in abuse at all.

The multi-state study of four batterer programs concludes that approximately a quarter of batterers appear unresponsive and resistant to batterer intervention. In this long-term study, based on victim and/or abuser interviews and/or police arrests, approximately half of the batterers reassaulted their initial or new partners sometime during the study's 30-month follow-up. Most of the reassaults occurred within the first six months of program intake. Nearly a quarter of the batterers repeatedly assaulted their partners during the follow-up and accounted for nearly all of the severe assaults and injuries. (p. 65)

Program Completion as a Marker for Successful Outcomes

Given that evidence does not show the robust effect of batterer intervention programs themselves, perhaps a better measure of effectiveness might be the preliminary findings related to program completion. Valuable data concerning the likelihood of future reoffending behavior might be generalized regardless of whether the batterer intervention program is itself effective, or is instead a correlate of the likelihood to reoffend. If program completion data predict the likelihood of reoffending, then these data can be potentially valuable in guiding future intervention strategies for a particular offender.

Different batterer treatment programs have variable rates of completion. The most recent estimate analyzing a series of different studies found that different rates of non-completion range from 25% to 89%, with the average being approximately 50% (Klein, 2009). This variance gives researchers the opportunity to determine whether completion of the program is correlated with future violence. This is important since program completion is highly correlated with reduced future violence; yet the programs themselves are not of significant value. Therefore, the importance of such programs might be that they serve as a highly effective predictor or marker of future violent behavior.

It does seem that program completion is a highly significant marker for future success defined as decreased or cessation of violence. A Chicago study of more than 500 batterers referred to 30 different programs found that recidivism after an average of 2.4 years was only 14.3% for those who completed the program, whereas recidivism for those who did not complete more than doubled to more than 34.6% (Klein, 2009, footnote 12). Even more importantly, the relative effect of program completion has been determined both long term and predictive of all forms of future violence.

A Massachusetts study found that, during a 6-year period, those who completed a certified batterer intervention program were significantly less likely to be rearraigned for any type of offense, including a violent offense or a protection order violation. (Massachusetts does not have a domestic violence statute, so researchers could not differentiate domestic from non–domestic violence offenses.) The rate differences for these offenses, between those who completed a program and those who did not, was as follows: 47.7 versus 83.6% for any crime, 33.7 versus 64.2% for a violent crime, and 17.4 versus 41.8% for violation of a protective order (Klein, 2009, p. 69; see footnote 18).

The importance of this research, therefore, is not so much that a particular batterer intervention program might make an offender less likely to offend, although as the preceding data show, some programs do seem to be more successful in preventing repeat acts of violence. The point, however, is that the differentiation of offenders by the simple form of monitoring compliance with batterer treatment programs themselves might prove to be a valuable tool in predicting reoffending. As such, program completion and/or more precisely noncompletion should become a key variable that judges use to determine final sentencing. This assumes that the sentencing structure and the judge are sufficiently flexible to include program completion as part of the mandated sentence. If the offender cannot control his behavior during the relatively short period of a batterer treatment program, the judge should assume that absent any other intervention strategy, he will reoffend and, therefore, should consider incarceration as a more radical intervention technique.

This could explain why court-mandated programs are important. They have higher rates of completion and ultimate success than those serving voluntary participants. We know that offenders can deny the criminal nature of their conduct. Without a judicial order, batterers might enter a voluntary program during the "honeymoon" or "remorseful stage" of a typical domestic violence cycle. When this mood changes, the voluntary offender might quickly drop out without some form of court or administrative sanction.

Evidence does suggest that batterers who are voluntary participants to treatment are more likely to reoffend than those who are court referred. Gondolf (1997) conducted a 15-month follow-up of 840 batterers in four cities and reported that 44% of voluntary participants reoffended compared with 29% of court-ordered participants who reoffended. Similarly, a San Diego study (Peterson & Thunberg, 2000) reported significantly increased program attendance after compliance hearings became routine. It is indeed possible that this differential offender response might be a result of the threat of further criminal justice involvement by offenders already in the court system rather than the treatment itself.

Quite frankly, it might be, as many have implied, that it is the imposition of a court-ordered metric, regular monitoring of the compliance with such treatment programs that become the key variable. One study (Bocko, Cicchetti, Lempicki, & Powell, 2004) showed that where specialized probation and aggressive monitoring were used, program completion increased to 62% compared with 39% when probation did not include such supervision (see also Klein, 2009; Rempel, 2009).

Hamberger and Hastings (1993) summarized the existing studies on the demographic profile of hard-core offenders. What is perhaps most disheartening, although not altogether unexpected, is that this profile mirrors that of the hard-core offender that the Minneapolis Domestic Violence Experiment (MDVE) replication studies suggested were not particularly affected by other interventions such as arrest.

Although completion rates are an important predictor of future conduct, the long-term and far more significant goal is to prevent offenders from reoffending. All programs have criteria by which they determine program success; however, there is an increasing and positive tendency to use competency-based criteria rather than simply that of mere program completion. If a batterer attends half of a 26-week course or attends irregularly, then he might not technically meet program completion requirements even if he did achieve the program goals of attitudinal changes. Contrast this with an offender who attended all sessions but who did not participate nor make any attitudinal changes, such as accepting responsibility for his actions. The latter would have technically "completed" the program, but success in changing attitudes is, at best, problematic (Bennett & Williams, 2001), even if the data do suggest that program completion is an important predictor of success.

Therefore, it might be wise to reconsider and orient program completion definitions. Should it be determined by the achievement of individual competency measures rather than the mere attendance at a set number of sessions? Alternatively, should psychological testing examine long-term personality or response change as it has been found to affect success rates? Deschner (1984), Hamberger and Hastings (1986), as well as Hawkins and Beauvais (1985) all reported that the mental health of the abuser at the end of the program seems to be important to long-range prospects for success. Similarly, future studies of the effect of such rehabilitative programs should assess offenders to determine whether individual characteristics of the offender—such as age, race, ethnic origin, histories of crime, and substance-abuse profile—significantly bear on rates of program success.

Although the two concepts are not the same, in addition to being only a measure of short-term success, program completion might provide a reasonably good indicator of future recidivism. Studies that have assessed the frequency of recurring violence as a measurement of program effectiveness have tended to show far different rates of recidivism for those who complete the program versus those who quit. Among program completers, the reported rates of recidivism have varied considerably across different studies. Hamberger and Hastings (1993) reviewed 28 studies for the effect of treatment programs on batterers. They noted that depending on whether success is defined as the complete cessation of violence versus reduction in frequency or severity of violence, the rates of recidivism ranged from 4% to 16% to as high as 47%. It also is noteworthy that several studies have not attributed much of an overall effect of treatment on subsequent rates of violence (Taylor, Davis, & Maxwell, 2001). Of course, it is possible that the variability in reported recidivism might be an artifact of several factors, including the studies' small sample sizes, the varying sampling techniques, the different measures of recidivism (including the time period being measured), and the fact that the people responsible for program implementation wrote much of the evaluative research, clearly presenting potential conflicts of interest. For example, Dutton (1987) freely acknowledged that the subjects in his 1986 study were batterers whose participation and treatment were determined in part by their willingness to participate in the treatment program. The low recidivism rate reported in his study might, therefore, be partially attributable to the self-selection of a group that was likely to be positively affected. Recidivism data in other studies originated in a national survey of violence abatement programs (Pirog-Good & Stets, 1986) or estimates of recurrence obtained from victims, batterers, and police reports. Thus, the variability in reported recidivism rates might reflect not only the probable success or failure rates of various programs but also the variance in treatment selection criteria and the sources of recidivism data.

Several small-scale studies that compared the recidivism of these two groups, however, have shown differences. Dutton (1986) as well as Hamberger and Hastings (1986) found significantly lower rates of recidivism among program completers compared with studies by Gondolf (1984), Halpern (1984), as well as Hawkins and Beauvais (1985), in which no truly significant differences were found between those who completed and those who dropped out of treatment programs.

It seems that until recently, much research in this area has reported the impact of treatment in isolation. This, of course, is merely an abstract of reality. More important is that mandated batterer programs might synergistically affect other aspects of the criminal justice system. For example, court-mandated counseling might have an indirect role in mediating the success of arrest. Dutton and Strachan (1987) found an apparent contradiction in the literature in recidivism after arrest. They reported that studies showing that arrest reduced recidivism used short-term measurements of success, often 6 months, as in Sherman and Berk's (1984a) MDVE. In their own study, however, they found that recidivism increased considerably, to almost 40%, within 30 months after the arrest, when no subsequent criminal justice action or batterer treatment followed the initial arrest. This was compared with an overall recidivism rate of 4% in the group that received counseling after arrest. In fact, they found that 84% of the wives of arrested and treated men reported no further acts of severe violence directed toward them during the entire 30-month follow-up period in the group in which the offenders were subjected to treatment programs. Consequently, a long-term decrease in recidivism might occur when arrest was paired with subsequent treatment (Dutton, 1986).

Therefore, Dutton's (1986) research suggested tentatively that although arrest had only a short-term deterrent effect, arrest plus an effective treatment program might have a long-term impact. Similarly, Ford and Regoli's (1993) research in Indianapolis found that court-mandated counseling as a condition of either diversion or probation reduced the chance of violence during the 6 months after case settlement (but before completion of counseling). It was no more effective than any other case outcome, however.

Regardless of the controversial impact of batterer intervention programs, it seems that they will continue to play a primary role in our judicial response to battering. Currently, legislative mandates are now imposed on the judiciary, and political realities and a lack of financially viable alternatives exist. Perhaps of greatest significance is that we lack evidence on effective strategies.

Types of Batterer Intervention Programs

We also should resist considering the category of treatment programs as a monolithic entity. Such programs vary enormously in structure and even in their purpose. This obviously might affect the rates of program success. For example, the sophistication and size of a program and the type of counseling (group versus individual sessions) intuitively would seem to have the potential to produce different rates of program success. Gondolf (1984) has already reported that the number and duration of sessions are determinative factors in the odds of successful batterer treatment.

Currently, the preferred approach to batterer intervention has been to focus on matching offenders with an appropriate program (Healey et al., 1998). As Saunders (1993) noted, treatment programs are likely to be more effective if they are designed to accommodate different types of batterers. For example, a treatment program that did not effectively deal with alcohol abuse might not fully address the unique problems of an alcoholic who is abusive when drunk. Although each treatment program is perforce unique, it is conceivable that programs might have differential rates of success depending on the qualifications or treatment pursued, style of the program (group or individual), as well as its length and duration. The dilemma is that current typologies based on personality types are not of great value because of both the comprehensive assessments needed and the lack of appropriate programs once these assessments are actually made (Healey et al., 1998). Furthermore, one study examining the utility of batterer typologies reported that many batterers were classified differently and that professionals had great difficulty selecting the appropriate subtype (Langhinrichsen-Rohling, Huss, & Ramsey, 2000). Because of numerous methodological issues—including high attrition rates, lack of statistical evaluations, lack of control groups, and nonrandom assignment to treatment groups—few definitive conclusions can be made. Perhaps we are now in the long, slow process of moving from the relatively sterile question of whether treatment works to a more productive exploration of the efficacy of many possible interventions with particular types of offenders.

As noted previously, batterer treatment programs of various types have been around for more than 30 years. Based on this, we would expect a well-developed empirically based literature that states what works and what does not work. This outcome would be expected in any intervention strategy. Unfortunately, one of the somewhat discordant facts that research has shown is that the type of batterer treatment program does not seem to affect materially the likelihood of success. The latest research has demonstrated that the type of batterer treatment program, whether it is "feminist," "psychoeducational," or "cognitive-behavioral," does not affect rates of reabuse (Klein, 2009; Saunders, 2009). Similarly, despite predictions to the contrary, programs that were culturally focused on particular groups of batterers (in this case, Blacks), had no greater success than nonfocused programs (Gondolf, 2005).

This does not mean that no aspects of customizing a program are significant. For example, the length of the program does seem to be correlated positively with successful outcomes (perhaps somewhat cynically simply because the offenders knew they were being monitored for a longer period of time) (Davis, Taylor, & Maxwell, 2000). However, it has been debated whether the length of the program is generalizable to all types of offenders (Gondolf, 2002, 2005).

When Should Batterer Intervention Programs Be Used?

In light of relatively modest indicators of success, some resources devoted to generalized batterer intervention programs might be more effectively targeted for specific groups of offenders, such as first-time offenders as well as their victims. Such programs could include victim counseling, early education, and family-based interventions. All batterer intervention programs have certain costs and administrative limitations. Treatment, other than on a group basis, is time intensive and expensive to an otherwise overloaded system. Meanwhile, research suggests that the most effective programs might require long commitments to therapy because differences in recidivism have been observed between shorter, less-intensive therapies and a 9-month program incorporating mental health and substance abuse treatments for the offender and even assistance to the victims of the original abuse (Gondolf, 1999). Moreover, the costs of batterer intervention programs are greatly increased by the large percentage of offenders who do not complete treatment.

Furthermore, the cost of counseling is but one component of this continued case monitoring. Case tracking by probation officers is both necessary and expensive. When an offender loses contact with the probation officer or the prosecutor's office, it is relatively easy for him to push the limits of a treatment program, gaining little real benefit. For this reason, the costs of counseling indigent offenders far exceed those for voluntary dismissals in which the prosecutor merely agrees to a negotiated plea followed by minimally supervised probation.

Many advocates do not necessarily understand this conflict over scarce resources. It can be argued that more funds are needed and should be provided for shelters and services for battered women rather than counseling for offenders. We recognize this position is morally difficult to refute. After all, the needs of victims of crimes should intuitively take precedence over those of an offender. The unfortunate reality is that shelters can realistically provide only a brief respite from abuse for some women, "harden targets," and sometimes help the victim make major life changes. If, however, an offender is not rehabilitated, then violence is likely to recur with either the same or another victim. For this reason, allocation of resources to offender counseling, if successful, might prove far more cost effective than shelters or, at the least, a good complement to them.

It also has been suggested that counseling could be more effective if it is part of a split sentence and coupled with incarceration to reinforce the importance of changing behaviors. Although incarcerating abusers might deter others by labeling this behavior as clearly criminal, surrounding abusers with other violent men in a prison environment might increase violent tendencies on their release. Indeed, some researchers have suggested that it might even teach them how to become "nonviolent terrorists" who can commit abuse effectively and legally (Gondolf, 1992), perhaps by stalking or through other forms of harassment. Alternatively, batterers form their own "support groups," reinforcing each other's behaviors.

Anecdotal information indicates that incarceration might have these unanticipated effects. For example, we have been told that the Quincy (Massachusetts) Probation Department has had cases in which batterers have continued to violate restraining orders and have harassed their victims from jail by using friends, relatives, or other proxies. In fact, two incarcerated abusers have been indicted in Massachusetts for hiring fellow inmates who were to be released to murder their spouses (Klein, 1994a).

California Online Batterer Intervention Program

Clearly, criteria vary for batterer intervention programs. Take, for example, California, where batterers can complete their program online in 10, 16, or 52 weeks: http://www.courtorderedclasses.com/?gclid=CKuK6uTSr5kCFQUWGgodzHkoJQ

Most evidence does not report that batterer treatment programs work effectively in outcome measurements. There are multiple possibilities to explain these findings. First, these could be the wrong programs. As we noted previously, many of the statutory guidelines for certified programs seem to be based ideologically on a theory of power and control. If that is not the real driving force behind many batterers, then we cannot expect that to be effective as a strategy. Therefore, it might be the curriculum that is being used.

Second, budgetary constraints might vitiate otherwise promising programs. For example, we noted that California has a 52-week program for its requirements. Now, it has implemented a 52-week online program. Although we understand that this is far less costly than a face-to-face initiative, we doubt that an online program can be tailor-made to meet the needs of an individual offender; it might be difficult to monitor and impossible to test if attitudes were changed.

Third, batterer treatment programs need to be examined in the context of the overall judicial response. Both Klein (2009) and Rempel (2009) suggest that the type of program and duration is less important than the fact that the offender is under judicial supervision. In short, monitoring the defendant's conduct during the program period might be the significant factor. Hence, the program's real value might be that it provides the ability for the judge and the probation department to check on the offenders more often.

SUMMARY

As we discussed, much attention has been given to providing a victim-oriented focus and to allowing for options other than formal case processing in the criminal justice system. Restorative justice has provided options such as mediation, in which a domestic violence incident is handled privately, not publicly, with a trained mediator. Alternatively, other approaches bring in the community and focus on the need to hold the offender accountable to both the victim and society.

Batterer intervention programs initially were developed as a way of addressing offender treatment needs with an emphasis on changing how they think. However, the focus has now shifted to ensure batterer accountability. Therefore, in some ways, the intended outcome of all these efforts is similar. The question remains, though, whether offender accountability through any of these strategies can ensure victim safety.

DISCUSSION QUESTIONS

1. Should all victims be provided with restorative justice options as opposed to traditional criminal justice case processing? What implications would this have for tracking and monitoring offenders who leave the community?

2. Is there more likely to be bias toward either victims or offenders in cases of domestic violence compared with a jurisdiction with detailed protocols and policies in place?

3. Should the criminal justice system invest more money into developing effective treatment programs for batterers, or should the focus merely be on monitoring their behavior? Could more batterers be treated successfully if existing services and programs were expanded and improved?

4. How do you balance money spent on victim services compared with the treatment of offenders?

Domestic Violence, Health, and the Health System Response

14

Chapter Overview

Every victim of partner violence requires medical care at some point, including the millions who never call police, enter a shelter, or go to court. A successful strategy to prevent or limit the consequences of partner abuse is inconceivable apart from the active collaboration of medicine and public health. Yet, until studies conducted during the late 1970s and 1980s showed the significance of domestic violence for women's physical and mental health, the health professions were largely unaware of the problem.

This chapter describes the health consequences of partner abuse, tracks the response of the health professions and delivery systems since the first shelters opened in the early 1970s, and identifies the major challenges to integrating the health system into a comprehensive community response. These challenges include the need to screen for partner violence as a routine part of medical care, broaden the health approach to partner abuse beyond a narrow focus on physical violence and injury, and help clinicians appreciate what it means to provide health services in the context of partner violence.

The Role of Health Services

Victims of partner violence use health services more often than persons who are not abused (Pakesier, Lenaghan, & Muelleman, 1998). Some insurance companies have responded to this fact by denying coverage to women known to be battered or for problems thought to be the result of abuse, a practice known as "pink lining." An informal survey in 1994 by the staff of the Subcommittee on Crime and Criminal Justice of the United States Senate Judiciary Committee revealed that 8 of the 16 largest insurers in the country used domestic violence as a factor when deciding whether to issue insurance and how much to charge.

Studies by the Insurance Commissioners in Pennsylvania and Kansas revealed that 24% of the responding companies reported using domestic violence as an underwriting criterion when issuing and renewing insurance (Fromson & Durborow, 2001).

The Health Care Reform Act of 2010 outlaws insurance discrimination against domestic violence victims. However, unless insurance practices are closely monitored and laws are strictly enforced, improving the identification of battered women in the health system could backfire, making it more difficult for victims to access services. All the challenges we discuss are circumscribed by the need to ensure access to health care, a problem battered women in the United States share with the millions of other Americans who are uninsured or underinsured.

> Discrimination risks are real. A 1998 joint report developed by the Pennsylvania Coalition Against Domestic Violence (PCADV) and the Women's Law Project reported that a woman from rural Minnesota was beaten severely by her ex-husband. After remarrying, she applied for health insurance and was told that she would not be covered for treatment relating to the abuse-related preexisting conditions of depression and neck injury.

The reason why battered women turn to medicine for help may seem self-evident. Hospital emergency rooms are the logical place to treat injury. This chapter shows why it is wrong to think of domestic violence largely in terms of emergent injury or to target intervention primarily at the sites where emergencies are treated and why the preferred approach is to make clinical violence intervention a routine part of primary care for women.

We have chosen to focus on the health consequences and experiences of female rather than of male victims of partner abuse. Some of what we say about female victims of male partners undoubtedly applies to male victims of female partner violence as well as to victims of same-sex partner abuse. Although we have extensive evidence of female partner violence from population surveys, only a few studies have attempted to compare the abuse experiences of males and females in the health system or differentiated among victims by their sexual identification or orientation. These studies report that the modal pattern of violence is bidirectional. A substantial proportion of women acknowledge having used violence against their partners even among those using shelters or other services for abuse victims. However, these studies also have documented significant differences in the dynamics and outcomes of partner violence by sex. In both surveys and clinical samples, female victims of bidirectional violence report higher levels of fear than male victims. We again emphasize female victimization, both because of the paucity of data on male victims in the health system and because male partner victimization of women is much more common and serious in its consequences than partner victimization of men.

Phelan et al. (2005) compared men and women presenting complaints of injury at a level 1 trauma center for emergency medical services and who reported being in a currently violent or abusive relationship. In this study, men reported significantly higher rates of violence initiation than women did. One hundred percent of the men reported they initiated violence between 50% and 100% of the time. In contrast, 91% of the women reported initiating violence between 0% and 20% of the time. Even in situations where violence was bidirectional, the women in these relationships were significantly more likely than the men to be injured by partner violence, to be injured more severely, to seek health care, and to experience a range of negative health impacts, including clinically significant levels of depression and posttraumatic stress disorder (PTSD). Based on these findings, the authors concluded that male partner abuse of women is qualitatively different than female partner abuse, not merely different in the degree of violence deployed.

Devising an appropriate health system response is vital to any overall strategy to manage or prevent domestic violence. Moreover, the knowledge base exists to implement such a response. At a minimum, this response would build on the core values of medicine and public health, particularly their emphasis on beneficence and nonmalfeasance ("do no harm") rather than on punishment; their willingness to embrace prevention; a capacity to take a nonjudgmental, holistic, and historical approach to health issues; and their distinguished history of addressing problems that most people would prefer to keep under wraps. Understanding partner violence as the context for a range of health problems that currently confound medicine would significantly improve intervention with female patients at all ages. In addition, a medical/public health perspective offers a vantage point to understand partner violence that complements and goes beyond the criminal justice framework we have outlined in earlier chapters.

Reforming the health response requires that we come to grips with what it means to treat health problems in the context of partner violence, incorporate clinical violence education into the education and training of health professionals and put screening tools and intervention protocols in place that reflect practice shown to be efficacious. However, as with policing, reforming the professional response involves much more than merely mandating that health providers change their behavior. Reform efforts should extend to confronting an institutional culture of medicine, a culture that has been shaped by many of the same sexist beliefs about women held by society generally, as well as to confronting the prevailing medical model. This model views societal problems through the narrow prism of their biomedical, behavioral, and mental health manifestations, making it hard to address root causes.

The Need for and Use of Health Services by Battered Women

Two things were clear by the mid-1980s: (1) Battered women use health facilities of all types for a range of problems related to abuse and (2) health personnel neither identify the problem nor treat its victims appropriately. This section addresses the first of these issues, whereas the next section examines the health care response.

Early state and national population surveys made it clear that a significant proportion of abused women sought medical assistance because of partner assault. For example, 17% of the abused women responding to a Kentucky Harris poll reported using emergency medical services, and in Texas, 358,595 women reported they required medical treatment at some point because of abuse (Stark & Flitcraft, 1988; Teske & Parker, 1983). Based on these and similar findings, the American Medical Association (AMA Council of Scientific Affairs, 1992) estimated that more than 1.5 million women nationwide sought medical treatment for injuries related to abuse each year, an estimate that proved extremely conservative. The cost of domestic violence–related injury has been increasing sharply alongside the overall costs of health care, from approximately $5.8 billion in 1995, to $8.3 billion in 2003, to more than $10 billion today. These estimates include both the direct costs for medical and mental health services and the indirect costs, primarily for productivity lost as a result of partner homicide or time off for health care (Centers for Disease Control and Prevention [CDC], 2003; Max, Rice, Finkelstein, Bardwell, & Leadbetter, 2004).

The estimates stated previously were largely based on reports from abused women about their need for health care, primarily for injury caused by assault. A more exacting set of studies examined the actual use of health services by battered women. Early estimates of health use by battered women were based primarily on medical record reviews. Hospital-based studies conducted in the 1970s and 1980s reported that between 18.7% and 30% of female trauma patients had a history of domestic violence (Stark & Flitcraft, 1996). Moreover, abuse-related injury was shown to be a major problem at each point in a woman's adult life cycle, accounting for 34% of the injuries to young women ages 16–18 years, for instance, as well as 18% of the injuries presented by older women 60+ years (McLeer & Anwar, 1989).

The largest of the early hospital-based studies was conducted at Yale-New Haven Hospital. In the Yale Trauma Studies, Stark and Flitcraft (1996) analyzed a random sample of medical records for more than 3,600 female patients who had come to the emergency room complaining of injury as well as for subsamples drawn from the child-abuse caseload, prenatal clinics, women who had been raped and attempted suicide, and from the psychiatric emergency service. The most startling finding from this work was that domestic violence was the most common source of adult injuries for which women sought medical attention. At the time, auto accidents were thought to be the most common cause of adult injury, but these data only accounted for slightly more than half as many injuries as abuse (11% versus 18.7%).

Once the availability of services made it ethically appropriate to ask female patients directly about their experience with abuse, researchers reported an even higher prevalence of abuse in the medical population. For instance, 54.2% of female patients disclosed a history of abuse in a multihospital study in Colorado (Abbott, Johnson, Kozial-McLain, & Lowenstein, 1995). A recent review of research in this area estimated that, on average, between 30% and 35% of women who visit the emergency service for injury are abused (Boes, 2007). It would be a mistake, however, to think that the emergency room is the only or even the best site for clinical violence intervention.

When researchers investigated primary care sites, they found that the proportion of female patients who identified themselves as abused was similar to or even greater than the proportion in the emergency room. In a large study of female partner abuse conducted in a primary care setting, 21.4% of the 1,952 women surveyed suffered physical and/or sexual abuse from an intimate male partner in their adult lives (Gin, Rucker, Frayne, Cygan, & Hubbell, 1991). Prevalence estimates from primary care sites fall between 7% and 29%, somewhat lower than estimates from emergency medical cites. However, some estimates from primary care are considerably higher. For instance, 55.1% of 1,443 women seeking medical care in two university-associated family practice clinics in Columbia, South Carolina, had experienced some type of intimate partner violence in a current, most recent, or past intimate relationship. Although most of these women (77.3%) experienced physical or sexual violence, 22.7% suffered the consequence of nonphysical abuse (Coker, Smith, McKeown, & King, 2000). Conversely,

38.8% of the women in a midwestern community-practice setting reported they had been abused (Hamberger, Saunders, & Hovey, 1992).

The fact that so large a proportion of female primary care patients has experienced abuse or is currently in an abusive relationship points toward the importance of identifying and responding to abuse wherever women seek medical care, not merely in the Emergency Room. Another rationale for intervening at primary care sites is that primary care medicine is predicated on the assumption of longitudinal responsibility for the patient regardless of the presence or absence of disease, and the integration of physical, psychological, and social aspects of health into a holistic understanding of a patient's needs.

The Significance of Abuse for Female Trauma

Medical research on abuse focused on trauma care initially because it was assumed that serious injury from physical and/or sexual assaults was the major reason women came to hospitals for help. Based on reviews in 1996 and 1998, the CDC reported that 40% to 60% of abused women were injured in the United States (National Center for Injury Prevention and Control, 2003). In a 2008 report, the CDC estimated that domestic violence resulted in approximately 2 million injuries to women and 600,000 injuries to men annually (CDC, 2008). In addition to the evidence on the extent of physical injury caused by abuse, anecdotal evidence that physical abuse was frequently accompanied by sexual assault was supported by findings that as many as a third of all reported rapes were committed by a current or former partner and that the proportion rose to one in two rapes if a victim was older than 30 years (Stark & Flitcraft, 1996).

Even at emergency sites, injury was not the only health problem presented by abused women. The Yale studies also showed battering to be a major context in which women attempted suicide. Battering was the context for 29.5% of all suicide attempts by women at Yale-New Haven Hospital, and for almost half (48.8%) of the suicide attempts by Black women (Stark & Flitcraft, 1996), making it by far the leading context in which Black women attempted suicide. Importantly, many of the abused women attempted suicide on the same day as or shortly after they had come to the emergency service for an abuse-related injury. Numerous emergency room visits also were prompted by other problems associated with abuse, including alcohol and drug abuse, psychiatric problems, HIV infection, and homelessness (Browne & Bassuk, 1997; Muelleman, Lenaghan, & Pakieser, 1998; Stark & Flitcraft, 1996). An indication of the potential benefits that might accrue because of intervention with women injured by abusive partners was that 41% of women killed by abusive partners had used the health system for abuse-related injury in the year prior to the fatality (Sharps et al., 2001, as cited by Plichta, 2004).

The Limits of Focusing on Emergent Injury

Responding to the serious injuries caused by abuse is obviously an important function of medical intervention. However, there are two important reasons why it is mistaken to equate abuse with emergent injury and so to focus intervention in emergency medical sites. The first reason why serious injury is a poor marker of abuse is that most partner assaults (well more than 90%) are noninjurious or cause only minor injury, even among abused women who come for help to the emergency department. Second, the most common and arguably the most devastating consequences of abuse for women's health include a range of general medical, behavioral, and psychological problems rather than injury. The prevalence of these problems explains why primary care visits play such an important role in the health-seeking by battered women. Although a small proportion of these problems can be linked directly to assault or to adaptations to the pain and fear associated with ongoing partner violence, most are rooted in other oppressive strategies.

The Nature of the Injuries Caused by Abuse

There is no need to minimize the seriousness of partner assaults to justify looking beyond injury when we consider how the health system should intervene. Alongside its association with rape, domestic violence frequently involves incidents of extreme violence, "beatings," choking, burning, torture, and the use of weapons that not only inflict severe injury but also can cause permanent disfigurement or death. In a British survey of 500 shelter residents, 70% had been choked or strangled at least once, 60% had been beaten in their sleep, 24% had been cut or stabbed at least once, almost 60% had been forced to have sex against their will, 26.5% had been beaten unconscious, and 10% had been "tied up." Because of these assaults, 38% of the women reported permanent damage (Rees, Agnew-Davies, & Barkham, 2006).

These dramatic events are not unusual. But even when incidents of severe violence occur in an abusive relationship, these are typically embedded in a long-standing pattern of minor violence that consists largely of pushing, shoving, grabbing, holding, shaking, arm twisting, hair pulling, slapping, punching, kicking, and so on. Thus, in the shelter sample from the United Kingdom mentioned previously, the women reported they were "shook or roughly handled" (58%); pushed, grabbed, shoved, or held (65%); slapped, smacked, or had their arm twisted (55.2%); and kicked, bit, or punched (46.6%) "often" or "all the time."

Of course, if someone falls down the stairs because they are pushed, serious injury can result. Moreover, in many states, these acts could be considered a domestic violence crime and result in arrest. Even so, from the perspective of the medical or criminal justice system, these assaults tend to fall near the bottom of the spectrum of severity. In the Yale Trauma Studies, for instance, of 2,123 visits to the emergency room by abused women who complained of injury, 9% involved no injury at all and the largest proportion, 58%, involved "contusions, abrasions or blunt trauma," "lacerations" and "sprains and strains." Although these terms refer to the mechanism of trauma rather than its severity, just 2% of these injuries required hospitalization or major medical care; this rate was no higher than among all other emergency service patients. Even when fractures or dislocations (9%), human bites (3%), and rapes (2%) were included, the data still showed that almost 90% of the injuries women presented would be classified as minor (Stark & Flitcraft, 1996). Similar findings have emerged from other sites where we might expect the severest outcomes of domestic violence to appear. In Connecticut cases where police made an arrest, for instance, only 3% of domestic violence victims were referred to medical care (Connecticut Department of Public Safety, 1999). Conversely, only 7% of substantiated cases that come to the attention of the military would be classified as severe enough to require more than one medical visit (Caliber Associates, 2002).

Abused women in the general population report even lower levels of injury than women who use the medical system. Among the abused women identified by a random population survey conducted by the Harris organization for the Commonwealth Fund, for instance, no woman reported she had been shot, stabbed, choked, or beaten up (Commonwealth Fund, 1999).

We can predict at least one implication of this evidence for health practice. Since most domestic assaults are noninjurious or cause only minor injury, if clinicians wait for serious injury before asking about abuse, they will miss as many as 90% of all cases. By contrast, routine questioning regardless of whether an injury is severe or even whether an injury is presented, will identify a much larger proportion of abuse cases.

The Secondary Consequences of Abuse

After the onset of abuse, battered women are at an increased risk for a range of medical, behavioral, and mental health problems that distinguish them from nonbattered women as well as from other classes of assault victims, including male and female victims of female partner abuse. Most battered women do not develop these problems, but the number of women who do is sufficiently alarming to affect the overall prevalence of these problems in the health system. Because of these secondary effects, the overall use of health services by victims of domestic violence is significantly greater than the comparable use by nonvictims, eliciting total annual health costs that are 19% higher than for women without a history of abuse (Rivara et al., 2007).

Battered women have an overall rate of physical health problems that is 60% higher than the rate for nonabused women (Campbell, 2002). Between 14% and 20% of these general medical problems are clearly related to assault or prior injury. The bulk of these presentations involve headaches from head trauma, traumatic brain injury, joint pain from twisting injuries, abdominal or breast pain after blows to the torso, dyspareunia or recurrent genitourinary infections from sexual assault, HIV or STDs as a result of partner sexual assault, dysphagia after choking, or chronic pain syndromes that often are exacerbated by the nonviolent forms of coercion and control that accompany physical abuse. Battered women also seek help for a range of problems that cannot be easily linked to abusive violence. These include functional gastrointestinal disorders, digestive problems, nutritional deficiencies, or central nervous system disorders. Up to 53% of female patients visiting pain clinics report physical and/or sexual abuse. Although many of these visits are clearly related to past and current injuries, battered women also are twice as likely as nonabused women to report pain unrelated to injury or "spontaneous" pain (Haber & Roos, 1985). Repeated somatic complaints also are a common presentation of battering, particularly among obstetrical patients, as are menstrual problems, sexual dysfunction, and pelvic pain. Not surprisingly, battered women are far more likely than nonabused women to rate their general health as fair or poor.

The psychosocial consequences of abuse are as important as the physical consequences. In the Yale Trauma Studies, Stark and Flitcraft (1996) compared a subset of 600 battered women with 600 nonabused controls. They found that the abused women were 5 times more likely to attempt suicide, 15 times more likely to abuse alcohol, 9 times more likely to abuse drugs, 6 times more likely to report fear of child abuse, and 3 times more likely to be diagnosed as depressed or psychotic. For example, 19% of abused patients attempt suicide at least once, and many make multiple attempts, whereas 38% were diagnosed as depressed or as having another situational disorder. Other common psychiatric problems presented by abused women include panic attacks, sleep disturbances, and agoraphobia. The absolute numbers of abused women with these problems were so significant that domestic violence emerged as a major context and, in some cases, with female suicide attempts, child abuse, and female alcohol abuse, for instance, as the major context in which these problems developed. Importantly, the incidence of these problems among battered women only became disproportionate after the onset of physical assault, unequivocal evidence that abuse was their context, if not always their proximate cause, rather than the result of a preexisting vulnerability.

Intimate partner violence also affects mental health. The CDC estimates that mental health services are provided to 26.4% of victims of partner violence. Numerous studies have found that victims of intimate partner violence report more symptoms and are diagnosed with psychiatric problems with greater frequency than nonabused women (Nicolaidis & Touhouliotis, 2006).

Abuse significantly increases a woman's risk of developing PTSD, depression, and a range of other psychological problems, perhaps by as much as 500% (Dutton et al., 2006; Golding et al., 1999). In the Yale studies, 1 in 10 abused women suffered a psychotic break.

One particular form of cognitive distortion widely thought to result from abuse is battered women's syndrome (BWS), which is a type of depression induced by repeated exposure to life-threatening violence. In its initial clinical description, psychologist Lenore Walker (1979) argued that victims experienced repeated "cycles of violence" consisting of tension buildup, an "explosion" of violence, and an apology (the "honeymoon phase"). If victims accepted their partner's excuses for violence and remained in the relationship, the cycle was repeated and they developed a profile of "learned helplessness," concluded that escape or turning to outside help was useless, and concentrated on survival instead. Walker's description has been largely discredited as a general account of how most battered women respond to abuse (Dutton, 1996). Research has demonstrated that most victims leave or attempt to break off the relationship, typically multiple times, and use outside resources. However, as many as 14% of abused women might exhibit BWS (Stark, 2007).

BWS often is classified as a subtype of PTSD, which is another common outcome of partner violence. The classic precondition for PTSD is exposure to an event that involves actual or threatened death or serious injury and that induces "intense fear, helplessness or horror" (*Diagnostic and Statistical Manual of Mental Disorders, IV-R* [*DSM-IV*], 1994). Recognizing that the traditional model failed to capture "the protean symptomatic manifestations of prolonged, repeated trauma" associated with abuse, psychiatrist Judith Herman (1992, p. 119) identified a pattern she called "complex PTSD" and applied it to victims of rape, incest, and partner assault. Complex PTSD is characterized by hyperarousal (chronic alertness), intrusion (flashbacks, floods of emotion, hidden reenactments), and constriction, "a state of detached calm . . . when events continue to register in awareness but are disconnected from their ordinary meanings" (Herman, 1992, p. 45). These symptoms are linked to a protracted depression not unlike that described by Walker as BWS. Several studies confirm that many battered women suffer from the symptoms of complex PTSD (as described by Herman) or classic PTSD (as outlined in the *DSM-IV*), particularly if they have been sexually and physically assaulted. Other studies suggest a higher than normal prevalence of psychosexual dysfunction, major depression, generalized anxiety disorder, and obsessive compulsive disorders among battered women, all of which are consistent with a PTSD framework (Dutton et al., 2006).

To some extent, the disproportionate risk of secondary health problems among battered women reflects their attempt to cope with or self-medicate the fear, pain, and stress associated with violent relationships. Whatever their etiology, however, many of these adaptive responses increase women's vulnerability to violence, compromise their decision-making ability, reduce their capacity to resist or escape abuse effectively, and cause a range of secondary medical and psychological problems. The destructive interplay between violence, at-risk behaviors, and subsequent negative health outcomes was illustrated in a study of teen violence. This work showed that the occurrence of sexual violence as well as both sexual and physical violence was associated with a victim's propensity for cocaine use, intercourse before 15 years of age, attempted suicide, heavy smoking, driving after drinking, binge drinking, laxative use and/or vomiting to control weight, pregnancy, and having three or more sex partners in the past 3 months (Silverman, Raj, Mucci, & Hathaway, 2001).

Exactly why male partner assault should elicit a unique problem profile in female victims is not clear. One explanation emphasizes the fear and stress elicited by the ongoing nature of the assaults they are experiencing. Another explanation highlights the effects of the nonviolent abusive tactics deployed by male partners to subjugate their partners in addition to assault, forms of intimidation, isolation, humiliation, and control that create a condition of entrapment akin to hostage taking. This strategy has been variously termed "patriarchal terrorism" (Johnson, 2008), "intimate terrorism" (Johnson, 2008), or "coercive control" (Stark, 2007). Whichever explanation we accept, it is clear that once the secondary effects of continuing domestic violence become the focus of women's health seeking, they reinforce their vulnerability to abuse, increase the probability they will engage in yet further high-risk behaviors, and increase the complexity of the health problems they present.

The Real Health Markers of Partner Violence and Their Cumulative Effects

The relatively minor nature of most domestic violence assaults does not mean that the abuse in these cases is minor, even in its health consequences. From the vantage of the medical system, the seriousness of abuse reflects its four hallmarks: (1) the frequency of assault, (2) the duration of abusive relationships, (3) its cumulative effects, and (4) the sexual nature of abuse.

The Frequency of Abusive Assaults

Dozens of studies have documented the frequency of assault in abuse cases. A few examples must suffice. In a Memphis study, 35% of the victims of violence in which an arrest was made were experiencing physical abuse daily (Brookoff, 1997). A Canadian study found that women who charged their husbands with assault had suffered an average of 30 previous abusive incidents (Jaffe, Wilson, & Wolfe, 1986a). Slightly lower frequencies are reported by population surveys. According to the National Family Violence

Survey, the National Violence Against Women Survey, and the National Youth Survey, for instance, persons who report a previous episode of abuse average between 3.5 and 8 assaults annually; many are beaten once a week or more, so-called serial abuse.

The frequency of abusive assault is reflected in the disproportionate use of health resources for domestic violence victims. Most adults have made one or two visits to the emergency room. At Yale's inner-city hospital, nonbattered women averaged 1.9 injury visits to the emergency medical service as adults. However, abused women averaged 5.7 injury visits and almost 1 in 5 had presented to the emergency room 11 or more times with complaints of injury (Stark & Flitcraft, 1996).

The Duration of Abuse

The frequency of assaults by partners takes its significance for health service use from the second marker of abuse, which is the duration of abusive relationships. From the perspective of the health system, partner abuse has a low "spontaneous cure rate." The adult medical records reviewed in the Yale Trauma Studies often covered 40 years or more. Nevertheless, if a woman in the sample had ever made a hospital visit related to partner abuse as an adult, there was a 92% chance she had presented at least one injury related to abuse in the last 5 years, which is the marker used to indicate that abuse might be a current concern. The average time span between the first abuse-related presentation to the hospital and the most recent was 7.3 years, which is called the "adult trauma history." Of course, since abuse might begin many years before a woman presents with an abuse-related injury to the hospital, her trauma history is a conservative measure of how long abuse had lasted. Many poor women use the emergency service for their primary care. Even so, at Yale, 80% of the adult women who had visited the emergency room three or more times had been battered. Combining estimates of frequency with the average duration of abusive relationships helps us understand how it is possible for abuse victims to have experienced hundreds of partner assaults.

The Cumulative Effects of Abuse

The frequency of partner violence in combination with its average duration elicits its third distinctive feature, the fact that health effects of abuse are the cumulative result of prolonged exposure rather than the by-product of discrete assaults. Many criminal populations commit multiple offenses of a similar kind. With abuse, however, the partner inflicts multiple harms on the same person. This means that the level of fear or the health or mental health problems observed in any particular encounter with a victim can only be understood in their historical context. Conversely, when a given level of fear or a behavioral, health, or mental health problem is *not* contextualized historically, clinicians can mistakenly conclude that a victimized woman is exaggerating (in the case of fear) or that the problem is from an internal disease mechanism rather than from abuse.

The fourth hallmark of abuse in the health system is its sexual nature. In one well-designed study, 37.6% of female primary care patients were identified as victims of partner violence. Almost half of these subgroup of abused women (18.1% of the total) also were sexually assaulted (Coker at al., 2000). In the Yale studies, battered women were 13 times more likely than nonbattered women to be injured in the breast, chest, face, and abdomen. The body map of abuse clearly identified its link to sexual power areas of the body frequently identified with female sexuality.

Many observers believe that the association of abuse and pregnancy also reflects the sexual nature of partner assault. Among battered women, physical abuse seems to escalate during pregnancy. Studies report that between 32% and 78% of pregnant women using the emergency medical service have been battered and that at least 15% of this group has experienced at least one partner assault during their current pregnancy (Datner, Wiebe, Brensinger, & Nelson, 2007).

The proportion of prenatal patients who are abused (21%) is even larger than the proportion of emergency patients (18.7%). Battered pregnant women are younger and less educated than their nonabused counterparts, are less likely to be married, and are significantly more likely to have trichomoniasis, report depressive symptoms, report high levels of psychosocial stress, and abuse substances. Not surprisingly, battering has been associated with a range of negative birth outcomes, including miscarriages.

The Cumulative Effect of Abuse

In his book *Coercive Control*, Evan Stark (2007) tells the story of Donna. One evening, shortly after she married, her husband tied her hands behind her back with a belt and "had his way with her" sexually. Fearing his reprisal, she never said no to his sexual demands again. Although he had only literally raped her once, she reported feeling as if she was being raped each time they had sex, and she suffered serious psychological deterioration as a result.

The Unique Contribution of Health to Defining and Measuring Abuse

The criminal justice system and health system take different approaches to how domestic violence is defined and measured. These different approaches reflect the different aims and paradigms from which criminal justice and health operate.

Domestic violence laws define abuse as a specific type of act and treat each instance of coercion by a partner as a separate offense. Whether this is the first arrest for an assault against a partner or the 500th makes no difference to his guilt or innocence for the particular crime. The four facets of abuse that are critical to the problems women present in the health system—its frequency, duration, cumulative effect, and sexual nature—have little or no standing in the criminal justice system. Furthermore, an offender's history of abuse or the likelihood that he will continue his abuse in the future is only marginally relevant to how his guilt or innocence for a particular act is assessed in the criminal court. The working definition of domestic violence in the health system is much broader than it is in the criminal justice system. Because there can be serious consequences for someone who is merely identified as a potential offender, the law and criminal justice strive to minimize the number of innocent persons included among those arrested, put on trial, or found guilty, even if this means that some real offenders go free. Translated into the terms used by epidemiologists, this means the criminal justice system tries to minimize "false positives" (persons who are mistakenly included in a category) even if this excludes some "false negatives" (those who should be included in the category but are not). This purpose is well served by narrow, incident-focused definitions of criminal conduct. By contrast, the health system operates out of an ameliorative framework. The medical assessment process is designed to minimize false negatives (persons with a particular problem who remain unidentified). Because there is usually little potential damage to a patient who is merely assessed for a health problem, clinicians cast the widest possible web, even if this means screening a large number of persons for problems they probably do not have. In the health system, domestic violence is a legitimate concern with any adult patient who complains of injury or other form of coercion or control by a partner or former partner regardless of the sex or sexual orientation of the parties, their living situation, or the status of their relationship. Even this broad definition might not capture most abused women who use health care, particularly those who visit primary care sites at which injury or the proximate consequences of coercion and control might not seem to be relevant concerns. The health system is interested in acts by others only insofar as this knowledge informs the victim's diagnosis, intervention, and prognosis for recovery, including the likelihood that a patient will suffer a similar problem in the future and can comply with both treatment and follow-up care. Police can make an arrest if they have probable cause to believe domestic violence has been committed regardless of the history of a victim's relationship to an offender. However, in the clinical setting, the history and context of a patient's problem is critical to determining the appropriate intervention.

Prevalence and Incidence

The importance of social and historical context for health gives medical care a unique vantage on how to measure domestic violence.

To mobilize and target health resources appropriately, public health distinguishes the incidence of a problem, the number of new cases that originate in a specified time period, which is usually a year, from its prevalence, the total number of cases in the population at a given point in time (discussed in Chapter 2). If we know how often new cases of battering occur, we can calculate the risk of being abused to any individual and evaluate prevention efforts, which are designed to reduce the number of new cases. Because prevalence measures the total burden a health problem poses to the community, it gives us a way to determine what resources are needed and whether interventions are effective in reducing a problem.

In most crimes and in minor illnesses like the flu, incidence and prevalence are interchangeable. The sentinel event—the robbery or the bout of sickness—is over shortly after it starts either because it resolves (the robber leaves the scene and the patient fully recovers) or the patient dies. In these instances, the number of "new" incidents is roughly the same as the total burden the problem places on the community. We need only to calculate incidence and prevalence separately if problems last for a nontrivial length of time while new cases continue to develop, increasing the total burden on the community.

Prevalence is calculated by multiplying the incidence (I) of a problem by how long it lasts on average, its duration (D), and it is expressed in the simple formula $P = I \times D$. Early in the AIDS epidemic, when patients died shortly after they contracted the virus, the incidence and prevalence of the problem were almost identical. As new drugs made it possible to manage AIDS medically, it was transformed into a chronic health problem in the United States. Although its incidence remains relatively low compared with many other diseases, as more persons who test positive for HIV live for long periods, its prevalence has sharply increased as have the costs of supporting its victims.

The duration of abusive relationships is disaggregated by criminal justice and is called "recidivism," as if each abusive assault was an independent event, like the flu. Because generally, researchers in the field have adapted a criminal justice rather than a health model, we have rarely distinguished the incidence from the prevalence of domestic violence. One result is that we still lack a definitive way to measure whether interventions are working, how to target resources most effectively to prevent new cases from developing, or help victims end abusive relationships.

The Yale Trauma Studies provided one of the vantages on this problem. Of the 18.7% of the female trauma patients who could be identified as battered women, half (54.5%) had presented at least one abusive injury during the target year and slightly less than 80% (14.6% of the total female patient population studied) had done so in the past 5 years; they used this figure to approximate the proportion of patients for whom battering was likely to be a current concern. This was the "institutional prevalence" of domestic violence since it reflected the population of patients for whom domestic violence intervention was appropriate. These women had been using the medical services for abuse-related problems for 7.3 years on average, which is an approximation of the duration of their abuse. Another well-designed study estimated that domestic violence continued for an average of 5.5 years (Campbell et al., 1998). Using the formula for prevalence, based on these data, Stark (2007) estimated that the annual incidence of domestic violence among all female trauma patients was between 2% and 3%. Translated into usage figures, of every 100 women who came to the emergency room for injury, approximately 15 were currently in abusive relationships. Two or three of these women presented a "new" case of abuse during the target year; the rest suffered ongoing abuse. Put differently, for every 100 abused women who used the emergency service, between 79 and 86 are in longstanding abusive relationships. These data suggested that early identification and early intervention could reduce the burden partner violence placed on the health system by as much as 85%, freeing up considerable resources to invest in primary prevention. Conversely, these figures meant that abuse would remain a significant health problem even if we could miraculously prevent any new cases from originating in the community.

These figures also remind us that partner violence has more in common with chronic illnesses like heart disease or AIDS than it does with the flu. Approaching domestic violence as a chronic health problem rather than as an emergent situation has far-reaching implications for intervention.

The Health System Response

Medical Neglect

When the first shelters opened, health and mental health providers were even less aware of the significance of partner abuse than the police were. This is illustrated by a 1985 survey of Injury in America (Committee on Trauma Research, 1985) conducted under the joint auspices of the National Research Council and the National Academy of Medicine. The final report reflected the prevailing understanding at the time—adult injury was almost exclusively caused by accidents. The report made no mention of domestic violence and covered other forms of interpersonal violence in only a few sentences.

As the Yale Trauma Studies showed, battered women sought assistance from health services in large numbers. Moreover, they did so even more promptly than victims of stranger assaults or car accidents. Within the medical system, however, they were largely invisible. In 1978, Hilberman and Munson reported that 30 of 60 women referred to them for consultation at a rural clinic in North Carolina were in abusive relationships, most for many years. However, abuse had been identified in only four of these cases. Meanwhile, at Yale, of 429 visits made by battered women to the psychiatric emergency service, abuse was identified correctly in only 25, an even lower rate of identification than in the North Carolina study, and never was listed as a diagnosis. The rate of identification in the emergency room was lower still. Emergency medical personnel correctly identified only 1 abused woman in 20 and linked only 1 injury to 40 suffered by abused women to partner violence. Clinicians would make an occasional note that a woman had been "beat up by boyfriend" or "kicked by foot." Even when domestic violence was mentioned, it made no difference in how clinicians intervened. Because the source of women's abuse-related problems was not identified, when they were again injured by the same "foot" or reported they had fallen "at bank," clinicians were stumped. The rate of identification did not change appreciably even when physicians reported that they believed it was their responsibility to identify domestic violence. A study of four Philadelphia emergency rooms identified a propensity for physicians to discredit victims who disclosed domestic violence and to avoid dealing with abuse even when they had been trained to identify battering and believed it was their responsibility to do so (Kurz & Stark, 1988). As late as 1991, only 20% of emergency departments in Massachusetts had a written protocol in place to identify domestic violence, and 58% reported that they identified five or fewer battered women a month, which represents a tiny fraction of research estimates (Isaac & Sanchez, 1994).

Some research suggested that the clinical response to abuse made things worse, actually increasing a woman's entrapment in the abusive relationship. After failing to identify partner violence, clinicians treated a woman's injuries symptomatically, which did little to address her underlying predicament. As abuse continued and she returned to the hospital, other problems began to appear on her medical record alongside injury, nonspecific pain, headaches, or somatic complaints, for instance. Typically, these problems were treated with sleep medications and anti-anxiety drugs; these medications were used subsequently by many in suicidal gestures or "cries for help."

Instead of recognizing persistent help seekers, clinicians misidentified many battered women as persons who were using the medical system inappropriately. Out of frustration, they then applied pseudopsychiatric labels to their aggressive help seeking, writing that these women were "frequent visitors," hypochondriacs, or "hysterics." The effect of applying these labels was to communicate to other clinicians that they should not waste valuable time on these women, which isolated them from vital resources even more. This reinforced the same message the abusive partner was giving the victimized patient: She was the problem, not him. Since the pills were given to her, clearly she was the crazy one. Her partner also had told her this was true. Without proper medical assistance, many women attempted to self-medicate, using alcohol or drugs to relieve the stress in the relationship. Now, a doctor or nurse might recognize that she was "beaten by boyfriend," but once the women appeared with "alcohol on breath" or a similar issue, their behavioral adaptations were taken as the primary cause of any abuse-related injury rather than as the consequence of domestic violence. Thus, women were referred for psychiatric or behavioral treatment, often with their abusive partner as an identified caretaker. Given these realities, it was not surprising that women rated medicine the least effective of all interventions (Bowker & Maurer, 1987).

Reforming the Health System

In the ensuing years, the health system response changed dramatically, although change occurred much more slowly and less consistently than the response of the legal or criminal justice system. Police, prosecutors, and judges are part of the state bureaucracy. They can be held completely accountable to legal and policy directives. By contrast, the health system in the United States is an amalgam of public, private, and nonprofit institutions, which are accessed by individuals largely through private contractual relationships financed by an eclectic mixture of fee-for-service, work-based insurance, and government funds. General standards of practice are set by the professional associations to which health providers belong, or by the associations that license hospitals and review their accreditation. Still, in the United States at least, the determination of which services will be delivered, as well as how, by whom, at what cost, and even which subgroups of patients will be served, are still a function of local markets, local administrative decisions, and the ability to pay. Meanwhile, physicians, who are the critical decision makers at points of service, are still largely self-employed and, therefore, are not directly accountable for the quality of care provided by hospitals or the costs of care. Most mental health providers also are private practitioners with similar limits on accountability to central policy directives and cost restrictions.

The earliest medical responses to domestic violence relied on individual, hospital-based initiatives by nurses and social workers. In 1977, building on the success of hospital–community collaborations in establishing rape crisis teams, the Ambulatory Nursing Department of the Brigham and Women's Hospital in Boston formed a multidisciplinary committee to develop a "therapeutic intervention" for abuse victims. The intervention at Brigham, like a parallel program at Harborview Hospital in Seattle, relied on a Social Service Trauma Team composed initially of volunteer social workers who met weekly with nursing staff. Although these largely volunteer efforts proved difficult to sustain, during the next decade, clinician-advocates who often worked closely with shelter or other women's groups in their communities, introduced free-standing domestic violence services at hospitals in Chicago, San Francisco, Philadelphia, Minneapolis, and many other cities.

Initial reform efforts emphasized developing domestic violence policies and protocols within hospitals and medical departments, primarily in emergency services, providing "guidelines" for practitioners at these sites, and training health practitioners to respond more appropriately. In 1986, under its Family Violence Prevention and Response Act, Connecticut established the Domestic Violence Training Project at the University of Connecticut's Health Center, which was one of the first publicly funded projects established to train health professionals in domestic violence intervention. Other states hosted similar projects, including Minnesota, Pennsylvania, Alabama, Colorado, New Jersey, and Wisconsin. In 1990, through its Office of Domestic Violence Prevention, New York became the first state to require that licensed hospitals establish protocols and training programs to identify and treat victims of domestic violence. The New York office also placed domestic violence advocates in all New York City hospitals. In 1994, Florida passed legislation requiring 1 hour of instruction on domestic violence as a condition of licensing and recertification for health providers. Shortly afterward, California mandated that hospitals and clinics screen all patients for domestic violence and required health personnel to report individual cases to authorities. In the wake of these changes, the San Francisco–based Family Violence Prevent Fund (FUND) and the Pennsylvania Coalition Against Domestic Violence selected six hospitals in California and six in Pennsylvania to test a new domestic violence resource manual for providers. Each hospital formed multidisciplinary teams (including a domestic violence advocate) and was given technical assistance to implement a comprehensive response. With funding from the Commonwealth Fund, the Domestic Violence Training Project (DVTP) mounted a similar initiative in Connecticut's 11 federally qualified community health centers.

As the knowledge base about the significance of abuse developed, local initiatives with hospitals were supplemented by attempts to mobilize the public health system and private practitioners. An unprecedented Surgeon General's Workshop on Violence and Public Health was convened by C. Everett Koop in 1985. This was followed by regional conferences on the same theme, as well as by a conference convened in Washington, D.C., by the American Medical Association (AMA) and cosponsored by 50 medical, legal, and social service organizations. Working with the CDC's National Center for Injury Prevention, Dr. Koop identified the unique importance of a health care response. He wrote:

> Identifying violence as a public health issue is a relatively new idea. Traditionally, when confronted by the circumstances of violence, the health professions have deferred to the criminal justice system. . . . Today, the professions of medicine, nursing and health related social services must come forward and recognize violence as their issue. (Koop, 1991, p. v)

The Workshop also emphasized the economic and social costs of violence and focused specifically on violence against women and children.

To the extent that private practitioners in the United States have responded to domestic violence, they have done so under the auspices of their professional associations. After a series of studies in Texas demonstrated that battering was a problem for many pregnant women, the American College of Nurse Midwives and the American College of Obstetricians and Gynecologists mounted national campaigns to educate their members. In 1991, the AMA followed suit, developing and disseminating diagnostic and treatment guidelines on child abuse and neglect, sexual abuse, domestic violence, as well as elder abuse and neglect. By the end of the 1990s, virtually every organization representing health professionals in the United States had identified domestic violence as a priority, some moved to action by advocacy groups within their profession. For instance, the American Nursing Association was pressured to adapt domestic violence as an issue by a newly formed National Nursing Network on Violence Against Women.

Many additional professional health organizations also took initiatives, including representatives for army medics, emergency medical personnel, psychiatrists and psychologists, dentists, pediatricians, and surgeons working with traumatic brain injury. Under the leadership of the AMA, a National Coalition of Physicians Against Family Violence was formed with institutional membership from more than 75 major medical organizations. The AMA's initiatives also emboldened state medical societies and groups in Colorado, Connecticut, Ohio, Maryland, and several other states to distribute diagnostic, reporting, and intervention guidelines to their membership. Illustrating these initiatives was a Physicians' Campaign Against Family Violence launched with a special issue on domestic violence by the Maryland Medical Journal. With seed funding from the state medical society, the Maryland program produced training materials, a physicians' manual, and patient information brochures, and the program stimulated legislation to develop on-site victim advocacy programs at four diverse hospitals.

In 1992, the AMA Council on Ethical and Judicial Affairs suggested that domestic violence intervention be rooted in the principles of beneficence and nonmalfeasance. In the same year, the Joint Commission on the Accreditation of Health Care Organizations (JCAHO) required emergency and ambulatory care services to develop domestic violence protocols. In 1996, the standards were upgraded to include objective criteria to identify, assess, and refer victims of abuse. The JCAHO standards provided a significant boost to training. McFarlane and her colleagues (McFarlane, Christoffel, Bateman, Miller, & Bullock, 1991) found that the implementation of a program for health professionals in a Texas obstetrical service resulted in a statistically significant gain in knowledge of domestic violence. Of those who completed training, 86% stated they intended to assess for signs of abuse among pregnant mothers. More importantly, at the 6-month follow-up, approximately 75% of the participating health service centers were assessing pregnant patients for signs of battering. The combination of community outreach, public education, and health professional training was linked to a noted increase in calls to information centers by battered women who had been referred by a health provider. When nurse interviews replaced reliance on patient self-reports, identification of domestic violence increased 20%. Other studies reported as much as a 600% increase in identification after an initial training of health providers (McCleer & Anwar, 1989). In part, these gains reflected the sorry state of awareness when training began. Without an ongoing institutional commitment to provide resources of clinical intervention with domestic violence victims, the initial gains from training were hard to sustain.

Medical education was another arena that was vital to reforming the health system response. By 1993, 101 of the 126 U.S. medical schools responding to a survey had incorporated material on domestic violence into required course material (Alpert, Tonkin, Seeherman, & Holtz, 1998). Other critical pieces of the health response included (a) major commitments to health research in rape and domestic violence by the National Institutes of Mental Health; (b) the establishment of regional Centers for Injury Prevention and Control with funding from the CDC to conduct translational research on violence prevention, including domestic violence prevention; (c) major funding commitments to domestic violence research and health interventions by private foundations such as the Commonwealth Fund and the Hilton Foundation; and (d) the designation of the San Francisco FUND as a national center to disseminate information on domestic violence–related health issues under the Violence Against Women Act (VAWA) (1994). Although the CDC had traditionally limited its role to surveillance, reporting, and epidemic control, in 1996, it launched a program to support Coordinated Community Responses to Prevent Intimate Partner Violence in several communities. Health care institutions played a vital role in these collaborations.

In 2000, a joint task force headed by the U.S. Attorney General and the Secretary of Health, Education, and Welfare issued an Agenda for the Nation on Violence Against Women. Among the 15 areas of focus, the health care system was prominent. A 10-point summary of the Health Care Systems section of the agenda is outlined as follows:

- Conduct public health campaigns
- Establish national task force on health and mental health care systems' response to sexual assault
- Educate all health care providers on violence against women
- Create protocol and documentation guidelines for health care facilities and disseminate widely
- Protect victim health records
- Ensure mandatory reporting requirements protect the safety and health status of adult victims
- Create incentives for providers to respond to domestic violence
- Create oversight and accreditation requirements for domestic violence and sexual assault care
- Establish health care outcomes measures
- Dedicate increased federal, state, and local funds to improving the health and mental health care systems' response to violence against women

For fiscal year 2000, $5.9 million was appropriated to support 10 projects administered by the CDC. In 2005, the reauthorized VAWA specifically targeted health professionals for support. VAWA recognized that, "Because almost all women see a health care provider at least once a year, the healthcare system is uniquely positioned to proactively reach out to women who are or have been victims of domestic or sexual violence. Health care providers, if trained and educated, can find safety long before she can turn to a shelter or call the police" (National Task Force, 2005, p. 5). Title V of the act sought to strengthen the health care system's response with programs to train and educate health care professionals about domestic and sexual violence, foster family violence screening for patients, and study the health ramifications of partner abuse.

The Challenges Ahead: Training, Screening, and Clinical Violence Intervention

Training

The interrelated components of reform efforts at the level of specific health institutions include routine questioning about abuse, training for providers, culturally sensitive and nonjudgmental support, addressing patient safety, documentation, and the provision of information about options and resources. With funding from the Commonwealth Fund, the DVTP completed a demonstration project that showed how a "training-the-trainer" strategy could implement this model with or without outside technical assistance from advocacy groups at Connecticut's 11 federally qualified community health centers (Stark, 2010).

Despite several state, national, and local efforts to make mainstream domestic violence questioning a facet of routine clinical practice, low levels of identification remain a major obstacle to access to health resources for victims. Research suggests that approximately 1 in 11 battered women are being correctly identified in the hospital setting today. This rate is an improvement since the Yale Trauma Studies were completed in the early 1980s, but it is still far from what advocates hoped to achieve.

The limited progress in identification is not hard to understand. Some abused women are too frightened or too ashamed to admit their partner is hurting them. Moreover, many clinicians are reticent to ask about or confront abuse for the same reasons police were traditionally arrest averse in domestic violence cases: They believe relationship violence is a "private" matter that falls outside their purview, that asking about relationship violence will open a Pandora's Box, and that it is pointless to confront abuse because they can do little to stop it.

These explanations are unsatisfactory for several reasons. First, most abused women report they would welcome inquiries about abuse from clinicians and are forthright when asked in a confidential setting (Caralis & Musialowski, 1997). Second, although issues of patient confidentiality must be handled delicately, physicians and nurses frequently elicit accurate information about other personal matters such as sexual activity or parenting practices. Finally, physicians routinely screen for problems for which no effective therapies exist.

Another explanation for low rates of identification highlights the discomfort physicians and public health practitioners feel about intervening in abuse. Some clinicians believe intervention to help battered women means discounting the competing rights of husbands. The implied involvement with the criminal justice system or child protective services also makes clinicians uneasy about clinical violence intervention. Nursing, social work, public health, and the allied health professions embrace more holistic concepts of health but are no less wedded to stereotypes that attribute blame to victimized individuals and preclude public advocacy where the roots of problems lie in politically charged issues such as sexual inequality.

Other obstacles to change are the status structure of medicine, its traditional male bias, and a commitment to a narrow disease paradigm that minimizes so-called social problems. Even when victims have financial access to health services, capitation arrangements and pressure for primary care providers to serve as gatekeepers can aggravate concern that asking about abuse will occupy more clinical time than these cases merit. Other challenges involve the absence of strong federal leadership in primary care or public health, and the huge number of families without adequate health coverage. Taken together, it is easy to explain why a health problem that affects 20% or more of the adult female population has elicited a medical response that is uneven at best, even from those practitioners specializing in injury.

Screening

Hoping to sidestep resistance to identification by individual clinicians, advocates shifted their emphasis to establishing routine "screening" as an institutional policy for hospitals and managed care organizations, a position endorsed by associations of health professionals like the AMA and American Nursing Association, as well as by JCAHO. Routine screening seemed eminently sensible given the high prevalence of abuse, its significance for a range of health problems, the reluctance of doctors to identify the problem on their own, evidence that early and effective intervention could lead to dramatic cost savings, and the low probability of harm caused by screening.

The San Francisco FUND developed screening guidelines and worked with providers to implant screening in diverse settings as part of a National Health Initiative demonstration project. Several studies suggest that screening in the context of supporting programs is extremely effective. Woman Kind in Minnesota and DOVE, which is known as Developing Options for Violence Emergencies, in Akron, Ohio, are two such programs.

It is surprising that proposals for routine domestic violence screening have excited so much controversy. Organizations such as the U.S. Preventive Services Task Force, the U.K. National Screening Committee, and the Canadian Task Force on Preventive Health Care have either withheld support for such recommendations or opposed them. The reasons given for their opposition range from the claim that domestic violence is not a disease per se to the fact that its risk factors are complex. However, the central and shared criticism is that there is a paucity of evidence that screening tools are accurate, that their application improves health outcomes for abused women, or that the services to which identified victims are referred have been proved effective. The traditional means of providing screening, comparing battered women who are screened with those who are not, violates the ethical imperative to inform all patients about the risks associated with abuse as well as about available resources. A survey of existing studies concluded that (a) although routine screening greatly increased identification, improvements waned with time; (b) asking one question was as beneficial as asking many; and (c) there was no evidence that improved identification led to better outcomes for victims (Ramsay, Richardson, Carter, Davidson, & Feder, 2002). One of the few randomized studies available reported that victims whose positive screen results were communicated to their physicians had no better outcomes than women who were simply given a referral card (MacMillan et al., 2009). Unfortunately, the retention rate in this study was too low to support its general conclusion, no evidence was provided from either study on whether physicians actually used the information they got from the screen, and a debatable statistical method was used to neutralize the reduction in harms that were found. Interestingly, more than four times as many abuse victims who were screened discussed violence with their physicians than abuse victims who were not screened (44% versus 10%), which demonstrates a remarkable effect of screening. None of these studies measured outcomes linked to health costs such as whether victims who were referred for support reduced their overall use of health services over time compared to abused women not referred for support.

Universal screening presents a shift in clinical practice from the more familiar professional norm of targeted screening, which involves asking only those individuals perceived by clinicians as high risk. Risk profiles are impractical with domestic violence because its prevalence is so high among all groups of female patients that any attempt to limit inquiry would produce too many false negatives to satisfy even minimal standards of care. Given their broad pattern of use, it would not make sense to screen only women at certain medical sites (the emergency room, for instance) but not at others.

It is questionable whether a demonstrable reduction in harm to abuse victims is the proper outcome measure of screening. First, it is naïve to assume that domestic violence can be reduced significantly or ended on any substantial scale unless the health care system actively collaborates with criminal justice or shelter services, relationships that many clinicians are reluctant to embrace. Second, clinicians routinely question patients about a family history of heart problems or other diseases as well as about a range of behaviors, such as smoking or sexual activity. These questions often have no immediate benefit for patients or, as is the case with asking about smoking, have not been shown to lead to beneficial outcomes. The principal function of these questions is to broaden the frame within which clinicians understand a patient's complaints, risks, and test results. Similarly, knowledge of abuse bears on how clinicians interpret and respond to a myriad of problems secondary to abuse, as well as to patient behaviors within the medical context, such as frequent visits, missed appointments, or reluctance to discuss the source of injury, to which they might otherwise apply stigmatizing labels. Domestic violence screening also is a form of patient and clinician education; this fact is illustrated by the dramatic increase in physician–patient discussions about abuse in the Canadian study. It also provides an institutional data set to help administrators allocate scarce resources and a baseline against which to judge the efficacy of intervention. Perhaps more importantly, although significant harm reduction might not result from hospital screening, compelling evidence suggests that not asking about or responding to domestic violence leaves victimized women at risk and elicits inappropriate and often harmful responses to the secondary effects of abuse from medical care.

Who should do the questioning, when, where, and with what questions are other issues in screening. Physician-oriented educational seminars do not seem to improve identification rates significantly, even when the annual physical is the setting for questioning, which is seemingly an ideal time to ask general questions about abuse (Soglin, Bauchat, Soglin, & Martin, 2009). By contrast, when nurses ask patients about abuse at check-in, the documentation of lifetime abuse improves substantially, although current abuse is often not reported. In a Canadian study, Thurston et al. (2009) found that 39% of all patients were screened on average and that the screening rate had risen to 52% during the last month of the 1-year study. Importantly, 16% of those screened acknowledged abuse, which is approximately the expected rate. In part, the improvement over time was a result of increasing comfort among nurses with questioning. In general, patients seem to prefer written and computer-based screens to face-to-face inquiry and provide complete information when they respond to questions in writing or on screen (MacMillan et al., 2006). Another alternative is the audio-based questionnaire. If they are interviewed, however, women express a preference for a female screener of their own race and for screeners who are in their age range, although age does not seem to concern older patients (Thackeray, Stelzner, Downs, & Miller, 2007). Only 7.9% say they would be angry or offended if they were questioned by their health care provider about intimate partner violence. Within particular services, screening can help identify high-risk subgroups. For instance, on the one hand, in the pediatric setting where screening is readily accepted, mothers who miss their well-child appointments have been identified as at risk for abuse (Phelan, 2007). On the other hand, victimized middle-class mothers might overuse well-baby services, reflecting the demands of a controlling partner.

Recent work on screening suggests that questioning patients only about physical violence might exclude many victims of coercive control, with approximately one in four women who present with the effects of being abused having never been physically assaulted (Lischick, 2009). Few screening tools contain specific questions about these broader dimensions of abuse, however, and the few that have been tested in a health setting seem to screen out nonabused women more effectively than they identify victims. Asking women general questions about whether they feel "safe at home," for instance, does not help identify women who experience low levels of physical violence at home.

Focus groups with patients have helped us understand victim preferences for screening. Factors that influence a victim's willingness to disclose information about abuse include (a) being treated with respect, (b) having some type of protection available, (c) documentation of injuries, (d) perceived control of the situation, (e) an immediate response, (f) providing options, (g) and the availability of future support (Dienemann, Glass, & Hyman, 2005). Victimized women also feel they should not have to disclose abuse to receive help and that an open-door policy should prevail, where help is available whenever a victim decides she needs it. Dictating to patients what to do rather than offering options can replicate the controlling behavior at home.

Although non-Hispanic Whites tend to favor screening more than other groups, evidence on whether low-income Blacks are more likely to be screened for domestic violence than other racial or sociodemographic groups is equivocal (Weeks, Ellis, Lichstein, & Bonds, 2008). Race impacts a survivor's experience in the health system, however, particularly given the relative lack of resources available for low-income Blacks.

Mandatory Reporting

Another challenge to the proper role of health providers involves whether they should be required to report abuse-related injuries to law enforcement much as they are to report child abuse, assaults involving deadly weapons, or other illegal acts. In the early 1980s, hoping to use reporting requirements to induce hospitals to invest in training, Wisconsin and Connecticut initially required medical services to compile monthly statistics on their census of battered women. These regulations were abandoned quickly, however, because reporting rates were extremely low since hospitals lacked a framework for identification and there were no sanctions for noncompliance. In contrast, Minnesota abandoned reporting requirements, in part because they implied a capacity to protect or otherwise protect these victims, which did not exist. Five states currently mandate individual reporting in certain instances of domestic violence (California, Colorado, Kentucky, New Mexico, and Rhode Island), and one state exempts victims of abuse from its general mandate to report certain injuries (New Hampshire). Supporters of these policies believe they facilitate prosecution of batterers, encourage clinicians to identify abuse, and improve data collection. Opponents argue that such policies reduce patient autonomy, compromise patient confidentiality, might increase women's danger, and can lead to a reluctance on the part of some victims to discuss abuse with their clinicians.

Equally controversial are policies that define domestic violence as a form of child abuse, which clinicians are already required to report.

Findings about whether most victimized women support mandatory reporting by health providers are mixed, although it seems that nonabused female patients are more likely to support mandated reporting than abused patients (Rodriguez, Craig, Mooney, & Bauer, 1998). Ariella Hyman, JD (1997), reviewed existing practices for the Family Violence Prevention Fund. In a policy paper for the FUND, she noted the following:

> The goals potentially served by mandatory reporting include enhancing patient safety, improving health care providers' response to domestic violence, holding batterers accountable, and improving domestic violence data collection and documentation will not necessarily accomplish these goals. Further, the implications of mandatory reporting for patient health and safety as well as ethical concerns raised by such a policy argue against its general application. (p. 11)

This is a conclusion we share.

Clinical Violence Intervention

Whatever kept individual clinicians or hospitals from responding appropriately to battered women in the past, experience suggests that health providers are willing to take violence as their issue when required behavioral changes are incremental and consistent with existing values, practices, and skills. The proper aim of clinical violence intervention is to prevent the progression of problems, largely by restoring a woman's sense of control over her material resources, social relationships, and physical environment; this process is referred to as *empowerment.*

As we have discussed, the most effective operational approach to identification in health settings involves an inclusive notion of coercion and control, regardless of marital or living status, sexual orientation, the severity of injury, or whether the presentation involves injury, medical, behavioral, psychological problems, or simply fear. Since the clinician's primary concern is future risk, the important distinction is between an anonymous assault, where ongoing problems are unlikely, and coercion and control by a partner.

The introduction of a brief screen into the basic interview with all female patients avoids the problem of relying on severe injury before identifying abuse. In one primary care setting, when a single question, "At any time has a partner ever hit you, kicked you, or otherwise hurt you?" was added to a self-administered health history form, domestic violence identification increased from 0% (with discretionary inquiry alone) to 11.6% (Freund, Bak, & Blackhall, 1996). After identification, a confidential assessment of service needs can progress from validating a woman's concern to a careful history of adult trauma. The "trauma history" would normally include an overview focused on the dynamics in the relationship that increase a woman's vulnerability to injury and other problems such as patterns of control, isolation, degradation, exploitation, and intimidation. It would also include a review of medical, behavioral, or mental health problems that might be associated with abuse and consideration of risk to children in the home.

Following from the general aims of clinical violence intervention is provider practice. Here, the aim is supportive empowerment, which is a strategy that emphasizes expanding a woman's options and facilitating individual choices rather than promoting a single course of action. This approach contrasts markedly with the protective service approach taken to abused children or victims of elder abuse, as well as with the strategies used to resolve family conflicts such as parenting education or couples' counseling. Supportive empowerment guides the health provider to safety planning *with* as opposed to *for* the victim, proceeding from how she has managed so far to what she views as the next step. Common interventions available involve shelter or other emergency housing, legal services, police involvement, treatment for substance abuse, ongoing physical therapy, job counseling, continuing education, and welfare or other emergency assistance. The critical point is that interventions evolve with each subsequent visit.

At the institutional level, clinical violence intervention builds on two principles: (1) mainstreaming, making clinical violence intervention part of routine care, and (2) normalization, building on the skills and patient education techniques clinicians successfully employ in other medical or behavioral health areas.

We have long understood that changing one facet of the system's response to domestic violence without changing others does little to help victims of partner violence and might even make things worse. An outstanding issue in moving the health response forward is how to broaden the traditional perspective of health care to recognize the strengths of parallel systems with alternative and even contradictory perspectives, and yet to maintain its core values and commitments. In practical terms, this issue is addressed through collaboration with shelters, police, and other community groups in a coordinated community response.

SUMMARY

This chapter has reviewed the health consequences of domestic violence as well as the history and status of the health care response. In contrast to the criminal justice system, which recognized domestic violence but minimized its significance, the health care system failed to identify the problem. Early research on the health consequences of abuse emphasized its importance as a source of female injury. However, it gradually became clear that abused women suffered disproportionate rates of a range of medical, mental health, and behavioral problems in addition to injury and that these problems typically emerged in the context of frequent, but generally low-level, violence combined with other tactics designed to isolate, intimidate, and control a partner.

The first interventions were mounted by volunteer teams of nurses and doctors in the hospital emergency room. As the base of knowledge about the health consequences of abuse expanded, however, virtually every major organization of medical, nursing, and public health professionals supported intervention; the education and training of health professionals was expanded to include domestic violence; and hundreds of hospitals and other health care organizations adapted protocols to identify, assess, and refer victims.

Despite these reforms, the health care system faces many challenges, including whether to screen routinely for abuse and with what instrument, and whether to report domestic violence assaults alongside other crimes that come to the attention of health providers. Understanding what it means to treat patients in the context of violence—clinical violence intervention—remains elusive.

Devising an appropriate health system response is vital to any overall strategy to manage or prevent domestic violence. Moreover, the knowledge base exists to implement such a response. At a minimum, it would build on the core values of medicine and public health, particularly their emphasis on beneficence and nonmalfeasance rather than on punishment; their willingness to embrace prevention; a capacity to take a nonjudgmental, holistic, and historical approach to health issues; and their distinguished history of addressing problems that most people would prefer to keep under wraps. Understanding partner violence as the context for a range of health problems that currently confound medicine would significantly improve intervention with female patients at all ages. In addition, a medical/public health perspective offers a vantage point to understand partner violence that complements and goes beyond the criminal justice framework we have outlined in earlier chapters.

Reforming the health response requires that we come to grips with what it means to treat health problems in the context of partner violence by incorporating clinical violence education into the education and training of health professionals. Screening tools and intervention protocols must be put in place that reflect practice shown to be efficacious. However, as with policing, reforming the health response involves much more than merely mandating that health providers change their behavior. It extends to confronting an institutional culture that has been shaped by many of the same sexist beliefs about women held by society generally, as well as a practice paradigm, in this case the medical model, which views societal problems through the narrow prism of their biomedical, behavioral, and mental health manifestations, making it hard to address root causes. Although the health system has much to learn from partnering with criminal justice and community-based services, it also has much to teach, particularly about what it means to take a holistic approach to a problem such as domestic violence.

How to Change the Health System Response

Researchers have identified the following interrelated lessons as the key to these efforts:

- *Accommodate the institutional culture.* This means responding to the unique skills, capacities, and organizational politics at each health institution.
- *Involve leadership.* The legitimacy of any intervention depends on strong signals from leadership.
- *Respect existing skills.* Practitioners should see the connection between clinical violence intervention and how they are approaching other important problems in their caseloads such as AIDS.
- *Build local capacity.* The most successful programs facilitate patient disclosure by garnering new resources for intervention, soliciting technical and training assistance from shelters and other local providers, and sensitizing all staff, including security, maintenance, and secretarial staff, to the importance of the issue.
- *Establish accountability for outcomes.* This might mean incorporating a domestic violence measure into existing quality-assurance procedures.

DISCUSSION QUESTIONS

1. Describe the health needs of battered women.

2. Why is injury a poor marker of abuse? Which markers are more appropriate?

3. Discuss why providing an intervention for battered women in the hospital emergency room is inadequate to meet their health needs.

4. Is domestic violence more like AIDS or the flu?

5. Compare the definition of abuse from a health perspective to the definition used by criminal justice? Which is more useful?

Domestic Violence, Children, and the Institutional Response

15

Chapter Overview

Until now, we have focused on adult victims, domestic violence offenders, and the institutional response, primarily by criminal justice. This chapter broadens the focus to the children present in the households where abuse occurs and to the response to the children's involvement in domestic violence by the two major institutions in our society responsible for child protection: the child welfare system and the family court.

The bases for this chapter are the growing body of empirical research showing that children are co-victims in a substantial proportion of domestic violence cases and might suffer short-term and even long-term harm as a result, as well as the descriptive evidence of the abusive dynamics in these cases. Complementing this literature is research documenting the failure of the child welfare and family court systems to respond appropriately to these cases. This chapter provides a critical overview of this literature and identifies the challenges to moving forward.

Population surveys and reports from abused mothers have generated a broad estimate that children are victimized in anywhere from 6.5% to 82% of all domestic violence cases and that the number of children affected in the United States is between 3.3 million and 10 million (O'Keefe & Lebovics, 1998; Rosenbaum & O'Leary, 1981; Straus & Gelles, 1990). Conversely, domestic violence might be the context for between 19% and 60% of the cases in which child abuse or neglect is identified by the child welfare system (Edleson & Beeman, 2000; Hangen, 1994; Stark, 2002). Different estimates reflect varying definitions of domestic violence and of the resulting harms to children, and these estimates are too discrepant to settle on a single number that can root a public policy or institutional response. All children exposed to adult domestic violence are harmed to some extent. But are these harms sufficiently widespread and serious to justify a generic intervention comparable with mandatory arrest policies? Should exposing children to domestic violence be defined as a form of child abuse, for example? Should we support policies that protect children even if the adult victim is left at risk? Can an abused parent remain a protective parent? Are there any circumstances in which a victimized mother should be held legally responsible for harms to her child caused by her abusive partner? What criteria should family courts apply to custody or visitation when they have evidence that a parent has abused a partner physically or otherwise? This chapter will provide a factual basis for debating these questions.

Even the lowest estimates of how frequently children are harmed by domestic violence suggest that the challenge facing those responsible for protecting or caring for children is formidable. Like the police response, the initial response by the child welfare and the family court systems to the "news" about domestic violence was denial. During the ensuing decades, these systems have generally acknowledged that domestic violence puts children at risk and have devised policies and programs designed to make special protections available for "dual-victim" families. Have these reforms been effective, and if not, why?

The first section of our chapter provides a broad overview of the nature and consequence of children's exposure to domestic violence. Early studies in this area documented the overlap between domestic violence and child abuse, highlighting the risk that children could be injured deliberately or inadvertently during a domestic dispute as well as the consequences of witnessing the abuse of a primary parent. Since this work was published, a large body of research has described children's experiences of parental violence as multifaceted, identified many scenarios in which child abuse and domestic violence occur together, and assessed the short- and long-term effects of domestic violence exposure on children's well-being. As our knowledge base has expanded, the focus on "witnessing" violence has been supplemented by an emphasis on "exposure," which is a broader term that encompasses the myriad ways in which children experience partner abuse. In addition to a child's visual and/or auditory perception of domestic violence, exposure includes children's intervention to protect a victimized parent, suffering physical abuse at the hands of a victim as well as of an offender, and being enlisted by an offending partner in the coercion and/or control of a partner. Children often become co-offenders as well as pawns in the extension of coercive control during a postseparation legal fight. They also are harmed as a secondary consequence of harm to their primary parent or because an offending parent has been removed from the family because of an arrest or a protective order, for instance. Much of the research on how children experience domestic violence comes from psychology. We have tried to make this work accessible to students with little background in psychology.

We close the first section by discussing new directions for research. The expansion of our understanding of partner abuse has raised a concern that researchers also need to assess how children are affected by exposure to forms of coercion and control other than physical assault. Meanwhile, the emphasis on child victimization has now been complemented by interest in resiliency factors in children, how batterer intervention and other counseling programs for offenders can be extended to include education about fathering, and research on the capacity for female victims to "mother through domestic violence" despite harm to themselves (Hester, 2004). There is a consensus that all children in homes where domestic violence occurs are affected to some extent, even when their parents believe they are not. These effects extend to children who are too young to verbalize their experience. No outside intervention is without consequences, however. So, it is important to weigh the relative benefits of dramatic interventions, such as the removal of children to foster care, against their risks (such as the trauma associated with removal or abuse in foster care) as well as against the risks of nonintervention or interventions that support victims and their children as a unit. Key considerations here are a child's resiliency and a victim's capacity to mother through domestic violence, which are two issues that have received only limited attention from researchers. Whether to help child victims of domestic violence is not the question. The issue is how to do so without doing more harm than good.

Part II considers the response to domestic violence by the child welfare system. Interestingly, more than a century ago, the agencies responsible for children's welfare approached domestic violence, child abuse, and child sexual abuse as part of a single constellation of illegitimate power exercised by men (Gordon, 2002). These so-called brutes often were arrested or otherwise removed from their families, and their wives and children were given public or charitable support. In the decades between the end of World War I and the establishment of statewide child-protection services in the 1960s, domestic violence and child sexual abuse had largely disappeared from the reform agenda. During this period, child abuse and neglect was redefined as a result of environmental stressors such as poverty, behavioral problems (such as alcohol or drug abuse), and deficits in parenting. The appropriate response was deemed to involve "service" rather than criminal justice intervention. Mothers were the targets of these services rather than the abusive fathers or father-surrogates. By the late 1960s, the proportion of child welfare cases involving neglect surpassed those involving physical or sexual abuse, and interventions consisted of some combination of individualized counseling and support for parenting (such as parenting classes), with foster placement as a frequently used second option. Except for the small proportion of cases in which sexual abuse is the identified problem, men still remain largely invisible in the child-protection system, with many jurisdictions continuing to classify cases in the mother's name even if she is deceased. Starting in the 1980s, however, the advocacy movement challenged the federally mandated child-protection agencies to change their purview once again to include the risks posed to women and children by abusive men in the home.

Part III deals with the family court response in disputed custody cases; the exposure of children to domestic violence has become a major source of controversy in this area. In most divorces that involve children, including those precipitated by abuse, couples arrive at custodial arrangements by either agreement or default. Partner violence is a factor in anywhere from a third or half of the cases in which custody is disputed (Stark, 2002). Based on evidence that domestic violence perpetrators pose an ongoing risk to their former partners and children even after separation or divorce, advocates have pressured family courts to limit access by abusive parents to their former wives or children.

The state is the plaintiff in criminal cases, and justice is sought by assessing the guilt or innocence of an accused party. However, in custody cases, justice issues resolved through fact finding are secondary to the mandate to identify and support a child's best interest. The prevailing conceit in these proceedings is that children are best served when their access to both parents is preserved to the maximum extent feasible. Indeed, 17 states plus the District of Columbia have statutory presumptions that favor joint custody (Bartlett, 1999). Given this mandate, it is not surprising that family courts regard claims of domestic violence with skepticism.

Domestic violence training for child welfare and family court personnel is now ubiquitous, and in most states and hundreds of communities, these systems have officially acknowledged domestic violence and many have devised specialized protocols or programs to respond to dual-victim families. Courts in most states are required at least to consider domestic violence as a factor in custodial assignment, and some state courts presume domestic violence victims will receive custody unless they are shown to be unfit. But have the prospects for victims and their children substantially improved as a result of these reforms?

The last section of the chapter describes the "battered mother's dilemma" created when the criminal court, family court, and child welfare proceedings send conflicting and even diametrically opposed messages about what must be done to preserve safety. An example of this is when child welfare threatens that a victim might lose her children if she allows her abusive partner access, while the family court orders her to provide him access under the threat of contempt. So often do the responses to domestic violence of the various judicial venues differ or conflict that one observer has described these systems as separate "planets" (Hester, 2009).

I. Domestic Violence and Children's Well-Being

The most widely researched and publicized effects of domestic violence for children involve its association with child abuse, child sexual abuse, and the psychological trauma of witnessing the abuse of a primary parent. The effects of exposure can also be profound and long lasting even when children are not assaulted and do not witness the abuse directly. Los Angeles' Dodgers' manager Joe Torre and his siblings were never assaulted by their father and never actually saw him beat their mother. But they overheard his rages throughout their childhood. On the Web site of Safe-at-Home (http://www.JoeTorre.org), which is the foundation Torre started to help children exposed to domestic violence, he describes how just seeing his father's car in front of his house filled him with fear, made him a "very nervous child," and caused him to hide at a friend's house rather than return home after school.

Domestic violence harms children in three ways. First, children are harmed directly, as an immediate consequence of an assault on them and/or their primary parent. Second, children suffer indirectly, as a secondary consequence of exposure to adult partner abuse or because of its effects on or consequences for caretakers. Last, because of modeling or a related form of learning, children may adopt the negative behaviors to which they have been exposed.

Direct Effects of Domestic Violence on Children

Child Abuse

Early research revealed a significant overlap between domestic violence and child maltreatment. Whether we start with battered mothers or with samples of children darted for abuse or neglect, domestic violence might be the most common context for child abuse and neglect. Stark and Flitcraft (1996) reviewed the medical records of all mothers whose children had been "darted" for suspicion of child abuse or neglect at Yale-New Haven Hospital during a single year. Forty-five percent of the mothers in the sample had a documented history of being battered. Compared to the children of the nonbattered mothers, the children of the battered mothers were more likely to have been abused physically (rather than neglected) and to have been abused by their father or a father substitute, who was typically the same man who was abusing the mother. Indeed, whereas the battered mothers were more likely than the nonbattered mothers to be responsible for a child's abuse, abusive fathers or father substitutes were three times more likely to have abused the children than in cases where domestic violence against the mother was not identified. A replication of this study at Boston City Hospital's Pediatric Department reported that the mother was battered in almost 60% of the cases (McKibben, Devos, & Newberger, 1989). Since this early work, more than 30 well-designed studies using a conservative definition of child abuse showed a robust link between physical and sexual child abuse and domestic violence, with a median co-occurrence of 41% and a range of 30% to 60% (Appel & Holden, 1998; Fantuzzo & Mohr, 1999; McCloskey, Figueredo, & Koss, 1995). Equally important is the link between woman battering and sexual abuse.

In addition to being abused, children are frequently harmed during an assault on a mother, either inadvertently, while she is holding an infant for instance, or when they try to intervene. One large, multicity study found that children were involved directly in adult domestic violence incidents from 9% to 27% of the time (depending on the city) and that younger children were disproportionately represented in households where domestic assaults occurred (Fantuzzo, Boruch, Beriama, Atkins, & Marcus, 1997). The dynamics in these cases often involve children trying to referee, rescue their mother, deflect attention to themselves, or otherwise distract the abuser, protect younger siblings, or call for outside help. Crenshaw (1991) reported that 63% of all young men between the ages of 11 and 20 years who are imprisoned for homicide have killed their mothers' batterers.

The seriousness of injury involved in these cases cannot be determined with certainty. In Connecticut, according to a report by the Connecticut Department of Safety (1999), children were identified as "involved" in approximately 17.6% of the incidents in which police were called to a domestic violence scene, but offenders were charged with risk of injury to children in 441 of 15,060 incidents (slightly less than 3%). By contrast, a study of child welfare cases involving domestic violence in New York City found that 12.7% of the women suffered medically significant injuries and an identical percentage of children suffered injury as well (Mitchell-Herzfeld, 2000). Because domestic violence in a relationship often involves dozens and sometimes hundreds of assaultive incidents, we can conservatively estimate that children are physically injured in between 25% and 30% of domestic violence cases. Estimates based on interviews with women in shelters are considerably higher.

Child Sexual Abuse

The overlap between domestic violence and incest or child sexual abuse also is widely documented. A male batterer is approximately four to six times more likely than a nonbatterer to abuse his children sexually. Conversely, incestuous fathers are more likely than other fathers to abuse their wives (Paveza, 1988). Truesdell, McNeil, and Deschner (1986) reported that 73% of the mothers of incest victims had been physically abused, which is approximately the same proportion as is found for fathers who physically abuse their children. In a historical study of the records of the Massachusetts Society for the Prevention of Cruelty to Children, Linda Gordon (2002) reported that 38% of the incest victims were the daughters of mothers who also had been abused. When researchers reviewed the medical charts of 570 children of battered mothers, they found that 93% had been exposed to domestic violence and that 41% had been physically abused, almost all by the same man who was abusing their mother. Eleven percent also had been sexually abused (Avery, Hutchinson, & Whitaker, 2002).

Witnessing

Much of the research on children's response to domestic violence focuses on the psychological, behavioral, and cognitive harms caused by witnessing parental assault (Margolin, 1998). It must be assumed that any child in a home where abuse occurs has witnessed the use of coercion and control tactics, particularly when we consider the repeated and ongoing nature of violence and control in these relationships. Although 70% of abused women report their children had witnessed their father's violent behavior, adults dramatically underreport children's exposure. As Jaffe, Wolfe, and Wilson (1990) found, children often provide detailed recollections of events they were not supposed to have witnessed. Supporting this finding, O'Brien, John, Margolin, and Erel (1994) found that 78% of the children in a community sample reported observing violence by fathers against their mothers when at least one parent reported that no violence occurred or that their children had not viewed such events.

Most children who are exposed to domestic violence do not suffer significant long-term harm as a result. Still, children who witness domestic violence have a considerably higher risk of experiencing difficulties than those who are not exposed. These difficulties can be grouped into the two major categories associated with recent exposure: (1) behavioral and emotional functioning and (2) cognitive functioning and attitudes. Children who witness domestic violence exhibit more aggressive and antisocial behaviors (externalized behaviors) as well as fearful and inhibited behaviors (internalized behaviors) when compared with nonexposed children (Fantuzzo et al., 1991; Hughes, Parkinson, & Vargo, 1989). Exposed children also show lower social competence than other children (Adamson & Thompson, 1998) and show higher than average anxiety, depression, trauma symptoms, and temperament problems than children who were not exposed to violence at home (Maker, Kemmelmeier, & Peterson, 1998). These are many of the same reactions classically identified with physical or sexual abuse. Indeed, some research suggests witnessing is more harmful than child abuse, particularly for younger children, because the anxiety associated with harm to a protective parent or fear of the unknown can be even more damaging than physical harm. Other problems identified with witnessing include low self-esteem, social withdrawal, and depression; lower cognitive functioning (and poor school performance), lower verbal and quantitative skills, and limited problem-solving skills; poor peer, sibling, and social relationships; lack of conflict resolution skills; conduct disorders, generally high levels of behavioral problems, disobedience, and psychopathology; impaired social problem skills; trauma-related symptoms; and belief in rigid gender stereotypes (Fantuzzo & Mohr, 1999; Stark, 2009a).

The relationship of the child to the violent adult influences how a child is affected by witnessing abuse. A study of 80 shelter-resident mothers and 80 of their children revealed that an abusive male's relationship to a child directly affects the child's well-being without being mediated by the mother's level of mental health (Sullivan et al., 2000). Violence perpetrated by a biological father or stepfather has a greater impact on a child than the violence of nonfather figures (e.g., partners or ex-partners who played a minimal role in the child's life). Researchers believe "there may be something especially painful in the experience of witnessing one's own father abuse one's mother" (p. 598).

Some research indicates that the effects of witnessing domestic violence differ depending on whether the exposed child is male or female. Whereas increased aggression and behavioral problems have been identified among exposed children regardless of sex, the general belief is that exposed females are more likely to experience low self-esteem and turn aggression inward and that boys are more likely to act out their aggression and to exhibit reduced social competence, depression and anxiety, feelings of helplessness, powerlessness, fragmentation, and anger. Mazza and Reynolds (1999) found that school-age boys' posttraumatic stress disorder (PTSD) symptoms were related to depression and self-esteem, whereas girls' symptoms were not.

Developmental Age: Special Risks to Infants and Preschool Children

All children repeatedly exposed to parental abuse are likely to exhibit emotional insecurity as characterized by (a) high levels of emotional reactivity; (b) regulation of exposure to parental conflict including both active avoidance and attempts at intervention; and (c) negative/hostile representations of interparental relationships. However, there is a growing consensus among researchers that children's responses to partner violence are developmentally specific and that the psychological and behavioral risks associated with exposure are mediated by the age-specific developmental tasks that are delayed, disrupted, or distorted.

The highest rates of domestic violence are reported by women between the ages of 20 and 35 years. So it is not surprising to find that younger children are represented disproportionately in households where domestic assaults occurred (Fantuzzo et al., 1997). Researchers believe that the stress-induced fear associated with witnessing violence is sufficient in itself to evoke psychological and behavioral problems in children in these age groups, largely because of separation fears. The healthy development of preschool and young children requires a sense of security in a continuous bond with a caretaking parent who exercises reasonable control over the child's immediate universe, including control over the boundaries separating the caretaking relationship from the outside world. Because many abusive partners violate the psychological, physical, and social boundaries of the primary caretaker, younger children exposed to domestic violence often experience their immediate universe as unpredictable and unsafe. This can generate a frightening sense of the world, which they might project outward onto others, producing nightmares for instance, or internalize in the form of low self-esteem.

The main mechanism of trauma to infants is the threat violence poses to their emotional security. The emotional security hypothesis suggests that differential exposure of children to the severity of the abuse will moderate the effect of maternal trauma on infant trauma. Thus, although an infant's temperament might modify the effects of exposure at lower levels of violence, severe violence seems to override any modifying effects of temperament. Descriptions of infants exposed to domestic violence note problem behavior that is consistent with trauma symptoms such as eating problems, sleep disturbances, lack of normal responsiveness to adults, mood disturbances, and problems interacting with peers and adults. Several clinical studies report that exposed infants have poor health, poor sleeping habits, are highly irritable, and exhibit high rates of screaming and crying. Osofsky and Scheeringa (1997) examined the case records of infants exposed to various traumatic events, including abusive violence. Threat to a caregiver, compared with other traumas, was most likely to result in specific symptoms such as hyperarousal, fear, and aggression; more severe symptoms; and the diagnosis of PTSD. In one study of infants exposed to domestic violence (Bogat, DeJonghe, Levendosky, Davidson, & von Eye, 2005), nearly half (44%) displayed at least one trauma symptom in the 2 weeks after an episode, and the number of episodes to which a child was exposed was directly correlated with the total number of infant trauma symptoms.

Alternatively, because preschool children think in egocentric ways, they are more prone than children at other ages to attribute violence to something they did. Physical independence (such as learning to dress themselves) is another developmental task specific to preschool-aged children. The instability associated with exposure to violence has been found to inhibit the development of physical independence and to elicit regressive behavior. Preschool- and school-aged children are frightened and sometimes terrified by witnessing abuse. They tend to express their insecurity through clinging, crying, nervousness, and a constant vigilance over where their mothers are and may also display a range of somatic problems, including insomnia and other sleep disorders, eating disorders, bed wetting, ulcers, and chronic colds. Exposed preschool children have been found to be more likely to suffer from a failure to thrive, developmental delays, and socialization deficits. A recent meta-analysis suggested that effect sizes for trauma symptoms in preschool children occurring as a result of exposure to domestic violence were greater than those for other forms of internalizing behaviors (Spilsbury et al., 2007).

Even though children who experience domestic violence in their homes are at high risk for physical injury and psychological or behavioral problems, it cannot be assumed that most exposed children suffer long-term or severe consequences. As Crooks, Jaffe, and Bala (2010) emphasized, whether serious problems will develop depends on the resilience of a particular child, the available support system, the child's developmental age, and the nature and extent of abuse to which children are exposed, with the probability of harm increasing sharply if abuse is chronic.

Even if they do not exhibit behavioral or cognitive difficulties, children who live with abuse are actively engaged: They interpret, predict, and assess their roles in causing "fights"; worry about the consequences; engage in problem solving; and/or take measures to protect themselves, their siblings, and their primary parent physically and emotionally. Intervening to protect an abused mother is a common source of physical harm to children as well as of guilt, when their intervention "fails." Psychological defenses might be at work even when children seem unresponsive. For example, Peled (1993, p. 122, as cited in Edleson, 1999) offers this chilling account: "I wouldn't say anything. I would just sit there.

Watch it. . . . I was just, felt like I was just sitting there, listening to a TV show or something. . . . It's like you just sit there to watch it, like a tapestry, you sit there."

Indirect Effects of Exposure to Domestic Violence on Children

Children also might be harmed as an indirect consequence of how abuse affects the parent–child relationship; how it affects the health, mental health, or behavior of one or both of their parents; or because the offending parent might enlist them in the abuse.

Separation

Virtually every child exposed to domestic violence experiences separation from a primary parent for at least some period during the course of abuse, and frequent separations are commonplace. Because few current interventions are particularly effective in ending abuse, a large proportion of victims use repeated temporary separations as a tactic to secure short-term safety for themselves and/or their children or to negotiate for a reduction in violence. For children, the risk of separation trauma is acute when a primary parent is killed, disabled, deported, or incarcerated as the result of abuse, or when a child is placed in foster care. Attempted suicide, depression, substance abuse, and many other physical, behavioral, or psychosocial health problems caused by abuse can also lead to periods of separation. But perhaps the most damaging facet of abuse in this respect is the more diffuse fear of separation occasioned by the chaos and unpredictability that typifies homes where abuse is chronic. Here again, the harms resulting from separation are developmentally specific. Younger children, for whom bonding and continuity of caretaking are most important, experience the highest levels of trauma. This is illustrated by the fact that young children who accompany mothers during a shelter stay often refuse to leave their side, following them even to the toilet, for instance, and they might experience the world of the shelter as far more alien than their mothers do, particularly if they have managed the fear of separation at home by hiding in a familiar place or surrounding themselves with familiar objects. But older children also might experience high levels of separation fear or guilt and often will find excuses to miss school or socialize rather than "abandon" a primary parent.

Diminished Capacity for Caretaking

Many of the same medical, behavioral, or psychological problems experienced by victims as a consequence of abuse also can compromise their capacity for caretaking. A vicious cycle is often initiated: A victimized parent may self-medicate the stress caused by abuse with alcohol or drugs, reducing her capacity to meet her children's basic needs for food, clothing, or medical care and increasing the feelings of anxiety and failure she associates with drinking. Furthermore, parenting might be compromised if a victimized mother is chronically fearful or if the abusive partner constrains her access to money, transportation, the phone, or other resources vital to caretaking. Abuse has a major impact on the victim's income, earning capacity, and employability, all of which are critical factors to children's support. In a randomized sample of low-income women, Susan Lloyd (1997) from the Joint Center for Poverty Research in Chicago found that those who had been physically abused, threatened, or harassed by a male partner in the 12 months prior to the study had lower employment rates and lower income, and they were more likely than nonabused women in the sample to exhibit depression, anxiety, anger, and other problems that affect their labor market experience over time.

There is general agreement that the effects of abuse on the mother, and particularly whether she exhibits symptoms of trauma or depression, for instance, might be important predictors of whether infants exhibit trauma symptoms. Depression is believed to affect maternal caretaking behaviors by contributing to reduced attention and interest in the child, including not assisting the child in emotional regulation. There is also evidence that maternal depression and trauma symptoms in the mother are related directly to the severity of the abuse to which she is subjected. Sabotage of birth control, which is a frequent facet of coercive control, can also lead to unwanted pregnancies and births, which overwhelm a mother's caretaking abilities.

Changes in Parenting

Perhaps the most dramatic changes in the relationship between a victimized mother and her children involve attempts by the offender to regulate how she parents. Although the man who is abusing his partner is the primary cause of child abuse in abusive relationships, battered mothers are slightly more likely to abuse their children than nonbattered mothers. Maternal abuse has complex roots in the context of domestic violence. Offenders might coerce a partner into using forms of discipline she knows are inappropriate, for example, by telling her that if she does not "properly" punish her child, he will do worse. Or, he might demand she enforce rules about noise in the house or other conditions that are unrealistic given the ages or disposition of the children. In each case, the "or else" proviso creates a dilemma for his partner, either to act in ways contrary to her nature or to risk harm to herself or the children. As the children mature, many will recognize that their mother selected what she believed to be the safest option, even when she hurt them; this behavior is an example of what Stark and Flitcraft (1996) termed "control in the context of no control."

An abused mother might change her parenting style in response to her abuser's parenting style. For example, she might become too permissive in response to the authoritarian parenting of an abuser because she is trying to keep children from annoying the abuser, or because she believes the children have been through so much; she might make age-inappropriate or unreasonable demands on children to placate the abuser or because she is constrained from meeting her needs for affection in more appropriate ways; or she might assume the demanding parts of parenting while he gets the "fun" parts.

Conversely, when an abusive partner insults a mother's intelligence or judgment, or undermines her parental authority in other ways such as failing to support or openly mocking her attempts at discipline, she might conclude that nonviolent forms of discipline are no longer effective. Because the children might not be aware of the level of threats and violence to which their mother is responding, they might mistake her compliance or dependence on the abusive parent as weakness, devalue or feel shame about their mother for "letting" herself be abused, or simply disregard her rules because they observe she is powerless to enforce them. A study of 95 battered mothers indicated that abusive partners undermined these mothers' authority with their children, making effective parenting more difficult. In the context of coercive control, some children also come to view their mother as a legitimate target of abuse. Finally, children might be angry at a mother for failing to protect them, to evict the abuser, or to comfort them when they are distressed. In some of these cases, children become "parentified," assuming caretaking roles for their mother or other siblings that are inappropriate for their age. Many abused children identify with the aggressor and become alienated from their mother to protect themselves either by an alliance with the stronger parent or as a magical way to protect their mothers.

Changes in the Victimized Parent

Coercion and control of their mother also might induce less tangible changes in the nonoffending parent that affect children. For example, a victimized woman might come to believe she is an inadequate parent because she has been portrayed by the abuser consistently as an unfit mother or as the cause of children's deficits. In several cases in which Dr. Stark has been involved, abusive fathers insulted the mother in front of the children or forced her to do embarrassing things while they watched (Stark, 2007). These situations might involve the offender timing her performance of routine activities (such as cleaning, dressing, or using the toilet), forcing public apologies, or even admissions that she is responsible for provoking her husband.

Mothering Through Domestic Violence

Early research in the field tended to overemphasize harms to children and the maternal deficits induced by abuse. There is a growing tendency to complement the emphasis on child victimization by interest in (a) resiliency factors in children, (b) how batterer intervention and other counseling programs for offenders can be extended to include education about fathering, and (c) research on the capacity for female victims to mother through domestic violence despite harm to themselves (Radford & Hester, 2006).

There is little truth to the belief that mothers typically become more abusive to their children in response to their own abuse. A study of battered women in shelters by Sullivan et al. (2000) concluded that mothers' experience of physical and emotional abuse had no direct impact on their level of parenting stress or on their use of discipline with their children. Both by their own and their children's reports, most mothers in this study were emotionally available to their children (98%), continued to value parenting (91%), and provided appropriate supervision and discipline (91%), typically using timeouts, grounding, and taking away privileges. Seventy-three percent of the battered mothers in this study reported spanking or slapping their children. Yet only 59% of the children reported ever being spanked or slapped. Although the proportion of battered mothers who employ corporal punishment might seem relatively high, it is actually smaller than the comparable proportion among American parents generally (Stark, 2002). Perhaps the most telling findings are that children of battered mothers in battered women shelters reported relatively high and stable scores on their self-concept across time and exhibited overall adjustment that fell within the normal range.

Perpetrator's Use of the Child as a Tool

Perpetrators of domestic violence also use children to extend their control over their mother, a pattern called "child abuse as tangential spouse abuse" (Stark, 2002). Thirty-six percent of the women in a British study and 44% of 207 battered women in a U.S. study reported that their partners threatened to hurt the children or to report them for abuse (Rees et al., 2006; Tolman, 1989). This pattern often is prominent during a separation or after divorce, when the perpetrator might no longer have direct access to his victim, and it is a common dynamic in custody disputes, when children might be used as spies, as proxies for an abuser's anger or manipulation, or as pawns in the endless extension of court battles. This phenomenon is known as "litigation abuse." A child's compliance in continued parental control might be elicited directly by threats to hurt the child, a pet, or their mother or, passively, by an offender's threat to hurt or kill himself, or his "forgetting" to provide basic safety or medical care for the child.

Offender Interference in a Victim's Parenting

A common control tactic involves interference with a woman's parenting. In a study that is quickly becoming seminal to our understanding of abuse, Bancroft and Silverman (2002) argue that men who batter systematically undermine and interfere with their partner's parenting and that this interference often extends into the postseparation period. Other researchers found that battered mothers were more likely than nonbattered mothers to alter their parenting practices in the presence of their partner, largely to appease him and to avoid abuse. Recent work also has looked at how nonviolent forms of coercion and control as well as exposure to physical violence might harm children (Stark, 2009a).

Modeling

Modeling involves the extent to which children internalize or otherwise learn the values, attitudes, and behaviors of the significant others in their lives, particularly parents, and replicate them as adults. This process is known as "intergenerational transmission." It is widely believed that modeling is a major cause of adult domestic violence, that children exposed to parental violence become violent adults, and that most perpetrators of domestic violence were abused or exposed to abuse as children. There is some truth to these claims. According to the National Family Violence Survey, children exposed to the severest forms of parental violence—involving knives or guns, for instance—are many times more likely than nonexposed children to become violent adults. However, because only a tiny proportion of children are exposed to such severe violence, it is impossible to generalize from this evidence to the risks faced by children in the general population. In fact, most exposed children (more than 70%) do not become violent adults (Kaufman & Zigler, 1987). Just as importantly, most abusive partners (between 80% and 90%) have neither been abused as children nor been exposed to violent adults (Stark, 2002).

Even if the crudest formulation of intergenerational transmission theory is a myth, modeling nonetheless plays a significant role in how exposure to parental abuse affects childhood development. For one thing, the proportion of exposed children who become abusive adults, which is reportedly 20% to 30%, is much greater than the proportion of children from nonviolent homes who become violent as adults; modeling parental violence is only one of many possible causes of this "transmission." In addition, batterers influence children's values and belief systems in several ways. Even if they do not use it with their partners, children might learn that violence is an acceptable means of getting their way; it is justified because it is "provoked" or rationalized as the result of alcohol or because "she deserved it." They develop rigid beliefs about gender roles, come to think that the degradation or domination of women is acceptable, believe abusers do not suffer the consequences for their actions, believe that violence is a legitimate response to frustration or anger, or conclude that women are weak, incompetent, or stupid, or conversely, that men need to be violent to retain or regain control. Abuse victims also might communicate attitudes and values that contribute to increasing children's willingness to accept violence. Some abused mothers believe their partner's excuses for abuse and reinforce them with their children. In many instances, mothers tell children abuse is their own fault and that they must change or improve their behavior. In other instances, because of the coercive control, mothers communicate their responsibility or guilt about the effects of abuse on children, excuse abuse because they think it is caused by alcohol use or the stress the partner faces at work, believe and teach that the abuse of women is culturally or religiously appropriate, or believe that men and boys should have more privileges and power in the family.

Evidence is mixed about whether modeling has different effects based on a child's gender. Boys raised in families with domestic violence are likely to overidentify with the batterer and to exhibit a greater degree of aggressiveness and bullying with their peers. Girls raised in families with domestic violence are likely to have self-image problems and to confuse love with violence, and they might not believe men can have a nonviolent, respectful relationship with them. In situations where girls have been the objects of violence or sexual abuse as well as their mothers, they might mimic their mother's reaction to violence (playing "the good little girl," e.g., or becoming violent themselves with partners); identify with the aggressive parent (by scolding or yelling at their mother or her surrogate); or try to relieve their anxiety about impending violence by acting in ways calculated to elicit a violent or disciplinary parental response. There also is a growing literature suggesting that girls exposed to domestic violence are more likely to be victimized as adults, particularly if they also are sexually abused, possibly because abusive partners look "familiar," even if they find violence repellant. Girls who are exposed to parental domestic violence also might be more tolerant of violence in partners, more likely to define themselves as caretakers who can "fix" violent men, and therefore, more likely to stay in an abusive relationship and more likely to be violent themselves.

The Limits of the Research and Future Direction

There are many problems with the research on how domestic violence affects children. Early work in this field relied on vague definitions of child abuse, on small or unrepresentative samples such as mothers in shelters, on population surveys with no confirmation of a parent's report, or on outcomes based on psychological tests rather than on evidence of behavioral or psychological malfunction. As we have observed, children often report having witnessed or been aware of parental abuse even when the parents deny such awareness. Little effort was made to distinguish the effects of different types of exposure or to differentiate the harms caused by witnessing alone from those presented by children who had been sexually or physically abused also. Several studies have shown that children's risks increase with the number of domestic violence incidents to which they are exposed and have compared exposed children with children from nonviolent homes. But only a few studies have considered the factors that mediate whether and how exposed children are harmed, such as their developmental age, resilience, or available supports. Similarly, few studies have differentiated children according to characteristics of the abuse to which they have been exposed, including its nature, severity, duration, and its consequence for a primary parent, what might be termed the "dose" to which they are responding.

Putting Exposure in Context

Perhaps the most serious challenge to researchers is to differentiate the effects of exposure to parental abuse from how children are affected by other adverse, traumatic, or violent events. Depending on how violence is defined, most children in the United States are exposed to violence in some form annually, and many are exposed to multiple adverse events. The National Survey of Children's Exposure to Violence conducted between January and May 2008 measured the past year and lifetime exposure of children 17 years and younger to various forms of victimization, including child maltreatment, conventional crimes, school and peer violence, as well as community and family violence (Finkelhor, Turner, Ormrod, Hamby, & Kracke, 2009). More than 60% of the children had been exposed in some form. Importantly, compared with the 9.8% of children who had been exposed to adult partner violence, almost half (46.3%) had been physically assaulted during the year, and more than 1 in 10 had been injured in an assault, with the risk of having been injured rising as children age. Multiple victimizations also were common; 38.7% of children reported two or more direct victimizations in the previous year, and more than 1 in 10 experienced five or more direct victimizations.

Furthermore, older children were more likely to witness violence at school or in the community than in the family. Indeed, exposure to family or intimate partner violence was found to be a significant risk factor only among infants (where it was third in importance) and in early adolescence (where it was fifth in importance). Moreover, since multiple exposures are typical, children only exposed to partner violence at home might differ from "typical" children in other respects as well.

Another important limit of current research is its almost exclusive focus on physical abuse. Stark (2007) estimated that between 60% and 80% of the women who seek outside assistance from shelters, police, or courts are experiencing a broader pattern of abuse rather than physical or emotional abuse alone. Variously referred to as intimate terrorism (Johnson, 1995, 2008), psychological maltreatment (Tolman, 1989), and coercive control (Stark, 2007), in this pattern, a history of physical and/or sexual assaults is accompanied typically by a combination of tactics to intimidate, humiliate, exploit, isolate, and control a partner. In a typical case of coercive control, violence involves frequent, even routine, but generally minor assaults (such as pushes, slaps, shoves, or grabs), often accompanied by coerced sex. Intimidation tactics can run the gamut from blatant threats through various forms of surveillance to more subtle tactics whose significance is only understood by the victim. Isolation tactics involve attempts to cut off the victim (and often children as well) from family, friends, helping professionals, and other sources of support and assistance. Control tactics also encompass a broad spectrum from constraints on a victim's access to basic necessities (such as money, food, or transportation) to the micromanagement of a victim's daily routines of cooking, dressing, toileting, cleaning, and so on.

The coercive control model of abuse suggests that domestic violence more closely resembles a chronic rather than an acute stressor such as assault and that its effects are cumulative and include harms to autonomy, decisional discretion, personhood, and basic rights (such as the right to speak or go and come freely), and liberties. Although the unique effects of coercive control on children have not been studied, given the prevalence of coercive control in partner abuse cases, it is clear that many harms attributed to physical violence alone are actually elicited by exposure to a combination of abusive tactics among which violence (because it often is low level) might not always be the most important. Even though children can be traumatized by witnessing a severe assault, their more typical experience is prolonged exposure to repeated, but minor, assaults and to the combination of violence, intimidation, isolation, and control. This type of multifaceted exposure causes psychological, behavioral, and cognitive harms that are not adequately encompassed by traditional trauma models and are unlikely to be ameliorated by interventions designed to relieve acute, incident-specific stress. Moreover, the more diffuse pattern of coercive control might elicit less tangible signals of distress in children than are associated with exposure to violence. Witnessing harms to liberty and autonomy might affect children's political as well as their gender identity and might extend to basic aspects of how they experience personhood.

II. The Child Welfare System

Next to policing and the legal system, the child protection or child welfare system (Child Protective Services [CPS]) has the greatest influence on domestic violence victims, particularly among the low-income, immigrant, and minority women and children who comprise most of its clientele. Women typically encounter child welfare services along the quasi-judicial continuum that extends from an initial complaint of abuse or neglect through the termination of parental rights. The proportion of child welfare cases in which battering is a background factor ranges from 16% to 60% (Stark, 2002). As we discussed previously, the highest percentages have been identified by reviewing the medical records of mothers whose children were darted for abuse or neglect in the pediatric setting. Estimates generated from the child welfare system are a function of whether the local child welfare agency has a screening tool in place, whether the organization supports intervention, and whether the host community perceives it as responsive to its safety concerns. An initial record review revealed that, during a 7-month period, approximately 32% of CPS cases in Massachusetts involved domestic violence. Yet, when caseworkers included a stated goal of protecting adult victims, the proportion of cases in which domestic violence was revealed increased by almost one third (48.2%) (Hangen, 1994). Even the lowest estimates of its prevalence indicate that domestic violence is a more common issue in child protection cases than is substance abuse, homelessness, mental illness, or other comparable problems to which considerable resources are devoted.

Despite its importance for children's well-being, domestic violence was officially invisible to the child welfare system when the shelter movement began. Shelters were not adequately equipped to respond to the frequent harms to children in these cases.

In her study of the Massachusetts Society for the Prevention of Cruelty to Children, the historian Linda Gordon (2002) showed that domestic violence was a commonly recognized problem more than a century ago, when child welfare was still largely a function of private charitable organizations. Working closely with police, the preferred response of early 20th-century child savers was to arrest or otherwise remove the abusive men from the home and provide support for the mother and child. By the 1920s, the focus had shifted from "brutal men" to prescriptive parenting for "inadequate" or "neglectful" mothers, and domestic violence (and child sexual abuse) had largely disappeared as an issue as it had from the social science literature more generally. Following the recognition in the 1960s that deliberate and sometimes fatal assault by parents was a common source of childhood injury or fatality in the pediatric setting, the states passed mandated child abuse reporting laws directed largely at health providers. The federal Child Abuse Prevention and Treatment Act (P.L. 93-247) was passed in 1974, providing federal funding for wide-ranging federal and state child-maltreatment research and services. Although child protection became an official state function, the orientation that had dominated private casework remained largely unchanged. CPS continued to focus on mothers almost exclusively—with many states classifying all cases in the mother's name even after she was deceased—and offered a limited range of services and supports for parenting. Behind the rationale of intervening to stem neglect, the child welfare system greatly expanded the scope of family problems in which it intervened to include substance abuse, homelessness, and many other conditions associated with poverty. The result of expanding its client base without a corresponding broadening of available services was the frequent resort to foster care for families whose primary needs were for housing, health care, employment, or income supports.

The child welfare response to domestic violence contrasted markedly with the response of the shelter system. Approximately 2 million children in the United States accompany their mothers to a shelter stay annually. Shelter advocates typically took an empowerment approach to victimized women that emphasized their capacity to make independent decisions, even when these decisions seemed mistaken. This approach clashed with the philosophy of child welfare at many points. Advocates emphasized a mother's needs as a woman, for instance, based on the belief that only through her own safety and empowerment can she protect her children or parent effectively. This approach was anathema to a system whose public mission was child safety and that, in the eyes of the advocates, treated abused women solely as transmission belts to the problems of their children.

By the late 1970s, compelling evidence indicated that children were frequently harmed in the context of domestic violence. In response, and as part of their attempt to win public support for victim services, advocates stepped up local pressure on the child welfare system to respond. The leaders of CPS were reluctant to tackle domestic violence, however, less it open a political Pandora's Box or jeopardize federal funding for children's services. Moreover, policymakers in child welfare also feared that assuming responsibility for adult-to-adult violence would reverse a long-standing trend for child welfare to define its role in terms of support and service rather than policing.

With the passage of the Violence Against Women Act (1994) and other federal and state legislation providing funds for domestic violence intervention, many state and local child welfare agencies acknowledged the risks domestic violence posed to children and increased efforts to train their staff to assess clients for the problem. The initial CPS response was far from what the advocates had envisioned, however. With New York State as the leader, many state child welfare agencies joined with family courts to charge nonoffending abused mothers with "neglect" for "engaging in domestic violence" and removed their children to foster care. An important finding from the Yale Trauma Studies was that for any given claim of abuse or neglect, the children of battered women were significantly more likely than the children of nonabused mothers to be placed in foster care (Stark & Flitcraft, 1996). In a review of CPS records in Hennepin County, Minnesota, Edleson and Beeman (2000) reported that cases in which domestic violence was identified were twice as likely as cases in which it was not identified to be "opened" (45.6% compared with 24.4%), and half as likely to be "closed" (20.3% versus 38.5%) after investigation. Although physical child abuse, sexual abuse, or a specific form of neglect was identified in some of these cases, in more than a third (34.2%) of cases, the mother was cited for "failure to protect." Perhaps more telling: Domestic violence was involved in three of every four cases in which "failure to protect" was identified.

Mrs. Nicholson

Citing the punitive response to victims of abuse, the child welfare system was publicly challenged by a landmark class action lawsuit against New York City's Child Protection Agency, the Administration for Children's Services (ACS). In 1999, Sharwline Nicholson was assaulted by her husband in her apartment in New York City and sustained a broken arm (see box on p. 415). Although this was the first incident of domestic violence, and her son was in school and her daughter was asleep in another room, caseworkers removed the children and charged Ms. Nicholson with neglect for "engaging in domestic violence." Many other mothers stepped forward with similar experiences. In removing the children in these cases, ACS had failed to show that the children had actually witnessed any abuse, let alone that they had suffered harm as a result. After months of evidentiary hearings, Federal Court Judge Jack Weinstein certified the case as a class action and found that the evidence to date, including testimony from scores of witnesses and hundreds of documents, lent "substantial support" to the claims of battered mothers and their children that their constitutional rights had been violated (*Nicholson v. Williams*, 2001). He also issued an injunction outlining procedures and policies for the agency to follow in child welfare cases involving domestic violence, and in 2004, the New York Court of Appeals unanimously held that a mother's inability to protect a child from witnessing abuse does not constitute neglect, and therefore, it cannot be the sole basis for removal. An important aspect of the rulings concerned the need for CPS to weigh the harm to children of exposure to domestic violence against the psychological harm to the child that could be created by the removal itself, and only in the rarest of instances should this decision be made without judicial approval. Richard Gelles, a widely recognized authority on domestic violence and child abuse, was among the experts who testified that the harms of placement might be greater than the abuse itself. This echoed the early findings of psychologist James Kent and his colleagues (cited in Gelles & Straus, 1988, p. 173) showing that physically abused children who remained with their parents continued to be at risk for abuse but did not exhibit the same psychological deficits exhibited by the children placed in a series of foster homes.

Temporary removal might sometimes be appropriate in domestic violence cases when children have been harmed and/or interventions to remove offenders and protect the victimized mother and child have failed. But the trauma to children removed from homes where their mother is being abused can be particularly harsh because domestic violence has already made the bond to the primary caretaker fragile. Abused mothers whose children are removed often blame themselves for the placement and experience powerful feelings of guilt and self-loathing that can leave lasting scars. Moreover, children who are removed might become more fearful and guilt-ridden than they were previously and blame themselves for their inability to protect their mothers.

Interestingly, although battered women are at an elevated risk compared with non-battered women for a range of medical, behavioral, and psychosocial problems, within the multiproblem CPS caseload, they are actually *less* likely than other mothers to have a history of substance use, mental illness, or childhood experiences characterized by sexual abuse or violence (Stark & Flitcraft, 1996). This conclusion is further illustrated by a study of CPS cases in New York City, in which nonbattered mothers were almost 100% more likely than battered mothers to be identified with abusing drugs (19.4% versus 11.3%) or both alcohol and drugs (2.0% versus 1.4%). In fact, 84.5% of the domestic violence victims had no mental health problems (Mitchell-Herzfeld, 2000). When we combine evidence of their parenting capacity with data on the relatively low rate of psychological or behavioral problems among battered mothers, it becomes clear that battered mothers enter the CPS caseload largely, if not exclusively, because of their partner's abusive behavior. This evidence indicates that they can be approached as "partners" who need enhanced advocacy to support their capacity for independent decision making about their own and their children's safety.

Fortunately, a growing number of CPS agencies are partnered with battered women's groups to provide a range of community-based intervention programs for dual-victim families, offering a credible alternative to placement as the first response. Numerous states now include a domestic violence assessment in their investigative procedures and special cautions against revictimizing women in the ways that were publicized by the *Nicholson* case. Following model developed by Massachusetts, CPS agencies in several jurisdictions now employ domestic violence advocates for consultation to caseworkers who are unsure how to respond to abuse. Other innovative programs include running parallel support groups for mothers and children, a special service track for dual-victim families, and the integration of counseling for batterers to include information about fathering. These programs vary in their design and emphases but typically combine advocacy on behalf of the mother and children with independent safety planning for all family members placed at risk. This approach was pioneered by AWAKE at Children's Hospital in Boston.

Sharwline Nicholson first became a victim of domestic violence one winter afternoon while Destinee, her infant daughter, was asleep and her son Kendall was in school. The father of her infant daughter, Claude Barnett, lived in South Carolina and made monthly visits up to Brooklyn to see the children. On January 27, 1999, during one of Mr. Barnett's visits, Ms. Nicholson ended the relationship. Mr. Barnett had never previously threatened or assaulted Ms. Nicholson. While throwing objects throughout the house, he kicked, beat, and severely assaulted Sharwline, leaving her with a broken arm. With her head bleeding profusely from the attack, Ms. Nicholson called 911. She also made arrangements for a neighbor to care for her children while she was in the hospital. After learning she would stay at the hospital overnight, she gave officers the names of relatives who could care for the children in her absence. The next day, an Administration of Children's Services (ACS) worker called Ms. Nicholson at the hospital and informed her that the agency had taken custody of her children the night before. ACS claimed that the children were in "imminent risk if they remained in the care of Ms. Nicholson because she was not, at that time, able to protect herself nor her children because Mr. Barnett had viciously beaten her." ACS also filed charges of neglect against Ms. Nicholson for "engage[ing] in acts of domestic violence" in the presence of their child. On February 4, 1999, Family Court ordered that Ms. Nicholson's children be returned to her, but Ms. Nicholson continued to be listed on the State's records as a neglectful parent.

III. The Family Court Response

Domestic Violence in Custody Cases

Domestic violence is an issue in as many as half of all divorces in which custody is disputed. This translates into approximately 50,000 cases annually in the United States, affecting more than 100,000 children. In about half of these cases, between 15% and 25% of all disputed cases, there is substantiating evidence of physical abuse, such as a prior arrest for domestic violence, a criminal court finding, or court order (Kernic, Monary-Ernsdorff, Koespell, & Holt, 2005). In the rest, abuse claims are presented through the testimony of an alleged victim that can be confirmed by expert testimony of a domestic violence specialist and/or a mental health evaluator appointed by the court.

Mothers receive primary custody either by agreement or by default in most divorce cases. But where custody is disputed, the prevailing sentiment favors shared or joint custody. The preference for joint custody is justified by the belief that children benefit psychologically if contact with both parents is maintained after divorce. The research on this point is more equivocal than popular lore suggests, however, and it shows that supportive contact with one parent is usually sufficient for children to thrive and that the harms to children who are exposed to continued parent conflict or violence after a separation or divorce outweigh any benefits from ongoing contact (Radford & Hester, 2006). But shared custody also is favored as a matter of equity, with a strong body of legal opinion supporting parental rights. Given this preference and since disputed custody cases involve high levels of parental conflict by definition, the family court must determine whether the level of conflict presented justifies setting the default preference aside.

Nowhere are the prospects for future contact by both parents more in doubt than where one or both parties allege violence or other forms of abuse. No other problem encountered by family judges or evaluators is comparable with battering in its prevalence, duration, scope, dynamics, effect on personhood, or significance for the health of everyone involved, particularly the children. The fact that national legislation on domestic violence is titled the "Violence Against Women Act" (VAWA) illustrates how widespread is the belief that domestic violence is a gendered crime from which women and children particularly require institutional protection. Although this belief is widely accepted in policy circles, the criminal justice system, law, medicine, and social services, it remains highly controversial in the civil arena and particularly in the family court system. Here, the tenet remains strong that the private sphere of family life should be generally immune from the principles of formal justice that govern criminal law. As a result, domestic violence claims have formal standing in custody disputes only when they can be linked explicitly to a child's best interest or attached to monetary claims for damages. Resistance to a gendered analysis of abuse in family court and the tenacity with which decision makers in this arena cling to arguments long rejected in criminal court also reflect the financial stakes at risk in family proceedings. Furthermore, the families who typically engage in custodial disputes are relatively privileged both economically and politically compared with the men and women charged in criminal court or involved in child welfare proceedings.

Despite the frequency with which domestic violence is raised in disputed custody cases, the judges, lawyers, evaluators, and advocates who work with families remain sharply divided about the appropriate response, as do the litigants. Horrific stories are commonplace of women who have lost custody to abusive partners or been punished, even jailed, for disobeying court orders to provide unsupervised visitation to these men. Based on interviews with female custodial litigants in Massachusetts, the Battered Women's Testimony Project at the Wellesley Center for Women documented a pattern of discrimination, mistreatment, and arbitrary or biased rulings they framed as human rights violations (Slote, 2002). These findings were replicated by the Arizona Coalition Against Domestic Violence (Post, 2003). Responding to publicity about the failure of state courts to respond appropriately in domestic violence cases, Republican Congresswoman Connie Morella proposed and the Congress passed House Concurrent Resolution 172 in 1990 recommending that state courts give presumptive custody to victims of domestic violence. Some variation of this recommendation has been adapted by all but two states. Although the language of these statutes is gender neutral, it is widely understood that their primary beneficiaries would be battered women.

Fathers also tell dramatic stories about being unjustly accused of physical or child sexual abuse by their wives and exiled by the family court to a lifetime of alienation from their children. Building on these stories, fathers' rights groups and their supporters use their Web sites to insist that husbands, not wives, are the real victims of bias, to discount documented injustice to mothers, and to attack feminists, protective mothers, and their supporters. These groups claim that statutes favoring presumptive custody for victims have exacerbated the prevailing anti-male bias in the family court and have allowed women to gain advantage in custody disputes by (falsely) asserting they have been abused and thereby alienating the children against fathers (Dutton, 2005).

Some who oppose a greater emphasis on domestic violence in family court acknowledge that exposure to abuse harms children but insist that the type of violence observed in custody disputes is less serious than the abuse found in other service settings, such as shelters or criminal courts. Instead, they insist, much of this violence is new rather than long standing, and it reflects separation-engendered violence or postdivorce trauma elicited by the tension surrounding divorce (Johnston & Campbell, 1993). Despite claims to the contrary, there is no evidence that the abuse reported in custody disputes is different or less harmful to children than in the cases that come to criminal court or other service settings (Stark, 2009a). Researchers have identified three factors that increase a woman's risk of severe or fatal violence nine fold, for instance, separation, the presence of a weapon, and the existence of high levels of control (Glass, Manganello, & Campbell, 2004). Other commonly cited risk factors include threats to children, sexual abuse, violations of court orders, and financial exploitation. Since disputed custody cases involve separation and children by definition and since a high proportion of these cases include claims of monetary and other forms of control alongside allegations of abuse, there is good reason to suspect that, if anything, the types of abuse in the custodial setting are more dangerous than the types of abuse observed in other service settings, not less so. Even when violence is reported for the first time during a divorce proceeding, this is often because the victim was too fearful of reprisal to report abuse earlier or because the violence only began after the break up.

The Significance of Custody Decisions for Victims and Children

The importance of custody and alimony decisions in domestic violence cases is indicated by the frequency with which child contact is a context for reassault during the postseparation period (Shalansky, Ericksen, & Henderson, 1999). Leighton (1989) reported that one quarter of the 235 Canadian women he interviewed had been threatened or assaulted during child visitations. As many as one third of violations of court orders occur during child visitation exchanges (McMahon & Pence, 1995), and multiple violations are commonplace. Studies of so-called high-conflict marriages and divorce indicate that children continually exposed to abusive encounters between parents in shared custody arrangements or in noncustodial visits have more behavioral problems in childhood and early adulthood than children in sole custodial arrangements (Hetherington & Stanley-Hagan, 1999). When abuse continues through contact, children who had been initially enthusiastic about visitation become anxious and depressed (Radford & Hester, 2006).

In deciding which arrangements are in the best interests of children, family courts have become increasingly reliant on forms of therapeutic jurisprudence in which court-appointed psychological evaluators use a variety of psychological tests and interview techniques to determine the relative parenting capacities of the contending adults. Complementing the parenting evaluation is the appointment of a law guardian to decipher and represent the child's best interests. Typically, the law guardian follows the lead of the evaluator and both are assumed to be neutral with respect to the disputants.

A major difficulty with applying therapeutic jurisprudence in abuse cases is that domestic violence is typically an instrumental behavioral pattern rather than an expression of underlying psychological problems. There is neither a single psychological profile associated with abusive behavior or victimization nor a single test that can definitively identify its occurrence. As we discussed in the chapter on health, domestic violence has predictable physical and mental health consequences for victims and children and psychological evaluators can be trained to recognize these consequences as well as the typical forms of violence and control in abusive relationships. However, most victims do not suffer these consequences and abuse may be long-standing, multifaceted, and serious even in the absence of these consequences. Moreover, since domestic violence is a crime, perpetrators of abuse have a strong self-interest in concealment, much as they do in cases of sexual abuse. This means that false denials are far more common in these cases than false allegations. The typical court-appointed evaluator or law guardian is unprepared by training or experience to confront, let alone to penetrate, the wall of fabrication and victim blaming constructed by offenders.

The difficulties with using standard therapeutic jurisprudence are magnified in cases where physical abuse has been minimal or frequent but low level; where a victim has not reported the abuse until the couple are separated or a divorce action is initiated; and where the main dynamics of abuse involved tactics to intimidate, isolate, and control a victim rather than simply to hurt her or the children physically. Identifying the consequences of abuse by assessing children is more difficult still since the normal defense mechanisms children use to ward off the anxieties elicited by witnessing abuse often are exacerbated in the context of a custody fight, particularly when the abusive parent uses the children to extend their control into the period of separation. This pattern is known as child abuse and tangential spouse abuse. In cases of coercive control, where children present with problems in socializing and independence, as well as present with levels of fearfulness that seem to have no objective correlate in physical abuse, evaluators and law guardians often conclude that the children's fears are exaggerated and might even be instigated by a vindictive wife, a pattern known as parental alienation syndrome (PAS). Although the American Psychological Association and other professional organizations have questioned the validity of PAS as a scientific assessment, it has become a common stratagem to defend against allegations of abuse. To place these outcomes in their proper context requires a more sophisticated understanding of abuse than is likely to be present in the evaluation setting. Recognizing this, some custody courts insist that claims of domestic violence be assessed by evaluators with specific expertise or experience in this area rather than by traditional psychologists.

Another difficulty faced by those who work on behalf of children in these cases is the frequency with which they express a preference for the parent who poses a threat to their safety or deny witnessing abuse despite compelling evidence that they have. Explanations for a child's apparent closeness to an abusive parent range from identification with the aggressor and Stockholm syndrome (where a victim seeks the protection of and protects the person who has hurt them) to the child's belief that he or she can magically protect the victimized parent by placating an abusive father, perhaps in response to his threats to hurt himself if he loses custody or his plaints about abandonment or even threats of suicide. Children might deny abuse or express a preference for an abusive father simply because they share their mother's fear. Too great a focus on the child's wishes in these cases can prevent judges, evaluators, and children's attorneys from explicating the dynamics of parental abuse and how it shapes a child's expressed feelings or perceptions.

Given its prevalence and potential significance of domestic violence for children, routine assessment for abuse in disputed custody cases is a prerequisite for any reasonable determination of equity and a child's best interest. Once abuse is identified, the critical questions are which particular power dynamics are at work in a case, the ways in which these dynamics jeopardize the physical and psychosocial integrity of partners and their children, and how to protect all family members during separation and after divorce.

After the passage of the "Morella" resolution, all but two states changed their custody laws to favor abuse victims either by giving them the presumption of custody, instituting a rebuttable presumption against joint custody, banning sole custody or unsupervised visitation for perpetrators, or identifying abuse as an important factor that judges have to consider. The National Council of Juvenile and Family Court Judges has promoted the rebuttable presumption approach through its "Green Book" initiative. There is growing evidence that legislation has not affected actual judicial decision making in abuse cases, however, particularly relative to changes in the institutional response in other arenas. For example, sole physical custody was given more often to fathers than to mothers in states where statutes favoring joint custody or friendly parent (FP) statutes competed with statutes denying custody to perpetrators of abuse (Morrill, Dai, Dunn, Sung, & Smith, 2005). In New York, fathers were more likely to receive visitation when the mother had a protection order than when she did not (Rosen & O'Sullivan, 2005).

At best, family courts remain deeply ambivalent about the changing normative response to abuse. With marked exceptions, most family courts continue to interpret partner violence as different only in degree, but not in kind, from other types of animosities and family problems that bring disputants in custody litigation to court. The most relevant fact for our current purpose is that in a disturbing proportion of cases, abusive partners continue to be given primary or shared custody and to be allowed unrestricted access to protective mothers and children. Moreover, even where abuse is well documented, it rarely surfaces as a major determinant of case outcomes.

When asked, psychologists, mediators, and other professionals charged with evaluation in family court claim that they assess for domestic violence and make specialized referrals or protective recommendations when appropriate (Bow & Boxer, 2003). Studies of their actual practice suggest otherwise. Like the study in New York, research in Kentucky found that domestic violence was not only overlooked by evaluators as a general rule but also that it played no role in recommendations even when it was mentioned in the report (Horvath, Logan, & Walker, 2002). Moreover, studies in both Kentucky and California found that domestic violence couples were as likely as those without such allegations to be steered into mediation and that mediators held joint sessions in nearly half of the cases where domestic violence was substantiated in an independent interview, even though this was against the regulations (Hirst, 2002). In San Diego, mediators failed to recognize domestic violence in 57% of abuse cases. Perhaps more importantly, revealing domestic violence was found actually to be detrimental to outcomes for victimized mothers. In fact, mediators who said they were aware of abuse were less likely to recommend supervised exchanges than those who were not aware (Johnston, Lee, Olesen, & Walters, 2005).

Research in Seattle illuminates the current status of decision making in abuse cases. Kernic and her colleagues (2005) studied all couples with minor children petitioning for dissolution of marriage in the target year and merged the marital dissolution files with police and criminal court files. Then, they compared the outcomes for mothers with a documented history of abuse (as well as those with allegations of abuse in the dissolution file) with those without this history. Of the cases with a documented history of abuse, more than three quarters had either no mention of domestic violence in the marital dissolution file (48%) or only unsubstantiated allegations (29%). In other words, the court was made aware of abuse in less than one case in four where it could be documented. After adjusting for a range of potential confounders (such as allegations that the mother had used violence), mothers with a history of abuse were no more likely than the nonabused mothers to be granted child custody. Fathers whose abuse was substantiated in both criminal and family court files were significantly more likely to be denied child visitation and assigned to relevant services than comparison fathers. This outcome is consistent with recommended best practices. But most (83%) abusive fathers had no such restrictions. The outcomes in cases that involved fathers with a documented history of abuse but whose abusive history was not included in the dissolution file and those with a documented history whose abuse was included only as an allegation by their wives were no different than the outcomes for nonabusive fathers. This last finding is particularly disturbing because the low level of violence typical of domestic violence and coercive control rarely prompts an arrest or protection order.

The Seattle study found no support for the claim frequently made by opponents of a gender approach to domestic violence that fathers are being disproportionately denied visitation when their wives allege abuse. No special restrictions were being placed on visitation even in most cases where there was documented evidence of abuse. Some judges who possessed information about abuse were more likely to take protective action. This suggests that better communication between criminal and family proceedings might improve the response as would proper investigation of abuse allegations by evaluators. Still, the fact that most judges failed to respond to documented abuse points toward a systemic constraint on appropriate decision making in custody cases involving domestic violence that is not likely to be remedied by training alone.

Separate Planets?

British scholar Marianne Hester (2004) has dramatized the different and often contradictory assumptions that criminal and family courts bring to bear in domestic violence cases by referring to them as "separate planets." In criminal court, a woman who presents evidence of abuse is considered a strong and cooperative witness. But if she presses these same claims in family court, she risks being identified as vindictive or uncooperative with "friendly parent" assumptions. The criminal court addresses equity concerns by using its authority to redress the imbalance of power exploited through abuse; in family court, abusive fathers are assumed to have an equity interest in custody. The "perpetrator" of domestic violence might be renamed by an evaluating psychologist as "the good enough father." No-contact orders are commonplace in domestic violence proceedings, but they are extremely rare in custody cases, even in the face of evidence that is identical to the evidence provided to the criminal court. To the contrary, even victims who hold a no-contact order from another court might be held in contempt in family court if they fail to provide access to an abusive dad. At best, family courts can help couples set aside long-standing grievances for the sake of the children. At worst, the normative emphasis on cooperation leads court professionals to misread partner abuse as a form of "high conflict," rationalize unworkable proposals for contact, and then turn on victims when these plans fail.

The Battered Mother's Dilemma

The battered mother's dilemma refers to the choices an abusive partner forces a mother to make between her own interests, including her physical safety, and the safety or interests of her children. Victimized mothers report that their abusive partners threaten to take the children or to report them to CPS in 64% of cases and do so "often or all the time" in 40% of cases (Rees et al., 2006; Tolman, 1989). A particular incident can bring this dilemma into sharp focus, as when a woman realizes that she might be hurt or killed if she attempts to protect her child from her partner's abuse. In custody disputes, common examples involve abusive husbands who threaten extended custody battles unless the wife abandons all claims for financial support or threaten her with physical harm if she pursues custody. Typically, however, the battered mother's dilemma describes an ongoing facet of abusive relationships where the victimized caretaker is forced repeatedly to choose between taking some action she believes is wrong (such as using inappropriate forms of corporal punishment with her child), being hurt herself, or standing by while he hurts the child.

A related pattern involves child abuse as tangential spouse abuse, when offenders extend their coercive and controlling tactics to the children either because a victimized mother is no longer available or has stopped responding to threats and violence. In these instances, child abuse, child intimidation, and other harms to children cannot be separated from the coercion and control of their primary parent.

Institutional intervention often can reinforce these patterns. With respect to child welfare, for instance, current CPS practice can aggravate a mother's dilemma. Women realize that if they do not report domestic violence, then they and their children might be seriously hurt or even killed. But if they do report, then they might be charged with neglect or "failure to protect," and they can lose their children as a result. This practice was challenged in the *Nicholson* case. The same dilemma is reinforced when the family court fails to recognize the external constraints to which a caretaker is responding. This happens, for instance, when, instead of providing appropriate protections for an abused mother, a court threatens to shift primary custody to an abusive partner if she fails to facilitate his access to their child. In both instances, risk is enhanced whichever option she selects. In both instances, deciding to report (or in the case of a custody dispute to persist in claiming abuse) puts her at risk of losing her child. If she does not report (or insist the court protect her child), she and the child might be seriously hurt. Women can be paralyzed by these dilemmas and might place themselves at extreme risk by taking steps to protect their children directly, fail to intervene when an abuser hurts their children, or hurt or scapegoat their children themselves.

The Future of the Child Welfare System and the Family Court Response

Three decades of advocacy, professional education, and legal reform have greatly enhanced the response of hospitals, police, child welfare, the criminal court, and other services to battered women and their children. However, the child welfare and custody court systems remain outside this process to some extent. Despite the landmark ruling in *Nicholson v. Williams*, advocates continue to identify instances in which agencies cite battered mothers for neglect instead, removing their children to foster care, thereby revictimizing abused women. As illustrated by the research described in this chapter, in family court, even when a documented history of abuse from the criminal court makes it into the family file, this information is only deemed relevant to custodial assignment in a small proportion of cases. One consequence is that, despite state legislation to the contrary, abusive husbands are given sole custody, joint custody, or unsupervised access to children in a disturbing number of cases, leaving hundreds of thousands at risk.

Well-designed research in New York and California suggests something more, that victims and their children might actually fare worse in the family court when abuse is identified than if mothers remain silent about domestic violence; this is a dramatic example of the battered mother's dilemma. Stories abound of abused mothers who have been forced to provide access to perpetrators, have been given pseudopsychiatric labels because of their aggressive attempts to protect their children, have had severe constraints placed on their own access, have been ordered to supervised visitation, and have been denied access altogether or even jailed for their reluctance to cooperate.

In sum, although domestic violence is the most common cause and context of child abuse and the most prevalent and most serious threat to children in disputed custody cases, the child welfare system and family courts generally fail to recognize its significance and might even respond punitively to battered mothers. This remains true even when state policies explicitly direct judges or child welfare agencies to provide recognition, protection, and support to victims.

One explanation for these responses is structural. The family court and child welfare agencies occupy unique niches in the legal system because of their substantive concerns with personal life and character, their informal evidentiary procedures, and their decision-making processes that lack the sort of accountability to formal law, public scrutiny, and empirical validation that characterizes other legal, medical, or criminal justice institutions. To some extent, this reflects their functions, which are to protect children identified as at-risk for immediate harm in the one instance and to reconcile the conflicting needs and wishes of particular individuals with children's best interests in the other. In both instances, a governing assumption is that protecting children might require measures that clash with formal principles of justice or equity.

Another explanation for the inappropriate response by the child welfare system and family court is paradigmatic. With respect to CPS, the prevailing conceit is that child protection requires intervention largely with the mothers assumed to bear default responsibility for child rearing. Since mothers are considered largely in their role as conveyor belts to the problems of their children rather than as women with needs of their own, the occurrence of domestic violence is perceived as a failure in child protection rather than as an occasion to support dual victims against a malevolent other. In family court, the emphasis on co-parenting implies that fathers have an inalienable "right to contact" if they choose to exercise it. In the family court system, therapeutic jurisprudence recasts the same man who appears as a perpetrator in criminal court as a "good enough father," rationalizes this interpretation as in the child's best interest, and reframes women who persist in seeking protective interventions as "uncooperative" or worse, punishing them for vindictively alienating their children from their fathers and giving these fathers primary custody. A third explanation reflects the socioeconomic and political context in which decisions are made in child welfare proceedings and the family court. The disadvantaged status disproportionately occupied by most clients of child welfare allows for a range of quasi-judicial policies that would probably not stand the light of public scrutiny, let alone be tolerated by the caseworkers who implement them. Conversely, the relatively privileged status of those engaged in custody disputes constrains decisions in custody cases to follow the dollar, in this instance, by dismissing or disregarding allegations of criminal domestic violence in favor of "parental rights."

SUMMARY

This chapter has provided an overview of how a child's well-being is affected by exposure to domestic violence and the response by the child welfare system and the family court, which are two major institutions charged with evaluating children's risk and ensuring that their best interests are protected.

Early work in the field described the overlap of domestic violence and child abuse without identifying the dynamics in these situations; early research focused largely on "witnessing" as the major form of exposure, and results often were generalized from small, unrepresentative samples. More recent work has captured the nuanced and multifaceted nature of children's experiences of domestic violence and has begun to link their risks to the types of abuse involved, the nature and duration of exposure, their developmental age, and perhaps most importantly, their resilience and the capacity of victimized women to "mother through domestic violence." As we develop a broader appreciation of the range of tactics deployed in abusive relationships, researchers need to follow suit, considering the harms to children of being exposed to forms of coercion and control other than physical assault.

Considering the response to domestic violence by the child welfare and family court systems raises an important challenge, whether and how to intervene without aggravating the "battered mother's dilemma," which is the predicament posed when a victimized mother has to choose between protecting herself and keeping her children safe. Interestingly, over time, the focus of child welfare in cases involving domestic violence shifted from targeting abusive fathers to deficits in maternal parenting. This emphasis often led local child protection agencies to charge abused women with neglect and to remove their children to foster care. The challenge to this practice of revictimization by advocacy groups culminated in the *Nicholson* case, in which a federal court ruled that it was unconstitutional. The hope was that child protection would extend its purview to the safety of all family members, to partner rather than to patronize abuse victims, and to serve as a liaison with criminal justice as part of enhanced advocacy.

Like child welfare, the family court often reinforces the dilemma faced by battered mothers, in this instance whether to press the issue of domestic violence and risk seeming uncooperative or being labeled an "alienator," or to conceal it and risk an ongoing threat to themselves and their children. Congress, several states, and the national organization representing family court judges have moved the consideration of domestic violence to the center of custodial decision making. This has yet to change the outcomes in custodial disputes, however, largely because of conflicting mandates favoring shared parenting and a widespread but unsubstantiated belief that a significant proportion of women are using claims of abuse as a "sword" against men rather than as a "shield." Indeed, family courts seem to do little to protect children even in cases with hard evidence of a history of domestic violence. So discrepant are the responses by child welfare, the family court, and the criminal justice system to abuse that they have been described as separate "planets." Moving forward means reconciling conflicting approaches in ways that appropriately address the needs of victimized women and children for safety and autonomy.

DISCUSSION QUESTIONS

1. Based on the information in this chapter, do you think the exposure of children to domestic violence should be considered a form of child abuse?

2. Should domestic violence be considered a factor when a family court determines which custodial or visitation arrangements are in the children's best interests?

3. What are the relative advantages and disadvantages of limiting the discussion of how children are affected by domestic violence to "witnessing"?

4. Describe and give at least one example of the battered mother's dilemma. What steps might child welfare or the family court take to prevent putting domestic violence victims in this situation?

5. Describe three critical challenges you believe should be addressed by researchers interested in the effects of domestic violence on children.

References

Abbott, J., Johnson, R., Kozial-McLain, J., & Lowenstein, H. R. (1995). Domestic violence against women: Incidence and prevalence in an emergency department population. *Journal of the American Medical Association, 273*, 1763–1767.

Aboriginal Women's Action Network (AWAN). (2001). *Aboriginal women's action network (AWAN Policy): The implications of restorative justice in cases of violence against aboriginal women and children.* Retrieved June 18, 2007, from http://www.casac.ca/english/awan.htm

Abraham, M. (2000). Isolation as a form of marital violence: The South Asian immigrant experience. *Journal of Social Distress and the Homeless, 9*, 221–236.

Adams, D. (1994, September 25). Records show uneven domestic violence effort. *Boston Globe*, pp. 1, 28–29.

Adamson, J. L., & Thompson, R. A. (1998). Coping with interparental verbal conflict by children exposed to spouse abuse and children from nonviolent homes. *Journal of Family Violence, 13*, 213–232.

Advisory Committee of the Conrad N. Hilton Foundation Model Code Project of the Family Violence Project. (1994). *Model State Code on Domestic and Family Violence.* Reno, NV: National Council of Juvenile and Family Court Judges.

Akers, C., & Kaukinen, C. (2009). The police reporting behaviour of intimate partner violence victims. *Journal of Family Violence, 24*(3), 159–171.

Allen, P. (2010, January 6). Shouting at your wife may get you a criminal record in France. *Mailonline World News.* Retrieved August 5, 2010, from http://www.dailymail.co.uk/news/worldnews/article-1240770/France-introduce-new-law-banning-psychological-violence-marriages.html

Alpert, E. J., Tonkin, A. E., Seeherman, A. M., & Holtz, H. A. (1998). Family violence curricula in U.S. medical schools. *American Journal of Preventative Medicine, 14*(4), 273–282.

Alsdurf, J., & Alsdurf, P. (1989). *Battered into submission: The tragedy of wife abuse in the Christian home.* Downers Grove, IL: InterVarsity.

American Bar Association. (1998). *Unified family courts: A progress report.* Chicago, IL: Author.

American Civil Liberties Union. (1994, September 29). *Analysis of major civil liberties abuses in the Crime Bill. Conference report as passed by the House and the Senate.* New York: Author.

American Civil Liberties Union. (2005, July 27). Letter to the Senate Judiciary Committee Regarding the Violence Against Women Act of 2005, S. 1197.

American Psychiatric Association. (1987). *Diagnostic and statistical manual of mental disorders* (3rd ed., rev.). Washington, DC: Author.

American Psychiatric Association. (2000). *Diagnostic and statistical manual of mental disorders* (4th ed., rev.). Washington, DC: Author.

Ammar, N. (2007). Wife battery in Islam: A comprehensive understanding of interpretations. *Violence Against Women, 13*, 516–526.

Anderson, B. S., & Zinsser, J. P. (1989). *A history of their own: Volume I.* New York: Harper & Row.

Anderson, K. L. (2002). Perpetrator or victim? Relationships between intimate partner violence and well being. *Journal of Marriage and Family, 64*(4), 851–863.

Andrews, B., & Brewin, C. R. (1990). Attributions of blame for marital violence: A study of antecedents and consequences. *Journal of Marriage and Family, 52*, 757–767.

Andrews, D. A., & Bonta, J. (1994). *The psychology of criminal conduct.* Cincinnati, OH: Anderson.

Appel, A. E., & Holden, G.W. (1998). The co-occurrence of spouse and physical child abuse: A review and appraisal. *Journal of Family Psychology, 12*, 578–599.

Apsler, R., Cummins, M. R., & Carl, S. (2003). Perceptions of the police by female victims of domestic partner violence. *Violence Against Women, 9*(11), 1318–1335.

Armstrong, E. G. (2009). Gangsta rap and violence against women. In E. Stark & E. S. Buzawa (Eds.), *Violence against women in families and relationships* (Vol. 4, pp. 141–164). The Media and Cultural Attitudes. New York: Praeger.

Associated Press. (2007, March 23). Judge tells battered Muslim wife: Koran says "men are in charge of women."

Austin, J., & Dankwort, J. (1999). Standards for batterer programs: A review and analysis. *Journal of Interpersonal Violence, 14*(2), 152–168.

Avery, L., Hutchinson, K. H., & Whitaker, K. (2002). Domestic violence and intergenerational rates of child sexual abuse: A case record analysis. *Child and Adolescent Social Work Journal, 29*(1), 77–90.

Babcock, J. C., Green, C. E., & Robie, C. (2004). Does batterers' treatment work?: A meta-analytic review of domestic violence treatment outcome research. *Clinical Psychology Review, 23*, 1023–1053.

Bachman, R. (1992a). Crime in Nonmetropolitan America: A national accounting of trends, incidence rates, and idiosyncratic vulnerabilities. *Rural Sociological Society, 57*(4), 546–560.

Bachman, R. (1992b). *Death and violence on the reservation: Homicide, family violence and suicide in American Indian populations.* Westport, CT: Auburn House.

Bachman, R., & Coker, A. L. (1995). Police involvement in domestic violence: The interactive effects of victim injury, offender's history of violence, and race. *Violence and Victims, 10*, 91–106.

Bachman, R., & Saltzman, L. E. (1995). *Violence against women: Estimates from the redesigned survey* (BJS Publication No. 154–348). Washington, DC: Bureau of Justice Statistics, U.S. Department of Justice.

Balbernie, R. (2001). Circuits and circumstances: The neurobiological consequences of early relationship experiences and how they shape later behaviour. *Journal of Child Psychotherapy, 27*, 237–255.

Ballou, M., Tabol, C., Liriano, D., Vasquez-Nuttal, K., Butler, C., Boorstein, B. W., & McGovern, S. (2007). Initial development of a psychological model for judicial decision making in continuing restraining orders. *Family Court Review, 45*, 274–286.

Bancroft, L., & Silverman, J. (2002). *The batterer as parent: The impact of domestic violence on family dynamics.* Thousand Oaks, CA: Sage.

Bannon, J. (1974). *Social conflict assaults.* Unpublished report for the Detroit Police Department and Police Foundation. Detroit, MI: Detroit Police Department.

Bard, M. (1967). Training police as specialists in family crisis intervention: A community psychology action program. *Community Mental Health Journal, 3*, 315–317.

Bard, M. (1970). *Training police in family crisis intervention.* Washington, DC: U.S. Government Printing Office.

Bard, M. (1973). The role of law enforcement in the helping system. In J. R. Snibbe & H. M. Snibbe (Eds.), *The urban policeman in transition: A psychological and sociological review* (pp. 407–420). Springfield, IL: Charles C Thomas.

Bardach, E. (1977). *The implementation game: What happens after a bill becomes a law.* Cambridge, MA: MIT Press.

Barnett, O. W. (2000). Why battered women do not leave, Part 1: External inhibiting actors within society. *Trauma, Violence & Abuse, 1*, 343–372.

Barnett, O. W., & Fagan, R. W. (1993). Alcohol use in male spouse abusers and their female partners. *Journal of Family Violence, 8*, 1–25.

Barnett, O. W., Fagan, R. W., & Booker, J. M. (1991). Hostility and stress as mediators of aggression in violent men. *Journal of Family Violence, 6*, 219–241.

Barnett, O. W., & Hamberger, L. K. (1992). The assessment of martially violent men on the California Psychological Inventory. *Violence and Victims, 7*, 15–28.

Barnett, O. W., Lee, C. Y., & Thelen, R. E. (1997). Differences in forms, outcomes, and attributions of self-defense and control in interpartner aggression. *Violence Against Women, 3*, 462–481.

Barnett, O. W., Martinez, T. F., & Keyson, M. (1996). The relationship between violence, social support, and self-blame in battered women. *Journal of Interpersonal Violence, 11,* 221–233.

Barnett, O. W., Miller-Perrin, C. L., & Perrin, R. L. (1997). *Family violence across the life span.* Thousand Oaks, CA: Sage.

Bartlett, K. T. (1999). Improving the law relating to post-divorce arrangements for children. In R. Thompson & P. R. Amato (Eds.), *The post-divorce family: Children, parenting and society* (pp. 71–102). Thousand Oaks, CA: Sage.

Basile, S. (2005). A measure of court response to requests for protection. *Journal of Family Violence, 20*(3), 171–179.

Bayley, D. H. (1986). The tactical choices of police patrol officers. *Journal of Criminal Justice, 14,* 329–348.

Bayley, D. H., & Shearing, C. (1996). The future of policing. *Law and Society Review, 30*(3), 585–606.

Belknap, J. (1995). Law enforcement officers' attitudes about the appropriate response to woman battering. *International Review of Victimology, 4,* 47–62.

Belknap, J., Fleury, R. E., Melton, H. C., Sullivan, C., & Leisenring, A. (2001). To go or not to go? Preliminary findings on battered women's decisions regarding court cases. In H. Eigenberg (Ed.), *Woman battering in the United States: Till death do us part* (pp. 319–326). Prospect Heights, IL: Waveland.

Belknap, J., Graham, D. L. R., Allen, P. G., Hartman, J., Lippen, V., & Sutherland, J. (1999). Predicting court outcomes in intimate partner violence cases: Preliminary findings. *Domestic Violence Report, 5,* 1–2, 9–10.

Belknap, J., & Melton, H. (2004). *Intimate partner abuse?* Harrisburg, PA: National Electronic Network on Violence Against Women, Pennsylvania Coalition Against Domestic Violence. Retrieved August 13, 2010, from http://www.vawnet.org/DomesticViolence/Research/VAWnetDocs/AR_MaleVictims.pdf

Belknap, J., Melton, H., Denney, J. T., Fleury-Steiner, R., & Sullivan, C. M. (2009). The levels and roles of social and institutional support reported by survivors of intimate partner abuse. *Feminist Criminology, 4*(4), 377–402.

Belknap, J., & Potter, H. (2005). The trials of measuring the "success" of domestic violence policies. *Criminology & Public Policy, 4*(3), 559–566.

Bell, C. C., & Mattis, J. (2000). The importance of cultural competence in ministering to African American victims of domestic violence. *Violence Against Women, 6,* 515–532.

Bell, D. (1984). The police responses to domestic violence: A replication study. *Police Studies, 7,* 136–143.

Bennett, L. W., Goodman, L., & Dutton, M. A. (1999). Systemic obstacles to the criminal prosecution of a battering partner: A victim perspective. *Journal of Interpersonal Violence, 14*(7), 761.

Bennett, L. W., & Williams, O. J. (2001). Intervention programs for men who batter. In C. Renzetti, J. Edleson, & R. K. Bergen (Eds.), *Sourcebook on violence against women* (pp. 261–278). Thousand Oaks, CA: Sage.

Benson, M. L., & Fox, G. L. (2004, September). *When violence hits home: How economics and neighborhood play a role* (NCJ 205004). Washington, DC: National Institute of Justice.

Bent-Goodley, T. B. (2001). Eradicating domestic violence in the African American community: A literature review and action agenda. *Trauma, Violence, & Abuse, 16,* 84-98.

Berk, R. A., Fenstermaker, S., & Newton, P. J. (1990). An empirical analysis of police responses to incidents of wife battery. In G. T. Hotaling, D. Finkelhor, J. T. Kirkpatrick, & M. A. Straus (Eds.), *Coping with family violence* (pp. 158–168). Newbury Park, CA: Sage.

Berk, R. A., & Newton, P. (1985). Does arrest deter wife battery? An effort to replicate the findings of the Minneapolis spouse abuse experiment. *American Sociological Review, 50,* 253–262.

Berk, R. A., & Sherman, L. (1988). Police responses to family violence incidences: An analysis of an experimental design with incomplete randomization. *Journal of the American Statistical Association, 83,* 70–76.

Berk, S. F., Campbell, A., Klap, R., & Western, B. (1992). Beyesian analysis of the Colorado Springs spouse abuse experiment. *Criminal Law and Criminology, 83,* 170–200.

Berk, S. F., & Loseke, D. R. (1980–1981). "Handling" family violence: Situational determinants of police arrests in domestic disturbances. *Law & Society Review, 15,* 317–346.

Berman, G., & Feinblatt, J. (2005). *Good courts: The case for problem-solving justice.* New York: The New Press.

Berman, G., Rempel, M., & Wolf, R. (2007). *Documenting results: Research on problem solving justice*. New York: Center for Court Innovation.

Berns, N. (2000). Degendering the problem and gendering the blame—political discourse on women and violence. *Gender & Society, 15,* 262–281.

Biden, J. R., Jr. (1999). *Safer streets, safer homes: The success of the violence against women act and the challenge for the future.* A Report from Senator Joseph R. Biden, Jr. (pp. 5, 9).

Binder, A., & Meeker, J. (1988). Experiments as reforms. *Journal of Criminal Justice, 16,* 347–358.

Bittner, E. (1967). The police on skid row: A study of peace keeping. *American Sociological Review, 32,* 699–715.

Bittner, E. (1974). Florence Nightingale in pursuit of Willie Sutton: A theory of the police. In H. Jacob (Ed.), *The potential for reform of criminal justice.* Beverly Hills, CA: Sage.

Bittner, E. (1990). *Aspects of police work.* Boston, MA: Northeastern University Press.

Black, A., & Reiss, A. (1967). *Studies in law enforcement in major metropolitan areas* (Field Survey 3, 2 vols). Washington, DC: U.S. Government Printing Office.

Black, D. (1976). *The behavior of law.* New York: Academic Press.

Black, D. (1980). *The manners and customs of the police.* New York: Academic Press.

Blackwell, B. S., & Vaughn, M. S. (2003). Police civil liability for inappropriate response to domestic assault victims. *Journal of Criminal Justice, 31*(2), 129–146.

Blumstein, A., Cohen, J., & Nagin, D. (Eds.). (1978). *Deterrence and incapacitation: Estimating the effects of criminal sanctions on crime rates.* Washington, DC: National Academy of Sciences.

Board of Regents of State Colleges v. Roth, 408 U. S. 564 (1972).

Bocko, S., Cicchetti, C., Lempicki, L., & Powell, A. (2004). *Restraining order violators, corrective programming and recidivism.* Boston, MA: Office of the Commissioner of Probation.

Boes, M. (2007). Battered women in the emergency room: Emerging roles for the emergency room social worker and clinical nurse specialist. In A. Roberts (Eds.), *Battered women and their families: Intervention strategies and treatment programs* (pp. 301–325). New York: Springer.

Boffey, P. M. (1983, April 5). Domestic violence: Study favors arrest. *New York Times*, p. L1.

Bogat, G. A., DeJonghe, E., Levendosky, A., Davidson, W. S., & von Eye, A. (2005). Trauma symptoms among infants exposed to intimate partner violence. *Child Abuse & Neglect, 30*(2), 109–125.

Bonomi, A. E., Holt, V. L., Martin, D. M., & Thompson, R. S. (2006). Severity of intimate partner violence and occurrence and frequency of police calls. *Journal of Interpersonal Violence, 21*(10), 1–11.

Botuck, S., Berretty, P., Cho, S., Tax, C. A., Archer, M., & Cattaneou, L. B. (2009, June). *Understanding intimate partner stalking: Implications for offering victim services.* Document 227220. Award 2005-WG-BX-0007. Retrieved August 13, 2010, from http://www.ncjrs.gov/pdffiles1/nij/grants/227220.pdf

Bow, J. N., & Boxer, P. (2003). Assessing allegations of domestic violence in custody evaluations. *Journal of Interpersonal Violence, 18,* 1394–1410.

Bowe files for Chapter 11 bankruptcy. (2005, October 18). *Washington* Post. Retrieved August 20, 2010, from http://www.washingtonpost.com/wp-dyn/content/article/2005/10/17/AR2005101700809.html

Bowe let go – sort of. (2001, February 23). *Associated Press.* Retrieved August 20, 2010, from http://www.cbsnews.com/stories/2001/02/23/sports/main274277.shtml

Bowker, L. (1982). Police services to battered women. *Criminal Justice and Behavior, 9,* 476–494.

Bowker, L. (1983). *Beating wife beating.* Toronto: Lexington Books.

Bowker, L. (1988). Religious victims and their religious leaders: Services delivered to one thousand battered women by the clergy. In A. L. Horton & J. A. Williamson (Eds.), *Abuse and religion: When praying isn't enough* (pp. 229–234). Lexington, MA: Lexington Books.

Bowker, L., & Maurer, L. (1987). Medical treatment of battered wives. *Women and Health, 12*(1), 25–45.

Bowman, C. G. (1992). Commentary—The arrest experiments: A feminist critique. *The Journal of Law and Criminology, 83,* 201–208.

Boyer, P. (1978). *Urban masses and moral order in America, 1820–1920.* Cambridge, MA: Harvard University Press.

Boyle, C. (1980, Spring). Violence against wives—the criminal law in retreat? *Northern Ireland Quarterly, 31,* 565–586.

Boyle, K. (2005). *Media and violence: Gendering the debates* (pp. 123–160). London: Sage.

Bradford, J. M., & Bourget, D. (1986). Sexually aggressive men. *Psychiatric Journal of the University of Ottawa, 12*, 169–173.

Bradley v. State 1 Miss. (1 Walker) 156 (1824).

Brady, T. M., & Ashley, O. S. (Eds.). (2005). *Women in substance abuse treatment: Results from the Alcohol and Drug Services Study (ADSS)* (DHSS Publication #SMA 04-3968, Analytic Series A-26). Rockville, MD: Substance Abuse and Mental Health Services Administration, Office of Applied Studies.

Braithwaite, J. (2006). Setting standards for restorative justice. *The British Journal of Criminology, 42*(3), 563–577.

Breslau, N., Davis, G. C., Andreski, P., & Peterson, E. (1991). Traumatic events and posttraumatic stress disorder in an urban population of young adults. *Archives of General Psychiatry, 48*, 216–222.

Brookoff, D. (1997). *Drugs, alcohol and domestic violence in Memphis. National Institute of Justice Research Preview.* Washington, DC: U.S. Department of Justice.

Brown, S. (1984). Police responses to wife beating: Neglect of a crime of violence. *Journal of Criminal Justice, 12*, 277–288.

Browne, A., & Bassuk, S. S. (1997). Intimate violence in the lives of homeless and poor housed women: Prevalence and patterns in an ethnically diverse sample. *American Journal of Orthopsychiatry, 67*, 261–278.

Bruno v. Codd, 396 N.Y.S. 2nd 974, NY, Sup Ct (1977). Reversed in part 407 N.Y.S. 2nd 105 (1978).

Buchbinder, E., & Eisikovits, Z. (2003). Battered women's entrapment in shame: A phenomenological study. *American Journal of Orthopsychiatry, 73*(4), 355.

Bui, H. N., & Morash, M. (1999). Domestic violence in the Vietnamese immigrant community: An exploratory study. *Violence Against Women, 5*, 769–795.

Burris, C. A., & Jaffe, P. (1983). Wife abuse as a crime: The impact of police laying charges. *Canadian Journal of Criminology, 25*, 309–318.

Buzawa, E. (1978). *Traditional responses to domestic disturbances.* Paper presented at the Michigan Sociological Association, Detroit, MI.

Buzawa, E. (1982). Police officer response to domestic violence legislation in Michigan. *Journal of Police Science and Administration, 10*, 415–424.

Buzawa, E., & Austin, T. (1988). Perceptions and attitudes of domestic violence shelter victims towards social and criminal justice systems. *Justice Professional, 3*, 201–222.

Buzawa, E., & Austin, T. (1993). Determining police response to domestic violence victims. *American Behavioral Scientist, 36*, 610–623.

Buzawa, E., & Buzawa, C. (Eds.). (1990). *Domestic violence: The criminal justice response* (1st ed.). Westport, CT: Auburn House.

Buzawa, E., & Buzawa, C. (Eds.). (1996). *Domestic violence: The criminal justice response* (2nd ed.). Thousand Oaks, CA: Sage.

Buzawa, E., & Buzawa, C. (Eds.). (2003). *Domestic violence: The criminal justice response* (3rd ed.). Thousand Oaks, CA: Sage.

Buzawa, E., & Hirschel, D. (2010). Criminalizing assault: Do age and gender matter? (pp. 33–56). In M. Chesney-Lind & N. Jones (Eds.), *Beating up on girls: Girls, violence, demonization, and denial.* Albany, NY: SUNY Press.

Buzawa, E., & Hotaling, G. (2000). *The police response to domestic violence calls for assistance in three Massachusetts towns: Final report.* Washington, DC: National Institute of Justice.

Buzawa, E., & Hotaling, G. (2003). *Domestic violence assaults in three Massachusetts communities: Final report.* Washington, DC: National Institute of Justice.

Buzawa, E., & Hotaling, G. (2006). The impact of relationship status, gender, and minor status in the police response to domestic assaults. *Victims & Offenders, 1*(1), 1–38.

Buzawa, E., & Hotaling, G. (2007). Understanding the impact of prior abuse and prior victimization on the decision to forego criminal justice assistance in domestic violence incidents: A lifecourse perspective. *Brief Treatment & Crisis Intervention, 7*(1), 55–76.

Buzawa, E., Hotaling, G., Klein, A., & Byrne, J. (1999). *Response to domestic violence in a proactive court setting: Final report.* Washington, DC: National Institute of Justice.

CA A. 363 (1991).

CA A. 226 (1993).

CA S. 178 (1993).

Caesar, P. L., & Hamberger, L. K. (Eds.). (1989). *Treating men who batter.* New York: Springer.

Cahn, N. (1992). Prosecuting domestic violence crimes. In E. Buzawa & C. Buzawa (Eds.), *Domestic violence: The changing criminal justice response* (pp. 95–112). Westport, CT: Auburn House.

Cahn, N., & Lerman, L. (1991). Prosecuting woman abuse. In M. Steinman (Ed.), *Woman battering: Policy responses* (pp. 95–112). Cincinnati, OH: Anderson Publishing and Academy of Criminal Justice Sciences.

Caliber Associates. (2002). *Symposium on DV prevention research*. Washington, DC: Department of Defense.

California Gender Bias Task Force. (1996). *Achieving equal justice for women and men in the courts. The draft report of the Judicial Advisory Committee on Gender Bias in the Courts.* San Francisco, CA: Access and Fairness Advisory Committee, Administrative Office of the Courts.

California Penal Code, §646.9 (1992).

Campbell, J. C. (1995). *Assessing dangerousness: Violence by sexual offenders, batterers, and child abusers.* Thousand Oaks, CA: Sage.

Campbell, J. C. (2002). Health consequences of intimate partner violence. *Lancet, 359,* 1331–1336.

Campbell, J. C., Kub, J. E., Belknap, R. A., & Templin, T. N. (1997). Predictors of depression in battered women. *Violence Against Women, 3,* 271–293.

Campbell, J. C., & Soeken, K. L. (1999). Women's responses to battering over time. *Journal of Interpersonal Violence, 14,* 21–40.

Cannavale, F., & Falcon, W. (1986). *Improving witness cooperation.* Washington, DC: U.S. Government Printing Office.

Canton v. Harris, 109 S Ct 1197. (1989).

Caralis, P. V., & Musialowski, R. (1997). Women's experiences with domestic violence and their attitudes and expectations regarding medical care of abuse victims. *The Southern Medical Journal, 90,* 1075–1080.

Carlson, B. E. (1984). Children's observations of interpersonal violence. In A. Roberts (Ed.), *Battered women and their families: Intervention strategies and treatment programs.* New York: Springer.

Carlson, M. J., Harris, S. D., & Holden, G. W. (1999). Protective orders and domestic violence: Risk factors for re-abuse. *Journal of Family Violence, 14,* 205–226.

Carmody, D. C., & Williams, K. R. (1987). Wife assault and perceptions of sanctions. *Violence and Victims, 2,* 25–39.

Carter, J. (2009, July 12). The words of God do not justify cruelty to women. *The Observer.*

Retrieved August 10, 2010, from http://www.guardian.co.uk/commentisfree/2009/jul/12/jimmy-carter-womens-rights-equality

Carmichael, S. E., & Piquero, A. R. (2006). Deterrence and arrest ratios. *Journal of Offender Therapy Comparative Criminology, 50*(1), 71–87.

Casey, P., & Rottman, D. (2005). Problem-solving courts: Models and trends. *Justice System Journal, 26*(1), 35–56.

Cassidy, M., Nicholl, C., Ross, C., & Lonsway, K. (2004). The victim's view: Domestic violence and the police response. *Law Enforcement Executive FORUM, 4,* 135–152.

Castelan, A. (2009). Moby to do benefit concerts to fight domestic violence. *San Diego CW 6 News.* Retrieved September 8, 2010, from http://www.sandiego6.com/news/local/story/Moby-to-do-Benefit-Concerts-to-fight-Domestic/NhC-p-OglUCj6RjrvcuuiQ.cspx

Catalano, S. (2006). *Intimate partner violence in the United States.* Washington, DC: Bureau of Justice Statistics. Retrieved August 13, 2010, from http://www.ojp.usdoj.gov/bjs/

Catalano, S. (2007). *Intimate partner violence in the United States.* Washington, DC: U.S. Department of Justice, Bureau of Justice Statistics. Retrieved August 13, 2010, from http://www.ojp.usdoj.gov/bjs/intimate/ipv.htm

Catalano, S., Smith, E., Snyder, H., and Rand, M. (2009). *Female victims of violence.* Washington, DC: U.S. Bureau of Justice Statistics.

Cavanaugh, M., & Gelles, R. (2005). The utility of male domestic violence typologies. *Journal of Interpersonal Violence, 20*(2), 155–166.

Celebrities violence. (2008). Yahoo Groups. Retrieved August 20, 2010, from http://answers.yahoo.com/question/index?qid=20081010154007AAv83iw

Centers for Disease Control and Prevention. (2003). *Costs of intimate partner violence against women in the United States: Atlanta, Georgia.* Retrieved April 26, 2009, from http://www.cdc.gov/ncipc/pub-res/ipv_cost/IPVBook-Final-Feb18.pdf

Centers for Disease Control and Prevention. (2008). Adverse health conditions and health risk behaviors associated with intimate partner violence—United States, 2005. *Journal of the American Medical Association, 300,* 646–649.

Chalk, R., & King, P. A. (1998). *Violence in families: Assessing prevention and treatment programs.* Washington, DC: National Academy Press.

Chaney, C. K., & Saltzstein, G. H. (1998). Democratic control and bureaucratic responsiveness: The police and domestic violence. *American Journal of Political Science, 42,* 745–768.

Chaudhuri, M., & Daly, K. (1992). Do restraining orders help? Battered women's experience with male violence and legal process. In E. Buzawa & C. Buzawa (Eds.), *Domestic violence: The changing criminal justice response* (pp. 227–254). Westport, CT: Auburn House.

Chermack, S. T., Booth, B., & Curran, G. M. (2006). Gender differences in correlates of recent physical assault among untreated rural and urban at-risk drinkers: Role of depression. *Violence and Victims, 21*(1), 67–80.

Chesney-Lind, M. (1997). *The female offender: Girls, women and crime.* Thousand Oaks, CA: Sage.

Chesney-Lind, M. (2002). Criminalizing victimization: The unintended consequences of pro-arrest policies for girls and women. *Criminology & Public Policy, 1*(2), 81–90.

Chesney-Lind, M. (2006). Patriarchy, crime, justice: Feminist criminology in an era of backlash. *Feminist Criminology, 1*(1), 6–26.

Chesney-Lind, M., & Irwin, K. (2008). *Beyond bad girls: Gender, violence and hype.* New York: Routledge.

Chesney-Lind, M., & Pasko, L. J. (2004). *The female offender: Girls, women and crime* (2nd ed.). Thousand Oaks, CA: Sage.

Child Abuse Prevention and Treatment Act of 1974, Pub. L. No. 93-247.

Childress, S. (2003). Muslim American women are quietly coping with a tragic side ffect of the attacks—A surge in domestic violence. *Newsweek, 142*(5), 2.

Ciokajlo, M. (2006, June 22). $4 million offer told in suit on 911 call. *Chicago Tribune,* at 7.

Cissner, A., & Puffett, N. (2006). *Do batterer program length or approach affect completion or re-arrest rates? A comparison of outcomes between defendants sentenced to two batterer programs in Brooklyn.* New York: Center for Court Innovation. Retrieved September 16, 2010, from http://www.courtinnovation.org/_uploads/documents/IDCC_DCAPpercent20final.pdf

Civil Action for Deprivation of Rights, 42 U.S.C. § 1983 (1979).

Coates, C. J., Leong, D. J., & Lindsey, M. (1997, July). *Personality differences among batterers voluntarily seeking treatment and those ordered to treatment by the court.* Paper presented at the Third National Family Violence Research Conference, Durham, NH.

Cobb, S. (1992, May). *The domestication of violence in mediation: The social construction of disciplinary power in law.* Paper presented at the Law and Society Conference, Philadelphia, PA.

Cohn, E., & Sherman, L. (1987). *Police policy on domestic violence 1986: A national survey (Report 5).* Washington, DC: Crime Control Institute.

Coker, A. L., Smith, P. H., McKeown, R. E., & King, M. L. (2000). Frequency and correlates of intimate partner violence by type: Physical, sexual, and psychological battering. *American Journal of Public Health, 90*(4), 553–559.

Coker, D. (1999). Enhancing autonomy for battered women: Lessons from Navajo Peacemaking. *UCLA Law Review, 47,* 1–111.

Coker, D. (2000). Shifting power for battered women: Law, material resources, and poor women of color. *U.C. Davis Law Review, 33,* 1009–1055.

Cole, G. (1984). The decision to prosecute. In G. Cole (Ed.), *Criminal justice: Law and politics* (5th ed.). Pacific Grove, CA: Brooks/Cole.

Coleman, D. H., & Straus, M. A. (1986). Marital power, conflict, and violence in a nationally representative sample of American couples. *Violence and Victims, 1,* 141–157.

Commonwealth Fund. (1999). *Health concerns across a woman's lifespan: 1998 Survey of women's health.* New York: Author.

Commonwealth of Massachusetts Executive Department. (1997). Executive Order No. 398: Establishing a policy of zero tolerance for domestic violence. Retrieved August 20, 2005, from http://www.lawlib.state.ma.us/ExecOrders/eo398.txt

Congressional Record, 126 Cong. Rec. 24, 120 (1980).

Connecticut Department of Public Safety. (1999). *Family violence arrests annual report.* New Hartford, CT: Author.

Connecticut Department of Public Safety. (2000). *Crime in Connecticut: 2000 Annual report.* Middletown: Connecticut State Police.

Connecticut State Police. (2000). *1999 data.* Middletown, CT: Crime Analysis Unit.

Corvo, K. N. (1992). Attachment and violence in the families of origin of domestically violent men. *Dissertation Abstracts International, 54,* 1950A.

Costa, D. M., & Babcock, J. C. (2008). Articulated thoughts of intimate partner abusive men during anger arousal: Correlates with personality disorder features. *Journal of Family Violence, 23,* 395-402.

Coward, S. (2000). *Restorative justice in cases of domestic and sexual violence: Healing justice?* Retrieved June 14, 2007, from http://www .abusehelplines.org/resources/rs_conf_april2000 .htm

Crank, J. P. (1990). The influence of environmental and organizational factors on police style in urban and rural environments. *Journal of Research in Crime & Delinquency, 27,* 166–189.

Crank, J. P. (1998). *Understanding police culture.* Cincinnati, OH: Anderson.

Crenshaw, K. (1991). Mapping the margins: Intersectionality, identity politics, and violence against women of color. *Stanford Law Review, 43,* 1241–1299.

Cretney, A., & Davis, G. (1997). Prosecuting domestic assault: Victims failing courts or courts failing victims? *The Howard Journal, 36,* 146–157.

Crocker, A. G., Mueser, K. T., Drake, R. E., Clark, R. E., McHugo, G. J., Ackerson, T. H., et al. (2005). Antisocial personality, psychopathy, and violence in persons with dual disorders: A longitudinal analysis. *Criminal Justice and Behavior, 32*(4), 452–476.

Crooks, C. V., Jaffe, P. G., & Bala, N. (2010). Factoring in the effects of children's exposure to domestic violence in determining appropriate postseparation parenting plans. In M. T. Hannah and B. Goldstein (Eds.), *Domestic violence, abuse, and child custody: Legal strategies and policy issues* (pp. 22.1–22.52). Kingston, NJ: Civic Research Institute.

Crowell, N. A., & Burgess, A. W. (1996). *Understanding violence against women.* Washington, DC: National Academy Press.

Crumley, B. (2010, January 9). French bid to ban marital abuse that's psychological. *Time* [online]. Retrieved August 5, 2010, from http://www.time.com/time/world/article/ 0,8599,1952552,00.html

Dabbs, J. M., Jr., Carr, T. S., Frady, R. L., & Riad, J. K. (1995). Testosterone, crime, and misbehavior among 692 male prison inmates. *Personality and Individual Differences, 18,* 627–633.

Dabbs, J. M., Jr., & Dabbs, M. G. (2000). *Heroes, rogues, and lovers: Testosterone and behavior.* New York: McGraw-Hill.

Dabbs, J. M., Jr., Frady, R. L., Carr, T. S., & Beach, N. F. (1987). Saliva, testosterone and criminal violence in young adult prison inmates. *Psychosomatic Medicine, 49,* 174–182.

Dabbs, J. M., Jr., Jurkovic, G. J., & Frady, R. L. (1991). Salivary testosterone and cortisol among late adolescent male offenders. *Journal of Abnormal Child Psychology, 19,* 469–478.

Dabbs, J. M., Jr., Ruback, R. B., Frady, R. L., & Hopper, C. H. (1988). Saliva testosterone and criminal violence against women. *Personality and Individual Differences, 9,* 269–275.

Daly, K., & Stubbs, J. (2006). Feminist engagement with restorative justice. *Theoretical Criminology (Special Issue: Gender, Race and Restorative Justice), 10*(1), 9–28.

Daly, K., & Stubbs, J. (2007). Feminist theory, feminist and anti-racist politics, and restorative justice. In G. Johnstone & D. W. Van Ness (Eds.), *Handbook of restorative justice* (pp. 149–170). Portland, OR: Willan.

Datner, E. M., Wiebe, D. J., Brensinger, C. M., & Nelson, D. B. (2007). Identifying pregnant women experiencing domestic violence in an urban emergency department. *Journal of Interpersonal Violence, 22,* 124–135.

Davies, B., Ralph, S., Hawton M., & Craig, L. (1995). A study of client satisfaction with family court counseling in cases involving domestic violence. *Family and Conciliation Courts Review, 33,* 324–341.

Davis, K. E., & Freeze, I. H. (2000). Research on stalking: What do we know and where do we go? *Violence and Victims, 15*(4), 473–487.

Davis, P. (1983). Restoring the semblance of order: Police strategies in the domestic disturbance. *Symbolic Interaction, 6,* 261–278.

Davis, R. C., & Erez, E. (1998). *Immigrant populations as victims: Toward a multicultural criminal justice system. Research in brief.* Washington, DC: National Institute of Justice.

Davis, R. C., & Smith, B. E. (1995). Domestic violence reforms: Empty promises of fulfilled expectations. *Crime & Delinquency, 41,* 541–552.

Davis, R. C., Smith, B. E., & Nickles, L. (1997). *Prosecuting domestic violence cases with reluctant victims: Assessing two novel approaches in Milwaukee.* Washington, DC: National Institute of Justice.

Davis, R. C., Smith, B. E., & Nickles, L. (1998). Prosecuting domestic violence cases with reluctant victims: Assessing two novel approaches in Milwaukee. In *Legal interventions in family* violence: Research findings and policy implications (pp. 71–72). Washington, DC: National Institute of Justice and the American Bar Association.

Davis, R. C., Tichane, M., & Grayson, D. (1980). *Mediation and arbitration as alternatives to criminal prosecution in felony arrest cases: An evaluation of the Brooklyn Dispute Resolution Center.* New York: Vera Institute of Justice.

Dawson, M., & Dinovitzer, R. (2001). Victim cooperation and the prosecution of domestic violence in a specialized court. *Justice Quarterly, 18,* 595–622.

DeJong, C., & Burgess-Proctor, A. (2006). A summary of personal protection order statutes in the United States. *Violence Against Women, 12*(1), 68–88.

DeKeseredy, W. S. (1995). Enhancing the quality of survey data on woman abuse: Examples from a national Canadian study. *Violence Against Women, 1,* 158–173.

DeKeseredy, W. S., & MacLeod, L. (1997). *Women abuse: A sociological story.* Toronto, Canada: Harcourt Brace.

DeKeseredy, W. S., Saunders, D. G., Schwartz, M. D., & Alvi, S. (1997). The meanings and motives for women's use of violence in Canadian college dating relationships: Results from a national survey. *Sociological Spectrum, 17,* 199–222.

DeKeseredy, W. S., & Schwartz, M. D. (1998). *Woman abuse on campus: Results from the Canadian national survey.* Thousand Oaks, CA: Sage.

del Carmen, R. V., & Walker, J. (2003). *Briefs of leading cases in law enforcement* (5th ed.). Cincinnati, OH: Anderson.

DeLeon-Granados, W., Wells, W., & Binsbacher, R. (2006). Arresting developments: Trends in female arrests for domestic violence and proposed explanations. *Violence Against Women, 12*(4), 355–371.

Deschner, J. (1984). *The hitting habit: Anger control for battering couples.* New York: The Free Press.

DeShaney v. Winnebago County Dept of Social Services, 109 S. CT 998 (1989).

Dienemann, J., Glass, N., & Hyman, R. (2005). Survivor preferences for response to IPV disclosure. *Clinical Nursing Research, 14,* 215–223.

Dill, K. E. (2009). Violent video games, rape myth acceptance, and negative attitudes toward Women. In E. Stark & E. S. Buzawa (Eds.), *Violence against women in families and*

relationships. Volume 4: The media and cultural attitudes (pp. 125–140). New York: Praeger.

Divorcing couple shackled together by judge. (2002). *Women's News.* Retrieved August 25, 2010, from http://www.womensenews.org/story/cheers-and-jeers/020302/divorcing-couple-shackled-together-judge

Dixon, D. (1997). Law in policing. Oxford: Clarendon Press.

Dixon, L., & Browne, K. (2003). The heterogeneity of spouse abuse: A review. *Aggression and Violent Behavior, 8,* 107–130.

Dobash, R. E., & Dobash, R. P. (1979). *Violence against wives: A case against the patriarchy.* New York: The Free Press.

Dobash, R. E., & Dobash, R. P. (1992). *Women, violence and social change.* London: Routledge.

Dobash, R. E., & Dobash, R. P. (2000). Evaluating criminal justice interventions for domestic violence. *Crime & Delinquency, 40,* 252–270.

Dobash, R. P., Dobash, R. E., Cavanagh, K., & Lewis, R. (1998). Separate and intersecting realities: A comparison of men's and women's accounts of violence against women. *Violence Against Women, 4*(4), 382–414.

Doggett, M. E. (1992). *Marriage, wife-beating and the law in Victorian England.* London: Weidenfeld and Nicholson.

Dolon, R., Hendricks, J., & Meagher, M. (1986). Police practices and attitudes toward domestic violence. *Journal of Police Science and Administration, 14*(3), 187–192.

Domestic Violence Training and Monitoring Unit. (2001). DV cases arrests by gender. *Domestic violence and sexual assault reports (from 01/01/99 –12/31/00), DV# 04.* Retrieved July 5, 2002, from http://courts.state.ri.us/domesticnew/dvsa/reports_dloads.htm_

Dugan, L., Nagin, D., & Rosenfeld, R. (2001). *Exposure reduction or backlash? The effects of domestic violence resources on intimate partner homicide: Final report.* Washington, DC: U.S. Department of Justice.

Dunford, F. W. (1990). System-initiated warrants for suspects of domestic assault: A pilot study. *Justice Quarterly, 7,* 631–653.

Dunford, F. W., Huizinga, D., & Elliott, D. S. (1989). *The Omaha domestic violence police experiment: Final report to the National Institute of Justice and the City of Omaha.* Boulder, CO: Institute of Behavioral Science.

Dunford, F. W., Huizinga, D., & Elliot D. S. (1990). The role of arrest in domestic assault:

The Omaha Police Experiment. *Criminology, 28*, 183–206.

Dunford-Jackson, B. L., Frederick, L., Hart, B., & Hofford, M. (1998). Unified family courts: How will they serve victims of domestic violence? *Family Law Quarterly, 32*(1), 131–146.

Dunham, K., & Senn, C. Y. (2000). Minimizing negative experiences: Women's disclosure of partner abuse. *Journal of Interpersonal Violence, 15*(3), 251–261.

Durose, M. R., Harlow, C. W., Langan, P. W., Motivans, M. Rantala, R. R., & Smith, E. L. (2005). *Family violence statistics: Including statistics on strangers and acquaintances* (NCJ 207846). Washington, DC: Department of Justice, Bureau of Justice Statistics.

Durose, M. R., Langan, P. W., & Smith, E. L. (2008). *State court processing of domestic violence cases* (NCJ 214993). Washington, DC: Department of Justice, Bureau of Justice Statistics.

Dutton, D. G. (1986). Wife assaulters' explanations for assault: The neutralization of self-punishment. *Canadian Journal of Behavioral Science, 18*, 381–390.

Dutton, D. G. (1987, July). *The prediction of recidivism in a population of wife assaulters.* Paper presented at the Third International Family Violence Conference, Durham, NH.

Dutton, D. G. (1988). *The domestic assault of women: Psychological and criminal justice perspectives.* Boston, MA: Allyn & Bacon.

Dutton, D. G. (1998). *The abusive personality: Violence and control in intimate relationships.* New York: Guilford.

Dutton, D. G. (2005). Domestic abuse assessment in child custody disputes: Beware the domestic violence research paradigm. *Journal of Child Custody, 2*(4), 23–42.

Dutton, D. G., & Strachan, C. (1987, July). *The prediction of recidivism in a population of wife assaulters.* Paper presented at the Third National Conference for Family Violence Researchers, Durham, NH.

Dutton, M. A., Green, B. L., Kaltman, S. I., Roesch, D. M., Zeffiro, T. A., & Krause, E. D. (2006). Intimate partner violence, PTSD and adverse health outcomes. *Journal of Interpersonal Violence, 21*(7), 955–968.

Dutton-Douglas, M. A. (1992). Treating battered women in the aftermath stage. *Psychotherapy in Private Practice, 10*, 93–98.

Eaton, L., Kaufman, M. R., Fuhrel, A., Cain, D., Cherry, C., Pope, H., & Kalichman, S.C. (2008).

Examining factors co-existing with interpersonal violence in lesbian relationships. *Journal of Family Violence, 23*, 697–705.

Edleson, J. L. (1993). Advocacy services for battered women. *Violence Update, 4*, 1–10.

Edleson, J. L. (1996). Controversy and change in batterers' programs. In J. Edleson & Z. C. Eisikovits (Eds.), *Future interventions with battered women and their families* (pp. 154–169). Thousand Oaks, CA: Sage.

Edleson, J. L. (1999). Children's witnessing of adult domestic violence. *Journal of Interpersonal Violence, 14*, 839–870.

Edleson, J. L. (2001). Studying the co-occurrence of child maltreatment and woman battering in families. In S. A. Graham-Bermann & J. L. Edleson (Eds.), *Domestic violence in the lives of children: The future of research, intervention and social policy* (pp. 91–110). Washington, DC: American Psychological Association.

Edleson, J. L. (2007). Coordinated community responses in the United States: Promoting safety for battered women and their children. *Libro de actas I Congreso Internacional sobre Violencia de Genero* (pp. 128–139). Valencia, Spain: Toerlanciacero.

Edleson, J. L., & Beeman, S. K. (2000). *Responding to the co-occurrence of child maltreatment and adult domestic violence in Hennepin County.* Retrieved September 7, 2010, from http://www.mincava.umn.edu/link/finreport.asp

Edleson, J. L., & Brygger, M. P. (1986). Gender differences in reporting of battering incidents. *Family Relations, 35*, 377–382.

Eigenberg, H. M. (Ed.). (2001). *Women battering in the United States: Till death do us part.* Prospect Heights, IL: Waveland.

Eigenberg, H. M., Scarborough, K. E., & Kappeler, V. E. (1996). Contributory factors affecting arrest in domestic and non-domestic assaults. In H. Eigenberg (Ed.), *Women battering in the United States: Till death do us part* (pp. 269–326). Prospect Heights, IL: Waveland.

Eitle, D. (2005). The influence of mandatory arrest policies, police organizational characteristics, and situational variables on the probability of arrest in domestic violence cases. *Crime and Delinquency, 51*, 573–597.

Ellis, D. S. (1993). Family courts, marital conflict mediation and wife assault. In N. Z. Hilton (Ed.), *Legal responses to wife assault: Current trends and evaluation* (pp. 165–187). Newbury Park, CA: Sage.

Ellis, D. S., & Stuckless, N. (1996). *Mediating and negotiating marital conflicts*. Thousand Oaks, CA: Sage.

Ellis, J. W. (1984). Prosecutorial discretion to charge in cases of spousal assault: A dialogue. *Journal of Criminal Law and Criminology, 75,* 56–102.

Ellis, L. W. (2005). A theory explaining biological correlates of criminality. *European Journal of Criminology, 2,* 287–315.

Ellison, C. G., Bartkowski, J. P., & Anderson, K. L. (1999). Are there religious variations in intimate partner violence? *Journal of Family Issues, 20,* 87–113.

Ellison, C. G., Bartkowski, J. P., & Segal, M. L. (1996). Do conservative Protestant parents spank more often? Further evidence from the National Survey of Families and Households. *Social Science Quarterly, 77,* 663–673.

English, B. (1992, June 22). Billing abusers for the damage. *Boston Globe,* p. 15.

Eppler, A. (1986). Battered women and the equal protection clause: Will the Constitution help them when the police won't? *Yale Law Journal, 95,* 788–809.

Epstein, D. (1999). Effective intervention in domestic violence cases: Rethinking the roles of prosecutors, judges, and the court system. *Yale Journal of Law and Feminism, 11,* 3–50.

Epstein, S. (1987). The problem of dual arrest in family violence cases. In *The law enforcement response to family violence*. New York: Victim Services Agency.

Erez, E., & Belknap, J. (1998). In their own words: Battered women's assessment of the criminal processing system's response. *Violence and Victims, 13,* 251–268.

Erez, E., & Tontodonato, P. (1990). The effect of victim participation in sentencing on sentence outcomes. *Criminology, 28,* 451–474.

Erwin, P. (2004). *When is arrest not an option? The dilemmas of predominant physical aggressor language and the regulation of intimate partner violence*. San Francisco, CA: Battered Women's Project.

Fagan, J. A. (1988). Contributions of family violence research to criminal justice policy on wife assault: Paradigms of science and social control. *Violence and Victims, 3,* 159–186.

Fagan, J. A. (1996). *The criminalization of domestic violence: Promises and limits*. NIJ Research Report. Washington, DC: National Institute of Justice.

Fagan, J. A., & Browne, A. (1994). Violence between spouses and intimates: Physical aggression between women and men in intimate relationships. In A. J. Reiss & J. A. Roth (Eds.), *Understanding and preventing violence* (Vol. 3, pp. 115–191). Washington, DC: National Research Council, National Academy of Sciences.

Fagan, J. A., Stewart, D. K., & Hansen, K. V. (1983). Violent men or violent husbands? Background factors and situational correlates. In D. Finkelhor, R. J. Gelles, G. T. Hotaling, & M. A. Straus (Eds.), *The dark side of families* (pp. 49–68). Beverly Hills, CA: Sage.

Fals-Stewart, W. (2003). The occurrence of partner physical aggression on days of alcohol consumption: A longitudinal diary study. *Journal of Consulting Psychology, 71*(1), 41–52.

Fals-Stewart, W., Golden, J., & Schumacher, J. A. (2003). Intimate partner violence and substance use: A longitudinal day-to-day examination. *Addictive Behaviors, 28*(9), 1555–1574.

Family Violence Prevention Fund. (2009). *Door opens for battered immigrant women seeking asylum*. Retrieved August 13, 2010, from http://www.endabuse.org/section/programs/immigrant_women

Fantuzzo, J. W., Boruch, R., Beriama, A., Atkins, M., & Marcus, S. (1997). Domestic violence and children: Prevalence and risk in five major U.S. cities. *Journal of the American Academy of Child and Adolescent Psychiatry, 36,* 116–122.

Fantuzzo, J. W., DePaola, L. M., Lambert, L., Martino, T., Anderson, G., & Sutton, S. (1991). Effects of interparental violence on the psychological adjustment and competencies of young children. *Journal of Consulting and Clinical Psychology, 59,* 258–265.

Fantuzzo, J. W., & Fusco, R. (2007). Children's direct exposure to types of domestic violence crime: A population-based investigation. *Journal of Family Violence, 22*(7), 543–552.

Fantuzzo, J. W., & Mohr, W. (1999). Prevalence and effects of child exposure to domestic violence. *The Future of Children, 9*(3), 21–32.

Faragher, T. (1985). The police response to violence against women in the home. In J. Pahl (Ed.), *Private violence and public policy* (pp. 16–48). London: Routledge and Kegan Paul.

Farrington, K. M. (1980). Stress and family violence. In M. A. Straus & G. T. Hotaling (Eds.), *Social causes of husband-wife violence* (pp. 94–114). Minneapolis: University of Minnesota Press.

Faulk, R. (1977). Men who assault their wives. In M. Roy (Ed.), *Battered women: A psychosociological study of domestic violence* (pp. 180–183). New York: Van Nostrand.

Feder, L. (1996). The importance of offender's presence in the arrest decision when police respond to domestic violence calls. *Journal of Criminal Justice, 12,* 279–305.

Feder, L. (1997). Domestic violence and police response in a pro-arrest jurisdiction. *Women & Criminal Justice, 8*(4), 79–98.

Feder, L. (1998). Police handling of domestic violence calls: Is there a case for discrimination? *Crime & Delinquency, 44,* 139–153.

Federal Interstate Stalking Law, 18 U.S.C., Sec. 2261A (1996, 2000).

Feld, L. S., & Straus, M. (1989). Escalation and desistance of wife assault in marriage. *Criminology, 27,* 141–161.

Felson, R. B., Ackerman, J., & Gallagher, C. (2005). Police intervention and the repeat of domestic assault. *Criminology, 43*(3), 563–588.

Felson, R. B., Messner, S. F., Hoskin, A., & Deane. G. (2002). Reasons for reporting and not reporting violence to the police. *Criminology, 40,* 617–648.

Felson, R. B., & Outlaw, M. (2007). The control motive and marital violence. *Violence and Victims, 22,* 387–407.

Felson, R. B., & Paré, P. P. (2005). The reporting of domestic violence and sexual assault by non-strangers to the public. *Journal of Marriage and the Family, 67*(3), 597–610.

Felson, R. B., & Paré, P. P. (2007). Does the criminal justice system treat domestic violence and sexual assault offenders differently. *Justice Quarterly, 24,* 435–459.

Ferraro, K. (1989a). The legal response to women battering in the United States. In J. Hanmer, J. Radford, & E. Stanko (Eds.), *Women, policing, and male violence* (pp. 155–184). London: Routledge & Kegan Paul.

Ferraro, K. (1989b). Policing women battering. *Social Problems, 36,* 61–74.

Fiedler, D., Briar, K. H., & Pierce, M. (1984). Services for battered women. *Journal of Sociology and Social Welfare, 11,* 540–557.

Field, M., & Field, H. (1973). Marital violence and the criminal process: Neither justice nor peace. *Social Service Review, 47,* 221–240.

Finkelhor, D., Cross, T., & Cantor, E. (2005). The justice system for juvenile victims: A comprehensive model of case flow. *Trauma Violence & Abuse,* 45–59.

Finkelhor, D., Hotaling, G. T., & Yllö, K. (1988). *Stopping family violence: Research priorities for the coming decade.* Newbury Park, CA: Sage.

Finkelhor, D., Ormrod, R., & Turner, H. (2007). Poly-victimization: A neglected component in child victimization trauma. *Child Abuse & Neglect, 31,* 7–26.

Finkelhor, D., Ormrod, R., Turner, H., & Hamby, S. (2005). The victimization of children and youth: A comprehensive national survey. *Child Maltreatment, 10*(1), 5–25.

Finkelhor, D., Turner, H., Ormrod, R., Hamby, S., & Kracke, K. (2009). *Children's exposure to violence: A comprehensive national survey.* Washington, DC: Office of Juvenile Justice and Delinquency Prevention.

Finn, P. (1989). Statutory authority in the use and enforcement of civil protection orders against domestic abuse. *Family Law Quarterly, 24,* 43–73.

Finn, P. (1991). Civil protection orders: A flawed opportunity for intervention. In M. Steinman (Ed.), *Woman battering: Policy responses* (pp. 155–190). Cincinnati, OH: Anderson.

Finn, P., & Colson, S. (1990). *Civil protection orders: Legislation, current court practice, and enforcement.* Washington, DC: National Institute of Justice.

Finn, P., & Colson, S. (1998). Civil protection orders. In *Legal interventions in family violence: Research findings and policy implications* (pp. 43–47). Washington, DC: National Institute of Justice.

Fischer, K., & Rose, M. (1995). When "enough is enough": Battered women's decision making around court orders of protection. *Crime & Delinquency, 41,* 414–429.

Fisher, B., Cullen, F., & Turner, M. (2002). Being pursued: Stalking victimization in a nation study of college women. *Criminology & Public Policy, 1,* 257–308.

Fitzpatrick, D., & Halliday, C. (1992). *Not the way to love: Violence against young women in dating relationships.* Amherst, Canada: Cumberland County Transition House Association.

Fletcher, A. (1995). *Gender, sex and subordination in England 1500–1800.* New Haven, CT: Yale University Press.

Foa, E. B., & Riggs, D. (1994). Posttraumatic stress disorder and rape. In R. S. Pynoos (Eds.), *Posttraumatic stress disorder: A clinical review* (pp. 1333–1363). Lutherville, MD: Sidran.

Ford, D. A. (1983). Wife battery and criminal justice: A study of victim decisionmaking. *Family Relations, 32,* 463–475.

Ford, D. A. (1984, August). *Prosecution as a victim power resource for managing conjugal violence.* Version of the paper presented at the annual meeting of the Society for the Study of Social Problems, San Antonio, TX.

Ford, D. A. (1987, July). *The impact of police officers' attitudes toward victims on the disinclination to arrest wife batterers.* Paper presented at the Third International Conference for Family Violence Researchers, Durham, NH.

Ford, D. A. (1988, November). *Preventing wife battery through criminal justice.* Paper presented at the annual meeting of the American Society of Criminology, Chicago, IL.

Ford, D. A. (1990). The preventative impacts of policies for prosecuting wife batterers. In E. Buzawa & C. Buzawa (Eds.), *Domestic violence: The criminal justice response.* Westport, CT: Auburn House.

Ford, D. A. (1991). Prosecution as a victim power resource: A note on empowering women in violent conjugal relationships. *Law & Society Review, 1,* 313–334.

Ford, D. A. (1992). *Training project on family violence for Indiana law enforcement officers: Final report.* Washington, DC: Department of Justice.

Ford, D. A. (1993). *The Indianapolis domestic violence prosecution experiment. Final report submitted to the National Institute of Justice.* Washington, DC: U.S. Department of Justice.

Ford, D. A., & Burke, M. J. (1987, July). *Victim initiated criminal complaints for wife battery: An assessment of motives.* Paper presented at the Third National Conference for Family Violence Researchers, Durham, NH.

Ford, D. A., & Regoli, M. J. (1992). The preventive impact of policies for prosecuting wife batterers. In E. S. Buzawa & C. G. Buzawa (Eds.), *Domestic violence: The changing criminal justice response* (pp. 181–207). Westport, CT: Greenwood.

Ford, D. A., & Regoli, M. J. (1993). The criminal prosecution of wife assaulters: Process problems, and effects. In N. Z. Hilton (Ed.), *Legal responses to wife assault: Current trends and evaluation.* Newbury Park, CA: Sage.

Ford, D. A., Reichard, D., Goldsmith, S., & Regoli, M. J. (1996). Future directions for criminal justice policy on domestic violence. In E. Buzawa & C. Buzawa (Eds.), *Do arrests and restraining orders work?* (pp. 243–265). Thousand Oaks, CA: Sage.

Forrell, C. (1990–1991). Stopping the violence: Mandatory arrest and police tort liability for failing to assist battered women. *Berkeley Women's Law Journal, 6,* 215–263.

Fortune, M., & Enger, C. G. (2005, March). *Violence against women and the role of religion.* VAWnet Applied Research Forum.

Franklin, D. L. (2000). *What's love got to do with it? Understanding and healing the rift between Black men and women.* New York: Simon & Schuster.

Frederick, L., & Lizdas, K. C. (2003). *The role of restorative justice in the battered women's movement.* Minneapolis, MN: Battered Women's Justice Project.

Freeman, M. (1980). Violence against women: Does the legal system provide solutions or itself constitute the problem? *British Journal of Law and Society, 7,* 216–241.

Freund, K., Bak, S., & Blackhall, L. (1996). Identifying domestic violence in a primary care practice. *Journal of General Internal Medicine, 11*(1), 44–46.

Frey, S., & Morton, M. (1986). *New world, new roles: A documentary history of women in pre-industrial America.* Westport, CT: Greenwood.

Frias, S., & Angel, R. J. (2005). The risk of partner violence among low-income Hispanic subgroups. *Journal of Marriage and Family, 67,* 552–564.

Frieze, I. H., & Browne, A. (1989). Violence in marriage. In L. Ohlin & M. H. Tonry (Eds.), *Family violence.* Chicago, IL: University of Chicago Press.

Frye, V., Wilt, S., & Schomberg, D. (2000). *Female homicide in New York City, 1990–1997.* Retrieved September 20, 2010, from www.ci .nyc.ny.us/html/doh/pdf/ip/female97.pdf

Fugate, M., Landis, L., Riordan, K., Naureckas, S., & Engel, B. (2005). Barriers to domestic violence help seeking: Implications for intervention. *Violence Against Women, 11*(3), 290–310.

Gagnon, A. (1992). Ending mandatory divorce mediation for battered women. *Harvard Women's Law Journal, 15,* 272–294.

Gaines, L., Kappeler, V., & Vaughn, J. (1999). *Policing in America* (3rd ed.). Cincinnati, OH: Anderson.

Gall v. Gall, no. 1720 MDA (2002).

Gallup-Black, A. (2005). Twenty years of rural and urban trends in family and intimate partner homicide: Does place matter? *Homicide Studies, 9*(2), 149–173.

Gamache, D. J., Edleson, J. L., & Schock, M. D. (1988). Coordinated police, judicial and social service response to woman battering: A multi baseline evaluation across three communities. In G. T. Hotaling, D. Finkelhor, J. T. Kirkpatrick, & M. A. Straus (Eds.), *Coping with family violence: Research and policy perspectives* (pp. 193–209). Newbury Park, CA: Sage.

Garland, D. (2001). *The culture of control: Crime and social order in contemporary society.* Chicago, IL: University of Chicago Press.

Garner, J. (1990). *Alternative police responses to spouse assault: The design of seven field experiments.* Unpublished manuscript.

Garner, J., & Clemmer, E. (1986). *Danger to police in domestic disturbances: A new look.* In National Institute of Justice: Research in Brief. Washington, DC: Department of Justice.

Garner, J., Fagan, J. A., & Maxwell, C. (1995). Published findings from the spouse assault replication program: A critical review. *Journal of Quantitative Criminology, 11*(1), 3–28.

Garner, J., & Maxwell, C. (2000). What are the lessons of the police arrest studies? In S. Ward & D. Finkelhor (Eds.), *Program evaluation and family violence research* (pp. 83–114). New York: Haworth.

Garner, J., & Maxwell, C. (2008). Coordinated community responses to intimate partner violence in the 20th and 21st centuries [policy essay]. *Criminology & Public Policy, 7*(4), 301–311.

Gartin, P. (1991). *The individual effects of arrest in domestic violence cases: A reanalysis of the Minneapolis Domestic Violence Experiment: Final report.* Washington, DC: National Institute of Justice.

Gavin, C., & Puffett, N. K. (2005). *Criminal domestic violence case processing: A case study of the five boroughs of New York City.* New York City: Center for Court Innovation. Retrieved September 21, 2010, from http://www.court innovation.org/_uploads/documents/Citywide %20Final1.pdf

Geberth, V. (1992, October). Stalkers. *Law and Order,* 138–143.

Gelles, R. J. (1972). *The violent home: A study of physical aggression between husbands and wives.* Beverly Hills, CA: Sage.

Gelles, R. J. (1983). An exchange/social control theory. In D. Finkelhor, R. J. Gelles, G. T. Hotaling, & M. A. Straus (Eds.), *The dark side of families: Current family violence research* (pp. 151–165). Beverly Hills, CA: Sage.

Gelles, R. J. (1993a). Constraints against family violence: How well do they work? *American Behavioral Scientist, 36,* 575–586.

Gelles, R. J. (1993b). Through a sociological lens: Social structure and family violence. In R. J. Gelles & D. Loseke (Eds.), *Current controversies on family violence* (pp. 31–47). Newbury Park, CA: Sage.

Gelles, R. J. (2007). The politics of research: The use, abuse, and misuse of social science data— the cases of intimate partner violence. *Family Court Review, 45,* 42–51.

Gelles, R. J., & Loseke, D. (1993). *Current controversies on family violence.* Newbury Park, CA: Sage.

Gelles, R. J., & Straus, M. (1988). *Intimate violence.* New York: Simon & Schuster.

Gendreau, P., Cullen, F., & Bonta, J. (1994). Intensive rehabilitation supervision: The next generation in community corrections? *Federal Probation, 58*(1), 72–78.

George, D. T., Phillips, M. J., Doty, L., Umhau, J. C., & Rawlings, R. R. (2006). A model linking biology, behavior and psychiatric diagnoses in perpetrators of domestic violence. *Medical Hypotheses, 67,* 345–353.

George, D. T., Umhau, J. C., Phillips, M. J., Emmela, D., Ragan, P. W., Shoaf, S. E., & Rawlings, R. R. (2001). Serotonin, testosterone and alcohol in the etiology of domestic violence. *Psychiatry Research, 104,* 27–37.

Gibbs, J. (1985). Deterrence theory and research. *Nebraska Symposium on Motivation, 33,* 87–130.

Gibson-Davis, C. M., Edin, K., & McLahanan, S. (2005). High hopes but even higher expectations: The retreat from marriage among low-income couples. *Journal of Marriage and Family, 67,* 1301–1312.

Giesbrecht, N., & Sevcik, I. (2000). The process of recovery and rebuilding among abused women in the conservative evangelical subculture. *Journal of Family Violence, 15,* 229–248.

Gilbert, L., El-Bassel, N., Rajah, V., Foleno, A., & Frye, V. (2001). Linking drug-related activities with experiences of partner violence: A focus group study of women in methadone treatment. *Violence and Victims, 16*(5), 517–536.

Gilbert, R., Widom, C. S., Browne, K., Fergusson, D., Webb, E., & Janson, S. (2009). Burden and consequences of child maltreatment in high-income countries. *Lancet, 373*(9657), 68–81.

Giles-Sims, J. (1983). *Wife battering: A systems theory approach.* New York: Guilford.

Gin, N., Rucker, L., Frayne, S., Cygan, R., & Hubbell, A. (1991). Prevalence of domestic violence among patients in three ambulatory care internal medicine clinics. *Journal of General Internal Medicine, 6*, 317–322.

Glass, N., Manganello, J., & Campbell, J. C. (2004). *Risk for intimate partner femicide in violent relationships.* DV Report 9, no. 2, pp. 1, 2, 30–33.

Glass, N., Perrin, N., Hanson, G., Bloom, T., Gardner, E., & Campbell, J. (2008). Risk for reassault in abusive female same-sex relationships. *Journal of Public Health, 21,* 1021–1027.

Golden, J. F. (1987). Mutual orders of protection in New York State family offense proceedings: A denial of "liberty" without due process of law. *Columbia Human Rights Law Review, 18,* 309–331.

Golding, J. M. (l999). Intimate partner violence as a risk factor for MENTAL disorders: A meta-analysis. *Journal of Family Violence, 14*(2), 99–132.

Goldkamp, J. (1996). *The role of drug and alcohol abuse in domestic violence and its treatment: Dade County's domestic violence court experiment, Final Report.* Philadelphia, PA: Crime and Justice Institute.

Gondolf, E. W. (1984). *Men who batter: An integrated approach stopping wife abuse.* Holmes Beach, FL: Learning.

Gondolf, E. W. (1988). Who are those guys? Toward a behavioral typology of batterers. *Violence and Victims, 3,* 187–203.

Gondolf, E. W. (1992). Discussion of violence in psychiatric evaluations. *Journal of Interpersonal Violence, 7,* 334–349.

Gondolf, E. W. (1997). Patterns of reassault in batterer programs. *Violence and Victims, 12,* 373–387.

Gondolf, E. W. (1998). *Assessing woman battering in mental health services.* Thousand Oaks, CA: Sage.

Gondolf, E. W. (1999). Characteristics of court-mandated batterers in four cities: Diversity and dichotomies. *Violence Against Women, 5,* 1277–1293.

Gondolf, E. W. (2002). *Batterer intervention systems.* Thousand Oaks, CA: Sage.

Gondolf, E. W. (2005). *Culturally focused batterer counseling for African-American men* (NCJ 210828). Final report for National Institute of Justice, grant number 2001-WT-BX-0003. Washington, DC: U.S. Department of Justice, National Institute of Justice.

Gondolf, E. W., Fisher, E. R., & McFerron, J. R. (1988). Racial differences among shelter residents: A comparison of Anglo, Black and Hispanic battered. *Journal of Family Violence, 3,* 39–51.

Gondolf, E. W., McWilliams, J. R., Hart, B., & Stuehling, J. (1994). Court response to petitions for civil protection orders. *Journal of Interpersonal Violence, 9,* 4.

Gondolf, E. W., & White, R. J. (2000). "Consumer" recommendations for batterers programs. *Violence Against Women, 6,* 198–217.

Gonzales v. City of Castle Rock, 2001, U.S. Dist. LEXIS 2618 (D. Colo. 2001).

Gonzales v. City of Castle Rock, 307 F.3d 1258, 1261 (10th Cir. 2002), aff'd on reh'g, 366 F.3d 1093 (10th Cir. 2004), rev'd. 545 US.748 (2005).

Goodman, L. A., & Epstein, D. (2008). *Listening to battered women: A survivor-centered approach to advocacy, mental health, and justice.* Washington, DC: American Psychological Association.

Goodman, L. A., Koss, M. P., Fitzgerald, L. F., & Puryear-Keita, G. (1993). Male violence against women: Current research and future directions. *American Psychologist, 48,* 1054–1058.

Goodmark, L. (2004). Law is the answer? Do we know that for sure? Questioning the efficacy of legal interventions for battered women. *St. Louis University Public Law Review, 23*(7), 10–13.

Goodmark, L. (2008). When is a battered woman not a battered woman? When she fights back, *Yale Journal of Law and Feminism,* 57.

Goodrum, S., Umberson, D., & Anderson, K. L. (2001). The batterer's view of the self and others in domestic violence. *Sociological Inquiry, 71*(2), 221–240.

Goolkasian, G. A. (1986). The judicial system and domestic violence: An expanding role. *Response, 9,* 2–7.

Gordon, L. (2002). *Heroes of their own lives: The politics and history of family violence, Boston, 1885–1960.* Champagne-Urbana: University of Illinois Press.

Gordon, M. (2000). Definitional issues in violence against women: Surveillance and research from a violence research perspective. *Violence Against Women, 6,* 747–826.

Governor's Division for Prevention of Family Violence. (2001). *Fiscal year 2001 annual report.* Phoenix, AZ: Author.

Grace, F. (2004). *James Brown released from jail.* Retrieved August 20, 2010, from http://www.cbsnews.com/stories/2004/06/15/entertainment/main623180.shtml

Graetz, N. (1988). *Silence is deadly: Judaism confronts wifebeating.* Northvale, NJ: Jason Aronson.

Grau, J., Fagan, J., & Wexler, S. (1985). Restraining orders for battered women: Issues of access and efficacy. In C. Schweber & C. Feinman (Eds.), *Criminal justice politics and women: The aftermath of legally mandated change* (pp. 13–28). New York: Haworth.

Green, C. T. (2010). *Domestic violence rates rise, funding decreases.* Retrieved January 4, 2010, from http://legalmomentum.typepad.com/blog/2010/01/domestic-violence-rates-rise-funding-decreases.html

Green, H. W. (1984). *Turning fear to hope.* Nashville, TN: Thomas Nelson.

Greenfield, L. A., Rand, M. R., Craven, D., Flaus, P. A., Perkins, C. A., Ringel, C., et al. (1998). *Violence by intimates: Analysis of data on crimes by current or former spouses, boyfriends and girlfriends* (NCJ-167237). Washington, DC: U.S. Department of Justice, Bureau of Justice Statistics.

Greenfield, L. A., & Snell, T. L. (1999). *Women offenders* (NCJ 175688). Washington, DC: U.S. Department of Justice.

Groves, R. M., & Cork, D. L. (Eds.). Panel to Review the Programs of the Bureau of Justice Statistics, National Research Council. (2008). *Ensuring the Quality, Credibility, and Relevance of U.S. Justice Statistics.* Washington, DC: National Academies Press.

Gruber, J. (1987). *Controlling bureaucracies.* Berkeley: University of California Press.

Gundle, R. (1986). Civil liability for police failure to arrest: Nearing v. Weaver. *Women's Rights Law Reporter, 3/4.*

Guzik, K. (2007). The forces of conviction: The power and practice of mandatory prosecution upon misdemeanor domestic battery suspects. *Law & Social Inquiry, 32*(1), 41–74.

Guzik, K. (2009). Abusers' narratives following arrest and prosecution for domestic violence.

In E. Stark & E. Buzawa (Eds.), *Violence against women in families and relationships: Criminal justice and the law* (pp. 137–160). Newark, NJ: Rutgers University Press.

H.R. Con. Res. 172, 101st Cong. § 1 (1990).

Haber, J. D., & Roos, C. (1985). Effects of spouse abuse and/or sexual abuse in the development and maintenance of chronic pain in women. In H. L. Fields, R. Dubner, & F. Cervero (Eds.), *Advances in pain research and therapy* (Vol. 9). New York: Raven.

Haddad, Y., & Smith, J. (Ed.). (2002). *Muslim minorities in the West: "Visible" and "invisible."* Lanham, MD: Altamira Press.

Hall, R. (1991). *Organizations: Structures, processes and outcomes* (5th ed.). Englewood Cliffs, NJ: Prentice-Hall.

Halpern, R. (1984). *Battered women's alternatives: The men's program component.* Paper presented to the American Psychological Association, Toronto, Canada.

Ham, C. (2005, October). *Table of primary aggressor statutes.* Minneapolis, MN: Battered Women's Project.

Hamberger, L. K., & Hastings, J. E. (1986). *Characteristics of male spouse abusers: Is psychopathology part of the picture?* Paper presented at the American Society of Criminology, Atlanta, GA.

Hamberger, L. K., & Hastings, J. E. (1993). Court mandated treatment of men who assault their partner. In N. Z. Hilton (Ed.), *Legal responses to wife assault: Current trends and evaluation* (pp. 182–229). Newbury Park, CA: Sage.

Hamberger, L. K., Lohr, J. M., Bunge, D., & Tolin, D. F. (1997). An empirical classification of motivation for domestic violence. *Violence Against Women, 3,* 401–423.

Hamby, S. L., Poindexter, V. C., & Gray-Little, B. (1996). Four measures of partner violence: Construct similarity and classification differences. *Journal of Marriage and the Family, 58,* 127–139.

Hamel, J. (2005). *Gender-inclusive treatment of intimate partner abuse: A comprehensive approach.* New York: Springer.

Hamel, J. (2007). Toward a gender-inclusive conception of intimate partner violence research and theory: Part I—Traditional perspectives. *International Journal of Men's Health, 6*(1), 36–53.

Hamel, J., & Nicholls, T. (Eds.). (2006). *Family approaches to domestic violence: A guide to gender-inclusive research and treatment.* New York: Springer.

Hampton, R. L. (1987). Family violence and homicides in the Black community: Are they linked? In R. L. Hampton (Ed.), *Violence in the Black family: Correlates and consequences* (pp. 135–186). Lexington, MA: Lexington Books.

Hampton, R., Carrillo, R., & Kim, J. (1998). Violence in communities of color. In R. Carrillo & J. Tello (Eds.), *Family violence and men of color: Healing the wounded male spirit* (pp. 1–30). New York: Springer.

Hangen, E. (1994). *D.S.S. interagency team pilot project: Program data evaluation, Office of Management, Planning and Analysis.* Boston: Massachusetts Department of Social Services.

Hanmer, J., Radford, J., & Stanko, E. A. (1989a). Improving policing for women: The way forward. In J. Hanmer, J. Radford, & E. A. Stanko (Eds.), *Women, policing and male violence: International perspectives* (pp. 185–201). London: Routledge & Kegan Paul.

Hanmer, J., Radford, J., & Stanko, E. A. (1989b). Policing men's violence: An introduction. In J. Hanmer, J. Radford, & E. A. Stanko (Eds.), *Women, policing and male violence: International perspectives* (pp. 1–12). London: Routledge & Kegan Paul.

Hanmer, J., & Saunders, S. (1984). *Well-founded fear: A community study of violence to women.* London: Hutchinson.

Hare, R. D. (1993). *Without conscience: The disturbing world of the psychopaths among us.* New York: Pocket Books.

Harrell, A. (1991). *Evaluation of court ordered treatment for domestic violence offenders [final report].* Washington, DC: Urban Institute.

Harrell, A., Newmark, L., & Visher, C. (2007). *Final report on the evaluation of the judicial oversight demonstration, Volume 2: Findings and lessons on implementation* (NCJ 219383). Washington, DC: National Institute of Justice.

Harrell, A., & Smith, B. (1996). Effects of restraining orders on domestic violence victims. In E. S. Buzawa & C. G. Buzawa (Eds.), *Do arrests and restraining orders work?* (pp. 214–242). Thousand Oaks, CA: Sage.

Harrell, A., Smith, B., & Newmark, L. (1993). *Court processing and the effects of restraining orders for domestic violence victims.* Washington, DC: Urban Institute.

Harris, R. N. (1973). *The police academy: An inside view.* New York: Wiley.

Hart, B. (1990). Gentle jeopardy: The further endangerment of battered women and children in custody mediation. *Mediation Quarterly, 7,* 317–330.

Hart, B. (1992). *State codes on domestic violence: Analysis, commentary and recommendations.* Reno, NV: National Council of Juvenile and Family Court Judges.

Hart, B. (1993). Battered women and the criminal justice system. *American Behavioral Scientist, 36,* 624–638.

Hart, B., & Sussman, A. (2004). Civil tort suits and economic justice for battered women. *Victim Advocate, 4*(3), 3–9.

Hartley, C., & Frohmann, L. (2003). *Cook County Target Abuser Call (TAC): An evaluation of a specialized domestic violence court.* Final Report. Washington, DC: National Institute of Justice.

Hartman, H. H. (1999). *Aggressive prosecution requires money, not more mandates.* Domestic Violence Report. Kingston, NJ: Civic Research Institute.

Hartog, H. (1976). The public law of a county court: Judicial government in eighteenth century Massachusetts. *American Journal of Legal History, 20,* 282–329.

Hassel, K. D. (2007). Variation in police patrol practices: The precinct as a sub-organizational level of analysis. *Policing: An International Journal of Police Strategies & Management, 30*(2), 257–276.

Hassouneh, D., & Glass, N. (2008). The Influence of gender-role stereotyping on female same-sex intimate partner violence. *Violence Against Women, 14*(3), 310–325.

Hassouneh-Phillips, D. (2003). Strength and vulnerability: Spirituality in abused American Muslim women's lives. *Issues in Mental Health Nursing, 24,* 681–694.

Hastings, J. E., & Hamberger, L. K. (1988). Personality characteristics of spouse abusers: A controlled comparison. *Violence and Victims, 3,* 31–48.

Hatty, S. (1989). Policing male violence in Australia. In J. Hanmer, J. Radford, & E. Stanko (Eds.), *Women, policing and male violence: International perspectives* (pp. 70–89). London: Routledge & Kegan Paul.

Haviland, M., Frye, V., Rajah, V., Thukral, J., & Trinity, M. (2001). *The Family Protection and Domestic Violence Act of 1995: Examining the effects of mandatory arrest in New York City.* New York: Urban Justice Center.

Hawkins, R., & Beauvais, C. (1985). *Evaluation of group therapy with abusive men: The police record.* Paper presented at the American Psychological Association, Los Angeles.

Hazen, A. L., & Soriano, F. I. (2007). Experiences with intimate partner violence among Latina women. *Violence Against Women, 13,* 562–582.

Healey, K., Smith, C., & O'Sullivan, C. (1998). *Batterer intervention: Program approaches and criminal justice strategies.* Washington, DC: National Institute of Justice.

Heckert, D. A., & Gondolf, E. W. (2000). Predictors of underreporting of male violence by batterer program participants and their partners. *Journal of Family Violence, 15*(4), 423–443.

Hemmens, C., Strom, K., & Schlegel, E. (1998). Gender bias in the courts: A review of the literature. *Sociological Imagination, 35,* 22–42.

Herman, J. L. (1992b). *Trauma and recovery: From domestic abuse to political terror.* London: Pandora.

Hertel, B. R., & Hughes, M. (1987). Religious affiliation, attendance, and support for "pro-family" issues in the United States. *Social Forces, 65,* 858–882.

Hester, M. (2004). Future trends and developments—Violence against women in Europe and East Asia. *Violence Against Women, 10*(12), 1431–1448.

Hester, M. (2009). The contradictory legal worlds faced by domestic violence victims. In E. Stark & E. S. Buzawa (Eds.), *Violence against women in families and relationships, Volume I: The family context* (pp. 127–146). Santa Barbara, CA: Praeger.

Hetherington, E. M., & Stanley-Hagan, M. (1999). The adjustment of children with divorced parents: A risk and resiliency perspective. *The Journal of Child Psychology and Psychiatry and Allied Disciplines, 40,* 129–140.

HI H. 2712 (1992).

Highfield, R. (2007, February 2). Chimps hold clues to roots of domestic violence. *United Kingdom Daily Telegraph.* Retrieved August 12, 2010, from http://www.telegraph.co.uk/news/uknews/1541115/Chimps-hold-clues-to-roots-of-domestic-violence.html

Higley, J. D. (2001). Individual differences in alcohol-induced aggression. A nonhuman-primate model. *Alcohol Reseach & Health, 25,* 12–19.

Hilberman, E., & Munson, K. (1977–1978). Sixty battered women. *Victimology: An International Journal, 2,* 3–4, 460–470.

Hilton, N. Z. (1991). Mediating wife assault: Battered women and the new family. *Canadian Journal of Family Law, 9,* 29–53.

Hilton, N. Z. (Ed.). (1993). *Legal responses to wife assault: Current trends and evaluation.* Newbury Park, CA: Sage.

Hirschel, D., & Buzawa, E. (2002). Understanding the context of dual arrest with directions for future research. *Violence Against Women, 8*(12), 1449–1473.

Hirschel, D., Buzawa, E., Pattavina, A., & Faggiani, D. (2007). Domestic violence preferred and mandatory arrest laws: To what extent do they influence police arrest decisions? *Journal of Criminal Law and Criminology, 98*(1), 255–298.

Hirschel, D., Buzawa, E., Pattavina, A., Faggiani, D., & Reuland, M. (2007). *Explaining the consequences of dual arrest: Final report.* Washington, DC: National Institute of Justice, U.S. Department of Justice.

Hirschel, J. D., & Hutchison, I. W. (1992). Female spouse abuse and the police response: The Charlotte, North Carolina, experiment. *Journal of Criminal Law and Criminology, 83,* 73–119.

Hirschel, J. D., & Hutchison, I. W. (2001). The relative effects of offense, offender, and victim variables on the decision to prosecute domestic violence cases. *Violence Against Women, 7,* 46–61.

Hirschel, J. D., Hutchison, I. W., & Dean, C. W. (1992). The failure of arrest to deter spouse abuse. *Journal of Research in Crime and Delinquency, 29,* 7–33.

Hirschel, J. D., Hutchison, I. W., Dean, C. W., Kelley, J. J., & Pesackis, C. E. (1991). *Charlotte Spouse Assault Replication Project: Final report.* Washington, DC: U.S. Department of Justice.

Hirschel, J. D., Hutchison, I. W., Dean, C. W., & Mills, A. (1992). Review essay on the law enforcement response to spouse abuse: Past, present, and future. *Justice Quarterly, 9,* 247–283.

Hirst, A. M. (2002). *Domestic violence in court-based child custody mediation cases in California.* Research Update, Judicial Council of California, Administrative.

Hitchings, E. (2005). A consequence of blurring the boundaries—Less choice for the victims of domestic violence? *Social Policy and Society, 5*(1), 91–101.

Hoagland, C., & Rosen, K. (1990). *Dreams lost, dreams found: Undocumented women in the land of opportunity*. San Francisco, CA: Coalition for Immigrant and Refugee Rights and Services, Immigrant Women's Task Force.

Holmes, W. M., & Bibel, D. (1988). *Police response to domestic violence: Final report*. Washington, DC: Bureau of Justice Statistics.

Holt, V. L., Kernic, M. A., Wolf, M. E., & Rivara, F. P. (2003). Do protection orders affect the likelihood of future partner violence and injury? *American Journal of Preventive Medicine, 24*(1), 16–21.

Holtzworth-Munroe, A., & Anglin, K. (1991). The competency of responses given by martially violent versus nonviolent men to problematic marital situations. *Violence and Victims, 6,* 257–269.

Holtzworth-Munroe, A., & Hutchinson, G. (1993). Attributing negative intent to wife behavior: The attributions of martially violent versus non-violent men. *Journal of Abnormal Psychology, 102,* 206–211.

Holtzworth-Munroe, A., & Meehan, J. C. (2004). Typologies of men who are maritally violent: Scientific and clinical implications. *Journal of Interpersonal Violence, 19,* 1369–1389.

Holtzworth-Munroe, A., Smutzler, N., & Sandin, E. (1997). A brief review of the research on husband violence. Part II: The psychological effects of husband violence on battered women and their children. *Aggression and Violent Behavior, 2,* 179–213.

Holtzworth-Munroe, A., & Stuart, G. (1994). Typology of male batterers: Three subtypes and the differences among them. *Psychological Bulletin, 116,* 476–497.

Homant, J. R., & Kennedy, D. B. (1984). Content analysis of statements about policewomen's handling of domestic violence. *American Journal of Police, 3,* 265–283.

Horne, S. G., & Levitt, H. M. (2004). Shelter from the raging wind: Religious needs of victims of intimate partner violence and faith leaders' responses. *Journal of Religion and Abuse, 5,* 83–98.

Horton, A. L., Wilkins, N. M., & Wright, W. (1988). Women who ended abuse: What religious leaders and religion did for these victims. In A. L. Horton and J. A. Williamson (Eds.), *Abuse and religion: When praying isn't enough* (pp. 235–246). Lexington, MA: Lexington Books.

Horvath, L. S., Logan, T. K., & Walker, R. (2002). Child custody cases: A content analysis of evaluations in practice. *Professional Psychology: Research and Practice, 33,* 557–565.

Hotaling, G. T., & Buzawa, E. (2001). *An analysis of assaults in rural communities: Final report.* Federal Grant #MA0095–400. Washington, DC: U.S. Department of Justice, Office of Community Oriented Policing Services.

Hotaling, G. T., & Straus, M. A., with Lincoln, A. (1989). Intrafamily violence and crime and violence outside the family. In L. Ohlin & M. H. Tonry (Eds.), *Family violence* (pp. 315–376). Chicago, IL: University of Chicago Press.

Hotaling, G. T., & Sugarman, D. B. (1986). An analysis of risk makers in husband to wife violence: The current state of knowledge. *Violence and Victims, 1,* 101–124.

Huddleston, C. W., Marlowe, D. B., & Casebolt, R. (2008). *Painting the current picture: A national report card on drug courts and other problem-solving court programs in the United States* (Vol. II, No. 1). Alexandria, VA: National Drug Court Institute.

Hughes, H. M., Parkinson, D., & Vargo, M. (1989). Witnessing spouse abuse and experiencing physical abuse: A "double whammy"? *Journal of Family Violence, 4,* 197–209.

Humphreys, I. C., & Humphreys, W. O. (1985). Mandatory arrest: A means of primary and secondary prevention. *Victimology, 10,* 267–280.

Hurt, H., Malmud, E., Betancourt, L., Brodsky, N. L., & Giannetta, J. M. (2001). A prospective comparison of developmental outcome of children with in utero cocaine exposure and controls using the Battelle Developmental Inventory. *Developmental and Behavioral Pediatrics, 22*(1), 27–34.

Hutchison, I. W., & Hirschel, J. D. (1998). Abused women: Help-seeking strategies and police utilization. *Violence Against Women, 4,* 436–456.

Hyman, A. (1997). *Mandatory reporting of domestic violence by health care providers: A policy paper.* San Francisco, CA: Family Violence Prevention Fund.

Illinois Domestic Violence Act, 750 I.L.C.S. §§ 60/102 (1986).

Incite! Women of Color Against Violence. (2003). *Community accountability strategies for addressing violence against women.* Retrieved June 15, 2007, from http://inciteboston.blogspot.com/2006_08_01_archive

Infante, D. A., & Wigley, C. J. III. (1986). Verbal aggressiveness: An interpersonal model and measure. *Communication Monographs, 53,* 61–69.

Isaac, N. E. (1994). Men who batter, profile from a restraining order database. *Archives of Family Medicine, 3*, 50–54.

Isaac, N. E., & Sanchez, R. L. (1994). Emergency department response to battered women in Massachusetts. *Annals of Emergency Medicine, 23*, 855–858.

Jackman, M. R. (1994). *The velvet glove: Paternalism and conflict in gender, class, and race relations.* Berkeley: University of California Press.

Jackson, S., Feder, L., Forde, D., Davis, R., Maxwell, C., & Taylor, B. (2003). *Batterer intervention programs: Where do we go from here?* Washington, DC: National Institute of Justice.

Jacobson, N. S., & Gottman, J. M. (1998). *When men batter women: New insights into ending abusive relationships.* New York: Simon & Schuster.

Jacoby, J. (1980). *The American prosecutor: A search for identity.* Lexington, MA: Lexington Books.

Jaffe, P., Hastings, E., Reitzel, D., & Austin, G. (1993). The impact of police laying charges. In N. Z. Hilton (Ed.), *Legal responses to wife assault: Current trends and evaluation* (pp. 62–95). Newbury Park, CA: Sage.

Jaffe, P., Wilson, S., & Wolfe, D. A. (1986a). Promoting changes in attitudes and understanding of conflict resolution among child witnesses of family violence. *Canadian Journal of Behavioral Science Review, 18*, 356–366.

Jaffe, P., Wolfe, D. A., & Wilson, S. (1990). *Children of battered women.* Newbury Park, CA: Sage.

James, S. E., Johnson, J., Raghavan, C., & Woolis, D. (2004). I couldn't go anywhere": Social networks, violence and drug abuse. *Violence Against Women, 10*, 991–1014.

Jenkins, P., & Phillips, B. (2008). When catastrophe strikes (battered) women: Domestic violence in the context of disaster. *National Women's Studies Journal, 20*(3): 49–68. Special Issue on Hurricane Katrina.

Johnson, H. (2000). The role of alcohol in male partners' assault on wives. *Journal of Drug Issues, 30*, 725–741.

Johnson, H. (2001). Contrasting views of the role of alcohol in cases of wife assault. *Journal of Interpersonal Violence, 16*, 54–72.

Johnson, M. P. (1995). Patriarchal terrorism and common couple violence: Two forms of violence against women. *Journal of Marriage and the Family, 57*, 283–294.

Johnson, M. P. (2000, November). Paper presented at the Workshop on Gender Symmetry. Arlington, VA: National Institute of Justice.

Johnson, M. P. (2006a). Conflict and control: Gender, symmetry, and asymmetry in domestic violence. *Violence Against Women, 12*, 1003–1018.

Johnson, M. P. (2006b, November). *A "general" theory of intimate partner violence: A working paper.* Paper presented at the Theory Construction and Research Methodology Pre-Conference Workshop, National Council on Family Relations annual meeting, Minneapolis, MN.

Johnson, M. P. (2007). Domestic violence: The intersection of gender and control. In L. L. O'Toole, J. R. Schiffman, & M. Kiter Edwards (Eds.), *Gender violence: Interdisciplinary perspectives* (2nd ed., pp. 257–268). New York: New York University Press; reprinted in A. J. Cherlin (Ed.). (2006). *Public & private families, A reader* (5th ed.), New York: McGraw-Hill.

Johnson, M. P. (2008). *A typology of domestic violence: Intimate terrorism, violence resistance and situational couple violence.* Boston, MA: Northeastern University Press.

Johnson, M. P., & Elliott, B. (1997). Domestic violence among family practice patients in mid-sized and rural communities. *Journal of Family Practice, 44*, 391–400.

Johnston, J. R., & Campbell, L. E. G. (1993). A clinical typology of interparental violence in disputed custody divorces. *American Journal of Orthopsychiatry, 63*, 190–199.

Johnston, J. R., Lee, S., Olesen, N. W., & Walters, M. G. (2005). Allegations and substantiations of abuse in custody-disputing families. *Family Court Review, 43*, 283–294.

Jolin, A., & Moose, C. A. (1997). Evaluating a domestic violence program in a community policing environment: Research implementation issues. *Crime & Delinquency, 43*, 279–297.

Jones, A., & Schechter, S. (1992). *When love goes wrong.* New York: HarperCollins.

Jones, D. A., & Belknap, J. (1999). Police responses to battering in a progressive pro-arrest jurisdiction. *Justice Quarterly, 15*, 249–273.

Jones, L., Hughes, M., & Unterstaller, U. (2001). Post-traumatic stress disorder (PTSD) in victims of domestic violence: A review of the research. *Trauma, Violence, & Abuse, 2*(2), 99–119.

Joseph, J. (1997). Women battering: A comparative analysis of Black and White women. In G. K. Kantor & J. L. Jasinski (Eds.), *Out of darkness: Contemporary perspectives on family violence* (pp. 161–1690). Thousand Oaks, CA: Sage.

Kahn, A. S. (1984). The power war: Male response to power loss underequality. *Psychology of Women Quarterly, 6,* 234–247.

Kandel, E., & Freed, D. (1989). Frontal lobe dysfunction and antisocial behavior: A review. *Journal of Clinical Psychology, 45,* 404–413.

Kane, R. (1999). Patterns of arrest in domestic violence encounters: Identifying a police decision-making model. *Journal of Criminal Justice, 27,* 65–80.

Kantor, G. K., & Asdigian, N. (1997). When women are under the influence: Does drinking or drug use by women provoke beatings by men? In M. Galanter (Ed.), *Recent developments in alcoholism. Volume 13: Alcoholism and violence* (pp. 315–336). New York: Plenum.

Kantor, G. K., & Straus, M. (1987). The "drunken bum" theory of wife beating. *Social Problems, 34,* 213–230.

Kantor, G. K., & Straus, M. A. (1989). Substance abuse as a precipitant of wife abuse victimization. *American Journal of Alcohol Abuse, 15,* 173–189.

Kappeler, V. (1997). *Critical issues in police civil liability* (2nd ed.). Prospect Heights, IL: Waveland.

Kappeler, V., Blumberg, M., & Potter, G. (2000). *The mythology of crime and criminal justice* (3rd ed.). Prospect Heights, IL: Waveland.

Kaufman, C. G. (2003). *Sins of omission. The Jewish community's reaction to domestic violence.* Boulder, CO: Westview.

Kaufman, J., & Zigler, E. (1987). Do abused children become abusive parents? *American Journal of Orthopsychiatry, 57*(2), 186, 190.

Kaufman Kantor, G. K. (1996). Alcohol and spousal abuse: Ethnic differences. In M. Galanter (Ed.), *Recent developments in alcoholism.* New York: Plenum.

Kaufman Kantor, G. K., & Jasinski, J. (Eds.). (1997). *Out of darkness: Contemporary research perspectives on family violence.* Newbury Park, CA: Sage.

Kaufman Kantor, G. K., & Straus, M. A. (1990). Response of victims and the police to assaults on wives. In M. A. Straus & R. J. Gelles (Eds.), *Physical violence in American families: Risk factors and adaptations to violence in 8,145 families* (pp. 473–486). New Brunswick, NJ: Transaction.

Kaukinen, C. (2002). The help-seeking decisions of violent crime victims: An examination of the direct and conditional effects of gender and the victim–offender relationship. *Journal of Interpersonal Violence, 17,* 432–456.

Kaukinen, C. (2004). Status compatibility, physical violence, and emotional abuse in intimate relationships. *Journal of Marriage and Family, 66*(2), 452–471.

Kaysen, D., Pantalone, D., Lindgren, K. P., Clum, G. A., Lee, C., & Resick, P. A. (2007). Posttraumatic stress disorder, alcohol use, and physical health concerns. *Journal of Behavioral Medicine, 31*(2), 115–125.

Keilitz, S. L. (1994). Civil protection orders: A viable justice system tool for deterring domestic violence. *Violence and Victims, 9,* 79–84.

Keilitz, S. L. (2000). *Specialization of domestic violence case management in the courts: A national survey.* Washington, DC: NIJ Research Conference on Violence Against Women and Family Violence.

Keilitz, S. L. (2004). *Specialization of domestic violence case management in the courts: A national survey.* Final report for National Institute of Justice, grant number 98-WT-VX-0002. Washington, DC: U.S. Department of Justice, National Institute of Justice.

Keilitz, S. L., Hannaford, P. L., & Efkeman, H. S. (1997). *Civil protection orders: The benefits and limitations for victims of domestic violence: Executive summary.* Washington, DC: Department of Justice.

Kemp, C. H., Silverman, F. N., Steele, B. F., Droegenmuller, W., & Silver, H. (1962). The battered child syndrome. *Journal of the American Medical Association, 181,* 17–24.

Kent, J. (1976). A follow-up study of abused children. *Journal of Pediatric Psychology, 1*(2), 25–31.

Kernic, M. A., Monary-Ernsdorff, D. J., Koespell, J. K., & Holt, V. L. (2005). Children in the crossfire: Child custody determinations among couples with a history of intimate partner violence. *Violence Against Women, 11,* 991–1021.

Kilpatrick, D. G., Acierno, R., Renick, H., Saunders, B. E., & Best, C. L. (1997). A 2-year longitudinal analysis of the relationship between violent assault and substance use in women. *Journal of Counseling and Clinical Psychology, 65,* 834–847.

Kim, J. Y., & Sung, K. (2000). Conjugal violence in Korean American families: A residue of cultural transition. *Journal of Family Violence, 15,* 331–345.

Kingsnorth, R. (2006). Intimate partner violence: Predictors of recidivism in a sample of arrestees. *Violence Against Women, 12*(10), 917–935.

Klein, A. (1993, November 14). Batterer is walking time bomb. *Boston Globe*, p. 1.

Klein, A. (1994a). *Recidivism in a population of court-restrained batterers after two years.* Unpublished doctoral dissertation, Northeastern University, Boston, MA.

Klein, A. (1994b). *Spousal/partner assault: A protocol for the sentencing and supervision of offenders.* Boston, MA: Production Specialties.

Klein, A. (1996). Re-abuse in a population of court-restrained male batterers: Why restraining orders don't work. In E. S. Buzawa & C. G. Buzawa (Eds.), *Do arrests and restraining orders work?* (pp. 192–213). Thousand Oaks, CA: Sage.

Klein, A. (2005). *Rhode Island domestic violence shelter and advocacy services: An assessment.* Waltham, MA: BOTEC Analysis Corporation and Rhode Island Justice Commission. Retrieved September 9, 2010, from http://www.rijustice.ri.gov/sac/Reports/Final%20ShelterEval%209-20-05.pdf

Klein, A. (2008). *Practical implications of current domestic violence research. Part II: Prosecution.* Washington, DC: U.S. Department of Justice, National Institute of Justice.

Klein, A. (2009). *Special report: Practical implications of current domestic violence research.* Washington, DC: U.S. Department of Justice, National Institute of Justice.

Klein, A., & Tobin, T. (2008). Longitudinal study of arrested batterers, 1995–2005: Career criminals. *Violence Against Women, 14*(2), 136–157.

Klein, A., Wilson, D., Crowe, A., & DeMichele, M. T. (2005). *Evaluation of the Rhode Island Probation Specialized Domestic Violence Supervision Unit.* Final report submitted to the National Institute of Justice. Washington, DC: American Probation and Parole Association and BOTEC Analysis Corporation.

Klein, E., Campbell, J., Soler, E., & Ghez, M. (1997). *Ending domestic violence: Changing public perceptions/halting the epidemic.* Thousand Oaks, CA: Sage.

Klinger, D. (1995). Policing spousal assault. *Journal of Research in Crime and Delinquency, 32,* 308–324.

Knickmeyer, N., Levitt, H. M., Horne, S. G., & Bayer, G. (2004). Responding to mixed messages and double binds: Religious oriented coping strategies of Christian battered women. *Journal of Religion and Abuse, 5,* 55–82.

Knoll, J. L., & Resnick, P. J. (2007). *Insanity defense evaluations: Toward a model for evidence-based practice. Brief treatment and crisis intervention.* Oxford, UK: Oxford University Press.

Koehler, L. K. (1980). *Women of the republic: Intellect and ideology in revolutionary America.* Chapel Hill: University of North Carolina Press.

Koop, C. E. (1991). Foreward. In M. L. Rosenberg & M.A. Fenley (Eds.), *Violence in America: A public health approach* (pp. v–vi). New York: Oxford University Press.

Kosky, R. (1983). Childhood suicidal behavior. *Journal of Child Psychology and Psychiatry and Allied Disciplines, 24,* 457–468.

Koss, M. P. (2000). Blame, shame and community: Justice responses to violence against women. *American Psychologist, 55,* 1332–1343.

Koss, M. P., Bachar, K. J., Hopkins, C. Q., & Carlson, C. (2004). Expanding a community's justice response to sex crimes through advocacy, prosecutorial, and public health collaboration: Introducing the RESTORE program. *Journal of Interpersonal Violence, 19,* 1435–1463.

Koss, M. P., Goodman, L. A., Browne, A., Fitzgerald, L. F., Kita, G. P., & Russo, N. F. (1994). *Male violence against women at home, at work, and in the community.* Washington, DC: American Psychological Association.

Kracke, K., & Hahn, H. (2008). The nature and extent of childhood exposure to violence: What we know, why we don't know more, and why it matters. *Journal of Emotional Abuse, 8*(1/2), 29–49.

Kruttschnitt, C., McLaughlin, B. L., & Petrie, C. V. (Eds.). (2004). *Advancing the federal research agenda on violence against women.* Steering Committee for the Workshop on Issues in Research on Violence Against Women, National Research Council. Washington, DC: National Academies Press.

Kulwicki, A. D., & Miller, J. (1999). Domestic violence in the Arab American population: Transforming environmental conditions through community education. *Issues in Mental Health Nursing, 20,* 199–215.

Kurz, D. (1996). Separation, divorce, and woman abuse. *Violence Against Women, 2,* 63–81.

Kurz, D., & Stark, E. (1988). Not so benign neglect: The medical response to battering. In K. Yllö

& M. Bograd (Eds.), *Feminist perspectives on wife abuse* (pp. 249–268). Newbury Park, CA: Sage.

Labaton, S. (1989, December 29). New tactics in the war on drugs tilt scales of justice off balance. *New York Times*, pp. 1, 14.

Labriola, M., Bradley, S., O'Sullivan, C. S., Rempel, M., & Moore, S. (2009). *National portrait of domestic violence courts*. New York: Center for Court Innovation.

Labriola, M., Rempel, M., O'Sullivan, C. S., Frank, P., McDowell, J., & Finkelstein, R. (2007). *Court responses to batterer program noncompliance: A national perspective*. New York: Center for Court Innovation. Retrieved September 16, 2010, from http://www.courtinnovation.org/_uploads/documents/Court_Responses_March2007.pdf

Langan, P., & Innes, C. (1986). *Preventing domestic violence against women*. Washington, DC: Bureau of Justice Statistics, Department of Justice.

Langhinrichsen-Rohling, J., Huss, M. T., & Ramsey, S. (2000). The clinical utility of batterer typologies. *Journal of Family Violence*, *15*, 37–53.

Langhinrichsen-Rohling, J., Smutzler, N., & Vivian, D. (1994). Positivity in marriage: The role of discord and physical aggression against wives. *Journal of Marriage and the Family*, *56*, 69–79.

Langley, R., & Levy, R. (1977). *Wife beating: The silent crisis*. New York: Dutton.

Lanthier, S. (2008). *Documenting women's experiences with the Toronto police services in domestic violence situations*. Toronto, Canada: Women Abuse Council of Toronto. Retrieved September 16, 2010, from www.womanabuse.ca/resources/cf_download.cfm?file . . . pdf&path

Lawrenz, F., Lembo, R., & Schade, S. (1988). Time series analysis of the effect of a domestic violence directive on the number of arrests per day. *Journal of Criminal Justice*, *16*, 493–498.

Lee, R., Gollan, J., Kasckow, J., Geracioti, T., & Coccaro, E. F. (2006). CSF corticotropin-releasing factor in personality disorder: Relationship with perceived parental care and CSF 5- HIAA. *Neuropsychopharmacology*, *31*, 2289–2295.

Lehmann, C. (2002). Abuse said to interfere with child brain development. *Psychiatric News*, *87*(1), 28.

Leighton, B. (1989). *Spousal abuse in metropolitan Toronto: Research report on the response of the criminal justice system* (Report No. 1989–02). Ottawa, Canada: Solicitor General of Canada.

Lemon, N. (2000, October/November). Review of New York symposium on domestic violence. *Domestic Violence Report*, pp. 5–6.

Lempert, R. (1987, June 21). Spouse abuse: Ann Arbor rushed into arrest ordinance without studying side effects. *Ann Arbor News*.

Lempert, R. (1989). Humility is a virtue: On the publicization of policy relevant research. *Law & Society Review*, *23*, 145–161.

Lentz, S. (1999). Revisiting the rule of thumb: An overview of the history of wife abuse. In L. Feder (Ed.), *Women and domestic violence: An interdisciplinary approach* (pp. 9–27). Binghampton, NY: Haworth.

Leonard, K. E. (1993). Drinking patterns and intoxication in marital violence: Review, critique, and future directions for research. In *Alcohol and interpersonal violence: Fostering multidisciplinary perspectives* (NIH Research Monograph No. 24, pp. 253–280). Rockville, MD: U.S. Department of Health and Human Services.

Lerman, L. G. (1981). *Prosecution of spouse abuse innovations in criminal justice response*. Washington, DC: Center for Women Policy Studies.

Lerman, L. G. (1984). Mediation of wife abuse cases: The adverse impact of informal dispute resolution of women. *Harvard Women's Law Journal*, *7*, 65–67.

Lerman, L. G. (1992). The decontextualization of domestic violence. *Journal of Criminal Law and Criminology*, *83*(1), 217–240.

Lessons from chronic illness management. *Violence and Victims*, *21*, 101–115.

Leung, R. (2005, March 20). *Gonzales vs. Castle Rock: Supreme Court to decide if mother can sue her town and its police* [Online news story]. Retrieved August 26, 2010, from http://www.cbsnews.com/stories/2005/03/17/60minutes/main681416.shtml

Levesque, J. R. (1998). Emotional maltreatment in adolescents' everyday lives: Further sociolegal and social service provisions. *Behavioral Sciences & the Law*, *16*, 237–263.

Levinson, D. (1989). *Family violence in cross-cultural perspective*. Newbury Park, CA: Sage.

Lie, G. Y., Schilit, R., Bush, J., Montagne, M., & Reyes, L. (1991). Lesbians in currently aggressive relationships: How frequently do they report aggressive past relationships. *Violence and Victims*, *62*, 121–135.

Liebman, D. A., & Schwartz, J. A. (1973). Police programs in domestic crisis intervention: A review. In J. R. Snibbe & H. M. Snibbe (Eds.), *The urban policeman in transition* (pp. 421–472). Springfield, IL: Charles C Thomas.

Liederbach, J. (2005). Addressing the "elephant in the living room": An observational study of the work of suburban police. *Policing: An International Journal of Police Strategies & Management, 28*(3), 415–434.

Liederbach, J., & Frank, J. (2003). Policing Mayberry: The work routines of small town and rural police officers. *American Journal of Criminal Justice, 28*(1), 56–72.

Lipsey, M. W., Wilson, D. B., Cohen, M. A., & Derzon, J. H. (1997). Is there a causal relationship between alcohol use and violence? A synthesis of evidence. In M. Galanter (Ed.), *Recent developments in alcoholism: Volume 13, Alcohol and violence* (pp. 245–282). New York: Plenum Press.

Lipton, D., Martinson, R., & Wilks, J. (1975). *The effectiveness of correctional treatment.* New York: Praeger.

Lischick, C. (2009). Divorce in the context of coercive control. In E. Stark & E. S. Buzawa (Eds.), *Violence against women in families and relationships* (Vol. 4, pp. 191–224). The Media and Cultural Attitudes. New York: Praeger.

Litchman, K. E. (2007). Punishing the protectors: The Illinois domestic violence act remedy for victims of domestic violence against police misconduct. *Loyola University Chicago Law Journal, 38*, 765–832.

Lloyd, S. (1997). The effects of violence on women's employment. *Law & Policy, 19*, 159–167.

Logan, T. K., Shannon, L., & Walker, R. (2005). Protective orders in rural and urban areas: A multiple perspective study. *Violence Against Women, 11*(7), 876–911.

Logan, T. K., Shannon, L., Walker, R., & Faragher, T. (2006). Protective orders: Questions and conundrums. *Trauma, Violence, & Abuse* 7(3): 175–205.

Logan, T. K., Walker, R., & Leukefeld, C. (2001). Rural, urban influenced, and urban differences among domestic violence arrestees. *Journal of Interpersonal Violence, 16*(3), 266–283.

Logan, T. K., Walker, R., Stewart, C., & Allen, J. (2006). Victim services and justice system representative responses about partner stalking: What do professionals recommend? *Violence and Victims, 21*(1), 49–66.

Loulan, J. (1987). *Lesbian passion.* San Francisco, CA: Spinsters/Aunt Lute.

Loving, N. (1980). *Responding to spouse abuse and wife beating: A guide for police.* Washington, DC: Police Executive Research Forum.

Lyon, E., & Goth Mace, P. (1991). Family violence and the courts: Implementing a comprehensive new law. In D. D. Knudsen & J. L. Miller (Eds.), *Abused and battered: Social and legal responses to family violence* (pp. 167–180). New York: Aldine de Gruyter.

MacMillan, H. L., Wathen, C. N., Jamieson, E., Boyle, M. H., McNutt, L. A., Worster, A., et al. (2006). Approaches to screening for intimate partner violence in health care settings. *Journal of the American Medical Association, 296*, 530–536.

MacMillan, H. L., Wathen, C. N., Jamieson, E., Boyle, M. H., Shannon, H. S., Ford-Gilboe, M., et al. (2009). Screening for intimate partner violence in health care settings: A randomized trial. *Journal of the American Medical Association, 302*, 493–501.

Maiuro, R. D., Cahn, T. S., & Vitaliano, P. P. (1986). Assertiveness deficits and hostility in domestically violent men. *Violence and Victims, 1*, 279–289.

Maiuro, R. D., Cahn, T. S., Vitaliano, P. P., Wagner, B. C., & Zegree, J. B. (1988). Anger, hostility, and depression in domestically violent versus generally assaultive men and nonviolent control subjects. *Journal of Consulting and Clinical Psychology, 56*, 17–23.

Maiuro, R. D., & Eberle, J. A. (2008). State standards for domestic violence perpetrator treatment: Current status, trends, and recommendations. *Violence and Victims, 23*(2), 133–155.

Maker, A. H., Kemmelmeier, M., & Peterson, C. (1998). Long-term psychological consequences in women of witnessing parental physical conflict and experiencing abuse in childhood. *Journal of Interpersonal Violence, 13*, 574–589.

Malefyt, M., Little, K., & Walker, A. (1998). *Promising practices: Improving the criminal justice system's response to violence against women.* Washington, DC: National Institute of Justice.

Manning, P. (1978). The police: Mandate, strategies and appearances. In P. Manning & J. Von Mannen (Eds.), *Policing: A view from the street.* Santa Monica, CA: Goodyear.

Manning, P. (1988). *Symbolic interaction: Signifying calls and police response.* Cambridge, MA: MIT Press.

Manning, P. (1993). The preventive conceit: The black box in market context. In E. Buzawa & C. Buzawa (Eds.), The impact of arrest on domestic assault [Special issue]. *American Behavioral Scientist, 36*, 639–650.

Manning, P. (1996). The preventive conceit: The black box in market context. In E. S. Buzawa & C. G. Buzawa (Eds.), *Do arrests and restraining orders work?* (pp. 83–97). Thousand Oaks, CA: Sage.

Manning, P. (1997). *Police work: The social organization of policing.* Prospect Heights, IL: Waveland.

Manning, P., & Van Maanen, J. (Eds.). (1978). *Policing: A view from the street.* Santa Monica, CA: Goodyear.

Mansnerus, L. (2001, January 9). Family strife is subject of new courts. *New York Times*, p. B2.

Margolin, G. (1998). Effects of witnessing violence on children. In P. K. Trickett & C. J. Schellenbach (Eds.), *Violence against children in the family and the community* (pp. 57–101). Washington, DC: American Psychological Association.

Margolin, G., John, R., & Gleberman, L. (1988). Affective responses to conflictual discussions in violent and nonviolent couples. *Journal of Consulting and Clinical Psychology, 56*, 24–33.

Martin, D. (1976). *Battered wives.* San Francisco: Glide.

Martin, M. (1997): Double your trouble: Dual arrest in family violence. *Journal of Family Violence, 12*, 139–157.

Martin, S. E. (1993). Female officers on the move? A status report on women in policing. In R. G. Dunham & G. P. Alpert, *Critical issues in policing* (2nd ed., pp. 327–347). Prospect Heights, IL: Waveland.

Massachusetts Office of the Commissioner of Probation. (2001). *Massachusetts probation service, registry of civil restraining orders summary.* Boston: Massachusetts Office of the Commissioner of Probation, Field Services Division, Research Department.

Mastrofski, S. D. (1999). *Policing for people.* Washington, DC: Police Foundation.

Mastrofski, S. D., & Uchida, C. (1993). Transforming the police. *Journal of Research in Crime and Delinquency, 30*, 330–358.

Mastrofski, S. D., Worden, R. E., & Snipes, J. B. (1995). Law enforcement in a time of community policing. *Criminology, 33*(4), 539–563.

Mathews v. Eldridge, 424 U.S. 319 (1976).

Matoesian, G. M. (1993). *Reproducing rape: Domination through talk in the courtroom.* Cambridge, MA: Blackwell.

Max, W., Rice, D. P., Finkelstein, E., Bardwell, R. A., & Leadbetter, S. (2004). The economic toll of intimate partner violence against women in the United States. *Violence and Victims, 19*, 259–272.

Maxwell, C., & Bricker, R. (1999, March). *The nature of police and citizens interactions within the context of intimate and domestic conflict and violence.* Paper presented the Annual Meeting of the Academy of Criminal Justice Sciences, Orlando, FL.

Maxwell, C., Garner, J., & Fagan, J. (2001). *The effects of arrest on intimate partner violence: New evidence from the spouse assault replication program.* Research in brief. Washington, DC: National Institute of Justice.

Maxwell, C., Robinson, A. L., & Klein, A. (2009). The prosecution of domestic violence across time. In E. Stark & E. S. Buzawa (Eds.), *Violence against women in families and relationships: Criminal justice and the law* (pp. 91–114). Santa Barbara, CA: Praeger.

Maxwell, J. P. (1999). Mandatory mediation of custody in the face of domestic violence: Suggestions for courts and mediators. *Family & Conciliation Courts Review, 37*, 335–356.

Mazza, J. J., & Reynolds, W. M. (1999). Exposure to violence in young inner-city adolescents: Relationships with suicidal ideation, depression, and PTSD symptomatology. *Journal of Abnormal Child Psychology, 27*(3), 203–213.

McCleer, S. V., & Anwar, R. (1989). A study of women presemting to an emergency department. *American Journal of Public Health, 79*, 65–67.

McCloskey, L. A., Figueredo, A. J., & Koss, M. P. (1995). The effects of systematic family violence on children's mental health. *Child Development, 66*, 1239–1261.

McCold, P. (2006). The recent history of restorative justice: Mediation, circles, and conferencing. In D. Sullivan and L. Tifft (Eds.), *Handbook of restorative justice: A global perspective* (pp. 23–51). London: Routledge.

McFarlane, J., Christoffel, K., Bateman, L., Miller, V., & Bullock, L. (1991). Assessing for abuse: Self-report versus nurse interview. *Public Health Nursing, 1*(8), 245–250.

McKibben, L., Devos, E., & Newberger, E. (1989). Victimization of mothers of abused children: A controlled study. *Pediatrics, 84*, 531–535.

McLeer, S. V., & Anwar, R. (1989). A study of women presenting in an emergency department. *American Journal of Public Health, 79,* 65–67.

McLeod, M. (1984). Women against men: An examination of domestic violence based on an analysis of official data and national victimization data. *Justice Quarterly, 1,* 171–192.

McMahon, M., & Pence, E. (1995). Doing more harm than good: Some cautions on visitation centers. In E. Peled, P. Jaffe, & J. Edleson (Eds.), *Ending the cycle of violence: Community responses to children of battered women* (pp. 186–206). Thousand Oaks, CA: Sage.

Mears, D. P., Carlson, M. J., Holden, G., & Harris, S. D. (2001). Reducing domestic violence revictimization: The effects of individual and contextual factors and type of legal intervention. *Journal of Interpersonal Violence, 16,* 1260–1283.

Mederer, H. J., & Gelles, R. J. (1989). Compassion or control: Intervention in cases of wife abuse. *Journal of Interpersonal Violence, 4,* 25–43.

Mednick, S. A., Gabrielli, W. F., & Hutchison, B. (1987). Genetic factors in the etiology of criminal behavior. In S. A. Mednick, T. E. Moffitt, & S. S. Stack (Eds.), *The causes of crime* (pp. 74–91). Cambridge, UK: Cambridge University Press.

Meier, J. (2005, March 19). Battered justice for battered women. *Washington Post,* A25.

Meloy, J. R. (1997). The clinical risk management of stalking: "Someone is watching over me. . . ." *American Journal of Psychotherapy, 51,* 174–184.

Melzer, S. A. (2002). Gender, work, and intimate violence: Men's occupational violence spillover and compensatory violence. *Journal of Marriage and Family, 64*(4), 820–832.

MI H. 4308 (1994).

Miccio, K. (2000). Notes from the underground: Battered women, the state and conceptions of accountability. *Harvard Women's Law Journal, 23,* 133–166.

Miethe, T. D. (1987). Stereotypical conceptions and criminal processing: The case of the victim offender relationship. *Justice Quarterly, 4,* 571–593.

Miller v. California, 413 U.S. 15 (1973).

Miller, N. (1997). *Domestic violence legislation affecting police and prosecutor responsibilities in the United States: Inferences from a 50-state review of state statutory codes.* Alexandria, VA: Institute for Law and Justice.

Miller, N. (2000). *A legislative primer on state domestic violence-related legislation: A law enforcement and prosecution perspective.* Alexandria, VA: Institute for Law and Justice.

Miller, N. (2005). *What does research and evaluation tell us about domestic violence laws? A compendium of justice system laws and related research assessments.* Alexandria, VA: Institute for Law and Justice.

Miller, S. L., & Wellford, C. F. (1997). Patterns and correlates of interpersonal violence. In A. P. Cardarelli (Ed.), *Violence between intimate partners: Patterns, causes and effects* (pp. 90–100). Boston, MA: Allyn & Bacon.

Mills, L. G. (1997). Intuition and insight: A new job description for the battered woman's prosecutor and other more modest proposals. *UCLA Women's Law Journal, 7,* 183–199.

Mills, L. G. (1998). Mandatory arrest and prosecution policies for domestic violence: A critical literature review and the case for more research to test victim empowerment approaches. *Criminal Justice and Behavior, 25,* 306–318.

Mills, L. G. (1999). Killing her softly: Intimate abuse and the violence of state interventions. *Harvard Law Review, 113,* 551–613.

Mills, L. G. (2006). *Insult to injury: Rethinking our responses to intimate abuse.* Princeton, NJ: Princeton University Press.

Mitchell-Herzfeld, S. (2000). *The Adoption and Safe Families Act (ASFA) Study, The Evaluation & Research Unit of New York State's Office of Children and Family Studies.* Unpublished report.

Moe, A. M., & Bell, M. P. (2004). Abject economics: The effects of battering and violence on women's work and employability. *Violence Against Women, 10,* 29–55.

Moe, T. M. (1987). An assessment of the positive theory of "Congressional Dominance." *Legislative Studies Quarterly, 2,* 475–520.

Moffitt, T. E., & Caspi, A. (1999). *Findings about partner violence from the Dunedin Multidisciplinary Health and Development Study: Research in brief.* Washington, DC: National Institute of Justice.

Moffitt, T. E., Caspi, A., Rutter, M., & Silva, P. A. (2001). *Sex differences in antisocial behavior: Conduct disorder, delinquency, and violence in the Dunedin Longitudinal Study.* Cambridge, UK: Cambridge University Press.

Moffitt, T. E., Robins, R., & Caspi, A. (2001). A couples analysis of partner abuse with implications for abuse prevention policy. *Criminology & Public Policy, 1,* 5–36.

Mohr, W. M., & Steblein, J. (1976, January). Mental health workshop for law enforcement. *FBI Law Enforcement Bulletin, 45*(1), 3–8.

Moll, J., de Oliveira-Souza, R., Eslinger, P. J., Bramati, I. E., Mourão-Miranda, J., Andreiuolo, P. A., & Pessoa, L. (2002). The neural correlates of moral sensitivity: A functional magnetic resonance imaging investigation of basic and moral emotions. *Journal of Neuroscience, 22*(7), 2730–2736.

Moore, A. M. (1997). Intimate violence: Does socioeconomic status matter? In A. P. Cardarelli (Ed.), *Violence between intimate partners: Patterns, causes and effects* (pp. 90–100). Boston: Allyn & Bacon.

Moore, C. W. (1986). *The mediation process: Practical strategies for resolving conflict* (2nd ed.). San Francisco: Jossey-Bass.

Moore, S. (2009). *Two Decades of Specialized Domestic Violence Courts: A review of the Literature.* New York: Center for Court Innovation. Retrieved September 10, 2010, from http://www.courtinnovation.org/_uploads/documents/DV_Court_Lit_Review.pdf

Moore Parmley, A. M. (2004). Violence against women research post VAWA. *Violence Against Women, 10*(12), 1417–1430.

Moore v. Green 848 N.E. 2nd 1015 (2006).

Moracco, K. E., Clark, K. A., Espersen, C., & Bowling, J. M. (2006). *Preventing firearms violence among victims of intimate partner violence: An evaluation of a new North Carolina law.* Final Report. Washington, DC: National Institute of Justice.

Morash, M., Bui, M., & Santiago, A. (2000). Gender specific ideology of domestic violence in Mexican origin families. *International Review of Victimology, 1,* 67–91.

Morrill, J., Dai, J., Dunn, S., Sung, N., & Smith, K. (2005). Child custody and visitation decisions when the father has perpetrated violence against the mother. *Violence Against Women, 11*(8), 1076—1107.

Mosely, B. (2009, June 24). Arguing couple does no damage with Cheetos. *Shelbyville Times-Gazette.* Retrieved August 17, 2010, from http://www.t-g.com/story/1549895.html

Muelleman, R. L., Lenaghan, P. A., & Pakieser, R. A. (1998). Nonbattering presentations to the ED of women in physically abusive relationships. *American Journal of Emergency Medicine, 16*(2), 128–131.

Municipality of Anchorage. (2000). *Analysis of police action and characteristics of 33 reported domestic violence in Anchorage, Alaska ten year study, 1989–1998.* Anchorage, AK: Author.

Muscat, B. T., & Iwamoto, K. K. (1993). *Abused women in the restraining order process: A study of their likelihood of completion.* Unpublished manuscript, American Sociological Association.

Myers, M. A., & Hagan, J. (1979). Private and public trouble: Prosecutors and the allocation of court resources. *Social Problems, 26,* 439–451.

Nagin, D. (1998). Criminal deterrence research at the outset of the twenty first century. In M. H. Tonry (Ed.), *Crime and justice: An annual review of research* (Vol. 23, pp. 1–42). Chicago, IL: University of Chicago Press.

National Center for Injury Prevention and Control. (2003). *Costs of intimate partner violence against women in the United States.* Atlanta, GA: Centers for Disease Control and Prevention.

National Center for Victims of Crime. (2007). *The model stalking code revisited: Responding to the new realities of stalking.* Washington, DC: National Center for Victims of Crime. August 13, 2010, from http://www.ncvc.org/ncvc/AGP.Net/Components/documentViewer/Download.aspxnz?DocumentID=41822

National Criminal Justice Association. (1993). *Project to develop a model antistalking code for states. Final summary report for the National Institute of Justice.* Washington, DC: U.S. Government Printing Office.

National District Attorneys Association. (1980). *Prosecutor's responsibility in spouse abuse cases.* Alexandria, VA: National District Attorneys Association, National Criminal Justice Reference Service.

National Network to End Domestic Violence. (2009). *Census report.* Retrieved August 18, 2010, from http://nnedv.org/resources/census/2009-census-report.html

National Research Council. (1998). *Understanding violence against women.* Washington, DC: Author.

National Task Force to End Sexual and Domestic Violence Against Women. (2005). *Title V. The Violence Against Women Act.* Retrieved June 30, 2010, new.vawnet.org/Assoc_Files_VAWnet/VAWA2005-FieldSummary.pdf

Newmark, L., Harrell, A., & Salem, P. (1995). Domestic violence and empowerment in custody and visitation in custody and visitation cases. *Family and Conciliation Courts Review, 33,* 30–62.

Newmark, L., Rempel, M., Diffily, K., & Kane, K. M. (2001). *Specialized felony domestic violence courts: Lessons on implementation and impacts from the Kings County experience.* Report submitted to the Center for Court Innovation and the National Institute of Justice. Washington, DC: The Urban Institute.

Newmark, L., Rempel, M., Diffily, K., & Mallik-Kane, K. (2004). *Specialized felony domestic violence courts: Lessons on implementation and impacts from the Kings County Experience.* Washington, DC: Urban Institute.

New York City Domestic Violence Court Open House, Center for Court Innovation, March 24–25, 2009.

Nicholson v. Williams, 202 F.R.D. 377, 379 (E.D.N.Y. 2001).

Nicolaidis, C., & Touhouliotis, V. (2006). Addressing intimate partner violence in primary care:

Norlander, B., & Eckhardt, C. I. (2005). Anger, hostility, and male perpetrators of intimate partner violence: A meta-analytic review. *Clinical Psychology Review, 25,* 119–152.

O'Brien, M., John, R. S., Margolin, G., & Erel, O. (1994). Reliability and diagnostic efficacy of parents' reports regarding children's exposure to marital aggression. *Violence and Victims, 9,* 45–62.

Office of the Attorney General, State of California. (1999). *Report on arrest for domestic violence in California, 1998.* Sacramento, CA: Author.

O'Keefe, M., & Lebovics, S. (1998). Intervention and treatment strategies with adolescents from maritally violent homes. In A. R. Roberts (Ed.), *Battered women and their families* (p. 175). New York: Springer.

Oliver, W. (1999). *The violent social world of Black men.* San Francisco, CA: Jossey-Bass.

Olsen, L. N., Fine, M. A., & Lloyd, S. A. (2005). Theorizing about aggression between intimates. In V. L. Bengston, A. C. Acock, K. R. Allen, P. Dilworth-Anderson, & D. M. Klein (Eds.), *Sourcebook of family theory and research* (pp. 315–331). Thousand Oaks, CA: Sage.

O'Neil, J. M., & Nadeau, R. A. (1999). Men's gender role conflict, defense mechanisms, and self-proective defensive strategies: Explaining men's violence against women from a gender role socialization perspective. In M. Harway & J. M. O'Neil (Eds.), *What causes men's violence against women* (pp. 86–116). Thousand Oaks, CA: Sage.

Oppenlander, N. (1982). Coping or copping out: Police service delivery in domestic disputes. *Criminology, 20,* 449–465.

Osofsky, J. D. (1999). The impact of violence on children. *Domestic Violence and Children, 9,* 33–49.

Osofsky J. D., & Scheeringa, M. S. (1997). Community and domestic violence exposure: Effects on development and psychopathology. In D. Cicchetti & S. L. Toth (Eds.), *Rochester Symposium on Developmental Psychopathology, volume 8. Developmental Perspectives on Trauma: Theory, Research, and Intervention* (pp. 155–180). Rochester, NY: University of Rochester Press.

Osthoff, S. (2002). But, Gertrude, I beg to differ, a hit is not a hit is not a hit: When battered women are arrested for assaulting their partners. *Violence Against Women, 8,* 1521–1544.

Ostrom, B. J., & Kauder, N. B. (Eds.). (1999). *Examining the work of state courts, 1997: A national perspective from the court statistics project.* Williamsburg, VA: National Center for State Courts.

O'Sullivan, C. S., Davis, R., Farole, D., & Rempel, M. A. (2007). *Comparison of two prosecution policies in cases of intimate partner violence.* New York: Center for Court Innovation.

Pagelow, M. D. (1981). *Woman battering: Victims and their experiences.* Beverly Hills, CA: Sage.

Painter, K., & Farrington, D. P. (1998). Marital violence in Great Britain and its relationship to marital and non-marital rape. *International Review of Victimology, 5,* 257–276.

Pakesier, R.A., Lenaghan, P., & Muelleman, R. (1998). Battered women: where they go for help. *Journal of Emergency Nursing, 24,* 16–19.

Paris Adult Theatres v. Slaton, 413 U.S. 49 (1973).

Parnas, R. I. (1967). The police response to the domestic disturbance. *Wisconsin Law Review, 2,* 914–960.

Parnas, R. I. (1970). Judicial response to intra-family violence. *Minnesota Law Review, 54,* 585–644.

Pate, A., & Hamilton, E. (1992). Formal and informal deterrents to domestic violence: The Dade County Spouse Assault Experiment. *American Sociological Review, 57,* 691–697.

Pate, A., Hamilton, E., & Annan, S. (1991). *Metro-Dade Spouse Assault Replication Project: Draft final report.* Washington, DC: Police Foundation.

Pattavina, A., Hirschel, D., Buzawa, E., & Faggiani, D. (2007). Policy, place and perpetrators: Using

NIBRS to examine srrest practices in intimate partner violence. *Justice Research and Policy, 9*(2), 31–52.

Pattavina, A., Hirschel, D., Buzawa, E., Faggiani, D., & Bentley, H. (2007). Comparison of the police response to heterosexual versus same-sex intimate partner violence. *Violence Against Women, 13*(4), 374–394.

Paveza, G. J. (1988). Risk factors in father-daughter child sexual abuse: A case-control study. *Journal of Interpersonal Violence, 3*(3), 290–306.

Pearson, J. (1997). Mediating when domestic violence is a factor: Policies and practices in court-based divorce mediation programs. *Mediation Quarterly, 14*, 319–335.

Peled, E. (1993). *The experience of living with violence for preadolescent witnesses of woman abuse.* Unpublished doctoral dissertation. University of Minnesota, Minneapolis.

Pennell, J., & Burford, G. (1994). Widening the circle: The family group decision making project. *Journal of Child & Youth Care, 9*, 1–12.

People v. Guenther, 740 P.2d 971, 975 (Colo. 1994).

Perry, B. D. (2001). The neurodevelopmental impact of violence in childhood. In D. Schetky & E. Benedek (Eds.), *Textbook of child and adolescent forensic psychiatry.* Washington, DC: American Psychiatric Press.

Peterson, R. R. (2001). *Comparing the processing of domestic violence cases to non-domestic violence cases in New York City Criminal Courts: Final report.* New York: New York City Criminal Justice Agency.

Peterson, R. R., & Dixon, J. (2005). Court oversight and conviction under mandatory and non-mandatory domestic violence case filing policies. *Criminology & Public Policy, 4*(3), 535–558.

Peterson, W., & Thunberg, S. (2000). *Domestic violence court: Evaluation report for the San Diego County Domestic Violence Courts* (NCJ 187846). Report submitted by San Diego Superior Court to State Justice Institute, grant number SJI-98-N-271. San Diego, CA: San Diego Superior Court. Retrieved September 16, 2010, from http://www.ncjrs.gov/App/Publications/abstract.aspx?ID=1878

Pew Center on the States. (2008). *One in 100: Behind Bars in America 2008.* Retrieved August 19, 2010, from http://www.pewcenteronthestates.org/uploadedfiles/one%20in%20100.pdf

Phelan, M. B. (2007). Screening for intimate partner violence in medical settings. *Trauma, Violence, & Abuse, 8*, 199–213.

Phelan, M. B., Hamberger, L. K., Guse, C. E., Edwards, S., Walczak, S., & Zosel, A. (2005). Domestic violence among male and female patients seeking emergency medical services. *Violence and Victims, 20*(2), L87–206.

Pierce, G. L., & Deutsch, S. (1990). Do police actions and responses to domestic violence calls make a difference? A quasi experimental analysis. *Journal of Quantitative Criminology*, 17–42.

Pierce, G. L., & Spaar, S. (1992). Identifying households at risk of domestic violence. In E. S. Buzawa and C. G. Buzawa (Eds.). *Domestic violence: The changing criminal justice response* (pp. 59–78). Westport, CT: Greenwood.

Pierce, G. L., Spaar, S., & Briggs, B. (1988). *Character of calls for police work.* NIJ Report. Washington, DC: Department of Justice.

Piquero, A. R., Fagan, J., Mulvey, E., Steinberg, L., & Odgers, C. (2005). Developmental trajectories of legal socialization among serious adolescent offenders. *Journal of Criminal Law & Criminology, 96*, 267–298.

Pirog-Good, M. A., & Stets, J. (1986). Program for abusers: Who drops out and what can be done. *Response, 9*, 17–19.

Pirro, J. (1982). Domestic violence: The criminal court response. *New York State Bar Journal, 54*, 352–357.

Pleck, E. (1979). Wife beating in nineteenth-century America. *Victimology, 4*, 60–74.

Pleck, E. (1987). *Domestic tyranny.* Oxford, UK: Oxford University Press.

Pleck, E. (1989). Criminal approaches to family violence 1640–1980. In L. Ohlin & M. H. Tonry (Eds.), *Crime and justice: A review of research* (Vol. 11, pp. 19–58). Chicago, IL: University of Chicago Press.

Plichta, S. B. (2004). Intimate partner violence and physical health consequences: Policy and practice implications. *Journal of Interpersonal Violence, 19*, 1296–1323.

Polochanin, D. (1994, July 30). Programs to treat men who batter fall short of need. *The Boston Globe.*

Pontius, A. A. (2004). Violence in schizophrenia versus limbic psychotic trigger reaction: Prefrontal aspects of volitional action. *Aggression and Violent Behavior, 9*(5), 503–521.

Post, D. (2003). *Battered Mother's Testimony Project: A human rights approach to domestic violence and child custody.* Phoenix: Arizona Coalition Against Domestic Violence.

Potter, H. (2007). Battered Black women's use of religion and spirituality for assistance in leaving abusive relationships. *Violence Against Women, 13,* 262–284.

Pressman, B. M. (1984). *Family violence: Origins and treatment.* Guelph, Ontario: University of Guelph.

Prince, J. E., & Arias, I. (1994). The role of perceived control and the desirability of control among abusive and nonabusive husbands. *American Journal of Family Therapy, 22,* 126–134.

Ptacek, J. (1995). Disorder in the courts: Judicial demeanor and women's experience seeking restraining orders (Doctoral dissertation, Brandeis University, 1995). *Dissertation Abstracts International, 56,* 1137.

Ptacek, J. (1999). *Battered women in the courtroom: The power of judicial responses.* Boston, MA: Northeastern University Press.

Ptacek, J., & Frederick, L. (2009, January). *Restorative justice and intimate partner violence.* Harrisburg, PA: VAWnet, a projection of the National Resource Center on Domestic Violence/Pennsylvania Coalition Against Domestic Violence. Retrieved April 25, 2010, from http://www.vawnet.org

Punch, M. (1985). *Conduct unbecoming.* London: Macmillan.

Quann, N. (2007). *Offender profile and recidivism among domestic violence offenders in Ontario, Canada.* Ottawa, Canada: Department of Justice, Research and Statistics Division.

Quarm, D., & Schwartz, M. (1983). Legal reform and the criminal court: The case of domestic violence. *Northern Kentucky Law Review, 10,* 199–225.

Quinn, D. (1985). Ex parte protection orders: Is due process locked out? *Temple Law Quarterly, 58,* 843–872.

Radford, J. (1989). Women and policing: Contradictions old and new. In J. Hanmer, J. Radford, & B. Stanko (Eds.), *Women, policing and male violence* (pp. 13–45). London: Routledge & Kegan Paul.

Radford, L., & Hester, M. (2006). *Mothering through domestic violence.* London: Jessica Kingsley.

Raj, A., & Silverman, J. (2002a). Intimate partner violence amongst South Asian women in Greater Boston. *Journal of the American Medical Women's Association, 57,* 111–114.

Raj, A., & Silverman, J. (2002b). Violence against immigrant women: The roles of culture, context, and legal immigrant status on intimate partner violence. *Violence Against Women, 8,* 367–398.

Raj, A., Silverman, J., Wingood, G. M., & DiClemente, R. J. (1999). Prevalence and correlates of relationship abuse among a community-based sample of low income African-American women. *Violence Against Women, 5*(3), 272–291.

Ramsay, J., Richardson, J., Carter, Y. H., Davidson, L. L., & Feder, G. (2002). Should health professionals screen for domestic violence? Systematic review. *British Medical Journal, 325,* 314.

Rand, M. R. (2009). *Criminal victimization, 2007.* Washington, DC: Bureau of Justice Statistics.

Rand, M. R., & Rennison, C. M. (2004). How much violence against women is there? In B. S. Fisher (Ed.), *Violence against women and family violence: Developments in research, practice and policy* (NCJ 199702). Washington, DC: U.S. Government Printing Office.

Reaves, B. (2007). *Census of state and local law enforcement 2004.* Washington, DC: Bureau of Justice Statistics, U.S. Department of Justice.

Rebovich, D. (1996). Prosecution response to domestic violence. Results of a survey of large jurisdictions. In E. S. Buzawa & C. G. Buzawa (Eds.), *Do arrests and restraining orders work?* (pp. 176–191). Thousand Oaks, CA: Sage.

Reed, D., Fischer, S., Kantor, G., & Karales, K. (1983). *All they can do. . . . Police response to battered women's complaints.* Chicago, IL: Chicago Law Enforcement Study Group.

Rees, A., Agnew-Davies, R., & Barkham, M. (2006). *Outcomes for women escaping domestic violence at refuge.* Paper presented at Society for Psychotherapy Research Annual Conference.

Reiss, A. J. (1971). *The police and the public.* New Haven, CT: Yale University Press.

Reiss, A. J. (1986). Official and survey crime statistics. In E. A. Fattah (Ed.), *Crime policy to victim policy* (pp. 53–79). New York: St. Martin's.

Rempel, M. (2009). Batterer programs and beyond. In E. Stark and E. S. Buzawa (Eds.), *Violence against women in families and relationships, Volume Three: Criminal justice and the law.* Santa Barbara, CA: Praeger.

Rennison, C. M. (2001). *Criminal victimization 2000: Changes 1999–2000 with trends 1993–2000.* Washington, DC: U.S. Department of Justice.

Rennison, C. M., & Planty, M. (2006). Reassessing who contributed most to the decline in violence during the 1990s: A reminder that size does matter. *Violence and Victims, 21*(1), 23–47.

Rennison, C. M., & Welchans, S. (2000). *Intimate partner violence* (NCJ 178247). Washington, DC: Bureau of Justice Statistics.

Rennison, C. M., & Welchans, S. (2003). *Intimate partner violence 1993-2001* (NCJ 197838). Washington, DC: Bureau of Justice Statistics, United States Department of Justice. Retrieved August 26, 2010, from http://bjs.ojp.usdoj.gov/content/pub/pdf/ipv01.pdf

Renzetti, C. (1999). The challenge to feminism posed by women's use of violence in intimate relationships. In S. Lamb (Ed.), *New versions of victims: Feminists struggle with the concept* (pp. 42–56). New York: New York University Press.

Renzetti, C. (2009). Intimate partner violence and economic disadvantage. In E. Stark and E. S. Buzawa (Eds.), *Violence against women in families and relationships, Vol. 1: Victimization and the community response* (pp. 73–92). Santa Barbara, CA: Praeger.

Renzetti, C., Goodstein, L., & Miller, S. L. (2005). One size fits all? A gender-neutral approach to a gender-specific problem: Contrasting batterer treatment programs for male and female offenders. *Criminal Justice Policy Review, 16*(3), 336–359.

Rice, D. W. (2007). *Dual arrest and predominant aggressor: A survey of police attitudes in Franklin and Hampshire counties.* Unpublished manuscript.

Ridley, C. A., & Feldman, C. M. (2003). Female domestic violence toward male partners: Exploring conflict responses and outcomes. *Journal of Family Violence, 18*(3), 157–170.

Riggs, D. S., & O'Leary, K. D. (1989). The development of a model of courtship aggression. In M. A. Pirog-Good & J. Stets (Eds.), *Violence in dating relationships: Emerging social issues* (pp. 53–71). New York: Praeger.

Riggs, D. S., & O'Leary, K. D. (1992). *Violence between dating partners: Background and situational correlates of courtship aggression.* Unpublished manuscript.

Ringquist, E. (1995). Political control and policy impact in EPA's Office of Water Quality. *American Journal of Political Science, 39*, 336–363.

Rivara, F. P., Anderson, M. L., Fishman, P., Nonomi, A. E., Reid, R. J., Carrell, D., et al. (2007). Healthcare utilization and costs for women with a history of intimate partner violence. *American Journal of Preventive Medicine, 32*, 89–96.

Roberts, A. R. (1988). Substance abuse among men who batter their mates. *Journal of Substance Abuse Treatment, 5*, 83–87.

Robinson, A. L. (2000). The effect of a domestic violence policy change on police officers' schemata. *Criminal Justice and Behavior, 27*, 600–624.

Robinson, A. L., & Chandek, M. (2000a). Philosophy into practice? Community policing units and domestic violence victim participation. *Policing: An International Journal of Police Strategies and Management, 23*, 280–302.

Robinson, A. L., & Chandek, M. S. (2000b). Differential police response to Black battered women. *Women & Criminal Justice, 12*(2/3), 29–61.

Rodriguez, M. A., Craig, A. M., Mooney, D. R., & Bauer, H. M. (1998). Patient attitudes about mandatory reporting of domestic violence: Implications for health care professionals. *The Western Journal of Medicine, 169*, 337–341.

Roederer, C. (2006). Another case in Lochner's legacy, the court's assault on new property: The right to the mandatory enforcement of a restraining order is "a sham, nullity and cruel deception." *Drake Law Review*, 321–369.

Romero, D., Chavkin, W., Wise, P., & Smith, L. (2003). Low-income mothers' experience with poor health, hardship, work, and violence: Implications for policy. *Violence Against Women, 9*(10), 1231–1244.

Rosen, L., & O'Sullivan, C. (2005). Outcomes of custody and visitation petitions when fathers are restrained by protection orders. *Violence Against Women, 11*(8), 1045–1075.

Rosenbaum, A., & O'Leary, K. D. (1981). Marital violence: Characteristics of abusive couples. *Journal of Consulting and Clinical Psychology, 49*, 63–76.

Ross, J. M., & Babcock, J. C. (2009). Proactive and reactive violence among intimate partner violent men diagnosed with antisocial and borderline personality disorder. *Journal of Family Violence, 24*(8), 607–617.

Rossman, B. B. R. (1998). Descartes's Error and posttraumatic stress disorder: Cognition and emotion in children who are exposed to parental violence. In G. W. Holden, R. Geffner, & E. N. Jouriles (Eds.), *Children exposed to marital violence* (pp. 223–256). Washington, DC: American Psychological Association.

Rothman, D. J. (1980). *Conscience and convenience: The asylum and its alternatives in progressive America.* Boston, MA: Little, Brown.

Rothwell, G. R., & Baldwin, J. N. (2007). Ethical climate theory, whistle blowing, and the code of silence in police agencies in the State of Georgia. *Journal of Business Ethics, 70,* 341–361.

Rotunda, R. J., Williamson, G., & Penfold, M. (2004). Clergy response of domestic violence: A preliminary survey of clergy members, victims, and batterers. *Pastoral Psychology, 52,* 353–365.

Roy, M. (Ed.). (1977). *Battered women: A psychosociological study of domestic violence.* New York: Van Nostrand Reinhold.

Sabol, W. J., & Couture, H. (2007). *Prison and jail inmates at midyear 2006.* Washington, DC: Bureau of Justice Statistics.

Sachdeva, S., Iliev, R., & Medin, D. (2009). Sinning saints and saintly sinners: The paradox of moral self-regulation. *Psychological Science, 20*(4), 523–528.

Sack, E. (2002). *Creating a domestic violence court: Guidelines and best practices.* San Francisco, CA: Family Violence Prevention Fund.

Sack, E. (2004). Domestic violence across state lines: The Full Faith and Credit Clause, congressional power, and interstate enforcement of protection orders. *Northwestern University Law Review, 98,* 827.

Salamon, L., & Wamsley, G. (1975). The federal bureaucracy: Responsive to whom? In E. Rieselbach (Ed.), *People v. Government.* Bloomington: Indiana University Press.

Salmon, M. (1986). *Women and the law of property in early America.* Chapel Hill: University of North Carolina Press.

Sampson, R. J., & Wilson, W. J. (1995). Toward a theory of race, crime, and urban inequality. In J. Hagan & R. D. Peterson (Eds.), *Crime and inequality* (pp. 37–54). Stanford, CA: Stanford University Press.

Sanders, A. (1988). Personal violence and public order: The prosecution of "domestic" violence in England and Wales. *International Journal of the Sociology of Law, 16,* 359–382.

Sartor Hilburn, K. (2008a). Falling. In K. Sartor Hilburn & T. Q. Autrey (Eds.), *Beating Hearts: Stories of Domestic Violence: An Exhibit of Photographic Constructions and Text.* Retrieved August 10, 2010, from http://www.beating hearts.net/exhibit/falling.html

Sartor Hilburn, K. (2008b). The Stupid List. In K. Sartor Hilburn & T. Q. Autrey (Eds.), *Beating Hearts: Stories of Domestic Violence: An Exhibit of Photographic Constructions and Text.* Retrieved August 10, 2010, from http://www.beating hearts.net/exhibit/stupid_list.html

Saunders, D. G. (1993). Husbands who assault: Multiple profiles requiring multiple responses. In N. Z. Hilton (Ed.), *Legal responses to wife assault* (pp. 9–36). Newbury Park, CA: Sage.

Saunders, D. G. (1995). The tendency to arrest victims of domestic violence. *Journal of Interpersonal Violence, 10,* 147–158.

Saunders, D. G. (2009). Programs for men who batter. In E. Stark & E. S. Buzawa (Eds.), *Violence against women in families and relationships: Criminal justice and the law* (pp. 161–178). New York: Praeger.

Saunders, D. G., & Size, P. B. (1986). Attitudes about woman abuse among police officers, victims and victim advocates. *Journal of Interpersonal Violence, 1,* 24–42.

SC S. 1287 (1994).

Schaefer, J., Caetano, R., & Cunradi, C. B. (2004). A path model of risk factors for intimate partner violence among couples in the United States. *Journal of Interpersonal Violence, 19*(2), 127–142.

Schafran, L. H. (1990). Overwhelming evidence: Reports on gender bias in the courts. *Trial, 26,* 28–35.

Schechter, S. (1982). *Women and male violence: The visions and struggle of the battered women's movement.* Boston, MA: South End.

Schechter, S., & Gary, L. T. (1988). A framework for understanding and empowering battered women. In M. A. Straus (Ed.), *Abuse and victimization across the life span* (pp. 240–253). Baltimore, MD: Johns Hopkins University Press.

Schmidt, J., & Steury, E. H. (1989). Prosecutorial discretion in filing charges in domestic violence cases. *Criminology, 27,* 487–510.

Schneider, E. (2000). *Battered women and feminist lawmaking.* New Haven, CT: Yale University Press.

Schultz v. Schultz, 63 How. Pr 181 (NY Gen Term 1882).

Schwartz, M. D., & DeKeseredy, W. S. (1997). *Sexual assault on the college campus: The role of male peer support.* Thousand Oaks, CA: Sage.

Schwarz, C. D. (2004). Unified family courts: A saving grace for victims of domestic violence living in nations with fragmented court systems. *Family Court Review, 42*(2), pp. 304–320.

Scott, K., Schafer, J., & Greenfield, T. (1999). The role of alcohol in physical assault perpetration and victimization. *Journal of Studies on Alcohol, 60*, 528–536.

Scott v. Hart, No. C-76-2395 (N.D. Cal. 1976).

Seelau, S. M., & Seelau, E. P. (2005). Gender-role stereotypes and perceptions of heterosexual, gay and lesbian domestic violence. *Journal of Family Violence, 20*, 363–370.

Sellers, C. S. (1999). Self-control and intimate violence: An examination of the scope and specification of the general theory of crime. *Criminology, 37*, 375–404.

Shalansky, C., Ericksen, J., & Henderson, A. (1999). Abused women and child custody: The ongoing exposure to abusive ex-partners. *Journal of Advanced Nursing, 29*(2), 416–426.

Shelton, D. E. (2007). *The current state of domestic violence courts in the United States, 2007.* National Center for State Courts White Paper. Retrieved September 8, 2010, from http://works.bepress.com/donald_shelton/9

Sheptycki, J. W. E. (1991). Using the state to change society: The example of domestic violence. *Journal of Human Justice, 3*, 47–66.

Sheptycki, J. W. E. (1993). *Innovations in policing domestic violence.* Newcastle upon Tyne UK: Athenaeum.

Sherman, L. W. (1992). The influence of criminology on criminal law: Evaluating for misdemeanor domestic violence. *Journal of Criminal Law and Criminology, 85*, 901–945.

Sherman, L. W. (1993). *Policing domestic violence: Experiments and dilemmas.* New York: The Free Press.

Sherman, L. W., & Berk, R. A. (1984a). *The Minneapolis domestic violence experiment.* Washington, DC: Police Foundation.

Sherman, L. W., & Berk, R. A. (1984b). The specific deterrent effects of arrest for domestic assault. *American Sociological Review, 49*, 261–272.

Sherman, L. W., & Cohn, E. G. (1989). The impact of research on legal policy: The Minneapolis Domestic Violence Experiment. *Law & Society Review, 23*, 117–144.

Sherman, L. W., Schmidt, J. D., Rogan, D. P., Smith, D. A., Gartin, P. R., Cohn, E. G., et al. (1992). The variable effects of arrest on criminal careers: The Milwaukee Domestic Violence Experiment. *Journal of Criminal Law and Criminology, 83*, 137–169.

Sherman, L. W., Smith, D. A., Schmidt, J. D., & Rogan, D. P. (1992). Crime, punishment and stake in conformity: Legal and informal control of domestic violence. *American Sociological Review, 57*, 680–690.

Shimtuh (Korean Domestic Violence Program). (2000). *Korean American community of the Bay Area Domestic Violence Needs Assessment Report.* Oakland, CA: Author.

Short, L. (2000). Survivors' identification of protective factors and early warning signs for intimate partner violence. *Violence Against Women, 6*, 272–281.

Sigler, R. T. (1989). *Domestic violence in context.* Lexington, MA: Lexington Books.

Silverman, J. G., Raj, A., Mucci, L. A., & Hathaway, J. E. (2001). Dating violence against adolescent girls and associated substance use, unhealthy weight control, sexual risk behavior, pregnancy and suicidality. *Journal of the American Medical Association, 286*, 572–579.

Silvern, L., Karyl, J., Waelde, L., Hodges, W. F., Starek, J., Heidt, E., et al. (1995). Retrospective reports of parental partner abuse: Relationships to depression, trauma symptoms and self-esteem among college students. *Journal of Family Violence, 10*, 177–202.

Simons, R. L., Wu, C. I., & Conger, R. D. (1995). A test of various perspectives on the intergenerational transmission of domestic violence. *Criminology, 33*, 141–170.

Simpson, E., & Helfrich, C. A. (2005). Lesbian survivors of intimate partner violence: Provider perspectives on barriers to accessing services. *Journal of Gay and Lesbian Social Services, 18*(2), 39–59.

Skogan, W. G., & Frydl, K. (2004). *Fairness and effectiveness in policing: The evidence.* Committee to Review Research on Police Policy and Practices. Committee on Law and Justice, Division of Behavioral and Social Sciences and Education. Washington, DC: The National Academies Press.

Skolnick, J. H. (1975). *Justice without trial.* New York: Wiley. (Original work published 1966)

Slote, K. (2002). *Battered mothers speak out.* Battered Women's Testimony Project. Wellesley, MA: Wellesley Center for Women.

Smart, C. (1986). Feminism and law: Some problems of analysis and strategy. *Journal of the Sociology of Law, 14*, 109–123.

Smith, B. E. (1983). *Non-stranger violence. The criminal court's response.* Washington, DC: Department of Justice, National Institute of Justice.

Smith, B. E., Davis, R., Nickles, L., & Davies, H. J. (2001). *Evaluation of efforts to implement no-drop policies: Two central values in conflict: Final report*. Washington, DC: National Institute of Justice.

Smith, D. A. (1987). Police response to interpersonal violence: Defining the parameters of legal control. *Social Forces, 65*, 767–782.

Smith, D. A., & Klein, J. (1984). Police control of interpersonal disputes. *Social Problems, 31*, 468–481.

Smith, M. D. (1994). Enhancing the quality of survey data on violence against women: A feminist approach. *Gender & Society, 18*, 109–127.

Soglin, L. F., Bauchat, J., Soglin, J. F., & Martin, G. J. (2009). Detection of intimate partner violence in a general medicine practice. *Journal of Interpersonal Violence, 24*, 338–348.

Sokoloff, N. J., & Pratt, C. (Eds). (2005). *Domestic violence at the margins: Readings on race, class, gender, and culture*. Piscataway, NJ: Rutgers University Press.

Solender, E. K. (1998). Report on miscommunication problems between the family courts and domestic violence victims. *Women's Rights Law Reporter, 19*, 155–160.

Soler, H., Vinayak, P., & Quadagno, D. (2000). Biosocial aspects of domestic violence. *Psychoneuroendocrinology, 25*(7), 721–739.

Sonkin, D., Martin, D., & Walker, L. E. (1985). *Group treatment for men who batter women*. New York: Singer.

Sorenson, S. B., & Shen, H. (2005). Restraining orders in California: A look at statewide data. *Violence Against Women, 11*, 912–933.

Spaccarelli, S., Coatworth, J. D., & Bowden, B. S. (1995). Exposure to serious family violence among incarcerated boys: Its association with violent offending and potential mediating variables. *Violence and Victims, 10*, 163–182.

Special court is aiding home violence victims. (1991, December 26). *New York Times*, p. 17.

Spilsbury, J. A., Bellison, L., Brotar, D., Drotar, D., Drinkard, A., Kretschmar, J., et al. (2007). Clinically significant trauma symptoms and behavioral problems in a community-based sample of children exposed to domestic violence. *Journal of Family Violence, 22*(6), 487–499.

Spitzberg, B. H., & Cupach, W. R. (2002). The inappropriateness of relational intrusion. In R. Goodwin & D. Cramer (Eds.), *Inappropriate relationships* (pp. 191–219). Mahwah, NJ: Erlbaum.

Spitzberg, B. H., & Cupach, W. R. (2007). Disentangling the dark side of interpersonal communication. In B. H. Spitzberg & W. R. Cupach (Eds.), *The dark side of interpersonal communication* (2nd ed., pp. 3–28). Mahwah, NJ: Erlbaum.

Spitzer, J. (2010, February 17). Streets may be safer but relationships? Not. *Women's News*. Retrieved February 17, 2010, from http://www.womensenews.org/story/domestic-violence/100216/streets-may-be-safer-relationships-not

Stalans, L. J. (1996). Family harmony or individual protection? *American Behavioral Scientist, 39*, 433–448.

Stalans, L. J., & Finn, M. A. (1995). How novice and experienced officers interpret wife assaults: Normative and efficiency frames. *Law and Society Review, 29*, 287–321.

Stalans, L. J., & Lurigio, A. J. (1995). Lay and professionals' beliefs about crime and criminal sentencing. *Criminal Justice and Behavior, 17*, 333–349.

Stanko, E. A. (1982). Would you believe this woman? In N. H. Rafter & E. A. Stanko (Eds.), *Judge, lawyer, victim, thief: Women, gender roles and criminal justice*. Boston, MA: Northeastern University Press.

Stanko, E. A. (1985). *Intimate intrusions: Women's experience of male violence*. New York: Routledge.

Stanko, E. A. (1989). Missing the mark? Police battering. In J. Hanmer, J. Radford, & B. Stanko (Eds.), *Women, policing and male violence* (pp. 46–49). London: Routledge & Kegan Paul.

Stanko, E. A. (2004). A tribute to 10 years of knowledge. *Violence Against Women, 10*, 1395–1400.

Stark, E. (1984). *The battering syndrome: Social knowledge, social therapy, and the abuse of women*. Unpublished doctoral dissertation, State University of New York–Binghamton.

Stark, E. (1993). Mandatory arrest of batterers: A reply to the critics. *American Behavioral Scientist, 36*, 651–680.

Stark, E. (2002). The battered mother in the child protective service caseload: Developing an appropriate response. *Women's Rights Law Reporter, 23*(2), 107–131.

Stark, E. (2007). *Coercive control: How men entrap women in personal life*. New York: Oxford University Press.

Stark, E. (2009a). Rethinking custody evaluations in domestic violence cases. *Journal of Child Custody, 6,* 287–321.

Stark, E. (2009b). The battered mother's dilemma. In E. Stark and E. S. Buzawa (Eds.), *Violence against women in families and relationships. Volume II, The family context* (pp. 95–123). Santa Barbara, CA: Praeger.

Stark, E. (2010). Health care intervention with battered women. In C. Renzetti & J. Edelson (Ed.), *The sourcebook on violence against women* (pp. 345–369). Thousand Oaks, CA: Sage.

Stark, E., & Flitcraft, A. (1983). Social knowledge, social therapy, and the abuse of women: The case against patriarchal benevolence. In D. Finkelhor, R. Gelles, G. Hotaling, and M. Straus (Eds.), *The dark side of families* (pp. 330–348). Newbury Park, CA: Sage.

Stark, E., & Flitcraft, A. (1988). Violence among intimates: An epidemiological review. In V. B. Van Hasselt, R. L. Morrison, A. S. Bellack, & M. Hersen (Eds.), *Handbook of family violence* (pp. 293–317). New York: Plenum.

Stark, E., & Flitcraft, A. (1996). *Women at risk: Domestic violence and women's health.* Thousand Oaks: CA: Sage.

State v. Rhodes, 61 N.C. 453 (1868).

Steele, B. F. (1976). Violence within the family. In R. F. Helfer & C. H. Kempe (Eds.), *Child abuse and neglect: The family and the community.* Cambridge, MA: Ballinger.

Steffensmeier, D., Zhong, H., Ackerman, J., Schwartz, J., & Agha, S. (2006). Gender gap trends for violent crimes: A UCR NCVS comparison. *Feminist Criminology, 1*(1), 72–98.

Steinmetz, S. K. (1980). Violence prone families. *Annals of the New York Academy of Sciences, 347,* 351–265.

Steinmetz, S. K., & Straus, M. A. (1974). *Violence in the family.* New York: Harper & Row.

Stets, J. E., & Hammons, S. A. (2002). Gender, control, and marital commitment. *Journal of Family Issues, 23,* 3–25.

Stets, J. E., & Straus, M. A. (1990). Gender differences in reporting marital violence and its medical and psychological consequences. In M. A. Straus & R. J. Gelles (Eds.), *Physical violence in American families: Risk factors and adaptations to violence in 8,145 families* (pp. 151–166). New Brunswick, NJ: Transaction.

Straus, M. A. (1973). A general systems theory approach to a theory of violence between family members. *Social Science Information, 12,* 105–125.

Straus, M. A. (1977). A sociological perspective on the prevention and treatment of wife-beating. In M. Roy (Ed.), *Battered women* (pp. 196–239). New York: Van Nostrand Reinhold.

Straus, M. A. (1977–1978). Wife beating: How common and why? *Victimology: An International Journal, 2,* 443–458.

Straus, M. A. (1980). Wife beating: How common and why. In M. A. Straus & G. T. Hotaling (Eds.), *Social causes of husband wife violence.* Minneapolis: University of Minnesota Press.

Straus, M. A. (1983). Ordinary violence, child abuse, and wife beating: What do they have in common? In D. Finkelhor, R. J. Gelles, G. T. Hotaling, & M. A. Straus (Eds.), *The dark side of families* (pp. 213–234). Beverly Hills, CA: Sage.

Straus, M. A. (1990). The National Family Violence Surveys. In M. A. Straus & R. J. Gelles (Eds.), *Physical violence in American families: Risk factors and adaptations to violence in 8,145 families* (pp. 3–16). New Brunswick, NJ: Transaction.

Straus, M. A. (1996). Identifying offenders in criminal justice research on domestic assault. In E. S. Buzawa & C. G. Buzawa (Eds.), *Do arrests and restraining orders work?* (pp. 14–29). Thousand Oaks, CA: Sage.

Straus, M. A. (1999). The controversy over domestic violence by women: A methodological, theoretical, and sociology of science analysis. In X. Arriaga & S. Oskamp (Eds.), *Violence in intimate relationships* (pp. 17–44). Thousand Oaks, CA: Sage.

Straus, M. A., & Gelles, R. J. (1986). Social change and change in family violence from 1971 to 1985 as revealed by two national surveys. *Journal of Marriage and the Family, 48,* 465–479.

Straus, M. A., & Gelles, R. J. (1990). How violent are American families: Estimates from the National Family Violence Resurvey and other studies. In M. A. Straus & R. J. Gelles (Eds.), *Physical violence in American families: Risk factors and adaptations in 8,145 families* (pp. 95–112). New Brunswick, NJ: Transaction.

Straus, M. A., Gelles, R. J., & Steinmetz, S. K. (1980). *Behind closed doors: Violence in the American family.* Garden City, NY: Anchor.

Straus, M. A., & Hotaling, G. T. (Eds.). (1980). *Social causes of husband wife violence.* Minneapolis: University of Minnesota Press.

Straus, M. A., & Smith, C. (1990). Violence in Hispanic families in the United States: Incidence rates and structural interpretations. In M. A. Straus & R. J. Gelles (Eds.), *Physical violence in American families: Risk factors and adaptations in 8,145 families* (pp. 95–112). New Brunswick, NJ: Transaction.

Stuart, B. (1997). *Building community justice partnerships: Community peacemaking circles.* Ottowa, Ontario, Canada: Department of Justice Canada, Aboriginal Justice Section.

Sudderth, L. K. (2006). An uneasy alliance: Law enforcement and domestic violence victim advocates in a rural area. *Feminist Criminology, 1*(4), 329–353.

Sugarman, D. B., & Frankel, S. L. (1996). Patriarchal ideology and wife-assault: A meta-analytic review. *Journal of Family Violence, 11*, 13–40.

Sullivan, C. M., Tan, C., Basta, J., Rumptz, M., & Davidson, W. S., II. (1992). An advocacy intervention program for women with abusive partners: Initial evaluation. *American Journal of Community Psychology, 20*, 309–332.

Sullivan, C. M., Juras, J., Bybee, D., Nguyen, H., & Allen, N. (2000). How children's adjustment is affected by their relationships to their mothers' abusers. *Journal of Interpersonal Violence, 15*, 587–602.

Swan, S. C., Gambone, L. J., Fields, A. M., Sullivan, T. P., & Snow, D. L. (2005). Women who use violence in intimate relationships: The role of anger, victimization, and symptoms of posttraumatic stress and depression. *Violence and Victims, 20*, 267–285.

Swan, S. C., & Snow, D. L. (2002). A typology of women's use of violence in intimate relationships. *Violence Against Women, 8*, 286–319.

Swanberg, J., Logan, T. K., & Macke, C. (2005). Intimate partner violence, employment, and the workplace: Consequences and future directions. *Trauma, Violence & Abuse, 4*(10), 1–26.

Swanberg, J., Macke, C., & Logan, T. K. (2007). Working women making it work: Intimate partner violence, employment, and workplace support. *Journal of Interpersonal Violence, 22*(3), 292–311.

Syeed, N. (2009, September 27). DC-area sniper's wife tells all. *The Washington Times.* Retrieved August 12, 2010, from www.washingtontimes.com/news/2009/sep/27/dc-snipers-wife-tells-all/

Szinovacz, M. E. (1983). Using couple data as a methodological tool: The case of marital violence. *Journal of Marriage and the Family, 45*, 633–644.

Taxman, F., Young, D., & Byrne, J. (2003). Transforming offender reentry into public safety: Lessons from OJP's Reentry Partnership Initiative. *Justice Research and Policy, 5*(2), 101–128.

Taylor, B. G., Davis, R. C., & Maxwell, C. D. (2001). The effects of a group batterer treatment program: A randomized experiment in Brooklyn. *Justice Quarterly, 18*, 171–201.

Teran, L. J. (1999). Barriers to protection at home and abroad: Mexican victims of domestic violence and the violence against women act. *Boston University International Law Journal, 17*, 1–70.

Terrill, T., & Paoline, E. (2007). Non-arrest decision making in police-citizen encounters. *Police Quarterly, 10*(3), 308–331.

Teske, H. C., &. Parker, M. L. (1983). *Spouse abuse in Texas: A study of women's attitudes and experiences.* Huntsville, TX: Criminal Justice Center Sam Houston State University.

Testa, M. (2004). The role of substance use in male-to-female physical and sexual violence. *Journal of Interpersonal Violence, 19*(12), 1494–1505.

Thackeray, J., Stelzner, S., Downs, S. M., & Miller, C. (2007). Screening for intimate partner violence: The impact of screener and screening environment on victim comfort. *Journal of Interpersonal Violence, 22*, 659–670.

Theran, S., Sutherland, C. A., Sullivan, C. M., & Bogat, G. A. (2006). Abusive partners versus ex-partners: Understanding the effects of relationship to the abuser on women's well-being and social support. *Violence Against Women, 12*(10), 950–969.

Thistlewaite, A., Wooldredge, J., & Gibbs, D. (1998). Severity of dispositions and domestic violence recidivism. *Crime & Delinquency, 44*, 388–398.

Thoennes, N., Salem, P., & Pearson, J. (1995). Mediation and domestic violence: Current policies and practices (special issue). *Family and Conciliation Courts Review, 33*, 6–29.

Thomas, T. A. (2004). Ubi jus, ibi remedium: The fundamental right to a remedy. *San Diego Law Review, 41*, 1633.

Thompson v. Thompson 218 U.S. 611 (1910).

Thurman v. City of Torrington, 595 F. Supp. 1521 (USDC, CN 1984).

Thurston, W. E., Tutty, L. M., Eisener, A. C., Lalonde, L., Velenky, C., & Osborne, B. (2009).

Implementation of universal screening for domestic violence in an urgent care community health center. *Health Promotion & Practice, 10*(4), 510–526.

Tjaden, P., & Thoennes, N. (1998). *Prevalence, incidence and consequences of violence against women: Findings from the National Violence Against Women Survey.* Washington, DC: National Institute of Justice.

Tjaden, P., & Thoennes, N. (2000). *Extent, nature, and consequences of intimate partner violence: Findings from the National Violence Against Women Survey.* Washington, DC: U.S. Department of Justice.

Tolman, R. M. (1989). The development of a measure of psychological maltreatment of women by their male partners. *Violence and Victims, 4,* 159–177.

Tolman, R. M. (1992). Psychological abuse of women. In R. Ammerman & M. Hersen (Eds.), *Assessment of family violence: A clinical and legal sourcebook.* New York: Wiley.

Tolman, R. M., & Bennett, L. (1990). A review of quantitative research on men who batter. *Journal of Interpersonal Violence, 5,* 87–118.

Tolman, R. M., & Raphael, J. (2000). A review of research on welfare and domestic violence. *Journal of Social Issues, 56*(4), 655–682.

Tolman, R. M., & Rosen, D. (2001). Domestic violence in the lives of women receiving welfare: Mental health, substance dependence, and economic well-being. *Violence Against Women, 7*(2), 141–158.

Townsend, R., & Bennis, W. (2007). *Up the organization: How to stop the corporation from stifling people and strangling profits.* New York: Wiley.

Tran, C. G. (1997). *Domestic violence among Vietnamese refugee women: Prevalence, abuse characteristics, psychiatric symptoms, and psychosocial factors.* Unpublished doctoral dissertation, Boston University, Boston, MA.

Truesdell, D., McNeil, J., & Deschner, J. (1986). Incidence of wife abuse in incestuous families. *Social Work, 3,* 138–140.

Turmanis, S. A., & Brown, R. I. (2006). The stalking and harassment behavior scale: Measuring the incidence, nature, and severity of stalking and relational harassment and their psychological effect. *Psychology and Psychotherapy: Theory, Research, and Practice, 79,* 183–198.

Umbreit, M. S. (1995). *Mediating interpersonal conflicts. A pathway to peace.* West Concord, MN: CPI.

Uniform Crime Reports. (2006). *Homicide Trends in the United States.* Washington, D.C.: U.S. Department of Justice. Retrieved July 15, 2006, from http://www.ojp.usdojgov/bjs/homicide/homtrnd.htm

United States v. Morrison, 529 U.S. 598 (2000).

Ursel, J. (1995). *Winnipeg family violence court evaluation.* Working Document WD1995–2e. Department of Justice, Ottawa, Canada.

U.S. Attorney General's Task Force on Family Violence. (1984). *Final report.* Washington, DC: U.S. Government Printing Office.

U.S. Commission on Civil Rights. (1978). *Battered women: Issues of public policy.* Washington, DC: U.S. Government Printing Office.

U.S. Commission on Civil Rights. (1982). *Under the rule of thumb: Battered women and the administration of justice.* Washington, DC: National Institute of Justice.

U.S. Department of Justice. (2001). *Stalking and domestic violence: Report to Congress* (NCJ 186157). Rockville, MD: National Criminal Justice Reference Service.

U.S. Department of Justice. (2009). *Justice Department commemorates fifteen years of the Violence Against Women Act.* Press release. Retrieved September 22, 2010, from http://www.justice.gov/opa/pr/2009/September/09-ag-953.html

Utah Gender Bias Task Force. (1990). *Utah Task Force on Gender and Justice: Report to the Utah Judicial Council.* Salt Lake City, UT: Administrative Office of the Courts.

Valente, R. L., Hart, B. J., Zeya, S., & Malefyt, M. (2001). The Violence Against Women Act of 1994: The federal commitment to ending domestic violence, sexual assault, stalking, and gender-based crimes of violence. In C. Renzetti, J. Edleson, & R. K. Bergen (Eds.), *Sourcebook on violence against women* (pp. 279–302). Newbury Park, CA: Sage.

Van Hightower, N. R., & Gorton, J. (2002). A case study of community-based responses to rural women battering. *Violence Against Women, 8*(7), 845–872.

Van Maanen, J. (1973). Observations on the making of policemen. *Human Organization, 32,* 407–417.

Van Maanen, J. (1974). Working the street: A developmental view of police behavior. In H. Jacob (Ed.), *The potential for reform of criminal justice* (pp. 83–130). Beverly Hills, CA: Sage.

Van Maanen, J. (1975). Police socialization: A longitudinal examination of job attitudes in an urban police department. *Administrative Science Quarterly, 20,* 207–228.

Van Maanen, J. (1978). Observations on the making of policemen. In P. Manning & J. Van Maanen (Eds.), *Policing: A view from the street* (pp. 123–146). Santa Monica, CA: Goodyear.

Vaughan, S. R. (2009). Women's Advocates: The story of the shelter. In E. Stark and E. S. Buzawa (Eds.), *Violence against women in families and relationships. Vol. 1: Victimization and the community response* (p. 3). New York: Praeger.

Vera Institute of Justice. (1977). *Felony arrests: Their prosecution and disposition in New York City's courts.* New York: Author.

Victim Services Agency. (1988). *The law enforcement response to family violence: A state by state guide to family violence legislation.* New York: Author.

Vigdor, E., & Mercy, J. A. (2003). Disarming batterers: The impact of laws restricting access to firearms by domestic violence offenders. In P. J. Cook & J. O. Ludwig (Eds.), *Evaluating gun policy* (pp. 157–204). Washington, DC: Brookings Press.

Vigdor, E., & Mercy, J. A. (2006). Do laws restricting access to firearms by domestic violence offenders prevent intimate partner homicide? *Evaluation Review, 30*(3), 313–346.

Violence Against Women Act of 1994 (VAWA), P.L. 103-322. Reauthorized in 2005.

Visher, C., Harrell, A., & Newmark, L. (2007). *Pretrial innovations for domestic violence offenders and victims: Lessons learned the Judicial Oversight Demonstration Initiative.* Washington, DC: National Institute of Justice.

Visher, C., Harrell, A., Newmark, L., & Yahner, J. (2009). *The Judicial Oversight Demonstration: Culminating report on the evaluation.* Washington, DC: National Institute of Justice.

Von Hirsch, A. (1985). *Past or future crimes: Deservedness and dangerousness in the sentencing of criminals.* New Brunswick, NJ: Rutgers University Press.

Waaland, P., & Keeley, S. (1985). Police decision making in wife abuse: The impact of legal and extralegal factors. *Law and Human Behavior, 9,* 355–366.

Waits, K. (1985). The criminal justice system's response to battering: Understanding the problem, forging the solutions. *Washington Law Review, 60,* 267–329.

Walker, L. (1979). *The battered woman.* New York: Harper & Row.

Walker, L. (1990). Psychological assessment of sexually abused children for legal evaluation and expert witness testimony. *Professional Psychology: Research and Practice, 21,* 344–353.

Walker, R., Logan, T. K., Jordan, C. E., & Campbell, J. C. (2004). An integrative review of separation in the context of victimization: Consequences and implications for women. *Trauma, Violence, & Abuse, 5,* 143–193.

Walker, S., Spohn, C., & DeLeone, M. (1996). *The color of justice: Race, ethnicity, and crime in America.* Belmont, CA: Wadsworth.

Walters, G. D. (1992). A meta-analysis of the gene-crime relationship. *Criminology, 39,* 595–613.

Wanless, M. (1996). Mandatory arrest: A step towards eradicating domestic violence, but is it enough? *University of Illinois Law Review, 2,* 533–587.

Waul, M. R. (2000). Civil protection orders: An opportunity for intervention with domestic violence victims. *The Georgetown Public Policy Review, 6,* 51–70.

Weeks, E. K., Ellis, S. D., Lichstein, P. R., & Bonds, D. E. (2008). Does health care provider screening for domestic violence vary by race and income? *Violence Against Women, 14,* 844–855.

Weisheit, R. A., Falcone, D. N., & Wells, E. L. (1996). Rural crime and justice: Implications for theory and research. *Crime & Delinquency, 42,* 379–397.

Weisheit, R. A., Wells, L. E., & Falcone, D. N. (1995). *Crime and policing in rural and small-town America: An overview of the issues.* Washington, DC: National Institute of Justice.

Weisz, A. N. (1999). Legal advocacy for domestic violence survivors: The power of an informative relationship. *Families in Society: The Journal of Contemporary Human Services, 80,* 138–147.

Weisz, A. N. (2005). Reaching African American battered women: Increasing the effectiveness of advocacy. *Journal of Family Violence, 2,* 91–99.

West, C. (1998). Lifting the "political gag order": Breaking the silence around partner violence in ethnic minority families. In J. L. Jasinski & L. M. Williams (Eds.), *Partner violence. A comprehensive review of 20 years of research* (pp. 184–209). Thousand Oaks, CA: Sage.

West, T. C. (1999). *Wounds of the spirit: Black women, violence, and resistance ethics.* New York: New York University Press.

Westley, W. (1970). *Violence and the police: A sociological study of law, custom and morality.* Cambridge, MA: MIT Press.

Wetzel, L., & Ross, M. A. (1983). Psychological and social ramifications of battering: Observations leading to a counseling methodology for victims of domestic violence. *Personnel and Guidance Journal, 61,* 423–428.

Whetstone, T. (2001). Measuring the impact of a domestic violence coordinated response team. *Policing: An International Journal of Police Strategies & Management, 24,* 371–398.

Whitcomb, D. (2002, March). Prosecutors, kids, and domestic violence cases. *National Institute of Justice Journal,* 3–9.

Widiger, T. A., & Mullins-Sweatt, S. (2004). Typology of maritally violent men: A discussion of Holtzworth-Monroe and Meehan (2003). *Journal of Interpersonal Violence, 18,* 1396–1400.

Widom, C. S. (1989). The cycle of violence. *Science, 244,* 160–166.

Widom, C. S. (1992). *Cycle of violence: Research in brief.* Washington, DC: U.S. Department of Justice.

Widom, C. S., & Maxfield, M. G. (2001). *An update on the "cycle of violence" (Research in brief).* Washington, DC: National Institute of Justice.

Williams, K. R. (1976). The effects of victim characteristics on violent crimes. In W. F. McDonald (Ed.), *Criminal justice and the victim* (pp. 177–213). Beverly Hills, CA: Sage.

Williams, K. R., & Hawkins, R. (1989). The meaning of arrest for wife assault. *Criminology, 27,* 163–181.

Williams, O. J. (1999). Working in groups with African American males who batter. In R. Carrillo & J. Tello (Eds.), *Family violence and men of color: Healing the wounded male spirit* (pp. 74–94). New York: Springer.

Wills, D. (1997). Domestic violence: The case for aggressive prosecution. *UCLA Women's Law Journal, 7,* 173–199.

Willson, P., McFarlane, J., Malecha, A., Watson, K., Lemmey, D., Schultz, P., et al. (2000). Severity of violence against women by intimate partners and associated use of alcohol and/or illicit drugs by the perpetrator. *Journal of Interpersonal Violence, 15,* 996–1008.

Wilson, D., & Klein, A. (2006). *A longitudinal study of a cohort of batterers arraigned in a Massachusetts District Court 1995 to 2004* (NCJ 215346). Final report for National Institute of Justice, Grant 2004-WB-GX-0011. Washington, DC: U.S. Department of Justice, National Institute of Justice. Retrieved August 17, 2010, from http://www.ncjrs.gov/App/Publications/abstract.aspx?ID=236929

Wilson, J., Phillips, B., & Neal, D. (1998). Domestic violence after disaster. In E. Enarson & B. H. Morrow (Eds.), *The gendered terrain of disaster: Through women's eyes* (pp. 115–122). Westport, CT: Praeger.

Wilson, J. Q. (1968). *Varieties of police behavior.* Cambridge, MA: Harvard University Press.

Wilson, J. Q., & Hernstein, R. (1985). *Crime and human nature.* New York: Simon and Schuster.

Wilt, M., & Bannon, J. (1977). *Domestic violence and the police: Studies in Detroit and Kansas City.* Washington, DC: Police Foundation.

Winfrey, O. (Producer). (2009, May 8). *The Oprah Winfrey Show* [television series]. Chicago, IL: Harpo Productions.

Winick, B. J. (2000). Applying the law therapeutically in domestic violence cases. *University of Missouri at Kansas City Law Review, 69,* 33.

Wisner, B., Blaikie, P., Cannon, T., & Davis, I. (2004). *At risk: Natural hazards, people's vulnerability and disasters* (2nd ed.). London: Routledge.

Wolf, R. (2007). *Principles of problem-solving justice.* New York: Center for Court Innovation.

Wolfgang, M., & Ferracuti, F. (1967). *The subculture of violence.* London: Tavistock.

Wolfgang, M., & Ferracuti, F. (1982). *The subculture of violence* (2nd ed.). London: Tavistock.

Wood, B. D., & Waterman, R. W. (1991). The dynamics of political control of bureaucracy. *American Political Science Review, 85,* 801–828.

Wood, B. D., & Waterman, R. W. (1994). *Bureaucratic dynamics.* Boulder, CO: Westview.

Wooldredge, J. (2007). Convicting and incarcerating felony offenders of intimate assault and the odds of new assault charges. *Journal of Criminal Justice, 35*(401), 379–389.

Woods, L. (1978). Litigation on behalf of battered women. *Woman's Rights Legal Reporter, 7*(2), 35.

Woods, S. J. (1999). Normative beliefs regarding the maintenance of intimate relationships among abused and nonabused women. *Journal of Interpersonal Violence, 14,* 479–491.

Worden, A. P. (1993). The attitudes of women and men in policing: Testing conventional and contemporary wisdom. *Criminology, 31,* 203–237.

Worden, R. E., & Pollitz, A. A. (1984). Police arrests in domestic disturbances: A further look. *Law & Society Review, 18,* 105–119.

Worden, R. E., & Shepard, R. (1996). Demeanor, crime and police behavior: A reexamination of the Police Services Study data. *Criminology, 34,* 83–205.

Wuest, J., & Merritt-Gray, M. (1999). Not going back: Sustaining the separation in the process of leaving abusive relationships. *Violence Against Women, 5,* 110–133.

Wylie, P. B., Basinger, L. F., Heinecke, C. L., & Rueckert, J. A. (1976). *Approach to evaluating a police program of family crisis intervention in six demonstration cities.* Alexandria, VA: Human Resources Research Organization.

Yellot, A. (1990). Mediation and domestic violence: A call for collaboration. *Mediation Quarterly, 8,* 39–50.

Yick, A. G. (2000). Predictors of physical spousal/intimate violence in Chinese American families. *Journal of Family Violence, 15,* 249–267.

Yllö, K. (1984). The status of women, marital equality, and violence against wives: A contextual analysis. *Journal of Family Issues, 5,* 307–320.

Yllö, K. (1993). Through a feminist lens: Gender, power, and violence. In R. J. Gelles & D. Loseke (Eds.), *Current controversies on family violence* (pp. 46–62). Newbury Park, CA: Sage.

Yllö, K., Gary, L., Newberger, E. H., Pandolfino, J., & Schechter, S. (1992, October). *Pregnant women abuse and adverse birth outcomes.* Paper presented at the annual meeting of Society for Applied Sociology, Cleveland, OH.

Yllö, K., & Straus, M. A. (1990). Patriarchy and violence against wives: The impact of structural and normative factors. In M. A. Straus & R. J. Gelles (Eds.), *Physical violence in American families: Risk factors and adaptations to violence in 8,145 families* (pp. 473–486). New Brunswick, NJ: Transaction.

Yoshihama, M., & Dabby, C. (2009, September). *Domestic violence in Asian, Native Hawaiian and Pacific Islander homes.* Asian & Pacific Islander Institute on Domestic Violence. Retrieved August 13, 2010, from http://www.vaw.umn.edu/documents/factsandstats/factsandstats.pdf

Yoshioka, M., & Dang, Q. (2000). *Asian Family Violence Report: A study of the Cambodian, Chinese, Korean, South Asian, and Vietnamese communities in Massachusetts.* Boston, MA: Asian Task Force Against Domestic Violence.

Zahn, M. A., Brumbaugh, S., Steffensmeier, D., Feld, B. C., Morash, M., Chesney-Lind, M., Miller, J., Payne, A. A., Gottfredson, D. C., & Kruttschnitt, C. (2008). *Violence by teenage girls: Trends and context* (NCJ 218905). Washington, DC: National Institute of Justice.

Zalman, M. (1991, November). *A review of state statutes concerning the police role in domestic violence.* Paper presented at the American Society of Criminology Annual Meeting, San Francisco.

Zlotnick, C. K., Kohn, R., Peterson, J., & Pearlstein, T. (1998). Partner physical victimization in a national sample of American families. *Journal of Interpersonal Violence, 13,* 156–166.

Zoeller, B., & Schmiedt, P. (2004). Suing the abuser: Tort remedies for domestic violence. *Victim Advocate, 4*(3), 11–14.

Zoomer, O. J. (1989). Policing women beating in the Netherlands. In J. Hanmer, J. Radford, & B. Stanko (Eds.), *Women, policing and male violence* (pp. 125–154). London: Routledge & Kegan Paul.

Zorza, J. (1994). Woman battering: High costs and the state of the law (Special issue). *Clearinghouse Review, 28,* 383–395.

Zorza, J., & Klemperer, J. (1999). The Internet-based domestic court preparation project: Using the Internet to overcome barriers to justice. *Domestic Violence Report, 4,* 49–50, 59–60.

Zorza, J., & Woods, L. (1994). *Analysis and policy implications of the new police domestic violence studies.* New York: National Center on Women and Family Law.

Index

About the Authors

Eve S. Buzawa is a professor and chairperson of the Department of Criminal Justice and Criminology at the University of Massachusetts–Lowell. She received her Bachelor of Arts degree from the University of Rochester as well as her Master's and Doctoral degrees from the School of Criminal Justice, Michigan State University. She has authored and edited numerous books and monographs. Recent publications include *Violence Against Women in Families and Relationships: Making and Breaking Connections,* a four-volume set (co-edited with Evan Stark, 2009). Professor Buzawa has also served as a principal investigator on several federally funded research projects and has directed numerous state-funded research and training projects. She is past president of the Society of Police and Criminal Psychology, past president of the Northeast Association of Criminal Justice Sciences, and past board member for the Academy of Criminal Justice Sciences.

Carl G. Buzawa is an attorney in private practice. Currently, he is Senior Vice President—Contracts, Legal, and Compliance at Textron Systems. He received his BA from the University of Rochester, his MA from the University of Michigan, and his JD from Harvard Law School. With Eve S. Buzawa, he is the coauthor of numerous books and articles on the topic of domestic violence.

Evan Stark is a forensic social worker and award-winning researcher with an international reputation for his work on the legal, policy, and health dimensions of interpersonal violence. A founder of one of the first shelters for abused women in the United States, in the 1980s, Professor Stark codirected the Yale Trauma Studies with Professor Anne Flitcraft, which was path-breaking research that was the first to document the significance of domestic violence for female injury as well as its links to child abuse and a range of other health and behavioral problems. The findings from these studies appeared in *Women at Risk: Domestic Violence and Women's Health* (Sage, 1996). Professor Stark has served as an expert in more than 100 criminal and civil cases, including *Nicholson v. Williams,* a successful federal class-action suit against New York City that made it unconstitutional to remove children from mothers solely because the mothers had been victims of domestic violence. Furthermore, he has consulted with numerous federal and state agencies and has won several prestigious awards for his work. His book

Coercive Control: The Entrapment of Women in Personal Life (2007) won awards from the Association of American Publishers and the American Library Association and was recently the subject of a special issue of *Violence Against Women*. With a PhD from Binghamton University, State University of New York, an MSW from Fordham, and a BS from Brandeis University, he is a professor at the School of Public Affairs and Administration at Rutgers–Newark, where he is also Director of Public Health. Professor Stark holds a joint appointment in women and gender studies at Rutgers–New Brunswick and is a professor and Chair of the Department of Urban Health Administration at the University of Medicine and Dentistry of New Jersey's School of Public Health.

SAGE Research Methods Online

The essential tool for researchers

Sign up now at
www.sagepub.com/srmo
for more information.

An expert research tool

• An **expertly designed taxonomy** with more than 1,400 unique terms for social and behavioral science research methods

• **Visual and hierarchical search tools** to help you discover material and link to related methods

• Easy-to-use navigation tools
• Content organized by complexity
• Tools for citing, printing, and downloading content with ease
• Regularly updated content and features

A wealth of essential content

• The most comprehensive picture of quantitative, qualitative, and mixed methods available today

• More than **100,000 pages of SAGE book and reference material** on research methods as well as editorially selected material from SAGE journals

• More than **600 books** available in their entirety online

Launching 2011!

⑤SAGE research methods online